YORKSHIRE IN THE REIGN OF ELIZABETH I

John Rushton

BLACKTHORN PRESS

Blackthorn Press, Blackthorn House
Middleton Rd, Pickering YO18 8AL
United Kingdom

www.blackthornpress.com

ISBN 978 1 906259 02 0

ILLUSTRATION CREDITS

The publisher and author are grateful to the following for help with
providing illustrations: Colin Hinson.

Printed and bound by CPI Antony Rowe, Eastbourne

The Blackthorn Press History of Yorkshire

Vol 1   Prehistoric Yorkshire by Phil Abramson – *In Preparation*
Vol 2   Roman Yorkshire by Patrick Ottaway
Vol 3   Anglo-Saxon & Viking Yorkshire by Alan Avery – *In Preparation*
Vol 4   Yorkshire in the Middle Ages by John Walker – *In Preparation*
Vol 5   Early Tudor Yorkshire by John Rushton – *In Preparation*
Vol 6   Elizabeth Yorkshire by John Rushton
Vol 7   Yorkshire in the 17th Century by Jack Binns
Vol 8   Yorkshire in the 18th Century – *In Preparation*
Vol 9   Yorkshire in the 19th Century – *In Preparation*
Vol 10 Yorkshire in the 20th Century – *In Preparation*

CONTENTS

AUTHOR'S PREFACE

This volume attempts to introduce you to the county of Yorkshire in the reign of Queen Elizabeth I. This was much the same county that we know. The people were in some cases the ancestors of those about us. Some hold the opinion that human nature doesn't change. That may or may not be. Almost everything else seems to have changed, and never more rapidly than in the 20th and 21st centuries. We move further away from our past.

Getting to grips with history is an exercise of the imagination, both for writer and reader. The artefacts and places that you see, the books you read, and the documents that you explore can only open a window to an earlier age. What the history writer sees through the window is a very personal impression of a vanished experience. There is no definitive history for all time. This book offers my selection of things come across and my view of them. You would have done it differently. History is a changing story and the story told depends on who you are and where you stand.

We have known an age in which scholars sat in libraries, fortunate to find a rare book, copying out extracts in long hand. The student spent more time getting to some distant archive than they could ever spend inside it, and when there pored over treasures rarely seen. A new age dawns, as librarians and archivists muster their resources to make them accessible in the home, through undreamt of equipment. This new availability of sources, must make a difference. There are surely interesting times ahead.

Serious attempts at keeping better records, and the serious writing of English history began in Queen Elizabeth's reign. We are all indebted to those people, since then, who have collected, excavated, deposited, transcribed, translated, indexed, published and otherwise made available the records of the past. And books are built on other books as well as records. Those who wrote the histories of Yorkshire places, people, families and subjects have done us proud. There is much to build with.

May I express appreciation for the ever helpful support given by the archivists and librarians at the Universities of Hull and York, the Yorkshire Archaeological Society at Leeds, York Minster Library, the East Yorkshire, North Yorkshire, Sheffield and Sheepscar County Record Offices and particularly the Borthwick Institute of Historical Research. I am grateful to the librarians of the Whitby Literary and Philosophical Society, and the librarians, at Pickering, Malton, Bridlington, Northallerton, Ripon, Rotherham, York and Sheffield libraries. A particular debt is owed to Bryan Berriman and Jon Webster of Scarborough Library. Enthusiastic librarians are a blessing.

I would like to thank a group of people who have recently contributed documents, the loan of books, or other help and encouragement and in several cases all three.- Madge & Johnathan Allison, Carol and Jeff Andrews, Alan Avery, Ann & Paul Bayliss, Mike Benson, Jack Binns, Mrs Betty Blizzard, Barry Brooks, Robin Boddy, Marjorie Brame, Charles Brear, Gordon Clitheroe, Richard Crocker, Mark Dodsworth, Joan & Chris. Evans, Glynnis Fairbrother, David Futty, Bill Goodall, Henry Greene, Brenda Green, Frances & Christopher Hall, Jim Halliday, Barry Harrison, John Hobson, Keith Johnston, Linda & Nick Kemp, Colin Langford, Francis and Maureen Marsh, Julie

Wardle, Helen Thompson, Gail Nicholls, Geoffrey Otterburn, Trevor Peirson, Christiana & David Pybus, Joan & Bill Pyemont, Sarah Stocks, Sheila Thomas, Mark Vasey, Richard Walgate, Robin Wardle and Chris Wilson. I am most notably indebted to Sheila McGeown for reading and correcting of text. She bore it well, and I thank her. My daughters Geraldine, Erika and Emma have encouraged me, as they always do.

Maps and Illustrations

Tables

A NOTE ON WEIGHTS, MEASURES AND MONEY

The weights, measures and monetary values used in this book are the ones contemporaries used. These may be summarised as:

Money:

4 farthings	=	1d (penny)
12d (pence)	=	1s (shilling)
1s	=	5p
20s (shillings)	=	£1 (pound)
21s (shillings)	=	1 guinea

Weight:

16oz (ounces)	=	1lb (pound)
1lb	=	0.45 kilograms
14lb (pounds)	=	1 stone
1 stone	=	6.35 kilograms
2 stones	=	1qr (quarter)
1qr	=	12.70 kilograms
4qr (quarters)	=	1cwt (hundredweight)
1cwt	=	50.80 kilograms
20cwt	=	1 ton
1 ton	=	1.02 tonnes

Volume:

2 pints	=	1 quart
1 quart	=	1.14 litres
4 quarts	=	1 gallon
1 gallon	=	4.55 litres
2 gallons	=	1 peck
1 peck	=	9.09 litres
4 pecks	=	1 bushel
1 bushel	=	36.40 litres
8 bushels	=	1qr (quarter)
1 quarter	=	2.91 hectolitres

Distance:

12in (inches)	=	1ft (foot)
1ft	=	0.305 metres
3ft (feet)	=	1yd (yard)
1yd	=	0.91 metres
22yds (yards)	=	1 chain
1 chain	=	20.12 metres
10 chains	=	1 furlong
1 furlong	=	201.17 metres
8 furlongs	=	1 mile
1 mile	=	1.61 kilometres

Area:

30¼ sq yds	=	1 perch
1 perch	=	25.29 sq metres

40 perches = 1 rood = 1210 sq yds = 1011.56 sq metres
4 roods = 1 acre = 4840 sq yds = 0.405 hectares

Prepared by Stephen Harrison

INTRODUCTION

Elizabethan Yorkshire

Queen Elizabeth reigned in England from 1558 to 1603. She was the daughter of Ann Boleyn and King Henry VIII. She succeeded Mary, daughter of Katherine of Aragon and King Henry VIII who had reigned from 1553 to 1558, a mere five years. Mary had replaced the boy King Edward VI, son of Jane Seymour and Henry VIII who had reigned from 1547 to 1553. Elizabeth came to the throne on the 17th November 1558 and reigned for forty-four years until her death on the 24th March 1603. King Henry VIII visited Yorkshire once, briefly, in 1540, after a great rebellion.[1] His successors, his children Edward, Mary and Elizabeth ruled but did not visit the county.

Yorkshire in the reign of Queen Elizabeth I was an ancient county of England, with a heritage derived from generations of British, Roman, Anglian, Danish and Norse men and women, and with a culture carrying something from all of those peoples. New Norman, Breton and Flemish lords had reorganised the shire in the eleventh and twelfth centuries. Their expanding society had worked the many for the earthly benefit of the few, but had diverted great resources and effort to support prayer in monasteries and churches, by a few, on behalf of the many.

The great plagues of the late 14th century ended social and economic growth and dramatically reduced the population. Late mediaeval society survived at a lower level, compared with former times, but there was some population recovery by the middle of the sixteenth century, and this would continue, transforming a rather empty landscape into a countryside of farms and fields, full of folk. The old monasteries and many other church based institutions were swept away by the state, between 1536 and 1557. Their wealth and their incomes were diverted into more mundane pockets and purposes. The parochial church survived on a smaller scale but with expanded activity.

William Smith described Yorkshire, at the time, as the greatest of forty counties, almost as big as Wales. The shire was seventy miles in length from east to west and sixty miles broad from bottom to top. Here was the great city of York, forty five market towns, over thirty castles, six hundred and twenty one parish churches, forty four chapels and more than seven hundred villages.[2] The county occupied much the same terrain then as it does now, apart from marginal changes in the boundaries and some land loss along the coast. Durham and Westmoreland were to the north, Lancashire and a strip of Cheshire on the west, Derbyshire, Nottinghamshire and Lincolnshire southwards and to the east was the "German Ocean", their name for the North Sea. Thomas Fuller would call this "the best shire of England".

The moors, hills and dales, with broader vales and flatlands, set the scene. The heart of the county, as they saw it, was the Vale of York. That broad expanse is no longer experienced in the way of the Elizabethan traveller, slowly moving on horse or foot. The Vale of York was more obvious then. If we would experience their world, we have to set aside the changes of later centuries, which brought so much growth to the West Riding

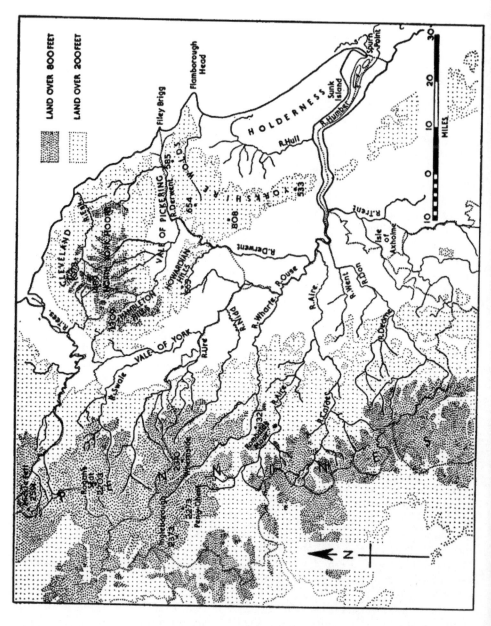

1. Physical Map of Yorkshire from *A History of Yorkshire* by Tate & Singleton

coal country and to the well-watered valleys beyond.

The well-travelled Bishop Cuthbert Tunstall of Durham had shown King Henry VIII "one of the greatest and richest valleys, fifty miles long and forty broad, that ever he found in all his travels through Europe". A few miles north of Doncaster, he waxed lyrical about this golden district, so full of activity. Within eight or ten miles of Hazlewood House, or a little more were "all these profits and pleasures, which are not to be found in so plentiful a manner in so small a compass, within all England". Here were one hundred and sixty five manor houses, the dwellings of lords, knights and gentlemen of the best quality, woods, some of five hundred acres, thirty two parks, two chases for deer, one hundred and twenty rivers and brooks, whereof five are navigable, upon which are seventy-six water mills for corn and stored with exceeding many salmon and other fishes, twenty-five coal mines, six market towns, and York, where three market days are stored with fresh fish from the sea, three forges for making iron, great store of corn and cattle sufficient for themselves and also the counties adjoining, hunting, hawking and fowling, flesh, fish, fowl, great store of meadow and pasture and excellent air".[3]

The remainder of the shire was thought to be very different. Here were the "great mountains and great hills, on the east side of the valley, known as York Wolds and Blackamore, and upon the west the high fells and the pleasant and fertile, valleys, or as we term them dales, named from rivers". York Wolds have since lost the association with that city but those chalk hills of the East Riding remain a distinctive, gentle, rolling landscape. Strangely, the stark Blackamore has now become known as the North York Moors. The Pennine fells and dales on the west are different again, now seen as one of the landscape treasures of England. There was already some pride in their peaks. Much of the land in the west and north was above eight hundred feet.

Roger Dodsworth recorded the local proverb,

"Penigent, Pendle and Ingleborrow,
are the highest hills all England thorrow."

William Camden rendered this as

"Ingleborrow, Pendle and Penigent.
Are the highest hills betwixt Scotland and Trent."[4]

The Humber, on the south of the county, was one of the four principal estuary rivers of England, absorbing the waters of the Trent from other counties and the Yorkshire rivers Hull, Derwent, Don and Ouse. Here was a route to the heart of England. The many rivers that fed the Ouse, including the Aire, Calder, Nidd, Ure, Rother, Wharfe, and lesser streams divided the western part of the county into its well-known dales. Their lower reaches in the Vale of York were often times navigable, giving cheap movement by ship and boat for the produce of the ocean, to supplement that of the land. The river Tees gave the shire its northern boundary. Small areas on the west of the Pennines drained towards the Lancashire and Westmoreland rivers, the Tame, Ribble and Lune.

The Elizabethan climate was a little colder than in earlier times bringing more severe winters and cool, wetter summers. There was skating on the river Idle in the winters between 1554 and 1563. The Thames was frozen over during the winter of 1564-65. As that winter drew to a close, the thaw in Yorkshire flooded rivers, and broke bridges. The tidal reaches of the river Ouse had a normal rise of two and a half feet on a spring tide. Men spoke of sixteen feet at York and nine feet at Cawood after heavy rain. There were cold northern winters in 1570, 1571 and 1574-75. The spring of 1587 was exceptionally cold. Seven York men were paid for breaking the ice at Clifton in January 1589-90. There was some terribly cold weather in the nineties when they say that thicker clothing came in. The Duke of Wurtemberg who toured the country in 1592 said that the English winter set in with snow in December and lasted till February.[5]

The Yorkshire weather was described by a contemporary, John Speed. He said of the North and East Ridings that "the air is subtle and piercing and not inclined naturally to contagious infections, which causes the people to live long and healthfully and not so subject to agues, fluxes and imperfections as those countries be that are more troubled with mists and vapours". Of the West Riding, he remarked that "the air, unto which this county is subject, is for the most part frigid and cold, much subject to sharp winds, hard frosts and other intemperate and winter like dispositions of weather; inasmuch as the people of the province are inured to maintain a moderate and ordinary heat in their bodies, by an extra ordinary hardness of labour and thereby become very healthful and not so often afflicted with infirmities, as others are that live more easily".[6] There were more local differences than that. Yearsley, a township on high ground east of the vale of York, exposed to chilling northern and eastern blasts, was a fortnight or three weeks later in vegetation than the valley below.

The Shire Organised

England's largest county was organised in three Ridings; North, West and East. These bore little relation to those administrative districts created in the twentieth century which are still with us. The Ridings were further divided into "wapentakes", virtually rural districts, which combined even earlier and smaller districts called hundreds. These wapentakes were used for such administrative necessities, as raising defence forces and levying taxation. A few "liberties" existed alongside these simple units, where great lordships had won exceptional privileges in early periods of history. The East Riding included the wapentakes of coastal Holderness, northerly Dickering and Buckrose, and on the west side "Ouse and Derwent", Howdenshire Liberty and Harthill. Hull with Hullshire was reckoned a county on its own.

The North Riding, from west to east, included the wapentakes of Hang, Gilling, the liberty of Allertonshire, wapentakes of Halikeld, Langbaurgh sometimes known as Cleveland, Birdforth, Bulmer, Ryedale, Pickering Lythe and the liberty of Whitby Strand. The West Riding held the wapentakes of Barkston, Ewecross, Osgoldcross, Staincross, Agbrigg, Morley, Skyrack, Claro, Staincliff, Strafforth and Tickhill. York was closely linked with the district west of the city towards Tadcaster, between the rivers Ouse and Nidd known as the Ainsty. York and the Ainsty were treated as a separate county. Several wapentakes had sub divisions, occasionally treated separately. Others like Agbrigg and Morley, Ewecross and Staincliff, and Strafforth and Tickhill were as often bracketed together.

The wapentakes were made up of smaller units called "townships". Each township had a name, which is usually though not always still familiar to us. The names are often those of the villages, but more accurately should be applied to the entire area of land off which a community lived. The community was not always a village. Each township had once sustained a largely self-sufficient agricultural community, but there had been mergers and sub divisions. The Victorians would later convert many surviving

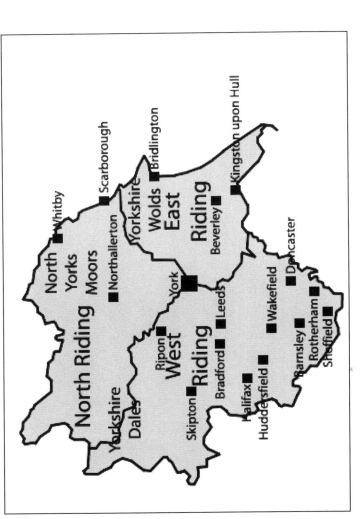

2. Yorkshire before the 1974 boundary changes.

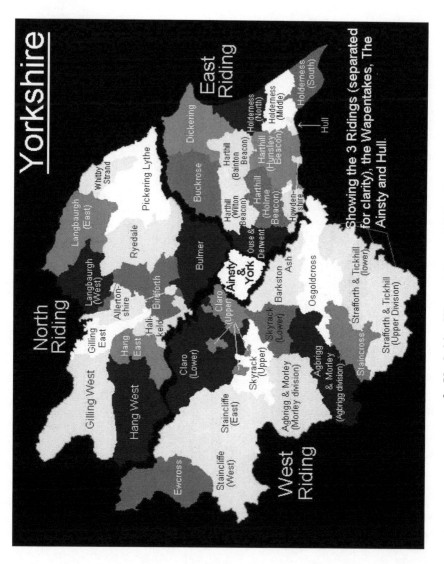

3. Yorkshire Wapentakes and Liberties

townships into the "civil parishes" of modern times. The community of a township could be housed in a town, a village, one or more hamlets, or in scattered farmsteads. Sometimes, one kind of settlement replaced the other, as crop or stock specialisation replaced self-sufficiency with production for markets. A village of ploughmen was needed for a suite of large arable fields but a shepherd could manage a flock in a pasture. The result could be a deserted village, in a township, still as large as it was before.

We can still see the different landscapes; the marshlands, the great Pennine dales and their uplands, the common field vales of York, Pickering and Cleveland, the smaller easterly dales, the hard rocky heights of the Moors, and the chalk Wolds. The early townships were in many areas arranged to cross the different terrains. Each normally contained some arable, pasture, meadow, carrs and moors, some closes and often woodland. They had some high ground and some low. The low carrs, and both low and high moors were often called commons, even sometimes inadequately described as wastes. The proportions of each differed widely from township to township and so did the balance of what was produced from them.

Most Yorkshire men, women and children were dependant, directly or indirectly, on what the "good earth" could be made to produce. Their principal resource was the land. Cultivation of crops was only one way of using land. Extensive marshes, moors, carrs and other rough pastures, often formed far more of a township than the cultivated land and chiefly supported stock and wild life. The hunter-gatherer tradition lingered strongest in sea and river fishing, but there was still much to catch, excavate or gather in the countryside, despite deer hunting having become a genteel pastime. The broad vales and dales were well provided with villages, hamlets, and farmsteads. Some of the higher ground and the steeper slopes were rough moorland, with patchy woodland and even mountainous terrain, almost empty of people.

New industries had already brought new settlement to some of the valleys and the dale slopes, cutlers' wheels on streams near Sheffield, mines taken down into the coal measures, iron and lead workings and most of all the rural cloth manufacture which was combined with small scale allotment farming. These things would continue. They were seen at the time as something of a marvel. James Ryther of Harewood could say that, "the inhabitants of Halifax are planted among our most stony and barren mountains" and yet "they surpass the rest in wisdom and wealth. These people have great liberty to enclose and build upon the wastes about them by reason they do for the most part appertain to the Crown".

Yorkshire remained a farming country, arable and pastoral, but with a growing industry outside the towns. Little food was imported except when harvests failed although much produce moved between districts of the shire. Land was the main source of wealth, created in foodstuffs, rents, profits, tithes, taxes and wages. Agriculture was the largest employer. From farming came the raw materials of the great leather and cloth industries. Mixed farming was general, but there were differences between the several districts of the shire. Whole groups of townships shared common situations, common pre-occupations, economies and culture, although each township had its own unique character and hence a local history.

John Leland had travelled much of the county, about 1540, though by no means all of it. He contrasted the low pastures of the East Riding, from Cottingham to Hull, Wallingfen to Beverley, Howden to Wressle with the stretches of good "champagne country", fertile, fruitful of corn and grass but with little wood. These were between York and Leconfield, from Beverley to Walkington, Malton to Sherburn and Seamer, and from Scarborough to Pickering in the North Riding. Similarly fruitful of corn and meadow was the West Riding country between Doncaster and Tickhill, from Conisbrough to Aberford, Ulleskelf to Tadcaster and Healaugh to York. Reasonable corn and pasture extended from Doncaster to Pontefract and from Crambeck to Malton. That part of Richmondshire, east of the high hills and dales grew plentiful wheat and rye, but had good meadows and woods. He was describing the common field countryside.[7]

James Ryther said that Yorkswold was "all champion, bearing good corn, meadow and pasture, especially good for sheep, yet so scarce of wood and fuel of any kind to burn, as their husbandmen use straw both for fire and candles."[11] William Camden in 1586 saw the difference that new industry was making. He said that the East and North Ridings had corn, cattle, veins of metal & iron, and an alum earth of sundry colours, from which some had lately begun to try very good alum & copperas. The West Riding mountain sides carried good grass in places while the bottoms of the dales were not infertile. Wensleydale had good ground where great flocks of sheep pastured but lead, stones, copper and pit coal could be found. Swaledale had plenty of grass, and some lead ore but lacked wood. How different was Walling Fen, sixteen miles in compass with many carrs in it and so big that fifty-eight villages lay either within or butted upon it. The ill-drained carrs filled the lower parts of the Vale of Pickering and were subject to annual flooding. A great area of poor carr formed the Humberhead levels.[8]

The number of people increased in the late sixteenth century. The proportion producing their own food and nothing else was falling. Those producing at least partly for the market would grow. The arable had to yield more crops, the pasture must support more stock. The yeomen were distinguished by the ownership of farming land from the husbandmen who were tenant farmers. Both welcomed new sources of income and many were involved part time in small industries. Other manufactures offered full time work which provided money for food and other purchases. Labourers and farm servants made up the bulk of the rural population.

There were a small but growing number of traders, and a larger body of craftsmen, including those handling transport. The nobility, gentry and clergy generally gave little time to farming or industry, but might give much to estate management. The definition of a gentleman was one who could live idly and without manual labour. Apart from the wealthy few, everyone else, who could, worked, whatever their age. Neither women nor children were seen as enjoying some right to leisure. Women were expected to be busy in both house and field.

T1 Table of Yorkshire Wapentakes and Liberties

	Towns	Rivers
York		
Ainsty	York	Ouse, Nidd, Wharfe
East Riding		
Buckrose	Derwent	
Dickering	Kilham, Bridlington,	Derwent, Harford, Gipsey
Harthill.	Beverley, Cottingham, Driffield,	Derwent, Coulney
	Weighton, Pocklington	
Holderness	Patrington, Hedon, Hessle,	
	Hornsea, Withernsea	
Howdenshire	Howden	Skell, Derwent, Coulney
Hull	Hull	Hull
Ouse & Derwent	Hemingbrough	Ouse, Derwent
North Riding		
Allertonshire	Northallerton	Wiske, Codbeck,
Birdforth	Thirsk	Willobeck, Codbeck
Bulmer	Easingwold	Foss, Derwent, Ouse
Gilling East		Wiske, Swale, Tees
Gilling West	Richmond, Reeth	Tees, Deepdale Beck,
		Lune, Marske, Arke,
		Greta
Halikeld		Swale, Ure
Hang East	Bedale, Masham	Swale, Ure
Hang west	Middleham, Leyburn, Askrigg	Swale, Cover, Ure, Semer
Langbaurgh	Guisborough, Skelton,	Esk
	Yarm, Stokesley	
Pickering Lythe	Pickering, Scarborough	Seven, Derwent, Harford,
		Costa
Ryedale	Malton, Helmsley, Kirkby	Ricall, Rye, Dove, Seven
		Derwent
Whitby Strand	Whitby	Esk
West Riding		
Agbrigg	Wakefield, Dewsbury,	Calder
	Huddersfield, Almondbury	
Barkston	Selby, Tadcaster.	Ouse, Aire, Wharfe
Claro	Knaresborough, Boroughbridge	Nidd, Skell, Ure
	Ripon	
Ewecross	Dent, Sedbergh	Wenning, Greta, Lune,
		Dee, Ribble
Morley	Halifax, Leeds, Bradford	Calder
Osgoldcross	Pontefract, Castleford	Ouse, Went
Skyrack	Leeds, Bingley, Otley, Ilkley	Aire, Wharfe
Staincliffe	Keighley, Barnoldswick, Skipton	Ribble, Aire, Wharfe
Staincross	Barnsley, Penistone	Dearne
Strafforth & Tickhill	Doncaster, Rotherham,	Don, Dearne, Rother
	Sheffield, Bawtry, Tickhill	

CHAPTER 1
GOVERNMENT

The Queen and the Privy Council

England and Wales were governed by Queen Elizabeth I, who ruled her kingdom with the help of a Council, a Parliament and the great Officers of State. She reigned from the 17th. November 1558 to the 24th. March 1603, some forty-four years. She could make war and peace, coin money and appoint people to the major offices in both church and state, by royal prerogative. She had no standing army. She was head of the Church of England. The Spanish ambassador in 1558 said that "she gives her orders and has her way as absolutely as her father did".

Elizabeth had been removed from the succession to the throne and declared illegitimate, after the execution of her mother Ann Boleyn for treason and adultery. When he died, her father King Henry VIII had restored her to the succession to the throne after Prince Edward and Princess Mary. Her half brother Edward died in 1552. While Mary was Queen, Elizabeth was briefly imprisoned in the Tower. Queen Mary died childless in 1558 and was succeeded by Elizabeth.

Queen Elizabeth was a very intelligent, and well educated woman. She made Sir William Cecil her principal secretary. She was urged to marry but remained a single woman, and never bore children. Her Catholic cousin Mary Stuart, Queen of Scots, was her most likely heir, and, while she lived, was a focus for Catholic opposition. Elizabeth won great authority in a male dominated society, as a strong minded, independent woman with an acceptance of national responsibility, and a keen sense of economy. She enjoyed visiting, music, dancing, and flamboyant dress. The Queen did not visit Yorkshire.

Those who entered the royal court, including the higher nobility, had the possibility of access to the Queen. Some other Yorkshire men and women were familiar to her. She was taught by Roger Ascham, a native of Kirby Wiske, from 1548 to 1550. He became her Latin Secretary in 1558. Owen Oglethorpe crowned her Queen. When her first Parliament met, she chose Sir Thomas Gargrave of Wakefield as its speaker. Her official artist was George Gower, possibly from Stittenham, near Sheriff Hutton. Frances Vavasour was her Yorkshire lady in waiting, Sir John Stanhope writing to Lord Talbot in 1599 of life at court said "our new maid Mrs Vavasour flourisheth like the lily and the rose."

The Queen chose her Privy Council, varying between nine and twenty members, from about sixty powerful men, some earls, more often knights. The Privy Council was an executive, issuing "orders in council" and channelling royal proclamations to the councils in the regions, to Lord Lieutenants, Sheriffs and Justices requiring its decisions to be implemented. Other people were commissioned for particular tasks. The Privy Council also served as a high court, with summary jurisdiction. As its business

1

4. Queen Elizabeth makes a State Progress through London

expanded, it met almost daily. The Secretary of the Council became the principal officer, although his duties were not tightly defined.

The great offices of state included the Lord Chancellor and Lord Keeper of the Great Seal, the Queen's representative in Parliament who presided over the House of Lords and directed the judiciary; a post held by Sir John Puckering from Flamborough from 1596 to 1603. The Lord Keeper of the Privy Seal managed the royal prerogative. The Lord Treasurer of the Exchequer was in charge of income and expenditure. The Principal Secretaries of State managed the council agenda, headed the diplomatic service and linked the Crown, Parliament and Privy Council

Sir William Cecil, as the principal secretary was the most frequent attender and through much of the reign gave focus and continuity to the work of the Privy Council. He was made Lord Burghley in 1571, Lord Treasurer the year after, and attended until his death in 1598. Other significant members of the council held such offices of state as Vice Chamberlain of the Royal Household, Comptroller of the Household, Lord Chamberlain, Master of the Horse, Lord High Admiral and Chancellor of the Duchy of Lancaster.[1]

The Queen's Council in the North

King Henry VIII had issued a new commission for the better government of the north after the northern rebellion in 1537 that was known as the Pilgrimage of Grace. The Duke of Norfolk acting as the King's Viceroy had been given the task of administering all the north of England, except Durham, Lancaster, Cheshire and the royal estates. His northern council met quarterly in York, Newcastle, Durham and Hull. This provincial council remained after the Duke's departure.

Later monarchs, and the privy council relied heavily on the Council in the North, both as their executive arm and as a high court. The Lords President were virtually viceroys and could determine all causes. Beyond the jurisdiction of the northern council, the Marches against Scotland remained under their Wardens. The system worked and the monarch need no longer visit the north in person.[2]

The earls and barons, archbishops and bishops were the natural leaders, available for controlling the north, including Yorkshire. After the Duke of Norfolk, two Archbishops of York, a Bishop of Durham, four Earls and two Barons would hold office as Lord Presidents of the Council in the North between 1537 and 1603. Apart from the Earl of Shrewsbury, and the second Lord Burghley, the earls and barons chosen were those with major estates outside Yorkshire. The office carried the use of Pontefract Castle, Sheriff Hutton Castle and the King's Manor, in the city of York. Ambrose, Earl of Warwick was ill and couldn't face a northern Winter. The second Lord Burghley was later made Earl of Exeter and Lord Sheffield would be made Marquis of Normanby.

T 2 Lords President of the Council in the North

Francis Talbot, 5th Earl of Shrewsbury	1549-1559
Thomas Henry Manners, 2nd Earl of Rutland	1561-1563
Ambrose, 3rd Earl of Warwick	1564
Archbishop Thomas Young	1564-1568
Thomas Radcliffe, 3rd Earl of Sussex	1568-1572
Henry Hastings, 3rd Earl of Huntington	1572-1595
Archbishop Matthew Hutton	1596-1599
Thomas Cecil, Baron Burghley	1599-1603
Edmund, Baron Sheffield	1603-1619

The other members of the northern council were chiefly knights and esquires, including several lawyers. Outstanding among the members was Sir Thomas Gargrave. This Wakefield man had attended the Inns of court. He served Thomas Lord Darcy as his steward till 1537, when he entered the service of Francis Talbot, 5th Earl of Shrewsbury. He gained a place on the Council in the North in 1544 and was a Justice of the Peace in all three Ridings from 1547. Gargrave was MP for York that year and M.P. for Yorkshire in 1553-55, and 1563-72. He survived Queen Mary and was elected speaker of Queen Elizabeth's first parliament and became Vice President of the northern council. There were long periods, in the absence of the Lord President, and under several occupiers of that office, when Sir Thomas Gargrave ran the Council. Lord Eure of Malton also served as Vice President of the northern council and later as Lord President of the Council in Wales.

It was provided in 1561 that the Vice President with one or more legal members, a secretary and a pursuivant, should always reside at York. This enabled the council to

5. Henry Hastings, Third Earl of Huntingdon

T3 Regular Members of the Council in the North

(L stands for "learned in the law.)

Shrewsbury's Sir Ralph Bowes(L), Sir Nicholas Fairfax, Sir William Babthorpe(L), Sir Thomas Gargrave (L), Sir Anthony Nevill, Sir Leonard Beckwith, Sir George Conyers, Sir William Vavasour, Robert Mennel, sergeant at law, Robert Rookbie, sergeant at law, Richard Belassis esq, Richard Norton esq, Robert Challoner esq (L) Henry Catyll esq, Francis Frobisher,esq. (L), George Brown esq (L), Christopher Estofte esq, John Rokeby Dr. of Laws, Thomas Eymes (Secretary (L)

Rutland's Sir Nicholas Fairfax, Sir Thomas Gargrave (L), Sir George Conyers, Sir William Pate, Sir Henry Gates, Robert Mennell sergeant at law, John Vaughan esq, Anthony Belassis esq, Henry Saville esq (L), George Brown esq, Francis Frobisher esq, Christopher Estoft esq, Robert Corbett (L) John Rokeby esq, Thomas Eymes (Secretary.L).

Young's Sir Nicholas Fairfax, Sir Thomas Gargrave, Sir Henry Gates, Sir John Constable, Sir John Foster, John Vaughan, esq, Anthony Bellassis esq, Henry Saville esq (L), George Brown esq, Christopher Estoft esq, Richard Corbet esq (L), William Tankarde esq(L), Alan Bellingham esq (L), Laurence Meers esq(L), John Rokeby esq, Thomas Eymes (L)

Sussex's Sir Nicholas Fairfax, Sir Thomas Gargrave, Sir Henry Gates, Sir John Foster, Sir George Bowes, John Vaughan esq, Alan Bellingham esq, William Tankarde esq, Laurence Meers esq, John Rokeby esq, Thomas Eymes (L)

Huntingdon's Sir Thomas Gargrave, Sir Henry Gates, Sir William Fairfax, Sir George Bowes, Sir William Mallorye, Sir Thomas Boynton, Sir William Bowes, Sir Thomas Fairfax (Denton), Sir Christopher Hillyard, Francis Wortley esq, Robert Bowes esq (Treasurer of Berwick), Laurence Meeres esq.

Burghley's Sir William Mallory, Sir Thomas Fairfax of Denton, Sir William Bowes, Sir Richard Mauleverer, Thomas Fairfax, jnr, Sir Thomas Posthumous Hoby, Sir Thomas Lascelles, Sir Henry Slingsby, Sir Edward Stanhope, (L), Sir John Mallory, Sir Thomas Fairfax, Sir Henry Griffiths, Sir Henry Bellasis, Sir Richard Wortley, Sir Thomas Hesketh, Richard Hutton esq, Charles Hayles esq, John Gibson esq, John Bennet esq, John Fearne secretary.

become a court of summary jurisdiction in both civil and criminal cases. There were regular and fringe members of the council. The Queen, in 1561, appointed the Archbishop, the Earls of Westmoreland, Northumberland and Cumberland, the Bishop of Durham, Lords Dacre, Gray of Wilton, Lumley, Eure, and Wharton, two Justices of Assize, the Dean of Durham, eight knights, Thomas Eymes as secretary, a sergeant at law and seven others to the council. The inclusion of the nobility and barony did not compel their attendance and it is unlikely that it was expected on normal occasions.

Some members were bound to continual attendance. The Queen gave instructions which required their behaviour to be according to their degrees and quality. She issued detailed instructions in forty-five articles to the Earl of Rutland as Lord President, and would do so again for later holders of the office. He was to administer justice, call people to further justice and punish evildoers. He had "a negative voice" in the council, virtually a power of veto. Salaries were paid to a number of those continually sitting, including Sir Thomas Gargrave, one hundred marks, Sir Henry Gate £20, John Ley £20,

George Brown £40, Christopher Estoft £50, Henry Saville £40, Francis Frobisher £20 and Thomas Eymes £33.6s.8d.[3]

Parliament

Parliament met to vote money to the Crown and to make legislation. The views and interests of the contending regional and local interests were coalesced into laws. Each Parliament was summoned and dismissed at the will of the sovereign. The Queen vetoed an average of just over five bills for each parliamentary session. The House of Lords included peers and bishops. The House of Commons at one session included three hundred and forty one gentlemen, lawyers and merchants. The total time of sitting was not great. Parliaments were only called for short periods. Parliament sat for only three years in all, during Elizabeth's reign. Sessions of Parliament were held in 1559, 1563-7, 1571, 1572-83, 1584-5, 1586-7, 1588-9, 1593, 1597-8 and 1601.

Yorkshire Speakers of the House were Sir Thomas Gargrave in 1559, Sir Christopher Wray in 1572, and Sir John Puckering in 1585. The consent of the House of Commons was necessary for the Crown to raise any new sources of revenue. The Crown otherwise relied on income from Crown lands, customs, the profits of justice, some feudal dues and since the breach with Rome, the first fruits and tenths from church benefices. Parliamentary taxation was low and only affected a minority. Most trading was free of taxation.

When the Queen came to her first Parliament, the Lord Keeper of the Great Seal, declared the Queen's pleasure to be that they should repair to their accustomed place and there to choose their Speaker. "At the common house, by the first motion and nomination of Mr. Treasurer of the Queen's House, the worshipful Sir Thomas Gargrave, knight, one of the Honourable Council in the North Parts and learned in the laws of the realm, was, with one voice of the whole house, chosen to be speaker and set in the chair". On Saturday next at one of the clock, he was presented to the Queen and confirmed, "after a notable oration which touched on the decays of the realm, and some suggested remedies."

The house heard a bill touching the felling of woods and trees in forests and chases and another for the thickening of caps and hats in mills. A subsidy was granted and the customs levies called tunnage and poundage. On 4th February, a request was made to the Queen that she marry. Mr. Speaker and thirty others attended on the afternoon of the 6th February and received a dusty answer. As the days passed, there were bills that York citizens might take apprentices despite statutes to the contrary, for the restitution in blood of Sir Henry Gate, for the preservation of fry of eels and salmon, for making the carriage of leather, hides or tallow overseas a felony, to revive the Act for the sewing of flax and hemp, and a bill against burning timber in the form of (char)coal to make iron. On the 8th March they attended the Queen. Forty two acts of Parliament were given the royal assent. The Parliament then dissolved.[4]

Yorkshire county freeholders, worth 40s a year, voted, at elections called by the High Sheriff, for two Yorkshire members of the Parliament called "Knights of the Shire". Other members of Parliament known as "parliamentary burgesses", were also elected from some Yorkshire boroughs; two each from Borough bridge, Hedon, Hull, Knaresborough, Ripon, Scarborough, Thirsk and York. Under Queen Elizabeth, some other boroughs were newly enfranchised, Aldborough, Beverley, Richmond, Pontefract, Malton and Northallerton.[5]

In practice, only major towns could afford to pay for two local burgesses to travel and remain in London for long periods. Many sent one local man and a country gentlemen. Noblemen and officers of state sought vacant seats for relations, friends and other nominees, some to build up influence in the Parliament. The House of Commons in 1584, had four hundred and sixty members, including two hundred and forty country gentlemen and fifty three townsmen. The rest were courtiers, officials, lawyers and similar nominees.

The Yorkshire election of 1597 was held in York castle courtyard, apparently with crowds reported as approaching six thousand present, many not entitled to vote. Sir John Stanhope, Sir Thomas Hoby, Sir William Fairfax, Sir Richard Mauleverer and Sir John Saville were nominated. Saville had the Sheriff read the statute saying that none should be chosen unless they were resident in the county. He rose to ask "Will you have a Mauleverer or a Fairfax". Shouting and uproar continued for more than two hours. Mauleverer was eliminated, leaving Saville and Fairfax against Stanhope and Hoby, who thought they had six to seven hundred supporters. Each side appointed a gentleman to view the crowd from an upper window.

These appraisers agreed that Saville and Fairfax had a majority of two or three hundred. Stanhope demanded a count, saying that five to six hundred of their opponents' supporters were not qualified to vote. The castle gate was shut and no more were let in. Two gentlemen scrutinised the voters in groups of twenty. Saville asked the under sheriff "what he was at". He said "though they would make you an ass, they shall not make me a fool". Saville and Fairfax then took him to dinner for three hours. On their return, he declared Saville and Fairfax elected. Sir Thomas Hoby sought a recount claiming that many in the crowd were not 40s. freeholders and hence were not entitled to vote. He took his case to the Privy Council and he lost.[6]

T4 A Summary of Major Parliamentary Legislation) [7]
1. Political
1559 Act restoring to the crown, the ancient jurisdiction over the state, ecclesiastical and spiritual.
2. Social
1563   Alms Act, for the relief of the poor...
       Statute of Artificers, JP's to set maximum wages. Apprenticeship of seven years compulsory for all urban crafts, but labouring poor excluded.

1571   Act sanctioning usury. 10% maximum interest rate.

1572   Vagabonds Act. Penalties placed on vagrants. JPs to list the poor and raise a rate to house the impotent and aged.

1576   Poor Relief Act. Houses of Correction for vagabonds and work schemes for the urban able bodied poor.

1597-8 Poor Relief Act. Overseers of the poor to be appointed by JPs and to lay parish rates to maintain them.
       Act for punishment of rogues-correction houses and whipping.
       Act clarifying Statute of Artificers. JPs to fix all wage rates.

1601   Act for relief of the poor. This codified poor relief legislation.
       Act to redress the misemployment of charitable donations.

3. Religion
1559. Act of Supremacy. The Queen as supreme governor of the Church of England to exercise the power by a commission. Oath of Supremacy required.

   Act for the uniformity of common prayer & divine service & the administration of sacraments.

1563 Oath of supremacy to be administered to graduates, schoolmasters & M.Ps.

1571 Treasons Act. This made denial of the Queen's Supremacy an act of treason

   Act against papal bulls.

   Act against fugitives overseas. Those without passports to lose goods.

   Subscription Act. Ordained clergy to subscribe to 39 articles of religion.

1581 Act to retain the Queen's subjects in their due obedience. Death penalty for those teaching papal supremacy. Fines and prison for those hearing mass. £20 a month fine for those refusing to attend church.

1584 Act for the safety of the Queen.

1585 Act against Jesuits & Seminary priests.

1592-3. Act to retain the Queen's subjects in obedience.

   Act against popish recusants

4. Agriculture
1563 Act to retain tillage. No tilled land to be converted to pasture. Land under the plough in 1528-63 to be kept under the plough.

1571 Tillage Act. Grain export allowed when price moderate

1592-3 Tillage Act repealed.

1597-8 Act ordering farmhouse repairs.

5. Maritime
1563 Act for maintenance of the Navy. English ships to be used for coastal and wine import trades.

   Wednesday made an extra fish day to support fishing industry

1584. Act deleting Wednesday as a fish day

Justices of the Peace

The county of Yorkshire was directly governed by those men who received the Queen's commission. The most important was the commission of the peace. The Justices of the Peace implemented statutes, royal proclamations and the instructions of the Queen's councils. They received a growing volume of orders and legislation from above. They had responsibilities for criminal justice and determined a wide range of causes. They had an administrative role, supervising constables, surveyors of highways and overseers of the poor. Many of those appointed were not active and the work was done by a quorum. They met in regular sessions, in every quarter of the year and at petty sessions when necessary. Their main duty was to maintain law and order, curbing lawlessness, riots and outrages. One of the quorum was appointed to keep the justices' rolls which recorded their orders, indictments and proceedings, known as the "custos rotulorum". The clerk of the peace was permanently appointed to advise on procedure and enter the records. The Justices, in a sense, ran local government.

A letter received from the Council in the North required their execution of stated articles. The Justices were to appoint overseers in each parish to enquire how all householders maintained themselves, to provide work and to persuade those without any means to work, and to imprison or whip the idle. They were to search for strangers and absentees, examine harborers and notice things amiss. They were to give due attention to the statutes licensing ale and tippling houses. They were to maintain archery, stop players of games, keepers of bowling alleys, regrators, forestallers and engrossers of corn and victuals, horse thefts, robberies, carrying of weapons, rebellions, bad behaviour in church and churchyard, and to maintain highways and watch keeping. This short reminder gave only part of their responsibilities.

The first help manuals for Justices were already in print. The "new book of the Justice of the Peace" of 1554 by Anthony Fitzherbert was largely a guide to the duties of justices, along with those of the bailiffs, escheaters, coroners and constables who executed their warrants and orders. Other volumes followed. The constables were the link between the local manor courts and both the local J.P. and the Assize court. The Attorney General, Sir Edward Coke in c 1600 prepared "articles" for constables. They were to answer for each wapentake at the beginning of every assize court. The matters for enquiry were vast, from felonies to vagrancy, recusants, trading offences, prices and wages, counterfeiting, desertion from the army, extortion, all the major crimes and a growing volume of offences against an increasing mass of legislation.

The appointment of High Constables was ordered in 1576 to mediate between local constables and the higher courts. Sometimes they were spoken of as Captain Constables. These new officials were to keep the peace within a division of the shire. They were appointed by the Justices of the Peace, from two literate and well favoured candidates in each wapentake of Yorkshire. It was envisaged that they would chiefly see to the labour and settlement laws and would manage the petty sessions. Some were chosen from the tax collectors, and continued to perform that office. The high constable of Barkston Ash wapentake failed to pay over all the moneys collected for a royal tax in 1598. Pontefract quarter sessions had him pay up a year later. Another captain levied more men for the musters than was needed and accepted bribes to let them go. He collected road repair money from the Selby country, for Friston causeway, but spent little of it on the necessary works. The high constables were sometimes physically attacked, when dealing with unpopular taxes and military levies. Edward Saville, acting as high constable, was assaulted in the public market at Leeds by six men. The high constable of Osgoldcross was attacked by other men at Pontefract market place.[8]

Manor Courts

It was in the manor courts that most people met the law, not only the law produced by Parliament, but an even wider range of local byelaws. To say that manor courts dealt with minor matters is to misjudge their role. Manor courts exercised a wide jurisdiction over local lives. They were the most local level of local government. Both cottagers and husbandmen might be required to attend as well as freeholders. Cropton and Danby freeholders, like many elsewhere, had to attend every three weeks. Most people appeared at no other court but their manor court. Useful incomes came from fines for non-attendance, but they kept meeting, even when the income from fines was not enough to cover the costs. Excuses were commonly accepted, known as essoins, including illness, absence elsewhere, and also "I cannot manage to come"

9

These courts enquired into breaches of statute law but also made and enforced the local byelaws known as pains. They supervised their own officers, including the constables, who carried a staff of office, made arrests and gave punishments. Jury foremen and constables appeared on oath. Many local problems were also discussed and resolved informally at their meetings which were attended by the new local officials overseeing the poor and the highways, and many other people. They applied a mixture of law and local custom, state law and byelaw. A visitor to the north west dales discovered that local custom was considered to rank above anything that Parliament might decide. Their nearest Justice of the Peace was some distance away.

There was an ancient distinction between a Court Baron and a Court Leet, though the two might be held together. A Court baron might meet monthly or twice a month to enquire if any of lord of the manor's lands, customs, rents, services, or royalties were withheld, whether there were encroachments on the lord's land or common, any overstocking, enclosing or digging the common, whether waifs or strays were withheld, or boundary stones and marks removed. The Court Leet had a wider remit, their charges echoing those required of the Justices of the Peace. The gravest offences were sent from manor courts to Quarter Sessions.

> **T5 Some Enquiries Required in Manor Courts**
> -scolds, brawlers, eaves droppers, barrators, breakers of the peace, rioters, unlawful assemblies, vagabonds who sleep by day and walk by night, those keeping thieves.
> -unlicensed and disorderly alehouses, haunters of alehouses and taverns without sufficiency to live on.
> -keeping bawdy houses, bakers, butchers and brewers making unwholesome meat and drink, or harbouring suspects,
> -highways encroached, un-repaired, obstructed by carrion, dunghills, dirt, diverted from their course, unfenced or walled. To see ditches scoured, trees lopped and bushes kept low near highways. Hedge breaking, water courses un-repaired, diverted or corrupted.
> -fraud and deceit in buying and selling by false weights and measures, sales of oats or hay at unreasonable prices, deceptive artificers, millers' tolls, use of unsealed cups and dishes for measuring, forestalling, engrossing and regrating markets.
> -breaking pounds and making rescues. Waifs and strays.
> -laying hemp in streams or ponds.
> -actions of officers, clerks of markets, surveyors of highways, leather and other market searchers, constables, ale tasters.
> -use of velvets, satins and furs on garments.

The steward of the manor sent a notice to the local bailiff, giving a few weeks warning of a court. The bailiff proclaimed it, requiring all over twelve years of age to attend. The jury were sworn not to favour or fear the rich, nor pity the poor. A charge was read to the jury stating the matters they must enquire into. At a Court Leet and Baron for the honour and manor of Skipton, the charge mentioned high treason, counterfeiting money, misuse of the great seal, petty treason, rapers and ravishers, murders, manslaughters, burglaries and robberies, felonies and petty larcenies. The Steward asked if anyone had information on any offences. The jury men took oath that nothing had been done, to their knowledge, within the constablewick since the last leet, contrary to any article in the charge to the jury, or else they made presentments of offences.[9]

The court rolls of the rectory manor of Dewsbury, also covering part of Hartshead, provide examples of what passed. Two reeves were elected for the year. A copyhold property was transferred from a deceased father to his fourteen-year-old son. New tenants paid entry fines as tenancies changed hands. Four men paid twopence for brewing and selling ale contrary to the assize of bread and ale, probably a good indication of how many alehouses there were. A building erected without permission was pulled down. Many men were fined 2d for assaults and affrays. When there was dispute about use of a water course, the jury decreed that one should have it one week and one the next. Men were fined for breaking the lock on the far watergate. Overseers were newly appointed for yoking and ringing swine for both the upper and the lower town. Swine were ordered to be ringed from Michaelmas to Candlemas and yoked from Candlemas to Michaelmas.

Manorial Bye-Laws

Manor court bye-laws reflected the past and present pre-occupations and problems of the court. They varied between those manors still managing their common fields and meadows and those where these had been enclosed. They were different for dales, field and marsh townships. Different problems occurred near to towns, along king's highways and on the sea coasts. A new bye-law could follow the discovery of a new problem and could be very specific. Robert Scott, the miller of Salton in Ryedale was ordered to keep the mill well and not to keep more than five hens and chickens there, with fines of 3s.4d. for either offence. All the bye-laws were entered in manor court rolls. These could get lengthy and even unread. The Loftus bye-laws were sometimes read out in church. Cases occur where a manor court made a bye-law, which had already been made at some earlier court.

Many bye-laws were concerned with agriculture, but others dealt with the many aspects of community life, where the action or inactivity of one person had consequences for others. Some bye-laws made national legislation more specific to a community. There was much concern about people gaining a settlement in places where they didn't belong and where they might become a burden, even a charge on the residents, who might have to support them if they fell out of employment. Acomb inhabitants were banned from keeping any person in their house, other than family members. A house owner who made two dwellings out of one cottage was subjected to a fine of twenty shillings. The Burton Agnes court allowed only one tenant in a cottage, except for a father or mother who were aged and single. They wouldn't suffer any idle person to dwell there. Many courts agreed that none should keep under settles under their roof. The fine for doing so at Acomb in 1581 was a pound.

Water supply for washing, drinking and use in households was a matter of general concern. The different uses had to be separated. Stream and well water were easily polluted and made filthy. The inhabitants of the west end of the village of Acomb, were told to scour the common well called Gaillwell before Whitsunday. William Shadlocke was banned from keeping any manure in his garden next to the well. Hemp was not to be retted in the East Field beck at Loftus. At Burton Agnes, none was to wash puddings, fish cloths or any filthy thing above the washing stone. At Ebberston drinking water was taken out well up the beck that lined the village street, and other things done further down stream. Salton manor had officers called "water graves". Blocked water courses could back up and flood higher land. Stokesley manor court required each inhabitant to scour the ditch before his front every fortnight. Hackness manor embraced several townships in a valley landscape, and required the Everley constable annually to open and scour all the water courses near the highway going to Everley bridge and the Dales constable to scour those near the roads to the Turfmoor.

Fire was a great risk, as more chimneys were built against cross passages and end walls, to replace the older central hearths. These had been open to the roof of the "firehouse", a name for the main room of an ordinary house or cottage. The smoke hoods above the new cottage hearths were often themselves flammable. Some manors had "searchers of houses". Hemingbrough had a serious fire in 1591. Acomb manor court decreed in 1580 that no inhabitant should dry hemp in fire houses or any oven, and four years later a man was charged for allowing a servant to heat hemp at his fire. Tadcaster ruled that none was to put straw or hay within three yards of a chimney, with a 6s.8d. fine for offenders. People were forbidden to thresh corn in barns by candlelight and were required to remove fodder and "elding" out of their fire houses. John Vesey at Holgate near York and Robert Towler of Paul, in the Humber estuary were ordered to repair chimneys for fear of fire. At Auburn, on the Dickering coast, in 1563 a man was charged with carrying fire in a pan.

A wide variety of byelaws reflected local issues. Middleton in Skyrack wapentake, ruled that tenants keeping "drabs, railers or women of evil gesture" for fourteen days should lose their tenement. They had Margaret Longfellow "dowked" in the "cuckstool". They required Thomas Marshall to bring his wife and cause her to be ducked. Ilkley stopped resident cottagers from leaving the township, for work in hay or harvest times, when they could be paid wages at home. The husbandmen were to take it in turns to have custody of the town bull, each being required to feed him well through the winter. The inhabitants of both Acomb and Holgate had to bury dead pigs within the hour and not leave them on the ground. North Loftus required carrion to be buried and Ilkley would fine those who cast dead birds in the water. Burton Agnes specified Bigot Hill for these interments and for any horse or mare that died in the pasture or the field.

Manor Court Offenders

A typical manor court, at Old Malton on the 13th of November 1577 dealt with four assaults, breach of a pound and two rescues from the pinder. Other people had failed to make up their fences, or had let their horses stray in wrong places. Some had kept pigs that were not ringed. At Goathland, the court recorded two men quarrelling but fined twenty-seven others 2d each for taking green wood.

T6 Some offences brought to Elizabethan Manor Courts in Yorkshire

Roos	unlawfully entertaining another at night time.
Gilling	John Brand's children carried away a hedge
Thwayte	William Oglesthorpe has enclosed a way
Ilkley	Bernard Hogg built a house upon the waste.

The court of Sir Nicholas Fairfax for Acaster Malbis in 1561 dealt with similar affrays, fences not made, a sike that needed scouring before St Andrew's day, pigs

12

getting into the fields, and another thirty eight people fined 2d for cutting wood. Since the Ilkley manor courts in 1583 fined another twenty five for taking greenhewe, and some for cutting oak saplings in the lords wood, we might conclude that small wood cutting was more a general activity providing court incomes than an offence.

Too strong an impression of lawlessness can arise from a perusal of manor court rolls. James Rither visiting Sedbergh, where gentlemen were rare and there was no JP within thirty miles, found only four disordered persons and some barrators haunting alehouses, but he admitted that "the great fault of this country" was the daily fighting. In Dent, on the other hand, only one man had been undutiful to his father, which he found remarkable among so many hundred householders. He thought that people among these wild mountains and savage hills, were generally well affected to religion, quiet and industrious, equal with Halifax in this respect, but excelling them in civility and temper of life and in abstaining from drink and other excesses.

The Higher Courts

The principal courts of the land formed a complicated system, some with overlapping jurisdictions. The Court of Common Pleas handled many civil suits between subjects. There were courts of King's Bench, Exchequer, Chancery, Admiralty and the Prerogative Courts of the Privy Council, namely Star Chamber and the Court of Requests. A Court of High Commission executed the royal supremacy on church doctrine, theology, church discipline and ceremonial in the church. There were several other church courts. The Duchys of Lancaster and York had their own courts, as did the Justices of the Forest.

Assize Judges visited their circuits three times yearly, to deal with crimes beyond the jurisdiction of the Justices of the Peace. These included theft, murder and treason. The Northern circuit took sixteen days in Summer, and seven in Winter, meeting at York and Lancaster respectively in the 1580's. Since the justices of the peace also attended, the higher courts were a channel for their instruction in the law. The visits of the Assize Judges saw some ceremonial, and Assize weeks became occasions for social gatherings of the gentry. Sessions took place with gaol delivery at York and occasionally as a one day Summer Assize at Hull. A Clerk of the Assize assisted the justices.[10]

The Council in the North also functioned largely as a court, perhaps the most significant for matters affecting Yorkshire. Its records have not survived. The sittings were on Mondays, Wednesdays and Fridays in the forenoon. Attachments were delivered to the Lord President three days before a sitting, with interrogatories. These were submitted by counsellors at law required to ensure that "all superfluous matters were omitted." There was a 20s fine on an attorney seeking delays. The attorneys were under orders "not to speak disorderly one to another". Decrees were issued and the parties were imprisoned or fined.[11]

A wide range of matters were dealt with. The Lord President ordered an enclosure pulled down at Wetwang after local complaint in c1553. The Vice-President put the York Mayor in gaol for failing to act against recusants in 1580. Matthew Metcalf of Bainbridge and Alexander Metcalfe of Countersett petitioned the Lord Treasurer in 1598 to direct the Lord President to determine the possession of East Witton mill. The Council reported to Sir Robert Cecil in 1598 on completion of a gaol delivery, the York gaol having been pestered with many poor prisoners. They found forty-one guilty out of fifty-six charged, but none were for notorious crimes, except a pedlar who counterfeited the Queen's Great Seal. Many were indicted for not going to church.

T7 Examples of Pleadings before the Council in the North

1557-8	Treason.
1567	Disputed right of way in Yeadon.
1572	Rights of the tenants of Haisthorpe manor to pasture cattle in the Turf Carr of Burton Agnes manor.
1578	Christopher Legard's removal of a dam at the west end of Julian Dyke.
1586	Robert Foxe against James Moyser on the manor of Wollas in Ainsty
1586	Boundary between Rawcliffe Low Moor and Clifton Moor.
1593	Whether Paneley Crofts belonged to the manor of Clifton near York, the Bootham ward pasture masters having impounded 96 Clifton sheep.

Men of the Law

Several Yorkshire men had distinguished legal careers. Sir Christopher Wray went from Bedale to Cambridge and Lincoln's Inn. He was a Justice of the Queen's Bench in 1572 and Lord Chief Justice in 1574. Wray was credited with a pregnant comment on estate management. He said that four things were necessary - "to understand it, not to spend it till it comes, to keep old servants and to have a quarterly audit."[12] John Puckering a younger son from Flamborough went from a lawyer's office to Lincoln's Inn, in 1559. He practised in Common Pleas and was employed by the Crown in state trials prosecuting for treason. He was knighted in 1592 and was Lord Keeper of the Privy Seal.

Sir John Saville one of three clever brothers from Bradley in Elland was educated by private tutors and at Brasenose College. He practised as a lawyer in the northern circuit from 1574 where he was made Justice of Oyer and Terminer. He became sergeant at law in 1594 and a Baron of the Exchequer in 1598. Sir John bought Methley and rebuilt the house. He was buried at St Dunstan's Fleet St but his heart and memorial came to Methley.[13]

A major contribution to legal practice was made by William West of Rotherham in his work called "Symbolaeography". This common law attorney collected and edited four volumes on "the art, description or image of instruments, covenants, contracts etc. of the notary or scrivener". His volumes were hardly light reading but they did represent part of the clarification of English law that was taking place. He was analytical about the meanings of words, while quoting Latin, Greek and modern authorities, Aristotle, Cicero and Sir Thomas More. West's instruments were the solicitor's tools, the covenants, bonds, contracts, feoffments, mortgages and letters of administration. He thought that scriveners should be skilful, diligent, moderate and keep secrets. He claimed that some parish clerks and schoolboys couldn't write one word correctly.

Crime and Punishment

What was punishable in Elizabethan Yorkshire is not always familiar to the modern ear. William West of Rotherham drew up standard forms of indictment for such offences as "absence from church for six months", for "drawing a dagger upon one in the churchyard to the intent to strike him", for cutting out of tongues, for "battery and maim by cutting off the right thumb", and "against the wife for poisoning her husband by putting arsenic and rosegree in his drink". These things sometimes happened. William Dickenson was charged with drawing his dagger in Church Fenton churchyard in 1575. There were cases, then as now, which became infamous. Calverley was said to have stained his progeny, consumed his estate by a riotous course, murdered his own children and stabbed his wife. He was riding to the nurse with intent to murder a son, when his horse stumbled and threw him. He was executed by pressing.

T8 Some Basic terms in West's Symbolaeography

jointure	an estate settled on a wife, to enjoy after her husband's death.
estate.	an interest a person has in land, of three types-freehold - of indefinite duration, leasehold by limited duration or copyhold held of a manor by special creation.
fee simple	an estate of inheritance, unqualified by knight service or socage.
entail	an estate settled without regard to the rules of descent.
easement	a privilege without profit.
tenement	land and or dwelling.
maritagium	a lord's right to dispose of a tenant's heir in marriage.
heredatiment	property that can be inherited.
fee tail	an estate in which inheritance is limited.

Thomas Wilson was indicted and condemned in July 1570 for the murder of George Walton, the retired Abbot of St. Mary's Abbey, York and for stabbing Archbishop Edmond Grindal. He made a hole through a prison partition, a brick and a half in width, passed through it to the St. Peter's chapel gallery and ascended ten feet, although his fetters weighed near fifty pounds and his maximum step was six inches. With a hooked nail and a sharpened piece of tin plate, he had cut his bed canvas into long strips and twisted them into a forty foot rope, to drop from the roof to the yard. He was heard crossing the roof and again secured. Wilson was put in a round dungeon out of reach of the walls under continuous watch. He made a lengthy address to the crowd before his execution.

Deference to those of high degree was normal. Offenders were firmly punished. John Gibson voiced "slanderous and opprobrious words of the Queen" at York in 1578. He had his ears nailed to the pillory on market day. He was whipped out of the city and sent back to Stockton. Johanna Howson, a Doncaster spinster was charged that "not, having the fear of God before her eyes, but seduced by the instigation of the devil contrary to her bounden allegiance" she "did on the 27th July, 1573, falsely maliciously and of her own imagination, utter divers false, unjust, seditious and scandalous rumours and statements concerning the aforesaid most serene and most dear lady, our Queen (of whom we are bound to think no evil) publishing, declaring, and stating forsooth, that our lady the Queen had borne, even if she still has them not, three bastard boys, to the great false, unjust, pernicious and malicious scandal of the said lady, our Queen." She was condemned to stand in a pillory, and unless willing to pay £100 in a month, was to have both ears cut off and to be imprisoned for three months.

There were different temptations, unfamiliar nowadays. You might milk someone else's cow. Isabella Mudie at Scarborough in 1598 saw a door open so she took a pot. Another house lost a table cloth and two napkins. Washing line theft was notorious. James Rither wrote to Lord Burghley from Harewood Castle in 1590, saying, "We have many Scottish wits among us. The borderer's property of taking more than his own, (for they never steal) is gotten so into use that cattle, sheep, horses were never so hard to keep from thieves' hands. Even in the heart of this shire, as now, the complaints are many and great, and the redress small." He spoke with keen prejudice of a neighbouring district, saying "the further north the less truth."

More considered offences hint at a criminal fraternity. Charles de Pascal, and others of Sheffield broke into a Stonegate warehouse to steal silks and drapery worth a hundred guineas. On the other hand, highway robbery might be a crime of opportunity in remote places. Francis Percy of Scarborough was pardoned for taking £26 from a London merchant's servant at Wetwang on the high wolds. A Pontefract yeoman was pardoned for theft of a gelding worth £3.6s.8d, and a labourer for theft of a black mare at Carlton, worth 40s. Wethers were stolen from the moors of Snainton and Ebberston. William Cliff, a Wakefield labourer, in 1590, assaulted his master William Hamshay with a three grained fork, from which Hamshaw died the next day. The judgement was self-defence.

Hanging till death was the sentence for felony, manslaughter, robbery, murder, rape and piracy. Offences against the state could result in being drawn to the place of execution on a hurdle or sledge, hanging till half dead, drawing and quartering. Peers judged guilty of treason by their peers were executed. Witches were hanged or burnt. Thieves could be hung, but were beheaded at Halifax. Executions at Tyburn outside York Micklegate Bar attracted great crowds to watch. Ten thousand were said to have watched the twenty-five year old coiner George Foster executed on April 8th. 1582.

T9 Some York Executions

1571   Highway robbery and attempted murder at Stockton on Forest by a Dover man

1572   High treason by the Earl of Northumberland.

1573   Coining by men of Scarborough, Hull, Driffield, Knaresborough, Pontefract, Wakefield and Wetherby.

1574   Wounding and attempted murder by three men at Skipton in Galtres.

1575   Coining by Hull and Keswick men in Thursday Market at York

1576   Issuing forged promissory notes at Leeds.

John Taylor saw the "fatal engine" used to behead thieves at Halifax in 1639. A royal grant had given permission to execute, when cloth was stolen from tenters. Conclusive evidence was "hand napping, back bearing or tongue letting" the last meaning confession. The engine was two tall timbers, an ell or yard apart, with a top cross piece, bearing a pulley and a rope with a heavy wood block fitted with an edge tool. The rope end was fastened to a pin, which the owner of the stolen goods had to cut, or lose the goods and see the thief pardoned. The beggars and vagrants litany held the saying "From Hell, Hull and Halifax, Lord deliver us". John Aubrey said that they feared the first least being the furthest away. Hull was terrible to them, as a town of good government, where vagrants met with punitive charity and were oftener corrected than amended." Halifax was formidable because thieves taken stealing cloth were instantly beheaded without benefit of law.

A great many people received pardons from the higher courts. Examples include Thomas Balwyne of Sheffield Park arrested at the Lodge after he killed yeoman John Wigley in self defence. Spinster Elizabeth Wilson of Kirkby Moorside, who broke into Francis Strickland's house and stole money, was pardoned. Robert Thackerowe a Bridlington smith charged with stealing John Waslings grey mare was pardoned, as was Gabriel Cootes who killed with an arrow, a boy watching the archers shooting at the targets at Northallerton. Richard Milner was pardoned for stealing money at Rither in 1597. Some thieves were burned on the left hand with a hot iron.

The stocks were widely used for petty thieves, who might sit there for two hours. When Richard Wiggoner at Whitby said that Justice Cholmley bound men over just to get fees, he had to spend an hour in the stocks and ask Cholmley's forgiveness on his knees or else go to York prison. Men and women were publicly whipped. Four men convicted of petty larceny were stripped from the middle upwards and soundly whipped at Wakefield in 1598. A man convicted at Hull in 1583 was to stand in the pillory on four market days.

The manor courts made extensive use of small fines, the scale of charges providing a good measure of how seriously they wished to deter the offence. Some constables kept a kidcote or small prison, somewhere to throw the drunk over night. Expulsion from a community was a last resort. A jury of twelve meeting in Gilling church ordered Ann Robinson to be expelled from Gilling and Sir Nicholas Fairfax backed them up, ordering her to go or be stocked. Scolds were ducked on ducking stools in stinking water. The Rotherham ducking stool was repaired in 1579 and again in 1592.

Officers of the Crown

The Crown had other agents active in the shire. Coroners were appointed to enquire into sudden or otherwise suspicious deaths. They set up inquests, with juries to take evidence. Escheators sought to maintain ancient feudal incomes, particularly when estates reverted to the Crown on the expiry of a family line or in cases of treason. The office of the Lord High Admiral had deputy Vice-Admirals in coastal counties, appointed to deal with marine causes, including wrecks, salvage and royal fishes. The Archbishop of York was the Vice Admiral for Yorkshire.

The transfer of several of the great honours and liberties from monasteries and noble families to the Crown, brought a considerable measure of direct control and local influence to the Privy council, even though the estates were often leased with their stewardships and bailiffdoms to members of the local knighthood and nobility. The King's will had been made to run in the Palatinate of Durham in 1536. The liberties of Crayke and Allertonshire, were taken from the Bishop of Durham by Act of Parliament in the first year of Elizabeth's reign.

The High Sheriff of Yorkshire was annually "pricked" by the sovereign from a preselected list of three candidates. The office was viewed as an expensive honour, but was unavoidable once the Queen had indicated her wishes. The Sheriff took precedence after the Lord Lieutenant and was expected to put down rebellion and disorder. He had a role in conducting county elections for Parliament. His regular duties included empanelling juries, execution of court sentences, arrests of heretics, and supervision of prisons. He collected payments to the Crown, fines, debts, distraints on goods where a debtor defaulted, and the taxes, or subsidies to the Crown, levied by Parliament.

Parliamentary taxation was usually levied on the income from land, or on goods, but at different rates. The income was assessed but usually this reflected rent less any deductions. Goods were assessed after harvest at their capital value rather than income. The tax payer only paid in one category, land or goods. Township assessors returned a list of tax payers, who were not numerous. The entire Ainsty wapentake held only two hundred and twenty two taxpayers in 1563. There was occasional corruption. The High Constable of Barkston was said to have increased the township rates by 20s and 30s a township, for himself.

T10 Some Assessments made on Parishes for Taxation

1595	Towards provisioning Her Majesty's ships with fat oxen
1597	Soldiers for service in Ireland (three times)
1597	For provisioning Her Majesty's household
1597	For Queens bench, Marshalsea and Hospitals
1598	For relieving the infected town of Scarborough
1598	For the council, for oxen, for Her Majesty's household
1599	For setting forth light horses with men and furniture [14]

Most people were assessed at sums of three, four and five pounds and paid three, four or five shillings at the 1590 taxation, which was called a Lay Subsidy, in Bulmer wapentake, the subsidy going to the Crown. Between three and eight people might pay tax in a village. Among 189 paying tax, 25 paid larger sums including Thomas Cundall at Huby, Thomas Gower at Stittenham, Francis Metham at Terrington, Sir Ralph Bouchier at Newton, Marmduke Cholmley at Brandsby & Stearsby, Richard Darley at Buttercrambe, and several other manor lords. Thomas Gower paid the entire tax of 26s.8d. at Stittenham.

T11 Numbers taxed in a Lay subsidy roll for Bulmer Wapentake 1590

Ten	-Easingwold
Eight	-Myton, Linton & Youlton, Sheriff Hutton
Seven	Huttons Ambo,
Six	Bulmer & Welburn, Sutton in Galtres, Alne, Newton, Buttercrambe & Aldby
Five	Tollerton, Helperby, Terrington, Huntington & Earswick, Clifton & Marygate, Brandsby & Stearsby, Craike, Marton & members, Thormanby, Stillington, Raskelf
Four	Skelton & Roucliffe, Stockton, Tolthorpe & Farlington
Three	Strensall & Earswick, Whenby, Huby, Haxby, Shipton, Holtby & Warthill
Two	Sand Hutton, Skewsby & Dalby, Heworth, Farlington, Osbaldwick, Foston & Thornton, Crambe & Barton, Harton & Claxton, Flaxton, Aldwark, Helmsley & Gate Helmsley, Wigginton
One	Scackleton Grange, Stittenham, Hinderskelfe, Conisthorpe, Ganthorpe, Heslerton

18

Early Challenges to the Crown

King Henry VIII had declared his daughters Mary and Elizabeth illegitimate. King Edward VI made a declaration in favour of Jane Grey in 1553. When he died, Lady Jane and her husband could not refuse the Crown handed to them. The reign lasted nine days. Mary came to power with little difficulty. She was proclaimed Queen and entered London in triumph on August the 3rd. Some of her opponents were executed. Others were pardoned. York Corporation sent a fulsome letter to the Queen and obeyed an order from the Council in the North for celebration bonfires.

Mary was a Catholic and she married the Catholic Philip King of Spain. There was a brief flurry on the Yorkshire coast when Thomas Stafford, younger son of Lord Stafford, with Captain Richard Saunders of Womersley, and John Sherles of Rouen sailed from Dieppe with a few supporters to land at Scarborough in late April. They quietly took possession of the castle. Stafford published a proclamation as "protector and governor of the English nation", claiming that Mary had forfeited her right to the throne by marrying a Spaniard. No local support appeared and he surrendered a few days later, to a small force, probably brought from Kirkby Moorside by the Earl of Westmoreland. Thirty-two prisoners were taken. Four were executed at York and the Frenchman was pardoned.

Queen Elizabeth faced problems with noble families of doubtful loyalty in Yorkshire from the start of her reign. Matthew Stuart, Earl of Lennox and Countess Margaret lived in Yorkshire from 1558 to December 1561 using Settrington, Whorlton castle and Temple Newsham. The earl was Catholic and third in line to the throne of Scotland. His wife Margaret Douglas was a niece of King Henry VIII, daughter of his sister Margaret, and thought of herself as a possible successor to Queen Elizabeth. Their son was Henry Lord Darnley. When the French king, husband of Mary Queen of Scots died, she considered her cousin Lord Darnley, only three years her junior, as a possible new husband. The Queen of Scots, Mary had a legitimate claim to the English throne which would pass to her descendants and would become effective if Queen Elizabeth did not marry.

Great ships were reported off the Yorkshire coast, on August 17th 1561. William Strickland wrote to the Lord President, the Earl of Rutland, about "two very great galleys", anchored a quarter of a mile off Flamborough pier. The largest ship had fifty oars on one side. Fifty-two more ships appeared. Each galley lowered two dowkers (swimmers) into the sea to test the depth of water. Robert Puckering was alarmed and set faggots on fire near Flamborough beacon. Two weeks later, Sir Richard Cholmley at Scarborough was told that Mr. Herynes, a fishmonger who took fish for the Queen, had sent his man on board a Flemish ship, anchored but going to Scotland. He had seen two fair gentlewomen in a handsome cabin, one laid on a cushion of gold. Mary was returning to Scotland.[15]

A group of Catholic nobility and gentry were in close touch with the Lennoxes. Margaret had lived at the Percy's Wressle castle. Their friends included Lord Westmoreland, Sir William Babthorpe, Sir Richard Cholmley, and Sir Richard Chamberlain, the keeper of Scarborough castle. Thomas Dolman of Pocklington, was their estate steward. Their house held three priests. Sir William Cecil, the Secretary of State, employed Thomas Bishop and a Lennox household servant to keep a close watch and report on the family.[16] The Earl of Lennox was imprisoned for a considerable time before eventual release, when he and his son returned to Scotland. Lord Darnley and the Scots Queen Mary married in 1565 and had a child. The countess was imprisoned in

England until 1567. During 1566 Lord Darnley was involved in the murder of a servant of Queen Mary, David Rizio. Darnley was himself killed the next year. Queen Mary remarried James, Earl of Bothwell but she was forced to flee to England on May 16th 1568. Bothwell fled to Denmark.

Mary was accommodated at Carlisle castle for two months in the custody of Lord Scrope, warden of the march and constable. Queen Elizabeth ordered her removal to Bolton castle in Wensleydale. Sir Francis Knollys was sent north to receive her. He wrote to Cecil on 27th May, of her meeting the Earl of Northumberland, Sir Nicholas Fairfax, his son Sir William and others "unsound in religion". Knollys rebuked the Earl for trying to take Mary into his custody and told Fairfax "that he would be taughte to attend upon Her Highnes' pleasure before he should attend upon the Queene of Skottes or upon my lord of Northumberland in such cases"

Mary stayed six or seven months in Bolton castle, in Wensleydale, waited on by forty servants, some of whom were housed in the village. "The Queen here is merry and hunteth and passeth her time in a pleasant manner" wrote Sir Francis Knollys. She wrote letters, and sewed embroidery, including a muslin apron with a floral pattern in coloured silks and a silk tapestry picture, and played Knollys and Scrope at chess. A court of inquiry was set up in October 1568 to investigate the charges made against Mary by the Scots, of complicity in Darnley's death. The Duke of Norfolk, the Earl of Sussex and Sir Ralph Sadler sat as Queen's commissioners. The court was ordered removed to London in November. Queen Mary was removed to Tutbury in January 1569. She remained a focus for conspiracies, but would later return to secure custody with the Earl of Shrewsbury at Sheffield.[17]

The Rising of the Northern Earls

The Earls of Westmoreland and Northumberland, with a small number of Yorkshire and Durham gentry led a rising in November 1569. The accounts of the rising are open to different interpretations. Some have argued that the State provoked the rising. Others debate the purposes and role of the main leaders, and how far they were influenced by real or imagined possibilities of overseas support.[18]

There had been the possibility of a rebellion in September, linked with a proposed marriage between the Duke of Norfolk and the Scots Queen, now exiled in England, a proposal on which the northern earls had been consulted. Some in the Privy council favoured Queen Elizabeth declaring Mary her heir to the throne. Queen Elizabeth's disapproval checked Norfolk, who wrote advising against rebellion. The Duke was sent to the Tower. Wild heads may have favoured rebellion but there are few signs that anyone was prepared for it.

Rumours of a likely rebellion persisted through October 1569. Lord Willoughby in Lincolnshire was told of people in arms in a rebellious manner about Kirkby Moorside. The northern council on October 1st warned a gathering of justices of the peace to keep good watch. Rumour claimed that the Lord President, the Earl of Sussex, would be seized in his house at Cawood. He summoned Westmorland and Northumberland from York but they vowed their loyalty and returned home. Sir William Ingleby was concerned enough to secure Knaresborough castle. The Privy Council wrote to Yorkshire gentry seeking to find the origins of the stories that were circulating.

The rumours died down in early November but Queen Elizabeth thought that the Earls should be in the tower. She told the Earl of Sussex to summon them to court. He called them to York on 4th November, meanwhile warning loyal gentry to be ready to seize York, Hull, Pontefract and Knaresborough, in the event of any show of force. Sir Henry Gate went to secure Scarborough castle. Sussex told the Lord Mayor of York to ask taverners, tipplers and innkeepers for news, tales and reports in the gossip of their houses. Northumberland on the 6th and Westmoreland at Brancepeth on the 7th sent their excuses. A second summons from the Lords President on the 9th brought a refusal whereupon Sussex ordered them to go to the Queen's Court.

The earls faced a stark choice. They must either submit and take their chances, flee the country or rebel. They were inadequately prepared, Northumberland was vacillating, Cumberland's position remained unclear and Westmoreland was less clear in his own mind than others of his family. These were difficult months to keep soldiery in the field. Sir Oswald Wilstroppe's troop of horse nearly caught Northumberland at Topcliff but he was able to ride off to Brancepeth, where he found Westmoreland, and some vigorous Catholic gentry, including the Nortons, Markenfeld, Tempest, Swinburne and Neville. The loyal Sir George Bowes at Streatlam on November 10th found that the rebel leaders were gathering forces, buying weapons and summoning distant retainers.

A royal proclamation was issued against them on the 13th. They caused mass to be said at Durham Cathedral that day and at Ripon a day or two later. They marched to Darlington on the 16th where they published their own proclamation. This claimed loyalty to the Queen, but spoke of evil counsellors about her, who had set up a new religion and would destroy the old nobility. They claimed that foreign powers would invade the land to restore the old religion, if action was not speedily taken. They summoned all between six and sixty to their side. The response was limited and came mostly from Durham, Richmondshire, Allertonshire, Birdforth and parts of Cleveland, along and near to the lines of march.

Rebels and loyalists lacked money and men. It was a commonplace that "Yorkshire never goes to war but for wages". Both sides sought to use the muster system. The rebel Earls called out musters at Richmond and Barnard castle "in the Queen's name". House burning was threatened at Leeming and Northallerton for those refusing. Sir Nicholas Fairfax entered Antony Catterick's house and took his two sons. Francis Norton raided John Sayer's house at Worsall for its armour. Crops were burnt at Danby Wiske. Christopher Neville rode for Kirkby Moorside to raise the earl's tenantry, and returned through Cleveland. The Earl of Sussex as Lord President warned the county justices to muster horse and foot. Sir Thomas Gargrave complained of lukewarm support with few horses coming in from some parts but good support from Protestant districts. He sent 200 to secure Hull and blocked the passage at Ferrybridge. Sussex sent for 800 from the East Riding.

The Lord President acted quickly to secure York, with good co-operation from the city. Mayor William Beckwith, the aldermen and councillors, from November 9th, inspected the bars, locked the posterns, and organised a night and day watch by trusty citizens. The Ainsty raised horsemen and 100 foot. Robert Stapleton was made captain of the city soldiers and John Ingleby commanded a levy of 1000 men. They were exercised, and arms and powder acquired. York was put in a state of defence. Within a fortnight walls and bars were repaired, and postern gates walled up. Ladders were ordered to be impounded from outside the walls, boats drawn into the city and guns over hauled. Landing places were fortified. By the 21st November, York was ready for a siege. Up to 3000 county levies were billeted in the city. Three hundred from Bulmer wapentake were quartered in Bootham, 100 under Lord Eure in Walmgate. On the 27th loans were ordered to be raised in York to pay the army.

Sir George Bowes had held Barnard castle for the Queen, and may have delayed movement south by the rebels. Two hundred horse reached Tadcaster capturing Mr. Tempest and 150 loyalists at Tadcaster. Larger forces reached Ripon on the 18th and Borough bridge on the 20th November, where a council was held in the manor house. By the 22nd they were at Clifton and Bramham moors. Various numbers were claimed for the Earl's, between 2000 and 4000 foot and 1200 - 1600 horse. The smaller numbers may well be the more accurate. They had passed through Richmond, Ripon, Knaresborough, Topcliffe and Wetherby. Outliers pressed towards Leeds but Gargrave closed the bridges at Ferrybridge, Castleford, Swillington and Leeds. Rebel patrols seem to have reached Cawood, Sherburn, Tadcaster and Selby by the 20th to 24th. The stop at Wetherby was over generously recorded in the ballad

> "At Wetherbie they mustered their host
> Thirteen thousand fair to see".

Sir Thomas Gargrave at Pontefract on the 25th thought the Earls had planned to seize Pontefract Castle, Wakefield and Doncaster to Winter. Westmoreland wanted to attack York west of the Ouse. Rumour said York had 5.000 defenders. Thomas Bishop warned "If you get repulsed, having no ordnance, it will discomfort your people. If you win that part it shall be with great loss of men". Had they taken York west of the Ouse, they would not have taken the city, merely some streets of it. Thomas Wentworth on the 28th said that "the rebels have bene lying between York and Tadcaster for a week or upwards. A great company of gents and soldiers are with the Lord President at York. Lord Darcy is at Doncaster, but needing armour and weapons. The country is sorely charged in making sundry kinds of musters and organised robberies under that name." The two Earls had already returned to Boroughbridge. Some expected them to divert their force into Galtres Forest, to attack York on the east side of the Ouse.

Sir William Cecil had been mustering a southern army of 14.000 men since the 19th. The Queen ordered the Earl of Derby to raise Lancashire and Cheshire. The Earl of Shrewsbury raised Nottinghamshire and Derbyshire. The Lord Admiral Clinton and the Earl of Warwick mustered Lincolnshire, Warwickshire and Leicestershire. Sir Edward Carey mustered the stewardship of Wakefield. Ordnance and munitions were moved northwards from the Tower of London. Receivers collected £2000 for Lord Darcy and Gargrave to take to York. Clinton reached Doncaster on December 12th. Christopher Neville and 300 rebels had secured Hartlepool, opening a port through which succour might come. Vessels were posted off the coast against any move from Flanders.

The two Earls were proclaimed traitors on 26th November at Windsor. On the 28th the Earl of Sussex as Lord President issued a proclamation claiming that the Earls only aim was to bring the realm into subjection to the foreign power of Spain. Some rebels forces went north, to besiege Barnard Castle, which, held by Sir George Bowes, saw the only serious fighting, in a siege which lasted eleven days before surrender. Sussex on December 7th wanted Clinton to march to relieve Barnard castle but his force was making slow progress on bad roads. On the 13th Clinton and Warwick reached Wetherby and Sussex marched to join them at Borough bridge.

Simon Musgrave, the Sheriff of Northumberland, came in to Northallerton with 400 horse on the 14th. With Warwick and the Lord Admiral at his back, there was talk of not refusing "if the rebels offer the fight". Clinton's army marched to Boroughbridge on the 15th and Ripon on the 17th. There was news the next day that the rebels had dispersed, the leaders towards Scotland. The army was at Darlington on the 19th. Sir Henry Gate led 300 men to recover Hartlepool. When they reached Durham there was only £1500 ready, not enough to pay the army if they were disbanded.

Harsh action was taken against the rebels and against areas which had responded to their appeals. Essex had long thought that the rebellion would provide the opportunity to "purge this country and other parts of the realm of the ill affected". The Crown accepted ransoms from the better off seeking to escape punishment in order to meet the considerable costs of the army. The Queen herself pressed for executions under martial law of the meaner rebels, with examples made at Ripon, Topcliffe, Wetherby and Tadcaster. Most of the affected villages saw a single execution. A number of petty constables were killed. Warwick's soldiers did much damage in Yorkshire and Lords Hunsdon, Sussex, and Scrope made punitive raids on villages each side of the Scots border.

> Full many a gallant wight
> they cruelly bereav'd of life
> and many a child made fatherless
> and widowed many a tender wife"

Discharging the army was urgent in view of the cost. Lancashire and Cheshire men were discharged on the 22nd, more two days later. Warwick and Clinton at Boroughbridge discharged six thousand on one day, and seven thousand more the next day, borrowing money to pay them off but they had to await the arrival of treasure to discharge the rest, which arrived on January 1st. On the 6th at Wetherby all were discharged but 1500. A cluster of prominent rebels were executed at York and a handful of estates changed hands. Westmoreland fled to Flanders, Northumberland was bought from the Scots for £2000 and executed.

Home Defence

Elizabethan England had kept no professional army, apart from palace bodygards and some small fortress garrisons. The revenues of the Crown were insufficient to pay for a regular army. Military forces were raised in several ways, when needed. The Crown had earlier relied on the feudal levies supplied by land owners who embodied their servants and tenantry. This system was replaced by selective contracts. Crown commissions were sent to picked land owners who enrolled people from their districts. An indenture or contract was drawn up to transport and accommodate them.

Most who served abroad were untrained volunteers, some free men, including gentlemen, or men drawn from the unemployed. Rogues were often taken up. Vagrants, the poor, the idle and criminals were enrolled. Pardons had been given in 1542 to sanctuary men dwelling in the liberties of Ripon and Beverley, so that they could be assigned for defence against the Scots. The military units were troops of horse and companies of foot. A troop of horse, fifty strong had a captain and an ensign. A company of foot with a hundred to a hundred and fifty men, had a captain, lieutenant and ensign.

Home defence was the responsibility of the county militia, a separate force mustered by wapentakes for service within the county, but beyond if there was an invasion.

Legislation of Phillip and Mary had enforced a liability on property owners and townships to provide horses and arms in proportion to their property. The Crown named a Lord Lieutenant for the county or for the north. He was charged to array and train the bands of men raised in his district and to command them. His commission allowed him to call up the men of his county, try them out, arm each according to capability and within the county "to repress, subdue, slay, kill and put to execution of death these enemies by all ways and means".

He appointed muster masters, and a provost marshall to administer martial law in case of rebellion or invasion. He had at his disposal the services of all justices of the peace, sheriffs and constables. He kept muster rolls and lists of arms. The Crown picked well affected landowners as deputy lieutenants who could array and train the levies, within the wapentakes. The Earl of Shrewsbury was given the Lieutenancy of Yorkshire and three other counties in 1565. The Earl of Huntingdon was Lord Lieutenant 1586-1595 followed by Thomas Cecil Lord Burghley.

The system of musters in peacetime was based on Mary Tudor's "Act for the taking of musters" of 1556-7, passed when a French invasion was feared. All able bodied men from sixteen to sixty were liable for military service within their county, and were obliged to equip themselves with arms according to their place in one of ten income groups. Coat and conduct money were provided, each man receiving a coat worth 3s.4d, eight pence a day and a halfpenny a mile, from the assembly point of the wapentake to the destination. There were heavy penalties for absentees, and those seeking exemption by bribes.

Property owners were liable to provide horses and arms. A man rated at £10 had to provide one bow and a harquebus. The duty to provide the weapons also meant finding the man to bear them. A man with £1000 or more in land had to provide six heavy horsemen (demi lances), ten light horses with equipment, forty corselets, 'almayne rivetts' and pikes, thirty longbows, sheafs of arrows and iron caps, twenty bills and twenty harquebuses and lorions. Townships also had to provide weapons, as agreed with the commissioners to equip the able bodied men too poor to be charged individually. These were kept by the constable. The cost of weapons and body armour fell on the individual or the townships but not the cost of powder and match.

The shire forces met once or twice a year, before hay harvest and after, usually on holidays and received 8d a day from the county. The able bodied men were listed with their weapons and body armour, both archers and billmen. The deputy lieutenants checked that weapons were in good order, that stocks of powder and match were complete and useable, and that carts picks, mattocks and shovels were ready. Most places had more men than equipment. From 1573 there was more stress on training selected men in the use of firearms. They were mustered separately, as trained bands, because access to firearms was limited. Light horsemen were also separately mustered. The Privy Council asked Lord Hastings in 1586 as Lord Lieutenant of the county to have 6000 footmen raised, enrolled and made ready, 2000 with calivers, 2000 pikemen, with corselettes, 1000 billmen and 1000 bowmen.

T12 Notes from the Constable's accounts at Stokesley May 25 - July 21, 1588. [19]

Journeys	to Stoxlay 4d; Gisbrughe 8d; Stoxlay & Allerton 20d; Constable for going once to Runckton, twice to Pottoe, twice to Swainbee, twice to Scarth wood 6d

24

Musters	Five to Barnebee moor 3s.9d
Guns	oyling a callever 1d; a lether to hing the flask in 2d; (powder flask); Wm Thomas for stocking the gun 2s.6d; James Sanders for mending the gun and nails wanting 10d; To Ric Ward for mending the gun 2d; Mowldes 6d (for casting bullets);To Ric Ward for the gun 2d,. carrying it 1d. Poyntes 3d (?possibly prickers for touch hole)
Instruction	trayning money 10s;
Weapons	sheaf of arrowes 2s6d, One dagger 18d; Armorer of Stoxley 20d; A dagger 16d; widow Richardson for a sword 2s; Wm Wetherell for a dagger 14d; Setting a cheap on a dagger 1d.
Warnings	repairing the beacon 2s.10d
Armour	cote of plate 14s; Wm Hewthwaite for a Sallett 2s (light helmet) & for a sword 2s; Armorer of Stoxlay 3s; One yard of harden 6d (for caps) (coarse linen). Two swerd girdels 12d; At plate cote burning 1d (burnishing) Leather for the archers jerkings 6s10d; One braser 2d. (arm guard for coat against bowstring). For making the cote of plate 3s.8d; Canvasse, thred, wax and rosell 4s; Covering the skull agane 9d;

The Warning system

The only means of giving early warning of an external military threat was by ship from some foreign informant, or a message sent by horsed messenger from the Council. The Yorkshire coastal beacons were lit when the enemy was already here and in sight. They served to inform the inland areas via a network of other beacons, which passed the message one to another. Erection of beacons was a royal prerogative vested in the Lord High Admiral or in the High Sheriff. They were erected in groups of three.

The brandreth or cresset was an iron basket to hold the fire. The beacon consisted of one pole with timber stays and a ladder or spokes to climb. Those in the East Riding in 1588 required a tar barrel to make dense smoke and might have one, two or three cressets. Rudstone beacon in 1573 was maintained by eight nearby townships. Thorpe and Carthorpe were to find the standers, Langtoft and Cottam the stakes, Burton Agnes the pins and whinns, Kilham the barrels and brandreths. Thornholme and Haisthorpe had to fire it and to keep it burning

T13 Beacons in the East Riding, (from south to north)

Holderness	Aldbrough 3; Dimlington 3; Barmston 3; Kilnsey 3; Withernsea 3; Waxholme 3; Grimstone 3; Welwick 1; Patrington 1; Mappleton 3; Hornsey 3; Skipsea
Dickering	Flamborough 3; Bridlington 3; Fraisthorpe 1(Beacon hill); Auburn 3; Reighton; Speeton 3; Rudstone 2 (Howe); Ruston 1; Muston 3 (Beacon Hill); Staxton 1 (Beacon Hill); Cowlam 1 (Kemp Howe); Wold Newton
Harthill	Bainton 2; Wilton 1; Holme 1; Hunsley 2; Bowerhouse Hill 1; Paule 1; Marfleet 1
Buckrose	Settrington 1 (Howe); Coleham 1
Bulmer	Whitwell

T14 Beacons in the North Riding.

Whitby Strand   Fying 3; Whitby 1; Sneaton 1; Suffield 1
Langbaurgh   Barmby 2; Hinderwell 2; Easington 2; Danby 1; Brotton 1 (Warsett hill); Rosebery, 1; Brampton; Marske 2 (sea bank & Burdley moor hill); Kirkleatham 1; Eston Nabb 1; Arncliff 1
Birdforth   Osmotherley 1; Somecliff 1(Birdforth or Husthwaite)
Ryedale   Ampleforth 1
Pickering Lythe   Pickering 1; Seamer 2; Wapnesse 1; Scarborough 3
Allertonhire   Bullamoor
Richmondshire   Onehill
Staincliff   Shardo (Gargrave)
Yewcross   Engeburgh
Claro   Fainesbergh [20]

Fresh orders were issued in 1588. The beacons were to be guarded by watchmen of judgment and discretion, two in the day and three in the night. Other honest householders were to keep watch for ships at sea or in the Humber, "suspicious by stay or altering course". The watchmen with the advice of the wisest were to set fire to one, if they saw a great number, then two, on shore and one inland. If an enemy was apparently invading, all three could be lit on the coast and two inland. Men were to resort to the first beacon lit. No bells were normally to be rung in church but upon the alarm being received all the bells were to be rung out.

T15 West Riding Muster Captains and Men, July 1602 [21]

The names ofthe Captains appointed by the L. Lieutenant for this county of Yorks with the numbers of men committed to them and the several places of their charge.

West Riding	Trained soldiers	
Michael Darry	300	Straford & Tickhill
Sr Thomas Fairfax	300.	Skyrack 200 Claro 100
Sir George Saville	200	Barkstone Ash
Sir John Saville	200	Agbrigg & Morley
Henry Goodricke	150	Claro
William, Ingilby	150	Claro
Robert Keye	100	Osgoldcross & Staincrosse
Hastings Stanley	100	Osgoldcross & Staincross
Richard Tempest	150	Staincliffe & Ewecross
Edmond Elltofte	150	""
John Talbot	100	""
Sir Henry Slingisby	200	York City & Ainsty
William Hildyard	100	""
	Total 2400	

West Riding	Private Soldiers	
Sir Thos Reresby	200	Strafforth & Tickhill
William Wentworth	150	" 100, Skyrack 50
Robert Swyfte	150.	Skyrack
Richard Gargrave	150.	Agbrigg & Morley
Ferdinando Fairfax	150	"

Thomas Wentworth	150	" 100 Staincross 50
Richard Wortley	150	Osgoldcross Staincross
Edward Stanhope	200	Barkston Ash
Maw Vavasor	150	Claro
John Mallory	200	Claro
John Yorke	150	Claro 50 Staincliff & Ewecross 100
Laurence Lyster	150	"
Stephen Procter	150	"
William Sunley	100	York City & Ainsty
John Bruffield	100	""
Lawrence Waad.	100	""
	Total 2400	

CHAPTER 2
HIGH SOCIETY AND LOW

Status or Degree

People lived in small communities. Even the towns were not large but the intimacy of community life was checked and channelled by recognised differences of wealth, income and status. Degree or status was expressed in many ways, including patronage and deference. Taken together, the whole society could seem like a pyramid of social distinctions, and in a way it was. Some spoke of four broad categories. There were the gentlemen, comprising titled nobles, knights, esquires and gentlemen by race, blood or virtue. There were the townsmen, free and often in different occupations. There were country yeomen who were free holders of land but there were other tenant farmers, on some scale and with similar status. The fourth group encompassed everyone else, day labourers, servants, town artificers, and poor husbandmen, "who had neither voice nor authority". There were more subtle groupings than that.

A stranger thought Yorkshire social differences less obvious than those elsewhere. James Ryther said of Yorkshire that "the common people of this country are by nature content and tractable, using more reverence and regard to strangers that pass among them, than those that live nearer the court. It is hard to know a serving man from a gentleman and a gentleman from a nobleman by apparel or outward appearance."[1] The differences were there, all the same. The strong social distinctions of the age were most clearly indicated in titles. There was rarely much uncertainty at the higher levels. You were called a gentleman or you were not. Local records made more of such terms of respect as mister, mistress, maister and dame.

The status differences that mattered most were those that governed behaviour within the community where you lived. Yeomen were separate from husbandmen, who held tenanted land, and both from grassmen and cottagers. Servants in husbandry were taken on for the year and had that security, while labourers came and went, taken on for a season or a task. Undersettles, paupers, vagabonds, and rascals completed the rural communities and those who moved outside them. The towns had merchants, aldermen, burgesses, freemen, artificers, journeymen, and apprentices, but many were known from their craft or occupation. The social classes were not castes and there was some mobility between the ranks, particularly those rising into the class of gentlemen. There were even legends of rags to riches, among them Thomas Ferris, the Glaisdale orphan who became Mayor of Hull.

A gentle man might receive deference but he knew his place and gave deference to those further up in the system. A gentleman, Mr. Hunter leased a Thornton Dale manor house from Lord Latimer. At his death, he left an ambling nag to the peer's daughter. Another gentleman Roger Dalton of Kirkby Misperton left the Earl of Huntingdon his Irish hobby horse worth ten pounds and bequeathed an Irish goshawk to Lord Eure. Some differences of status were enforced by law, especially if they were publicly

6. Elizabethan Noblemen and their Wives

challenged. John Ward of Bransdale would be charged for   making "contumelious speeches against Sir John Gibson." A woman at Crathorne would appear before the courts, not because in 1574 she complained of Rector John Scarth's dung heap in front of the Rectory House. The trouble was that, when he refused to appear, she opened his door and called him "nought but a kirtle prest that durst not come but sat still in the house." He sued her for defamation of character.

The Nobility

The noblemen and their families were at the peak of the pyramid of social rank. Their titles were treated as something more than honours. The dukes, earls, marquises and barons, were said to have "noble blood". This made their titles inalienable. The core of this high status group was the barony. The nation boasted only one duke. This was Thomas Howard, fourth Duke of Norfolk. The earls, viscounts, and the rare marquises were barons, with the addition of a second name dignity. Each commonly held a string of other titles, from their baronies. Henry Earl of Huntington was, Lord Hastings, Lord

Hungerford, Lord Bottreaux, Lord Molin and Lord Moyle. The Earl of Shrewsbury, usually given as "Salop", was Lord Talbot, Lord Furnival, Lord Verdon and Lord Strange. The title "Lord" was derived from the barony. The Privy Council sent letters to the Lord Keeper, the Lord Treasurer, one Marquis, eighteen Earls, two Viscounts and thirty-one Barons in August 1599.[2]

Yorkshire entered the reign with six earls who had a principal seat in the county. Such families commonly had several major houses with estates in more than one shire. When not required by the head of the family, the other houses were usually occupied by relations or stewards. The Clifford, Earls of Cumberland, the Manners, Earls of Rutland, the Neville, Earls of Westmoreland, the Percy, Earls of Northumberland, the Stuart, Earls of Lennox and the Talbot. Earls of Shrewsbury had significant Yorkshire houses and estates. The Howard, Earls of Surrey, and the Stanley, Earls of Derby had more modest estates, as did William Parr, the Marquis of Northampton.

The Earls of Cumberland held Skipton Castle and Londesborough, where a new house was built for Francis Clifford from 1589. The Earls of Rutland had their principal home at Belvoir, in Lincolnshire, converted from a castle to a house by the first Earl, but he quartered relations at Helmsley castle. The Earls of Northumberland held Topcliffe, Spofforth, and Wressle castles, with a house at Leckonfield, where Thomas Percy lived for twelve years. He had estates in five other northern counties. The Earls of Shrewsbury occupied Sheffield manor. Matthew Stuart, Earl of Lennox used Whorlton Castle and houses at Temple Newsham and at Settrington. The Earls of Westmoreland used Kirkby Moorside castle. The widow of the fifth Earl enjoyed her dower there, and her under age son lived there with his Uncle Christopher. Near the end of the reign, Thomas Cecil Lord Burghley settled at Snape castle. He would later become Earl of Exeter. Edmund Lord Sheffield settled at Mulgrave castle. He was made Marquis of Normanby in 1603.

The barons were marginally lower in status than the earls, but shared their pre-occupations and roles. The oldest son of an earl was known as a baron before succeeding to the earldom. The title "Lord" was commonly used of both. Barons with Yorkshire residences during the reign of Elizabeth included Lord Carey, Lord Conyers at Skelton, Lord Dacre at Hinderskelfe, Lord Darcy, Lord Eure at Ingleby Greenhowe and Malton, Lord Latimer at Snape castle and at Danby castle, Lord Scrope at Bolton castle and Lord Wharton at Healaugh Priory. Robert Carey took the title of Baron Leppington but evidence has yet to be found that he ever resided at that East Riding village. Several other barons entered into the history of the county. The members of some sixty noble families, often kin to each other, met at their homes, at court and in the Parliament.

The great noblemen drew more significance from their landed estates, their wealth, their high offices, their regional reputations and from Crown recognition, rather than from any fictions about blood. Lord Burghley's 1588 list of candidates for the peerage started with "knights of great possessions". The nobility exercised patronage and influence through their kin, their servants, their marriages, their connections, as landlords, and as the traditional leaders of society in peace and war. The Earl of Shrewsbury even took a feudal "aid" from his manorial tenants on the marriage of his eldest daughter Katherine. The custom looked back to a vanished past, but it brought a substantial sum, reluctantly paid.

The noblemen accepted important offices under the Crown. Their ancient power was modified rather than replaced by their involvement in the government of the north, through membership of the Queen's Privy Council, but more often and more directly in the vice-regal Queen's Council in the North. The most powerful northern office was that of Lord President of the Council in the North. This was a royal appointment, which brought another nobleman, Henry Hastings, Earl of Huntingdon into Yorkshire residence and virtual rule for almost half of the reign. The office gave use of Pontefract Castle, Sheriff Hutton Castle and the King's Manor at York. The earls and the major barons, the Archbishops of York and the Bishops of Durham were considered suitable candidates for the presidency. The Lords President during the reign were Francis Talbot, Earl of Shrewsbury, Henry Manners, Earl of Rutland, Thomas Young, Archbishop of York, Henry Hastings, Earl of Huntingdon, Thomas Cecil, Lord Burghley, and Edmund, Lord Sheffield. Other Earls and Barons were summoned to attend the council.

The appointment of noblemen to crown offices, reinforced their authority and their powers of patronage, while seeking to bind their loyalty to the crown. Some posts were sinecures, but most brought good fees, prestige and opportunities for profit. Francis Earl of Shrewsbury was Justice of the Forests, north of Trent, and keeper of the royal castles in Yorkshire and Nottinghamshire. Henry 2nd. Earl of Cumberland was constable and steward of Knaresborough and steward of Ripon. Henry Earl of Rutland was steward of Wakefield and Sandal, and from 1570 held the offices of constable of Nottingham castle, steward, warden, keeper and Chief Justice of Sherwood Forest, feodary of the Duchy of Lancaster in two counties and Lord Lieutenant of Nottinghamshire.

The reign was long enough for more than one member to enjoy the position of head of each of these noble families. The earldoms and baronies normally passed to the eldest son. The first marriage of these boys was arranged with the parents, or custodians of the wardship of daughters of other noble families. When second marriages occurred, they commonly drew more widely, on widows from the knightly class. The weakness of the hereditary system was sometimes manifest. It could produce both able custodians of family and fortune but occasionally those who, when presented with the trappings of power, wealth and great income, lacked the character to exercise the role wisely.

T16 Yorkshire Nobility of the Elizabethan Age

	Countess
Clifford, Earl of Cumberland	
-Henry, 2nd. Earl (1542-1581)	Ann Dacre
-George, 3rd Earl (1581-1605)	Margaret dtr of Earl of Bedford
Manners, Earl of Rutland	
Henry, 2nd Earl (1543-1563)	Margaret, dtr of Earl of Westmoreland
	Bridget, dtr of Lord John Hussey,
Edward, 3rd Earl (1563-1587)	Isabel, dtr of Sir Thomas Holcroft
John, 4th Earl (1587-88)	
Roger, 5th Earl (1588-1612)	Elizabeth dtr of Sir Phillip Sydney
Neville, Earl of Westmoreland	
Henry, 5th Earl (1550-1563)	Jane Manners, dtr of Thomas Earl of Rutland
	Jane, dtr of Sir Roger Cholmeley
	Margaret, dtr of Sir Roger Cholmley
Charles, 6th Earl (1563-1601)	Joane, dtr of Henry, Earl of Surrey

Percy. Earl of Northumberland	
Thomas, 7th Earl (1557-72)	Anne, dtr of Henry Earl of Worcester
Henry, 8th Earl (1572-85)	Catherine, dtr of John, Lord Latimer
Henry, 9th Earl (1585-1632)	Dorothy, dtr of Walter, Earl of Essex

Stuart, Earl of Lennox	
Matthew, 4th earl (-d1571)	Margaret Douglas, dtr of Archibald, Earl of Angus

Talbot, Earl of Shrewsbury	
Francis, 5th Earl (1538-1560)	Mary, dtr of Thomas, Lord Dacre of Gilsland
	Grace, dtr of Robert Shakeley
George, 6th Earl (1560-1590)	Gertrude, dtr of Thomas, Earl of Rutland
	Elizabeth, dtr of John Hardwick
Gilbert, 7th Earl (1590-1616)	Mary, dtr of Sir William Cavendish

Six Northern Earls[3]

The Earls of Shrewsbury

The Talbot estate reached its greatest extent under Francis 5th Earl of Shrewsbury (c1500-1560). Although centred on Sheffield, there were properties in seven counties, including the newly acquired Rufford abbey, and Worksop Priory estates. The Earl had lead and iron interests in Derbyshire, Herefordshire and Yorkshire. He served four monarchs, Henry VIII, Edward VI, Mary and Elizabeth, often commanding on the Scot's border, as in 1557-8, when his son led five hundred horse. Shrewsbury was Lord President of the North through the reigns of Edward VI and Mary He disapproved of the Elizabethan Act of Supremacy and the new church service books and retired to Sheffield, where he died two years later. His son George became the 6th Earl.

George Talbot was made Lord Lieutenant in the counties of Yorkshire, Nottinghamshire, Derby and Staffordshire in 1565. He was a privy councillor and a friend of Queen Elizabeth, who wrote to him about her smallpox in 1572. He was spoken of as "the greatest subject in the kingdom". His second marriage in 1568 was to the strong-minded Bess of Hardwick. The Scots Queen was committed to his care with £2000 a year for her maintenance, because he had "a spirit neither to be overawed or corrupted". She stayed sixteen years. His spending as her custodian depleted his fortune and his marriage to Bess of Hardwick depleted his spirit. The marriage collapsed in 1583.

The Earl made arrangements to provide estates for his younger sons and dowries for his daughters, alienating the Rufford estate with daughter Mary to Sir George Saville. The Queen made him Earl Marshall after the Duke of Norfolk's attainder. He returned from London to live at the manor in Sheffield Park in 1585, where four years later the Queen wrote to him affectionately as her "very good old man". He was full of gout and in a doting condition, supposedly under the influence of a servant Eleanor Britten. Arthur Mower wrote in his diary of the earl's funeral in November 1591. "The assembly to see was marvellous both of nobility, gentry and country folks and poor folks without number."

Gilbert Talbot gained the Earldom but quarrelled with both relations and neighbours. He wrote to his brother Edward in 1594 calling him a liar and a forger and challenged him to a duel with rapiers and daggers. He thought that his physician was "a most palpable Machiavellian", who sought his death with poisoned gloves. The queen tried to persuade him to ease the plight of his tenants.

The Earl of Lennox

Matthew Stuart, 4th Earl of Lennox was a friend of King Henry VIII. He was banished from Scotland, and his Scots estates were confiscated. From 1543 to 1564, he lived in England where the King gave him his niece Margaret in marriage, a pension and a grant of Yorkshire estates, taken from such Pilgrimage of Grace dissidents as the Percys at Hunmanby, Sir Francis Bigod at Settrington and Lord Darcy at Temple Newsham. The Countess was an ardent Catholic. Their son Henry Lord Darnley was born at Temple Newsham. The Queen allowed the Earl to return to Scotland where Darnley joined him. When the Queen ordered them back, they refused and their estates were confiscated. When Lord Darnley married his cousin Mary Queen of Scots in 1565, Queen Elizabeth put his mother and brother in the Tower. Darnley was murdered in 1567. The Earl was shot in 1571 and the dowager Countess was buried at Westminster abbey in 1578.

The Earls of Cumberland

Henry Clifford the 2nd Earl of Cumberland held Skipton castle, as well as the ruined New Malton and Brompton castles. He had many books and studied alchemy. His son and heir George Clifford was the 3rd Earl and the thirteenth lord of the honour of Skipton. He was Sheriff of Westmoreland by inheritance. George was raised at Battle Abbey, and saw some education at both Oxford and Cambridge. The Earl of Bedford held his wardship and married him to his daughter Margaret Russell in 1577. The third Earl was prominent at court, and as an expert jouster, served as the Queen's champion. He sat in the northern court in judgement on Mary Queen of Scots. He commanded a ship in action against the Spanish Armada and made several sea voyages, some at his own expense, attacking Spanish settlements. George Clifford was the first governor of the East India Company. He sold his Malton area interests to Lord Eure in 1599.

The Earls of Rutland

Thomas Manners, Lord Roos of Helmsley, was raised to the Earldom of Rutland in 1525 and rebuilt Belvoir as his principal seat. His son Henry Manners was the 2nd Earl from 1543 to 1563. His Yorkshire estate centred on Helmsley Castle, long a home of the Roos family, to which was added the Rievaulx Abbey estates including Bilsdale, the Kirkham Priory manors of Helmsley and Bilsdale, and Warter and Nunburnholme Priory lands in the East Riding. Henry was a marcher warden in 1549 and a general of horse in the French war of 1557. He favoured religious reform and had a reputation for learning. Henry was Lord President of the Council in the North, and an Ecclesiastical Commissioner from 1561 to 1563, when he died, possibly from the plague.

His son Edward Manners was the 3rd Earl, initially as a boy ward of Sir William Cecil, who wrote him instructions for his French tour. Edward held a command under the Earl of Sussex in the suppression of the northern rebellion. He was put on the northern Ecclesiastical Commission and in 1579 on the Council in the North. Edward rebuilt the western domestic wing which made Helmsley Castle into an Elizabethan residence. His only child, Elizabeth Baroness Ross married William Cecil, Lord Burleigh. Edward's brother John was briefly Earl in 1587-8 and John's son Roger became the 5th Earl. Cecil again advised the nephew in 1595, for his visits to Paris, Switzerland, and Italy. He spent some time at Grays Inn. He was a Colonel of foot in Lord Essex's Irish expedition in 1599 and he served against the Dutch.

The Earls of Westmoreland

The Nevilles of Staindrop & Raby in County Durham held the Castle and Manor of Kirkbymoorside and tenanted some Crown interests in the Pickering area, including Blansby Park. Henry Neville, 5th Earl of Westmoreland had grants of both the Keldholme and Rosedale Priory estates. He supported Queen Mary in 1552 and was a commander of horse in the northern army in 1557. The next year, he was made Lieutenant General of the North. He irritated Queen Elizabeth when he remarried a Catholic, apparently in some secrecy. She ordered proceedings against him in 1561 for keeping the sister of his former wife as his wife. The Archbishop saw him and reported him "strangely in love with his pretended wife". After his death, his widow had her dower at Kirkby Moorside, where her son lived under age and under the influence of his Uncle Christopher.

The elder son Charles Neville, 6th earl of Westmoreland, was probably raised mainly at Raby castle in Durham. He joined the Council in the North in 1569. He was a Catholic. There were rumours that he was moving towards rebellion and he was required to meet the Earl of Sussex at York but demurred. His uncle Christopher and 114 other rebels rose at Kirkby Moorside in 1569. Charles joined the rebellion and was attainted in 1571. After fleeing to Roxburghshire and then the Netherlands, with a dozen or so servants, he died an exile at Nieuport in 1601. The Countess stayed in England, pensioned with £300 a year by the Queen.

The Earls of Northumberland

The great Percy family had lost ground in the early 16th century. Henry Percy, the 6th Earl was obliged to abandon his love for Anne Boleyn and retire north. He arrested Cardinal Wolsey at Cawood for King Henry VIII. His brothers Sir Thomas and Sir Ingram Percy were executed for involvement in the Pilgrimage of Grace in 1536. Henry died without children and made his estate over to the Crown. Both the Earldom and his baronies were briefly extinguished. Queen Mary raised his nephew Thomas, son of Sir Thomas Percy as Baron Percy and 7th Earl of Northumberland. She restored some of the Percy estates still in Crown hands but he did not regain Seamer, Nafferton and Hunmanby.

At the accession of Elizabeth, Thomas was made Warden of the Scots Marches. He lived at Leckonfield and elsewhere in Yorkshire in the next decade. He was a professed Catholic and was heavily involved in the Rising of the North in 1569, after which he fled to Scotland. He was betrayed and executed at York in August 1572, avowing the supremacy of the Pope and saying that those obeying the Queen were no better than heretics. The title had been entailed to his brother Henry, the 8th Earl, also a Catholic, who was required to live in the south of England. He was suspected in 1585 of conspiracy in favour of Mary. He was put in the Tower and died in mysterious circumstances in June 1585.

Thomas's son became heir to his uncle at the age of eight, having been taught by a Church of England parson. Henry Percy, the 9th earl was known as the "wizard" due to his enthusiasm for science. He made the grand tour in 1581, succeeded at twenty-one to estates in eight counties, but was at loggerheads with his mother, heiress of the Nevilles, who remarried her steward Francis Fitton. The young earl gained close acquaintance with hawks, hounds, horses, dice, cards, fine apparel and mistresses but later encouraged scholars including the mathematician Thomas Harriot. The 9th Earl didn't visit the north after his uncle's execution. Petworth in Sussex became the main residence and Syon House in Middlesex was acquired in 1594. Henry married the widow Dorothy Devereux, sister of the Earl of Essex in 1594, but they were parted by 1599.

Some Yorkshire Barons

Lords Eure[4]

The barons Eure had long been active on the border with Scotland. William 1st Baron Eure of Witton in County Durham died in 1548-9, but his father Ralph survived him at Ayton Castle near Scarborough and was buried in Hutton Bushell church in 1551. William, the 2nd baron, was grandson of the first. He was contracted to marry Marjory daughter of George Lord Darcy, when he was eleven and she was four. This was set aside by decree in 1554 and he married Margaret daughter of Sir Edward Dymock of Lincolnshire.

Lord Eure was warden of the Middle March against Scotland under Edward VI, Mary and Elizabeth. As Captain of Berwick from 1558, he rebuilt its fortifications. He had a great double courtyard house at Ingleby Arncliffe in Cleveland and a house in York. He commanded a force at the city during the rising of the northern earls. He became Vice-President of the Council in the North. His wife was buried at Ingleby in 1591 as was he in 1594. He had a house at Malton by 1569. Robert Butler, buried in old Malton church in 1580 left property to "The Right Honourable my lord and master the Lord William Ewrie."

Ralph 3rd Lord Eure, was born at Berwick castle, attended St John's College, Cambridge and Grays Inn. When he married Mary, elder daughter of Sir John Dawnay of Sessay in 1578, Dawnay agreed to pay the father Lord William a £2000 dowry, in instalments of £400 over the first five years of the marriage. Ralph journeyed in France, Germany and Italy during 1582-83, corresponding with Sir Francis Walsingham for advice and giving accounts of his travels. He wrote to his father in law, complaining of his wife's unthriftiness during his absence. He was M.P. for Yorkshire in 1584.

Ralph Eure succeeded his father in 1593. He was made Lord Warden of the Middle March in 1595 and urged the Queen to appoint Yorkshire gentry to pacify the borders, where locals were obliged to tryst with outlaws. His enemies claimed he made unreasonable exactions. He sought relief from the duties in 1596. Lord Ralph is said to have removed lead, timber, fireplaces, glass and furniture from Ayton castle to Malton after succeeding to the estate. Five years later, he offered £675 to George Earl of Cumberland for his half of the manors of Welham and Sutton and his third of the castle and manor of New Malton. A rain head at the new house was dated 1602.

Lord Eure raised North Riding men to serve in Ireland in 1599. His wife was visited at Malton for two hours by Lady Hoby in her coach in September that year returning to Hackness via Rillington and Seamer. Lord and Lady Eure returned the visit He sailed from Margate on December 10th 1602, to take up an appointment as the Queen's ambassador at Bremen to the King of Denmark, the Emperor Rudolph and the Princes of the Holy Roman Empire. This was despite his claim that through lack of practice he had lost his command of foreign languages. The Queen said that an English nobleman who travelled in France and Italy was fit to meet the best of Germans. He was there when the Queen died.

Lords Latimer[5]

The third Baron Latimer used Snape and Danby castles, and halls at Sinnington and Thornton Dale. He once bought a gelding at Danby, and he left money to Glaisdale chapel. Leland said that at Sinnington, "Lord Latimer hath a fair manor place" and he sent a gelding from that village to Thomas Cromwell in 1534. He married Catherine daughter of Sir Thomas Parr of Kendall as his second wife and villagers would later claim that Catherine Parr once walked the village green. His son John was with King Henry VIII in France with one hundred foot in 1544, and served in Scotland in 1545.

John Neville, the fourth Baron was a seriously flawed personality. He was much at London where he was accused of assault and murder. After marrying Lucy, the Earl of Worcester's daughter in 1540, child births interspersed with lengthening separations filled the years till 1553, after which, fearing to go near him, she fled to her mother in Wales. She said he was driven to great lustiness and anger, cruelty and melancholy. He beat her, trampled upon her, kicked her, even when she was with child. He pulled her around by her hair and threatened to drown her in the fishpond. On at least three occasions in the fifties he was suspected of violence against other women, including ear slitting.

He was a prisoner in the Fleet in London in 1553-4 for misdemeanour towards a female servant. He quarrelled repeatedly with his neighbour Sir Thomas Danby of Thorp Perrow and wounded one of his men with a rapier. Thomas Edwards told the Earl of Rutland how "Lord Latimer would have ravished the wife of the house where he lay and struck the good man." Sir Henry Percy had married his elder daughter and tried to stop his spending, as mentally unfit, in 1561. The High Commission in 1562 investigated a dozen women accused of fornication with him. The Archbishop of York complained in 1563 of his "evil and misordered life", and said that he was not "a man of government". He died in 1577, after which his widow enjoyed five peaceful years.

The inscription on Latimer's effigy avoids these difficulties. "Here lyeth buried Sir John Nevell knight, last Lord Latimer, who died the 23rd of April 1577, who married the Lady Lucy, the eldest daughter of the Earl of Worcester and she lyeth buried in Hackney churche by London and by her left four daughters and heires, whose matches are hereunder expressed." The estate was divided between four daughter heiresses. The elder Elizabeth married Sir John Danvers of Dauntsey who gained Danby. When the dowager died in 1582 and was buried at Hackney she left her daughter Cornwallis her great chain of gold, twelve silver plates, five silver dishes, of which two were for boiled meats and some silver platters. Thomas Cecil, Lord Burghley married the coheir Dorothy and succeeded to Snape Castle.

The Knights[6]

The order of knighthood was not hereditary. Knighthood was a royal appointment. The rank was conferred by letter or by accolade from the monarch, or from a nobleman delegated to make knights, on the field of battle, or during a campaign. Some were named at the coronation. The Knights of the Bath and the Knights of the Garter were of greater estimation. Knights bannerets were elevated on the field of battle during a war. Suitably qualified gentlemen were expected to take up knighthood. The basic qualification was adequate money from land.

Sir Thomas Wilson in "The State of England" said that knights were usually made according to the yearly revenue of their lands. Persons returned as having lands of the yearly value of £40 had to compound for the order of knighthood in 1558, which meant that they paid not to be knighted. There were about five hundred knights in England, in 1600, for the most part spending between £1000 and £2000 yearly, but many of them were equal to the best barons and some not much behind many earls, able to spend yearly between £5000 and £7000.

The knights were great men in their day and are probably the best-recorded group in the shire. Those living in Yorkshire were not numerous at any one time. A list of 1572 giving Yorkshire residents of knightly status and above mentioned the Earl of Shrewsbury, Lords Darcy, Latimer and Eure, and only fifteen knights. There were two or three of them, reckoned "men of most power and worship" at any time, in each Riding. Over the reign, the knights were more numerous, because fortunes were variable, life was short and generation quickly succeeded generation. Not only the heads of families, but their sons, daughters, and even the cousinhood, shared in their local status. Their lives reveal some common themes as well as wide differences of biography. Some knightly families had great regional significance.

T17 Sir Thomas Gargrave's list of the principal gentlemen of Yorkshire, 1572

	Barons	Knights	Esquires	Gentlemen of meaner degree
East Riding		3	9	14
North Riding	2	5	15	10
West Riding	2	6	23	32
York		2	3	

Queen Elizabeth was sparing in her creation of new knights. Sir Thomas Reresby of Thrybergh in south Yorkshire, reflected that it was "very rare and consequently of great honour in those days". He claimed to be in debt due to "his following the Court without any recompense than empty knighthood." Among the new creations were men who featured much in county history; Sir Valentine Brown, Sir Charles Cavendish, Sir William Devereux, Sir Thomas Fairfax, Sir Thomas Gerard, Sir George Hart, Sir

Thomas Hoby and Sir John Sydenham. The Duke of Norfolk knighted Sir Arthur Gray and Sir William Fairfax of Gilling at Barwick in 1560. The southward journey of King James to take up the English throne in 1603, saw a jostle for knighthood as candidates rushed to his side. Knighthoods quickly became more plentiful. Within a year or two, sixty Yorkshire squires gained elevation, with such names as Bellasis, Cholmeley, Dakins, Davill, Eure, Fairfax, Gibson and Tancred.

The estates of the knights were more focused in a single county than those of earls and barons. They might hold one or more manors and they commonly held several scattered estates within Yorkshire. As a result, their interests were rarely parochial. Collectively, the knights owned a great deal of the shire. Many in a previous generation had invested in the lands of dissolved monasteries, including the Beckwiths, the Babthorpes, and the Constables. Sir Thomas Gargrave, perhaps the most famous knight in the county, bought the Nostel Priory estates in 1567 from Lord Mountjoy for £3,560.

T18 The Estates of some Yorkshire Knights

Sir John Constable
-manors of Burton Constable, Newton Constable, Uppawle, & Benningham, Lamwathe, Hackness, West Halston, East Halston, Upsall, Marton, Pawle, Benningham Grange, Thornebargh, S. Kilvington, Silpho, Suffield, Everley, Hackness-Dale, Harwood Dales, Burniston, Broxey, Barningham, Headon, Tunstall, Sheirley, Dowthorpe, Thorkleby, Pawleflete, Carleton, Wythornwicke, Flinton, Fytling, Marton, Fosham, and Tansterne, the Rectory of Hackness. There was also a Lincolnshire estate and two houses in Blake St. York.

Sir Thomas Danby 1593.
-manors of Masham, Mowthorpe, Mossa with lands at Scruton, Farnley, Cleckheaton, Scoles, Thorpe Perrrow, Watlass, Driffield, Wibsey, Pott Grange, S. Cave, Thirsk

Sir Robert Saville 1584.
-manors of Heddingley, Bramley, Burley, Armley & Denholme, site of monastery of Kirkstall, houses, mills and lands at Leeds, Calverley, Wyddergrange, Whitecote grange, Riggecote grange, Barne grange, More grange, Cullingworth, Horsforth and Adle.

Sir George Saville 1591.
-manors of Thornhill, Elande, Steyneland, Barkeslande, Rishworth, Norland, Waddesworth, Stansfelde, Skircote, Wyke, South Owram, Golcar, Bothomhall, Shelf, Ovenden, Tankersley, Mirfield, Thurleston, Hunsworth Sotehill, Rowtanstall, Haddlessey, Darrington and Emley.

The knights' incomes came mainly from their rentals but several were active in industry and others maintained substantial demesne farms. Sir Marmaduke Constable of Everingham had 159 cattle, 38 pigs and 1020 sheep in 1575 and Sir William Ingleby of Ripley had comparable stock, 178 cattle, 12 pigs and 1465 sheep in 1579. Sir William Bellasis made early enclosures. Sir Arthur Darcy and later Sir Stephen Procter at Bewerley, and Sir William Ingleby at Brimham had interests in lead working, Sir William Gascoigne mined coal, while Sir John Saville of Howley had the Kirkstall iron works.

38

T19 Yorkshire Knights Wealth, in inventories.

1575 Sir Marmaduke Constable	Everingham	£1202
1579 Sir William Ingleby	Ripley	£700
1582 Sir Thomas Boynton	Barmston	£2454
1588 Sir Cotton Gargrave	Nostell	£2714
1595 Sir William Fairfax	Gilling /Walton	£1072
1603 Sir Richard Wortley	Wortley	£1181

Crown service beckoned the knights, whether in Yorkshire, in other counties, at the nation's capital, or overseas. Many held Crown appointments, some sinecures, some full of duties, as castle governors, stewards, foresters, feodaries, escheators, and commissioners. The stewardship of Crown estates made a man greater in his district, giving power over honour, forest and manor courts. The Crown castles had lost some significance but the stewardships of the great estates focused on them, at Wakefield, Pontefract, Knaresborough, Conisbrough, Pickering and Richmond were as important as ever. Oversight was the expectation, with mundane duties passed on to others. The fees might be modest but there were often perquisites. Crown fees paid for the keeper of Scarborough castle were £16 and for Knaresborough castle £15.6s.8d, where the porter also had £6.1s.8d. a year. The Pickering steward had £10 and the riding forester £3.6s.8d.

Sir Thomas Gargrave was steward of Doncaster, deputy constable of Pontefract, receiver of Yorkshire, and "custos rotulorum" for the West Riding. He was a long serving Vice President of the Council in the North. Sir Henry Saville of Thornhill, served as steward of Pontefract & Wakefield. At other times, Wakefield was held by a Wentworth and a Tempest. Sir William Ingleby was steward of Knaresborough. Sir Thomas Wharton was steward of Crown lands in the East Riding and Steward of the Crown manor of Hemingbrough. Sir Richard Chamberlain was governor of Scarborough castle in 1568, but was dismissed for being obstinate in religion. He was replaced by Sir Henry Gate of Seamer, who had been made deputy steward and constable of Pickering castle, honour and forest in 1565. Sir John Constable was Scarborough castle governor from 1579 till his death in 1584, perhaps coincident with his residence at Hackness. Other stewardships were held in the service of the earls and barons. Sir Robert Constable of Flamborough managed the Howdenshire estates of the Bishop of Durham and had been steward of the Marshland for St. Mary's Abbey. Sir William Ingleby was steward of the Earl of Derby's Kirkby Malzeard estate.

Several knights served on the Council in the North. Sir George Calvert served in the capital as Secretary to the Lord High Treasurer. Sir Christopher Wray born at Bedale, was Lord Chief Justice of the King's Bench, and later Lord Privy Seal. Several Yorkshire men were trusted with ambassadorships, including Sir William Pickering, Sir Thomas Chaloner in Spain, Giles Talbot in France and Lord Eure in Denmark. The fortress captaincy at Berwick and the wardenships of the West, Middle and East Marches against Scotland were no sinecures, and often came to Yorkshire knights or barons. Henry Eure served as master of the ordnance at Berwick. Sir Henry Danvers, who had been a page to Sir Phillip Sydney, became a professional soldier in the Low Countries. The Earl of Shrewsbury wrote from Rouen to Sir Robert Cecil in 1596 to bring him to the attention of the Queen.

There were Queen's commissioners for sewers, and other temporary commissions to enquire into such matters as masterless men, or the lunacy of Guy Fairfax in 1559.

Among the more important Crown commissions were those issued to noblemen, bishops, sergeants at law, and knights to serve as justices of the peace in the Yorkshire Ridings, though some were dropped on account of their Catholic religion. The 1564 commission of the peace enlisted these trusted members of the knighthood:-

West Riding - Sir Thomas Gargrave; Sir William Vavasour; Sir Thomas Danby; Sir William Ingleby; Sir Edmund Mauleverer,

North Riding - Sir Thomas Gargrave; Sir Henry Gates; Sir Christopher Danby; Sir George Bowes; Sir William Bellasis; Sir Nicholas Fairfax.

East Riding - Sir Thomas Gargrave; Sir William Vavasour; Sir Henry Gates;

The social peak of a lifetime for a knight, or a rich esquire, could be selection as High Sheriff of Yorkshire, some of whose official functions were an occasion for ostentatious hospitality and display. They said that Sir Christopher Metcalfe of Nappa, when High Sheriff in 1555, rode out of York to meet the Justices of Assize on circuit, with a retinue of three hundred men, of his own name and family, clad in his cloth or livery, all well mounted on white horses, to conduct them to York. Sir Robert Stapleton of Wighill, picked as Sheriff in 1581, greeted the judges with one hundred and forty men in suitable liveries, and entertained them with great magnificence. The Sheriff was personally selected by the Queen and acted for the monarch for one year. Sir Thomas Fairfax, as Sheriff in 1571, had to remove the Duke of Norfolk's goods from Hinderskelfe castle. The next year, he made an estimate for the repairs needed at Sheriff Hutton castle. The office came with high costs. Sir William Mallory of Studley said that he was unsuited for the office in 1582 and Sir Cotton Gargrave pleaded exemption on account of his father's debts.

T20 Yorkshire Knights who served as High Sheriff of Yorkshire, 1557-1603
Sir William Bellassis. (Newbrough.1574-5).
Sir Henry Bellasis (Newbrough, 1603-4)
Sir George Bowes (Streatlam, 1562-3)
Sir Robert Constable (Everingham, 1557)
Sir John Constable (Halsham, Kirkby Knowle, 1566-7)
Sir Henry Constable (Burton, 1586-7)
Sir Thomas Danby (Farnley Hall, 1575-6)
Sir John Dawnay (Sessay 1572-3, 1589-90)
Sir Ralph Ellerker (Risby, 1558-9)
Sir William Fairfax (Gilling, 1577-8)
Sir Nicholas Fairfax (Gilling, 1561-2)
Sir Thomas Gargrave (Nostell Kinsley, North Elmsal, 1565-6 & 1569-70)
Sir Christopher Hildyard (Winestead, 1570-1, 1595-6)
Sir William Ingleby (Ripley, 1564-5)
Sir William Mallory (Studley, 1592-3)
Sir Richard Mauleverer (Allerton, 1588-9)
Sir John Neville (Liversedge, 1560-1) (attainted 1571)
Sir Robert Stapleton (Wighill, 1581-2)
Sir Henry Savile (Thornehill, 1567-8)
Sir William Vavasour (Hazlewood, 1563-4)

Neighbouring members of the knightly class knew each other well. Some pride was taken in hospitality. Lady Hoby rode out from Hackness to visit her Linton estate and to call at Snape Castle and Nunnington Hall. Sir Thomas Wharton offered another knight the use of his house. The household account books of Sir William Fairfax of Gilling Castle show between thirty and fifty commonly dining in the hall, with great eating on days when their were visitors. Many were servants but the guest list at a supper in honour of the Earl of Rutland, included Sir Robert Constable and Sir William Bellassis. A party of gentry arriving at Sir Thomas Hoby's house expected to be given hospitality and it was given.

Conspicuous expenditure marked out the knights. Many rebuilt their houses. Sir Nicholas Fairfax bought estates to settle on his numerous children and left them sixty pound to spend on basins and ewers for heirlooms bearing his coat of arms. Sir John Constable allotted five hundred marks for a tomb for his dead son and himself in 1579. Sir Henry Belllassis put up a tomb in York minster with effigies of himself, his son and two daughters during his own lifetime. He kept fifty-one servants compared with the thirty of Sir Ralph Babthorpe at Osgodby. Many had portraits painted, or miniatures prepared by the fashionable painters Nicholas Hildyard and George Gower.

There were other roles to play. A knight might be a "gentleman born" but he could gain recognition in some more ideal sense. Sir William Pickering, sometime Knight Marshall to King Henry VIII, is said to have kept house at Byland Abbey. His son died at Oswaldkirk in Ryedale in 1575. He was described as "a brave, wise and comely English gentleman". He was once thought likely to have married Queen Elizabeth. "He was of tall stature, handsome and very successful with women, for he is said to have enjoyed the intimacy of many and great ones." His wardrobe included, twenty-five best shirts, a black satin woman's gown with hanging sleeves and several womens' silk waistcoats.

Sir Phillip Sydney who was "equally addicted to arts and arms" was reckoned by some of his peers, to be the "common rendezvous of worth in his time." Sir Robert Stapleton, of Wighill, in the Vale of York, according to Camden, was "a person, well spoken, comely and skilled in the languages." He was said "to have scarce an equal, except Sir Phillip Sidney and no superior in England." Francis Cholmley of Whitby was "a valiant and complete gentleman, except that he was so exceedingly over topped by his wife." The scholarly Sir Henry Saville was "an extra ordinary handsome and beautiful man, no lady had a finer complexion."

Sir Robert Swift of Doncaster and Rotherham was a great swordsman and an elegant speaker. He was a legend in his lifetime. Abraham de la Pryme described him as an ingenious, witty and merry gentleman, concerning whom Hatfield had many traditional stories. When he found Mr Slack of Cantley stealing a king's deer, he accompanied him to prison. They took lodgings on the way, where they told merry tales, with so many pots of good ale that Swift passed out. Slack put a verse in his pocket and left

> "To every creature
> God has given a gift.
> Sometimes the Slack
> does over run the Swift:"

More robust descriptions of the knights were couched in the psychology of the time. Sir Henry Carey was "choleric but not malicious". Sir Richard Cholmeley had "a haughty spirit naturally choleric", but was "well natured". Fuller made Sir Martin Frobisher "very valiant but withal harsh and violent". Sir Thomas Hoby, to one observer, was a "fine justice of the peace". Others saw him as "the busiest sauciest little jack in the country", a "scurvy urchin" and a "spindle shanked ape".

Esquires

The "Academy of Armoury" described the rank of esquire as including "all sons of dukes, marquises and earls, the eldest and younger sons of all viscounts and barons, and the elder son of the younger sons and their elder sons for ever, and the eldest son of a knight and his eldest son forever." Here again was that emphasis on the blood line. The knight who founded the line might not have any special blood but his descendants did. There were also "esquires of the Queen's body" and the Queen could create one by the gift of the collar and the silver spurs. The title of esquire, like others, might pass to eldest sons forever but there was a little flexibility. At the fringe, there were esquires by office, and by repute, which simply meant an ancient family and a considerable estate. Counsellors at law, along with bachelors of divinity, law and physic were also allowed the title.

Esquires were not all that numerous, probably not more than a hundred or so in the county at any one time. Many had roots in the knightly class of the middle ages, including those whose surnames were the same as the name of the place where they resided. The most obvious distinguishing feature of an esquire was his possession of a coat of arms. These were shown on house doorways, chimney pieces, silver plate, signet rings, memorials, on seals, clothes, windows, vehicles and harness, on counterpanes and bed heads. A memorial of 1590 in Brompton church shows a coat of arms and cheerfully recalls the service to the Crown by one esquire.

> "Heir lieth James Westrop
> who in wars to his greit charges
> sarved oin king and tow quenes
> with du obediens and withowt recumpens"

Outstanding esquires gained appointment to the expensive role of High Sheriff of Yorkshire. Another outstanding group were those appointed to the Council in the North. Among them were the professional sergeants at law including Thomas Fairfax of Steeton, Robert Mennell of Hawnby and Robert Rokebie. Other Council members who had been to the Inns of Court were recorded as "learned in the law". The office of custos rotulorum for the East Riding was filled by esquires. Christopher Estoft c1558-66, John Vaughan c1573-77, Ralph Rokeby 1577-c1584 and later Thomas Knyvet. Esquires filled many offices serving those higher up the social scale. Roger Radcliffe of Mulgrave was constable of Raby Castle for the Nevilles. Robert Dolman of Pocklington was steward of the Lennox manor of Hunmanby.

T21 Esquires as High Sheriffs of Yorkshire, 1557-1603
1559 John Vaughan (Sutton on Derwent) 1568 Richard Norton (Norton Conyers)
1570 Christopher Hildyard (Winestead)   1571 Thomas Fairfax (Denton)
1572 John Dawnay (Sessay)   1573 Marmaduke Constable (Cliffe)
1576 Thomas Boynton (Barmston)   1578 Christopher Wandesforth
                    (Kirklington)

1579 Richard Goodricke (Ribston)   1580 Ralph Bouchier (North Grimston)
1582 Thomas Wentworth (Gawthorpe)   1583 Cotton Gargrave (Nostell)
1584 John Hotham (Scorborough)   1585 Bryan Stapleton (Carleton)
1587 Robert Aske (Aughton)   1590 Phillip Constable (Everingham)
1591 Richard Goodricke (Ribston)   1593 Ralph Eure (Malton, Ingleby)
1594 Francis Vaughan (Sutton)   1596 Francis Boynton (Barmston)
1597 Thomas Lassells (Breckonbrough) 1598 Marmaduke Grimston (Grimston)
1599 Robert Swift (Doncaster)   1600 Francis Clifford (Skipton)
1601William Wentworth (Wentworth)   1602 Thomas Strickland

T22 Esquires on the Council in the North (LL-learned in the law)

Anthony Belassis 1561; Alan Bellingham LL 1564,1568; Robert Bowes LL; 1572; George Brown LL155?, 1561,1564. Richard Corbett LL 1561, 1564, Christopher Estoft LL 1555, 1561, 1564, Thomas Eyms secretary 1555, 1561, 1564,1568; Francis Frobisher LL 1555, 1561, Laurence Meers. 1564, 1568, 1573, John Rokesby Dr, 1561, 1564; Henry Saville 1561, 1564, William Tankarde. LL 1564; John Vaughan 1561, 1564, 1568 and Francis Wortley 1572.

Gentlemen

The "gentlemen" and the "gentlewomen" formed a much larger group than the esquires, but they were still a small proportion of the whole population. Not only the head of a house, but the elder son, when he came of age, could carry this title of respect, and be addressed as mister or maister. Younger sons and daughters usually lost the status. Gentility was really rather open ended. William Harrison explained in 1577 that "there are comprised under the title of gentlemen, whosoever studies the laws of the realm, who abideth in university or professes physic and the liberal sciences, or beside his service in the room of a captain in the wars, or good counsel given at home, whereby his commonwealth is benefited, can live without manual labour and thereto is able and will bear the port, charge and countenance of a gentleman."

The nub of it was "to live without manual labour". The ranks of the gentlemen included "all ecclesiastical persons professing religion, all martial men that have borne office and have had command in the field, all students of arts and sciences and by our English custom, all inns of court men, professors of the law, it skills not what their fathers were, whether farmers, shoe makers, tailors or tinkers." You could join the ranks of the genteel, but there was both resistance and resentment. Officials called heralds registered gentility and could speak of "usurpers of the name and title of gentleman." In practice, in day-to-day life, there was a fluctuating group, whose names didn't always enter the herald's records, who claimed the title of gentleman, or were so credited by their peers or neighbours.

Most villages had an esquire or a gentleman, and his family were often at the hall or manor house. Large villages with several manors could have several. Many were manor lords but many were not. An expanding gentry acquired freeholds and leases of monastic granges, and the properties that had sustained friaries, hospitals, guilds and chantries. Some acquired rectories and owned advowsons, giving them the right to appoint the clergy to local churches. The towns had clusters of gentlemen, including those from the growing professions and the second generations of some who had simply done well in one sphere or another. Families rose and fell, prospered or died out, were well remembered or just forgotten.

T23 The Gentlemen of Yorkshire (in Glover's Heraldic visitation, 1584-5) [7]

	knights	esquires	gentlemen
East Riding			
Buckrose		4	18
Dickering		6	7
Harthill		12	30
Holderness	1	11	28
Howdenshire Liberty			11
Ouse & Derwent		6	6
North Riding			
Allertonshire Liberty	1	2	5
Birdforth	1	4	16
Bulmer	1	4	21
Gilling east		2	15
Gilling west	2	8	10
Halikeld		2	5
Hang east		3	6
Hang west		4	15
Langbaurgh liberty		11	34
Pickering Lythe		4	14
Richmondshire liberty			
Ryedale	1	8	12
Whitby Strand liberty		5	2
West Riding			
Agbrigg & Morley	2	27	38
Ainsty	3	6	6
Barksotn Ash	1	9	19
Claro	3	11	16
Clifford fee liberty		7	9
Osgoldcross liberty		5	20
N Pontefract		6	8
Knaresburgh liberty		4	6
Ripon liberty			6
Skyrack		6	16
Staincliff & Bowland		6	8
Staincross		9	9
Strafforth		8	16
Tickhill Liberty		8	41
Yewcross		1	6

The clergy were a shrinking body, for the present, but the other professions were expanding. This was a litigious age. The Inns of Court were attractive to younger sons and to others seeking to retain status or simply to find a gainful career. Estate management was a rising profession. Land surveying was emerging and even architecture. Quite apart from stewardships, there were excellent prospects opening up in the service of the Crown, the nobility, the boroughs, and notably in the courts. Most estates had a bailiff as well as a steward. Gentleman, Thomas Wood of Kilnwick Percy spent his life in administration and dying on the 23rd of October 158, left this memorial.

> "Thomas Wood, gentleman, who in warfare hath be
> He fought in Scotland, in royal arms three
> Lyeth now, buried in this grave hereunder
> Of Boulogne when it was english, clerk-comptroller
> of the ward court, six and twenty years together
> Deputy receiver of Yorkshire, once Eschetar,
> Clerk of the Statute in London noble city
> Collector of Selby with £10- yearly fee
> For thought, words and deed, which to God or man were ill
> Of both he asked forgivenes with glad heart and will
> He built the house hereby to this church, brought in good case..
> God grant his wife and sons to passe a godly race. Amen

There were practical advantages in having a higher status. Oxford University allowed the eldest sons of esquires and the younger sons of knights, and those of loftier rank, to take a bachelor of arts degree in a shorter time. The Inns of Court would order that none be admitted that was not a gentleman by descent. And there was influence. Ralph Eure accused George Dakins of Foulbridge of assisting in the murder of one of his servants and complained of his influence in high places that allowed him to go free. Mr. Conyers of Whitby was said to be uncontrollable, "being of great birth". William Seagrave the Helmsley Steward sent John Thornton to the Earl of Rutland. He said that he "would very gladly be vicar of Helmsley" and had offered to keep a school to maintain himself. Richard More of Grantham wrote to the Earl of Shrewsbury in 1584 wanting to change the position of his church pew "most unfriendly placed, amidst boys and apprentices".

All too often, early death carried off the head of a gentry household before any male heir had reached maturity. The wardship of possible heirs became a kind of property. The Court of Wards was virtually a department of state for selling control of the assets of under age heirs. Purchase of the wardship could give some years of custody of an estate, and even disposal of the heir and his brothers and sisters in marriage, with their child's portions. The further possibility of the heir's death carried the value of wardship to these other members of the family. In the not uncommon event of a failure in the male line, there could be a division among co-heiresses. Francis Alford offered four hundred marks in 1588 for custody of Sir William Fairfax's son, if the knight died. Sir Ralph Bowes bought the wardship of the young co-heiress Elizabeth daughter of Roger Aske of Aske. She married his son Richard, who thereby received South Cowton.

John Legard was eleven at his father's death in 1589. Only when he reached maturity in 1597-8 did Lord Burghley, as Surveyor of the Court of Wards and Liveries transfer the Ganton estate to the boy. The next year he married Elizabeth daughter of William Mallory of Studley, by whom he had six sons and three daughters. Edward Fairfax, holding the wardship of William Westrop, moved into his Cornbrough house with his wife Elizabeth, and with slight exception used his furnishings as his own. The Queen told Lord Bacon to take order in the case of Edward Saville. He had been conveyed away by his base brother Robert and married to a simple poor woman.

Heralds and Lineage

The upper end of the status system was supervised from the 1530s by officials called heralds. The Earl Marshal was assisted by Garter, Clarenceux and Norroy Kings of Arms, who with six heralds and four pursuivants made up the College of Arms, which had been given a new charter in 1555. William Flower, Norroy King of Arms was the son of a corn merchant in the parish of All Saints Pavement at York. Laurence Dalton of Kirkby Misperton was appointed Norroy King of Arms in 1557, for £20 a year and his livery, but Robert Glover, a successor, described him as "one Dakins, the late lewd usurper of the office" and required the insignia that he issued either justified or cancelled.

The heralds visited each county, every few decades, to separate the titles of gentility claimed by those who were "worthy" from any adopted by "the baser and vulgar sort" which were not due to them. Those who claimed gentility had to appear when summoned and pay a fee, 25s for a gentleman, 35s for an esquire and 55s for a knight and they had to provide proof that they were entitled to bear arms, either by a grant, or long usage of eighty years or more.

The lesser gentry and some rising men were caught in a pedigree craze. The heralds used the shield of arms as the symbol and proof of gentility. It was best to appear with a pedigree of descent from someone with a clear grant to use arms. However, the heralds could also register anyone of free birth with £10 a year in land or £300 in moveable goods, and could issue new coats of arms when they thought necessary. George Earl of Shrewsbury complained of some pedigrees issued by the Heralds. Other critics spoke of gentlemen being made good and cheap.

Heraldic coats of arms offered a shorthand guide to family connection. The Earls had huge pedigrees made, on long rolls, or in manuscript volumes, some for use in the law courts. Crests, supporters and mottoes were added to shields. William Flower granted Edward Hutchinson of Wykeham a crest to augment his family arms. Esquire Arthur Dakins adopted the somewhat obscure motto "strike Dakyns, the devil's in the hemp". An establishment roll of 1578-80 recorded the heraldry of sixty-four peers, with roundels of paper set on wood, the arms on one side and crests on the other. Yorkshire and the north were represented by Henry Percy, George Talbot, Edward Manners, George Clifford, Henry Hastings, Henry Scrope, John Lumley, John Darcy, Henry Wentworth, Phillip Wharton, Edmund Sheffield, and Henry Carey.[8]

The best chamber at Gilling Castle displayed four hundred and fifty painted shields, hanging from painted trees, in a four foot deep frieze, virtually a "who's who" of genteel families, in the entire shire, wapentake by wapentake. The fireplace had the Queen's arms and those of the Fairfax knights. The new glass windows proved an ideal setting for richly coloured armourial glass, showing the heraldry of their Fairfax, Stapleton and Constable relations. The Somerset Herald sketched a record of the glass of the Aske family in Aughton Hall. One hundred and seventy three shields were painted on the walls of the Moyser family chapel at Lockington. St Leonard's Church, Thrybergh in 1584 held a vast array of heraldic shields in glass.

The cult of long lineage could reach peaks of romantic absurdity, with fancy supplementing or supplanting fact. Christopher Stapleton's crest was a Saracens head, supported by the story that three kings of England, France and Scotland had witnessed a Stapleton ancestor win victory in combat with a giant Saracen. More popular versions made him an ogre living on an offshore English island, given his end moment, with a

T24 A Yorkshire Elite, The 1590 Yorkshire Book of Arms, Esquires and above

West Riding

Agbrigg	Bradford, Bunny, Kay, Saville; Waterton, Wentworth
Ainsty	Sir William Fairfax of Walton, Sir Robert Stapleton of Wighill
	Fairfax, Ingleby, Lawson, Newarke, Vavasour, Wilstrope
Barkston	Babthorpe, Beckwith, Beverley, Gascoigne, Hungate, Stapleton,
	Vavasour
Claro	Sir Wm Mallory of Studley, Sir Thomas Fairfax of Denton
	Bernard, Coniers, Drax, Goldsbrough, Goodrick, Ingleby, Lindley,
	Mauleverer, Middleton, Palmes, Plumpton, Righlay,
	Rosse, Saville, Slingsby, Tankard, Vavasour , York.

Ewecross & Staincliffe .George Clifford, Earl of Cumberland

Catherall , Clapham, Eltofts, Lambert, Lister ,Tempest

Morley	Beiston, Calverley, Coplay, Hopton, Saville, Tempest
Skyrack	Arthington, Ellis, Foliambe, Gascoigne, Hawkesworth, Mauleverer,
	Norton, Oglethorpe, Ryther

Staincross & Osgoldcross

Barnby, Bosville, Burdet, Eastoft, Everingham, Gargrave, Haldenby,
Mearinge, Nevill, Radcliffe, Rockely, Skerne, Stanley, Wentworth,
Woodrowe, Wortley

Strafforth & Tickhill Gilbert Earl of Shrewsbury, John Lord Darcy of Aston

Anne?, Bosville, Copley, Drax, Pollington, Portington, Reresby,
Rokesby, Scargill, Swift. Wentworth, Wombwell, Worrall

North Riding

Bulmershire, Sir Ralph Bouchier of Beninmgbrough,

Cholmley, Darley, Gower, Mettam, Redman, Thwinge

Birdforth & Allertonshire Sir Wm Bellasis of Newbrough, Sir John Dawney of

Sessey, Lassells, Mennell, Talbot

Gilling East	Sir Thomas Cecill, Sir William Bowes,
	Bulmer, Dakins, Green, Place, Vincent, Warcoppe, Wandesford
Gilling West	Bowes, Catherick, Gascoigne, Pudsey, Bowes, Rookby, Wicklifffe
Hang East	Phillip Lord Wharton.
	Conyers, Darcy Girlington, Lawson, Wicliffe
Hang West	Henry Lord Scroop of Bolton
	Scroope, Soulby, Thoresby, Wyvill

Langbaurgh & Whitby Strand. Wm Lord Eure.

Constable, Crathorn, Layton, Radcliffe, Rookby, Salvine, Sayer
Strangewayes, Tochitts

Ridall & Pickering Lythe Roger Manners, Earl of Rutland

Atterton, Cholmley, Dakins, Dalton, Evers, Gates

East Riding

Buckrose & Dickering

Bambrough, Dakins, Captain Gourley, Griffiths, St Quintin

Harthill	Henry Percy, Earl of Northumberland,
	Bethell, Constable, Darell, Ellicarr, Hotham, Hungate, Legard, Rudston
	Thirkeld, Thwing, Vaughan
Holderness	Sir Christopher Hildyard of Winestead, Sir Henry Constable
	Alford, Alured, Appleyard, Boynton, Cresswell, Frodingham, Grimstone,
	Holme, Legard, Moore, Strattery, Wright

Ouse & Derwent

Babthorpe, Aske, Gates, Hussey, Metham, Palmes, Portington,
Saltmarsh, Stillington, Vavasour

47

sword thrust up his armpit. The Crathornes claimed descent from one Henry, supposed to have held hides of land from Siward Earl of Northumbria, long before the Normans came. He mightily resisted the Conquest, till reconciled with the Conqueror by Bishop Reimgil of Dorchester, when his Cleveland estate was restored to him, or so they said.

The Chaloners claimed descent from Trahayrne the Great, son of Mayloc Kwrme, one of the fifteen heads of the tribes of North Wales, by marriage with Gwenllyan, daughter of Howell Koedmore, who was lineally descended from Griffith son of Llyllan ap Jerworth, Prince of Wales. The Langdale's were given a genealogy back to Sir Lancelot Langdale of Langdale in the time of King John. a figure otherwise unknown. His grandson married Goditha daughter of Patrick Aislaby. Oddly Goditha was the name of the not far distant Wykeham corn mill. In the end, what could be thought to matter, was not what you were, nor even who you were, but who you were descended from. A brass plate at Seamer church recalled Dame Lucy, wife of Sir Henry Gate. This told you nothing of the lady but traced her descent from Thomas Plantaganet, Duke of Gloucester, youngest son of King Edward III. She was significant in death, only for her ancestors.

William Mauleverer of Ingleby Arncliffe kept two versions of his descent, one of 1591 signed "Per me Lancaster Herald at Armes". This started with Sir Richard Mauleverer, who came over with the Conqueror and by him was appointed "Master of the forests, parks and chases, Trent northwards." Another record of 1601 was "collected and contrived out of myne auncient and newe evidences". The first version was fiction, the second accurate, or so they said. A pedigree inscribed on three skins of parchment and sewn together at Burton Agnes, listed fifteen generations before Francis Boynton of c 1585. A note on the back in faded ink said "this is false". A brass at Otley showed Mr. Palmes of Lindley on a mattress with the names of his ancestors in a tree above. Here was

> "No figment of the herald's craft,
> not venally procured.
> These ancient monuments declare
> a race of worth assured:"

Some families did keep accurate personal records. An old volume contained "A note of the birth and christenings of all Sir William Belassis children such as are now living" in 1571-2, including the christenings at Awkeland 1551, at Coxwold 1553-55, at Newborough 1559 and at Henknowl 1562. Five had died while very young. A first edition of Chaucer was used to register Wentworth family births. An entry for Thomas, the eldest son said that he was "born at London on Good Friday the 13th of April about 12 of the clock at noon, his godfathers Sir Edward Saville and Mr. Atkinson, his godmother the Lady Digby, Anno Domini 1593 in Chancery Lane, at the house of grandfather Robert Atkinson, a bencher at Lincoln's Inn".

Family trees could run from two generations to fourteen for a Conyers, a Mauleverer, or a Thornton and for many others. Redman of Fulford showed six generations, Palmes of Naburn seven and Acclom of Moreby thirteen. Descent from the younger sons of great mediaeval barons had left scatterings of Conyers, Percys, Mennells, Constables, and Cliffords, all around the county, many no longer gentry. The Grays had been at Barton le Street manor since the 13th century. Crathornes, Nawtons and Westrops still held manors in the townships whose names they bore. Just occasionally, irritation broke through these assurances. Richard Dutton of Cloughton remarked that, "the Dutton blood was fully as good as that of Cholmeley, if not better". One of the Legards recorded a conversation with a man claiming Norman descent. A local remarked "Mine was here when they coomed."

As great gentry tombs were placed in chancels, displays of wealth, and personal biography began to challenge the displays of heraldry and descent. The Knaresborough church was given the monument to Sir Francis Slingsby and his wife, showing her hair combed back under a lace-bordered cap. The arms of Percy and Brabant were on her skirts but the inscription gave his story and was a sort of tribute. "Under this tomb are interred Francis and Mary Slingsby. Francis leaving the University served under King Henry VIII as captain of horse, at the siege of Boulogne; and afterwards at the Battle of Musselberg, was a general of the horse; in the reign of Queen Mary, he commanded a troop of horse; and in the following reign of Queen Elizabeth, he was sent unto the north, sole commissioner for settling disputes with the Scots. He died 4th of August 1600 aged 78 years."

Mary, no less distinguished by her virtues than by her birth was the only sister of Thomas and Henry, Earls of Northumberland. "She was so sincerely devoted to the service of her master as to be justly called a heavenly star of piety. In the 66th year of age she yielded her body to mortality and resigned her soul to immortality. This pair had twelve children nine sons and three daughters, the daughters died young. Of the sons six arrived to manhood, followed the court and were employed in various negotiations in foreign parts, in France, Spain, Portugal, Italy and as far as India, the seventh taking holy orders and being a bachelor in divinity became rector of Rathburne in Northumberland. Henry Slingsby their heir erected this monument in 1601 to record the nobility and mortality of his relatives."

A Suitable Marriage

Men of property usually made marriages within their status. They might go outside it, for material gain. The same surnames occur in pedigree after pedigree across the county. Marriages by those of widely different status could be thought of as a dishonour to you and your descendants. The highest status marriages were arranged by the heads of families. Elder sons and daughters bore the full weight of the system. Younger brothers and sisters seem less well recorded and were probably a little less controlled. The 5th Earl of Shrewsbury's sister Margaret Talbot wed Henry Earl of Cumberland, another, Mary wed Henry Earl of Northumberland, while Elizabeth married Lord Dacre. Generally speaking, the elder sons of knights married daughters from the same or a higher cadre, at least for first marriages. Sir William Belasyse of Newbrough married Margaret daughter of Sir Nicholas Fairfax & Jane Palmes. William son of Sir Nicholas Fairfax wed Anne daughter of George Lord Darcy of Brayton. The daughter Jane wed Sir Thomas Boynton of Barmston.

The gentry practice of sending young people to other gentry households for upbringing helped establish such links, but the final key was the arranged marriage, and the settlement. Lord Dacre of Gilsland wrote to the Earl of Shrewsbury in 1554. His daughter Anne had agreed to marry the Earl of Cumberland. He asked "Will he take her with a thousand pounds". He couldn't afford more owing to his large family and many lawsuits. Roger Manners in 1586 wrote to John Manners asking "would you like Sir Henry Darcy's daughter for the son George. Least to give will be £2000." John Dawnay paid Lord Eure a £2000 dowry for his daughter, in instalments.

Sir Henry Percy wrote to Sir William Cecil in 1562 saying that "having himself married a daughter of Lord Latimer, he recommended the second at fifteen years as a suitable wife for Cecil's son Thomas, who was reported as of "ill behaviour". They "both should be matched in a great house, as also the likelihood of possessions to come thereby." The girl had "beauty very well, her hair brown, yet her complexion very fair and clear", and "the favour of her face everybody may judge it to have both grace and wisdom."

Considerable pressure could be brought to bear to secure a marriage. The Queen addressed the rich widow Olive Talbot in 1579 commending her sometime ward, Robert Stapleton. She wrote saying "Dear and well beloved. We greet you well, upon knowledge of an earnest and great affection that our trusty and well beloved Sir Robert Stapleton beareth for you, tending to a godly purpose of matching you in marriage, we have been pleased by our letters to commend his suit unto you to that end." She would bring him £1200 a year for thirteen years. Robert Carey came from a family of seven sons and three daughters raised by tutors and governors. He stated openly that "I married a gentlewoman more for her worth than her wealth, for her estate was but £500 a year jointure and she had between five and six hundred in her purse." He had only £100 a year and was nearly a thousand pounds in debt.

Bequests were made to maintain marriages within appropriate degrees. Lord Edward Rutland left four hundred marks for Sir Thomas Manners' daughter Mary "so as she marry a gentleman having three hundred marks a year land or be heir to a gentleman so endowed." Sir Henry Cholmleley made extensive sales to John Lighton and Ralph Hodgson at Pickering in 1596-98, in order to raise £2600 for daughters' portions, so that they would make suitable marriages. Unable to sell entailed estate to clear debt, he took his eldest son Richard from Cambridge University and married him to the sixteen-year-old Susanna Legard of Ganton who had a marriage portion of £2000. Then he sent the boy back to college. The girl was well shaped, her hair chestnut, her eyes grey. She had a shapely face and a clear complexion. Half way to Cambridge, the boy decided that Ganton offered a better vision in prospect than the University and turned his horse homewards.

Romantic love was known. They called it fantasy or fancy, a thought that lingered in the "fancy man" of later days. Where the fact was socially impossible, idealism mounted to dizzy heights. Fancy thrives on frustration. Barnaby Barnes wrote to an out of reach noblewoman, "Beautiful lady, the Lady Bridget Manners, rose of that garland, fairest and sweetest of all those sweet and fair flowers, pride of chaste Cynthia's rich crown." Occasionally, love did challenge parental approval. Sir John Forster wrote in 1586, "I understand by Sir Thomas Gray that there is a contract of marriage between him and Lady Katherine Neville, one of the daughters of the late Earl of Cumberland (sic) and I perceive that he has such a good liking for her and she of him that they have such a contract between themselves that they cannot go back again but are man and wife before God." Perhaps the Earl of Rutland made his own choice for his man Seagrave wrote from Helmsley, "I trust you have chosen well and I am sure of it, if the report be true that she fears God, loves the Gospel and hates Popery."

Sir Richard Cholmley of Whitby had paid £1000 down as part of the marriage portion for his favourite daughter to marry Lord Lumley. Come the day, Katherine, on her knees before him, said that she could never love Lumley because she loved another. He fondly bowed to her wishes, saying, "Rather than marry thee against thy liking, I will lose my money." She had fallen for a lesser gentleman, a younger son, one Dutton, employed about the house to teach her to sing. She married him and the father left her five or six hundred pound a year anyway. The same Sir Richard took a different view when his son Francis married without his approval, choosing Mrs. Jane Bulmer "of good family", "but no good fame", of a "humour he liked better for a mistress than a wife." So he entailed his estate.

Gentlewomen

Young gentlewomen seem less likely to have survived childhood than their brothers. Those who did so, went to stay in other gentry houses. Great ladies commonly maintained a group of young gentlewomen, including young girls, in their households, as part servants, part companions. Arthur Dakins, a wealthy esquire of Linton grange near Wintringham, sent his daughter Margaret to be raised in the sternly Puritan household of Catherine Countess of Huntingdon, wife of the third Earl, where her companions included Walter Devereux and his sisters Penelope and Dorothy. The Countess was the daughter of John Dudley, Duke of Northumberland and sister of Robert Dudley, Earl of Leicester. Margaret Dakins would later marry Walter Devereux. During her third marriage to Sir Thomas Posthumous Hoby, she kept a similar household where she would allow time to "talk with her maids".

Margaret Countess of Cumberland lost her natural mother, when young. She would write that, "we were scattered and put to the disposal of friends, which kindness of friends hath continued more happiness to me than all the things of this present life. Yet many accidents follow frail friendships." The first seven years saw many sicknesses. She next moved to her father's house to live under her mother-in-law. She loved her father but feared his new wife. Death took a brother and she herself had the green sickness for two or three years. Cumberland showed a liking for her, but her father, whose ward he was, wanted him to marry the older sister Elizabeth. Margaret now fourteen years old was matched to another, "though our minds met not, but in contraries and thought of discontentment". She was twenty-eight before she married the Earl.

Elizabethan epitaphs can strain a point to destruction but they do include some remarkable tributes to gentlewomen. A brass in Kirkby Moorside church of 1600 shows Lady Brooke kneeling at an altar, with six sons and five daughters. The inscription reads "Here lyethe the body of my lady Brooke, who, while she lived, was a good woman, a very good mother and an exceeding good wife." Alderman Robert Brooke found in his wife, "great love to me and all my friends. She was always wise and discreet and had the fear of god before her eyes." Jane was "always a natural mother to our children and very careful for their godly education." The sober dame of Thomas Ingram portrayed in Langton church, was "a wife, as one would wish, be this her pride, she nere displeased her husband till she died."

At the peak of society, household management must have been largely supervisory but the lady's role could extend to managing the entire estate in a husband's absence. It was a commonplace that, "a virtuous wise woman was a great support to a family." James Crathorne of Crathorne said of his wife "she knoweth in every part what I owe." A mother's son would say that, "she was a very virtuous religious woman, a loving wife and understanding in the management of her husband's affairs, both domestic and out of doors, in his absence. By her goodness and wisdom, she had got a great influence over him." Her death was a great loss to the estate and the family.

This was not always so. "It is hard to wive and thrive all in one year", said the proverb. Young Ralph Eure touring the continent, wrote in 1581 to "my very good wife Mary Eure", at home with the servants. Twelve months later, he complained to her father. "At my last departure out of England I willed that Nelson's rent of forty mark by year should be paid to your daughter, not doubting but your good example in husbandry will make her thrifty and use the same the better. Considering likewise her charge is so small, having no wages to charge her withal save herself and her maids, I think she may content herself therewith. I conceive she is discontent with those whom I did appoint to wait of her and doth refuse likewise the service of all those whom I wage." Her "toys and light behaviour" needed amendment.

Matrimony in any age can become exemplary, tolerable or abysmal. The Earl of Shrewsbury, in early days said of his wife " Of all the joys I have under god, the greatest is yourself" and "I long daily for your coming." They married in 1568 but he came to judge it "an evil hour". Conflict was well established by 1578, and separation in 1583. She called him knave, fool and beast and mowed at him while he told her "she was a byword for rapacity, from which imperfections he rescued her by marrying her." By 1590 the Bishop could tell him that "The Countess is a sharp and bitter shrew and therefore like enough to shorten your life, but if shrewdness or sharpness may be the just cause of separation between a man and wife, I think few men in England would keep their wives long."

The proverbial culture of men contained much that assumed difficulties in later married life. There was the saying that "woman was an angel at ten, a saint at fifteen, a devil at forty and a witch at eighty." Squire Robert Roos married a daughter of Sir Nicholas Fairfax but a life of lawsuits and his "lewd wife" led him to resign his inheritance into the hands of the Earl of Rutland, in return for his debts paid, a modest payment for life, and a chamber at South Dighton, whence a meal was sent from the table of Mr. Manners who lived at the vicarage.

> "Thy youth in folly have thou spent,
> Defer not now for to repent.
> Anon I taste your wine and a cordial flower,
> And prove as women sometimes sweet and sour."

Such sentiments, whether cynical or jocular, were enshrined on five inch diameter wood roundels.

> "A woman that is wilful is a plague of the worst.
> As good live in hell, as with a wife that is cursed."

Women responded with such sayings as "There's no such thing as leading apes in hell."

Gentlewomen were no more favoured than any others in their relationships. Bitterness from genteel women about their men is well evidenced. The Countess of Westmoreland "a woman of spirit", could "burst out against her husband with great curses". Katherine St Quintin at Harpham in 1597 claimed maltreatment against her husband George. The Earl of Cumberland and his wife were reconciled, but only on his deathbed. While Sir Martin Frobisher voyaged to find Cathay by the north-west passage, his wife Isabel sat in a poor Hampstead room, "ready to starve". She described herself as "the most miserable poor woman in the world". She told Walsingham that her former husband Thomas Riggats of Snaith had left her wealthy and her children with good portions. Captain Frobisher had spent it all and put them to the wide world to shift.

Jane Bulmer was secure in the affection of her husband Francis Cholmley but opposed by his family. He felt it necessary to stress, in his will, how freely he made bequests to her. He spoke of her good wisdom and called her his "most trusting and loving wife." Others saw him as so overtopped and guided by his wife that they thought she did it by witchcraft. They said that she led her husband into law suits to regain family portions and persuaded him to settle his disposable estate on her after his death. She had him build a house of old fashioned timber rather than stone at Whitby, saying it would serve good enough for her time, as she had no children. She put her initials before his on the lintel stone. When he died, she moved his body for burial at Beverley rather than Whitby. Then she remarried a young man of mean quality and gave him the estate.

Sir Richard Cholmeley married as his second wife, Katherine daughter of Henry first Earl of Cumberland and widow of John Lord Scrope of Bolton. She kept her title from the first husband, Lady Scrope, throughout her marriage to the second. When some differences arose between them, they parted beds, and did not cohabit as man and wife for years, until coming to a gentleman's house, where they were straight of lodging, "or did not take notice of the difference", they were fitted but with one chamber for them both, where lodging together, it pleased god that the lady that night conceived, which child proved a son, and was named Henry." After this, "they lived kindly together."

Francis Bacon thought Sir Thomas Hoby well married saying "No man may better conceive the joys of a good wife than yourself." Lady Margaret Hoby could write to her husband in 1599, "Dear heart and good jewel, I confess you to be an exceeding good husband and to deserve a better wife than my wit will serve me to be but I will draw as nigh to the high degree as I can." They were married thirty-seven years at Hackness. Hoby later reflected on "the extra ordinary affection that was between her and myself in our lifetime."

The Hobys kept a Puritan household. She prayed privately and publicly. She wrote notes in her testament, read chapters of the bible daily and meditated on them. She heard lectures from her chaplains and would write out the sermon into her book. Her diary tells of her having speech with "the poor and ignorant" and "instructing Thomson's wife on the principles of religion", just as she instructed her entire household. Once a day, she walked about the house, the barn or abroad in the fields. She would take the air in her coach or exercise her body at bowls, which she "found good". She ate breakfast, dinner and supper, took order for the meals, and for things from the granary. She gathered apples, preserved quinces, wound yarn, did wrought work and managed her bees. She ran a daily surgery for ailing tenants before breakfast and would dress a poor boy's leg or go out to a wife in travail of child. She had no time for idleness. She was ever "busy about the house".

Widows at a Premium

Widows were sought after in all levels of society, wherever there were widowers with estates to run, households to manage, and families to rear. Those with dowries or a settlement could have more than personal attraction. Sir Gervase Clifton of Alwoodly had more wives than Henry VIII, but he did not move far in social station, wedding three honourables, three right worshipfulls and one wellbeloved. Others chose second brides, outside the rigid boundary lines of their own status. Many a nobleman chose a knight or esquire's widow for a second marriage.

The heiress, Margaret Dakyns was married to Walter Devereux, but she lost him. The Earl of Huntingdon urged his nephew Thomas Sidney on the widow and Lord Burghley's candidate had to wait his turn. When Sidney died at Hull in 1595, Sir Thomas Hoby tried again. He arrived hotfoot before the widow, too quick for good manners. He was bid to retreat but did better on a second visit when he brought. jewels and pearls and letters of support from Lord Burghley and the Earl of Huntingdon. Thomas Meynell at Ingleby Arncliffe recorded that "having condoled two years and being about the age of forty-one, I married Martha widow of James Thwaites of Marston, an esquire, whom I found so answerable to my other wife in virtue, huswiferie and almost all condition that I have great cause to thank the almighty God who had great clemencie towards me."

Widows had claims on a third of the joint estate. William Raybankes, preparing for burial in Danby church in 1596, wrote into his will "The dues of Margaret my wife I need not speak of, for her right in the thirds of that I have, will be given her by the laws and customs of the realm." Yet he feared that they being so small they would soon be wasted "without great husbandry." He urged her to take the advice of her "good and wise friends" and compound with the supervisors of the will for a yearly annuity.

Norton memorials recall a twice married and much valued lady. Anne Strange of St Albans married William Gourley, a soldier who served in the 1566-7 Irish campaign.

> Here worthy captain William Gourley lies
> Who served the emperor Charles, fifth of that name
> Henry the Second, King of France, likewise
> And lost his leg, in Ireland, with fame
> In service of the Queen, his sovereigne Dame
> Courteous he was and faithful to his friend
> Valiant his life and Godly was his end. Obit 17 June 1591

Anne remarried another soldier at Langton in 1591, memorialised at the same church in seventeen verses.

> Here lies the corpse of Thomas Westrop esquier
> A valiant soldier in camp, a faithful servitor
> in court, and a bountiful housekeeper in the country
> His worthy parts my muse might more commend
> But virtue from oblivion will defend
> And in despite of time, preserve and keepe
> His praise in memory, though his person sleep.
> Obit 12 die Aprilis 1604

The widow, Ann Strange was remembered with

> Virtue, bounty, wit, sweet favour, comlie grace
> United were in her, whose corpse lies in this place
> Ann Strange her name, which birth and baptism gave
> But twice estrang'd from Strange as hymen's hest did crave
> Brave minded Gourley did her youth possess

Westropp her age with equal happiness.
Obit 19 December 1604.

Stewards

Stewards ran the great estates on behalf of their lords. Good lordship fostered an atmosphere of mutual loyalty and traditions of good service. Stewardship of such properties went far beyond mere household duties, offering great responsibility over broad estates, and considerable power over their tenantry, not least when the landlord was himself an absentee. The steward was rewarded with fees and perquisites, with a great house and a share in his lord's local social status. Few men enjoyed more local significance than a steward. The role varied with the scope of the task but typically a steward would decide policy for demesne farming and leasing, receive all moneys from a receiver or bailiff and take the decisions about making provisions, paying bills, paying wages, and buying corn cattle and sheep. He had to look into the work of under-officers and speedily reform any fault.

The sixth Earl of Northumberland had six stewards for his Yorkshire lands, and could fee men of the status of Sir Thomas Wharton, Sir Stephen Hamerton, Sir William Babthorpe and the esquire Robert Lascelles. Officers from his estates in three counties had fixed times of the year to wait upon him. Another steward William Ferrand was granted a coat of arms at the request of his master Francis Earl of Cumberland in 1586. William West steward to George, fifth Earl of Shrewsbury was able in later life to build Firbeck Hall near Roche. Sir John Constable of Kirkby Knowle left his son Joseph a parsonage and the office of the stewardship of his manors and the lordship of Holderness for life, with a £20 rent from the estate.

The ninth Earl of Northumberland required his Steward to have a knowledge of the "tenure of lands and customs in the area, how to receive revenues in money or kind, what assurances the tenant had, to and from the lord, leases for years and lives, annual rents or fines or both, the services owed, the manner of sales, assurances and mortgages, the rates at which sold, measuring by the acre or other common measure, the qualities of ground whether sandy, clay, black moulds, heathy, stony, woody and the dry yield of whins, grass or grains, by the acres."

The Earl was well aware of the temptations affecting those around him. His treatise on officers and servants suggested the principles by which his son should understand his estate better than any one of his officers. He advised him never to suffer his wife to have power in management of his affairs. He should let his gifts and the bestowing of his actions be his own without intercession of others. The Earl considered that all men loved their own ease and themselves best. Habit was the enemy of good service because men would not easily be removed out of a track of life once entered into.

A brass plate in Danby church recalls Samuel Raybankes, steward of Henry Earl of Danby. This paragon left his earthly stage, possibly Cannon Hall on the old Guisborough Priory estate, for his musical destination, age sixty-six on December 14th 1635.

> His life was an academy of virtues
> His conversation was a precedent for piety
> His estate was a storehouse for charity
> His good name a palace for innocence
> His death a passage to eternity

His eternity a perfection of glory
where he now sits, triumphs and sings,
with angels and archangels,
and cherubims and seraphims.

Estate Management

Estates ranged from single tenements, with or without land, and small manors up to the overlordships of great multiple manors organised in honours. The return of much monastic and chantry property to lay ownership broke up those long established estates, often widely scattered, into many small properties, some mere lists of rents to be gathered annually. There was a wave of speculative buying followed by much local buying and reselling. The more vigorous land market was sustained as old leases fell in, needing renegotiation throughout Elizabeth's reign and as inflation encouraged new policies of estate management and significant sales.

Knights and other rising men bought or leased estates, with a tendency to concentrate in one county, selling off those at a distance. Sir Phillip Constable bought the manors of Thorp le Street, Drax, Arras and more for about £3000. Sir Christopher Danby and his heir purchased the manors of Low Ellington, Healey and Sutton in Mashamshire. Sir Thomas Danby acquired the manors of Bramham Biggin, Scruton, Pot Grange, Ellingstring and South Cave. These purchases were at least partly financed by sales elsewhere. Sir Richard Cholmley bought lands that he already had in lease, including the manors of Whitby, Whitby Lathes, Larpool, Stakesby, Hawsker and Fyling for £5000. He added the Crown's Fyling estate in 1563 for £1120, while selling lands in Kent and Pickering Lythe. Ralph Bouchier sold most of his Staffordshire estate between 1568 and 1575 and moved to Beningbrough, into a house three hundred yards south east of the present Hall. He was High Sheriff of Yorkshire in 1580.

T25 Some Major Yorkshire Estates
1544. Earl and Countess of Lennox.
Manors of Whorlton, Brigton, Grenehagh, Temple Hurst, Temple Newsome, Silkeston, Beckhay, Settrington, Hunmanby, Kirk Levingtson, Wandesford, Gemling, Nafferton, Scrafton & granges at Scrafton, Castleton, Lazinby and Tunstall
1581 Earl of Rutland
Ampleforth, Beadlam, Bilsdale, Bransdale Boltby, Carlton, Cowhouse, Harum Haugh, Helmsley, Hesketh, Howsham, Hunmanby, Linton, Oswaldkirk, Pockley, Pottowe, Ravensthorpe, Rievaulx, Seamer, Skiplam, Sproxton, Thirleby, Thornham, Turnham, Upsall castle, Wombleton
1588. George Earl of Cumberland licence to sell
Manors of Conondley, Gisburn, Gigglewick, Preston, Langestrothdale, Threplande, Crakowe, Woodhowse, Appletreewick, Litton, Littondale, Haltongill, Fountance Skalle, Stodderhall, Coishe Foxhoppe, Over Hesselden, Nether Hesselden, Sleghtes, Storthes, Hesselwood, Draughton.

Among the greatest estates were the Crown honours of Pontefract, Pickering, Knaresborough, Richmond, Conisbrough and the Manor of Wakefield. Some were liberties with such privileges as the exemption of the tenantry from tolls and freedom from attending the sheriff's county court. Another cluster of estates centred on Sheriff Hutton were organised under the Dukedom of York. The Queen in right of her Duchy of Lancaster was chief lord in Pickering Lythe, with manors at several villages and demesne properties leased out at several more. The office of joint receiver and bailiff of the honour of Pickering was held in succession by Lord Neville, Sir Robert Dudley, Henry Earl of Huntingdon, Sir Thomas Knyvet and esquire Richard Etherington during the reign. Only the last lived locally at Ebberston, central to the estates.

The management of large estates was a professional task. There was a movement from customary arrangements and understandings to written contracts. Surveys were made to record assets and rents paid. Old rentals were perused for vanished incomes. Queen Elizabeth appointed William Tusser in the second year of her reign to enquire by oath into those Crown tenants throughout Yorkshire who were paying small rents or nothing at all. He was to agree new rents or entry fines and if they wouldn't agree, he could find new tenants, at better rents, "suitable to the goodness and quantity of the property". The Stewards were to grant copies of court rolls to persons delivered by Tusser, and admit them according to the custom of the local manor. The payments were to be no less than four pence yearly rent and a ten shillings entry fine for every acre, a sixpence rent and twenty shilling entry fine for every house, five shillings rent and forty shillings fine for every mill or mine.

The drive to raise incomes occupied many Stewards in the face of inflation. Their challenges to the customary rights of freeholders were bitterly resented. For the landowner, a fixed rent roll in a period of inflation was the ticket to disaster. Some men, especially those in debt, granted very long new leases for a heavy down payment. Others looked to the future and reduced the length of time for leases to run. Raising entry fines or raising rents was the principal choice. Sir John York, the Treasurer of the Mint, and purchaser of the Whitby monastery estates, put up the rents in 1555 before selling the property to Sir Richard Cholmley. Leasing the park or the demesne land were other options. The Earl of Rutland leased one of his two Helmsley parks for twenty-one years to gentleman William Seagrave in 1560. The other park remained a charge on the estate paying £3.10s a year to the keeper. Two hundred and fifty acres of demesne land, a mill and cottages were leased to the Steward for £5 a year. The Helmsley estate fines were raised between 1597 and 1600.

This was an age of surveys. Esquire Edward Stanhope surveyed the manor of Almondbury in 1578, posting a written notice in the church twenty days beforehand, "so that tenants have their evidences ready". A long list of articles to enquire into, included the boundaries of the manor and of the townships of Huddersfield, Honley, Metham, South Crosland, Slackthwaite and Quick, as well as single houses elsewhere which came under the jurisdiction of the manor court leet. The castle had long since decayed, and the manor house was farmed by esquire Francis Samwell. The Hall-Bower mansion with thirty-eight acres was let to Edmund Blackburn and a new house at Almondbury Park was tenanted by John Lockwood. There were twenty-three freeholders.

Maps made a new contribution to estate surveys. Robert Saxton, the pioneering cartographer, prepared the maps of the Percy's Spofforth estate in 1606 and 1608. He used different symbols to record land use, for arable, demesne, meadow, pasture and others, not fully explained, showing the relative quality of the land. His Manningham map was commissioned, with a written survey, for legal proceedings. The bounds were given in great detail, while the houses were shown conventionally.

The broad variety and range of the different estates can only be suggested in a few examples. The 1608 survey of Hackness reveals an estate covering several villages working fields and commons and two dales. The Hackness demesne included a manor house, stables, park, orchard and hop yard, two corn mills, a quarry, a smithy, sheep houses and sheep sties, and a mustard seed close. There were twenty-seven acres of coppiced wood, and one hundred and thirty-five acres of other wood. One freehold had nineteen acres. Within the estate were the six townships of Hackness, Silpho, Everley, Broxa, Suffield and Dales, with at least sixty-one tenements and twenty-three houses.

A survey of Kirkby Knowle recorded the "mansion house of great height and length, passing beautiful of itself and fair of prospect. Including one goodly hall, great chamber, parlour and bed chamber, with a number of other pleasant lodging chambers, one study, chapel and amories, gallery, kitchen, buttery, cellar, pantry, wine cellar, porter lodge, bake house, brew house and larder in proportion, quadrant, covered with lead and well glassened." This had been begun by Sir John Constable. Other features were given values, some nominal, including the court leet, view of frank pledge and all regalities; with the court baron, held yearly for claims of debt.

The park held "great store of fallow deer and wood of all sort, oak, birch and alder, six hundred and forty five acres and one perch of marvellous, pleasant meadow and pasture, every acre well worth 3s.4d." The park seems to have included old closes and pieces of the West, Steney and South Fields some held by the lord and some by tenants. A mill which stood in 1590 had burnt down and never been rebuilt, the site in the grass near the church with the dam and the hollow of a mill race. The squire had the donation of the parsonage of Kirkby Knowle and Bagby with a good house with hall, chamber, parlour, buttery and other houses, an orchard and two gardens in metely repair, standing near the pale of the park occupied by George Welles the parson there with glebe land. There were ten other tenements.

Household Servants

The great families of noblemen and knights, and even some merchants and other gentlemen needed the labour of household servants to sustain them. The greater the house, the greater the number of servants, especially men servants. Some performed the functions of laundry and cooking, of brewing, malting and baking, of fuel supply, stabling and house repair. Others were servants of the body, and some were for show. Personal service was one of the most appealing rewards of wealth. Servants and the means to house and feed them were a very visible expression of status. Male household and estate servants had also been used as retainers for war. Latterly personal armies had been discouraged but the 1504 Statute of Liveries had exempted from penalties those who retained persons as their household or manual servants. The Crown could still licence retainers for service in war.

The household book of Henry fifth Earl of Northumberland detailed an establishment of one hundred and sixty-six servants, in the early part of the century. Many were liveried. Twenty of them waited on him in his great chambers in the morning, eighteen in the afternoon and thirty in the evening. Sir Nicholas Fairfax kept thirty or forty serving men at Gilling castle in 1555-6. Sir Richard Cholmeley lived in great port, at Roxby near Thornton Dale, until his death in 1583, "having a very great family, at least fifty to sixty men servants about the house." There were occasions when arriving late, he could find none of the twenty-four pieces of meat which had been put in the pot. The third Earl of Rutland visiting London with the Countess in 1586 was accompanied by forty-one servants, including a chaplain, a trumpeter, gardeners and an apothecary.

Francis Clifford at Londesborough in 1597 had twenty-three to twenty-five servants entitled to two meals a day and another eleven or twelve given one meal daily. Fifteen of these were counted genteel as well as the younger Cliffords and their children. Lady Grissold had three gentlewomen and four ladies of her chamber. Sir Ralph Babthorpe of Osgodby, and Charles Stuart son of the Earl of Lennox at Settrington, each kept more than thirty household servants. Sir Henry Bellasis had 51 servants at Newbrough, giving a wages bill of £24.16.8 a quarter in 1609.

George Constable prepared "A Book touching the order and government of a nobleman's house, divided in three sorts" for his kinsman Sir Phillip Constable of Everingham in 1608. He wrote that "There belongeth to a noble man, that intendeth to keep an honourable house in order, these particular officers", listing a treasurer, a comptroller, a receiver-general, a surveyor-general and the auditor of the household. These should be assisted by "two gentlemen ushers, a gentleman of the horse, two chaplains, two secretaries, a clerk controller and a clerk of the kitchen."[9]

Inferior officers included yeomen of the ewrye, the cellar, the great chamber, the pantry, the buttery, the wardrobes, the horse, the larder, the garner, the bakery, the brewery, the scullery, the wood yard, the cellar, a slaughter man, the master or usher of the hall and two master cooks. Four children might attend the cooks. Others could be taken on "at the lords pleasure", including gentlemen waiters, yeomen waiters, two gentlemen of the bed-chamber, two pages, gentlemen for the hawks, and for the hounds, and four footmen. Then, there might be grooms of the bedchamber, the hall, the wardrobe, and the stable, one for every two great horses, or three geldings. There was a laundry, spaniels to be seen to, yeomen of the leash and falconers.

Everyone's duties from the principal steward down to the "least and meanest "were specified, along with their diets. The gentleman usher governed everything above stairs or in his lord's presence, except in the hall. The hall might be marshalled by the steward and the comptroller, bearing white staves. They would countenance the meat from the dresser to the lord's table. The yeoman porter was told to stop country people at the gate, who wanted to speak with anyone in the house. He blocked the gates before dinner, supper and prayers, and when it was growing dark.

When the Fairfax family were being served in the great chamber at Denton, "the steward and chaplain must sit down in the hall and call unto them the gentlemen, if there be any unplaced, and then the servants of the strangers as their masters be in degree. All the servants must be ready upon the terrace at such times as the strangers do come to attend their alighting" and "when prayers shall begin (or a very little before) the gates on all sides shall be shut and locked and the porter must come into prayers with all the keys." Hugh Rhodes' "Book of Nurture" of 1577 advised on expected behaviour at table. "Sup not loud of the pottage. Take salt on your knife, not by dipping your meat in it. After pottage wipe your spoon. Don't scratch your head when you eat meat. Don't pick your teeth with your knife. Don't spit over the table and don't blow out crumbs as you eat."

The servants were most concerned with food and drink, all vouched for by tallies, with weekly checks of what had been spent and what remained. Laying the hall tables might require a trencher, napkin, cup, loaf and spoon for every man. Sharp knives were at hand to cut meat. There were basins and ewers to wash hands at table, voiders to clear away morsels left on the trenchers, once they had been removed with a trencher knife. The household daily work included making beds, cleaning fireplaces and the candle boxes, and leaving shut doors open to freshen the house. The entire house would be swept and dusted weekly.

T26 Household Servants of Henry Earl of Huntingdon, with half year wages 1564

Gentlewomen & chamberer - Mrs. Guildforde, Mrs Beaumonte, Mrs Pyster, Dorothy Vernon

Gentlemen   George Devereux, George Bouchier, John Burley, Thomas Estwick, Thomas Cotten, John Cholmeley jnr, Thomas Sill, George Secheverrell, Thomas Sloughter, Robert Harver, seven at 26s.8d.

Clerk of the kitchen	Robert Pykes
Yeomen	twenty-five one nothing, two 26s.8d., rest 20s
Grooms of the stable	six at 16s.8d. each
Gardeners	four, at 30s, 23s.4d., 13s.4d. and 10s. respectively
Armourer	Robert Claver at 20s.
Waynmen	two, at 20s. and 10s.
Carters	two at 20s. and 16s.8d.
Slaughterman	Richard Large at 13s.4d.
Children of the kitchen	four "their apparel found by my lord"
Laundry maids	two
Menders of Arras	one and a boy paid weekly
Tiler	one at 20s.
Woodherd	one at 13s.4d.
Men	nine, two at 26s.8d. one 13s.4d. rest 20s.

The literature idealised the model servant, who kept his master's secrets, was swift on errands and bore his wrath. Some households levied fines for oaths, or dirty garments. Gentry children grew up knowing servants better than parents. A main reason for sending sons to travel was to wean them from familiarity with serving men. There was hierarchy in a household and promotion was possible for the literate, who could keep wage lists and kitchen checkrolls. Servants were rewarded with board, clothes, shoes and candle ends. Ann Lutton at New Malton in 1551 could leave a cousin a feather bed but her maid servant Jane Wharton had a mattress, three coverlets, a pair of line sheets, a pair of harden sheets, a brass pot, three pieces of pewter, her holiday gown, a sage kirtle, a pair of blankets, a cod and a laten candlestick. The Fairfax servants had their bedsteads over the middle gates, in the porter lodge, over the far gates, in the stable, over the stable, in the dairy, some fortunates warmly by the kiln near the lead cistern and two in the oxhouse. The retired Londesborough servants formed a sort of local elite, occasionally called upon. James Pennyman in 1635 at Ormesby made ten shilling bequests to servants that sat in the hall at meat and five shillings to servants that sat in the kitchen.

The Conflicts of Great men

Some Elizabethan personalities seemed larger than life. Many of the nobility and gentry retained great freedom of action, even as the state expanded its power against mighty subjects. Wrong choices in religion or disloyalty to the Crown could bring personal and family disaster. Several of the highest in Yorkshire society came before the highest courts. A few spent time in the Tower of London. Some were even exiled or executed.

Personality clashes and family feuds occurred as well as differences of political loyalty. Lord Latimer, undoubtedly a difficult man, threatened formal complaints against the Earl of Cumberland in 1557, and complained to the Council in the North that Sir Thomas Danby and his men had attacked him at Snape. It says much that Latimer was indicted. A few months later, he sought the arrest of Sir Oswald Wilstrop, Mr Thomas Markenfield and five others, accused of abusing him while hunting, attacking him and his servants and pulling down three roods of his park pale. Latimer was in the Fleet Prison within the month.

The Privy Council told the Earl of Cumberland and the Marquis of Northampton to settle their differences. When Sir John Constable of Halsham was feuding with John Bellow and the pair were ordered to keep the peace, it was claimed that when Sir John took against a man, he didn't care what harm he did him. Constable was removed from the Council in the North and bound over to keep the peace after quarrelling with two other members Sir Henry Gate and John Vaughan. Quarrels could become family feuds, lasting more than a generation. The Earl of Westmoreland wrote to the Earl of Rutland saying that his enemies tried to trap him, during the horse running day at Gatherley moor in May 1554. Christopher Neville of Kirkby Moorside went to see his horse run, but there were many Bowes and Rokebys there and in the fracas one was killed. Retainers of the Talbots and Gargraves had one of a series of affrays at Pontefract sessions in 1598.

Sir Stephen Proctor of Fountains Abbey claimed that he was plagued for eight years with frivolous suits by Sir John Mallory, Sir William Ingleby and others. Procter secured a Catholic priest near Ingleby's house within his park, on a warrant from the Privy Council. Mallory had him set upon at Smithfield in London, saying he would take an arm or leg immediately. Procter claimed an attempt to lure him and murder him on Kirkby Malzeard moor, and that his opponents had hoped to cast him into a coal pit. There were riotous assemblies at Grewelthorpe moor, assaults on his men at the coal mines, coals set fire to, a coal pit filled in, pistols fired at windows and his servants were "pulled by their lugs".

The young Countess of Shrewsbury sent Sir Thomas Stanhope a message in February 1592, that he was a reprobate, and his son John a rascal. Her servant Williamson was sent to elaborate on the theme. "My lady hath commanded me to say thus much to you, that though you be more wretched, vile or miserable than any creature living, and for you, wickedness become more ugly in shape than the vilest toad in the world and one to whom none of reputation would vouchsafe to send any message" yet she didn't wish his death, but "that all the plagues and miseries that may befall any, may light upon you." She felt sure he would be "damned perpetually in hell fire". There were affrays by the Earl of Shrewsbury's followers on Stanhopes men in Fleet Street in 1595.

The greatest scandal of the reign arose from a quarrel between Sir Robert Stapleton and Archbishop Sandys of York. Stapleton and Sir William Mallory had investigated complaints against Sandys, back in 1578, when he was Dean of Durham. There was some public quarrelling, when Sir Robert met the Archbishop by chance, at the Bull Inn, Doncaster, on May 10th. 1582. During the night that followed, William Sysson, the innkeeper roused the house, and forced the door of the Archbishop's chamber. Stapleton and others rushed in, to discover the innkeeper's wife naked in the bed. Sandys gave Stapilton money to bribe Sysson to keep his silence.

When the story leaked out, Lord Burghley employed Dean Matthew Hutton and Archdeacon Robert Ramsden to "boult out the truth". There were attempts to omit certain evidence. The dispute ended before the Court of Star Chamber. Sissons was said to have offered Stapleton a way to get even. Stapleton was accused of connivance at least and of persuading the innkeeper at worst, while he claimed to be merely an onlooker. It was said that the Archbishop had given Sissons £500, and Stapilton £200, a loan, and a lease worth £2500. Sissons had a violent dispute in the garden at Bishopthorpe, when he demanded another £800.

Syssons and his wife were pilloried, fined, imprisoned and lost their ears. Stapleton was fined heavily, and told to make an apology on his knees. The apology was written for him. He delivered it in so haughty a manner that he was put into prison. Current opinion was divided. Some thought that it was decided to clear the Archbishop at Stapleton's expense. He was soon released at Burghley's request who wrote to tell the Archbishop that his "long continuance in prison would be attributed to motives of revenge". The Queen thanked Burghley for his handling of the issue.[10]

CHAPTER 3
RELIGION

The Church before Queen Elizabeth

The Christian church had existed for more than 1500 years. A hierarchy of officers, clergy, priests or ministers and others managed buildings called churches and chapels, in which they provided religious services for the faithful, and said prayers for everyone. The Church had fostered a wide range of behaviours, institutions and beliefs. Yorkshire was part of a church district called the Diocese of York, which contained several hundred smaller districts called parishes, each with at least one paid priest and other voluntary officers. The church sought to promote a Christian culture, while offering a variety of frameworks for living, with the approval of the secular authority.

The main church buildings were available to serve parishes, which were of very different size. The parish had a priest, either a rector or a vicar, the latter word meaning substitute. The rector received the great tithes and the vicar the lesser tithes, which were together a tenth of any increase of the produce of the soil. Rectories had often been given to monasteries. The Parish church was the place where baptisms, marriages and burials were held. They were rarely allowed elsewhere. Parish clergy were thought of as having the "cure of souls". They could hear confessions. Other religious services were provided. The parish churches were supplemented by chapels, almost one to a village, which were used for some services. The dales were served by scattered chapels. There were monasteries and nunneries, friaries and hermitages for those who adopted the religious life, as a vocation. The monasteries, nunneries and friaries had churches, those of some Augustinian priories doubling as parish churches. Many castles, manor houses and maison dieus held private chapels, while others of a more public nature were at some hospitals, bridges and shrines.

Church courts exercised supervision of wills, morals and much else. The landscape held many crosses at road junctions, market places, and boundaries. There were religious guilds and church public houses. The Church owned massive landed estates, from which income flowed to finance the religious life, and the activities of the priesthood, which included some charity. The church taxation called tithe, and mortuary bequests came from everyone able to pay, along with voluntary gifts from those minded to give them.

The York province of the Christian church included most of the East, West and North Ridings of Yorkshire, together with Nottinghamshire, Cumberland, Westmoreland and parts of Lancashire. The York Diocese was organised under an Archbishop of York, in archdeaconries, deaneries and parishes, each with their own officers. The archdeaconry of York included deaneries of the Christianity of York, of Ainsty, Craven, Doncaster, and Pontefract. The archdeaconry of Cleveland held deaneries of Bulmer, Cleveland and Ryedale. The archdeaconry of the East Riding included deaneries of Buckrose, Dickering, Harthill and Holderness.

7. Edmund Grindal, Archbishop of York

A new Chester Diocese had been formed from Lancashire, Cumberland and Westmoreland with parts of the West and North Ridings of Yorkshire in 1541. Those parts of Yorkshire taken into Chester diocese, formed the archdeaconry of Richmond, with its deaneries of Boroughbridge, Catterick and Richmond. Yorkshire also included small parts of the deaneries of Retford, Ashton under Lyne and Lonsdale.

The English Church formed part of the broader organisation of Latin Christendom, embracing most of western Europe, but distinct from other Christian connections in

Eastern Europe. The English church was organised as part of the Roman Catholic church, of which the Pope in Rome was the head. The Church nominally included everyone but what most people actually believed and what they practised in the sixteenth century is not at all obvious. The written records of that time and later were largely produced by churchmen. Even so, older beliefs and behaviours of a pagan or non-Christian character were an important part of the broader culture and would surface again. Many ideas and practices of pagan origin had even been taken into the life of the church.

A movement critical of many church beliefs and practices, known as Lollardry, had taken root in England in the broad period of the plague outbreaks of the late fourteenth century. An Oxford University teacher from Yorkshire, John Wyclif had questioned papal authority, arguing that the only sure source of authority was the bible, which he thought of as divinely inspired. He believed that the church was too wealthy and questioned the need for people to pay tithes. His followers arranged for a translation of the bible into the English language instead of Latin. The Lollards questioned whether priests were necessary. They challenged the strange, almost magical doctrine, known as "transubstantiation", that during the service called the mass, bread and wine were actually turned into the body and blood of Jesus Christ. Lollardry was persecuted and went underground. The continuing impact of the movement in sixteenth century Yorkshire remains uncertain. Only isolated cases reached the church courts.[1]

A new critical movement spread from central Europe to England in the early sixteenth century. The German monk Martin Luther criticised many of the existing beliefs and practices of the Church, including the sale of indulgences to finance the rebuilding of St. Peter's Church at Rome. The indulgences purported to offer sinners remission of the time they would spend in "purgatory", after death, purging their sins. Luther and others went on to question many other beliefs and practices, which had become central to the life of the church, but for which no precedent could be found in the Christian Bible. Luther stressed the faith of believers and the role of divine grace in the "salvation" of individuals.

John Calvin at Geneva developed other ideas that proved influential in England. He considered souls to be pre-destined either to salvation or damnation. He envisaged a reformed church as a company of elect believers, not a communion that included everyone but rather consisting of those predestined to belong. Anabaptists rejected all links between church and state and required a church composed of adult members. Others sought to replace the religious service called the mass by bible exposition. The making holy of supposed saints and their relics, of popes and bishops, images and shrines, of certain days and even of churches themselves, was called into question.

The new movements came to be thought of as "Protestantism". Many of the old ideas and practices that they criticised came to be seen as "superstition". English Protestants in the reign of King Henry VIII and that of King Edward VI made great changes in the English church. The king's minister Thomas Cromwell licensed Yorkshire man Thomas Coverdale to make another revised English translation of the bible. Copies began to be placed in parish churches.

King Henry VIII wanted a divorce from his Queen Catherine of Aragon in order to marry Anne Boleyn, a woman who he thought might give him a male heir. The Pope would not grant permission. The King initiated measures in 1532-33 which resulted in him being confirmed by Parliament under the 1534 Act of Supremacy, as "Supreme Governor of the Church in England". This ended the role of the Pope in the English church. The Convocation declared that scripture gave no sanction for the exercise by the Pope of Rome of any jurisdiction higher than that of any other bishop. There were a few voices raised in protest and some clergy went into exile overseas. A Jervaulx man who said the Pope alone was head of the church was executed at York in August 1535.

The Loss of the Monasteries[2]

A huge monastic establishment had been settled in Yorkshire in the 12th and 13th centuries, and there were a few later additions. Here was a church within a church, for those seeking refuge in a full time "religious" life, which was originally based on chastity, obedience, order, poverty and prayer. Several orders of monks, nuns, canons and friars had offered different emphases of organisation, role and pre-occupation. The number of inmates had once been huge. There had been over a hundred monks and several hundred working lay brothers at Rievaulx Abbey alone. By 1534, much of the early zeal had gone and the total number in the entire shire was only about a thousand.

Monasteries and nunneries had become part of the established social landscape and not very much more. They served their members. The monks and nuns enjoyed a good life, with enviable accommodation, regular food and drink, duties that were not too onerous and a living standard better than most. The religious men and women were recruited within twenty or thirty miles of each house, from the middling and upper ranges of society. They employed considerable numbers of servants. The small priory of Keldholme with six inmates had twelve servants, Drax with ten inmates employed twenty-nine servants and boys. The small Priories of Marton and North Ferriby each employed more than thirty people, to do the work. Some of the houses may have provided a little education, much charity and some places of retirement for those able to afford them.

The monasteries remained great owners of property with incomes from great tithes, rents, courts and much else. The Lord of Settrington and Mulgrave, Sir Ralph Bigod had mingled with Lutherans and he published a treatise in c1535, criticising the system whereby parish incomes were used to support distant religious houses. He wanted their incomes diverted to sustain a preaching clergy within the parishes. King Henry VIII and his advisers wanted the monastic wealth and incomes for the state. Religious and moral reformation was made an excuse for the abolition of monasteries. Two Commissioners were sent to appraise and value the religious houses in 1536. They looked for fault, and they found it. They condemned forty-seven Yorkshire monks and canons for relations with women, nine as homosexual and ninety-two for 'self-abuse'. Fourteen nuns had children and two more were unchaste.

The King secured an Act of Parliament in February 1535-6 dissolving the small monasteries with incomes of less than £200 a year. Pensions were given to heads of houses. A proposal to transfer inmates to larger houses proved impractical. Protests against these abolitions formed a part, perhaps not the major part, of the wider protests against many changes made, threatened and rumoured, which were the basis of the Yorkshire rebellion known as the Pilgrimage of Grace in 1536-37. One rumour was that parish churches might be destroyed and their possessions confiscated. The rebels gathered from many wapentakes, marched to York and on to Doncaster, where they were persuaded to disperse with false promises. The leaders were executed. The larger wealthier monasteries were dissolved in 1539 under a second Act of Parliament.

Thirty-five Yorkshire abbeys and priories for men, twenty-one nunneries, the double house at Watton for men and women, the large hospitals at Northallerton and York, and nineteen friaries were closed. Six hundred and ten monks and canons and two hundred and thirty nuns and sisters returned to ordinary life, with pensions and two hundred friars without pensions. An account of the dissolution of Roche Abbey, written later, as a reminiscence, claimed that no sooner had the visitors turned the monks out and the servants left, than the plunderers were in at the door, including the writer's uncle. That day "every person had every good thing cheap: locks and shackles were plucked away; doors, service books, windows, iron hooks from walls, lead, choir seats and pewter vessels were taken". Tombs were broken up. "Every person bent himself to filch and spoil what he could".[3]

T27 Yorkshire Monasteries & Friaries Dissolved 1536-38 (with numbers of "religious", where known)

York & Ainsty
St. Clement's (8), St Mary's (49), Holy Trinity (11), St. Andrew's (4), Austin friars (14), Black friars (11), Grey friars (21), White friars (13).

East Riding
Bridlington, Ellerton (5), Hull (13), Kirkham (18), Meaux (24), North Ferriby (6), Thicket (12), Watton (21), Warter (10), Wilberfoss (11), Yedingham (10), Hull Austin friars, Hull whitefriars, Beverley blackfriars, Beverley greyfriars

North Riding
Arden, Basedale (11), Byland (25), Grosmont (5), Guisborough (25), Hackness (4), Handale (10), Keldholme (6), Malton (10), Marton (8), Moxby (8), Middlesbrough, Mount Grace (27), Newburgh (18) Richmond, Rievaulx (22), Rosedale (10), Whitby, Wykeham (13), Northallerton whitefriars (11), Richmond greyfriars (15) Scarborough blackfriars, Scarborough greyfriars, Scarborough whitefriars. Yarm blackfriars (12)

West Riding
Arthington (9), Bolton 15), Coverham, Drax (10), Easby (18) Eggleston (9) Ellerton, Esholt (11), Fountains (31), Haltemprise (10), Hampole (14), Healaugh Park (6), Jervaulx, Kirklees (8), Kirkstall, Marrick, Monk Bretton (14), Nostell (29) Nunburneholme, Nunkeeling (12), Nun Appleton (19), Pontefract (13), Roche (18), Sawley, Selby (24), Snaith (2) Sinningthwaite (10), Swine (20), Doncaster greyfriars. Doncaster whitefriars, Pontefract blackfriars (7) Tikhill Austin friars (8), Knaresborough Trinitarian friars (11)

There had been few bequests to monasteries in recent years, although the friars, more out and about, had kept some popularity. It is not evident that many lamented the passing of the religious vocation. It had offered a good life, with a sense of purpose, for some dedicated men and women who believed in its value, and possibly some others who didn't. The monasteries soon faded from memory. Their unending petition of prayer ceased, significant only if you shared a belief in the necessity for delegated prayer.

Society kept its rather cynical proverbs. "He swears like an abbot". "Friars, boys, dogs and chickens never have their bellies full", and even more cynically " Beware of the fore part of a woman, the back part of a mule and all sides of a monk." The Catholic Queen Mary who followed would make little attempt to restore the world of monks, friars and nuns

The Changing Church[4]

Many more changes were introduced to the churches, in the later years of King Henry VIII and King Edward VI which bore more directly on the lives of ordinary churchgoers and believers. It is difficult for us to be at all sure of how many of these there were and what role the church played in their lives. It could be that many, perhaps even most people took their religion lightly, and that some didn't bother with it very much at all. The church may have formed the accepted background to life. Religion is not always a matter of burning interest to everyone. That situation is well evidenced in world history, not least in 21st century England and this may not be as novel as it seems. The record of sixteenth century change is better than the record of what was there before it.

The new Articles of Religion adopted by state and church in 1536 repudiated indulgences. The English bible translated and revised by Coverdale was to be issued and made available to all. The book was to become central to parish church life. Archbishop Lee of York urged parishes to provide a chained English bible in the parish church. Every curate and priest was to read four chapters daily of his own New Testament, and do his best to understand it. Clergy and parishioners were to rehearse the Pater Noster, the Ave Maria, the Creed and the Ten Commandments on holy days. The Easter communion was to be confined to those who could recite these statements of their faith. He wanted the clergy to give four solemn sermons a year.

The use of intermediaries in prayer between men, women and their God, had been an important and popular element of Catholic religion. The months of the year were peppered with days dedicated to saints. The landscape held holy wells, churches and chapels dedicated to saints. Church walls were painted with pictures from their lives. St. George, St. Christopher, St. Catherine and others are displayed in the surviving wall paintings at Pickering church. If some had a fictional quality, like St. Pulcre, from the word sepulchre and St. Alkelda of the many springs, and others had embellished lives, more miraculous than saintly, this hadn't prevented their serving as centres for devotion. Now, authority had turned against them and the cult of saints was ended.

The Latin mass was replaced by less frequent holy communion services based on the English Book of Common Prayer. There were some moves towards raising a more educated, preaching clergy. Royal injunctions and those of Archbishop Holgate of York, issued in 1547, required clergymen to study the New Testament, to read lessons, epistles and gospels in the English tongue and to preach. Privy Council orders of 1548 abolished the lighting of candles for the dead and any adoration of shrines or images. Pictures of saints were to be removed. Erasmus's Paraphrases and other books of catechisms and homilies were to be placed in every church. Rich coloured vestments were to give way to a white surplice. An order of 1550 required altars to be replaced by communion tables.

These changes were imposed from above. Robert Parkin, the curate of Adwick le Street complied, but he disliked the changes. He said that in 1548 "candlemas saw no candles sanctified, nor ashes in Lent and images, tabernacles, crucifixes were abolished.

68

On rogation day, no procession was made about the fields, but cruel tyrants did cast down all crosses standing in open ways despitefully". "In the month of December 1550, all altars of stone were taken away and a table of wood set in the choir". Others seemed to welcome the changes but some mocked them. William Bull a Dewsbury shearman told a York court in 1543 that "he would rather be baptised in a running river than a stinking font", and rather "confess to a layman than a priest". Three Halifax men were accused of sacrilege against the sacrament. Old Lollardry may have entered into these responses. A man from York was prosecuted as a Lollard in 1555.

Churchwardens' accounts record a modest impact on parish church life. There were the usual mundane payments for repairs by wrights, plummers casting leads, for candles, surplices, bell strings, gloves, lanthorns, besoms, hooks and snecks, to clerks for writing, and to organ blowers. This was as it was before and mostly it was how it was afterwards, apart from the candles. The Masham churchwardens still paid out to set the rowell candle before the rood, and for wax for candles to mark the "Assumption of Our Lady", as well as for organ tuning, maintaining the clock, and fetching lead from Pateley Bridge in 1542. Novelties came and changes were made. The wardens of St Michael, Spurriergate, York, bought two books of the new processions and lessons in 1544 and in the next year or two took down the saints, and led away the angels wings. The Sheriff Hutton churchwardens replaced the altar with a table of wood, and two years later a full communion table. They paid 5s.4d. for "the book of new service for ministration of the communion".[5]

The clergy were allowed to marry, from 1549 until 1554. About ten per cent seem to have done so, including Miles Coverdale and Robert Ferrar, once Prior of Nostell and now a Bishop. Archbishop Holgate of York married Barbara Wentworth in 1549, daughter of esquire Roger Wentworth. She had been plighted to Anthony Norman eighteen years earlier, at Adwick church, when he was seven, and she was five. They had lived in her father's house at Adwick but the union had been nullified. Parkin wrote "that Christen masse week after, was published the banns of matrimony both in the parish churches of Bishopthorpe and Athwyk by the streatt in Yorkshire".

The City of York voluntarily dissolved eight chantries under a Statute of 1536. Their rent incomes had declined below the level necessary to maintain the services. Statutes required a priest with the cure of souls to be paid six marks a year and five marks if he lacked that role. The City also secured an Act of Parliament for the union of parishes in 1547. Fifty parish churches in York were reduced to twenty-three. The Archbishopric of York also lost old feudal franchises and forty or so manors to the Crown in exchange for the grant of thirty-three impropriations and advowsons that had belonged to monasteries.[6]

York Minster saw changes that same year. The appointment of the Dean passed from the chapter to the Crown. Bibles were placed throughout the building. The Minster clergy were urged to study at a new library and to preach. Archbishop Holgate regularised the preaching, when the new prayer book of Edward VI was issued in 1552. He started lectures in divinity, with monthly examinations for the Minster clergy, scripture reading and memorising for vicars-choral and deacons. Bible texts replaced wall paintings of the saints. The organ was closed and singing confined to plain song on Sundays and at festivals.

The minsters of York, Beverley and Ripon, and several other endowed collegiate churches had supported large numbers of clergy. Estates called prebends had supported individual canons and other officers. Most of the officers served functions which are not obvious in retrospect and contributed little to society at large. They were swept away or only allowed to remain in truncated form. The Dean and Chapter of York Minster suffered less than others. York had six prebendaries. The Treasurership and its prebend at Bishop Wilton went to the Crown in 1547. The prebends of Salton and Bramham were suppressed, along with the priories at Hexham and Nostell which had held them. The Chapter kept the remaining prebends and some jurisdiction in its own extensive possessions.

The incomes of Beverley Minster had sustained a provost, nine canons, seven parsons, nine vicars, fifteen chantry priests, four sacristans, two incense bearers, eight choristers and twenty-two others. Seventy-seven shared an income of £900 from lands and tithes, of which £109 supported the provost. Between 1544 and 1547 this staff was reduced to a vicar and three curates, and in Elizabeth's reign to a vicar and one curate. Ripon Minster was dissolved under the second Chantry Act and was for some time reduced to a parish church. By 1546 there was only one resident canon. The church property went to the King the next year. The Minster was only refounded in 1604.

The End of the Chantries

Chantries had been formed during the late Middle Ages by wealthy men who wanted prayers to be said for their souls, for ever, after their death. A chantry had an endowment, sufficient to provide for priests, who would continue this petition of prayer, and have lights burning at an altar, dedicated to a saint. The underlying belief was that sinful souls would be helped in their passage through purgatory, to heaven rather than hell, in an after life. The chantry often had a chapel building and the parish gained an extra priest, sometimes with a better income than the vicar. Such a priest had few duties and time on his hands which often went in teaching school. The Malton St James chantry even raised funds for bridge repair. York Minster held some forty-seven chantries, and another forty-one were in nineteen of the city churches.

Commissioners recorded the possessions of four hundred or so Yorkshire chantries and other endowments supporting stipendiary priests in 1546. Two Acts of Parliament in 1545 and 1549 abolished the chantries, most of the hospitals throughout the county, also the religious guilds, and with them collegiate foundations, including St William's college and the college of the vicars-choral of the Minster at York. Howden college with five prebends vanished and other collegiate churches were reduced or swept away at Kirkby Overblow, Lazenby, Lowthorpe, Middleham, Pontefract, Sutton in Holderness and Rotherham.

The collegiate church of Hemingbrough which had belonged to Durham Priory, was dissolved in 1540. The provost's house was sold. and he was given a pension of £13.4.6 instead of his £40 salary. Pensions of four marks a year were given in 1549 to the three surviving canons and £6 a year to three vicars. Two more had died and another was appointed as a curate. This became a poor living. The College of Acaster, St Andrew had a school which was continued with a single master and curate at £8 a year.

Prophecies and rumours of more changes brought a local rising in 1549 in parts of Dickering and Pickering Lythe, at the same time as rebellions in Devonshire and Norfolk. The chantry dissolutions were in progress and there was a prophecy that King, nobles and gentry would be swept away and replaced by four representative governors and a Parliament of the commons. Talk at a Wintringham alehouse alerted the Lord President but the Seamer parish clerk and an East Heslerton yeoman, William Ombler, lit the Staxton beacon causing a local muster. An official investigating the future of the chantries was killed. The rebellion was suppressed. Pardons were followed by executions.

Catholic again under Queen Mary[7]

Queen Mary came to the throne in the Summer of 1553. She was Roman Catholic. Parliament responded by ending the Royal Supremacy. The Church of Rome once again encompassed the church in England. The majority of clergy and laity acquiesced in yet another change. Some Lutheran clergy left the country for exile among the changing continental churches. The heresy statutes against the Lollards were revived. The Queen sent articles to York Minster authorising the deprivation of clergy who were guilty of misconduct or heresy and for marriage, especially those who had once sworn celibacy. Priests could profess abstention with their wives' consent and there was leniency if a wife had died. A handful of married clergy were disciplined or deposed. One or two gave up their wives and returned to office.

York Minster returned to a Catholic style of worship. A large sum was spent on altars, tabernacles, candlesticks and redecoration. Parkin said that by early September mass at the minster was once again in Latin. The pageants in the city were revived, including the portrayal of the Assumption and Coronation of the Virgin Mary. There was no serious attempt to restore the vanished monasteries, chantries or guilds. Indeed, the Queen granted the city £157 a year of college and chantry revenues. Wyatt's Protestant rebellion of 1554 failed, but in the aftermath, the south of England saw nearly three hundred Protestant martyrs burnt at the stake. John Leaf from Kirkby Moorside had gone to London as a tallow chandler's apprentice. He died at the stake after denouncing transubstantiation in 1555. He could neither read nor write.

Archbishop Holgate of York was deprived of office but the policy of his successor Archbishop Heath was moderate. Irreverence to the sacraments, and other possible signs of Protestantism were reported at Hull, Halifax, Wakefield, Scarborough, Leeds, Beverley, Ampleforth and Oswaldkirk. Two Wintringham men who had mocked the priest carrying a crucifix had to do public penance, bare foot, bare legged and bare headed. Christopher Kelk was charged with Lollardry before a church court in 1555 but there were no prosecutions at York for heresy. The Lutheran Robert Ferrar, a Halifax man, lost the Bishopric of St Davids because he was married. He refused to subscribe to the articles, and so was condemned as a heretic and burnt at Carmarthen. Richard and John Snell of Bedale were imprisoned by Archdeacon Dakyn of Richmond, now in Chester diocese. After some of his toes had rotted away, John agreed to hear mass. He was freed but drowned himself in the river Swale. Richard was burnt to death in Richmond market place, the only Protestant martyr in the county.

The Sheriff Hutton wardens bought books "for to say and sing the old service according to the Queen's grave request." They carried the rood back from York to set it up again. Soon the rood cloth was sewn, shaped, painted and nailed on. Other small things were bought at York, a pulley for the "sacrament", a mass book and a pair of censers. The chrismatory, the organs and the sepulchre were mended. They paid four pence for the pope's pardon. At Masham, the wardens paid out small sums in 1554 for setting up a rood and an altar and for mending the vestments. The next year, their organ was repaired and rowell candles were made. Easingwold mended their Easter sepulchre,

71

and set up their altar and a rood loft with a crucifix and figures of St. Mary and St. John. They bought a little mass book and a holy water can.

It was not to last. The uncertainty of the times appeared in the will of Richard Malthous of Roclyff in July 1558. He wanted burial in St Michael le Belfry church at York and left them a silk and gold wrought case, with a corporax inside. He gave a blue chequered silk vestment with stole and fannon with crosses of velvet, to Salley chapel. He added a rider, transferring the gift to his wife and children, "if the use of vestments do cease in churches or chapels or if the chapel be pulled down".

The Elizabethan Church Settlement.

Queen Mary died in November 1558. Archbishop Heath of York called a Parliament and proclaimed Elizabeth as Queen. He opposed the new Acts of Supremacy and Uniformity, which made the monarch, now a woman, head of the church. He was deprived of office and imprisoned but was released in 1563 and lived on till 1579. William May, Dean of St. Pauls was named for the Archbishopric in June 1560 but died on the day of his election.

The Elizabethan "Act for the uniformity of common prayer and divine service in the church and the administration of the sacraments" made a fresh attempt to secure uniform standards of behaviour, and belief in church life. The Queen's Injunctions of 1559 went further. The Queen's supremacy in the church under God was to be declared by clergy four times a year. Images, relics and miracles were to go, so that superstitions "devised by human fantasy" might vanish. Sermons were to be preached monthly and when there was no sermon, the paternoster, creed and ten commandments were to be read in English. Homilies were to be read every Sunday and within three months, the large English bible provided. The youth were to be taught the catechism every second Sunday. Church processions were stopped, lest they offer distraction.

Every person in England and Wales was required to attend church on Sundays and holy days. Absence could lead to a fine of two pence, levied by the church wardens for the use of the poor. Once again, churchwardens in the parishes did what the state required. The Masham churchwardens bought a communion book and a psalter in1559. The Sheriff Hutton wardens obtained a large bible, a communion book, the injunctions and the articles .

Some Roman Catholic clergy sought exile. The Archdeacons of York and Richmond were deprived of office, along with six York prebendaries and Robert Pursglove, the suffragen Bishop of Hull. A scattering of other clergy departed from the archdeaconries, five under York, six from the East Riding, three under Cleveland and three for Richmond. The rectors of Romaldkirk and Ripley went from the Chester archdeaconry. Some Protestant clergy who had been deprived of office were restored to their livings. William Coverdale returned from Geneva and would preach till his death in 1568. John Best of Hutton Cranswick, a zealous Protestant became Bishop of Carlisle.

Royal commissioners toured the Yorkshire deaneries, summoning clergy and churchwardens to answer fifty-six specific enquiries. Was there obedience to the Queen as head of the church? Did parishioners know the faith and the commandments before taking communion? Were prayers said in English and homilies plainly read? Were the Lord's Prayer, the creed, and the ten commandments said in English on holy days? Was scripture reading encouraged? Did the minister avoid superstition? Had the images, shrines, tables, candlesticks, paintings and other monuments of fained miracles, pilgrimages, idolatry and superstition been removed and destroyed? Was there talking in church and what of heresies, drunkards, adulterers, brawlers, and sorcerers? The answers were less dramatic than the questions. The main complaints were of poor buildings, lack of prayer books and bibles and reports of people living unlawfully together, about one couple to a parish.

The prospect for Catholicism looked bleak, but there is doubt whether Protestantism had yet achieved a firm hold in Yorkshire. The first Protestant Archbishop of York was Thomas Young. He was a married man, who had been a refugee in Germany. He arrived in February 1560-61 and was also appointed Lord President of the Council in the North, a remarkable conjunction of offices. He was commissioned in May to administer the Oath of Supremacy throughout the Diocese. Clergy who would not take the oath were deprived of office. Thomas Robertson, the vicar of Wakefield who had helped compile the Edward VI prayer book and had been Dean of Durham under Mary refused the oath.

Archbishop Young held office until 1568 and there was a two years vacancy after his death. Very few of his clergy showed signs of either Protestant or Catholic fervour. Many people seemed indifferent to the changes. All that impressed the Londoner, John Stow, when policies changed, was that Latin gave way to English in services and there were new preachers. Yet, there was Privy Council concern about the northern leadership. Something of a gulf seemed to be opening between the gentry and others. Young reported his diocese quiet but thought that the nobility, gentry and clergy were still to be feared. At York, eleven out of thirteen aldermen were no favourers of Protestant religion. Sir William Cecil wrote in 1565 that "hardly a third of the whole number of justices was fully assured to be trusted in the matter of religion". Some prominent Catholics had their movements limited, including Robert Pursglove, suffragen bishop of Hull, who was confined to Ugthorpe, "very wealthy and stiff in papistry and of estimation in the country". There were noblemen and gentry who carried on their Catholicism unchanged. Outward conformity was enough for the present.

The church was moving from a culture of images and flickering candles to a culture of the spoken word, but old habits died hard, helped by nostalgia, inertia, and even confusion. The mass, the Latin liturgy, the old calendar, the doctrine of trans-substantiation and much more had gone. There was some pressure to end the private use of rosaries, crucifixes and relics. And yet, the Holderness visitation found four or five vicars still saying communion for the dead. Fifteen or more churches had copes, tabernacles, a holy water stoup or some other survival of the past, supposedly proscribed. York Minster wasn't cleared of its Marian redecorations until 1567 when Matthew Hutton became the Dean. Robert Hype, the old vicar of Kilnwick Percy in 1562 still left the church a white cope to be used on our lady day in her honour. James Fox a layman of Thorpe le Willows in Ryedale made a will which spoke of the blessed Virgin, Saint Marie and all the celestial company of heaven.

Here and there, a stronger stand was taken. Gabriel St Quintin of Harpham was accused of wilful absence from sermons and hindering his tenants' attendance, but he submitted in the end. Two Hedon men did "utterly mislike the estate of religion now established and never use to come to church, but do speak very unseemly words against Christ's word and the ministers". They were excommunicated. There was a flurry at Ripon church. A parish clerk scoffed at the Queen's proceedings. The vicars refused to read the service in the body of the church. They took the church keys from the sacristan one night and conveyed some holy images to a hiding place.

The Archbishop's concerns tempered with the passage of time. He wrote from Cawood to Lord Rutland in 1567 "doubting not but, although the raging enemies of Christ's gospel do something more than other triumph and show their stoutness, but no further than's God's will is; yet God of his great mercy, for the defence of his elect and for the free passage of his holy word, will so temper the matter that in the end all shall be to his glory and the comfort of his people."

A Diminished Church[8]

The Protestant church slowly removed the relics of the Catholic past, but there were few signs of any other improvement. There were far fewer clergy. There was a substantial loss in services to parishioners. Within the mediaeval parishes, almost all villages and many dales had maintained a small chapel, usually without any burial, baptism or marriage rights, but where other services and local functions could be held. This was a meeting place that united church and parishioners. These chapels had attracted small endowments to maintain lights, services, occasionally a full chantry with a priest, and often smaller gifts. The West Riding at mid century had almost as many chapels as it did parish churches. Over a hundred had vanished. The local chapels had been abandoned wholesale. Most were closed and converted to other uses, in the face of compulsory attendance at parish churches. A long time passed in the West Riding before some were re- opened in the industrial districts and the dales.

The loss of religious guilds may have been the greatest break of all. Their role in maintaining lights, and sustaining saints' day services was perhaps less significant than the over all connection that they maintained between the church and the community. Guilds, as voluntary organisations, drew on the better off and were inevitably somewhat divisive, but they were numerous and were the only voluntary societies, apart from urban craft guilds. Many owned guild houses, which must have functioned something like clubs. These steadily fell into private hands. Society was the poorer with group life confined to the weekly meeting of everyone in the church and whatever the common alehouse could offer.

The church was badly hit by the loss of monastic control of many rectories. The monasteries had undertaken responsibility for chancel repair or passed this on to rectory lessees. The rectories were good investments and were now bought or leased by unsupervised laymen. The new investors sought to maximise their tithe incomes, and minimise their costs. Many tithe cases were taken to the courts as they pressed for new payments. Meanwhile, the chancels generally fell into decay. The larger the chancel the more likely was its ruin. Some collapsed. Much of the religious significance of the chancel had gone, with communion tables moved into the body of the church. Chancel maintenance and repair was the duty of rectors. Seventy-five chancels were decayed by 1575 and not a few entire churches.

The problem could have been overcome by maintenance clauses in leases. Rolland and Richard Hutchinson of Skelton, two yeomen, leased Marske church and parsonage, at twenty marks a year, to James Phillips on condition that he find a curate and uphold the parsonage house and chancel. More often, the decay continued for decades. The Weaverthorpe church wardens reported the church in decay in 1578, the chancel and parsonage in decay in 1591 and the chancel windows in 1596. Snaith church had a "chancel in extreme ruin and decay and very loathsome for any to see" by 1607. At one church of the dean of York "they thought Mr. Dean should repair it in 1568. Two years later, they said "it had been that way for a long time and they didn't know who should repair it. By 1600, choir, chancel and windows lacked repair and "to their knowledge the fault is the dean".

T28 1575. Decayed chancels in the Yorkshire Deaneries[9]

York	5	Ainsty	11	Craven	3
Pontefract	9	Doncaster	6	Bulmer	7
Ryedale	1	Cleveland	7	Allerton	2
Buckrose	3	Hull	2	Holderness	9
Beverley	1	Harthill	1	Howden	2
Dickering	5				

There was some pressure to raise clergy standards. The Cockan chapel clerk in Bransdale was charged with not reading divine service plainly and distinctly. They said he did "mumble the up the same". Examined at York Minster, this proved to be true. He was ejected. Marmaduke Atkinson was accused of incompetence by his curate. At the altar he was unable to find the gospel of the day, wasn't sure when he had found it, and read it out wrongly. They said of John Birkbie, rector of Moor Monkton and chaplain of Lord Latimer that "He is of very dissolute life and lewd conversation and uses very indecent apparel, namely great breeches, cut and drawn out with sarcenet and taffeta, and great ruffs laid on with laces of gold and silk". He appeared to take divine service at Ripon in a coat with a long sword. He was suspected to be a fornicator. He had been taken divers times at night in Ripon by the wakemen with lewd women. He danced at alehouses and marriages.

The Catholic Crisis[10]

A recusant was a man or woman who refused or neglected to attend the worship of the Established Church on Sundays and the appointed holy days, in breach of the statute. Either the pressure to enforce the law was modest or most people conformed occasionally and sufficiently to escape the attention of authority through the early years of the reign. There was little vigourous assertion of the Roman Catholic faith and little persecution. Active catholics dwindled to small clusters, chiefly at the gentry level and higher who practised their own modes of worship in private. They included the Earls of Lennox, Northumberland and Westmoreland and the Lords Dacre and Wharton.

A stiffening of Catholic attitudes may have preceded a limited Catholic rising in 1569. An important step was the formation by William Allen, of a Catholic college at Douai in the Netherlands to educate the sons of gentry and to train missioners for work with English catholics. He had been a York Minster canon in Mary's reign. During the year or two before the first men returned, the Elvington rector, an Escrick curate and the Vicar of Stillingfleet were accused of distributing "seditious, papist literature ". Edward Sandall, clerk of the parish of St Martin, Micklegate York, was heard to say that he "trusted to see the day when he should have off the heretics' heads that now be in authority."

The Catholic Rebellion was led by the Earls of Westmorland and Northumberland, with a small group of gentry, who attracted some hundreds of others in November and December 1569. They wrote to the Pope for support on 7th. November and may have had strong early hopes of assistance from overseas. None was forthcoming. Nor was there any general rising outside their spheres of influence and the line of march. The rebellion was a manifest failure. The East Riding and most of the West Riding were barely affected. Men would rise to support Catholic Earls and knights who were their landlords but not otherwise. The state responded vigorously. A wave of persecution was directed against those who had taken part. Examples were made across areas, which had given support. The leaders either fled or were executed.

The Pope issued a Bull of Deposition and Excommunication, "Regnans in Excelsis" on February 25th 1570, directed against the Queen. She suppressed the Bull, so that few saw it but the message filtered through. It came too late to strengthen the rebels. The Bull was a political disaster. It made conformity to the national law a matter of excommunication for Catholics. This aroused active Catholic opposition to the state on the one hand and brought active State opposition to Catholics on the other. It virtually guaranteed the persecution of Catholics. Put another way, it made treason a requirement for Catholics. Its practical effect was to stiffen the well placed and strong hearted into sustaining a secret underground religion. For others it meant conformity and giving up their Catholicism. It has also been argued that the bull fostered the birth of a strong anti-Catholic movement. This was a turning point.

Acts of Parliament against the Papacy and revised articles of Religion were introduced in 1571. The same year saw the first men from the missionary colleges arrive in England. Henry Simpson of Darlington, who had met the exiled Earl of Westmoreland, landed at Whitby in October. He was soon taken prisoner at York. The Parliament passed new laws to destroy the missions. It became an act of treason to go abroad to a seminary or to stay in England having been there. It was treasonable to be reconciled with Rome, to aid a priest, or to bring in Catholic literature or devotional objects. It was a felony to hear mass, to own devotional objects or send children overseas for a catholic education. A refusal to attend parish church services was subject to a fine of a shilling a person a Sunday, or £3.15s. a year. Refusal to take the Oath of allegiance could lead to loss of property and fines of £20 a month.

Archbishop Edmund Grindal

Edmund Grindal, a native of Cumberland, had been a chaplain to King Edward VI, and one of the six men to whom the Forty-two Articles of Religion had been submitted for approval in 1553. He was exiled at Strasbourg and Frankfurt during Mary's reign and met Martin Luther. He returned from the continent on the Queen's accession. Grindal became Bishop of London and was translated to York in June 1570. His arrival was delayed by the "ague" and he reached Cawood, fearful of the air of the place, "very moist and gross," and was told his Bishopthorpe palace was "an extreme cold house for winter".

Grindal met Sir Thomas Gargrave and Sir Henry Gate, only to learn "that the greatest part of our gentlemen are not well affected to Godly religion and that among the people there are many remnants of the old". They kept holidays and fasts that had been abolished. They offered money, eggs and candles at the burial of their dead. They prayed with beads. This seemed to Grindal to be, "as it were, another church, rather than a member of the rest". His conclusion was to "see in them three evil qualities, which are great ignorance, much dullness to conceive better instruction and great stiffness to return to their wonted errors".

Archbishop Grindal immediately launched a programme of reform. His injunctions were issued before his first visitation. There was the familiar call for the destruction of altars, vestments, mass books, and chalices, with rood lofts stripped of beams and figures. He wanted pulpits facing the people and a new reading desk in the nave, for morning and evening prayer in the larger churches. Ministers were only to provide the marriage service for those who could say the catechism by heart. They were to read chapters from the old and new testaments daily and catechise youth, servants and women weekly. Unmarried ministers were prohibited from keeping any woman under sixty in their house. He told laymen to shut shops in time of prayer; he banned minstrels at rush bearings and he wanted to stop people leaving little wooden crosses at graves. He directed more reforming articles to the Dean and Chapter of York.

Grindal used the church wardens to press for the results he sought. Bell ringings, fasts, confessions, candles at Candlemas and much more that was traditional would disappear from view. The real problem was his clergy. His 1571 visitation made him aware of the small stipends and of the ignorance of many of his ministers. "Oftentimes where there are a thousand or fifteen hundred people in a parish, there is neither parson nor vicar but only a stipend of seven or eight pounds for a curate". Richmond shire held many churches which had heard no sermons since the start of the reign. As a Puritan, Grindal lacked nothing in determination to bring about change but the obstacles were formidable. It was his good fortune that the same year brought him an ally. Henry Earl of Huntingdon "a pious and sincere Protestant" was appointed Lord President of the Council in the North. Strype said of them "They cordially loved one another and drew the one way". Grindal wanted a new commission with the Lord President put into Derby and Lancashire "where the most part of the lewdest sort had remained and were cherished".[11]

T29 Sir Thomas Gargrave's list of Protestant, Evil, Less Evil and Doubtful Gentry 1572[12]

East Riding

Worst	Sir Wiliam Babthorpe (Babthorpe Hall), Peter Vavasor (Bellasize)
Mean	Sir Marmaduke Constable (Everingham), Robert Aske (Aughton)
Doubtful.	Sir John Constable (Burton Constable)
Protestant	John Vaughan (Sutton on Derwent), Christopher Hillyard (Winestead); John Hussey (North Duffield), John Hotham (Scorborough), Rauf Boucher (Grimston), Thomas Boynton (Barmston), Edward Ellerker (Risby)

North Riding

Worst	Sir Thomas Danby (Scruton), Roger Tockettts (Langbaurgh), William Wycliff (Whitby), Francis Wycliff, Mr. Pudsay, Christopher Wyvell (Osgodby)
Mean	Sir Richard Cholmley (Roxby), John Sayer (Worsall)
Doubtful	Francis Wansforth (Kirklington), Christopher Rokeby (Merston), Richard Aldburgh
Protestant	Lord Eure (Malton), Sir Henry Gate (Seamer), Roger Radcliffe (Mulgrave) Thomas Layton (Saxham), John Constable (Dromanby), Thomas Gower (Stittenham), Thomas Savile (Welburn), Lord Latimer (Snape)

Worst   Bryan Stapleton (Wighill), Walter Calverley (Calverley), Richard Gascoigne (Lasingcroft)

Mean   Sir Richard Stapleton (Carlton),.Sir William Mallory (Studley Royal), John Vavasour (Weston), Thomas Wentworth (Wentworth Woodhouse), William Plumpton (Plumpton)

Doubtful   Lord Darcy, Sir Ingram Clifford, Sir William Ingleby (Ripley), Francis Wortley (Wortley), William Tankerd (Boroughbridge), George Saville (Haselden Hall), Edward Eltofts (Farnhill), William Hungate (Saxton), William Hammond (Scarthingwell), Thomas Reresby (Thribergh), William Lister (Midhope), John Beverley (Selby)

Protestant Earl of Shrewsbury, Sir Thomas Gargrave, Sir Simon Musgrave, Richard Tempest (Bowling), Thomas Fairfax, Richard Mauleverer, Francis Slingsby (Scriven), Thomas Waterton (Walton), Francis Woderoffe (Woolley), John Lambert (Carlton), Richard Beaumont (Whitley)

Gentlemen of meaner Degree

East Riding

Mean   Marmaduke Constable (Cliffe), Thomas Dolman (Pockington),

Doubtful   Robert Wright (Patrington), Robert Hawdenby (Haldenby), Bryan Lacey (Folkton), Marmaduke Lacey, Gabriel St Quintin (Harpham), Mr.Constable (Carthorpe), Robert Sotheby (Pocklington), Anthony Smethley

Protestant. Arthur Dakyns (Linton), William Strickland (Boynton), George Dakyns (Brandsburton), Christopher Legard (Anlaby)

North Riding

Worst   Robert Rokebye (Manfield)

Mean   Anthony Cateryck (Carlton), Henry Scrope (Danby), Michael Wansforth (Kitlington)

Doubtful   Roger Burghe (East Hawskwell), Simon Dodsworth (Thornton Watlass)

Protestant Roger Dalton, John Place. Avery Uvedale, William Davell (Cowold)

The County of the City of York

Doubtful   Sir Oswold Wilsthorpe, Gabriel Fairfax (Steeton), Mr Vavasour (Hazelwood), John Ingleby

Protestant Sir Robert Stapleton (Wighill)

West Riding

Worst.   William Hawkesworth (Hawkesworth), John Hamerton (Monkroyd), Henry Oglesthorpe (Beaghall), Wiill Gascoigne (Caley), Martin Anne (Frickely)

Mean   John Hamerton (Craven), Thomas Draper, Robert Ley (Hatfield), Mr.Stanley (Womersley), Henry Gryce (Sandall), Christopher Elson, Christopher Hopton (Armley)

Doubtful   Laurence Kythley (Newell), Matthew Redman (Harewood), John Lacy (Levethorpe), Henry Tempest (Broughton), Robert Rockely (Rockley), Mr Bosville (Ardesley), William Frobisher (Finningley), John Holmes

(Hampole), James Washington (Adwick le Street), Bartholomew Trygott (South Kirkby), (many more evil and doubtful)

Protestant Richard Bunny (Newland), Hugh Saville (Wrenthorpe), Robert Bradfurth (Stanley), John Lacy (Brerelay), William Wombwell (Wombwell), John Kay (Woodsome), John Kay (Oakenshaw), William Vavasour (Weston) Bryan Bales

A Preaching Clergy

Grindal wanted a body of clergy who could bring about a reformation. He sought learned preachers. He would appoint clergy who showed signs of a conversion experience and those who had been to University. He even hired refugee Scots priests. There were few Puritans when he arrived. Now came his new men imbued with Calvinist theology. "Therefore while he was at York, he procured above forty learned preachers and they graduates, within less than six years, to be placed in the diocese (a great number in those times), besides those he found there, and there he left them." He told the Queen they would make obedient subjects. It was his opinion that "by frequent preaching the Word of God, two very good things would prevail among the people, viz; true religion towards God and obedience and loyalty towards the Prince". He considered the point proved by the loyalty of the town of Halifax, in the rebellion. That parish had seen much good preaching and it sent four thousand armed men to quell the rebels.

The clergy felt the weight of more supervision, from the new High Commission, and from the Archbishop, his Archdeacons and the churchwardens. The more typical poorer clergy were instructed, where possible and corrected. Archdeacons examined them for diligence in their study of the bible and a few approved texts. Visitation questionaires invited the lay church wardens virtually to spy on the clergymen. They were to enquire "whether he observed or allowed any holy days or fasting days not in the new calendar. Did he keep an alehouse? Was he a hawker, dicer, carder, or given to naughty women? Did he resort to suspect houses? Did he give at least four sermons a year and say the homilies?" Many were incapable of preaching the sermons.

Grindal used the new men to train the rest. His device was study meetings called "prophesyings", where two or three men, stated the faith, rather than debating it, but could draw an audience together. At the prophecies, two young men would each expound some piece of scripture. After one hour, a more learned graduate preacher would moderate, for a second hour. The laity did not speak. Some meetings were weekly, some monthly, but probably many areas were not reached. Harrison thought these occasions turned ministers away from visiting alehouses, for tables, dice and cards as they had done in the past. The meetings eventually raised official opposition, as the emerging Puritans questioned still surviving practices as being popish and even wondered whether bishops were scriptural.

There were other regular fortnightly open air preachings in market places. Further afield, there was serious debate about the faith. Calvinist beliefs about "election" challenged the opinions of more moderate men. Puritan groups were meeting in the universities and at London. The publication of Foxe's "Actes and Monuments" in 1563, based on Grindal's notes, recalled Lollardry and hailed the Protestant martyrs. It proved the best seller of the reign. William Strickland of Boynton, the M.P. for Scarborough, who had known Puritans at Cambridge, launched the Parliamentary campaign for reforming the Book of Common Prayer. He said that "the book of common prayer is drawn very near to the sincerity of the truth, yet there are some things inserted, more superstitious or erroneous than in so high matters be tolerable, as namely the administration of the sacrament of baptism, the sign of the cross to be made with some ceremonies and the ministration of that sacrament by women in time of extremity and some such other errors:" He wanted "to have all things brought to the purity of the primitive church and the institution of Christ.

The general picture was more mundane. When Archbishop Grindal examined his visitation returns from more than five hundred parishes and chapelries in Yorkshire in 1575, he may have found little comfort. A good proportion of the parishes answered little more than "all's well", possibly but not necessarily, a sign of vigour. Over a hundred and fifty parishes or chapelries reported not having the required sermons, many having none at all. Decayed chancels abounded, but absentees from church numbered less than a hundred people across the shire. Moral offences were most numerously reported, illegitimacy, fornication, living apart and the like. There was still little sign of vigorous religion, whether conformity or non-conformity.

The new clergy would make an impact in time, where they gained appointments in the parishes. They read themselves into their livings. Bryan Sharpe, the new vicar of Braithwell, in south Yorkshire, read his testimonial from Dr.Gibson and all the ten articles of religion in the church, when he was welcomed by two gentlemen and the rest of his parishioners. Giles Wigginton would come from a Cambridge fellowship to Sedburgh vicarage in 1579. Such men made more of the bible and in doing so, weakened the old respect for church tradition, as the source of authority on disputed matters. Conversion religion re-emerged. Elizabeth Aske married Richard Bowe, a landed proprietor at South Cowton near Northallerton. After having twelve children and reaching the age of fifty, she and her husband heard John Knox preach during a visit to Berwick. Her life was changed. She even went to Geneva to meet Calvin.

There was opposition. There was some exasperation with the new "religion of sermons". John Wiseman of Thirsk in 1571 said that he would come to church "when he would and thought best". There was disagreement about beliefs, organisation and modes of service. The bible was now in English, a volume open to many interpretations. Informed comment could not be confined to clergymen nor even to churchwardens. The whole notion of uniformity sat ill with discussion. Some found within the pages of the bible the gathered churches of believers, without parishes or bishops, or even buildings, which would become the inspiration for an emerging non-conformity. Some clergy failed the test themselves and bore the brunt. Paule Mayson vicar of Bishopthorpe in 1571 left his "base begoten doughter" a yewe and a lamb, "the first that doth lambe". Folk would say something about that. One critic thought the curate of West Heslerton was "more mete to keepe a herd of swyne than to serve a cure".

Preaching Chambers

Compulsory church attendance brought more use of the parish church nave. Chancels were neglected. The new communion table and the reading desk were placed in the nave. Loss of outlying chapels meant more use of the parish church. Full attendance could mean crowding in a small building. The available church wardens' accounts do show steady attention to nave repairs. Even the monastic churches converted to parish use were modified to meet the need. The walls of Guisborough church were made up around a nave still floored with earth. A new roof was raised in 1595, its crevices tightly packed with moss picked by the infirm poor, to keep out the snow. There are stories of Marton village church being rebuilt, after the decay of that Priory. Bridlington and Malton churches had to be cut down to size.

The weak had always gone to the wall in church naves, which were sometimes lined with stone wall seats in earlier times. Rows of seats in chancels for clergy and favoured laymen were not new. Pews in the body of a church even gained occasional mention in the 15th century. The edict of 1559 requiring a pulpit for the parson and fixed seats for congregations was repeated by Archbishop Grindal in 1573. The naves would gradually fill up with furniture, called stalls or pews. Wath on Dearne had oak pews in a side chapel inscribed "John Saville caused this to be made on the 19th day of September in the year of our Lord God 1576." Nicholas Medd & John Stonas of Hartoft joined together to build a stall on the north side of Rosedale chapel. Goathland chapel gained stalls in 1594 and a pulpit in 1602.

Pews became personal and the seats were soon thought of as properties. William Kirby at Winestead in 1585 wanted burial "at my stall end". Gentleman Anthony Hunter of Thornton Dale asked for burial in the chancel by the place where he was accustomed to sit in common prayer. William Chancie made a bequest for mending the church stalls at Brompton by Sawdon, "where the young men sit." James Winde was accused of pushing another from his stall in Glaisdale chapel. Pew disputes led to assaults at Kellington in 1573. Sir Thomas Fairfax and James Moyser argued about the pews at Bolton Percy church in 1597. Robert Jackson of Ganthorpe had a stall in Terrington church for ten years, but when Dorothy wanted one, he pulled it up and threw it about.

Outlying townships claimed parts of church naves and transepts as their own, so that they could sit together. Parts of Huddersfield church belonged to Clayton and Byron, while Quarmby folk sat opposite. John Gledhill of Barkisland had made a family stall and another for his sons at Ripponden by 1594. His tenants knelt at the long stall next to the wall. Squires often chose to occupy pews, separate from the rest, and some old side chapels virtually became private chapels for a gentry family. The language of the building changed. Altars and consequently aisles and chapels had been dedicated to saints. The names lingered for a while and then they were forgotten. George Conyers of Pinchinthorpe still asked to be buried in a "place called the lady choir" in 1570. William Plompton could ask to be buried in "Plompton choir where his ancestors did lie" in 1602. The end result was often, as at Kirkby Moorside, serried ranks of pews, in social status rows, gentlemen at the front, labourers at the rear, and the poor near the door, in the draught.

It was not long before colourful memorials of the gentry came in place of the images of the saints. The tombs reflected social degree. They showed fine costume and they proclaimed heraldry and genealogy, while the portraiture slowly began to show individuality. Sir Nicholas Fairfax in a will proved in 1572, wished to raise a tomb in Gilling church, "according to his degree", the value to be thirty or forty pounds and "his first wife's children to be pictured and graven on it." Londesborough church boasted a monument to a gentleman in Francis Clifford's household, who died in 1600. The crowded chancel at Coxwold, would end with barely enough room for the vicar to make his way between gentry memorials.

T30 Some 'Elizabethan Tomb' Monuments

Kirby hill	John Dakyns	1558
Hornby	Lord Darcy	1578
Coxwold.	Sir William Bellasis.	1603
Methley	Sir John Saville	1606
Kirk Heaton	Sir Richard Beaumont	1631
Hazlewood	Sir Thomas Vavasour	1632
Healaugh	Thomas Lord Wharton	1568
Roxby	Lady Boynton	1634
Kirklington	Sir Christopher Wandesford	1590
Sheffield	Earl of Shrewsbury	1590
Well	Lord Latimer	1596
Wentworth	Sir Thomas Wentworth	1587
Winestead	Sir Christopher Hildyard	1602
York	Anthony Bellassis	1603

A few churches and surviving chapels were rebuilt, extended or renovated, largely as a result of new patronage. As Protestantism took hold, closed chapels were re-opened, during the latter years of the reign, particularly in the dales districts of hamlets and scattered farmsteads and in the industrial areas of the West Riding. Muker chapel was licensed for marriages, christenings and burial in 1581 and gained a curate. Glaisdale had the date 1585 on its tower. John Kaye and others rebuilt their local chapel in 1593. Brafferton chapel held an inscription to pray for Ralph Neville, described as its founder. A bell also inscribed to him was dated 1598. Sir Richard Shearburne of Stonyhurst built a chapel at Mitton in1600. Birdforth church was partly rebuilt in 1585.[13]

At St Michaels Malton the register recorded William Aire as the "first that was baptised in the fount after it was made" in December 1591. Bells to summon attenders were more important with compulsory attendance. Some carrying dedications to saints were broken up. After recasting, they were given salutary inscriptions such as "Remember thy end and flie" made in 1598 for Raskelf and "Jesus be our speed" at Settrington. For those who answered the call, the churches had become preaching chambers. Where they lacked a preacher, as was often the case, the homilies and the bible were read out by the parish clerk. Sermons, that could be measured by the new hour glasses, were in English and comprehensible but they invited debate. and even derision when unbelievable text was read, or was given a wrong emphasis. One man slammed the book shut on the reader at Pickering church. The apparent mystery of religion in the Latin language was lost but soon forgotten. This was bible religion now.

Changing Beliefs

A Skipton woman of the late 15th century in her will had called on the holy company of heaven, angels, archangels, patriarchs, prophets, apostles, martyrs, confessors and virgins. The belief that deceased saints could intercede on behalf of living Christians had been challenged. An Act of Parliament had forbidden payment to priests for singing masses for the souls of the dead. The tanner John Ripley of Pickering still desired the blessed lady saint Mary and all the saints in heaven to pray for him in 1556. Edward Salven of Newbigging, near Whitby, a Catholic, in 1558 still spoke of "the time to come". Some still believed in the ability of prayer to alter the possibility and nature of an after life. Many remained concerned with an afterlife but such appeals lingered in a declining proportion of wills, written by surviving Catholics and their priests.

The Elizabethan church encouraged belief in the efficacy of prayer, but less in bringing about things asked for, than for securing a sense of forgiveness for things done. For those who believed in Calvin's notion of election, you could not pray your way into that state. But old traditions died hard. Lady Hoby of Hackness reported that she applied for divine pardon, both for sins of omission and commission, "wherein I found myself guilty" and "It pleased the lord to give her sure testimony of his favour "On another occasion, "it pleased the lord to deal mercifully with her. "After her "diligent attention to her lector", "the lord did hear my prayer, by removing all wanderings which use to hurt me, so that I received much comfort."

Others showed that worried preoccupation with sin which would run strongly through future centuries. Esquire Thomas Saville of Welburn said that "all my thoughts, words and actions are nothing else but abominable sin and wickedness in the Lord's sight". He had undoubted faith and hope, and was penitent. He wanted this confession declared in open sermon at his funeral by some godly preacher. Archdeacon Gregory of Kirkby Misperton took a similar view of himself. He wanted "to wash his foul soul". Humbled by his own sinfulness, he sought "only the lowest room in the heavenly house." His body had always been "in rebellion, conspiring with the lewd affections of an evil mind."

Doctrinal matters occasionally broke into the personal record, certainly a consequence of the new bible teaching and preaching. John Carlill of Thornton Dale was convinced that older sins governed his fate. He saw himself as "born in sin, descended of the stock of our old father Adam, guilty of his fault and fall, and subject thereby to damnation, yet of mere mercy redeemed". Robert Taylor left his soul in 1587, "into the merciful hands of almighty God my maker and former and to Jesus Christ my saviour and redeemer, and to the holy ghost my sanctifier, whom I confess to be three different persons, but yet one, true, immortal, only, wise and everlasting God."

There was an expectation of a Judgement Day. They said that Dame Margaret, wife of Sir William Bellassis, "was called forth of this world to the mercy of almighty God." Some expected to take their bodies, others their spirits, into an after life. Ralph Westrop relied on "the infinite mercy of God, the merits and passions of his dear son, to enter the everlasting fellowship of his blessed spirits, taking my wretched body from this transitory life". George Dakyns of Foulbridge hoped that "his omnipotent power and his precious blood would save his body," which was to be buried wherever he was called to God's mercy. He trusted that at the general Day of Judgement, "I shall be one of the number to whom Jesus Christ shall say, Come ye blessed children of my father and possess the kingdom, prepared for you since the beginning of the world". Brompton labourer Henry Harrison died in 1588 waiting with a sick body "till the coming of Jesus Christ, who would restore it glorious, though it was now weak". Lady Jane Brooke at Kirkby Moorside was sure that, "though worms destroyed her body, she would see God in the flesh".

Some found certainty, convinced that they were the "elect" of God, a pre-ordained chosen people. Gentleman Leonard Mauleverer of Hawnby in 1566 bequeathed his soul to God, Jesus and the Holy Ghost who had sanctified him and "the elect people of God." John Green of Silkstone, a husbandman in 1584, suffering bodily sickness, which he saw as being "visited with the hand and mighty power of God", "trusted to have full pardon and forgiveness of his sins" and to "enjoy the place of felicity provided for me and all the elect people of God from the beginning". John Fletcher of Hagg House in Bilsdale spoke of "the holy ghost who has sanctified me and all the elect people of God" in 1588. George Saville of Wakefield, while bequeathing church tithes to his relations could declare, "I am of the number of the faithful and elect children of God". Matthew More of Thornthorpe lived "in certain hope of resurrection."[14]

Life and death events were attributed to divine influence. Some made sickness the "messenger of God." Death came when you were "called by God" or "visited by the hand of God". We read in the Braithwell register of Elizabeth Pigott "marvellously slain in her masters house with the thunderbolt, as it pleased the lord", in July 1595. George Conyers of Pinchinthorpe in 1569-70 was concerned about "what meditations a man's mind should be occupied in extreme sickness and at point of death".

In time, the wills became less personal. William West of Rotherham produced a model will for lawyers in 1590. It read "I do most joyfully commit my soul into the hands of Almighty God my creator, whom I most humbly beseech to accept the same, and to forgive me all my sins, through his mercy, and by, and for the passion, death and merits of our Lord, and only saviour Jesus Christ, who in his infinite mercy and love hath redeemed me from the bondage of death and everlasting damnation, that made full satisfaction to my heavenly father for all my sins".

T31 Parishes with Puritan Ministers

Agbrigg/Morley-	Batley 1602; Bradford 1568-96; Elland 1588; Emley 1584; Wakefield 1598; Halifax c1592, Sowerby 1591
Ainsty	Bolton Percy 1575
Allertonshire	Birkby 1565-86, Sessay 1579
Birdforth	Thirsk c 1606
Buckrose	Thorpe Basset 1582
Bulmer	Newton on Ouse
Dickering	Bridlington c1602; Carnaby c1589; Ganton 1574; 1582;
Harthill	Beverley St John 1603, Hessle and Hull 1561-91; Hull.c1578; Watton; Huggate 1572; Cherry Burton 1579;
Holderness	Beeford 1594; Withernwick 1592.
Langbaurgh	Easington 1583
Osgoldcross	Badsworth 1599; Owston 1598, South Kirby 1579, 1592
Pickering Lythe	Hackness 1599 or earlier; Scarborough c1593, 1602;
Ryedale	Slingsby 1591
Skyrack	Bingley 1577; Guiseley 1581;
Stai/Ewecross	Gargrave 1576; Gigglewick 1576; Gisburn;.Bolton by Bowland 1598; Skipton 1587; 1591. Marton in Craven c 1591; c160?; Long Preston 1588; Kildwick 1572. c1586; Broughton 1603; Staincross Felkirk 1583; High Hoyland 1576-93, 1592, 1592; Tankersley 1587, 1595
Straff/Tick	Bolton on Dearne 1587; Braithwell 1600; Conisbrough; 1591; Dinnington 1591; Doncaster

	1579 1596; Fishlake 1589; Cantley 1593; Rotherham 1577; Sheffield 1598; Sprotborough 1596; Kirk Sandall. 1597; Todwick 1579; 1591; Treeton 1594; 1575 Penniston 1602; Rossington 1591; Stainton 1592
York	York St Crux, 1599

Catholicism-Treason and Martyrdom[15]

The recusancy laws were more strictly applied after 1577. The £20 fines were exacted without mercy. Those unable to pay were put in York Castle, at their own charge. Between 1578 and 1582 recusancy was found much more widely than before. The numbers of recusants and non-communicants charged rose rapidly. New Jesuit missionaries arrived in 1581. The Treason Acts were tightened again, with the first really heavy fines levied for non-attendance at church. An Englishman reconciled to Rome became guilty of treason. A levy of £20 a month became possible against proven Catholics over sixteen, who failed to attend church regularly. All goods and two thirds of lands could be confiscated, if the sum wasn't paid. In 1593 £10 a month was the fine for sheltering a recusant. Only the wealthy could pay such penalties and they not for long. Most conformed immediately.

The Catholic church in England had become a mission, directed from overseas, with cadres of young men, brought in through the Yorkshire coast. Some were arrested soon after arrival. At the prisons in York and Hull, Protestant clergy sought to change their opinions. The missionary priests had the support of a significant part of the aristocracy and could expect to find refuge and employment in their homes. Priests arriving at Whitby, bare of clothes or money were sent on by Margaret Babthorpe, wife of Sir Henry Chomley equipped with both, to inland Grosmont in a remote moorland dale "notorious for receiving priests and fugitives". Upsall in Richmondshire and Kirkby Knowle were other havens. If they could reach the home of some great nobleman or knight, or even anonymity in York, they might rest secure.

It became a kind of internal war. Since, it was high treason for an Englishman ordained as a Catholic priest to be in England they were hunted down. All Roman Catholic priests were judged to be traitors and to be sentenced to death. Some of those arriving were younger than the old priests. The Jesuits were imbued with a burning zeal. Some were ready to die. The Earl of Huntingdon and others of the northern council actively opposed them. Catholic gentry, still too many to be unseated, gave them protection. The Privy council used Sir Francis Walsingham's spies and paid informers to find them. Some rejoiced in martyrdom. One told the judge that "he looked upon himself as a wretched sinner and infinitely unworthy of so great an honour as that of martyrdom

T32 Some Roman Catholics executed at York in the 1580s (L-layman, p-priest)

1580	John Robinson (L) James Way (p)
1582	William Lacey (p) Richard Kirkham (p) James Thompson (p) Luke Kirby (p)
1583	Wm Hart (p) Richard Thirkeld (p)
1584	John Finglay (p)
1585	Hugh Taylor (p) Marmaduke Bowes (L)

1586	Margaret Clitherow (L) Frances Ingleby (p) Robert Bickerdyke (L) Alexander Crow (p) Richard Langley (L) John Fingley (p)
1587	Edmund Sykes (p) George Douglas Scot
1588	Edward Burdon (p) Richard Ludlum (p) Richard Simpson (p)
1589	William Spencer (p) Robert Hardisly (L) John Amias

Lord Eure took Hugh Taylor prisoner after searching a house Father Ingleby was observed being given marks of respect waiting to cross the Ouse. Robert Bickerdyke was arrested in an alehouse. Eleven priests and a sub deacon were sent to Hull prison from York in 1585. Laymen were brought to book, some families ruined, others survived. The Council in the North heard an account from two yeomen warranted to levy goods from offending recusants. They had demanded what was due from Henry Fairfax of Dunsley, not far from the Whitby coast. He refused, threatened them with a gun, and with eighteen men bearing staves, pitchforks, bows and arrows. Grosmont Priory was attacked and searched but to no avail. Catholicism became a minority movement concentrated in limited areas. By 1590 some 365 recusants out of a total of 806 were concentrated in twenty-one of the 600 parishes. By 1604, the total of recusants and non-communicants was 2412 from a total communicants population of 200.000.

T33 Concentrations of Catholics. Parishes where 20 or more were presented in 1604

Bulmer	Brandsby
Claro	Ripley, Ripon, Kirkby Malzeard
Gilling	Melsonby Stanwick, Forcett, Barningham, Kirkby Ravensworth
Hang	Grinton
Howdenshire	Hemingbrough
Langbaurgh	Brotton, Egton, Eskdale, Guisborough, Kirk Levington, Loftus, Lythe, Stokesley
Ryedale	Hovingham
Whitby Strand	Fyling, Whitby,
anon	Masham Bariwkc near leeds, Carlton by Snaith, Bubwith, Hemingbroughgrinton with Muker, Masham,

'Superstitions"[16]

Towards the end of the 16th century, Yorkshire had well recorded individuals and families, who were well imbued with the beliefs of emerging Puritanism and others retaining catholic beliefs. The majority of people were probably not yet in either group. They were given sermons or readings regularly, weekly in many parishes, embracing the beliefs acceptable to the Protestant church of the nation. The young were catechised. There are indications of indifference, where people left the building for the games outside as divine service or the preaching began. Compulsory church attendance, with everyone present, whatever their condition, must have had many problems. Silence will have been an achievement, general interest a triumph, humanity a distraction.

The Roman Catholic religion offered an explanation of human history, an account of the possibilities for the individual life, and a source of moral injunction to guide behaviour and belief in that life. The church had suggested ways of influencing personal fortune in this life and in an after life. These had included confession of sins, prayer, miracles, blessings, imitating the lives of saints, pilgrimage to shrines, burning candles and many other minor rituals using the sign of the cross, rosaries and holy water. The core of accepted Christian belief changed in protestant England. Many, though not all, of these practices and the beliefs that sustained them were labelled "superstition". At the time, this seems to have meant unbiblical, even unreasonable, and perhaps just no longer acceptable beliefs about things unknown.

A protestant might see the use of holy water or some other consecrated thing as virtually the use of magic. A whole cluster of supposed holy relics were swept away. Howden church had claimed a piece of wood from the cross; another piece from the cross of St Andrew, some dust from the bones of St John the Baptist, the hand of St. John the Evangelist; the robe of St. Lawrence, the bones of St. Theodore, St. Sebastian and St. Clement, hair of the Virgin Mary, a piece of the Lord's cradle and vestments of St. Thomas Martyr, St. Leonard and St. Cuthbert. Other churches and monasteries had similar fragments.

A protestant came to see much of Catholicism as superstition. The word conjuror was sometimes used for a recusant priest. The visitation articles put to the York Minster canons in 1573 asked whether any in their parish had mass books, vestments, albs, tunnicles, stoles, pixes, hand bells, sacring bells, sencers, chrismatories, crosses, candlesticks, holy water vats, images, 'relics of superstition or idolatry'. They were questioned whether anyone prayed upon beads or knots, or any Latin primer, whether they burnt candles in church superstitiously, resorted for shriving to auricular confession to a priest, superstitiously wore crosses or said prayers for the dead. This was a wholesale rejection of past behaviours as "superstitious".

Quite separate beliefs and practices from different traditions were viewed in the same light. Much had been taken into Christian culture from older religions and other beliefs. The days of the week and the months of the year still bore the names of old pagan gods. There were holy sites that were not Christian, from Rudstone churchyard to the Devil's Arrows, and there were pagan wells continued under a saint's name. At the same time, over many centuries, the bishops had condemned old gods, and some old beliefs and practices. The continuity of condemnation suggests that they were not altogether successful. Catholic Christianity had not really denied the existence of the older gods, but had relegated them to the status of evil spirits. This allowed a continued belief in them.

An Act of Parliament in 1542 had condemned practices called conjuration and witchcraft, sorcery and enchantment. Witchcraft became an offence punishable by hanging until the legislation was repealed. Archbishop Cranmer of Canterbury ordered his clergy to report anyone using charms, sorcery, enchantment, witchcraft, and soothsaying, and any like craft invented by the devil. The issue was raised again in the Parliament of 1559 and in 1563 came the Witchcraft Act. This was a statute against conjurations, enchantments, witchcraft, fond and fantastical prophecies, invocation of evil spirits, charms and sorcery. The justices would deal with the witchcraft and the church courts with the other condemned behaviours.

The lawyer William West of Rotherham was acquainted with legal charges brought in his day. He distinguished:

Mahitians - those who by uttering of certain superstitious words conceived, attempt things above the course of nature, by bringing forth dead men's ghosts, as they falsely pretend, in showing of things either secret or in places far off; and in showing them in any shape or likeness. They have taken themselves to the devil.

Soothsaying wizards - a kind of magician who divines and foretells things to come and raises up evil spirits by certain superstitious and conceived forms of words and answer by voice or else set before their eyes in glasses, crystals, stones or rings, the pictures or images of things sought for.

Diviners,   - manifest who has stolen things and tell where things lost or stolen be.

Jugglers and sleighty curers of diseases. - use words or writings called charms or spells hanged about part of the body

Enchanters   - by words, images, herbs think they can do what they list.

Cases of such kinds brought before the Yorkshire courts were not all that numerous but they did persist. We are left to wonder whether they really were that rare or whether we see the tip of the iceberg. It is rarely clear whether things said and done represent a burning faith or a mild and trivial mental habit. The volume of folklore in later centuries suggests such practices may have been widespread, but that the labels given them were sometimes too dramatic. The folklore, recorded later, makes it likely that people were reluctant to abandon any help that unseen powers might give. Most folk did not separate magic, religion, science, prayer, ritual, or the beliefs behind them. They tried what they were advised to try, and if consequences ensued, particularly if things improved, placed faith in them. Since it was difficult to discern improvement and even more difficult to find the cause, faith could flourish, even in the face of failure.

Witchcraft was reported from Little Driffield, while a Rotherham wizard used charms to cure the sick and had dealings with a familiar spirit in the 15th century. A Knaresborough wizard was consulted by a York merchant in 1509 about recovering a runaway servant. There was witchcraft at Newbald in 1510, and at Bishop Wilton in 1528 when three women took fire to running water, lit a wisp of straw, set it on the water and invoked Benedict against flue and night fevers. Occasional cases occurred in Elizabeth's reign, at Fishlake, at Hull in 1583, at Beverley in 1587 and at Collingham in 1597. Four were executed at Hull in 1604 and others brought to book in the new reign at Bolling, Rossington, Rothwell, Tadcaster and Wakefield. William Witham Esq of Ledstone Hall was popularly supposed to have been bewitched to death by Mary Pannal. For this and other sorceries, she was arraigned and convicted at York in 1603 & burnt to death.

Charms to bring hoped for results or to protect against evils remained part of the common culture. Branches of rowan tree or mountain ash were gathered on St. Helen's eve, with a careful ritual. She was the mother of the Emperor Constantine and credited with the rediscovery of the true cross. Branches were placed on lintels above house doors, on byres, and bed heads. They were used as gads and small pieces were carried in the purse. Witch posts were installed at the entry from the threshold to the firehouse in cruck framed homesteads, sometimes of rowan tree and marked with a diagonal St. Andrew's cross and other symbols to protect against witches or other evil spirits. Naturally occurring limmel stones with a hole in, were supposedly disliked by witches. Those from the lead workings in Richmondshire were called witch stones. Larger holed stones, were crept through at Ripon and Roseberry Topping .

Rogers of Danby had prepared charms, part of the stock in trade of supposed witches and wisemen. One charm against all diseases, written on lambskin, with ink mixed with the blood of a white dove, was to be pinned to the "sark" of a woman when "child begotten". Earlier it had to be laid under the pillow of a bride who was a true maiden, "at her husband coming to her arms". Other charms would supposedly guard cattle from the murrain, a horse from being witch-ridden and one would cure the palsy.

Magical tables cut on lead, were found in a burial mound in Middleton Tyas, embodying a curse condemning four members of a Brignall family to beggary and "nothing joy or prosper with them in Richmondshire". They were inscribed with planetary marks, scratches and rows of numbers one to eighty one, in tables so that the totals diagonally and perpendicularly added to 369. The tables derived from books of occult philosophy by Cornelius Agrippa published in 1532 but the man condemned was alive in 1575.

James Rither of Harewood said of Yorkshire that "the common sort delight greatly in old prophecies, which commonly come to pass before they are spoken of. "Forecasting" or prophecy was widely accepted. Queen Elizabeth consulted Dr Dee on the propitious day for her coronation. He cast horoscopes for her, seriously weighing supposed good and baleful influences from the planets. The prophecies of mother Shipton of Knaresborough had been made in Henry VIII's time and though not yet published may well have circulated widely by word of mouth. Ellen Spinke of Buttercrambe "declared the destinies of her neighbours, by taking on hands."

Simpler means of prophecy were known in the Fairfax family. If a sick person was given a penny weight of land cress to eat for three days, while fasting, followed by a drink of water or wine, the patient who cast it up could be expected to die. Tormentil, bayberries and finely powdered mirre mixed in stale ale were just as good. Keep it down and you lived. Cast it up and you died. The berries purged, the tormentil voided all venom and raw meats in the stomach, while the mirre suffered no corruption in man's body, or so they said.

Omens, the notion that one event foretold another of greater significance, were widely viewed with confidence. Even the Puritan Archbishop Grindal was superstitious about earthquakes. On 26th February 1574 about five at night an earthquake shook Yorkshire, Nottinghamshire and other northern counties, "It did no harm but the concussion much terrified the people, fearing that some public calamity might follow". Casting some sort of spell to influence future events was another step. Evil wishing was reported at Thirsk in 1611, when Elizabeth Cooke's cursing of her neighbours and their goods preceded damaging events. Elizabeth Creary at Northallerton was believed to have damaged a black cow and her calf by enchantments and charms.

CHAPTER 4
ELIZABETHAN PEOPLE

Men and Women[1]

Sir Thomas Elyot portrayed sixteenth century man as "fierce, hardy, strong in opinion, covetous of glory, desirous of knowledge, appetiting by generation to bring forth his semblables." Women he thought were "mild, timorous, tractable, being of sure remembrance and steadfast." Others used the contemporary psychology of the humours, to portray men as hot and dry, women as cold and moist. Men's awareness of the significant differences sometimes gained interesting expression. Dealtry commenting on the medicinal virtues of the Knaresborough well, thought "females as ever more apt to be deluded." John Donne gently concluded that, "women have a motion of their own which men are unable to fathom."

Elizabethan society was made up of households, centred on a family, of which a man was normally the head. If there was a chair he sat on it. The name, the status and most of the property passed from generation to generation within the family, the elder son usually the principal beneficiary of inherited estate. Younger sons might inherit if the elder died, and other provision was sometimes made for them. Many departed to make their own way in the world. Younger brothers commonly made few claims on elder brothers but some of the western dales may reveal a different approach, the so-called "partible inheritance", where younger sons received a share in a property.

Women had little legal authority. The parent or husband was responsible for a woman's debts and she needed permission to make a will. Even in York and the borough towns, very few women became sole traders able to be in debt and enter contracts, even though many were brewsters. York did allow widows to carry on their husband's businesses. Those women who did gain the freedom of York, paid twice the charge of twenty shillings, levied on men who became free by apprenticeship. Of the free women recorded before 1566, six were victuallers. Women gained a greater role in handling property at seaports, where men were often away at sea, and death at sea was not uncommon.

Women's wills and inventories showed a different sense of values from men. They selected different items for individual bequest. Lady Ann Conyers in 1557 left her son William a beryl glass, set with feet of silver and gilt, while Henry had a gold ring with a stone in called a crapon, and five silver spoons "that go daily about the house", a salt cellar, a coffer with a weaving stool in it, all the working stuff and samplers, and some silk, woollen and linen cloth. Custance Aked of Tadcaster in 1562 picked out her sameron and harden sheets, a thrown chair, a dough trough, "one gilte pige with wattells under the chine" and a stone of hemp.[4] Margaret Wyvell of Burton Constable left french hoods, six ells of linen cloth, her best cloth gown, a diaper table cloth, a velvet hat, and a workday kirtle petticoat. Her maidens received smocks, kerchiefs and rails, being garments for the neck.

Courtship

We might think that the principal decision a woman took in her life was to choose a husband, and for a man to choose a wife. At all levels of society, there was advice on the selection of the life partner. Lord Burghley told his son Robert that the decision was one from which "may spring all future good or ill." He suggested enquiries into her disposition and how her parents had been inclined in her youth, but "not to choose uncomely for wealth, not a dwarf or a fool, there being nothing more fullsome than a she-fool." More ordinary people faced more limited choices. Those of a similar age in a small village or dale would be very few. There might be no choice at all, if you followed the old adage "it is better to marry over the midden than over the moor." The parish church gatherings and the local markets were important marriage marts.

Young people showed much interest in divining the best choice, or prophesying who they would marry. The popular methods included throwing nuts in the fire on nut crack night, to answer any question. You asked, "would he be dark or fair?" If the nut cracked left or right, you had the answer. The county folklore was full of ways of finding your marriage partner, particularly in dreams. Rosedale women were told to gather graveyard moss in the night and then walk backwards to their house and place the moss beneath their pillow. A woman might dream of her intended. He might even turn up at the window.

Elizabethan proverbs contained much useful advice for men, such as, "never choose a woman or linen by candlelight." It was a common opinion to judge a daughter by the mother. Homely advice on appearances came from that wise man Thomas Ogle of Scarborough,

> "Beware of the lass, with a well shaped head,
> and truthful een,
> whose leg is thinne but shapely,
> whose teeth are small but unseen,
> whose hands are thin but deft withall.
> She is selfish and passionate.
>
> Beware of the lass, whose nose is flat
> and een nigh together,
> whose feet and face are flat and flabby,
> combined with an unseemly breast
> She is lazy and untrustworthy.
>
> Beware of the lass, whose lips are full
> and turned outwards,
> whose hips run backward to swell her buttocks,
> whose hair is red or crisp black
> Such are of a libidinous nature."[2]

John Marston left his famous ideal of feminine good looks, but added "If nature fails thee, see what art can achieve." "The face should be ruddy and round, forehead smooth, high and white, eyebrows, small delicate and marked with pencil, lips coral or like cherries, eyes lamp like and downcast, chin dimpled, cheeks showing the rose and the lillie in combat and dimpled. The space between the shoulders must be wide, breasts high, fair and round, hands small and white with long fingers and red nails, waist slender, hips large, legs straight, feet small with high instep." But, you could "paint the face, dye or bleach the hair, pluck and darken the eyebrows, redden the lips, drop belladonna into the eyes with a feather, pencil in blue lines on a whitened bosom, remove speckles and spots, wear a mask, wash the teeth and hair, lace the waist and pad the hips. A pomander would help, if your breath was too valiant."[3]

Trothplight was the early expression of a serious commitment. Walks were taken along "love lanes". A couple would exchange gifts. Love tokens commonly given and received included handkerchiefs, coins, hair combs, stay busks, knitting sheaths, or spoons hand carved with messages and promises. A couple would plight their troth at some recognised place, sometimes an old oak tree, secretly or before witnesses. There were written trothplights. Ann Conyers had a ring of gold with a trothplight in it. Garters were given by boys to girls, tied on in secret and worn on the left leg at the knee. Some were charms, made from stook straw while the harvest moon was shining, and given supposed power by "witching", only to be untied on the wedding day.

Where there was little property involved, trothplight marked a first stage towards matrimony but not all worked out. Betrothal contracts were thought binding, if undertaken in the present tense, but not in the future tense. "I take thee" not "I will take thee." Childhood contracts were only legal if consent was renewed when the boy was fourteen or over and the girl twelve. A gentry boy called Ralph Eure was betrothed in 1548 to the daughter of a Snainton gentleman Robert Sellowe. When he was eleven and she was seven, or eight. Ralph would call her wife and kiss her when he came home from school. Later he claimed that, "he would take her in his arms and kiss her for good manners not as his wife." The contract did not prove permanent. She married Roger Langdale of Ebberston.[4]

Friends were used as go-betweens during long courtships. Robert Stanehouse of Old Malton was courting Joan Coats in 1558. His friend, a Wykeham husbandman John Spencer acted as intermediary. The girl was living with her mother and her step-father Stephen Jerome. John was despatched for a definite answer, or the return of the pledges that Robert had given her. He asked the mother if Robert was welcome to her. She said that, "If another had twice as much, he would not be as welcome as Robert." They found Joan making the fire in the kiln house and he said "here is Robert Stanehouse and if you think you may find it in your heart to have him and forsake all other, you may tell him or else give him back his gifts." She said that, "if Robert had her father's good will, she was content." Robert replied, "Thou knowest that I had thy father's will well enough and look, whatsoever I give thee from this day forwards it shall be in the way of matrimony." Come Lammas, at Malton, Robert offered her a silver cross, which she accepted. At Lady day Robert sent Robert Fell of Old Malton to give her an old groat, asking would he be as welcome as before. She said that he would and so the wooing went on.

With long delayed marriages, friends were allowed an important role in giving marriage advice. The ailing James Westrop willed that his three daughters "be advised of their friends, with Seth Edwards and their mother for their marriages, or else forfeit their portions to their two brethren." Robert Fletcher a Tripsdale husbandman wanted his heir Richard to get the Bilsdale farm but decreed, "he shall not marry a wife but such as John Fletcher of Westerdale and John Farrer of Bilsdale and other friends are contented withall." Should Richard refuse counsel, his brother John was to have all the right. On one point he was very firm. "My will is that Richard shall not marry any of the Kirkes

8. A Merchant and Wife

nor none of that name." There were other considerations. Edward Robinson of Cloughton made a bequest but "not if he marry Elizabeth Bigging, who is a Papist." Dame Mary Skargill a Tunstall widow left three hundred marks to daughter Thomasin towards her marriage but only if she married some one whose inheritance in fee simple was £200 a year.

The popular proverbs said much about marriage. It was acknowledged of women that, "they make the ease of men", but that "women be wilful if they be not first sought unto." They said that "courting and wooing brings dallying and doing" and "faint heart never won fair lady", but "love is blind." There is wisdom in the saying that "there belongs more to marriage than four bare legs in a bed." William Camden wrote the proverbs down in his "Remains concerning Britain." "Women like hens desire only to lay where they can see nest eggs." A good Jack maketh a good Jill" but "Love grows soon cold when want calls at your door" and "Time will tell you of many imperfections in her, that plenty must plasters for." In the end "age and wedlock tames man and beast." There was an opinion that "England was a paradise for women, a prison for servants, and a hell for horses." In reality, any marriage could be "for fairer or for fouler."[5]

Arranged Marriage

Arranged marriages were normal among gentry, yeomen and husbandmen, where property was involved. Henry Best wrote a famous account of the customs used in arranging a marriage, in the middling ranks of society in the East Riding of Yorkshire, about 1641. The arrangement was not as forceful as it might at first appear. There was parental involvement, but the young people had their say.

A young man, or his father, might write to a maid's father to discover whether a visit would be welcome. A mere thank-you, or an excuse, in reply meant no. This might conceivably come from the father or the maid. The next stages were between the young people. He would call twice "to see how the maid standeth affected." If she was "tractable and her inclination was towards him", he would give her a ten or twenty shilling piece of gold or a ring of that value on the third visit, the next time a pair of gloves of 6s.8d. or 10s worth and each time thereafter some toy or novelty of less value. These visits continued every three or four weeks over a half year. Only when the young folks agreed and were contracted, did the maid's father take her to the young man's house "to see how they like of all." The two fathers met to treat of dower and jointure for the woman and to set the day of marriage for three or four weeks later. This allowed time

93

to get wedding clothes, to arrange the wedding dinner at the maid's father's house and to buy gloves.[6]

There was no sense that marrying for money had any drawbacks. Life was a very material matter and a marriage portion improved a girl's material prospects. Portions depended on who your father was. Sir Henry Gate's eldest daughter had Hunmanby rectory as her portion. Matthew Hutton of Marske gave £1900 to his son Timothy on marriage with Elizabeth Bowes in 1592. Ralph Westrop in 1605 left William Westrop's three daughters £400 each at twenty-one or when they married. George Conyers at Whitby gave his daughter Margaret a hundred marks of good leather in his bark house. Richard Simpson of Edstone left one girl with twenty marks, two oxen, two kye, two silver spoons and her grandmother's next best girdle, towards her marriage. Two other daughters received two hundred wethers pasturing at Hartoft and two silver spoons each.

John Bulmer of Scrayingham gave daughter Agnes a significant portion; "two oxen, two kie, two stirkes, six yowes, with their lambs and ten hogges, one great cauldron and one arke, one credell, one girdle" and "then she to be forth with her portion." The other daughters had nominal bequests, Elizabeth one girdle, Isabel a pair of beads and the youngest daughter ten shillings "because she has neither girdle nor beads." Husbandman Thomas Barker of Newton sent his daughter to matrimony with her father's aumbry, cauldron, dishbink and cressett. It was a charitable thing to help those with little to take into matrimony. John Ledum, a Whitby merchant, gave £4.6s.8d. to thirteen poor maidens' marriages, while merchant Robert Bushel gave his servant Alice 13s.4d. and two yards of red cloth for her wedding.

Human urgencies have always sat ill with legal contracts and social conventions. John Etherington was born at Wheldrake of Francis Etherington and Ann Hansbie "in lawful contract, before their marriage." Widower John Elyot of Bridlington would argue that he was drunk at his betrothal in 1584. He addressed the curate "Sit down and I'll give you a pot of ale", before confiding a wish to marry widow Margaret Clarke at church the next Sunday. He took her to wife "handfest" and plighted troth, drew hands twice and kissed, and then took her home and gave her possession of his house and his kiln before witnesses. He was married, drunk or not. Some were more careful. Even the pre nuptial agreement was not unknown. The Tadcaster vicar noted that when Thomas Nicholson wed Alice Grange; "It is promised by Nicholson before the marriage that Alice his wife shall have half his farm during her widowhood."

Weddings

The Edward VI prayer book required banns of marriage to be called on three Sundays by a priest in the church, in the presence of many people. The clergy were regularly asked if they had married any couple without banns, or any couple within the degrees of consanguinity or affinity forbidden by the law. These were listed in a table of degrees posted in the church. Those who wished to avoid calling banns could obtain a marriage licence. A formal statement was made, usually by the groom, called an allegation, that there was no lawful impediment to the marriage. The groom and a friend had to enter a bond to forfeit a sum of money if this proved to be untrue. After the third reading of the banns, the congregation shouted "God speed them well."[7]

A pair of gloves was given to each of the bride and groom's friends on the wedding day morning, when they were almost ready to go to church. The groom took the bride by the hand and said "Mistress I hope you are willing" and kissed her. Then it was off to church, the other young men ushering the maids. Vows were exchanged in the church porch, perhaps at one time simply the familiar "if thee tak I, I tak thee", followed by a blessing inside. The Prayer Book took them into the body of the church for a solemn ceremony. The address told them that matrimony was not to be lightly or wantonly undertaken "to satisfy men's carnal lusts and appetites, like brute beasts that have no understanding." Then came the "rough music", the teasings and testings of the day. A man from away might get rams horns on his head, hinting at a little hostility. The race for the bride's garter was run from the church to her home. The garter on the left leg, symbolised virginity, or at least commitment, and had been placed there earlier by the groom. This was awarded to the winner of the race.

Their friends tended them at the wedding feast. Robert Stevenson of Arras in 1561 gave John Jackman a fat wether "to his wedding." Then came the bedding. Turf might be stuffed down the chimney, a bush put in the bridal bed and sand thrown over the guests' shoulders, backwards towards the shared bed, the first to hit being the next bride. Henry Best says that the husband fetched her home about a month after the bride's portion was paid. Men friends and neighbours came too and others met them on the way, for some jollity and ale, perhaps staying for dinner, supper and breakfast the next day. Other accounts have the bride riding on a brideswain, a four wheeled vehicle stacked with her own goods, and her marriage portion, gathering gifts of small furnishings from other houses on the way.

The parish register at Roos contained a notice in Latin hexameters giving the canonical seasons for marriage, with a translation, signed by the minister and two churchwardens.

> "Advent doth forbid the bans,
> and Hilary sets them free again,
> Septuagesima saith yee nay.
> Eight days after Easter saith yee may,
> Rogation bids thee to contain.
> But Trinity set thee free again.

T34 Atwick Parish, 1558 to 1597 Monthly Baptisms, Marriages and Burials

	Jan	Feb	Mar	April	May	June	July	Aug	Sept	Oct	Nov	Dec
Marriages	12	7	0	7	13	8	13	6	3	17	53	4
Baptisms	20	14	16	27	28	24	15	17	30	19	20	20
Burials	13	9	8	16	11	15	17	17	16	14	19	24

The Moral Concern

It may well be that the new Protestant church supervised the morals of courtship and marriage more closely than in other periods of history. This can hardly be proved but much was now heard about sexual morality. The practice of private confession to a priest followed by private penance had been well established before the breach with Rome. The church had never lacked realism on day-to-day matters. Dr. Layton had claimed in 1536 that the nuns of the north had potions to procure abortions. Now, public denunciation, public confession before the congregation in the church and public penance replaced private confession for moral lapses.

Betrothal could be early and marriage late. Couples could be betrothed at seven years of age but had the right to dissent when they came of age. The minimum legal age for marriage was twelve for women and fourteen for men. In practice, the time of marriage was far later than that. A few might marry early but the average age of marriage was in the twenties. The world expected you to be able to maintain an independent family, in a separate household, when you married. The law made transfer of property depend on a church wedding. In some circumstances, with short life spans, this could mean waiting until the farm became available. Others had to find paid work bringing enough money to rent a vacant house, and then wait till one was available. Living- in may have been more common than we know.

Sex might begin at some point after trothplight and before a church wedding. Perhaps five per cent or sometimes more women were pregnant at marriage. Many births were entered in parish registers as "base born", "a natural child" or "a merry begot", while a woman might be labelled a "fornicatrix". The vicar of the large West Riding parish of Halifax spoke of "burnt bottoms". There was a growing concern about those who "lived incontinently "or who were "being naughty together." The Puritans actively discouraged sex before or outside marriage. Charges of sexual immorality were frequently made in the church courts.

The peculiar court of Masham required Lawrence Johnson of Healey to do penance in 1583, having begot a child with Jane Buckle six years earlier. There were six or seven other fornications to consider. John Walker allowed women to have a child in his house and then leave. Alice, daughter of Jane Dixon was "base begotten at Old Malton." Humfrey Gillome, a salt petre man who passed through was supposed to be the father of a child there in 1598. Sex before or outside marriage was also evident in the not uncommon provision made in wills for illegitimate children. Whitby merchant Robert Bushell left "Robert Tate called Robert Bushell, as some say, son of George Bushell", three pounds at the age of twenty one.

Family Life

Marriage came late in short lives but could last fifteen or twenty years. Women moved from being daughters to become wives, although a high proportion of brides had already lost their fathers and many were married from service. Most women expected to marry, with child bearing as an obligation. Women left one family at marriage to enter another, one household for another, normally moving into an established house. If the single woman was a servant, matrimony led to a higher status but not one equal to her husband.

Authority, at least in theory, belonged to the male head of the household but his wife would stand next in line. The balance of relationships was well suggested by the epitaph accompanying Anne Bennet's alabaster of 1601 in York Minster. "She was a woman of the fairest character, of singular modesty and uncommon piety, the best and most dutiful of wives." In widowhood, a woman might have a powerful position, for a time. Robert Kendall, a Bolton Percy labourer, left his house to his wife while she remained unwed, and then to which ever of his two sons "doth please and favour my wife better."

Gervase Markham said that the housewife was subordinate to the husband, being of lower rank. He still portrayed her as a partner, needing many household and other skills. Both partners worked, she especially at the home, the dairy, the garden, the malt house, the loom, the spinning wheel and the still. Family members were heavily dependant on each other and most problems were solved within the family. He urged husband and wife to make reckonings to each other of any spending. He advised the wife, with a husband behaving irresponsibly, to call him home from his error, "with mild sufferance, rather than with anger, to abate the least spark of his evil."[8]

A strong sense of kinship was evident in family life. No doubt this was tested and tried by the stress of incompatibilities, strong characters, the mothers in law and step-mothers portrayed in the nursery rhymes. Wills commonly showed small bequests to many family members. John Frank at Hutton in the Hole in 1575 decreed that, "my brethren and sisters shall occupy all things together as we have done, so long as they can agree." John Hall, the Wood Appleton yeoman, ordered that his sons John and Thomas should occupy the same farm, if Agnes his wife agreed, half going to her and half to them for the time being, but added that "the farmhold shall never go out of the name of Hall but is to go to any kinfolk that bear that name." A surprising number of sons and daughters didn't marry.

Sir Antony Fitzherbert gave us the classic sixteenth century account of a woman's work in a yeoman or husbandman's household. He remarked that, "seldom does the husband thrive without leave of his wife." He briefly stated what works a wife should do.

"First in a morning when thou art waked and purposeth to rise, lift up thy hands and bless thee and make a sign of the holy cross, and when thou art up and ready, then first sweep thy house, dress up thy dish board, and set all things in good order within thy house; milk thy kye, suckle thy calves, sye up thy milk, take up thy children and array them and provide for thy husbands breakfast, dinner, supper and for thy children and servants and take thy part with them. And to ordain corn and malt to the mill, to bake and brew withall when need is. And meete it to the mill and from the mill and see that thou have thy measure again beside the toll, or else the miller dealeth not truly with thee, or else thy corn is not dry as it should be."

"Thou must make butter and cheese, when thou maist, serve thy swine both morning and evening and give thy poleyn meat in the morning and when time of the year cometh, thou must take heed how thy hens, ducks and geese do lay and to gather up their eggs, and when they wax broody, to set them there as no beasts, swine nor other vermin hurt them". "See that they be well kept from the gleyd, crowes, fullymartes and other vermynne. In the beginning of March, or a little before, is time for a wife to make her garden. As often as need be, she must weed it." The wife would sow flax and hemp, weed, pull, water, wash, dry, beat, brake, taw, heckle, spin, wind, wrap and weave hemp. She would make sheets, board cloths, towels, shirts, smocks, and "let they distaff be always redy for a pastime, that thou be not idle."

It was a wife's occupation to "winnow all manner of corn, to make malt, to wash and wring, to make hay, shear corn, and in time of need to help her husband to fill the muck wain or dung cart, drive the plough, to load hay, corn and such other. And to go or ride to the market, to sell butter, cheese, milk, eggs, chickens, capons, hens, pigs, geese and all manner of corn." She would buy necessaries for the household, keep accounts and make her husbands clothes.[9]

Children

Women married in their early and mid twenties and might have children well into their thirties. Rich women may have had shorter intervals between births, which came closer to once a year. For working women, it was more often once every two years, with six or seven a rough maximum. Despite this, the usual size of families remained modest, kept small by infant deaths. There were exceptional families and one or two large families could raise the local average. John Pek who died in 1558-9 and his wife Jane of Wakefield had nine sons and nine daughters. Most households were of modest size at any one time. The largest households were those of highest status. The perils of childbirth were all too evident in the records of births, marriages and deaths. Many children died in their infant years and many mothers in pregnancy, whatever their social position. The monasteries had maintained some items supposed to be helpful during pregnancy. Newburgh Priory offered the supposed girdle of St. Salvatoris to assist lying in women. Rievaulx Abbey had St. Ailred's girdle and the nunnery at Keldholme Priory could lend St. Stephen's finger. These things had gone but the belief persisted that similar charms might help in what was then a very dangerous time.

The linen for the child-bed was treasured. Elisabeth, widow of Alderman Robert Askwith of York in 1608, left her son in law, a christening sheet sewn with black and two fine linen sheets belonging to "my bed when I laid in child bed." One was plain white, while the other had fair laid cut work. There were a few midwives, licensed by the church, but friends gathered for a birth. Lady Hoby rode over to Ayton Castle for Mistress Dawnay's labour in May 1600. When Bridget, wife of Robert Lunde of Reedness, was laying in her chamber, "at the time of the travaill," John Taylor's wife Ann "disquieted her neighbours", by calling them witches and scorning Bridget when she cried with pain. William Woodruff at Hollywell grange in Thurnscoe parish wrote to tell Mrs. Plumpton that "my wife hath not yet laid her belly but remaineth at her wits end. Since my being with you, I have not had three day's health."

The clergy thought that a child was open to evil forces, between birth and baptism, being not yet cleansed of inherited sin. The baptism of the child and the "churching" of the mother were a kind of ritual purification. The gap was rarely more than a week. Baptism was usually on the first holy day after the birth, for fear of the child dying unbaptised. Friends gathered again for a baptism, some as god parents, usually two women and one man for a girl. William Walker the minister at St Michael's Church, Malton regularly listed three or more witnesses at baptisms. William son of Lord Eure, Captain Thomas Westrop and Mrs Margery Constable of Newsham appeared for William the son of gentleman John Heslerton. A sense of responsibility towards god children persisted. Robert Stevenson of Arras left every one of his god children four pence in 1561. Richard Simpson of Edstone in 1568 gave twelve pence to each person in the parish but gave one ewe sheep to every godchild that he had christened.

It was all too common for a couple to die before their children became adult. Their under-age children passed into other households as orphan cousins, or were taken into a second marriage. John Symonson the Helmsley tanner, in an earlier decade, had left one son to Rievaulx Abbey with a child's portion, another to Byland Abbey and he had hoped that the bailiff of Nunnington would accept the third. Henry Eden at Lund Cote, Kirkdale in 1560 bound his wife Jane and his elder sons William and James to nourish and bring up four other children until they were twenty. Some elder children and young adults received their child's portions in material bequests designed to establish them in the world. At Kirkdale in 1556, John Walker had received an ox, a cow, five sheep and a chest, while another son was given as many spokes and fellies as would make a pair of wheels.

Difficult children were as familiar then as now. William Laing, a Bilsdale yeoman, in 1559 said that after his widow's death, his dwelling house would go to son John, "so that he be diligent to please his mother and help her to work the farm." She could allow him to occupy a part of it, after his good behaviour. He added "if any of my children are disobedient and will not be ruled and rodded by my wife," she had the discretion to alter their inheritances. Thomas Hugill of that same long dale in 1564 required his three children to be ordered by their mother and she to put the farmhold to one or two of them that pleased her best. The son Thomas was to have his portion and no more, and depart from the farmhold immediately after his father's death.

Perhaps there was a more general problem of adolescence. James Ryther blamed "the remiss education of indiscreet parents" in Yorkshire, because their sons "fall to rude pastimes before they learn civil behaviour." Robert Brookes was twice Mayor of York and his wife Jane died aged sixty-eight in 1599. Their epitaph at All Saints Pavement said that they had sixteen children and left eleven, adding "not naughty were they, as children now are, but all perchance good." Sir Cotton Gargrave of Nostell when he appointed his eldest son Thomas as his executor, remarked of him, "At this instant, understanding by his most intolerable and monstrous pride that thereby he is drowned into the forgetfulness of his duty to Almighty God and is fallen to a most loose, licentious, blasphemous, prowd, wasteful and contentious life."

Challenges to Marriage

"The principal duty of a wife is to love her husband", said Fitzherbert. Reality could take a different course. Ann Unthank at Crathorne in 1586 refused to sleep with her husband. Anthony Sandwith beat and otherwise abused his wife at York in 1590. Melchior Smith, the vicar of Hessle, who had married Elizabeth not long before, was brought to court in 1561 for using her uncharitably. She ran from him to the river Hull and leapt over the staith into the water. He wasn't the mildest of men. He once pulled a Hull mariner's beard and fisted his face. He would only admit that, "he did not at all times agree with her as perfectly as he might."

The proverbs cautioned that "hot love is soon cold", and "it is better to be a shrew than a sheep." "Many kinfolk could mean few friends" and there was the cautionary "hold fast when thou have it." "Many kissed the baby for the nurses sake."

But, "change of women makes bald knaves" and it could be "like the flounder, out of the frying pan into the fire." "The cuckold is the last that knows it" and "every man can rule a shrew save he that hath her" while "need maketh the old wife trot." Sixteenth-century glass in York Minster and in the church of St Michael le Belfrey showed the "adulterous kiss."

The canons of the church standardised the moral enquiries to be made at visitations. People had to be presented at church courts, who were guilty of adultery, drunkenness, usury, whoredom, swearing, incest, ribaldry and disturbing divine service. Nearly ten thousand men were summoned on sexual charges in Elizabethan Essex. The accusations were based on ill fame, suspicion and gossip as well as evidence. They did penance in their churches.[10] Many were charged at the Yorkshire church courts. Two adulterers were to do penance in Askrigg market place one Thursday, at Askrigg chapel on the

Sunday next and at Aysgarth church the Sunday after that. Elizabeth Knowles, alias Simeon alias Pearson, "moved by a spirit of wickedness" in 1592-3 at Hedon called Richard Ingram "a whoremaster, whoremonger and warlet" who lay in bed with another man's wife or maid He claimed, that he was honest, chaste and never married. The Halifax vicar identified several women, two of them blind, as whores with between two and five bastards. The Ilkley bye-laws of 1583 promised any tenant who kept drabs, railers and women of evil gesture for fourteen days or more, with loss of their tenement.

Marriage break-up could follow. While William Beckwith of Clint was serving as a captain in Ireland, his wife Jane was unfaithful. He repudiated her, married Mary Salmon, and had five children. Thomas Lambe of Pocklington was charged in 1591 with not remaining with his wife according to the order of the law. The local officers gave their opinion, "The fault is we think in the woman." He claimed that his wife Elizabeth went away from him with another man about Whitsunday last and came not to him again. Sexual laxity could seem a threat to the married women. A famous 17th century case was well recorded at Castleton in Danby. A woman was stripped naked to the sark, and walked through the street behind the crier, who proclaimed her a common drab. Wedded dames beat her buttocks with hazel twitches along the way. On another occasion, in another place, mariner and husband William Roper of Halifax and Agnes Jeffrayson, wife of a cordwainer were publicly accused of their sin. Widow Katherine Thomson was charged as a "bawd" for allowing their use of her house. They were carted together about the town on a Saturday, one with a paper on her head marked with great letters.

Reputation was jealously guarded in small communities. Scandal was of great interest. Accusations and more casual abuse used the language of sexual laxity. You could be called "a pocky scurvy queen", "a false perjured harlot", an adulterer, fornicator, cuckold, whore, or a Wakefield drab. We hear of a "paltry queen" at Doncaster. A clergyman could remark "She is lord huntsman's whore and further than that, she has a wart on her belly". At Darlington, in the next county, a woman taunted Elizabeth Oswald with having her first child, thirty five weeks after the marriage, adding "thou are a deformed drab, a filthy testrel, a stinking minded, brazen faced queen, and thy children are loathsome to look upon." At a drinking party of weavers, tinkers and pedlars with their wives, they told each other "thou are a piper's whore, a piper's judy, a piper's bitch" and "she should be fellow to a piper's whore as long as she lived."[11]

The word bawd was a term of abuse. The bawd was the go between. The occupation cannot always be ascribed to those so labelled. Bordellos are mentioned in several of the larger Yorkshire towns before 1550. Prostitution in town bawdy houses was well established in Elizabeth's reign. Scarborough had at least two brothels. Christopher & Alice Dickson at Scarborough harboured those of naughty behaviour. James Garstang and Jane Sharrocke harboured "incestuous persons and other evil livers."[12] A woman in St John's parish at York was said to be a scold, a slanderer and a common bawd in 1575, who allowed naughty persons to repair to her house. Ralph Blesdaill and Bridget Horn were said to be whore-mongers. He had fled from Harewood where he had fornicated with four. A couple were called whore-mongers at Almondbury.

A Hull bawd of 1562 was eloquently described by Abraham de la Prymme. "The devilish impiety of one Isabel West, the wife of one Thomas West, a tailor", arose from them "both finding their trade to be dead and themselves to be troubled with the evil of idleness. They laid their heads together and plotted how they might live better and he agreed with her that she should be a whore and that he would be witness of it, and that she should wash and paint and attire her head and look out of the window and entice and allure strangers, apprentices and young men to lie with her and that he should hide himself in the room and as soon as they were got to bed, he should start out with a drawn sword in his hand and make them redeem their lives with good sums." "This beastly and devilish trade the two carried on a long time to the ruin of a great many young men and apprentices but they being at last discovered and brought before the mayor and aldermen, he was disenfranchised and his name erased out of the book of burgesses. The jailer took both into custody, to keep on bread and water for a month, after which they were to ride through town in a cart with a paper on their heads, declaring their crime, then to be banished from the town for ever."[13]

A Young Society

The age groups in Elizabethan England were balanced very differently from our own. This was a youthful society, in the sense that children and young people made up a far greater proportion of each community, than is familiar in the 21st. century. Older people were rarer and formed a smaller part of the whole. Roughly half the people were under twenty compared with less than a third today. Each generation saw a steady erosion losing many members to death year by year. The youthfulness of people had a great bearing on Elizabethan life. Children and young people will have been a perpetual experience, in the home, at work, on the street and in church, where attendance was compulsory. Nonetheless, childhood in the modern sense of prolonged upbringing and education was confined to very few. Elizabethan childhood ended early for the great majority, with participation in work. Some stayed home and some went to work as servants in other houses.

The older age groups were small in proportion to the whole. Less than ten per cent were over sixty. We live a little longer, most of us. Today that figure is much higher. Their expectations were different. If they were believers, heaven and hell were a little closer. There were always a few exceptions. St Michael le Belfry church at York had a memorial of 1591 to "a devoted, charitable and most patient man, unwilling to hurt or offend by word or deed, a rare example in these days, whose good life, a comfort and pattern to posterity, ended when he had lived about 83 years." Old age could be a status, when the length of life was low. You knew the way of things. You might remember where it was or how it had been said and done. Sir William Ingleby took depositions from three "aged men" at Lindley to discover the bounds of Leathley common in 1575. They were seventy-seven, sixty and fifty-six. Robert Prudome of Glaisdale, high in the North York Moors, in 1595 left ten pence to each child, "which I am grandfather to."

A few reached a stage that might be called retirement. For most, stopping work meant poverty. A farmer might provide against that. William Kendall of Askwith, bequeathed two whye stirks to his son James, "to be kept of my farmhold," and all else to his sons Nicholas, Richard and James "on condition they shall honestly keep me in sickness and health, find meat and drink during my life." They were to have the goodwill of his farm, tenanted from Sir William Fairfax. He had already provided for a son who was married. Thomas Stevenson a husbandman of Arras, on the Wolds, gave his son the farmhold in 1553, but reserved for himself, "a chamber, the house under it, sufficient finding Winter and Summer for one horse, ten sheep and for one milk cow on the pasture, only in Summer." The son was to pay forty shillings a year. The father was to have food and drink and "two pence in his purse to spend every Sunday when he goeth to church." Thomas gave twenty marks to divide between his four children on May Day as their portions, but, to avoid discord, Agnes was not to dwell with Thomas.[13]

There were a few people who claimed exceptional longevity. Bolton on Swale parish register recorded the death of Henry Jenkins in 1670. He claimed that his mother had said that he was born in 1500. Supposedly, he became butler at the age of thirty to Lord Conyers of Hornby Castle, who died in 1557 and he lived till he was one hundred and sixty nine. Mrs Anne Saville wrote to Sir Richard Graham saying, "When I first came to live at Bolton, it was told me, a man lived in the parish near one hundred and fifty years old." He had sworn as a witness in a cause at York to one hundred and twenty years. She questioned him, when he begged at her door. He couldn't read or write but he offered a few memories that she tried to check. Some, who were a hundred years old, said he was elderly ever since they knew him. He walked to York assizes and swam in rivers when over a hundred.[14]

There were other legendary figures. Bridlington claimed a memorial tablet to Thomas Newman, who died in 1542, aged one hundred and fifty three. Roger Brook of Halifax, who died in 1568 was supposed to be one hundred and thirty. Margaret Metcalfe died, aged one hundred in 1579. She was born at Cogden in Swaledale, daughter of Simon Robinson, and married Anthony Medcalfe of Wensleydale. The couple had twelve children of whom eleven died before her. "She had a good stomach, was very pleasant, merrily conceited, and used to use sundry pretty taunts and nyppes and had her answers ready at every objection. She sore repented of her former life, idly spent and evil, sorry that she was superstitiously and popishly bent in times past."[15]

A More Numerous People

No Census returns tell us of the growing population between 1558 and 1603 but people were well aware of the change. There had been a great fall in England's population between the late 14th century and the 1520's. Contemporaries in the next two decades still spoke of a people that had once been more populous, and was now greatly decayed. Some might have noticed a small and growing increase of baptisms over burials, by 1546-56. By the seventies and eighties, there was talk of the great increase of people, and even a shortage of employment.

Parishes were required to keep registers of baptisms, marriages and burials. These were transferred from paper to parchment after 1597, the copies to go back to the start of the reign. Some of those transcriptions were full and carefully made. Others suffered a little in the process. Those at Preston in Holderness abbreviated female entries and ended with such statements as "Lancelot Collman was married November 7th 1598", removing all information about his wife. Despite such inadequacies, the registers have provided modern scholars with the basis for considered estimates of the scale of population change.

England may have had five to six million people before the great pestilences of the late 14th century. By 1520 the national population is estimated to have been two and a half million. Thereafter the number is believed to have risen to over four million by 1603. It has been suggested that two periods of growth in the 16th century were separated by two decades of stagnation. A nation wide epidemic gave heavy mortality in the last two years of Queen Mary's reign, halting earlier expansion in the period 1548 to 1563. There were more epidemics, particularly in the towns, but baptisms out-stripped burials strongly in the period 1576-1586 and more modestly for the rest of the reign.[16]

Communities

People lived in towns, villages, hamlets and single farms. Towns were few and far between but they were rarely large enough to lose a sense of community. Most people lived in a house in a village, but the scattered farmsteads of the dales often had no focal settlement, no gathering place, unless it was an isolated chapel, the manor house, a mill or an alehouse. The shared relationships, the concerns, the talk and the accepted rights and obligations would differ in a dale from a village or town. It was a longer walk to borrow something. It would be harder to muster enough men to haul vertical the timbers of a cruck house. These things would be done, nonetheless.

Villages varied much in size, layout and character. It is striking that each wapentake had a range of large, medium and small settlements. Many were far smaller than we know them and an effort of the imagination is needed to reveal their past. Filey, in the Armada year, was a modest village which saw ten baptisms, seven weddings and twenty one burials. Ebberston, in the Vale of Pickering, was a large village with three parts, each with a name, Upperby, Netherby and Kirkdale, virtually three villages in one, and in a dale of the higher ground, were the scattered farmsteads of Bickley and Deepdale. Where the fields met the moor was a single farmstead called Malton Cotes, once a Malton Priory grange. All were part of one township, within a single boundary. You can still discover old Ebberston but you must search for the old village within the town of Filey.

Most villages were communities of ploughmen and labourers, with their families, who worked the common fields. Houses stood around a green, at a crossroads or along a single village road, usually on both sides, with crofts running away to back lanes or ditches, which separated off the ploughland. Even the town of Northallerton was "nothing but a long street", with its crofts stretching to back lanes. Gate Helmsley, near York, was exceptional, subject of the proverb "all of a side like Gate Helmsley", because the far side of the road was in another Riding, and lacked houses. The simple road layout with houses each side, a sort of one strip ribbon development went with the single manor. Where there were several parts of a village, there were usually several manors with tenants houses built along their own roads, as at Thornton Dale. Other villages had discrete parts, with road twists and turns, like Bainton or the less regular villages of Holderness.

Village size depended on the extent of field, and meadow, but the presence of a great house, or of some other rural asset could provide employment and expand the number of households. Estate villages, where one owner held a substantial demesne, or an extensive rental, had a different history to those communities with several freeholds. The social dominance of the great estate holder, whether resident or acting through a steward, often limited any independence of spirit and action. Even a single freeholder could inject an alternative point of view into village affairs. All village communities have a local history, but this is a little more evident where there are freeholds or where the appointment of the clergyman was in other hands than those of the main landowner.

Normally, the larger villages had at least one independent property, comprising the local interest of the church rectory including its tithes, or another formed by the vicarage, with the small tithes and any glebe land of the church. Where these came on to the market, they were often leased by the main landowner. Villages which housed a parish church had regular gatherings at the church from outlying townships, and this might foster a little trade, support a craft or two, and give a community focus for outlying farmsteads. The parishes could range in scale from a single township, to the vast parish of Halifax, containing several townships. Pickering parish church in one decade welcomed six families, coming for baptisms, marriages and burials, from the shrinking village of Kingthorpe on the dry limestone hills, eight more from the scattered farms of the wet Marishes and four from the distant dale of Goathland. That would be a long way to carry a coffin.

Some Yorkshire Villages

A few examples must suffice to contrast different Elizabethan village communities. There was the village with the great family house or mansion. Settrington on the fringe of the chalk Wolds near Malton, was a large village with seventy-seven houses. There was the Manor with its farm, which saw the family and household of the Earls of Lennox a parsonage, a market house, and a chantry house There were sixteen freeholders, fifteen husbandry houses, fourteen grass farms, with insufficient lands to make husbandries, and another twenty-eight cottages, with no land at all, but with rights of common of pasture.

Sheriff Hutton, on the edge of the limestone hills, north east of York, had fifty-six houses, in two blocks. One was near the church on the east, where the early motte and bailey castle had been abandoned but the large church and parsonage remained. A second larger regular block was along the road to the west. The castle, built on the south side of the road had a sizeable demesne and a large park. The Earl of Huntingdon knew it well but, without a resident family it would soon lose its significance. The common furnace and forge decayed, perhaps due to lack of estate work. For the moment, this was a village of husbandmen, with few freeholds.

The village where there had been a monastery was different again, once dominated by the unusual household at the principal house. Nun Monkton in 1538 had thirty-three tenements and the monastery. A 1567 survey and a map of 1607 recorded all the houses and fields. "West from the site of the said late monastery is the towne of Nun Monkton seated; whereof the south row of the same butteth upon the common towards the north and the common field called the town field on the south." Thirteen cottages were in South Row, thirteen more in West Row, and seventeen in North Row, forty-three in all. Beyond the village stretched the Town, Middle and West fields.

Where common fields had been abandoned for pasture, the villages shrank or became deserted; visited only by the shepherd and his flock. Usually a single farm remained. The shrunken village was a commonplace on the Wolds but could exist alongside populous villages elsewhere. They were the result of human decisions not of epidemics. Good land would come back into use after a plague. Shrunken villages were rarer elsewhere in the county, but not unknown. Some places that were later depopulated were still thriving villages. Hinderskelfe, where Castle Howard and its park would one day be laid out, had an older castle site and twenty-four houses in 1564, fifteen north of the village street and nine on the south. There were twenty-two tenants at will in 1593.

Community Life and Strife

Much of the regulation of community life was in the hands of the manor and of the church. It commonly fell to the manor courts or parish churchwardens to insist on community obligations being fulfilled but problems that reached the courts as breaches of law or bye law in some places, failed to do so elsewhere. Many local byelaws were passed as a response to a particular local problem. Elsewhere, we must wonder whether the record or the facts were different. Neighbours had to work together. This was especially so in busy seasons; at the harvest which needed all hands, and for such major tasks as cleaning out the church, quelling a fire, taking dung out to the fields, repairing a shattered harbour pier, or following the hue and cry. Neighbours gave each other their reputation. Four witnesses were often enough to make good evidence, to supervise a will, or value goods for an inventory. Men would clear themselves of charges on the oath of four honest neighbours. A dispute at Egton was settled in chapel by just such a group in 1585.

Communities had less formal, customary ways of expressing disapproval and of regulating behaviour. Setting horns on the door was one way, recorded at Faceby. A man might gape at a woman and put out his tongue. The difficult individual could be sent to Coventry, or otherwise isolated. This was earlier described as being "put outside the community of the vill." A jury of twelve in Gilling Church ordered the expulsion of Ann Robinson. The manor lord, Sir Nicholas Fairfax backed them up, telling her to go from Gilling or be stocked. The Halifax vicar wrote character assessments in his register after folk had died. "This George Boulton was a common drunkard and a lecher. He sold his land, drank it, fled the county and was slain." Gregory Paulde was an "arrant hypocritical rogue", while Thomas Wilkinson Orde "was a great whoremonger in his youth and boasted of it in his last sickness, whereof he died."

"Riding the stang" occurred across the county in this century and later. A representation or effigy of an offender was mounted on poles and danced up and down the street, outside his house, by men or lads, crying "a rang a tang tang, we're riding the stang, old so and so beat his woman." During 1609 on a Sunday morning in hay time Gabriel Houseman was carried on a stang into Bolton Percy churchyard during the time of divine service, with a great clamour and crying and shouting, by many people. Gabriel shouted "Ellen Winde hath bett her husband and that is the cause why I now ride." He had been hired to do so by Robert Tate.

Community life could be disturbed by the individual or family who publicly rejected other peoples' values. Richard Lawson of York ended before the church courts and was fined ten shillings. He was "a very noisome and contentious person, using scolding, quarrels and brawling." He would challenge his neighbours to fight and sew dissension between man and wife." The people of Burythorpe presented Bartholomew Wightman as "a frequent swearer, drunkard, ribald, contentious, uncharitable, a common slaunderer of his neighbours, a railer and sewer of discord." Margaret Sheles, a vagabond, was a notorious and defamed person, who, for ten years loitered about York, "after a very roguish manner" disquieting Thomas Colthurst and Katherine with "wrongful and clamourous exclamation." She had been whipped, burnt through the ear, and was a beggar. They gave thirty shillings for her to depart the city.

Women were often times charged with scolding. The judgements were usually made by men, but the discord added to community life was real enough. Ann Tailor of Redness scolded with her neighbours calling them witches. She was known as "a common scold, curser, banner, envious person, blasphemer, a sower of dissension and sedition, a daily backbiter of all her neighbours." She had to do penance. Thomas Haxoppe and James Wycliffe had wives who were scolds at Bishopthorpe in 1575. Five Acomb men were warned not to allow their wives to chide and scold with their neighbours in 1577. Henry Mason at Upper Poppleton in 1594 wished the devil would bridle Henry Spink's wife. Jane Haxlop was drawn through York in market time and had to ask forgiveness from those offended by her tongue. A Marston man used too much chiding with his mother. Another gave lewd and unseemly words to his father. At Acaster Malbis in 1600, Alice Atkinson was judged a common scold with her neighbours, but especially with John Scots's wife.

Fights and rows in the streets brought many before manor courts charged with affrays. Hurled insults were part of day-to-day life. Much weight was given to defamation of character, and many took their case before the bawdy courts to defend their honour. There was a rich language of insult. John Purvis scoured the cause papers of the York Diocese, finding such terms of abuse as; dog, cormorant, brabener, swiller, foxface, greedy guts, witch, scold, false knave, hobthursk, madcap, piller and poller, redhead, Scottish man, toadfast and papist. A York man called another "false traitor and a midden knight". The long border wars had left a distrust of Scotland. James Ryther claimed, "they are a nation by nature delighting in fraud and treason." A witness at Thwing was deprecated in 1563 as being a "Scottisheman".

Voluntary Groups

The association, voluntarily joined for its shared purposes had yet to find a new way in England. The mediaeval clubs called "religious gilds" had once been numerous, often more than one to a parish, and were sometimes linked with a chapelry or a township.

We only know of many guilds through chance mention in wills or at the moment of dissolution. Their formal purposes were to maintain altars and lights, and to celebrate saints days, but they gave support for members, involved the priest in a wider social life, enjoyed annual feasting and turned out their members at funerals. Their social functions may well have out weighed their official purposes. At the same time, since voluntary association excludes some while it includes others, the guilds may well have divided communities.

Possibly, the greatest change to social life in town and countryside in the sixteenth century, was the abolition of these guilds in 1547, which enabled the state to seize their endowments and properties. Doncaster lost a dozen guilds. Remote Goathland in the north eastern moor dales had a guild. At a stroke, the tradition of rural associations for specific purposes, which would be so influential in later centuries, was, for the time being, swept away. The revival of Protestant chapel life in dales townships late in the reign drew on similar well springs. A good number of guilds seem to have maintained a guild house. Bridlington had at least two guild houses. Guild houses at Kilham and Foston had kitchens. Hornsea had three guild houses and perhaps another at Hornsea Burton on the coast. Robert Metham had left a quarter of barley for beer to all four Hornsey Guilds in 1528.

Economic associations survived in the few urban craft guilds and in the rare, new merchant, maritime and industrial companies. Their common interests gave a strong sense of purpose and they learnt to wield influence. They made rules for their members. Here were arenas where opinions gained expression, and they sparked other opinions from those they excluded. The Hull Trinity House was an association of master mariners, which heard some "very bad and unseemly speeches." An alderman's wife was abused by a brother in drink. An excluded mariner William Skelton of Hull railed against the governors of Trinity House. They were all "cozeners and mainsworne men and he wished the house were on fire on their heads." The new town corporations were often as much common interest groups for the traders and craftsmen who dominated them as they were organs of local government.

Departure

The end of life was often a family occasion, and funerals could see a community gathering, though customs were necessarily abandoned in those years when villages saw recurrent deaths due to sweeping epidemics. Life held many events which could bring death, suddenly, rapidly, unexpectedly or otherwise. There were plagues and wars, as well as the more ordinary endings of life spans. Folk gathered at a deathbed. Emmot Allan of Wood Appleton made bequests by word of mouth from her bed. Her daughter Jane, wife of Will Thorpe said to her "Mother we owe you forty shillings, which you said you would forgive us. What say will you do it?" She answered, "Yes, Yes, I do forgive it."

The mediaeval church had treated the dead as if they were still there, in some other "world". There was prayer for the dead and prayer to dead saints. Church teaching seemed much preoccupied with destinations after death. It is not too much to speak of a cult of death and the dead. Great families continued to arrange great distributions of alms at their funerals, which once had sought to gain the prayers of poor men, though whether it was now for prayers, show, charity or mere custom is unclear. At the funeral of the Earl of Shrewsbury in 1591-2 there were, "by the report of such as served the dole unto them, the number of 8,000 and they thought that there were almost as many more that could not be served through their unruliness. Yea, the press was so great that divers were slain and many hurt, and further it is reported of credible persons that well estimated the number of all the said beggars that they thought there was about 20,000."

Sir William Fairfax, a Catholic buried at Bolton Percy, paid for fourteen poor men in black gowns to carry fourteen torches. Sir Robert Ughtred of Kexby was buried at London in 1590 "being on a Tuesday at even tide by torchlight." Lesser gentry valued a decent turn out. Richard Simpson buried at Edstone church in 1568, left every priest at the funeral eight pence, every parish clerk four pence, every poor body a penny and three shillings and four pence for the prayers of the curate of Sinnington.

John Bonville of Spaunton represented a more Protestant position. He sought burial "without any pomp." He left his soul "to Jesus Christ my maker and redeemer" and he expected his tenants "to do the duties usually done in the town." He gave a quarter of wheat to be baked and distributed to the poor folks of the village. William Ellis of Kiddall in 1573 wanted "no pomp or sumptuous funeral." Thomas Spencer of Old Malton in 1574 gave each son, one and a half yards of black cloth, at ten shillings a yard, to make a coat and each daughter two and a half yards of cloth to make a gown. Much later, in 1638 that religious man, Thomas Wilson, the Danby clerk, left his soul to god, "in assured confidence that none shall pluck it out of his hand." He wanted no charges for a funeral, beyond a sermon, and to give moderate refreshment to those who accompanied him to church. He said that the " reason is chiefly because the kingdom of god is not meat and drink" adding "I know the good will of my most loving neighbours will willingly afford me this last Christian duty, without recompense."

The custom of the community was the wake or arval feast, continued from earlier centuries. Agnes Care of Welburn, near Kirkby Moorside, in 1587 left her sisters and son one bacon flitch, the old name for a side of bacon, and another bacon flitch to the poor people of Welburn to be divided among them. William Cox in that same year gave thirteen shillings to the poor people of Leconfield and Arras on the Wolds, and a further six shillings and eight pence to the poor people of Bewley, after the Arval day. William Sproxton left bread, ale and cheese for the poor at his burial. Others gave the customary cakes, cheese and ale. A testator of 1554 had left a sum to the good wives in Castlegate in York to "make merry withall."

Poverty

9. Rich and Poor

As the Elizabethan population grew, the poor became even more numerous, far exceeding any expansion in the opportunities for paid work. There was obvious unemployment. "Our poor are without number or order" said Yorkshire man James Rither, "We breed of all sorts much faster than they do further south." The Lord President in 1577 spoke of that great and troublesome number of poor, pitiful to behold and some slander to the magistrates of the city of York. Towards the end of the reign, everyone was aware of the great number of beggars and vagabonds. Privy councillors in 1598 were baffled as to how the vagabonds managed to survive.

108

The old system had supported the travelling poor at monasteries and hospitals, walking distances apart, around the county. Since its foundation, Bridlington Priory had been required by the founder Walter de Gant, to give every tenth loaf from the four hundred quarters of wheat that the monastery used each year, making forty quarters given away in alms. They had to give every tenth gallon of ale, fifty quarters out of the five hundred quarters of malt they used. On St. Valentines Day, the Priory had given out another forty shillings worth of white bread and white herring.

Many Yorkshire monasteries and hospitals had offered a night's stay, a herring, bread and ale to the travelling poor. Some hospitals were near the gates of borough towns, others at remote half way places on king's highways. Most borough towns had at least one hospital close at hand. The poor knew where to go. The abolition of these houses ended food handouts at their gatehouses and over night stays at their hospitals. Only a few of the almshouses called "maison dieus" had survived, specifically endowed to help the local town poor, aged and diseased.

> "If you go to Nun keeling,
> you shall find your body filling,
> of whig or of whey.
> Go to Swine
> and come betimes,
> or else you go empty away
> But the Abbot of Meaux
> doth keep a good house
> by night and by day."

Attitudes to the poor were changing. Help for poor men, women and children had been a Christian duty but distinctions were already made between the worthy and the unworthy poor. Man the master of his soul, could be blamed for his own poverty but many had tempered that hard judgement. Some blamed the numbers of the poor on the existence of measures taken to assist them. The Duke of Norfolk at Sheriff Hutton in 1537 had told Thomas Cromwell that the large numbers of vagabonds in the northern counties were due to the many alms they had from religious houses and to the slackness of justices. Fuller observed that places with abbeys swarmed with poor people. Now, the abbeys had gone but the poor remained.

Legislation of 1531 required the aged, poor and impotent to be licensed by a justice so that they could beg in their own parish, while "the whole and mighty in body" could be tied to a cart and whipped through a town till their bodies were bloody. When parishes were made responsible for their own poor in 1536, the intention was to employ the able, help the disabled and punish the idle. Those between five and fourteen were to be put to a master. Voluntary parish funds would be raised to assist the unemployed. Branding was decreed for persistent vagrants in 1547.[17]

Bishop Ridley, preaching to Edward VI in 1551 examined the duty of those in authority to "be merciful to the poor" and "to comfort and relieve them." He spoke of nine kinds of poverty. The poor by "impotency", embraced the fatherless child or the child of the poor man, the aged, the blind and the lame, and those diseased by leprosy or dropsy. The poor by "casualty" included the wounded soldier, the decayed householder, those visited with grievous disease, and those poor by thriftlessness. Then there was the rioter that consumed all, the vagabond that would abide no place and the idle or strumpet.

Under Queen Mary, John Hamerton had petitioned for the re-edifying of the college and hospital of St Trinity, Pontefract. He claimed that this was desired "by the whole inhabitants and the poor of the hospital." The town had held "an abbey, two colleges, one house of friars preachers, one anchoress, one hermit, four chantry priests and one guild priest." Now they had "an unlearned vicar, who hires two priests for he cannot else discharge the cure and has under forty marks. The proctors catch at most of the property and the needy get none at all, so that the town is in great misery, ghostly and bodily, since the sanctuaries of God have been so misused and defiled."

The increase in the number of the Elizabethan poor brought a movement from charity to compulsory rates, as voluntary giving proved inadequate to cope with the problem. Clergy and churchwardens were in 1551 required annually to appoint two able persons to gather alms for the poor. The 1556 poor law made some provision for those who couldn't work and required those who wouldn't work, to be made to do so. Justices were soon empowered not only to restrain alms giving, but to compel all to make reasonable regular donations. Beggars' licences were banned in 1572 and the twenty shillings penalty for alms giving was renewed. From 1597-8 the justices appointed parish overseers of the poor with defined duties.

York had the biggest poverty problem in the shire. Each ward had master beggars, given gowns and birching rods for the King's visit of 1541. Constables and churchwardens of the city parishes gathered a sum from each parish called a "benevolence", the moneys from which were paid to the four city wardens to relieve poor people in 1550. These officers listed the inhabitants by parishes in 1560-61, and visited them on Sundays to ask gently what extra contribution they would give weekly to relieve the needy, impotent and aged. They could compel contributions from the more remiss, if the total wasn't enough. Inn holders were told not to charge the poor more than four pence for a meal of bread, drink, herring and salt fish with some kind of pottage.

Contributions of eight pence were levied from each aldermen and four shillings from the twenty-four councillors in 1566. The next year webbing was set up for the idle and children of the aged and poor to work. Beggars were sought out by the constables, for return to their parishes of birth in 1569. The St. Thomas's hospital near Micklegate Bar, St. Anthony's Peaseholme Green and the Trinity hospital in Fossgate were brought back into use as places where the poor could work at weaving. Six thousand turves were brought as fuel for the three workhouses.

St George's house became a House of Correction for others of the city poor in 1576. Borrowed funds were used to buy a stock of wool for the poor to work in 1577 and two mills were installed at St Anthony's. William Pink was allowed the disused chapel to teach children. The loitering poor were becoming a threat to public order. No more head beggars were chosen after 1583. Throughout the changes, York gave poor relief in hundreds of cases. City policy was reviewed in 1587.

The changing attitudes and the requirements of new legislation worked their way through the other major towns. Moneys were raised for a House of Correction at Beverley in 1591. Rotherham was giving "benevolences" to over one hundred and forty poor people in 1597, usually sums of two pence, three pence and four pence but with more substantial interventions to buy clothing and to pay for accommodation for children The old St Thomas Hospital at Scarborough was made into another House of Correction in 1598. That year Malton was said to be greatly over charged with the poor.

There were tragedies throughout. Katherine Pape "a poor wench which hath her feet almost rotted off" was allowed a shilling at Aldborough.

T35 Expenditures for Rotherham Poor; Graves Account. 1597[18]

Laid forth for Thos Graves clothes. Two yards and a half of sacking for to make a doublet for the said Thomas   2s.4d

For ale and bread for the pore children when measure was taken of them to make their coats.   5d

To Robert Okes for 3 yards of hardinge to line the pore folks clothes within the bodyes.   18d.

To Henry Garrett for making the clothes for 6 pore children and for girkyn and hose for Thos Roe with a pair for old Milforth   4s.5d

To Widow Jones who keppeth two pore children   4d

The poor appear in whatever records survive at less populous parishes throughout the shire. An "Elizabeth Nobodie daughter of Nobodie" was baptised in 1573, the son of a "strange woman" in 1591, "a poor bastard" in 1596 and "a poor woman" was found dead in a calf house in 1598. The winter months were the worst. "Whereas", the courts were informed that a poor woman and a young child came begging for four or five days in North Owram "the woman fell sick, so the constable carried her into a poor man's house in Shelf township where she died." The child under one year of age was still there. The justices ordered that Owram was to pay a shilling a week and Shelf four pence towards the relief and education of the child. A child was found abandoned on the common, south east of Sowerby. Francis Marten of Thirkleby took it in. Six years later there was a quarrel as to who should pay for the child, because land was inter commoned between Sowerby, Bagby Balk and Thirkleby. The justices decided that the parishes with common rights ought to pay the cost.

Population growth, harvest failures and inflation, with rising prices, rising rents and low wages, were producing a national crisis. A bill was put before Parliament in 1585 that every man's best garment at his death should be taken to erect banks of charity in London, York, Norwich and other main cities. It was rejected. The great Poor Law Acts of 1598 and 1601 made it a general duty of churchwardens and overseers of the poor to maintain the poor unable to work, to provide materials and work for the poor that could work and to levy a poor rate on all inhabitants. The overseers of the poor were four substantial householders named yearly by the justices of the peace. They could apprentice poor children. They could give relief in food, fuel, house rent and clothes to the lame, impotent, blind and others not able to work. Begging was forbidden outside the parish where you lived and made punishable by whipping. . Where there was no church or chapel, the constable would perform the role.

The problem remained. A survey was made by the twenty-four men of Sheffield for Gilbert earl of Shrewsbury early in January 1615. It was recorded that, "There are in the town 2207 people of which most are poor artificers, their children and servants but 725 are not able to live without the charity of their neighbours, all begging poor; 160 householders not able to relieve others. These are such (though they beg not) as are not able to abide the storm of one fortnight's sickness but would thereby be driven to beggary. 100 householders who relieve others. 1222 are children and servants."

T36 The Concentration of the Poor, Seventy years later in the1670s.
(householders discharged from paying hearth tax)
Large towns Wakefield 517, York 434, Hull 261, Scarborough 186; Beverley 187; Halifax 150, Bridlington & Quay 122; Guisborough 111
Market towns Helmsley 97; Malton 83, Doncaster 81, Richmond 89, Driffield 76, Pickering 72, Sheffield 77, Northallerton 61, Pontefract 65, Bainbridge 52, Thirsk 55, Hunmanby 57, Howden 50, Ripon 50, Patrington 44, Easingwold 46, Sheriff Hutton 48; Pockington 43; Thorne 44; Stokesley 48; Rotherham 40, Leeds 41, Selby 35
Fishing communities Fyling 65, Filey 60, Flamborough 59, Lythe 55

The New Charity[19]

The scale of poverty forced a change in official attitudes to charity. It was made compulsory, as a poor rate. Before that happened and afterwards, charity remained a "good work", assumed as an obligation by some. The new charity revived the mediaeval tradition of the "maison dieu", some of which had indeed survived, including one at Tickhill and another outside the north bar at Beverley which was bequeathed two milk kine by Stephen Smailes in 1584. The word almshouse sums up the new foundations which sought to provide residential accommodation with some measure of other relief for "the deserving poor" in old age and poverty. A Doncaster almshouse was for those "of good fame, poor by sickness or misfortune."

A new almshouse was a practical form of conspicuous charity requiring substantial endowment to provide and maintain buildings and staff. Margaret Countess of Cumberland founded the Beamsley Hospital securing royal letters patent before parochial relief became statutory. A round stone chapel thirty feet in diameter was built in 1592-3, for a poor matron and twelve poor sisters, chosen by the Clifford family, subject to annual visitation, audit of accounts, enquiries into offences and expulsions when necessary.[20]

The benefactors of almshouses sought specific and often highly individual arrangements. John Freestone wanted his seven aged men from Warmfield and Normanton to receive twelve pence a week, the oldest an extra sixpence, the vicar to have sixpence for a service and a laundress twelve pence. Robert Thornhill of Woodall House left timber to build the almshouse on Walkingham common, the seven little houses each to have a chamber and a chimney, and their inmates £1.2s.2sd a quarter. Henry Saville provided gardens and asked for the prayers of the poor.

The administrators of charities enjoyed considerable powers, and they were easily open to charges of favouritism. Their selection could be as difficult as selecting inmates. The elaborate arrangements for deciding who would be wardens of Kirkby Hill hospital in the parish of Kirkby Ravensworth, became known as "Kirby hill races". Under the will of John Dakyn, in 1555, each of four churchwardens nominated a candidate, the Vicar one and all together another one. The names on sixty-seven pieces of white paper, were wrapped in brown paper, then in a small ball of cobblers wax. These were dropped hot, cracking into a bowl of water. The first two taken out were elected. (7)

Other charities sought to assist people in their own houses. Rents from land gave a secure endowment. Trustees or the vicar and churchwardens usually gained the responsibility for selecting those who received the relief. Several charities were broad enough to help the poor in several places. Queen Elizabeth's dole saw a sum of

£17.13s.4d. granted out of the rectories of Hooton Pannal and Thorp Arch, £2.6s.8d to the poor of the city of York; and similar Christmas doles to Thorp Arch, Collingham, Otley, Calverley, Bardsey and Pannal. Thomas Wood of Kilnwick Percy had done well in London, as Clerk of the Statutes and he left money to benefit forty-four places. Dame Mary Bolles of Heath Hall in 1602, bequeathed £500 to be spent on land, some of the profits to go to binding Warmfield children as poor apprentices, and sums of £200 each for the poor of Royston and Sandall. Richard Sunderland of High Sunderland in 1574 gave £6.13s.4d. to the poor of Halifax, £3.6s.8d. to the poor of Northowram and £3. 6s.8d. to the poor of Howarth.

T37 Some Elizabethan Almshouses in Yorkshire

Date .	Place	Founder	
1557	Walkingham	Robert Thornhill	seven poor people
c1570	Wakefield	Henry Saville	six poor people
1590	Wakefield	Leonard Bate	
1593	West Ardsley	Richard Greenwood	three poor women
1594	Warmfield	John Freestone	seven aged men
1595	Kirkthorpe	John Freestone	poor women
1595	Hull	William Gee	ten poor people

Work charities mimicked the arrangements of the towns in buying stock for the poor to work on. Thomas Basforth of Thormanby in 1586 provided £5 a year to buy wool, flax or hemp for the poor to work into cloth. After sale, the wardens kept a twentieth and the rest went to the poor. Bryan Leedes of North Milford left £40 in 1560 for the Vicar and churchwardens of Kirkby Wharfe to pay a sum to any inhabitant of the parish having to pay "garsons" for his house or farm and not able to pay. Others could "be helped who were poor" for lack of corn for their family, or a cow for a poor man or woman, or even a yoke of oxen. The Earl of Shrewsbury provided £200 for the Sheffield wardens to make loans up to £10 for three years, at interest of a shilling on the pound

T38 Some Endowed Poor Charities

Adwick le St	William Adams	1593	£1 p.a.
Arksey	Cartwright's dole	1593	£1.6.8.d to two poor of Arksey and Bentley
Easingwold	Ralph Stringer	1599	Foss bridge house for two poor
Kirkby Underdale	Thomas Wood	1568	£10 p.a. rent charge to the poor of 44 parishes
Brandsby	Anthony Hardwick	1600	to the poor
Pocklington	Thomas Wood	1568	£1 p.a.
Pontefract	Leonard Healaugh	1600	20s out of a house in Neat Market
Wakefield			
Rothwell	William Lyley	1602	£5 rent charge
Sowerby	Robert Wade	1592	£4 pa. to Sowerby poor
Tickhill	Godfrey Holmes	1581	£1.10s pa. to six poor families
Wakefield	Henry Burgh	1601	£2 to Wakefield poor for five years
Wigganthorpe	Francios Metham	1595	£4.p.a. out of Terrington land to The poor

Once only donations for the local poor are evident in most wills of the period, perhaps seen as a normal obligation to the local community. Some seem to hark back to the desire for the prayers of the poor at a funeral but could equally be seen as abiding by custom. Mr. Rabanckes gave four or five suits to the Danby poor and a penny a piece to those at the burial "according to ancient custom" in 1596. Other examples of small charity at the time of departure are endless and a few illustrations must suffice.

T39 Charity at Death

Lord Eure	1592	£40 for poor people of Ingleby Stokesley etc
John Goodyear of Beckhouse.	1553	4d to every house in Cropton
William Peirson of Westerdale	1574	2d to every house in the dale
Nicholas Clayton Greasbrough	1576	3s for the "poor men's box at Rotherham
Thomas Dawon of Sceckling	1558	6s8d to the poverty within town
William Bolton of Bolton	1558	peck of rye to every house.
John Bonville of Spaunton	1582	quarter of wheat baked for Spaunton poor
James Waddesworth of Hull	1558	linen cloth in shirts and smocks to the poor

CHAPTER 5

FARMING

Farming Ways

The principal products of Yorkshire agriculture were corn, cattle and sheep. There was farming for subsistence, and there was farming for sale to local and distant markets, either directly or through middlemen. The shift from one to the other was not easily achieved but some townships were becoming specialised, producing what they were best suited for and selling their surpluses for cash or for credit. The expanding population of the Elizabethan age increased the demand for foodstuffs. The massive growth of London exerted a great pull on parts of the country remote from the capital, including Yorkshire. Within the county, population growth was greatest in several areas where new industries were making subsistence agriculture a secondary pursuit. They drew raw materials and some foodstuffs from districts further afield.

Each township normally contained arable, pasture and meadow, along with open commons and often some woodland. Manor houses, farmsteads and cottages stood in small private closes. A few other closes held improved pasture. The proportion of cultivated land differed widely between townships, giving each its own balance of what might be produced. The arable field areas where crops were grown had expanded from the eleventh to the late thirteenth centuries. The meadows, commonly known as ings and holmes, provided a valuable hay crop, used for feeding stock. The commons, sometimes badly described as wastes, included low carrs, both low and high moors, and in parts of the Pennines a mountainous terrain. They provided extensive rough pasture, wild fowl, brackens, whins and fuel. There were still areas of marshland awaiting reclamation. The old woodland had been permanently reduced at quite early dates, but would see some recovery in this reign, as a result of coppice management and localised field enclosures using hedgerows.

Most farming was mixed farming, in the sense that both crops and stock were produced. Sir Anthony Fitzherbert in 1534 said that "A husband can not well thrive by his corn, without he have other cattle, nor by his cattle, without corn, for else he shall be a buyer, a borrower or a beggar." He thought that sheep were the most profitable stock that a man could have. The lowland and vale farmers grew some fodder crops, as well as grain and pulses. They also needed animals to maintain the fertility of the cornfields. Animals manured the field land as they fed in the fallows and on the stubble of harvested plough land. In the higher country and in the narrower reaches of the upper dales, cattle and sheep were the main assets of the farmers. They concentrated on rearing sheep and cattle, and when favourable, fattening them, or, on dairying, pig breeding and horse keeping. They kept sheep for their wool but many sold their young cattle for fattening in lowland pastures.[1]

10. Churning Butter

There were several different farming situations. We might call them common field, compact farm and part time farming. Village farmers in the "common field" countryside, including the home farms of their manor halls and rectories, lived one way of life, in one kind of landscape. Their townships were distinguished by large shared fields. These might be altered by enclosures, by conversion of arable to pasture, by the establishment of outlying ring fence farmsteads and even by village collapse. Where gently sloping land prevailed, the common fields of one township abutting another, seemed to a distant viewer like great belts of arable. Elsewhere, in the Vales of York, in Ryedale, and in the lower reaches of many West Yorkshire river valleys, the common fields were like islands of cultivation, set amidst great tracts of unbroken common. Both fields and common were managed in a communal way.

A different way of life had long continued in the compact enclosed farms, which characterised many of the upper dales, whether the western dales of the Pennines, or the smaller dales of Blackamoor. The dale might be full of scattered farms. The farmstead stood among its own arable and pasture closes. The higher slopes of the dale, beyond the edge of the farm enclosures, were open commons, and were shared. The enclosed land belonged to the farm and was privately managed. The moors, in so far as they were managed at all, were communally controlled. If there were any common fields, as there were at Danby, Egton, Westerdale and Urra in Blackamoor, they would support a village, but they remained a small part of the largely pastoral landscape. The separate farms had grown far beyond them in the valleys and up the slopes. Elsewhere, as at Rosedale or Farndale, a monastery or a mill had sometimes become the focus for a small hamlet. Other small dales within large townships, distant from the common field village, developed their own single farmsteads, as at Bickley and Harwood Dale. There was little visible sign of dramatic change in these landscapes in the age of Queen Elizabeth.

On the one hand, we have the situation at Settrington, a common field township centred on a large village of the East Riding wold edge. The village held some seventy-eight houses and cottages working two thousand seven hundred acres of common fields. The entire township produced corn crops and could support 240 oxen, 550 cows and 550 sheep.[2] On the other hand, Rosedale west side, which had belonged to the Abbey of St. Mary's at York, part of its Manor of Spaunton, had no village in 1601. There were seven farmsteads, each with between four and ten closes, one cottage and a mill. Rosedale east side, a separate township which had housed a small nunnery, now converted to a gentleman's house, held a further seventeen separate farms, and one cottage. The manor farm, a bake house and a mill formed a small hamlet. Rosedale grew rye and oats, kept dairy cattle, reared oxen and sold some of them, along with butter, timber, woodworks and hemp, miles away at coastal Scarborough.

The third kind of farming landscape existed wherever small scale farming of new intakes of land was subsidiary to industries, in the mining of metals and coal, near river side cutler's wheels, or in the homes of the cloth making districts. These industries were established where the raw materials existed, and where fast flowing streams provided waterpower. The farm holdings, often intakes, were founded near at hand, made available on easy terms, often on Crown estates. There could be old villages, but there were many new hamlets or scattered settlements. The large Pennine parishes west of Doncaster, were partly composed of isolated farms and small hamlets, where farming was combined with cloth making northwards and with cutlery further south.

Towards the end of Elizabeth's reign, there was more discussion of farming management, as the pressure on food supplies increased. Much of this concerned the compact demesne farms owned by the gentry, who could enforce new rules for crop rotation, frequency of manuring, or other proposals on stewards and tenants, without the restraint of the custom of the common field. Most farmers would remain untouched by such developments, striving in traditional ways to make a living and relying on village bye laws to maintain agreed local standards of good husbandry. There was a prejudice that the cornfield signified industry and the cattle and sheep pastures meant idleness but good pasture was at a premium, and innovations were sometimes agreed in the use of leys, conversion of arable to pasture, and the enclosure of commons.

Crops

The dominant field crops varied around the shire, though most were grown in the larger common fields. Drayton spoke of "rich Holderness, I have, excelling for her grain." Cleveland would be noted for wheat and Ryedale for good oats, locally known as haver. "Bere" was a coarse inferior barley and "bigg" a poor, hardy barley. The Wolds were already a barley country, from Flamborough to Sledmere. Rye was grown on low damp land at Wykeham near Malton, at Welburn and Harum in Ryedale, and on the poorer soils of the moor edge, but was also sewn mixed with wheat as maslin, one of several mixtures of grain, sometimes called "blend corn". Rye may have been the most general bread corn.

Robert Kirk a husbandman at the isolated Spout House in Bilsdale grew haver and rye in 1577. A man at Newbrough, near Coxwold, in 1568 had "sodden grain" and "evil rye". A rent at Crow grange, once a property of Meaux Abbey was paid in wheat and in quarters of dredge, a mixture of oats and barley. Oats were the most successful cereal on poor wet soils. They were also the main crop of the dales, used for making oat bread, oatmeal, oat cake, porridge, gruel, and hasty pudding. Oats fed horses as well as men. The varieties were white, black and red but Tartarian oats were already known in Westmoreland and would spread to Yorkshire.[3]

Farm inventories might yield a fuller picture, but they are seasonal, survive patchily, and have only been studied in a few areas. Field crops are often described as hard corn, Winter corn, corn in the barn, corn sewn, or even oxgangs sewn. Wheat and rye were called "hard corn", barley and oats were "ware corn". Husbandmen at South Cave in the East Riding, between 1558 and 1577, mentioned wheat and rye sewn in their fields, but also quarters of barley, barley malt and blend malt, pecks of wheat, and some quarters of peas. Thomas Marshall had five different crops gathered as well as six rooks of peas, straw, and nine oxgangs sewn in the fields. He owed other people in nearby villages, for purchases of oats, barley, peas and malt.[4]

Farmers at Falsgrave, whose fields edged wind blown coastal Scarborough bequeathed quarters of barley, bushels of wheat and rye, "the crop of a land of beans and peas" and "a quarter of wheat, rye and barley out of an oxgang", not yet harvested. At Halsham, there were bequests of wheat, barley, malt, rye and peas. At Swaledale in the pastoral country, the inventories mentioned crops more rarely, but haver and bigg, wheat and rye, were grown in the lower dale. At Sedbergh, amid the mountains, there were pecks of bigg.

Regular crop rotations were maintained in many common fields of the Vale of York, first winter corn, then spring corn or pulses followed by a fallow. Parts of East Yorkshire knew a two-course rotation, one field fallow in one year, the other field divided into furlongs with a Spring sewn crop and others with a Winter sewn crop. Hunmanby near the coast had "three fields, west, south and north-west, all arable." A surveyor reported that, "Of the three fields aforesaid, one doth lye fallow, one sown with winter corn and another with ware corn." There was an unstinted common moor and three large areas of meadow. The demesnes were let to tenants. A stook of wheat at Strensall in 1567 was worth twelve pence, compared with ten pence for maslin, sixpence, for barley, four pence for haver or oats, and a penny for peas.

Little is known about yield, the return on what was sewn. That Elizabethan Thomas Tusser said that a three fold return, giving seven and a half bushels to the acre was good.[5] Another man of the time, William Harrison said that in ordinary years each acre

118

of rye or wheat, well tilled and dressed, would commonly yield sixteen or twenty bushels. An acre of barley would give thirty-six bushels. An acre of oats could give four or five quarters. He thought that yields were less than that in northern parts. Allison Harrison in November 1569 had half a quarter of wheat, rye and barley from her oxgang in Ebberston. The Healaugh estate demesnes in 1568 gave Lord Wharton thirty-five quarters of corn, twenty-three quarters of malt, and a hundred loads of hay for forty-five cattle, fifteen horses and seventy two sheep.[6]

Good and bad harvests were a main determinant of well being. The harvest failures of 1555 and 1556 are said to have given general starvation. Too great a crop could have effects as dire. When corn prices fell below statutory limits in 1565, a Crown proclamation allowed local export of five hundred quarters of wheat, a thousand quarters of barley and malt and a thousand quarters of peas and beans, through Hull and Bridlington provided that prices didn't rise. There were poor harvests in the years 1594-1597 with corn rising to eighty shillings a quarter in 1596 and one hundred and twenty shillings in 1598. Another poor harvest came in 1600, but 1601 was a better year and prices fell again.

The introduction of a new crop into the common fields needed general agreement, if there were several freeholders. Flax and hemp were often grown in house crofts. Indeed the general name for the land behind a house plot in parts of the county became the "hempgarth". Tithes of flax and hemp were taken at Knottingley in 1564. It is said that the short liquorice plant was introduced to Pontefract about 1562, by sets and not seed. Another tradition claims its cultivation was begun by the mediaeval friars. Yet another unlikely story has the Mediterranean plant introduced by a Yorkshire schoolmaster who in 1588 received a bundle of liquorice sticks from a wrecked Spanish galleon. He birched the boys with them. They bit into them to lessen the pain. The roots, sliced and boiled, dried and rolled into sticks became Pontefract cake and this was used for stomach complaints.

The Farmer's Tools

Arable land was usually ploughed two or three times, from April to August in the fallow year, to prepare for sewing a crop. Men spoke of three ploughings for barley, at fallowing, stirring and sowing. They said that "the more furrow, the more corn" so a deep square furrow was recommended. Heavy land was ploughed into high ridges with deep furrows. It was harrowed to break up the clods and then sewn .The harrow tore at the earth again, as it was dragged over the sewn corn, to cover the seed and stop the birds eating it. The ox drawn harrow was six pieces of ash or oak, two yards long and the width of a lower leg, slotted together in a framework. Each timber held six sharp pieces of forward sloping iron. The horse harrow was slighter, with five timbers. Where boulder stones were found in the soil, in the Ripon district, Sir Anthony FitzHerbert saw young ash wood used instead of iron.

There was already debate about the relative merits of oxen and horses in the plough. Fitzherbert said that horses were quicker in the plough than oxen, on light soils and on even ground, but they were more costly to keep. They needed both hay and corn in winter to eat and had to have straw for litter. They must be well shod on four feet and they used more costly gear. The ox had no shoes but needed a good pasture, hay and straw. Oxen went to the butcher when their years were done. The horse only gave a hide. William Harrison a Wombleton husbandman who died in 1604, kept three horses and five oxen, some or all of which were his plough animals. He had two ploughs with their gear, two horse harrows and one ox harrow. John Smothing of Gembling, near Bridlington, apparently combined horses and cattle in a yoke of "white neat with two mares". 'Neat' were hornless cattle.

Fitzherbert knew a variety of ploughs, some with wheels, and up to five foot long. The plough beam was the long, slightly bent top tree and the share beam was the lower tree, which carried a piece of oak morticed into both beams and the plough share or sock, a piece of iron set firm by wedges. This cut the earth to a suitable depth and breadth. The ploughman held the plough tail in his hands, into which the plough beam was slotted so that it could rise up and slide down. The coulter was an iron blade set in the front of the plough share to make a first cut in the soil. A mouldboard behind the plough share turned the furrow over.

When William Wraye a Coneysthorpe husbandman died in 1558, he carefully listed his plough, his coulter sock, a bolt, three teams, three yokes and other gear. The teams were the harness that attached the animals to the yoke, the curved bar of wood which coupled the oxen together. John Hagstaine of Stainton in Downholme in 1589 owned "plowe and wayne gear, three teams, four yokes ironed, one sock, one coulter, one buckle shackle, one plough shackle, two ploughs, two sledges, a pair of iron bound wheels", as well as two boarded carts called coups and two pair of "coup stangs". In all, his farm equipment was worth thirty-three shillings and four pence.

Husbandman Robert Bewshawe at Brompton in the Vale of Pickering kept his implements in the heck and within his inner house doors. Scattered around Mr. Tancred's manor house at Boroughbridge were six timber trees, wain shelvings, a pair of unbound new wheels, five gauge of fellies and two of spokes, twelve mould boards and a pair of wain blades. Sheep bars were stored in a chamber. He had three iron bound wains and three coups. The unbound wheels were without an iron tyre while fellies were lengths of a wheel rim. Many inventories listed the small tools of farming, including wombles, gripes (forks), axes, mattocks (picks), muck rakes, iron forks, pea hooks, spades, mittens (gloves), scythes, clodding beetles, weed and reap hooks, pitchforks, rakes, flails, drags (muck harrows), gavelocks (crowbars), and stees (ladders).

The farmers' seed corn was carefully stored in the house or sometimes bought from far afield, chosen with care and steeped in brine, lime, or urine to reduce rotting. Corn was sewn and then harrowed in, or ploughed under. The seeds might be sewn by hand, called dibbling or setting, with a setting board. Different crops were thought to favour different grounds, a matter given much thought by men who knew their lands well. Lady Hoby supervised the sewing of a field in her husband's absence, one October, walking to set some wheat, and had five pecks of rye hand sewn. Hay, barley and oats were mown with the scythe, and wheat was reaped with a sickle or a hook. When gathered, twenty-four sheaves of corn set up together made a thrave. Then the fields were gleaned by the poor, picking up any ears of corn, left by the reapers. At Acomb near York, the manor court required them to wait till the sheaves had been taken from the fields to the barn.

Farm Buildings

Elizabethan Manor houses in the arable belt were often well-equipped farmsteads. John Legard bought the manor of Ganton from the younger Marmaduke Lacey. A survey of 1585 recorded his "new builded" manor house, with walls of chalk stone and a slate roof. The farm buildings included a long barn of timber forks containing eight rooms, meaning eight bays. The west side of the courtyard was a long house containing a stable and a beast house, a hay house with a little chamber over the stable for poultry to set in, and one little roost joining the hay house. The east side of the court was another long house, containing a stable, two little storehouses and another stable for plough horses, with a chamber and two storehouses over. A new house built for a kiln contained four rooms. A stone dove house was covered with slate. There was a garden, an orchard, two closes, a coney garth, a windmill on the east side of the village and the demesne was sixteen oxgangs of land.[7]

Many manors had far less. The Holme on Spalding Moor manor house, on lease to Arthur Dakins in 1565 had a milk house, stables, and hay house in the outer court, with an ash garth and garden. Lund manor had a stable, two barns and a kiln house. Some dissolved monasteries and their granges had very good, specialised farm buildings. Esholt Priory on the Aire, north of Bradford, had two fair barns. Each one had a stone wall, standing a yard and a half high, with narrow boards above, nailed on upright studs. One barn was one hundred feet by thirty-two feet with good doors, and a slated roof. The other was sixty feet by thirty-five feet, and in height forty feet from roof to eaves.

An oxhouse, eighty feet by thirty-three feet, doubled as a house for rearing cattle. This had taller stone walls, two and half yards high, which supported twelve cattle stalls. There was a wain house, a cow house, a lime house, two stables, a wood house, a charcoal house and a swine house. Basedale Priory, now a lonely farmstead, in a remote North York Moors valley had a hay house. The Kirklees Priory buildings included a round dovecote and a two story corn barn seventy-two feet by thirty feet. At Handale Priory the cow house, the barn, the calf house, stable, kiln and brew house were all thatched but the garner over the refectory had a lead roof. An Esholt Priory wainhouse was converted into a dwelling before the end of the reign. Buildings to house cattle and working oxen were fitted with stalls, called bowses, the front boards known as the skellbowse. Above were wooden hecks or hayracks and stand hecks, racks for fodder with parallel bars. Helms were field sheds for cattle sometimes with a straw loft above the helm balk.[8]

The incoming laymen valued such buildings. The Rosedale Priory or manor yard was still surrounded by two storey buildings that included a stable, two lathes or barns, two cow houses, and a kiln, as late as 1650. A small orchard and a water mill stood apart. The largest known barns were the wool and grain stores of the larger monasteries, and the church tithe barns in some large parishes. The great lead covered barn north of Bridlington Priory in 1537 was one hundred and seventeen paces by twenty-seven paces. Excavation of the foundations in the 1930s revealed lower walls made of sandstone blocks, with opposed doorways in the north and south walls, to give a through draught, suitable for threshing corn. The Duke of Norfolk said it was the longest, widest and deepest roofed barn that he ever saw.

Godfrey Bosville of Gunthwaite, who married Bess of Hardwick's sister, built the famous black and white, eleven bay timber barn, fifty-five yards by fifteen yards, and forty-five foot high. The huge oak structure was held by wooden pegs, and without nails, but had three threshing floors. Tradition claimed that an apprentice spent his whole seven years making its wooden pegs. The door was wide enough for a wain and six oxen to turn in.[9] Stakesby manor house, near Whitby, had a great barn called wheat laithe and another barn called haver laithe in 1596. Rievaulx abbey's Dereholme grange, down in the Pickering vale marshes, was more modest and perhaps more typical of many farmsteads. The ancient house was described in 1647 as a small tenement built in the manner of a cottage, with a very small barn, both thatched with straw, and in reasonable good repair, which had a fold yard, half of a small parcel of ground called carrot garth and a close of pasture.

The ring fence farmsteads of the dales were necessarily equipped with storage space for straw, hay for wintering stock and cover for farm vehicles. Rosedale was full of detached farmsteads, three of them in North dale. Of the thirty-five holdings, none under ten acres, thirty-three had barns and twenty-eight had cow houses by 1650. Only two farms had stables and one a bake house. Together, these worked seventeen hundred acres, of which one hundred and three acres were meadow.[10] The eighty-four tenements in Bilsdale in 1637 had forty-one oxhouses, thirty-eight cow houses, sixty-one hay houses, six wain houses, four stables and twenty-three kilns. The Abbotside survey of 1613 recorded the field houses, so characteristic of the western dales.

T40 Some Cracowe Farm Buildings 1586 (some were new, some ready to fall)[11]

firehouse	barn	hayhouse	other	other	tenant
4 pair ash crookes.	5 pr oak crooks.	3 pr oak	3 pr ash.	2 pr ash.	S.Kitchen
6 pr ash	3 pr oak	2 pr oak			T. Toppon
3 pr ash	4 pr oak	2 pr oak			J. Cockson
4 pr oak	4 pr oak		2 pr ash		J. Westwood
4 pr ash	4 pr oak		2 pr ash		W. Howson

Muck, Marl, Lime and Fallow

Crops took much out of the earth. The fruitfulness of the soil could be partly restored by pasturing cattle and sheep on the land. Resting or fallowing the ground returned it to grass which could also be ploughed in. A fallow break between cultivation did much to control weed growth. New vigour could be attained by carting and spreading manure, lime or marl. Harrison could speak of "soil grown more fruitful". Many materials were added to achieve that result. Fold yard litter could be added to a heap of stubble and fired. Turf was pared up and burnt into ash. Sea sand and seaweed were spread on the ground near the coast and peaty moor earths in the high country. FitzHerbert in his 1534 Book of Husbandry recommended all these courses. Manures improved the yield of most arable crops. Barley gained most from a rich manure.

Muck was the Yorkshire name for house and farm manure. The household waste was sometimes gathered in dung pits or dung heaps in the road or outside houses. York had a dung cart in each of the four wards and a place outside each barr or postern gate for ward dung to be laid. Country husbandmen could call there to carry it away. The dung of cud chewing cattle was reckoned good, thinly laid dove droppings the best and horse dung the worst. Sheep dung was good, strong and readily available. FitzHerbert favoured muck spreading on land after it was first stirred at every ploughing, in small heaps close together, evenly spread and mixed with the earth. Many mucked in September. In Hallamshire and northwards towards York and Ripon, dung was loaded up, directly after harvest.

Soil conditions and natural drainage varied widely. The high limestone townships had an alkaline soil, free draining and easily worked but prone to drought. The fertility of more acid soils was sometimes improved by mixing in other earths. They might be clayey, limey or old naturally occurring deposits, which had proved fruitful, sometimes

.a calcareous clayey soil known as marl. A poem of advice on husbandry speaks of "mellow grounds which had been spread with marl", in February. A soft marl was used about Knaresborough. A rich yellow marl was spread over the fields, in the Aire valley near Pontefract, enabling them to bear corn for years together. Marl closes and pits appear in that area, but also at Tanshelf as early as the fifteenth century and later at Kirk Heaton, Whitley and Lepton. The Cleveland township of Ormsby had marl pits in 1550 and Roundhay Park held some in 1628.

The commonplace book of John Kaye of Woodsome near Huddersfield recorded his distribution of well over a hundred loads of marl on his demesne fields between 1577 and 1582. He mentioned eighty-eight loads of Pomfret marl. In his own words, "In 1582 I set thirty loads of marl in the Spring ings bank". He would lime the same fields, using ten load of marl to one of lime. Marl was often applied to newly cleared ground. His son said that he "marled and stubbed Rishworth Ing and the Milner Hill to the double ditch and made it ploughable and set in it of marl and lime thirty-three loads."[12] Gypsum was used from Lazenby and shells, sand and sea rock instead of marl in Cleveland, making "the good husbands of the low towns fat in the purse and merry in the hearts."

Camden noticed that limestone was already being burnt to manure the land in the Elmet district, near Sherburn and Leeds. He was "credibly informed that, within a few miles of Pontefract, no less than twenty thousand pounds worth of this coarse commodity is yearly made and vended in the vicinage. It is a great fertiliser of ground, if judiciously disposed of. Indeed the laying of lime on light and sandy ground will soon burn out the heart thereof; which bestowed on cold and chill ground brings it to a fruitful consistency, and prudently ordered, it will for a long time retain the same." Sir George Wentworth of Woolley leased out the Notton manor house and lands in 1637 with covenants on the tenant not to convert to tillage unless he laid two wain loads of lime or twenty-four horse loads on every acre. The tenant wasn't to take above three crops without liming again.

Common Fields

The arable land in a "common field" township was arranged in several large fields, usually next to the village, whose residents held shares in the fields. There were usually three or four fields, but some small Pennine hamlets had just one town field, and other villages had two.[13] The fields were formed of furlongs, furshotts or flatts, which were essentially groups of strips, although odd pieces were also known, and balks and headlands might separate and give access to the furlongs. The furlongs, were clusters of strips, often going in the same direction, but called flatts if they had been or were still in single ownership. Both were composed of strips, which were also known as lands, selions, acres, and by many other names. One farmer's share in the strips, in all the furlongs of the fields, was his "oxgang". Either fields or furlongs could be used as the units for rotating crops and for ensuring regular fallows to rest the land.

The fields in many townships were laid out on grounds which had been cultivated for centuries. Their arrangement varied widely with the terrain, but taken together, they gave a broadly simple landscape. Along the hill slopes of many parts of north east Yorkshire, including Pickering vale and Ryedale, the cultivated fields formed an almost continuous belt, broken only by small wooded vales and streams, roads and drove ways, leading to the commons above. Elsewhere, sloping belts of cultivation were less evident. Small islands of cultivation occurred on the high limestone, but also, in low-lying central

Ryedale. Larger islands of field land, divided among several townships occurred along the broad Vale of York. Near the city, in the old Forest of Galtres, the plough land formed fingers of cultivation pointing towards York, separated by belts of common grazing. Some of the western dales, had modest lines of arable fields in their valley bottoms, quite dwarfed by the pastures of the slopes above, and some of these had already been broken up into closes.

Much of the chalk Wold country of the East Riding was worked with a variation of the common field system. The Wold edge fields spread further, into the high ground, of the thinly soiled chalk hills, giving two sets of fields, high and low. The higher out-fields were only ploughed occasionally. They supplemented the infields near the villages, which were more continuously worked and gained most of the muck. Consequently, the entire land of the township was ploughed at some time or another, the infield frequently and the outfield every few years. Butterwick in the high wold valley was entirely under fields. "They have no sheep pastures or common moors or heaths but only the common arable fields as they lay them. The soil is not fruitful of pasture or meadow but good for corn which the tenants uttereth (send) to the barren corn towns near there about. And they buy all their hay for the most part." The inhabitants had no neat's pasture or oxpasture "but as they cut off a corner of their fields of their arable lands ends." When the pressure for arable crops had eased in the fifteenth century and later, some townships turned their outfields on the high wolds over to sheep walks.

Fields had names but the names didn't always have the permanence shown by furlong names. Tinsley, in south Yorkshire was said to have had three fields, a wheat field, presumably sewn that year with winter grain, a war field for spring sewn grain and a fallow. These are not permanent names, but they do show the fields being used as units for the rotation of crops. Hard corn was winter sewn and ware corn was spring sewn. However, the landscape was more fixed than land use. Furlongs could also be used as units of rotation or could be put down to grass when need arose. Many fields were known from the points of the compass, north, south, west and east. When Christopher Saxton mapped Shafton for Lord Talbot in 1597 he mentioned the Lydgate field, Eshbarrowe and Townend fields north of the village, going from west to east, while to the south were Nether field on the west and Head field on the east of the road to Shafton common. New laid fields or furlongs were rare but not unknown. Thirteen acres of "newly broke land" are mentioned at Aldburgh in the Vale of York in 1558.

Each township had a local geography. Amotherby in Ryedale had six fields. There were low and far east fields, near and low west fields, west greets and middle gavels in 1563. Barton le Street had arable lands in low and high fields, and even in the low pasture. That township had three moors, where those farmers with beast gates had rights to pasture and take whins. The common fields were unchanging in outline, well fixed in the landscape. The land under tillage at Pickering in 1676 was in six fields which with two ox pastures included 2516 acres. When the cultivated land there was to be enclosed in 1785, there had been little change. It was estimated as 2376 acres. The Tadcaster survey of 1613 recorded acres in Tonge field (124 acres), Humell field (63 acres), Inholme field (111 acres), Newton field (69 acres), Hargarth field (88 acres) and Nether field (60 acres), along with several other flatts and ings. The low moor was 127 acres and the high moor 506 acres.

T41 Common Arable Fields in some Elizabethan Townships

Ainsty	Healaugh	Church, Kellock & Mill fields.
Agbrigg/Morley	Heptonstall	North & South fields.
Allertonshire	Sessay.	SE, East, NE, & North fields.
Birdforth	Sand Hutton	Howe, West, & Middle fields.
	Thirsk	Three fields, each of 3-400 acres
Dickering	Staxton	West, Middle &East fields
	Flixton	West, Middle, East Fields.
	Butterwick	North & South fields.
Gilling	Aldbrough	Corn, winter corn & fallow fields.
Hang	West Witton	High, Low & East fields.
Langbaurgh	Eston	North, South & West fields.
Pickering Lythe	Kirkkby Misperton	Kinnercliff, Hungrill & Bridge fields
Ryedale	Kirkby Moorside	High, West Mill & Dove fields
Staincliffe/Ewecross	Grassington	West, East & South fields.
Staincross	Shafton	Lydgate, Ashbarrowe, Town End, Nether, Mill & Head fields
Strafforth/Tickhill.	Mexborough	Nether, Middle & Wood fields.
	Ravenfield	Wood, Kirk and Nether fields

Oxgangs

Villages, common fields, and oxgangs go together. The existence of the one usually implies the existence of the other, with only occasional exceptions. The entire arable of a township had anciently been assessed as so many oxgangs, and within the total figure, owners and tenants held their share of the field land as a number of oxgangs. They can almost be thought of as ox-goings, for that is where they went. One or two oxgangs could form a typical holding in some districts, but larger holdings were more typical on the Wolds. Within Pickering Vale, the Friar Hill grange at Sinnington, once worked by Malton Priory had six oxgangs in 1599-1600, "dispersed promiscuously in the fields of Sinnington." Whitby Strand, in 1626, included such townships as Hawsker where fourteen houses worked thirty oxgangs, Stainsacre with thirteen houses working twenty-six oxgangs but the hamlet of Normanby consisted of the manor working land reckoned as six oxgangs.

One of the more frustrating features of English history is the variable character of old measures. The linear measure called the perch was different from place to place. The statute perch was sixteen and a half feet, but the Thorp Arch perch was twenty feet. The oxgang was worse. It had a fixed meaning at any one place and time, but any reduction or expansion of cultivation would alter its size, over time, so that an oxgang could not be readily converted into any standard measures of acreage. Its extent in one township was rarely identical with that in another. Oxgangs could range from six to thirty or more acres in different places. An oxgang at Barnby in Cleveland at this time was 26 acres and 14 perches. Every oxgang on the east side of the river at Pickering contained twenty-four acres of arable and meadow with four gates in the east side oxpasture. The oxgangs west of the river were about half that, with twelve acres more or less and two oxgates. Each side had sixty-six oxgangs. The late 17th century surveyors noted that with sales, gifts and exchanges, not one oxgang was left entire.

An oxgang at any one time and place was a definite number of strips of field land, often dozens of them. The oxgang referred to the arable, but it also carried rights in the meadow, and commons. Once the crops had been lifted from the oxgang land, as well as in a fallow year, the fields reverted to use as common pasture. At Staxton, near Filey, four oxgangs in the three fields was equal to thirty-one acres and two roods. Every oxgang kept an ox or horse in the oxpasture, or horse carr, and had unstinted cattle in the neat pasture called the carr. Each oxgang had the keep of twenty sheep and each "housestall" had another twenty. Turf rights were also related to the oxgang. At nearby Folkton the oxgang carried pasture rights for twenty sheep, two oxen, three kyne, two horses and two young bullocks.

A manor house might often have six to sixteen oxgangs nominally held in demesne, but the amount retained for working from the home farm was often less. The strips of the demesne oxgangs had sometimes been compacted together in flatts at early dates. Additional land had been brought into cultivation, outside the bounds of the ancient common fields in the late Middle Ages, variously called assarts, intakes, inhames, offnames, riddings, and foreland. This land was not always included in the oxgangs and so was recorded in acres. Where old arable began to be inclosed and fields divided into closes, or where fields were put down to pasture, oxgangs could vanish as the field sharing system of working the land was given up. At Cropton, north west of Pickering, in a dry limestone country, only thirteen oxgangs remained out of forty, for a conversion to pasture was under way.

Villages without oxgangs were rare in earlier days but boroughs, fishing villages like Robin Hood's Bay and Staithes, and industrial settlements, all without shared arable land had become well known. Oxgangs without a village could occur, where scattered farms shared a common field, but the arrangement was unusual. Where scattered farmsteads had always prevailed, it was a different world. The survey of the Honour of Skipton made in 1603 had oxgangs at Littondale, Grassington, Eastby and Threpland but they were not mentioned for the farms at Upper and Nether Hessilden, Halton Gill, Halton and Connonley.

Strips

When oxgangs were mentioned, they usually referred to scattered strips of land in the fields. Just occasionally the word continued in use to refer to awarded plots received in exchange for the strips under an enclosure. The strips that made up an oxgang could vary in width, some called broad lands and others narrow lands. When an oxgang was divided, often by the splitting of an inheritance, the language of the half oxgang commonly gave way in documents to a full description of the strips held. Such strip lists are invaluable for reconstructing a vanished field landscape, as each strip is located by the field, or at least the furlong within the field where it is sited, and often by the names of the strips and their owners abutting it on each side.

A strip list from Falsgrave, near Scarborough, in 1629 shows half an oxgang to include fifteen lands in several different furlongs. Some of these strips or lands were known to the owner and his fellows, from the name of the furlong in which they stood, such as maske lands, wranglands, and elsebutt wandells. Natural abbreviation led Pickering freeholders to own "wispas", the name derived from a furlong of that name. Danby had a small field system but also many enclosed lands, so that How House farm in 1575 consisted of a three acre house plot, a croft, two lands in a new close, nine other lands, of which two were called leas, a three rood piece of meadow and six "ingswathes", the last being meadow strips. A Hackness husbandman tenanted eight lands in Suffield from Sir Thomas and Lady Hoby in the Merycks, Lunds, Gayrebrow and Keldgate furlongs, together with twenty-six beast gates on Hackness head and common rights in the waste grounds. The furlong names are often descriptive of the terrain as it had been at some time in the past.

T42 Arable Strips or Lands on John Westwood's 12 acre farm at Cracowe, 1586

croft on backside with garth and fould
four lands in Crakbar
one butt in Fowleforth
two lands on Aldthorne
two lands called Over Wharton
three lands on Langdales
one land called Nether Turgaytes
two lands called Lang Langdales
two short Langlands
two lands on Thistle Gryme
three lands on Rossaw

three lands on Windle
three lands on Pearlands
two lands on Bawderflatt
one butt on Dickland heades
two lands on Morein
two lands called Crowk
four buttes in Morein Ing
two in Burble Kell
one in Nether Dicklandes
two lands on Caplandes
two on Capland Rayne
one land called syeckes

A complete estate survey gave an incredibly detailed picture, with every owner or tenant's strip shown by its field, its furlong, and its abuttals with neighbours on every side. A terrier or land list was made for the common fields of Old Malton. This description moved around the High field, Low Field, Brows and Braydale fields, the Priest Ing field, East Field, Spital field, and the "field between towns", going through each flatt, furshott or furlong, giving the length and width of every strip, for example fifteen foot by eighty foot, mentioning unploughed "balks", boundary "raines", ways and "stinting" lands.

The High Field on the west side of Malton butted on Brows lane and the town on the south, and "upon Spittlefield on the north." The survey continued with the meadows, at Priest Ing and Long Ings, and the Bracon How field, Wood field and Low Field of Wykeham, a small township which shared commons with Old Malton. The Lord Eure's demesne land was mostly intermixed with that of other freeholders but there were some demesne "flats" and some clusters. The record filled thirty-six sheets. The yeoman or husbandman of the time will have known much of it, in his head.

A manor lord owning an entire estate might speak in different words, saying little of oxgang shares, but speaking rather of flatts and 'day works'. William Wyvell of Cayton on the Scarborough coastline had a flatt of twenty lands, meaning strips, in the fields of nearby Osgodby. Christopher Saxton's written survey of the Thornhill demesne, in west Yorkshire in 1602, started with the old enclosures, including the site of the manor in the moat, the washing garth, the orchard, the old orchard and the bowling place. The arable land was all measured in acres, roods, day works and perches. A description of day works by Robert Rayner at Liversedge, had "A note of every man's lands according to days work, where every ancient messuage is accounted for two days and cottages for one day, where also three days mowing of meadow is set against five days work."

127

Cattle

Meat was a principal object of husbandry, both from cattle and sheep, with their hides and fleeces hardly less important. The dairy was more significant in some districts than others. The common field farmers kept animals as well as raising crops. Oxen and horses were used as work animals. The dunging by other animals was essential to maintain the fertility of the common arable fields. Those parts of the shire, pastured cattle and sheep seasonally on uninclosed common land, and on the common field and meadow, once their crops had been lifted. The dales graziers could seem to occupy a different world, the improvement of pasture, their main pre-occupation.

English oxen and cows drew the notice of overseas visitors. Gervase Markham described Yorkshire as one of seven counties known for breeding fine cattle, again generally black with large horns. The Yorkshire long horn had a square stately body, short legs, black hair, large white horns tipped with black, and was good for tallow, hide and horn, a good milker, and strong in labour. The next county, Lincolnshire had white cattle with tall bodies and small crooked horns. Short horns of Dutch breed, could also be found, and were said to be good for the pail. There was a tradition of a wild herd of cattle at Rimington,

T43 Descriptions of Cattle on Elizabethan farms

Robert Easterbie	Sproxton	a white rigged cow
William Readhead	Brompton	a crumble headed brownwhye & a black tagged cow
William Baulke	Humbleton	a black pied cow, a rygilde cow and a white cow.
Robert Hudson	Falsgrave	a white ox and a brown cow
Robert Thompson	Scarborough	a red cow and a brown whye
Thomas Wilson,	Danby	two black oxen and two black whies
Agnes Care	Welburn	a tagged cow, a red branded whye

The stockman's language has become unfamiliar. The why, or whie, was the heifer, or young cow, up to three years old or until calved. She became a ky or kie, a cow, after the milk of the first calf was finished. A drape cow was dry, or barren, especially if she had had three or more calves. Bucket, skeeled, bowl or finger calves were pail fed. The stirks were young cattle, one to two years old, of either sex. The steer was the younger ox, usually under two years. The stotts were the young male cattle, one to four years old.

Great herds as well as great flocks had been managed by the larger monasteries even towards the end of their days. They ran from granges and vaccaries or stock farms, some of which were distant from the mother house. Whitby abbey in 1394 had 2659 sheep and 394 cattle. Fountains Abbey at one time had 2356 horned cattle, 1326 sheep, 86 horses and 79 swine. The monasteries often gave stock and land leases to tenants. Bramley farm, once a grange was leased with twenty cows in 1524 to John Man who paid twenty calves and forty stone of butter and cheese, as well as a money rent. The Archbishop of York still had nine 'vaccaries' in Nidderdale in 1532. The great monastic farms passed into other hands

Lordly demesne farms still managed animals on a large scale. Sir William Fairfax on a demesne farm at Steeton in November 1558 numbered his animals with their values. Here were twenty-two kye (£32), twelve fat stotts (£26), two fat oxen (£4), four fat quyes (£5.6s.8d), six quyes (£10), twenty-six calves (£6), six bulls (£7.8s.4d), sixty-six wedders (£8.4), seventy-two yowes (£12), one hundred lambs (£10), fifteen swine, one hundred sheep and several horses, He held eighty quarters of wheat and rye, twenty-four of barley, sixteen of oats and three of rye.

T44 Animals in Elizabethan Farm Inventories

Bedale	-1558 John Tennant. 175 sheep, 79 cattle, 19 oxen
Aiskew	-1568 Richard Nelson. 80 sheep, 7 cattle, 15 oxen, 6 horses
Wombleton	-1604 Wm Harrison. 10 sheep, 5 beasts, 3 horses, 4 oxen
Grinton	-1570 Janet Metcalf. 3 kine, 3 calves, 1 quie, 1 stirk, 10 ewes, 1 tup, 4 hogs
South Cave	-1592 Ambrose Tenant. 9 oxen, a whie, 8 kine, 8 young beasts, 14 horses, 60 ewes & lambs, 60 geld sheep, 8 swine

There were mixed farming men, with cattle on a larger scale, in the West Riding. Nicholas Butler of Rawcliffe in Osgoldcross in 1577 had eighty-three beasts, twenty-eight draught oxen (worth £79), one hundred and sixty sheep and lambs, twenty-five horses and some swine. His gathered crops included wheat, barley malt, oats, rye, hay and peas, worth in all £102. 6s. 8d. The standing crops were rye, barley and oats. He had marling wains, muck wains, corn and turf wains and stored twenty quarters of salt. In his house were twenty feather beds, twenty-two mattresses, eighty-two coverlets seventy blankets and sixteen bolsters. His total inventory was worth £367 2s.8d.

T45 The Annual Produce of John Peckett's farm at Farlington 1550-54

	sheep	sow	calves	lambs	fleeces	pigs.	loads hay
1550	16	1	3	10	13	10	8
1551	15	1	3	10	13	10	7
1552	15	1	3	10	9	12	6
1553	15	1	3	9	12		5
1554	15		3	8	12	10	4

Many cattle were sold to the butcher at local markets. Beasts were also being raised in the dales and fattened in the lowlands. Calves needed a good start so they ran with the cows for a year. They would be fattened for the butcher, near York. The lowland farmers bought stock from August to October and fattened them for sale in winter or spring. Barren cows and oxen used for draught also found their way to the butcher. Cattle fairs serving the long distance trade already flourished, especially at Northallerton, Rotherham and Wakefield, as dales stock breeding expanded and as the Scots drovers began to bring their animals south. By King James time, vast numbers of beasts were said to gather yearly on Bowes moor. Cattle from Middleham fair reached Sheffield. Men from York made sales at Chesterfield and Market Harborough. A Northallerton cattle man sold twenty-one oxen at Harborough, fifteen oxen at Elye and forty fat oxen at London in 1585.

Dairy Cattle

The cow was the main producer of milk, although ewes and goats were also used. The dairy was in large measure seen as the woman's province. Thomas Tusser remarked that,

> "From April beginning till Andrew be past,
> So long with good housewife, her dairy doth last.
> Good milch cow and pasture, good husbands provide.
> The residue, good huswives best know how to guide."[14]

A good cow for winter and another for Lent was ideal. Yield could rise from two gallons to five gallons a cow, if they were put out to good grass all day. Calves were weaned at two to eight weeks, after which the cow might give milk through the summer and winter. Extra feed was needed when the summer grass was thin, and through winter, when cattle might be kept in over night, or all the time, as the weather worsened.

Christopher Briggs of Gargrave from June to November 1552 kept eighteen milk cows and had fourteen calves from them. He used twelve wainloads of hay. The value of the milk was 28s.8d. Each calf was worth five shillings but a wainload of hay cost 6s.8d. Thomas Corney had a small mixed farm in Rosedale in 1601. His five kye had two calves and they gave two gallons of milk a week. Single cows were kept, especially in the towns for house use and to provide butter or cheese for local sale.

A dairymaid might manage ten cows. Most farms had under fifteen and a usual herd was about five. She fed them, and hand milked them into a wood kit or pail. The milk was sieved and poured into broad wood bowls where the cream rose to the surface. This was skimmed off into the cream pot. The milk was shaken for hours in a churn, until butter separated from the buttermilk. The butter was scooped into a wood skeel or bucket, washed, beaten to exclude air and salted. A gallon of milk might make a pound of cheese. Rennet also called "keslops", from a dried calf's stomach boiled in water, was added to curdle the milk. The curds were broken, put in a cheese cloth, in a cheese vat and pressed. The whey was drained into siles. The dairy was sometimes a separate room, or a lean to with butter tubs, cheese trough, churns, the sinkers which were weights for pressing cheese, butter and cream kitts, and a sieve for straining the milk.

Good maid servants for the dairy were at a premium. The price of a badly run dairy was white dry cheeses, too salty, burnt, puffed up, tough, and full of spots, hairs and whey bugs. The bad housewife or slovenly maid was said to have,

> "her milk pan and cream pot so slabbered and sost,
> that butter was wanting and cheese half lost.
> Where some of a cow do raise yearly a pound,
> with such seelie housewives no penny was found."[15]

Henry Best, in 1651, said that Wolds butter was locally bought and sold, by the pound or the cake, two pounds in every cake. The price fell through the season from early Lent, ten pence down to five pence by mid May. Country folk took it to market. Larger scale dairying gained some encouragement from the new trade of cheese mongers. Camden met them in Sussex and London cheese mongers were in Yorkshire by the 17th century, when Whitby and Cleveland began to export butter and cheese to

London and Newcastle in firkins. The local ash firkins hooped with hazel, held fifty-six pounds of butter.[16]

Meadow

Meadow was the principal source of winter feed for cattle. Only where the hay was very poor or scarce was a Michaelmas slaughter of animals necessary. Good meadows were highly valued, often two and three times the worth of arable land per acre. Those meadows called ings were usually well laid out, flat areas of low ground, lining the rivers and major streams, particularly in their lower courses. They were annually flooded from the watercourses, but were drained by ditches, at both sides and rear, which allowed rapid removal of the water. The floodwaters deposited silt which refurbished the land. Other meadows called holmes were more irregular closes alongside lesser streams, often in higher ground. The word ing was also used in the higher townships, clear of streams, to indicate areas cleared and improved to give the best possible crop of grass fit for mowing.

The riverside ings were man made, or at least improved, and were only valuable as long as the ditches were kept clear. Throughout the vales and lower dales of the shire, the ings or water meadows of one township ran onto those of the next, so that the principal rivers and many minor streams were bounded on each side by long belts of ing land, separated by boggy carr from the arable of the fields. The Ings were ploughed and might be divided into strips called swathes. Alternatively, the hay crop was taken up communally and shared amongst those with oxgang rights in the fields. Mowing was the act of cutting down hay with a scythe. A swathe was as much as the scythe cut at one stroke of the mower. Hay was tedded or pitch forked out of the rows for stacking and would sweat in the stack.

Meadow rights were jealously guarded. Management varied widely from meadow to meadow. The Castle Ings on the Rye riverside near the Marishes of Pickering vale were a demesne meadow reserved for foddering the horses of Duchy of Lancaster officials at Pickering Castle. The swarth was burnt about February to encourage a lusher growth. Not far away, Knapton had meadows subject to too much water, and slow to drain. The meadow strips were re-allocated annually at some townships. At Dringhowe, on the Holderness coast, the strips were "laid forth by the gadd, of fifteen foot length." One man was allowed a broad land and two gadds of a narrow land. There were one hundred and fifteen gadds making one thousand seven hundred and thirty two and a half feet in all. Fordon in the well-drained chalk Wolds had no meadow of its own but each arable oxgang had half a days mowing in the Ing and a quarter of a days mowing at Twillings and Ings Barf in nearby Hunmanby, where the resident farmers had one and a half days mowing.

T46 John Westwood's Meadow strips at Cracowe, 1586, (in all making 9½ acres, 3 perches)

three lands on Wiloo landes	one on Cald Thornay
three lands called Crofts	two on short Sharrowes
two lands in Elshowe Gill	one land on Thornar Leyes
one land on lang Headlandes	two lands called Tripes
one land on Potlandes	three lands on Lythowes
two butts on Whem Banck	dale of meadow in Crackbar

one on Whem

one on Whem Knott

two lands on the Far Sett

two lands in the Gilles

three lands called Sharrowes

two dales in Dawdthorne

two dales in Langdale Ing

one dale in Thavidale

one piece meadow in Thackdales

Pasture Closes

A different farming system prevailed in some of the western dales, where large pasture enclosures covered sloping valley sides, and even valley bottoms, while the arable fields had never been extensive. The thinly soiled limestone produced finely turfed green hills, contrasting, not only with the common field countryside, but also with the moorland terrain and poor pasture of the areas of grit stone. Even in the 13th century, Wytheside in Swaledale, about Grinton and Ryther had been praised as "a large pasture in severalty so clean and healthy that sheep there will always be clean from the scab." Leland and Camden found Swaledale, Wensleydale, Coverdale, Arkengarthdale and Uredale, full of good grassland. Cattle rearing and dairying were the main tasks. An acre or two gave oats and rye for bread corn. Most of High and Low Abbotside was a pastoral manor, virtually without arable, but with great pasture enclosures for cattle, apart from the moor. Middleham's cultivated land was 7% arable, 55% meadow and 37% pasture.

The more modest dales of north-east Yorkshire showed a similar farming style but in a smaller way. A flat-bottomed dale made excellent valley pasture and some had been developed as demesne pastures or stock farms. Some five hundred and sixty beasts of the Earl of Salisbury had been nourished on the Danby pastures, in the fifteenth century, some already sold into distant Scarborough and Holderness. Such pastures could be let to paying graziers, as "agistments", locally "geists". The Hole of Horcum was a "geist" and Fryup dale was another. Queen Elizabeth's agent, William Tusser converted "Horcombe geist" into several stock farms. He granted one hundred and eighty acres "according to forest measure" from the Crown estate to Sir Richard Cholmley with "liberty of enclosing and occupying the same in severalty at all times of the year and to build upon." Another ninety acres were granted to five Lockton men the next year, while Scalby hay, originally a deer preserve, became a new agistment.

A new pasture close in the common field country was the ox pasture. Fitzherbert discussed whether plough horses or plough oxen did better and reasonably concluded that some did better in one place and some in another. The plough oxen needed good sustenance over night. An oxpasture was essential if the animal was to tackle hills and stiff clay land. Horses could be tethered on a balk head but were costly because they needed shoeing, hay and corn to eat and straw for litter. Oxen ate straw and a little hay, but needed no shoes and were more profitable. Many townships set aside an area of good land near the village as an oxpasture, and occasionally a horse pasture. The surveyor of Staxton in 1563 said that every oxgang holder could keep one ox or horse in the oxpasture, now called the horse carr. John Whiteacre at Hinderskelfe in 1574 reserved a close to feed the ten demesne oxen, each April and planned to send a few nags there for the winter, with a load of hay laid to serve them in the hard weather. Welburn in 1562 had a common oxpasture, newly enclosed from the moor, where each tenant had the right to keep two beasts for every oxgang.

Sheep

Sheep were a prime consideration on farms over much of the county. FitzHerbert distinguished black and white varieties. The moorland breeds, both white and black faced, were small horned. They gave good mutton and fine wool. The Swaledale blackfaced sheep were big boned with twisted horns. Sheep were known by sex and age, as tups, ewes, wethers or riggons. The ram was locally known as a tup. A castrated or cut male was a wether, wedder or wither and an under sexed male sheep, with only one testicle, was a rigolt or riggon. The wether had formerly been a tup but being gelded, was clean if both stones were taken away. A close tup had both stones in the body, in the ridge of the back, while a riggon tup had one dropped in the cod and one in the ridge. The hung tup had both down and was ready for breeding.

The female lambs when twice shorn became ewes or yowes. The ewe and her lamb were described as a couple, and an orphan lamb reared by hand was a cade. A lamb from weaning to first shearing was a hogg, a female in the same phase from spring to first midsummer was a gimmer lamb, then a gimmer hogg from weaning till first shearing, then a gimmer shearing between first and second shearings, and only a ewe after she was twice shorn. A geld or gelt was a barren ewe. Sheep were marked to show what progress they had made.

Shepherds in Yorkshire used ancient counting systems, with variations from one district to another of the numbering up to twenty,

> "yan, tan, tethera, methera, pimp,
> sethera, lethera, hovera, dovera, dick,
> yanadick, tanadick, tetheradick, metharadick, bumfit,
> yandsbumfit, tanabumfit, tetherabumfit, metherabunfit, and jiggit."

Some of the largest flocks had belonged to mediaeval monasteries. Fountains abbey may have had up to eighteen thousand sheep on Malham moor and in the dales. Meaux Abbey had rights to pasture eight hundred sheep in Myton, eight hundred and sixty at Warter, three hundred in Beeford, and two hundred at Hatfield. Rievaulx had pasture for one thousand sheep in Folkton parish alone. Kirkstall abbey once had four thousand sheep and six hundred cattle. Witnesses at the dissolution of Byland Abbey said the monastery flocks included five hundred ewes at Great Murton, one thousand at Old Murton, seven hundred at Wethercote and more at Old Byland.

Laymen had tenanted some of these pastures; long before the dissolution of the monasteries. Thomas Westropp kept two thousand seven hundred sheep centred on a single Malton Priory grange at Ebberston in 1366. After the years 1536 to 1538, all the monastic pasture rights went to laymen, a massive shift in ownership, all over the shire. A modest example must serve. The Challoners of Guisborough acquired the right to pasture three hundred sheep on Birdley moor at Upleatham. Archbishop Holgate at Cawood and his other demesne manors on occasions recorded four hundred muttons, as well as one hundred and twenty beasts in the 16th century. He may have had two thousand five hundred sheep.

The stock accounts of John Baron Scrope of Bolton in 1536, show the considerable consumption of a great household. From his three hundred and eighty-six sheep, some three hundred and thirty-three went to the kitchen. There were seven hundred and fifty one lambs. Thomas Rokeby of Mortham in 1567 had more than eleven hundred sheep, divided into separate flocks, pasturing in several parts of his estate at Mortham moor, Rokeby moor, Gilmonby and at Stonesdale. Sir William Ingleby of Ripley in 1579 had one thousand four hundred and sixty-five animals in seven pastures. William Segrave the Helmsley estate steward had three hundred and five sheep going on the common till 1560, among those of his master, the Earl of Rutland. The Earl left six hundred wethers and five hundred ewes, in his will to Lady Isabel in 1583.

Five or six fleeces made a stone. Costs were modest and a thousand sheep could make £80 to £200 a year from wool sales. The Earl of Shrewsbury had £1200 offered for his wool in 1580 at eleven shillings the stone, well washed and in good condition, even though bought before clipping. Many yeomen and husbandmen kept flocks of about a hundred animals. Eight hundred sheep from several farmers' flocks grazed over the lands of the deserted village of East Tanfield in the North Riding. Other men kept many more. Thomas Yoward at Westerdale in Blackamoor in 1554 had twelve score wethers, forty ewes and lambs, two hundred and ten ewes and shearings and eighty-nine lambs. John Brotton the Westerdale curate kept at least twenty yews. When his inventory was drawn up in January 1556, he had a cow and a whye, six stirks and four calves, a mare and its foal, two beehives, one hundred sheep and a land of corn in the field, the whole valued at £17.16s. George Harker of Hawnby in 1598 left twelve stone five pounds of wool.

The chalk wolds had already seen much land converted from field to sheep walks. This was a sheep country. Wolds man Henry Best wrote thirty pages on sheep and barely mentioned cattle. Kilham had a notable sheep fair. Francis Wandesford of Hipswell kept nine hundred and fifty-four sheep in 1559. Sir Mark Constable at Everingham in 1575 had a thousand and twenty. The Countess of Lennox had eight hundred in the care of three people at Settrington in 1580. John Thorpe of Appleton took four hundred and sixty ewes, three hundred wethers and three hundred and sixty hogs to pasture at the almost deserted township of Wharram Percy in 1543. Parliament ordered a census of sheep by parishes in June 1549, intending ewes on enclosed ground to pay three pence a head, wethers and shear sheep twopence and other sheep a penny halfpenny each, for those pasturing on commons or enclosed tillage. Men with flocks under twenty would have paid less. The returns are patchy but Silvester Eads had a flock of eight hundred at Mowthorpe and a Settrington flock that was over a thousand.

The sheep farmer chose ewes for breeding in August and thinned them so that they were lean to mate. The rest were slaughtered. The tups were in with the ewes in September, early or late depending on the quality of pasture available, lest there was not enough milk. They said, "the lamb shall not rot as long as it sucks, except the dame want meat." They grazed through November and were given extra food in the Winter months. The ewes were brought nearer to the farm for lambing in March. The lambs were given extra food in April and had their tails removed against insects. The sheep moved to new pastures in May, were sheared and dipped in June, then clipped and dipped in July, when the lambs were taken from their mothers and the unwanted ewes sold. The lambs might be sold to lowland men for fattening.

The sheep were washed before shearing, often at regular sheep washes and held by the head against drowning. A thorough wash was needed, not just a dip in running water and a thorough drying before shearing.

"Wash sheep for the better, where water doth run,
and let him go cleanly and dry in the sun.
Then sheer him and spare not, at two days an end,
The sooner the better his corps will amend."

Any pricking was treated with salve from the tar box. Foot rot and scab were the common enemies, throughout the year. Damp land and weedy fallows were best avoided. "One scabbed sheep will marr the whole flock" said the wiseacre. FitzHerbert used a sheep salve, prepared from a sheet full of broom crops, leaves and blossoms seethed in a twenty gallon pan with running water, mixed with two pounds of molten sheep suet, "a pottle of old piss" and another of salt brine. This was a cheaper alternative than tar mingled with oil, goose or capon grease.

Sheep might graze by themselves, without shepherds, through much of the Winter and Summer, where there were ample commons. They would keep to a "heeaf" or stray, but were no respecters of man-made boundaries. A shepherd could reduce losses. He would drive them into a yard for fodder, in snow or hard frost. The animals were marked with township brands, the more necessary where commons merged without fencing, and where sheep were moved between pastures.

The bye-laws of North Loftus required every man to mark his sheep with his house mark. The flocks were folded on field land, more for some crops than others, moved around daily, sometimes stopping quite briefly and raised up on arrival "to stand, dung and piss", before being moved elsewhere. The number of sheep allowed on a common was sometimes limited or "stinted". The pasture field at Potter Brompton was restricted to four hundred sheep in 1570. The Thirkleby manor court laid down that "children and servants were to have no more than four sheep on the common."

The proverbial wisdom took a benign view of sheep. "A good man can no more harm than a sheep", but "It was better to be a shrew than a sheep." Wool was the main marketable product, but there was also mutton, tallow and skin. "As soon goeth the lamb skin to the market as the old ewes." and "He loveth well sheep's flesh that wetteth his bread in the wool." and "It is better to give the fleece than the wool." The heaviest wethers could weigh sixty pounds, others forty or fifty. The best could sell for twenty shillings, others from six to ten shillings. The small moor black face gave a coarse fleece of only three or four pounds weight, but they fed cheaply. The skins of the best sheep were worth a shilling when the worst were eight pence and a pound of wool was worth twelve pence. Ewes' milk made a moist, mellow cheese.

Commons

The low commons were known as carrs. They were boggy, rough grazing land, some with water not far below the surface. The commons of the high ground were often but not always moorland. Camden called Blackamoor "a land black and mountainous, being with crags, hills and woods up and down it, rugged and unsightly," adding that among the mountains nothing was remarkable except " rambling brooks and rapid torrents." He said of Richmondshire towards the border with Lancashire, "the prospect among the hills is so wild, solitary, so unsightly and all things so still, that the borderers have called some brooks that run here Hellbecks, that is to say Hell or Stygian rivulets." Here was safe living for goats, deer and stags. Among craggy rocks and vast mountains, only some valley sides offered "pretty rank grass." The bottoms and valleys were not altogether unfruitful but there were few plough lands. The inhabitants of Aysgarth parish said it was "very mountainous with nothing to live on but the increase of cattle and sheep."

Such portrayals over state the case for some parts of the moors. At Kirkby Moorside, they said that there were "many wealthy men around Kirkby due to the great commons, but in Kirkby all are poor people." Much land described as commons was neither mountainous nor craggy. Nor were the commons confined to very high or very low ground. The commons were huge and they were everywhere, outside the tracts that had been carved from them for cultivation or improved pasture. A considerable effort of the imagination is necessary to realise how huge they were. Later centuries of enclosure, drainage and urban sprawl have confined them much more narrowly. There were small townships which had tiny commons, but through much of the shire, the commons dwarfed the cultivated land. And they were not waste-lands. These vast common grounds were rough pasture, of great service to sheep and even cattle. Their fringes and much of the valley sides of the dales had been changed by centuries of pasturing to good grass. Taken together, the open commons were extensive beyond our dreams.

Pickering low commons were Eastgate low carr (455 acres) and Westgate low carr (338 acres). The Pickering high commons were Scallomore and Howdale (110 acres), Haugh rigg, West moor, Kelldale moor and Yates (865 acres) and in all, there were one thousand seven hundred and sixty eight acres. There were two hundred and thirty five common rights held by separate people, each a right to use the commons, so each common right in theory was about seven and a half acres. When an Elizabethan surveyor said that he believed them to be "capable of improvement", he meant that part could be converted into other uses, and yield a better rent return for the Crown. He was right but the commoners were tenacious of their rights and resisted the proposals.

The moors of one township ran into those of another, only separated by some stream or a string of boundary marks. Some of the largest commons were used by more than one township. This was known as "intercommoning". Scalby parish commons were shared by three townships until their division in the 18th century. Several townships used the high commons of Middleton parish, and yet the low carrs were divided into township areas, using small streams as boundaries. Tenants of Husthwaite and Baxby had "bite of mouth together with their cattle" in the three fields, and "in Husthwaite woods and commons". Forty-eight townships held stints or shares in the intercommons of Walling fen, where an annual court made and enforced the rules.

T47 Some Elizabethan Commons

Bulmer — Sutton in Galtres. 1500 acres, part good, part barren, common for 1500 sheep and the oxen pulling thirty-six ploughs. A.shortage of grass.

Dickering — Fordon. Commons only in high hills, too steep and too stony to be ploughed. The main pasture was the open field, when fallow. Each house had three cows and a cottage one. Sheep allowed at 24 per oxgang.

Ouse & Derwent — Heslington, Fulford, Wheldrake, Dunnington and Elvington had inter-commoned one tract of common Escrick, Skipwith, Riccall, Osgodby, Cliff & Duffield had inter-commoned another.

Shared commons made for disputes, as pressure on the pasture increased. Wheldrake and Eskrick men had a great affray on Wheldrake moor before an agreement

136

was made in 1542 giving equal rights to each village. Easingwold men took Raskelf tenants to the Duchy of Lancaster courts for intrusion into pasture and turbary at the Launde in Galtres Forest. Sir William Fairfax wrote from Gilling to the Lord Treasurer of "great contentions" between the Queen's tenants of Stonegrave and Cawton and those of Mr. Atherton's Hovingham lordship, "whereof hath ensued divers murders and one of them of very late days." He asked for a commission to divide the common between the two townships, "to their most commodity and great quietness." This was done in 1575. The Duchy of Lancaster set up inquisitions for bounding the townships of Lockton, Allerston, Dalby and Troutsdale and the agistments of Horcombe and Wheeldale in the heart of Blackamoor.

T48 Some Elizabethan Commons Boundary Settlements

Over Helmsley and Warthill	1564
Marske and Marricke	1569
Yearsley Peel common	1570-71
Hartshead & Liversedge	1587
Lindley & Leathley	1575
Hovingham and Stonegrave	1575
Appletreewick manor	1587
Bingley & Priestthorpe	1592
Westerdale & Stokesley.	1596

The new map making techniques were used to record boundaries. Christopher Saxton was employed by Sir George Saville in 1594, to map the boundary between the manors of Wadsworth and Midgley, west of Halifax. His "platt of the bounders of the Manor of Waddesworth" made in 1594, gave the scale in furlongs, half furlongs and miles. The boundary ran from Oxnop Common to Fosterclough Heades, and Calder Flue, east of Mythamroyd Brigg. "The disputed turf pits were marked and in Foster Clough was a note "here hath been a pinfold." Even so, a second "platt of Wadsworth Common" had to be made in 1602 naming bounder marks at High Brownestone, Greenewood Stone, Merestones, Ferrer Merestone and Reasbye Meare.

Some disputes were referred to the Lord President and the Council in the North. Thomas Earl of Sussex gave judgement in 1569 after a dispute between Arthur Phillipson of Marske and John Sayer of Marricke about the great waste, believed to be a thousand acres, stretching from Bradowbeck northwards to Skelton moor and from Whitegate eastwards to the bounds of Marske. Quarrels between Westerdale men and Lord Eure ended in a lawsuit to settle the bounds of the moor between Stokesley and Westerdale in 1596. Sir Henry Constable's Hackness tenants had ancient pasture rights in Hutton Bushell woods and commons. When Roger Conyers of Hutton made enclosures in 1580, he was ordered to pull down a house hedges and fences, with a proviso for any future disputes to go to the Lord President.

Danby moor had private "fotheringsteads" from which individual common rights were exercised. Other townships employed shepherds for sheep and neat herds for cattle. Stray cattle or sheep were gathered by a township "pindar" and impounded in a pound or pinfold, for recovery by their owners at a price, or for sale if they were unclaimed. Drifts were made over the common every year at Liverton and many other townships. When Huntington men impounded York cattle going to Stockton common in 1571-4, the city authorities retaliated by banning the inhabitants from having any dung or manure from the city and its suburbs. Commons boundaries were marked with standing stones, often called "man" stones, or ran along streams. They were perambulated so that they were known and maintained. When Kepwick boundaries were ridden in 1633, over fifty went, including sixteen boys.

Where commons were modest or were under pressure, townships limited their use by stinting. A Snainton man could keep twenty sheep in the fields, after the crop had been lifted for every oxgang he held. A house gave the right to keep ten sheep and no more on the common pasture. A Snainton grass man could only keep sheep on the township moors but not, by right, in the fields. He could only have sheep within the acre dike or flattes by reason of his grass house "by sufferance of his neighbours." Where commons were more extensive, steady intaking was possible. South West Yorkshire saw steady encroachment on the commons. Sir Thomas Gargrave led a commission to ascertain what extent of heath and waste had either been granted out by Bradford manor stewards or had been encroached since the first year of Henry VIII's reign in the graveships of Bradford and Stanbury. It emerged that several hundred acres had been granted to tenants.

T49 Some Elizabethan Commons Boundary Marks

<u>Kepwick</u>	Hangman's stone, Catt stone, Gallowe howe, from 'man to man'
<u>Bilsdale Rievaulx</u>	Wetherwath, Megg in the mire stone, the street, three howes, a beacon, Donna cross, Ropey cross, Pedderstone,
<u>Masham</u>	Roger cross, Woolswath, Sinderhowe hill, Eller cross, Roger cross, Kettlestang cross, High cross, Hellwath, Studelystone, Clotherholme cross, Ridley causeway, Mowbray wath, Old marche stones
<u>Cogden</u>	Great horrocke of stones, Whitestone, another hurrocke, the stone man on the height between Wensleydale and Swaledale.

The commons were often the sole source of fuel, stone and litter. There was a new awareness that they might also hold valuable minerals. All these things could be a source of dispute. A case of trespass was brought against Christopher Lepton by Thomas Brandsby at Kepwick, for digging and taking nine cart loads of turves and thirty cart loads of ling and heath. A Marske yeoman and labourers were charged at quarter sessions for assault at Cockhowe in Skelton on two others and theft of their turves in May 1566. The Malham tenants asked Londoner John Robinson, lord of the manor to "take some good order for managing the moor." The lead mines were reserved to Robinson. Arbitrators restored widow Katherine's common rights to cut whins on Ganton common, when she was stopped by squire Marmaduke Lacey.

The Farmer's Year

Sir Anthony Fitzherbert in the early 16th century and Thomas Tusser later in the century recorded summaries of the farmer's year, the latter in verse. Farming activities varied with the kind of farming, with local custom and with manor court decisions. A Yorkshire Steward's view of the farmer's year comes from an estate management volume of the Constable family of Burton Constable, given here in brief summary form.[17]

January/February.
-Fell woods for faggots, billets, block wood, white and black charcoal and timber .
-Plough land for peas, beans, oats, though not in rain or snow, which impoverishes the ground.
-Cleanse fallow ground from such rubbish as brier, bramble, blackthorn and shrubs which will faggot up as good fuel for brewing and baking. Cleanse ground where cattle went last Winter. Throw mole hills abroad for better growth of grass.
-Take up colts to be broken and managed for the saddle.
-Sew beans, peas and oats in suitable ground

March/April
-Sew barley seed.
-Pare summer cattle pastures, from 25th March to 1st May, giving them time to grow.
-Put cattle in meadow and low ground till May day, then cleanse & furrow them.
-Sell fat cattle and sheep, using the money to buy lean cattle.
-Mark store and bought cattle, with burn or brand, along with horses and sheep.
-Repair houses as the days lengthen and the weather dries.
-Sort cattle for summer pasturing by Mayday, putting each kind by themselves, draught oxen, milk kine, weaning calves, yearlings, two, three and four year olds. Put larger, fairer cattle together, horses with geldings, mates with foals, colts, hackneys, draught horses, in suitable pastures.
-Put ewes and lambs into ground fit to feed lambs. As they are killed off, feed up the ewes to be sold.
-Make wood into faggots.

May/June
-Wash sheep, pasture them for several days until dry, shear wool, wind it, weigh it and lay it up in lofts. Put your own house muttons in better pasture.
-Cleanse winter corn from thistles and weeds, with nicked wood tongues for pulling up by roots, or a weeding hook and forked stick to cut them.
-Roll barley to smooth it.

July/August
-Mow grass for converting into hay, and take it to barn or stack
-Wean lambs from ewes in August and pasture them in good ground. Later fatten them by themselves in the best pasture.
-As it ripens, harvest your corn and move it to barn or stacks.
-Put draught horses and oxen into the "average". Put hogges into the average after the cattle are taken out.
-Gather crab apples in the woods and hedgerows for making of verjuice and to store.
-Gather all fruit in due time.

September/October
-After harvest is ended, mostly in September, have all ploughs and harness made fit for the next sewing of all seed, wheat, rye, meslin, and vetches, so that no time is lost at seed time.

-Gather or buy hops.

-Graze beef cattle in fitting ground for winter or else stall feed them.

-See that young cattle bought for store, steers and whyes or those of three or four years are well wintered with grass or straw at the barn doors

-Rear calves for breeding, from October to May.

November/ December

-Sort sheep, so that wethers, weaning lambs and breeding yews are kept apart

-Put rams to sheep after St Lukes Day or lambs will fall before the end of March, when grass is scarce and cold weather might kill or crook them.

-When the rams are done, put them in good pasture or to chaff.

-Put mares with foals into fitting ground, where there is a hovel, with rack and manger to feed them on corn or oats.

-Take draught cattle and pasturing cattle into the house before storms.

-Dry flitches of bacon, and preserve lard in pickle.

-Give fresh straw to draught cattle at the stand hecks or the barn doors.

Much farming in common field townships was regulated by custom and the decisions of the manor court. The common practise might be spelt out or even altered by manor court bye-laws, which were called 'pains'. They show something of the problems of the common management of fields, moors and carrs. Times had to be agreed for sewing, ploughing, harrowing, lifting crops, for open average, and for gleaning.

Dewsbury had four common fields, called Crackenedge, North, Mylne and Croft fields. Preservation of the growing crops was a main concern. The Rectory manor pains required the fencing of land ends, and the repairing of gates. A pain was laid that "no man shall fetch or drive any cattle through Crakenedge except they take two sufficient persons to help to drive them, for safeguard of the corn." The court decreed that "no man shall tether nor gait on our bierdoll field until all the corn be rid out of the same" and "any person that had any unreasonable sheep or cattle was to yoke and keep them orderly."

Breaches of custom gave rise to new bye-laws. North Loftus tenants were ordered to make up their hedges before St Helen's Feast. No foals were to be kept loose in the cornfield after midsummer, and no one was to drive horse or cattle to destroy grass meadow or corn afterwards. Certain ways were stopped, when corn was on the ground. Gleaning during harvest was banned until the corn had been led away. Then came the open average time, which was proclaimed by the bellman at the appointment of the bylawmen. It was usual to run animals on the aftermath about Lammas, otherwise August the first.

Where common field farming was over or had ceased, the manor court remained concerned with management of the commons. At Bridlington, St Helen mass, the third of May, was fixed as the day to start grazing the moor with beasts. Loftus men were not to take garsel from a neighbour's hedge nor oak or ash from the woods, while common brackens were to be collected and divided equally and not taken individually. At Middleton in Skyrack wapentake, the preoccupation was now entirely with trees and pastures. There were prohibitions on shaking down acorns from trees, and gathering acorns in other people's closes. Hedges were to be repaired at the gapsteads, none were to flayte or chase other people's sheep with dogs, nor were they to put any sheep on the common from other lordships, feed swine in the lord's wood, or pull down the park pale.

Changing the Fields

Common fields covered much of the best land in Yorkshire. They could be changed in several different ways. The strips in the fields could be rearranged to give more compact clusters under one man's management. Alternatively, part or all of the fields, could be inclosed and divided anew, replacing all the scattered strips with compact blocks of land, and ending rights of pasture on the aftermath, so that the newly allocated land could be fenced in.

Consolidating strips into manageable groups under single ownership was known even in the Middle Ages. Many manor lords had established blocks of strips, called flatts, and even sometimes fenced them. This could still happen when one estate owner owned everything within the fields. Since there was normally a church interest, this required the promoter of the project to have ownership or tenancy of the tithes as well as the estate, or at least the agreement of the person who did. Where the demesne land in a township was already compact, enclosures could be confined to the demesne. Sir Ralph Bigod gave husbandman Thomas Hardy his long-standing tenant of the manor place and twenty-four oxgangs at Bainton, licence to enclose or dike the demesne lands in 1531. Sir Ralph Bouchier was both lord of the manor and lessee of tithes and glebe land at Kirkby Underdale, when he enclosed the entire township in 1583.

Enclosure was often a prelude to the conversion of arable to pasture. An early enclosure at Northstead, a Crown demesne holding near Scarborough, had by 1650, left only thirty-one acres of arable and meadow, as against four hundred and twenty-four acres of pasture in closes. Enclosure could also be a means of improving arable cultivation by ending communal management of the fields, leaving the farmer free to make his own decisions. Fitzherbert saw enclosure as a way to control manuring and to use fallow herbage to the best advantage for stock. Compensation always had to be given for any church rights in the crops produced, and at least in theory for any common rights lost by others. A farmer could control slightly less land when the enclosure was complete, than he held in his strips before it.

Where there were only two owners, a field division could have much the same effect as an enclosure. Two years after Sir William Fairfax of Gilling in 1581 had bought Roger Dobson's manor of Cawthorn, near Pickering, for £200, he boundered the Normans wood and Scrogdale common, and joined with his neighbour to divide the fields between the two owners. A field system gave way to two estates, and the village quickly contracted to two farmsteads. One owner sold his Cawthorne interest to William Horsley of Skirpenbeck, lord of nearby Cropton, for £500.

Where there were many freeholders, and a passive or absentee manor lord, exchanges were inevitably numerous and could take place over a long time. Piecemeal enclosure within the open fields could result. An undated document mentions fifty-seven closes amounting to two hundred and eighty-one acres made in five fields and in the west ings at Pickering by piecemeal enclosure. Ingleby Arncliffe freeholders achieved some consolidation by granting each other leases which were perpetually renewable. An agreement between the lord of the manor and the freeholders in 1595, was based on "the desirability of having their land together, the several grounds in the township lying dispersed."

The complete division and enclosure of a township's common fields saw compact blocks of land awarded in place of scattered strips. The enclosure extinguished common rights over land, especially common grazing. The stubble or aftermath was no longer

141

surrendered after harvest to the use of the entire township. Owners could then use the new closes how they would. Many such enclosures had taken place long before, where ownership was in a few hands. Values often rose. Norden made the point, when saying that one arable acre enclosed was worth one and half in the common field. Thomas Tusser remarked,

> "More profit is quieter found,
> Where pastures in several be.
> Of one silly acre of ground,
> Than champion maketh of three."

Strangely, the term "severalty" meant individual ownership. The champion or champagne landscape consisted of small enclosures, severally owned. Much common field enclosure was delayed till later centuries. On an estate manor, belonging to one lord, with no freeholds, both enclosure and conversion of arable to pasture could take place without any disturbance of other men's rights and often little record. If the population was already low it was perhaps easier still. There might be considerable social loss, as the ploughman's village faded away. Ganthorpe near Henderskelfe was inclosed, mostly for pasture with no common fields remaining in 1563. Soil deterioration might provide a motive. Village desertions were already familiar on the poor ground of the high Wolds but a scatter of desertions resulted from conversion to pasture in the West and North Ridings.

Wharram Percy amidst the high Wolds was almost deserted after much earlier contraction. A further one hundred and twenty-four acres were laid to pasture by the lord, four ploughs put down and four houses decayed before 1517. The township virtually became a single enclosure. By 1543, the pasture was let to a grazier, who kept near twelve hundred sheep, where ploughs had ceased to cultivate. Not even the shepherd lived locally in 1556. It was said that, "If the vicar might be permitted to plow his arable ground through the fields, his two oxgangs were able to bear sixteen loads of corn." Enclosure could bring complaint and might even be reversed. George Leppington of Wetwang refused to pay tithes to the vicar for some crofts in 1554. He said they were on land enclosed by Robert Cocket but that the enclosure was pulled down by order of the Lord President of the North, after complaint by the inhabitants.

Quarter Sessions jurors said that Maunby, Gristhwaite and North Kilvington near Thirsk were enclosed and depopulated during the reign of Queen Elizabeth. Salton in Ryedale fields were enclosed about 1583, and by 1607 the village was described as pitifully depopulated. Air photographs show a truncated village but there was still a village. A 1563 Act of Parliament required all lands in tillage for four successive years since 1529 to be kept in tillage. A later act for the maintenance of husbandry and tillage required lands converted to sheep pasture or the fattening and grazing of cattle since the first year of the reign to be restored to tillage. Further conversions were banned.

Complete field enclosures were the result of local estate owners' decisions. The inclosed and the uninclosed townships could co-exist, side by side, for centuries. The fields were brought into ring fence farms at Whorlton and Swainby in Cleveland, where almost the entire 8200 acres belonged to the Strangeways family, but Potto, Carlton, Faceby and Ingleby nearby still had common fields and oxgangs. Some of the new closes and intakes were named after their tenants of Armada times. When the Ingleby Arncliffe open fields were enclosed in 1595, the chief lords land and each free holders lands were laid separately and in each case, the tillage lay by itself, the meadow by itself and the pasture by itself.

In the western dales, where the arable fields were a very small proportion of the whole, enclosures had come early. Many settlements had emerged as clusters of cattle farms. At Middleham where graziers had large herds and flocks, 93% of the cultivated land was under pasture. Much of the Ripon area was more suited to pasture than arable. Dent fields were mostly enclosed. Hay houses were built in the enclosed pasture fields. The town fields of Askwith in mid Wharfedale were divided by piecemeal enclosure by 1596 into small closes, with a few uninclosed strips remaining in the lea field. A surveyor at Bowes and Hawes said that, "the greatest part of these two lordships consists of meadow and pasture and out commons, with a small quantity of arable land, it being not able to bear corn for the coldness of the soil and the length of winter there." Their meadow was rated in three sorts, worth 5s, 2s.6d. and 1s an acre their pasture 3s.4d. 1s.6d. and 4s, and their arable 4s. 2s. and 1s.

Some would claim that arable farming was beyond memory. A surveyor in 1639 found sixty-four tenants at Marsden, all copyholders "but what number of acres they contain, we could not learn of the tenants, for they will not acknowledge that they can tell what an acre of land is and indeed there is little plowing in this manor, but the most part of the arable land which they sow with oats, they dig, having no other corn growing and there is scarce a team in the town, but we conceive there are about seven hundred acres. They are very poor yet either very cunning or fearful and suspicious. They insist upon certainty of fines. If they are, the manor is worth little."

Changing the Commons

Commons enclosure was a very different thing, with quite different results. Small areas of common were already being enclosed. Several kinds of enclosure were undertaken. Land was newly enclosed and ploughed on Rawdon moor and at Horsforth moor in 1564. There was some enclosure of common at West Upsall near Ormsby in 1586 Commissioners awarded half of Scagglethorpe moor adjoining the manor house called Red House to the owner Francis Slingsby, and compensated the Upper Poppleton tenants for lost rights in 1574. There was a Liverton moor enclosure in 1584 and a moor enclosure at Carperby in 1592. A commission enclosed and divided Ruswarp Carr, near Whitby after a local agreement among the freeholders in 1602. Previously, there had been pasture and eatage for pigs and cattle in one hundred and thirty beast gates.

The township of Grindleton petitioned to be allowed to enclose part of their commons in 1587 in the Manor court of Slaidburn. They said that, "the town is greatly increased in buildings and dwelling houses, and thereby much more populated than heretofore it hath been, by reason whereof, the ancient grounds used and employed to pasture, meadow and tillage, are in no sort able or sufficient to maintain our said freeholders and copyholders, whereby much poverty doth daily increase among them." The upper slopes soon gained rectangular fields, of one to three acres, even up to eight hundred and a thousand feet, with a building to every five or six fields. The old open field in the valley was turned to pasture. Badgers brought grain in for sale from the markets to the east.

Smaller enclosures from the wastes and commons were called intakes. Areas of good pasture, attractive to the encloser, were to be found on many moor fringes. The process was of long standing in the West Riding. A modest expansion of people took place into many of the uplands. An enquiry made in 1557 for the Earl of Cumberland revealed a long list of unlicensed minor encroachments over the past ten years within the manor of Silsden in Craven. Enroachments were made with or without the permission of manor courts, notably within the Crown manors. Intakes were taken from the high commons in Wensleydale between 1544 and 1603 with new houses built by tenants of the Countess of Lennox. Thirty years after one Earl of Northumberland had enclosed a hundred acres called Parsons haggs at Spofforth, the tenants claimed common there from a different Earl and pulled up the fences in the night.

Pickering Lythe intakes on the south side of Blakey moor were still dealt with under Forest Law by officers of the Duchy of Lancaster. Over the centuries, Goathland in Blackamoor had become a community formed out of such intakes. Lands there called intakes in 1559-60 held seventy acres in at least fifty parcels, all described as closes, and with six houses built on them. Sir Richard Cholmley was charged with intaking three hundred acres at Black Bush in 1573 and he built a house on Haugh Rigg. Esquire William Metham made three intakes, erected two haystacks and built two houses at Lockton. These intakes were presented at Forest courts and fines imposed.

The Duchy of Lancaster itself licensed some intakes, under improving leases. They took a different view of those made by others. The Duchy surveyor Edward Stanhope in 1580 listed those gentry who had made "waste" in Pickering Forest, including intakes at Dalby, Troutsdale, near Cockrah Cross on Hutton moor, Coombe hills, Newton Dale, Keldale, Snainton and forty acres near Beckhouse at Cropton. Other freeholders vigourously opposed the intakes, on the grounds that their common rights were being lost. John Read and others were charged in 1583-4 with "riotously and maliciously "setting fire to hedges in five places" at night, burning two hundred roods around ten score acres held by tenants of Sir Richard Cholmley, the principal man in the district.

The Queen, under her Duchy of Lancaster seal, empowered William Tusser in 1580, to seek out new enclosures made in all her Yorkshire estates, which lacked a proper title. Those in possession could compound with him to keep the intakes, for a rent of four pence a year per acre, and a ten shillings fine per acre, a six shillings rent and twenty shillings fine for a building, a five shillings rent and four shillings fine for a mill. Half the fine went to Tusser himself. The properties were entered as copy holds of inheritance in manor court rolls. Levisham freeholders bought their manor in 1585-6 with a clause allowing them to inclose and take in moors and to make a coney warren. The Wheeldale agistment was enclosed shortly afterwards.

The Duchy even considered a more general enclosure of parts of the moors and commons in the forest of Pickering in 1600. It was thought that the lower commons would be worth five shillings an acre but might be worth double after twenty years if the Queen would allow wood for building houses. Sir Thomas Hoby and Thomas Selby agreed to make enclosures at Broxa in 1601. They set up tenements and intakes at Barnscliffe and Hingles, and inclosed part of Hallgate wood, which had already been taken in from the common. A Hartoft deed of 1601-2 shows small enclosures quietly made on Sinnington moor, the Horsley intakes on Beckhouse riggs, carrs and cliffs and intakes at Marton head near Riseborough hagg.

Low commons were not exempt. There were "two closes newly enclosed from the summer pasture at Holme on Spalding moor", some twenty acres in 1577. James Hebblethwaite was accused of enclosing Norton common, near Malton against the wishes of tenants with common rights. A house was built on Norton out gang by 1585. Many intakes were created to give improved pasture closes. Henry Best's father in the high Wolds had let pasture at two shillings a land, rising to three shillings, but being enclosed, it let for three times that. Quite different again were the intakes to convert pasture to arable. Rawden moor had been "a barren waste and heathy ground" of little profit until 1559 when part was enclosed by Michael Rawden, digging up stones, stubbing and digging up heath and burning it on the seventy acres of inclosed ground to make it fertile. It gave corn "indifferent good" after seven years. Others said it was a good pasture before.

New enclosures could be set about with quick set hedges, white thorn and crab tree in woody country, oak ash and elm elsewhere, provided that the young growth was protected from sheep and cattle. Fitzherbert described hedge making using oak, crab tree, blackthorn or eller stakes, or reed withy in marshes, pleaching it after some years and filling gaps. Dry stone walling spread in some districts. There was much skill in laying a good wall, without mortar. Use of a guide frame could give neat walls of the same profile for miles. Stones were selected and laid, with a broad base, strengthened by regular through stones, and careful structuring to give everlasting walls.

Drainage

Important small scale drainage works were inherited from the past over much of the county. The great Yorkshire ings, or water meadows, lining every major river, had been created by making water drains around them. Within Pickering Vale, where the waters of the rivers Derwent and Rye had a limited way of escape, cross dikes had been made for Cistercian monks in the old fenny area called the Marishes. It fell to manor courts to maintain these ditches and to keep field furrows and meadows clear of excess water. Holderness was another marshy district with many meres and small drainage works of some antiquity.

The coastal manor of Cleeton made bye-laws for the Hallfield dike, New dike and all the other "sikes", from time to time, ordering tenants to make up dikes quickly or face sixpence fines. The flat lands around the lower courses of the principal rivers, notably around the Don, Ouse, Derwent and Humber, south east of York were poorly drained but had patches of cultivation, supporting small villages. Howdenshire, and the lower reaches of the river Hull had ill drained tracts. Some extensive areas of marsh and fen were inundated through Winter, but there were sheepcotes in Keyingham marsh, near the Humber

A Statute of Sewers was passed in 1531-32. New authorities were created with powers over areas broader than the single estate or township. The Crown appointed Commissioners for the main marsh areas of the country drawn from among the local land owners, each required to have lands or tenements of a clear yearly value of forty marks, freedom of a corporate town or recognised legal knowledge. Some were members of the Council in the North. The commissioners were made responsible for inspecting drains and banks, deciding who was responsible for any defects. They could fine them if they were not put right. They decreed times of scouring and were empowered to maintain them if necessary.

A Court of Sewers met for the area "from Ravenspurne up all Humber side and Hull water unto Hull Bridge, and both sides of Ouse and Derwent in the East and West Riding to York." A Court of Sewers for the East parts of the East Riding, dealt with Holderness and the Hull river. They took action to maintain dikes and banks, and kept an eye on dams and mills. They ordered repairs to river banks at Drypool during the reign. A third commission meeting at a court at Hutton Bushell had a twenty-four man jury and probably covered Pickering vale and Ryedale. The courts worked chiefly by putting pressure on manor courts.

A commission of inquiry into the ancient water sewers on the common carr in Aldeburgh called many knights and other witnesses in 1594 to give evidence on how the sewers ought to run from the head springs at Uskell Head, Whyte Well, Leakemire and Stockwell, and how they had been blocked. They ordered streams cleansed out, and levied twenty shillings fines. Christopher Legard petitioned for removal of the Julian dike at Derningham but eventually took action himself to remove the dam at the west end of the dike in 1578. There were enquiries about the drain in Bond Burstwick and other Holderness sewers later in the century. There appears to have been some supervision from the Council in the North.

Where the many waters of the Idle, Torne, Aire, and Went flowed, and with the Don in two tidal branches, moved towards the Humber river, several distinct broad tracts of land were only a few feet above sea level and were annually flooded. The greater part was too low for arable cultivation. Here was the Marshland, Thorne Moor anciently Inclesmire, Dykemarsh, the Isle of Axholme and Hatield Chase, where the King had hunted in 1541. Camden found the Marshland a fenny tract producing a very green rank grass, which was good for cattle. Hatfield manor embraced a rank moor fifteen miles in circumference, where you could thrust a pole down ten or fifteen feet.

Thorne Waste was reckoned twenty-five miles around. Twelve Yorkshire townships from Adlingfleet to Snaith and Ayrmin took turf there. Thorne men drained land for corn, meadow and pasture but this was a fowler's country, rich with hares, partridge, black moor-game, ducks, geese, curlews, snipes and foxes. There were plenty of cranberries, and an "odiferous shrub called gale, sweet willow, or Dutch myrtle." Fifty-three copyhold fishings were rented from Hatfield manor and more from the lords of the manors of Epworth, Croul, and Wroot. Stovin said the inhabitants maintained the banks, clews and sewers, and many poor people were maintained.

Leland had described Walling Fen, with its many water-logged carrs "as so big that fifty-eight villages lay in or abutted on it. The fen had a separate administration by forty-eight men. It was claimed in 1666 that "the court or congregation of Wallingfen hath been kept after the same order and form that it now is, ever since the 4th year of King Henry VI." (1426) They met at the eight and forty house. A cheering legend spoke of forty-eight witches, who all perished one night in drunken debauch, leaving the ditty

> "We're eight and forty jolly girls,
> though witches we may be,
> we live upon the best of food
> and, like the air, we are free.

The Isle of Axholme held a north-south ridge rising to one hundred and thirty three feet, which occupied the central quarter of fifty-one thousand acres, of which the rest was permanently or periodically flooded, between the rivers Trent, Idle, Torne and Don. Villages and hamlets on the ridge produced arable crops but such a small part was cultivated, that dairy and other cattle prevailed. Half of the tenants at Westwood held less than five acres. An Act of Parliament which was passed in 1600 led to the drainage by Vermuyden, which sought to substitute an arable economy for one based on pasture and fowling.

Pigs and Poultry

Outside the main branches of farming, rabbits, doves, swans, pigs, geese and occasionally other animals and birds were reared. Each added to the meat diet. Most were confined to the few. Pigs ate most things, including household waste, and could be foraged on the woodland floor in forest areas, where pannage payments for pigs were still made. The charge for "pannage" was a normal manorial fee for tenants to run pigs in the woods, where they fed on acorns, beech mast, crab apples, hazel nuts and the litter. Large scale farmers kept pigs for market. A swineherd at Whitwell drove his master's swine at Hardye flat, towards Welburn then drove them back to Whitwell field. Small farmers kept one or two pigs to fatten and kill for bacon and ham and a sow for her litter.

When things matter, there is a word for everything. Pigs became hogs after one year and swine after two. Pigs were gelded. The hogs were castrated males. The boar was an uncastrated male. Gilts were young female pigs until their first litter. Brimming was when a sow was ready to take the boar. Richard Gatenby at Well in 1577 kept poultry and a sow and seven pigs. The next year, Bedale brewer Robert Justance had ten swine but no other stock. No doubt they could feed on the brewer's waste. The happy pig, cheerful on the third or fourth strainings of the brewer's mash was a familiar figure of fun in earlier centuries. The pig was a good scavenger but there had to be something for him to scavenge on.

It is almost a commonplace that the pig was the poor man's main source of meat in past centuries. Whether this was true in Elizabethan times is not obvious. They would consume household waste, dairymen's whey, pulses or chaff, but it is a bit moot whether the cottager or small husbandman had enough waste to feed them. The pig gave meat which hanging in the roof, kept better than most. Bacon was in great demand at York and numbers were kept in the vale to supply the city. Even the parson of St Saviours, York kept a pig. The York ward motes required pigs taken into the house, and constables to see the footways made clean every Saturday and the muck and filth taken away.

Doves ate other people's crops. A pair of birds could consume four bushels of grain a year, foraged from the cornfield. They were particularly welcome in winter as a fresher option than salted meat. Dovecotes had been a manorial prerogative, but the right had often passed to chantries, monasteries and their granges. The St James chantry in Malton castle had its own dovecote in 1553. Thomas Fox at Thorpe le Willows in 1557-8 had his dovecote where the great Byland Abbey wool house had been. As they came into laymen's hands, the manorial monopolies broke down. The great dovecotes with nesting boxes for two hundred to two thousand birds, remained at the greater mansions, but a small cote could be broken into a more modest gable end. John Milbourne of Hinderskelf had a dovecote at his Helmsley burgage. So did William Harte a tenant of the Earl of Rutland at Helmsley, the dovecote adjoining his house and kiln.

Nature offered other supplements to the produce of the farmland. A rich and varied wild life occupied the countryside. The Sheffield Manor in 1637 had hares, red deer, roe deer and fallow, pheasant and "great store of partridges and moor game in abundance, both black and red, as moor cocks, moor hens and young pootes upon the moors, as also mallard, teal, hearnshawes and plover." The rivers that passeth through had "great store of salmons, trouts, chevens (chubs) eels and other small fish." Everywhere, gentry consumption of wildfowl was considerable. The ordinary catcher, as in later times, could get reward by delivering things caught to the mansion door.

Rare birds were taken in elaborate traps. Bridlington Priory had kept a warren of herons at Little Kelk. Hatfield chase held sixteen swanneries which supplied the monarch. Ordinances for preserving the king's swans and signets, fish and fowl had been issued under Henry VIII. The Earls of Northumberland had duck decoys at Seamer Mere and at Arram Car near Leckonfield which passed on to new owners. The Earl had a great mark of swans in Leconfield carrs, and many wild swans bred there yearly. With much other fowl and fishing, in the carrs, he kept four overseers and bought out the rights of commoners who disturbed the wild swans breeding.

Villages with large greens, became known as "goose villages". Geese could be raised in yards, but they liked a broad common and would walk the greens and roadways, greeting a visitor and following him to the other end of the village. A grass man, Henry Drawen of Bolton Percy in 1578 gave his daughter Jane "all my geese about the house". The manor court of Sand Hutton near Thirsk in 1630 allowed two geese for each husbandman and one for every grass man or cottager. The fine for a breach was five shillings. A newly domesticated bird was the turkey brought to Europe soon after the conquest of Mexico and said to have been introduced to England by one of the Yorkshire Stricklands. William Strickland, son of Roger Strickland of Marske was on a ship in Sebastian Cabot's voyage. The family adopted the turkey cock as their crest.

The Duke of Wurtemberg, a visitor to England in 1592, spoke of vast numbers of rabbits or coneys, everywhere to be found, escaping from enclosed warrens into fields and woods. Rabbits gave meat at six weeks and saleable fur. Richard Hakluyt named black coney skins as a principal export. Small coney warrens had been set up near Yorkshire manor houses since Norman times. The animals were kept within bounds by a good turf wall, ample feeding and prepared soft burrows. A neglected warren allowed the animals to spread and to become a catch for the working man and a pest for the field farmer. Sir Ralph Ryther asked Sir Robert Plompton for "two couple of coneys to the stocking of a little ground that I make at Ryther" saying that "the bringer hereof my servant may have the coneys and Jesu keepe you." He offered a buck killing in exchange.

A new movement established much larger warrens on commons in the 16th and 17th centuries. By 1536 there was a large warren on Hutton moor near Ripon, leased by Sir William Mallory to the Warrener for ten marks rent and thirty couple of conies a year. The warren provided two thousand couple annually. A coney warren was established on Killing hall moor in Knaresborough Forest by 1554. A new rabbit warren was begun at Middle head on the moors above Pickering by the Duchy of Lancaster. A four acre Conyhill was on the waste near old Ravenser at Spurn in 1566 and a rabbit warren at Ganton in 1585. Robert Theakstone the warrener at Newbrough was partly paid with an allowance of the profit of conies, some twelve score couple. Ebberston had a warren by 1613, probably that at Scamridge common, high above the village, twenty years later. At Deighton in Allertonshire haberdasher William Rocliffe of Dighton Hall had a coney warren with a warren house, and leased the right of killing and keeping conies and collecting strays to Jamie Pinkney of Eskrick in 1603.

Many farmers and others had a few chickens in the yard. Thomas Etherington, the Driffield gentleman who grew corn on fifteen and half oxgangs worth £140 and held eighty loads of hay worth £26.6s.8d, had six swarms, eighteen turkeys, thirty geese, cocks, capons, ducks and drakes. James Spenslay of Marrick in 1549, a much less prosperous man, kept one swine, a cock and three hens. Some kept a verjuice press for crab apples, but common presses could be kept by a community. Honey was the only form of sweetening for most people. Bees were kept in rye straw skips or hazelwood hives. John Carvine of Patrington left four beeskeps, "one next to the garden gate." A Kirkby Grindalythe man in 1570 had a swarm of bees worth eight shillings, a gallon of honey 3s.4d, and a pound of wax 10d. Christopher Hewardine at Kirkby Moorside left three hives in another man's garth, suggesting that they were moved around. Hives were frequent around the edge of Blackamoor.

Tithe Collection

The church had anciently collected its tithe through the centuries, a tenth of any increase in the produce of the land, whether in stock or crops. The major tithes were now in the hands of laymen. Tithes were a property to their owners and a tax burden on those who had to pay them. Small tithes sometimes still went to support a local clergyman but the others yielded nothing of any communal advantage. Their collection in kind brought endless conflict. The new tithe owners proved quite grasping, noting new crops and making levies never before taken. Jane Goldell, a Burstwick woman who farmed the tithes, pursued John Frankish for the tithe of five thousand kids of whins in the Twyer in Elsternwick, their value 33s.4d. Tithe of whins was claimed at Flamborough and tithe of eggs, bracken and rakins at Firby in Westow.

The Rectors of two parishes claimed the tithe of the sheep at Great Wareholme in Thixendale, where William Hungate kept three or four hundred animals from April to July 1556-7. The fleeces were worth between four and thirteen pence each. At Welburn near Bulmer, every tenth stook of barley was marked with a "dockan" for the tithe collector. At Husthwaite in 1584, it was the "laudable custom that every man having any tithe corn and especially oats, or haver, ought, after shearing the corn, to bind the same into sheaves, as well the tenth part as the rest, to stook the same and to put ten sheaves in every stooke, then at the leading of the said stookes, they ought by custom to leave every first, second, third and fourth stooke, one sheaf called a corner sheaf for the tithe, or other sheaf standing upon the ground supporting the hoode sheafe and at the leading of every fifth stook they ought to leave a hoode sheaf." Thomas Holme of Husthwaite, a webster, at the last harvest helped load eight loads of rye which were, "truly tithed, because he did caste forth every tenth sheaf."

Compact Farmsteads

The compact farm, where the farmstead stood among a small group of its own closes was well established in many parts of Yorkshire. There were several kinds. The largest group were dales farms, stood among their own closes, apart from any villages. The bigger Pennine dales were replete with single farmsteads, either in the valleys or scattered along the dale sides, at roughly similar contours. These farmsteads shared the high commons and sometimes large stinted pastures. There was still an element of manorial control in the management of the moors.

Compact farms sometimes occurred as the home farms of some manor demesnes, in very small townships, where the terrain had never allowed village growth. Other developments could leave an isolated hall, even a castle, or a park lodge converted to farming. Old monastery granges could be broken up into smaller tenancies. Another group were at places where total enclosure and conversion of a suite of fields to pasture, had reduced a village to a hamlet or single farm. Classical common field enclosure in a freeholder village rarely resulted in the creation of compact farms, for freeholders were compensated with some of each kind of land, and the village farm usually ended with several scattered closes distant from the farmstead.

With many townships showing distinctive local histories, a varied landscape was already evident in the Elizabethan age. Watton township in the East Riding already had outlying farmsteads called Watton Carr, Loande house and Swinckild in 1559. Bolton Percy west of York had Street House, standing alone on the king's highway running through the north end of the township. New farms of this kind could emerge as investments on fresh moor edge intakes.

Compact farms offered a different system of farming, a more self-sufficient way of life and a different landscape. The farmstead stood within a cluster of small closes, arable or pasture. This was the landscape of those small dales nominally part of the townships around the North York Moors. Here were farmsteads, like Bickley in Ebberston or Darncombe in Brompton. The stream broken landscape along the coast near Whitby and Fyling carried a scattered farm settlement, despite occasional common fields. Stainton dale at the coast had seventeen customary tenants in 1542, occupying four messuages, seven cottages, two tenements, a hall, a house and a mill. Thirteen men bought freeholds in 1557 and four bought the lordship five years later. There were no common fields.

The larger dales at Farndale, Bransdale, Rosedale, Bilsdale and Eskdale could each have more than one township within them but only Urrah in Bilsdale and a few Eskdale townships had ancient common fields, some forming a minor part of the local landscape. Bilsdale had forty named farmsteads by the 17th century. The farmers kept sheep and cattle pretty evenly. There may also have been some movement of stock seasonally in and out of the dale. Bequests show rye dominating over oats, as the bread corn. Goathland in 1599 consisted of thirty-three properties, most clinging to the dale edges, some divided into two tenements, and many with a hayhouse. Danby and Egton combined modest common fields, with many scattered farms. Egton had a village near the common field but Castleton developed late as the village for the scattered farms of Danby. Bramblecarr and Howe farms still had strips in common fields and swathes in the ings. Other farmsteads there had neither.

Perhaps the most important of the new farmsteads were the small- holdings that were created, to be worked jointly with industrial activity in the south Pennines west of Halifax and Leeds. Where there were common fields, these had often been enclosed early, even before the sixteenth century. Pasture intakes followed often with cottages built on them, and the plots were quite small. The 1565 commission recorded substantial acreages allotted as intakes at Bradford, Stanbury, Holmfirth, Hipperholme, Sowerby, Ovenden and Halifax. The Halifax survey of 1589, found forty-two out of two hundred and one copyholders holding land recently enclosed.

Grange Farms

A significant group of single farmsteads, out side villages, some in the dales and some elsewhere were the early monastic granges. A line of new farmsteads were founded where field met moor in the 12th or 13th centuries in Pickering Lythe. A mere sheepcote was sometimes elevated to a farmstead to manage large flocks and offer winter cover. Here were the Wykeham and Bodale granges distant from Wykeham village, Malton Cotes, Wyedale cotes, and several more. In the low ground, Rievaulx

Abbey, Little Marish Priory and Foulbridge Preceptory occupied the old Viking settlements and new sites in the Marishes. Further west, Rievaulx abbey had several granges in Bilsdale, where the number of isolated farmsteads was increased as the granges were broken up and farms let to tenants. Many monasteries took this step long before the dissolution.

Monastic leases were still falling in during Elizabeth's reign. The granges seemed very attractive investments and even residences for emerging gentry and prospering yeomen, detached from villages and outside the common field system. Here, you could farm in whatever way you chose. There was a distinct drift of gentry into many of these well-equipped farmsteads. The grange gentry for a time formed a recognisable group, but in isolation proved less tenacious of their social distinctions than some others. The Kirkby Moorside area was an example. Gentleman William Eddon lived at Skiplam, an old Rievaulx abbey grange near Kirkby. His will made in 1549 recorded his standing bed in the parlour, his silver spoons, great chairs, counter and fire hook. He bequeathed to his daughter two salt salmon to be taken yearly in his waters at Preston on Tees. His neighbours included Richard Maddock at Keldholme and Richard Dobson at Old Malton's Freear Hill grange on the west bank of the stream at Sinnington.

Many granges were well used to producing for a mother house and could easily be adapted to supply the market. Often their interests were in more than one township. Aislaby Grange of Malton Priory in the hands of gentleman Ambrose Beckwith had seven field oxgangs at Aislaby but also pasture for three hundred sheep in Cropton. The great sheep runs of Malton Priory at Malton cotes, Ebberston went to Mr. Langdale. John Gibson built Welburn Hall around the lath and plaster Rievaulx Grange and repopulated a village that Rievaulx had depopulated in the 12th century. Gentry called Hunter, Burton, Cholmeley, Seloes and Eure moved into Marishes granges. The Templar House at Foulbridge remains today, a timber structure where Ralph Eure gave way to George Dakins at the hall with its fair chambers, parlour, dovecote, garth and closes,

Farming and the Towns

The towns exerted a strong demand on surrounding farming districts. Those once founded as newly planted boroughs had no fields but usually had some access to rough grazing, while cows, pigs and chickens were familiar in town streets. New Malton burgesses had no fields, but did have a right of way along the out gang, to the commons of old Malton moor, where they had pasture rights. Such boroughs might draw heavily on the crops of the township in which they had been formed. Other boroughs had been grafted on to villages and some towns had grown out of villages. Those communities had their own fields and commons.

The city of York had exceptional pasture rights in the commons and in some of the fields, of several neighbour townships once the crops had been harvested. Leland was told that there were four miles of great plain common north of York that served both for feeding beasts and for supplying turves for fuel. The York liberties were the more remarkable for extending into the Forest of Galtres, which included the suburbs of Bootham, Gillygate, Paynelathe croft, Newbiggin, Monkgate and Barkerhill. Town artificers kept a milk cow or two, summering in the commons, and wintering on hay. When the cows returned to town, men stood aside. The northern adage said "Take him for a tall man, that dare by force take the wall of a prentice in London, of a scholar in

Oxford or a cow in York." Hull families were limited to two cows within their walls in 1576.

The York citizens enjoyed three kinds of pasturage. The freemen of some city wards intercommoned the moors and carrs of the nearby townships of Clifton, Huntington, Rawcliffe, Wigginton, Stockton and a common called the Tilmire. They kept one cow per person, for the whole year, from sunrise to sunset, under a cowherd. Other men had half year rights, called average, over certain open fields, closes and meadows in the suburbs of the city and the adjoining townships, usually from the end of October to the end of March, basically from the time of harvesting corn to the mowing of hay, shared with the commoners of those townships. York also had its own grazing for cows and horses on Heworth moor and part of the Knavesmire while it shared Hobmoor with Middlethorpe and Dringhouses. The Knavesmire was enclosed in 1545-6 and thereafter agisted at sixteenpence for a cow and two shillings for a horse.

Scarborough had bought the neighbouring manor of Falsgrave in 1253 and allocated part of its fields and commons to the borough. The Corporation acted as a manor lord, letting the field land to tenants and supervising the commons. They paid £18 for a common bull in 1618, which was wintered in Weaponess pasture, where a neat herd supervised the cattle for those with grazing rights. Sheep were excluded from the fields within the acredykes and confined to the commons. Twenty-one people were presented on one occasion for running pigs in the streets of the town. Cows were also kept. Elizabeth Lenwood once went up stairs to her chamber to get hay for her cow. Coming down, the stairs broke beneath her and she fell on her head.

Yeomen Farmers

The farmers were called yeomen, husbandmen or grass men. Yeomen were the free men, owning some freehold land, which gave them a measure of independence. Freeholders had a secure title, and could sell or bequeath their property without hindrance. In practice, things were less clear cut. A yeoman could tenant other land beside his freehold, while substantial leaseholders and copyholders, with fifty acres or so, might be spoken of as yeomen, for it was also a term of status.

Thomas Wilson found yeomen with six kine and as many plough horses, who were able to spend three to five hundred pounds a year but the son "must skip into his velvet breeches and silken doublet and getting to be admitted into some inn of court or chancery must ever after think scorn to be called any other than gentleman."[18] This sounds loftier than many Yorkshire yeomen could aspire to but they were men of a recognised status, who served as jurymen, and filled local offices. "Better head of the yeomanry than tail of the gentry", said the proverb. Harrison for the south of England said that "this sort of people have a certain pre-eminence and more estimation than labourers and the common sort of artificers. They have working servants and "often setting their sons to the schools, to the universities and to the inns of the court or otherwise do make them gentlemen. They are called by their names or sometimes 'Goodman'."

Yeomen could be men of substance. Much depended on the size of a holding, how many oxgangs in the corn country. Thomas Foxcroft a yeoman of New Grange in the parish of Leeds made bequests of a silver tun, sealing and glass in his windows and an iron bound chest in 1599. Malton yeoman John Cootes in 1585 had assets worth £84.6s.7d. and was owed £27.19s.4d beside. He owed more than eight pounds himself

152

and had £29.6s.8d. in his pocket. His hall had a chair and painted cloths and he had three pairs of breeches Yeoman Edward Robinson of Cloughton was buried in Scalby church choir. He had invested in the tithes of Staintondale. He left a whie to Lady Etherington, the wife of he local Crown steward. His bequest to his lad was conditional, "not if he marry Elizabeth Bigging who is a papist."

Richard Simpson the Great Edstone yeoman had a holding that would have done credit to any gentleman. He expected a burial inside the church and he left his son Roger in 1568, a gold signet ring, and the corn on the twelve oxgangs belonging to the hall. He had bushels of wheat and rye, and two hundred wethers pasturing in the hills at Hartoft and at least twenty kye. He seems to have reached some kind of retirement for his two full teams of eight oxen each were being worked by two other men. His farm equipment included a wain, a coup, a plough, yokes, and teams. There was firewood in the garth and in his orchard. The house had a great counter in the hall, a great brass pot and two great spits. The grandmother's bed covering and her best beads were passed down in his family.

Yeoman had a strong sense of kinship. John Burletson the Brompton yeoman, who spoke of his "mansion" house, bequeathed a great chair, forty shillings to the vicar for a bible and a shilling yearly rent, to be given "to my kinfolk of my own name." John Frank, a Hutton in the Hole yeoman of 1595 could say "My will is my whole tenement should never go out of the name of Frank" so long as there are lawful male heirs. Yeoman John Hall of Wood Appleton in 1583 said that his farm hold "shall never go out of the name of the Halls." It was "to go to any kinfolk that bear that name." He had painted cloths in the house and a balance for weighing wool with lead weights.

These freeholders were jealous of their rights. When Richard Cholmeley tried to inclose twelve acres at Horcum, some two hundred roods were maliciously burnt down in the night. It was said of Pickering, a place full of freeholders, that they "permit no fence to stand about their haggs, to the end they may usurp the herbage of them for their cattle in Scallamore." "Order must be taken to restrain them, being a refractory company, nothing can curb but the rigour of the law." Scalby freeholders successfully challenged Thomas Williamson's lease of the manor of Scalby, in the courts, to defend their older rights. Groups of freeholders even bought manorial rights. Four freeholders representing others acquired the manor of Levisham, in 1585-6 including its rights of hawking and hunting.

Husbandmen

Husbandmen held tenanted farms, although the yeomen with tenanted land and the husbandman with a small freehold elsewhere could be found. Substantial husbandmen were known for the size of their holdings, but many husbandmen held just a half oxgang or a single oxgang. Some worked for their landlords at harvest or did other labouring to make extra income. Harrison has them living on a diet of bread, cheese, bacon and beer, and liable to be wiped out in a poor harvest. He said that a thirty acre farm might make a profit of fourteen pounds a year, of which eleven pound would be needed to feed the man, his wife and four children.

Husbandmen held their land in various ways. The tenant for life, lives or years paid a rent, and a fine when the tenancy was renewed or transferred, which could be increased by his landlord, unless he could prove "fines certain". The fixity or otherwise of fines on different estates was a controversial matter, as landlords sought to increase estate revenues, and was often settled in the courts. Fixed fines were a great boon to a tenant. The Earl of Rutland raised the fines at Helmsley between 1597 and 1610. Copyholders held land by virtue of an entry in the manor court roll and tenants at will were even less secure.

Tenancy agreements were getting more precise, to ensure no loss of assets to the owners. Robert Wright had a twenty-one years lease at £37 a year on the manor, demesne and rectory of Welwick. At the end of the term, he was to leave forty acres of wheat sewn, forty acres of peas, drage and oats and twenty acres of barley, at a price of five shillings an acre. All other arable land was to be ploughed and fallowed, "as should seem good" to four Crown appointed appraisers. A cottage at Baxby held by spinster Elizabeth Richards in 1568 was let for twenty-one years, subject to the proviso that the landlord could enter and take up roots of all apple trees. Another clause decreed, "Nor shall she marry a husband" without his special licence in writing.

A distinctive group of tenant farmers were those who leased lords' demesnes. They rarely took the whole of a manor demesne, but were often farmers on some scale. Richard Maddox the demesne tenant at Kirkby Moorside had sixteen acres in each of three open fields, twenty-four beast gates, a pasture close, nine acres in an arable field new laid to pasture, and thirty acres of meadow. He also tenanted the market tolls. Yeoman William Deane in Halifax parish in 1586 provided his younger son with the messuage there lately builded with a laithe or barn and seven closes part of the demesnes north of the lane to Halifax and leased at £6 a year.

Husbandmen making wills were careful with their husbandries. A Welburn husbandman in 1548 left a daughter's portion to her grandame "if she be contented to bring her up to the increase thereof." A Helmsley man in 1553 provided that "if Richard should manure one acre of Winter corn and one acre of ware corn, he should have them." "No children were to tavern or put away any part of their bequests." A Wombleton husbandman with "broadlands" in 1573 left bushels of wheat. His mother had a land in each field. He made arrangements for providing her with seed corn, a sack of oats, and a cow gate winter and summer for life. Will Layng of Bilsdale in 1559 laid down provisos "if any of my children are disobedient and will not be ruled and ordered by my wife."

'Grass men' appear as a separate group in some places, where there was ample pasture. They could be farmers on a similar scale to the husbandmen though often with smaller houses, and without oxgang lands. John Millington a grass man at South Cave held no arable but he had sheep and cattle, kept bacon flecks and six cheeses, and had a well stocked house with assets worth £38.12s.8d. The township of Sutton on Derwent held twenty-two husband houses and thirty-eight grass houses. The grass men were distinct from cottagers.

T50 Farmer's Inventory. Wombleton .Thomas Chapman. 16 November. 1587

personal;	purse, girdle and apparel	13s4d
farm stock	two kye & calves	£5
	hawked whys	20s
	a whye & a young stott	26s.8d
	two mares	£3
	two foals	20s
	eight swine	33s.4d
	geese and pullons	10s
farm crops	corn in the barn	33s.4d

	corn in the field 40s
	hay in the barn 20s
rent	lease of an oxgang of arable land in Nawton field 40s
household	a canter and a great pott 8s
	five brass pots, four candlestick, two chaffing fishes 26s8d
	six pannes 10s
	sixteen pieces pewter, three salts 18s
	pair racks, pair cobirons, dripping pan, spitt, cresset, frying pan, grail
	iron 6s
	two kettles, two pans 13s.4d
	three reckons 2s
	iron hammer, axe, wimble 12
	five tubs 15s
	wort trough, skeels, a swill and other implements 5s
	ten bowls 3s.4d
	an ark 2s
	six stands and a reamer 4s
	a salting fat, drink pots 3s.4d
	two kits of salt butter, seven drinking skals 9s
furniture	eight cushions, two chairs 8
	bed & furniture, two chists 3s.4d
	two bedsteads and furniture 16s
	two chists, spinning wheel, 2 bords 2s.8d
	2 carts, ropes & 2 sauers
	verjuice barels 16d
	2 mawdes, 2 skuttles, a riddle, a syve flaskett 12d
	2 bedsteads and other furniture 20s
	pair of sheets hemp and harden 24s
	4 bordclothes 12 table napkins 9s
	9 codwaires 7s
	2 chests 3s
	wood and other implements 12s
other goods	dung about the house 6s.8d
	two paire wagon ropes, 2 pair mytan 2s.8d
	fifteen wayne spencks, 16 plow steerings heads and sheaths 7 stear
	tres, one handle one oxton, one horse harness 3s
	two gang of fellows, one nafe 9s
	hay in the barn, hackna saddle 4s
	rye in the barn 30s
	five pair of broken wayne blaides a hopper ton with all other of coks
	and firewood 13s.4d
	all the cornpaste so full about the house 13s.9d
	eleven yards of hemp lin cloth 6s
	some yards of harden cloth 7s
	hemp growing on the ground, a bridle and halter 2s.6d
sum	**£32.11.4**

155

1. OAK CHEST EARLY 16TH CENT.

2 PANEL, CARVED WITH THE HEAD OF A WARRIOR KING. DATED ABOUT 1530.

3. ARM-CHAIR. ABOUT 1530.

4. BEDSTEAD. INLAID WALNUT DATED 1593

5. BENCH-END. EARLY 16TH CENT.

6. OAK SETTLE. REIGN OF HENRY VII.

7. OAK DRAW-TABLE. 1600.

8. SIDE-TABLE OR BUFFET EARLY 16TH CENT.

9. OAK CUPBOARD. ABOUT 1500.

11. Tudor Furniture
(From 'The Story of Tudor & Stuart Britain' by C W Airne)

Farm workers

Farm servants were hired at Martinmas to serve for the year. These were the "servants in husbandry" quite distinct from other labourers, often cottagers, taken on for shorter terms in harvest and other busy seasons. Henry Best described the hiring fair, albeit fifty years after the end of the reign. The chief constable notified the petty constables in the townships, a fortnight before Michaelmas. They told the masters and servants the dates of the justices "sittings", the "statute days" or "statute fairs" as they called them, held in each wapentake. Servants, both men and women, stood in the churchyards, at Kirkburn, Kilham and Sledmere in the Wolds country. Farmers, stewards and hinds looked them over.

Henry Best's advice to the farmer was to make sure, first of all, that the servant was at liberty. The next task was to discover whether the man or woman was "addicted to company keeping", and for the maid, whether she was a good milker. The sluggish and sleepy maids were to be avoided, as liable to cause fires. His final advice was "don't hire too near their friends." A youth had to be able to hold the plough and load a wain and carry bushels to the barn. Henry warned of the fingers of peevish and ill disposed servants, and recommended the hirer to "keep as much as you can under lock and key." Wages could be paid yearly or quarterly at Candlemas (2 February) Saint Helen's day (3 May) Lammas (1 August) and Martinmas (11 November).

Bargains were struck at hirings between master and servant, so much money and perhaps a pair of breeches, an old hat or some shoes, an apron or a smock for maids, even the wintering of a sheep, to seal an agreement. Some small "fest" money was given to conclude the bargain. This was called a "god's penny" and was a sum between sixpence and three shillings by mid 17th century. James Rither said of the Elizabethan Yorkshire men, "they change their masters yearly, seeking after more wages and lesser labour." Two or three days after Martinmas, servants left their old masters to visit home or friends for two or three days. This was the time of the butter loaves feast, when a loaf, with a top hole filled with butter was left on the table for hospitality. People went to their new master on the fifth or sixth day. Sunday was avoided and they said "Monday flitt never sitt."

Farm servants might live in, or come in daily from their homes. Members of the farmer's family lived and worked alongside them. A servant's bed might be in the stable. The family was all there was on many farms and for most members of the family, their life was like that of farm servants. Rither regretted the great familiarity between Yorkshire masters and their men. A large farm might employ a foreman, some men, youths and maid servants, all contracted for the year. Henry Best's foreman had to be able to sow, stack peas, go well with four horses, and go to market. He trusted him with the sowing of all the seed. The plowman was in charge of the working oxen, and had to feed them and muck them out at the start of the day, to rub them down, take them to water and see to their harness. He yoked them up, went with them to the field and ploughed. At the end of the working day, he brought them home, rubbed them down, cleaned and fed them. Then he prepared the feed for the next day and carried it to the barn.

The Statute of Artificers of 1563 provided that no person should be hired or taken into service to work for terms less than a whole year, in any science, craft mystery or art as "clothiers, woollen cloth weavers, hosiers, tailors, shoemakers, tanners, glovers, saddlers, cappers, hat makers, felt makers, pewterers, cuitlers, spurriers, smiths, farriers, bakers, brewers, butchers, cooks, millers, bowyers, fletchers, turners and arrow head makers. Everyone between twelve and sixty not being lawfully retained, nor an apprentice, nor a gentleman born, nor a university student or in school, not having lands or being an heir to someone living with goods worth £40, not having a farm would be compelled to serve in husbandry by the year if required, with any husbandman of the shire." Faced with rapid price rises, after many years of stability, Parliament passed the statute in 1563 requiring justices of the peace in each shire to fix wages. .

T51 Agricultural Wages in York and Ainsty[19]
Servants and artificers in husbandry

Bailiff	Wages by the year	30s	clothing	6s
Hind, shepherd		22s		5s
Servant		20s		4s
Woman servant		10s		5s
Children under 16		10s		3s4d
		or 1s	& meat, drink & clothing	
Apprentices		6d	& meat, drink & clothes	

Harvest folk

Mowers	Wages by the day with meat	4d no meat	9d
Reaper, shearer, carter		3d	5d
Woman		1d	3d

T52 Servants in Husbandry, Hiring Wages in the East Riding. 1593[20]
Yearly Wages

Bailiff or overman, for a gentleman or yeoman that puts his whole charge to his servants.   33s.4d, meat and drink, a livery or 6s.8d

Chief servant of a husbandman that oversees servants/chief shepherd to a gentleman
26s.8d. meat and drink, livery or 6s.8d

Miller,   26s.8d, livery or 6s.8d

Servant in husbandry, that can mow or plow well, 23s.4d, meat, drink, livery or 6s.8d

Other common servant in husbandry   20s and livery or 5s

Young man, 12-18,   16s, meat, drink, no livery

Woman servant that takes charge of brewing baking kitchen milkhouse or malting hired with gentleman or yeoman whose wife does not take the pains and charge upon her   61s, meat, drink, livery or 4s

Woman servant of husbandman or freeman   13s.4d, livery or 3s.4d

There were also day labourers, taken on for shorter periods, for the task or the harvest. They might or might not be fed. When Henry Best employed thatchers he paid them less than they could get elsewhere, because he gave them three meals a day. Some villages were well populated and held a ready supply of workers. Sherif Hutton parish had twenty-four families of husbandmen but forty-eight families of grass men. Dales areas seemed to lack a pool of labour outside the families. Workers went from the towns into the countryside to help with the harvest.

T53 Day Labourers, East Riding, Hiring Wages 1593

Harvest work

Mower of grass or corn, with meat and drink 4d a day; without meat and drink		10d
Shearer or binder of corn	2d	5d
Man mowing an acre of meadow	1d	8d

Other Day work

Common labourers for ditching, paling, railing, hedging, threshing etc.

All Saints to 1st March, with meat and drink 1d without meat and drink		4d
1st March to All Saints	2d	5d
Threshing a quarter of hard corn	8d,	
quarter of peas or beans	5d	
quarter of barley	4d	
quarter of oats	3½d	

No man shall take for casting or setting a ditch, having good wood ready, for 1 and 3/4 yard broad and an ell deep   3d a rod

To make a dry stone wall, the stone laid beside him, wall 1 yard high and 1 yard thick   12d a rod without meat and drink

James Rither voiced what may have been a stock complaint of the times that many idle serving men were more adept with the flattery than diligent deeds. Speaking apparently of Yorkshire men generally, he said they took courtesy rather than gave it, and were prone to move from amity to enmity, and were more apt to envy than emulation." Further north among the mountains on the west side of the county, he found "a true simple plain people, yet living without any great labour or riches, for they rely more upon their milk and sheep; their grain they have growing is oats only, of which they make both bread and drink. These are strong, tall people; they have much fine and fertile pasture and meadow, amid the fells."

"The Yorkshire man being rather the bigger of stature, lyker of lym to be stronge every way, yet with more paine and straininge doth use to lyft but half a quarter of corn than the Hertfordshier man a whole quaryter and seldomer is he seen to do it. This humour erectith and maintayneth manye alehowses, the hatchers of ill rule and harberers of our worst disposed persons. Servants though few good, yet all daintie and ill to please. They change their masters yearly hunting after more wages and less labour till they remove to the rope or beggary."

A more realistic view of the farm servants' life is revealed in surviving fragments. Michael Waughe, eventually a husbandman of Howe House on the edge of Old Malton moor, had moved from Settrington to Ryton at the age of four, where he was "brought up in husbandry till he was twelve." He moved four miles to Eddlethorpe, staying for eighteen years, moved to Bulmer eight miles for the next seven years, back to Ryton for fourteen years. While he was at Ryton, he went half a dozen times a year to see, his father, mother and friends. John Hoggard of Stokesley later a husbandman lived with his father William, till he was about thirty, when he married a girl a quarter of a mile away at Kirkby. He helped his father in the fields from age ten to thirty.

Wills occasionally throw up a moment of truth. A Sutton Bonnington bequest to a woman servant in 1562 was a yearling cow calf, "my brother Henry to winter it in until May Day." When widow Emott Allan of Wodappleton was dying in 1598 her daughter Jane said "Mother we owe you forty shillings, which you said you would forgive us, what say, will you do it." She answered, "yea, yea, I do forgive it." Labourer Thomas Dickson made a will by word of mouth in 1602. Two neighbours visiting said, "Thomas it were good for you to dispose of your goods and to bestow them who should have them." His reply was "To whom should I give them but to this old woman my wife?" Mary Dickson.

CHAPTER 6

INDUSTRY

The Old Crafts

The towns held small groups of specialist craftsmen, weavers, dyers and fullers for cloth, tanners and glovers for leather, bakers and butchers, metal smiths and others. A scattering of other craftsmen lived in the villages. Most worked on a small scale, husband, wife and sometimes children, perhaps a servant or two, using the home or out buildings as a workshop, only rarely adapted for retailing by a lowered shutter that became a counter. Sizeable workshops and workplaces were rare, apart from tanneries, corn mills and some kilns. There were specialised tools around the house but no machinery more complicated than a loom or a spinning wheel. The principal raw materials were wool, hemp and line, hides, horn, fats and skins, the metals, vegetable dyes, wood, stone, turf, ling and bracken from the commons, the crops of the field, and the by products of meat and fish.

Monasteries and the greater churches had sustained some of the specialist crafts, especially plumbers and stonemasons. A monastery normally had a range of semi-industrial buildings, including the malthouse, brew house and bake house. Some outlying granges had been industrial, working iron. Yedingham Priory had a kiln house with a malting floor. Bridlington Priory had a tannery called the bark house. Whitby abbey employed four cooks, and a brewer. Kirkham Priory employed a plumber, a fuller and a goldsmith. Malton Priory in 1526 had a cooper, two brewers, a cook, a cheeser, fisherman, maltster, smith, carpenter, four bakers, three kitcheners, a farrier and kept a wool store. These employments had been swept away. Some of the greater gentry houses kept a range of craftsmen among their servants.

York was a major centre for small-scale craftsmen. Thirteen crafts and trades were represented on the common council in 1579 by two councillors. These were the merchants, mercers, drapers, grocers cum apothecaries, goldsmiths, dyers, skinners, barbers, fishmongers, tailors, vintners, joiners, and glaziers. Another fifteen crafts sent one member only, namely the hosiers, vestment makers, bowers, inn holders, wax chandlers, weavers, walkers, saddlers, bakers, glovers, ironmongers, masons, butchers and pewterers. Other crafts were not directly represented or were in guilds under other occupations. These York craftsmen were freemen of the city, masters of trades, with some privileges not available to strangers. They employed apprentices and servants.[1]

T54 Crafts and Trades active in the City of York in 1579
cordwainers, tanners, curriers, parchment makers, bottle makers, horners, skinners, saddlers, glovers, cobblers, lorimers
potters, glaziers, tilers, painters, masons, tilemakers,
sheremen, cappers,

merchants,

mercers, drapers, dyers, tailors, hosiers, vestment makers, weavers, walkers, hatters girdlers,

bladesmiths, and cutlers, pinners, blacksmiths and locksmiths, founderers, goldsmiths, ironmongers, pewterers, spurriers, plumbers

coopers, cartwrights, joiners, turners, pattenmakers, fishers, fishmongers, mariners, cooks, millers, grocers, vintners, inn holders, bakers, butchers, saucemakers apothecaries, barbers, bowers, wax chandlers, minstrels, fletchers, bookbinders & text writers, cardmakers, ropers, tapiters, porters, featherbed makers, stringers and labourers

York, Beverley, Hull, Scarborough and a few other large towns had sufficient craftsmen in some trades to form associations called craft guilds. The guildsmen joined together to seek advantages for their members. They tried to maintain standards of workmanship, and to keep the demarcation between their craft and others. They discriminated against country craftsmen. Entry to their craft was restricted and they tried to maintain prices. Craft Guilds also provided companionship and some charitable services. York guilds had substantial memberships but in the smaller towns there were only a handful of members. On occasions, the Scarborough baker's guild had five members, and the smiths' guild nine. One or two crafts would combine together in a small borough, the combinations merely to suit local convenience. Even in Beverley, the carpenters company included bottle makers in 1596.

T55 Some Craft Guilds in Yorkshire Boroughs

Ripon	1607	14	spurriers, lorimers & armorers, saddlers, merchants & mercers, haberdashers, felt makers & saddlers, tanners, cordwainers, glovers, curriers, inn holders, butchers, dyers, apothecaries & barbers
Scarborough	1467	19	Porters, shoemakers, barkers, barbers, chandlers, wrights, painters, sclaytors, chandlers, masons, weavers, walkers, stringlayers, glovers, bladesmiths & shearmakers, bakers, butchers, smiths, merchants

Apprenticeships were served in crafts with or without guilds. York required every craftsman to take a freeman's son as an apprentice in 1594. Breaches of the conditions of apprenticeship came before quarter sessions. A typical indenture of apprenticeship required Hugh Croslay, son of a deceased Balk yeoman to put himself apprentice to Anthony Bell the village webster, from Whitsunday 1583 for seven years. "He was to keep his master's secrets, and everywhere do his lawful and honest commandments. He was to commit no fornication within or without his master's house, do his master no hurt, nor consent to it, but rather to warn him. He was to shun taverns except on his master's business. He was not to play cards, dice and unlawful games, nor waste his master's goods." He would be taught the webster's trade, chastised for wrong doing, and provided with meat and drink, and cloth, linen and woollen.

Hours of work had been fixed by statute in 1515 "Every craftsman and labourer shall be at work between the middle of the month of March and the middle of the month of September, before five of the clock in the morning. And that he have but half an hour

12. Tudor Industry
(From 'The Story of Tudor & Stuart Britain' by C W Airne)

163

for his breakfast and an hour and a half for his dinner, at such time as he hath season for sleep, appointed to him. And at such time as it is herein appointed that he shall not sleep, then he is to have but an hour for his dinner and half an hour for his noon meat. And that he depart not from his work till between seven and eight o' clock in the evening and for the rest of the year they shall be at their work in the springing of the day and depart not till night of the same day.[2]

The Leather Crafts

The Yorkshire leather industry was on a considerable scale. Hides and skins were profitably converted to leather in many small tanneries. They were concentrated at the market towns. Tanners were spread around the countryside, more or less regularly, normally on streams and within reach of the butchers and farmers who supplied them. The tanner needed a stock of hides in all stages of the process, which took many months to complete, so his capital was tied up for long periods. Legislation of 1563-4 stated that leather intended for the soles of footwear should stay in the tan pit for at least a year. The tanner's stock in trade consisted of hides, oak bark, pits, vats or tubs, lime, turves, and chopping and scraping knives.

Tanning was the process by which raw ox, cow, calf and other hides were converted into durable leather by prolonged immersion in oak bark. A water supply was essential. The bark was gathered, dried, crushed and softened, by soaking in leaching tubs or pits lined with plank and clay. Tubs may have been used as often as earth pits. Hides were scraped clean of hair and fat, soaked in lime, washed and then hung from battens on the edge of the tan pits, steeping for periods up to two years, in a series of pits, with bark fluids of increasing strength. The skins became leather as the gelatinous part combined with the oak bark. They might then be cured with tallow to replace natural oils.

Tanning had long been concentrated at Beverley and at York, despite the city having to obtain supplies of bark from distant west Yorkshire woods. The later expansion of the county beast stock may have encouraged more local tanneries. Most towns had a tannery. Urban tanneries were commonly sited near the fringe of the built up area. John Pykerd built a new tannery on the Guisborough waste in 1551. Scarborough had a tannery outside Newborough gate by 1515 and others recorded later in St Thomas gate and St Nicholas gate, both near the outer town ditch. Tanner Richard Wolfe gave one son his St Thomas street house and the other use of the stock of leather and bark in the tubs, with the lime, the chopping knives and working gear. A Richmond tanner had a lime pit garth in 1561. The Bedale tanner, Thomas Metcalfe in 1623 had stocks of bark, leather and hides distinguished as odd hides, bend leather hides and horse hides. His equipment comprised apron, working knives, shutting, say and scouring tubs, a handling sleck, a sleck trough and a kimlin.

A great many tanners were prosperous enough to make wills. Matthew Coates the Malton tanner had shipping interests and was in touch with London and Hull traders. He had a hogshead of salmon and a goshawk. He left hides to his son. Working tools and leather commonly feature in tanners' wills. John Tyndall of Helmsley left a barker clout hide to each of his two apprentices, a pair of shoes for each maid and two tubs to William Tyndall. A husbandman of Worsborough, John Addy, left two dicker of leather in 1558. A dicker was ten hides, and a last was twenty dickers. James Simpson left bark tubs at Sinnington in 1578 and Thos Addy of Ederthorpe in Darfield in 1569, all "the tubs and vessels belonging to the art of a tanner." William Robinson at Lastingham in 1587, left a tan tub to each son and two white hides to his servant.

T56 Some Elizabethan Tanners in Yorkshire

Agbrigg/Morley	Drighlington, Huddersfield 2, Hunslet, Morley, Gt Sandall, Wakefield, Wortley, Stanley, N. Owram,
Ainsty	Dringhouses
Barkston Ash	Selby 5, Cawood, Stutton 2, Thorp Arch,
Birdforth	Brandsby, Thirsk 3,
Bulmer	Sheriff Hutton
Claro	Ripon 9, Sawley, Spofforth
Dickering	Bridlington, Flamborough
Harthill	Beverley 27, Cottingham 4, Hull
Holderness	Hornsey, Pattrington 3,
Langbaurgh	Briscoe, Egton, Guisborough, Lythe, Stanghowe, Upleatham, W. Barnby, Yarm, Lease Rigg, Swainby
Osgoldcross	Norton
Pickering Lythe	Falsgrave, Rosedale, Pickering 2, Scarborough 5, Sinnington
Ryedale	Helmsley 2, Hovingham, Hutton, Keldholme, Kirkby Milnes, Kirkby Moorside 2, Lastingham, New Malton 4
Skyrack	Collingham, Middleton, Horsforth.
Staincliff/Ewecross	Addingham
Staincross	Barnsley, Royston, Woolley
Strafforth/Tickhill	Doncaster 3, Ecclesfield, Rotherham 3, Sheffield, Tickhill, Ecclesall, Fishlake 2
Whitby Strand	Ugglebarnby, Whitby
York	York 23.

The skinners were concentrated at York where their guild ordinances were revised in 1582.[3] They had demarcation agreements excluding tailors and glovers from their work, which dealt with many lamb skins and conies, a hundred at a time, for furring gowns, collars and cuffs. They also used the skins of martins, minckes, beavers, otters, foxes and cats. York had parchment makers who would only take sheepskins complete with ears, neck and cheeks. The softer skins of deer, sheep and pigs could be dressed with alum, or tawed with tallow by a currier, but specialist tawyers are rarely recorded and it is likely that tanners took all the skins that they could get. There was a white tawyer at Methley.

The hides of the larger animals were used for the soles of shoes and wherever thick solid leather was needed. Elizabethan legislation decreed that bull and horsehides should not be converted into boots, shoes or slippers. Tanners were stopped from selling hides or skins that were gashed or cut, putrefied, rotten or tainted. A hide was not to lie longer in lime than would make the hairs fall off and was not to be steeped in things like "culverpoo" or "henpoo". Several Manor courts kept leather searchers and levied fines on offenders.

Leather was used for clothing, boots, shoes, gloves, saddlery, purses, bottles, belts and buckets. Many villages had someone working with leather if only making boots. Some leather was imported through Turnbridge and Bawtry to the clothing districts of the West Riding. Cordwainers made the best kinds of shoes, but corvisers or shoemakers seem as numerous. The terms were used more loosely outside York, where a city ordinance of 1582 decreed that shoemakers could sole and vampet boots, old and new, only with black leather but not red or bend leather. They were only to sole or vampet but were not to spetche, dowt or cobble any boot. The cobblers repaired old shoes. They could "sell, amend, clowtre and cobble all old shoes", after they had been worn once, but only with red and bend leather, and not with black leather.[4]

The glovers are believed to have made many other light leather goods. Their numbers, often in rural locations, suggests that gloves were widely used in agriculture, for many hand tasks. They are sometimes called mittens. Scarborough still had a glovers' guild in 1608, and a glover's pit at Peaseholme. There were lorimers at Ripon, something of a centre of leather working amidst a horse and cattle rearing country. Saddler Thomas Benson of Rotherham in 1600 left Thomas Baynes his "hackney saddle with girths and stirrups", but gave his apprentice Christopher Brigham one great hammer, the best small hammer, a pair of the best shears, two of the best bodkins, two of the best garnisses, a paring knife and a fine heckle.

T57 Yorkshire Leather workers' wills, 1558-1603[5]

Cordiner's   York 20, Hull 9, Beverley 6, New Malton 5, Ripon 5, Scarborough 3, Pontefract 2, Kirkby Moorside 2, Cottingham 2, Helmsley 2, Bridlington 2, Hedon, Cawood, Snaith, Thirsk, Otley, Grantley (Ripon), Foulrice (Whenby), Skipton (Craven), Brandsburton, Wetherby, Middleton (PL), Sheffield, Normanton

Shoemakers   York , Selby 3, Pontefract 2, Kirkby Moorside 4, Patrington, New Malton, Wakefield, Wetherby, Rimmington, Thorpe (Ripon), Hedon, Slaidburne, Newby (Gisburn), Swine, Kirkham, Tockwith, Easington, Sheffield 2, Robin Hood's Bay

Glovers   York 12, Beverley 17, Hull 9, Doncaster 5, Yarm 4, Cawood 2, Ripon 2, Bridlington 2, Whorlton, Barnsley, Brandesburton, Bridlington, Burley (Otley), Churwell (Batley), Cottingham, S Dighton, Easingwold, Egton Bridge, Ferrybridge, Gilstead, Hardwick (Wragby), Hedon, Helmsley, Hessle, Horsford, Humbleton, Kirkby Overlow 2, Leaven, Methley, Pontefract, Rocliff (Snaith), Saxton, Scarborough, Spofforth, Thirsk, Topcliffe, Wansford, Wetherby, Wheldrake, Whorlton, Wistowe, Woolley 2, Whitby

Saddlers   York 11; Hull 2, Beverley, Emley, Helmsley, Ripon, Rotherham

Skinners   York

Curriers   Barnsley

Blacksmiths

Blacksmiths were well spread around the county. Near a hundred communities are known to have included a working smith, apart from those who excavated the iron. On a through road, villages a mile or so apart might each have a smith, Middleton in 1552-3 and Wrelton the next village but one in Ryedale by 1589. The bloomsmiths made the iron, the blacksmiths made the artefacts, in growing quantities, the horse shoes, stirrups, knives, edge tools, locks, and much more. Hardly an inventory lacked some iron-work, if only at the hearth. Labourer Bartholomew Bird had a frying pan, kettles, little pans, a reckon, hearth tongs, a fork and a spade in 1558. There was some specialisation mainly in the towns, but most smiths could turn their hand to anything, including mending farm tools and craft equipment.

Blacksmiths received a rough bloom, sometimes half finished, to be worked up at the hearth. The smith's anvil or "stithie" was a block of iron set on a wood trunk. Edward Copley of "Woddersome", left Avery Copley "a stithie and all my smithy gear" in 1548. His tools would include hammers and tongs, punches, chisels, swages and formed tools to produce repetitive shapes. He might build up a stock of hinges, iron tips for wood spades, combs for wool, axes, baker's peels, flesh hooks and cart clouts. A Rievaulx smith in 1576 left bellows, stythie, hammer and fuel.

Increased transport gave a fillip to the smiths. Edmond Cape the blacksmith at the busy village of Seamer in 1604 was owed money for shoeing horses. He left hammers, two great nail coyles, a pair of balances, some old iron and some new iron worth 13s.4d. He owed men of York and Scarborough for the iron. New smithies were set up at busy junctions and on highways. A Ferrybridge house, the Dust hall had its gatehouse converted into a smith's shop. A piece of land in Ackworth high Moor had a smithy built on it in 1588.

The smiths' guilds at the larger towns could include specialists who concentrated on some single product. York had locksmiths who made locks and keys, girdlers producing dagger chapes, purse knoppes, dog collars and girdles, spurriers, rowel makers, lorimers, armorers, wire drawers, pinners, nail makers, bladesmiths, furbours, ferrours, and shearmen. Their journeymen worked at a daily rate for the master and some remained wage earners all their life. Metalmen and ironmongers at York and Hull suggests that there was wholesale trading in iron and iron products.

York silversmiths had their own guild mark. They travelled widely to markets and fairs. Silversmith Thomas Symson was at Stoubridge Fair in the Midlands during the plague of 1562 and the Guild Searcher was allowed expenses of four pounds to go there five years later. Alan Alanwyke who kept the silversmith's shop in Stonegate, at York left his tools to a kinsman, provided that he kept on good terms with the widow.[6] Silver plate featured in the wills of the wealthy. Silver spoons were seen to hold their value and were a common bequest. One with a London goldsmith's mark of 1510-11 was found in the thatch of Harum Hall, when the house was moved to the Ryedale Folk Museum. This fine spoon was six inches long, with a shallow fig shaped bowl, it had been hammered from a single piece, but with a gilt knop soldered into the end of the hexagonal stem.

The goldsmiths' shops of London's Lombard Street and Goldsmith's Row at Cheapside were nationally known and their products reached Yorkshire. The York Goldsmiths met the Mayor and council at York on Ouse bridge to agree their own ordinances, in 1561, including their touches and the town, year and maker's marks. They touched their products with the pounce of the city, called the "half peard head and half flour de luce." They agreed not to work worse gold than the "touch of Paris" unless in rings or small jewels brought for repair nor a worse alloy than sterling. Martin Soza the goldsmith who died in 1560 had been born in Spain and served as city Sheriff. The church demand for wrought gold had been reduced but after 1560 chalices were being replaced by communion cups. Peter Carlill of Hull supplied several churches in 1591-92.[7]

Potteries

Pot making was an age-old industry. Suitable clays were widely available and mediaeval kilns have been identified, some by excavation, at Baildon, Brunthwaite (Silsden), Conisbrough, Cowick, Newby near Scarborough, Potterton, Shadwell, Ripon,

Thorner, and Upper Heaton. Documents suggest others at Altofts, Bramham, Oulton, Pontrefract, Potter Newton, Roundhay and Wetherby. Potters were mentioned at Emley, Horsforth, Rawdon and Wilsden. Continuity with the later industry is not well evidenced but some early potteries continued working into the 16th century.

The later kilns seem to be less scattered but included Grimstone, Potter House, Helmsley moor, Osmotherley, Potterton, Potovens and Stearsby. Clay pits occur at Ossett in 1525 and Huddersfield in 1588. The early 16th century Yorkshire kilns produced the curiously named "Cistercian" wares including the finely made small cups and beakers, in a hard red fabric, with a treacle brown glaze, inside and out, found at York, and others in a cream fabric with a yellow glaze, later evolving into black and yellow wares.[8]

An Elizabethan "Ryedale Ware", came from kilns at Grimstone manor, Stearsby and Potter Hill, north of Helmsley. Fragments of the cisterns, jugs, bowls, tripod pipkins and plates, have been found as far afield as Hull and York. The glazing often lapped inside for easy cleaning. The Stearsby kiln occupied a roughly oval rock basin, faced with flat stones, and with traces of clay walls and a clay-lined flu sloping uphill. The Newby kiln was fifteen to sixteen feet across. Snargate wood had traces of two or three kilns.[9]

The products varied from kiln to kiln but included two handled mugs called tygs, jugs, large two handled jars or cisterns, some with bungholes above the base, watering jugs with perforated spouts, bowls, spouted pitchers, flanged bowls and colanders. Stoneware was imported through Hull and Scarborough from the Rhineland potteries around Cologne, including ale mugs, and bellarmines, the stoneware bottles with the face of Cardinal Bellarmine on the neck and a medallion on the body. Low countries pottery came in and less commonly "Tiger ware" and "Martin camp ware" from near Dieppe.

Corn Mills

The countryside held a great many small water mills in the corn districts supplemented by windmills in waterless areas like the Wolds or where river movement was slow, in the low grounds. They held the only machinery most people ever saw. Many manor lords owned a water mill for grinding corn, with rights of soke, which required use of the mill by tenants of the manor, a virtual monopoly. Mills could exist to avoid paying charges to the mill in another lordship. There were different lordships in west and east Rosedale, in Blackamoor, so each had a mill.

The water mills stood on age-old sites, often on fast flowing valley streams, some on more sluggish waters, usually apart from the villages they served, and reached by well-worn rights of way. Major water courses had several mills along their length. The banks of the streams had to be neither too high nor too low, to house a water wheel. Rivers in a flat country, like the Swale at Topcliffe could rise and fall frequently, and the flood could render a mill inoperable for weeks. The weir of a new mill built at Driffield about 1580 raised river levels and flooded meadows.

A mill race gave a measure of control of the water supply feeding a mill. A weir across the main stream diverted sufficient water into a short channel called a leat or goit, which led to an undershot wheel and vented to a tailrace. The banks of the millrace needed dry-walling or other strengthening. A pond for a fishery could be made by widening the head race. Breast shot wheels needed a more definite head of water, supplied to a higher point of the wheel. A head race taken along the contour in a narrow valley could gain sufficient height to feed an over shot wheel. This would need maintenance. The channel would be lined with puddled clay, to reduce loss by seepage but roots could break up the clay.

Most mill wheels were undershot, the stream driving the wheel by acting against the lower paddles. Sir Anthony FitzHerbert's Book of Survey of 1538 praised the efficiency of breast shot and over shot mill wheels, and he knew of the use of buckets to add gravity. Advice on water wheels formed part of the renowned publication "De Re Metallica" by "Agricola", which was known in Britain during the reign. Mill structures were among the very few buildings of the time which might have more than one storey. They were built with stone or heavy timber to withstand vibration. The water wheel operated one or more pairs of grindstones by the use of shafts and gearing. The lower stone was fixed and the upper stone driven. The corn fed through the eye of the upper millstone, and was radiated along the furrows of the lower stone.

Iron was introduced for parts subject to wear such as gudgeon bearings. The millwrights were virtually the first engineers. Harum in Ryedale had a millwright in 1583. Millstones were sometimes imported and were moved long distances. The Cloughton quarry near Scarborough is said to have provided millstones. Some were brought from near Malton to Hackness. Settrington mill was leased by the manor lord, in 1600, but he was obliged to provide millstones when required as well as materials for the repair of the mill. Christopher Gryme bequeathed his lease of the Green mill at Richmond to his son in 1557 with the implements and a pair of new millstones he had half paid for and a timber tree placed near the mill for repairs.[10]

Manorial mills enjoyed monopoly rights through out the manor. They took a levy in kind called multure, as payment for the right to use the mill. This was a proportion of the corn ground. Such payments in kind were sometimes replaced by money. When Malton burgesses used the manor lord's mill to grind their corn and malt there was a sliding scale for multure. When a quarter of corn sold for four shillings, it was multured at the sixteenth vessel. If the price rose to between four shillings and sixpence and six shillings, the multure was at a twentieth and beyond six shillings it was charged as a twenty-fourth. The burgesses maintained a sworn page to keep an eye on the two millers. The miller's hand in your sack was a problem at all times. The Almondbury manor tenants paid multure at one sixteenth but not on any corn that they bought.

Many monastic mills passed to the Crown and were soon on the market, including ten Whitby abbey mills, and six Priory mills in Bridlington parish alone, of which two were watermills and four windmills. Nun Monkton Priory had four grain mills on the river Nidd. The important Castle mills on the river Foss at York passed from St Leonard's Hospital to the Crown in 1539 and were sold to Francis Guilpyn for twelve pounds in 1570. The St Mary's abbey mill on the Foss was leased from the Crown by York Corporation for £6.6.8 a year in the nineties.

The greater Crown lordships had clusters of mills for letting. The manor of Wakefield had mills at Warley, Sowerby and Holmfirth, Horbury and Sandal. As mills were leased and sold separate from manors and from dissolved monasteries, it became more difficult to maintain the mill soke monopolies. Decay of soke rights could close a badly sited mill.[11] Several law suits resulted in the fast growing town of Leeds. A commission was issued to the Leeds manor Steward in 1574 to amerce tenants "for withdrawing their suit from the Queens mills there." An ancient exception was still made for residents on old Knight Templar estates.

High maintenance costs were often passed on to tenants. The Hemingbrough mill needed repairs costing £7.14.4 in 1568. The surveyor argued that the tenants should be bound to repair it, since the Queen had no timber, stones or iron there. The mill was leased to the Howdell family for the rest of the reign.

A Crown jury decided responsibility for repairing Wakefield chantry mill dam in 1571. The Queen was responsible for the first rood, described as seven yards long from the clue, and seven yards towards the fulling mills. The second rood was repaired by landowners, Woodhall and Newton, the third by Sir Thomas Gargrave, the fourth by Susan Palmer for Snapethorpe land, and the fifth by Robert Radford for Stanley's Colley hall.

Builders of new mills were taken to court for breach of soke rights. Nicholas Fairfax built a new mill on the wastes of Brompton by Sawdon. Another was erected in nearby Troutsdale where the area of cultivation was modest but existing mills were either distant or in other estates. The Duchy of Lancaster as overlord disputed the rights of the lesser manors. The Duchy did agree to let an acre at the Hurst in Easingwold moor for thirty-two years, for Thomas Driffield to build a mill on "the fosse called the goate of Kyle water."

Mill properties were tightly defined, along with limited rights of access. When a new water mill was built at Hooton Roberts, a prior agreement allowed just sufficient of Thomas Wentworth's Hooton moor to make a milldam, with piles and withies, hedges at the ford, and a right of way across the moor, for corn brought to be milled or cloth to be walked. The tenants of the manor house were to be "hopper free" and to have a twentieth of the corn ground as multure. Barmston water mill was let in 1597 with the house, a close and twenty foot of ground. Little Kelk mill had a right of road, sixteen feet broad from Sheepsbrigg, through the cultivated land.

Mills were valuable properties and could be profitable. York Corporation fixed charges for flour and malt at all the wind, horse and water mills in the city, suburbs and precincts. New uses could multiply mills. Aislaby mill on the prolific waters of the river Costa near Middleton, was adapted for corn and cloth fulling by 1600. Almondbury had a water corn mill, with a decayed fulling mill sited on its tail race or goat, and a second fulling mill annexed to a new corn mill built by William Ramsden. Owners could employ a miller or lease the mill. Two water mills and a walk mill at Hackness were let at sixty shillings and 6s.8d. for the year. Three water corn mills tenanted by Widow Pinder at Tadcaster paid £30 a year in rent. All the Tadcaster tenantry were bound to grind their corn there. Bransdale mill serving a modest number of farms was held by George Cowper with "course, suit, soke and multure", for twenty-one years at ten shillings a year.

Windmills had become more numerous since their introduction in the 12th century. They clustered around York and other populous places, but could stand alone in the low flat lands south of York, between the rivers Ouse and Derwent. Fulford and Deighton had windmills, while Escrick had four windmills, one watermill and one horse mill. There was more wind than water in the high Wolds, where a flowing stream was hard to find. The Dickering wapentake, behind Bridlington had dry wold valleys and Bridlington itself was only fed by the irregular Gipsey race. Villages large and small like Argam, Bempton, Bessingby, Carnaby, Flamborough and Ganton had windmills. A coastal sketch of 1570-80 shows many mills along the Yorkshire coast, highly visible as landmarks to sailors.

Maltings

Malt was made from barley. This was soaked in water in a cistern for three days and nights. The water was drained off and the malt spread out on a clean floor in a round heap. When it was ready to shoot, the malt was spread more evenly and turned several times a day. For twenty-one days, the malt was spread ever more thinly. It was spread again in a malt kiln, and gently heated, using a fire of wood, straw, furze and broom, and turned until dry. The more it dried, the sweeter and longer lasting it became. The malt was ground at the mill or by using hand querns. Malt kilns were built on a small scale and were scattered through the country districts. William Billingham of Harome in 1557 gave his son William the things in his kiln, a steepfatt, a kiln hair and all the wood.

The 1548 Act of Parliament for the "True making of Malt", gave justices of the peace, borough bailiffs and constables, the power to fine maltsters for breaches of the law, and maltsters were bound by recognisance. The malt was to dry for at least three weeks. Malt was often made too quickly and if not properly dried, it weighed more but soon deteriorated. Offenders included those who mixed good and bad malt, or who added dust. Large scale malting had been done by monasteries and on great lords demesnes. The Fountains Abbey malt house was sixty foot square with an eighteen foot diameter steeping vessel. The Bridlington Priory malthouse was seventeen yards by forty-four yards, doubling as a dining chamber for the harvest men. The kiln house at Grosmont was thirty-five feet by fourteen feet. These malt kilns passed to laymen.

York imported barley from a wide area, which was malted in many small kilns for town and country use. Richard Layton told Thomas Cromwell in 1540 that malt kilns had caused the decay of York. Every merchant made a kiln and employed his corn and timber to make malt. The city then had between forty and a hundred malt kilns. They brought barley from Lincolnshire and out bid country buyers to get the entire local supplies. A few years later, in 1549, the shortage of wood in the city led the council to agree that no malt kilns should be occupied or exercised in the city or its suburbs for two years. Ward masters were warned in 1550 that malt kilns were to be done away with. The citizens complained of lack of drink that year. An ordinance of 1584 required free citizens keeping kilns to enter bonds, with sureties, that they would not make or cause to be made any malt for strangers, but only for free citizens of the town, without a mayor's licence. The number of malt kilns was again limited in 1590.

Large scale malting developed in a similar fashion at the ports of Scarborough and Bridlington, for trading with the north east coalfield and with London. Bridlington was licensed for the export of malt and grain in 1565. Thomas Lawson tenanted the old Priory brew house and malt house at Bridlington Priory in 1585, a year in which twenty-five ships and hoys were laden at the quay with nearly fifteen hundred quarters of grain for Berwick and elsewhere. Bridlington ale became as famous as Whitby butter. Seamer, a village which at one time had six malt kilns of its own, complained that the Scarborough burgesses had given up their old callings and taken to malting and engrossing corn, "in which they were mightily engaged." The beer brewers of Newcastle complained of great quantities of malt brought there from Scarborough. which was "deceitful and evil, all the strength sprouted forth and damp." The Scarborough malt shipments for the north east coal field, recorded in February 1595 were made by eleven traders, in the vessels Primrose, Greyhound and Providence, in quantities varying from one to sixty-seven quarters, but this included Seamer and other country malt.

Breweries

Ale was a basic foodstuff for everybody, only recently supplemented by beer. Andrew Borde said that "ale is made of malt and water & they which do put any other thing to ale than is rehearsed, except yeast, barme or godisgood, doth sophisticate their ale. Ale for an Englishman is a natural drink. It must be fresh and clear. It must not be ropy nor smoky nor must it have no weft nor tayle. Ale should not be drunk under five days old. New ale is unwholesome for all men, and sour ale, and dead ale, the which doth stand a tilt is good for no man. Barley malt makes better ale than other malt or any other corn does. It doth engender gross humours but yet it makes a man strong."

Brewing ale was a local industry everywhere. Ale did not travel well or keep well, so brewings had to be frequent and the product needed drinking up. Nor could yeast, better known as "godisgood" be stored for more than a few days. Standard brewing equipment included a mash tub, some kind of fire or furnace, a sieve, a cauldron, a trough, a cooler called the wortlead, small tubs and a quern. Monastery, castle, mansion and merchant brew houses were probably the best that existed. The Sheriff Hutton brew house and bake house in the outer ward of the castle was served by two yeomen and six grooms. When the brew house was newly fitted out, a great copper kettle was brought from York. Vast quantities of wine, ale, beer and five and half hundred weight, twelve pounds of hops, with many empty barrels were once kept at the Castle. Grosmont Priory had a stone and slate brewery, forty foot by fourteen foot, beside the inner court wall. The Basedale Priory brew house was attached to the upper end of the stone Low Hall, where the Prioress had her upper chamber, on the west side of the cloister.

The Earl of Northumberland had his own breweries and malt kilns at Wressle. He took Wressle malt by water to Boroughbridge and then on wains to Topcliffe and occasionally bought more ale from Ripon, in the early part of the century. When his officers paid two pence a gallon, this was reckoned dearer than making their own. On occasion, they bought malt at Topcliffe to brew. Six quarters of malt cost 6s8d the quart. Six pounds of hops were a penny halfpenny a pound, while faggots at five a penny cost twenty pence. The expenditure of 43s.5d allowed them to make twelve hogsheads, each containing forty-eight gallons of strong ale.

Every member of the Earl's household had a quart of ale or beer a day, including Lord Percy age ten and Master Percy age eight. A quart of beer and a quart of wine were served at breakfast on flesh days for the Earl and his lady, the beer presumably for him and the wine for her. A quart of ale seems to have been an accepted daily requirement for everyone. Corrodies often gave a gallon of good ale a day and a second gallon of weak ale. These were different strengths, made from successive strainings of the mash, certainly taken up to thirds. Women and children may have been given the weaker strengths. Swineherds had the mash residues. Harrison could call the old ale thick and fulsome. His wife and her maids made a single brew once a month to provide the best part of two hundred gallons. He used wheat meal and oats in his liquor and added bayberries and pepper

Some places already had a reputation for good ale. Mary Queen of Scots staying at Tutbury in 1584 had ale from Burton on Trent three miles away. Brewing alehouses seem to have provided most of what was drunk in the towns. A critic of York expressed the view that "for all their use of drinking inordinately, yet no such faculty exists as a common brewer in their city, by which their beer is not good nor wholesome. Their ale in many places is mingled with resin to make it strong, in some parts with urine." It is

172

not clear how far home brewing extended below the substantial farmers, in the countryside, possibly not very far, leaving the numerous alehouses as the source of ale and beer for village people. .

Borough and manor courts everywhere appointed ale tasters, as required by the ancient Assize of Bread and Ale. A bye law at Hutton Pagnell required brewers to send for the ale taster before any was sold. The drink had to be clear, taste well and be wholesome. Malton burgesses chose an ale taster in their own court. He tested the ale of all common brewers weekly, together with the sub-bailiff. Three Acomb women, as common brewsters were fined eight pence for not submitting new ale to the ale tasters in 1557. Every brewer of Acomb and Holegate in 1572 had to send for the ale taster when brewing or pay a shilling. Their brewers were ordered to "brew good ale wholesome for men's bodies" or pay ten shillings. Two men who failed the test were only fined four pence.

Beer had been imported as early as the fourteenth century. The new drink used hops, serving as a flavouring and as a preservative. A common jingle, in various versions and of dubious accuracy made this claim.

> "Hops, turkeys, cards and beer.
> Came into England all in one year."

Beer was differently prepared, using a copper as well as the mash tun. Bridlington Priory at its dissolution had three keeling vessels, ten barm tubs, two sweet wort vats and a tonning vat, a copper lead and kettles in what was already called "the beerhouse". Four mawnds of hops were kept elsewhere. Four pounds of hops could make ten score gallons.

Hull had seven known beer brewers, between 1514 and 1553 while Bridlington Quay and Patrington had one each, suggesting that maritime influences were decisive in spreading the taste. During Queen Elizabeth's reign, five more beer brewers were known at Hull, and one each at Bridlington, Scarborough, Hornsey and at Winestead The York freeman's roll shows beer brewers enrolments increased from two in 1500-1520 to ten in the 1540s and 50s .Not everyone was pleased with beer. Some thought that hops dried up the body and gave melancholy. Andrew Borde saw beer as the natural drink for a Dutchman. Others claimed that beer swelled the belly.

Forests

The Yorkshire "forests" were bounded districts, set aside in the Norman middle ages, for the preservation of the major game, the deer and the wild boar, along with the woodland that gave them cover and fodder. The forests were created partly for hunting, but more particularly to supply venison to the tables of the monarch, major churchmen and some barons. A considerable area of Yorkshire was declared royal forest in the 12th century. Entire districts, including their fields, meadows, woods and commons were brought under distinctive forest law, with harsh penalties for those who killed deer and felled major trees. The word forest did not just mean woodland. The forest was an organisation.

Kings Richard I and King John disafforested many forests, including those covering the entire wapentakes of Ryedale, and Ouse and Derwent. The Forests of Galtres, Knaresborough and Pickering survived as royal forests into Elizabethan times. The

Crown had also granted rights of forest to a few barons and lesser rights of chase and private warren to certain barons, knights and churchmen, both inside and outside the royal forests. The chases embraced some broad districts, in the wilder dales and the Hatfield lowlands, where deer still ran free. A grant of warren usually preceded the creation of a private deer park, some small area of wood and pasture, strongly fenced and ditched to keep the deer within and the people out. The parks remained in the sixteenth century.

Sir Thomas Smith's contemporary list speaks of the Yorkshire forests of Swaledale, Applegarth, Lune, Bowland, New Forest, and the chases of Hatfield, Langstrothdale, Barden and Bishopsdale. Some of these were in transition from forest to pasture. Langstrothdale had been a Percy family chase, but was largely given over to cattle grazing. A number of other areas still showed some sign of forest organisation. Danby in Blackamoor and New forest or Arkengarthdale were still spoken of as forests and there were chases at Ingleborough and Wharncliffe.

Drayton's picturesque Yorkshire map of 1622 showd Pickering, Galtres and Knaresborough Forests but west of Richmond, he indicated Applegarth and New Forests with Swaledale Forest further south. Barden Chase and Hatfield chase stood alone in very different terrains. Hatfield Chase had its boundaries perambulated during Elizabeth's reign. The Crown surveyor-general was its chief officer and the legendary Sir Robert Swift of Street Thorpe was the bowbearer. The ancient customs of the forest of Knaresborough were confirmed by a decree of 1563 and again enrolled at forest courts in 1577.

The royal forests were the best known. They had their own code of forest law, administered by a hierarchy of officers. Forest courts met under Justices of the Forest. There was a master of the game, and foresters, bow bearers, and verderers responsible for woodland, agisters for pasture and regarders for maintaining boundaries. These officers were drawn from the local gentry, some holding estates in return for performing forester duties and they had significant perquisites of office. The Galtres Forest master of the game, enjoyed rights of herbage, pannage, browsing, netting woodcocks, pitting, windfall wood, fishing and fowling. He held the Laund house and herbage, Siward close, and some fees. Sir Thomas Knyvet followed the Earl of Westmoreland, Lord Latimer and John Vaughan in that office. Thomas Vavasour had a life grant of the offices of foot forester and mounted forester of Galtres in 1589, following his father, in rewards not confined to the fee of four pence a day.

The early Forest administration had inhibited the expansion of common field farming in the interests of the deer, restraining the intaking of new land, and the felling of timber. This was in the past. Things had changed and there was more concern now with raising revenues by granting intakes and by selling timber and small wood. The forest calendar and customs remained but the purposes were different. The number of deer had fallen and the wild boar had gone. Even the woodland had been eroded by centuries of use. The forest courts now enforced few limitations on farming different to others. It was a question of what yielded the best return.

As good timber became scarce, some effort was devoted to retaining what there was. Woodland rights were more tightly defined. Galtres forest freeholders could have substantial timber, called housebote, plow bote and cart bote but only at the view of foresters. They held customary rights to lesser wood called fire bote, hedge bote and haybote for fencing, but young spring wood was not to be touched and timber trees were never to be used as fuel. Galtres forest tenants could take rammel wood - small hedge wood, between Michaelmas and Lady Day at four pence a load. Easingwold and Huby tenants claimed an entitlement to an annual load of garsel wood for sixpence for their farmhouse and lathe walls. But this was not notably different to elsewhere. Outside the forest, in Ryedale, green hue wood was allowed at a fixed charge at two shillings an oxgang and one shilling a house at Welburn. At Ganthorpe a standard charge was levied, unless the villagers swore that they hadn't taken any.

Crown surveyors held enquiries to detect any spoiling of wood at Sutton in Galtres in 1577. They asked what woods there were and how many trees had been felled by the roots since Humphrey Barwick came to live there. They listed the numbers taken for timber and separately those removed for firewood, and by whom. There was little good timber left and none to spare beyond what was needed for maintenance of the houses. Since the Queen's deer would not suffer from any enclosures made, they suggested that forty acres could be enclosed each year for six years, to grow spring wood, bringing the township into line with what was required by statute.

Although the deer in the royal forests were few, pasture was still restricted in the traditional seasons. Easingwold men could pasture beasts and swine in the forest, between Michaelmas and St. Helen mass, provided there was no permanent destruction of browse or herbage. Browse was the young twigs of trees and underwood and was banned to cattle between St. Nicholas Day and Candlemas, virtually midwinter. A Forest manor lord had the right to cut reasonable amounts of fern or bracken, within eight days after Michaelmas. No-one could enclose his own grounds without a justice's licence but in practice new intakes attracted a rent at a level which the justice assessed. Pigs were banned from the woodlands in the fence month, from 14th June to 14th July but ran there in the mast season from 14th September to 18th November, paying charges called pannage.

The royal forests were not the distinctive districts they once had been. They were going through a transition from one sort of exploitation to another. Galtres was disafforested in 1630 when lands were assigned to fifteen townships in lieu of their common rights. Pickering Forest petitioners at mid seventeenth century claimed that forest laws stopped them keeping sheep on the commons, and getting wood and turf, while the old woods were largely destroyed and the park was big enough for the few deer remaining. Disafforestation came shortly afterwards.

Parks

Parks were another way of managing deer and woodland, on a more local scale than in the early forests, by confining the deer instead of limiting the agriculture. An Elizabethan park could still give a good return in venison and timber from what was often rough valley land. The earliest park-like enclosures had been made as "hays" within the forests, as safe havens for the deer to breed. With early disafforestation, grants of warren were made which allowed the hunting of minor game and small parks were created to keep fallow and roe deer.

Yorkshire had more parks than any other county, varying in size from less than a hundred acres to several thousand. The deer park was usually close to the house that it fed, but Mulgrave Castle had a deer park in each of the four quarters of the estate, Julian Park, Cukewald Park and Butter Park, north and south of Egton, and Newbiggin Park near Aislaby. The Lord Eure's Ingleby Greenhow manor had fallow and red deer parks. More parks were made as the more remote chases came into new ownership. Upper

Wharfedale was ranged by numerous half wild herds of deer, when the Threshfield estate passed to the Clifford family about 1580. Several parks were established with keepers appointed to maintain them. Threshfield Park held a herd of one hundred and twenty fallow deer by 1603.

The management of herds of deer had been the core of the forester's craft for centuries. They had their own skills. The foresters knew the lair of the great stag, could gauge his weight and size from his "fewments" or droppings, and detect his course from his fraying and his slot or footprints. Specialised dogs were used to hunt by sight or smell. Some large herds remained. Westerdale in 1539 was thought to have 610 fallow deer and 60 red deer. Kirkby Knowle in 1570 still had great stock of fallow deer in the park but Wakefield park in 1574 was bushy and barren with little timber and only a few deer, "neither buck nor soar", as the fencing had decayed. Hatfield chase had a thousand red deer in 1607 and Sheffield Park in 1637 still claimed a thousand head of fallow deer and two hundred "deer of antler". More typical were the smaller parks. Spofford in 1607 with one hundred and seventy-five fallow deer and Kippax with forty-five in 1604.

T58 Some Yorkshire Parks in the reign of Queen Elizabeth
East Riding
Catton, Constable Burton, Burstwich, Leckonfield (3), Newsham Risby, Wressell
North Riding
Bignall (Greta), Bolton, Blansby, Byland, Carlton, Danby (3),Douthwaite, Egton, Farndale, Fyling, Gilling, Glaisdale (Budick), Guisborough, Helmsley (2), Ingleby Greenhow, Kildale (5), Kilton, Kirkby Moorside, Liverton, Mulgrave, Normanby, Ripon, Tanfield, Topcliffe (2), Thorn Park, Whorlton
West Riding
Aston, Bolling, Brierley, Caley, Calverley, Conisbrough, Denholme, Denton, Farnley, Goldsbrough, Greasbrough, Harewood, Hatfield, Hazlewood, Healaugh, Kinsley, Kippax. Kiveton, Knaresborough, Plumpton, Pontefract, Rothwell Haigh, Selby (4), Sheffield, Spofforth, Tankersley, Wakefield (2), Walton, Wighill, Woodsome, Wortley, Ribston, Sheffield; Skipton, Stockhill, Threshfield, Thribergh, Wortley

Parks could be leased to tenants for hunting, for timber or for conversion to stock pasture. John Lord Darcy of Aston had a grant of Roundhay Park in 1599. The Earl of Huntingdon granted the Sheriff Hutton Park to an official Richard Pollard, who sublet some to others, himself pastured several hundred sheep and probably sold much of the timber. Royal forest officers could be allowed use of a forest park. This was a sufficient reason to take office. The Earl of Westmoreland kept a lodge at Blansby Park near Pickering, as well as his manor house at Kirkby Moorside, not far distant, and immediately west of his own recently enlarged park. Martin Frobisher enjoyed the keepership of Ackworth Park. Francis Slingsby was granted the offices of keeper of Bilton Park, porter of Knaresborough castle and forester of Wardale, Swynden, Okeden, Harlowe, and Fulwith in the Forest of Knaresborough. He would employ deputies to do the work

Park keepers were well paid and enjoyed substantial perquisites. Charles Earl of Westmoreland appointed William Barike to keep the park, deer and wood at Kirkby Moorside in 1561. In addition to the annual fee he had pasture for ten kine and two horses and three acres of hay. Christopher Thorpe had £4 a year as keeper of Kirkby

Knowle Park. Park lodges were used for hunting forays, as well as residences for park keepers. The Manor Lodge at Sheffield Park was virtually a second home, with long gallery, tapestries and hangings of great value, quite distinct from three keepers' lodges. Fencing the park boundary was a major continuing expense. A survey of Howden in 1561 said that "there is a park, wherein no deer, which is let forth by lease to the Lady Tunstall for twenty nobles rent by the year. It is a mile and half about." This park contained cattle and horse pastures, fishponds, an orchard and a stone store house for fruit. Parks kept for deer usually contained a few closes. Blansby Park had twenty-four acres of meadows which were mown to provide feed for the deer in winter.

T59 Notes from the Queen's Survey of Pontefract Park. 1588

Area	Within the park pale 700 acres
Land use	No meadow, 100 acres thought suitable for arable. Remainder pasture. Meadow in Allerton ings belonged to the park, worth 3s.4d an acre
Timber trees	1370, the 400 best worth 10s each, 400 more 6s.8d each, the rest 5s
Fuel trees	1760, 500 worth 6s.8d each, 500 worth 5s each, the rest 3s.4d.
Other trees .	400 saplings worth 16d each.100 ashes worth 16d a piece
Underwoods	Worth £60, of thorn, maples, hazels, alders etc
Mines	None
Deer	300 in first year of reign, now 595
Fees	Keeper for his fee £1.6.8. and for carriage and making pales 13s.4d.
Lodges	Three, two in good repair, one in decay and a barn to lie hay for the deer.
Closes	New or vicars close. in the park, also Carr close, tenant William Mallet Esq

Poaching was treated seriously by park owners and by the courts. A deer killed in Kimberworth park was reported to the Earl in 1586. Yeoman Edward Morley of Adlingfleet was formally charged at Wakefield sessions that on the twentieth day of December 1599, he "with a dog called a greyhound unjustly and illicitly broke and entered the free chase of our lady the Queen called Hatfield Chase at Adlingfleet and with the dog illicitly and unjustly chased and hunted a deer in English called a stag and the same stag with the same dog did kill and carry away without authority or licence."

Great timber trees were not confined to parks, although the parks held some of the best. Sheffield Park was famous for its huge old oak trees. Haugh Park in 1637 was still full of excellent timber of very great length and very straight, some of them sixty feet before you came to a knot. Travellers said in awe that they had not seen such timber in all Christendom. Timber felling has always been a temptation for a hard pressed estate owner. The Crown was always hard pressed. and great clearances did occur. Conisbrough park timber was felled and sold locally for £1900 in 1575. Eight hundred trees and over three hundred stumps were sold in small lots from Beverley Westwood in 1584. One tree might bring from 2s.6d. to 5s.4d., stumps 1s.2d. to 3s.6d.

T60 Timber in Topcliffe Little Park, 1577

Dalton Hagg	64½ acres	320 oaks.	
Elmer Hagg	54½ acres	306 oaks.	
Chamber close	13acres	94 oaks	
Manor wood		310 oaks	
In the body of the park		220 oaks.	
Total trees in little park		1250 priced as	
oaks of best sort 100	at 6s.8d	£33.6.8	
oak of 2nd sort 250	at 4s	£62.10.0	
oaks of the 3rd sort. 350	at 3s.4d	£58.6.8.	
oaks of the 4th sort 1050	at 2s.6d	£131.5.0	

(There were 9809 mostly big trees and more little oaks worth £300 in the Great park and another wood on the east, containing 1000 oaks was worth £100)

Parks were something of a luxury, wasteful without good wood and pasture management. Several parks were converted to other uses. Liversedge park was disparked, soon after it passed to the Carey family, about 1578. Timber felling seems to have been the cause. Fyling park was replaced by a new park, closer to the new mansion at Whitby. The estate Steward reported on the state of the park at Hinderskelfe. This was very barren ground but the park pale, or fence, was in good repair and staunch. Alas, the profit of the herbage wouldn't keep the hedges and the rent wouldn't pay for the fence. He said that they needed a keeper, or the wood would be stolen. When forty or fifty tenants destroyed the manor house at Golsbrough in Claro in 1586, they pulled down the park fence, allowing the deer to escape. The parker was killed by a pike thrust into his thigh.

Managing the Woods

There was national concern about maintaining supplies of heavy timber. Much monastic land had come into the hands of the Crown. King Henry VIII appointed surveyors of woods north of Trent and from 1554 a Surveyor General of Woods, Forests, Parks and Chases. During the reign of King Edward VI, Robert Hennidge recorded jury returns of wood sales, whether from old oaks or springs of twelve years growth, by the Crown woodward William Ramsden and his deputies for the king's woods in the northern parts. The returns showed extensive felling and selling across the parts of the shire that were recorded, especially in the West Riding, in woods from Bramham to Laughton, and Wakefield to Headingley. The chalk Wolds were largely devoid of timber apart from small copses, but the narrow limestone belt west of the Wolds was still wooded. and saw some felling.

Good timbers were so scarce that they were moved long distances. Many townships lacked the timber to repair their own houses. When oak, ash and esp trees were felled in some quantity at Settrington in 1581, they were sold deep into the chalk country, one hundred and thirty trees to Kilham, seventy-two to distant Rudstone, and all together to thirty-seven villages, from Langtoft and Weaverthorpe on the east to Kirkby Grindalythe on the west. Heavy timbers were needed for ship building, harbour works and house construction. Scarborough could still get oaks from the nearby Raincliff and Langdale valley in Blackamoor, but wayneblades were brought from Rosedale. Bridlington had to send to Nunburnholme, for large timbers for harbour works. When six score timber trees

178

were needed to make the gallery at Roxby house, near Thornton Dale, they were sawn and framed in Goathland by wright George Bernard before carriage across the moors.

Woodland management to provide steady supplies was becoming a major objective. Trees grow to their height, then broaden out. Heading was combined with winter lopping and cropping to provide browse wood for deer and small bows which were kidded and sold in hundreds. Large trees were topped three or four foot above the timber. Lesser trees were headed thirty or forty foot high so that they would bear much more wood and bows. Bows were cut from the bottom up to avoid damage and not to spoil the bark.

Acts of Parliament in 1559 and 1570, prohibited charcoal burners from using timber trees. Charcoal was the fuel of the older furnace industries, especially iron working, giving a high temperature, no smoke and little ash. This was prepared by piling cut wood in regular heaps, and covering them with turfs. Air holes could regulate the rate of firing. The smoke escaped by a central chimney hole and .the charred wood sank to the bottom. Prunings and thinnings from young trees were used as well as coppice growth. Mid Winter was the best time for making charcoal. When Derbyshire and Ossett smiths bought spring wood at South Anston in 1553, they had "the turf and hilling for the coaling of the wood" but were to "leave young waivers, woodman like, and waives oak, thirty inch in compass, one ell high, for refencing." The use of wood as an industrial fuel was stopped in1615.

The coppice, locally called a hagg, was essentially a way of treating wood as a crop. An Act of Parliament of 1483 had legalised the enclosure of coppices in forest districts after felling. They could be kept fenced until seedlings of beech and oak had grown again. The system of "coppice with standards" meant that many new trees were cut back close to the ground, while selected trees were left at intervals to achieve full growth. The stools of the cut trees produced a plentiful growth of pole timber, which could be cut regularly on a cycle of five to twenty-five years. Other woods were coppiced without standards. The steeper Wold slopes at Settrington carried two hundred and thirty-five acres of woodland in eight haggs, that were cut in rotation.

George Constable advised his uncle, Sir Philip Constable on a programme of woodland management in 1608. Timber was felled for building, and wood for faggots, bavin or brushwood, billet, block wood, and charcoal in January and February. Sticks and stakes were cut for hedging. Wood for sale to tanners for its bark was felled when the sap put forth the bud, and some leaves showed at the tree tops. Fuel wood was sorted and brought home, the charcoal to be kept dry in the house, bavin and faggot well stacked, for baking and brewing, billet and log wood piled in large stacks for house use. This was the time to make fences or hedges for closes and to see ditches well cleansed and scoured. Coppices, springs and other wood ground that had been felled that winter were strongly fenced in March and April to stop cattle and horses breaking down new grown wood. They were kept fenced for seven years. New felling came with November and December to provide browse either for deer or cattle. The new year brought faggotting for the house.

There was a growing demand for wood for furniture, barrels and butter firkins. Small ashes went to coopers, great ashes to wheelwrights and mean ashes to plow wrights. Ash was used for bowls, dishes and hoops, larch for gates, beech for chair legs, springy ash for many tools and oak for wheel spokes. Small wood was needed for domestic fuel, for thatching spars, for fencing stakes and hurdles, and for fuel in brewing, iron and glass working. Inventories listed "boards" as common items of house furniture.

Carpenters and more rarely coopers and joiners were scattered around the shire, a few in towns and others near countryside woods. Specialised turners were rare. One at Sneaton Thorpe produced wooden vessels. A Langdale forester, whose perquisites in 1568 were 4s.8d. worth of oaks, ran a timber yard and workshop in his five bay barn at Broxa, supplying boards, ash spars, bowls and dishes. He sold trees with favourable grains, which Henry Awden, Francis Ducheman and Roger Fox of Troutsdale and Sawdon made into twenty gangs of whole timber. A shilling oak went to make an axle tree for John Braithwaite's corn and bran mill. A Bickley oak, valued at 2s.6d had "in it three pair of wayn blades." The husbandmen also made their own tools, toys and household objects

T61 Sir Antony FitzHerbert on "How forks and rakes should be made

"A good husband hath his forkes and rakes made ready in the Winter before and they would be got between Michelmass and Martinmas and "beyked" and set even, to lie upright in thy hand and then they will be hard stiff and dry. And when the husband sitteth by the fire and hath nothing to do, then may he make them ready and "tooth" the rakes with dry wethywode and bore the holes with his wimble, both above and under, and drive the teeth upward fast and hard and then wedge them above with dry wood of oak, for that is hard and will drive and never come out and if he get them sappe-time, all the baking and drying that can be had shall not make them hard and stiff, but they will always by "plyenge", for they be most commonly made of hazel and withee and these be the trees that bloom and specially hazle, for it begins to bloom as soon as the leafe is fallen and if the rake be made of green wood, the head will not abide upon the "stele" and the teeth will fall out, when he has most need of them and let his work and lose much hay. And see that thy rake and fork lie upright in thy hand for and the one end of thy rake, or the side of thy fork, hang downward, then they be not handsome nor easy to work with."

Quarries[12]

Stone had been quarried for centuries originally at natural inland outcrops and from the sea cliffs of Scarborough, Whitby and Filey Brigg. The county had broad districts with different rocks. The west of the shire had carboniferous limestone, much of it capped by millstone grits. The East Riding held the chalk hills of the wolds, and north east Yorkshire its grits, sandstones and different limestones. The Vale of York held red sandstones and the narrow but important belt of magnesian limestone. These terms were not used in the Elizabethan age. There was no "geology" yet.

Stone was costly to extract, to work and even more costly to transport. The carriage of stone could double the costs of extraction over a few miles, unless the quarry was near a navigable water course. This kept many quarries small and local. The largest early quarries supplied the Romans with road and building stone. The great quarries at Hildenley, Pickering, Stonegrave, Aislaby near Whitby, Malton and in other places may go back to those times. Quarries at Huddlestone south of Tadcaster supplied Roman and mediaeval York by water, along with the Vavasour quarries at Hazlewood. In later ages, old buildings were always robbed to provide stone for the new.

Stonemasons were mobile, working for the duration of a contract at a building site. They used traditional tools, such as iron wedges, iron rods, gavelocks or crowbars, iron hammers, poleaxes, brochaxes and shovels. On building sites, swinging platforms called cradles, and windlasses were used for raising men and materials. Mediaeval stone houses were rare, largely confined to castles, some manor houses, churches and monasteries. A modest local quarry near the building site could often provide all that was needed. Stone roofing tiles, foundation stones, mill and bake stones were used more widely. Cloughton quarry north of Scarborough supplied early millstones and tombstones. York Minster drew on quarries at Thevesdale, Huddleston and Tadcaster for magnesian limestone. Hazlewood had the famous "delph" called Peter's post.

Quarries are mentioned at many places in the 16th century, including Brackencliff in Ackworth, Hampole, Terrington and Yeadon. Ecclesall drew on the quarry at Brincliffe Edge. Roofing flags came from Elland and millstones from Rawdon. Westow on the Wold edge had a slate quarry, the word then meaning a limestone roofing flag. Grindstones were found in the sea cliff near Whitby and bake stones in the dales of Blackamore. The navigable river made the difference. Newton quarry near Tadcaster sent stone to York Guildhall. Hampole quarry fed Kings College Cambridge in 1513. Christopher Beane of Tadcaster was required to get capstones for a new piece of York city wall, replacing a stretch that had fallen near St Leonard's landing in 1602. A surveyor said in 1623 of the "Tadcaster quarries, the stone whereof is very hard and therefore costly to be gotten but being gotten is a very good and durable stone to make any building withal."

Masons prosperous enough to leave wills in the Elizabethan period were recorded at York, Barnborough, Bridlington, Stock near Braithwell, Cawthorne, Darfield, Hassel Clough at Ecclesfield, Gildersome, Over Guiseley, Swillington and Todwick, Wallers were near Dewsbury, Halifax and Ecclesfield, slaters at Doncaster, Farnley, Horsforth, Lepton and Thorner. There was a plasterer at Brightside near Sheffield. How far timber houses were given stone cladding below the level of gentry and the richer clothiers is unknown. When it happened, the local geology would give different areas their characteristic building stones. Top layers of rubble had to be removed to reach good blocks in many quarries. Bramham quarry yielded blocks of durable, load bearing stone. The Wolds had chalk which was not durable and needed periodic replacement. Limestone and freestone were plentiful around Ryedale. Houses had been built in the old vertical quarries at Pickering Undercliff by 1622.

Alabaster, a soft, white rock, easy to work, was carved into figures and reliefs at York until the mid 16th century. When unsuitable for carving it was burnt and made into plaster The York Minster obtained plaster from Buttercrambe, east of the city. There were alabaster quarries at Fairburn near Ledsham, used for carved memorials in the 16th century, when both Ledstone, and Ledsham had "plaster pits". Nicholas Stone used alabaster at Gilling, Knaresborough and Otley, but his monument to Sir William Belassis of 1603 bears the inscription "Thomas Browne did carve this tombe, himself alone of Hesselwood stone." Gypsum was also dug in quantity from the Isle of Axholme. A plaster pit paid a rent of 26s.8d. a year at Holme on Spalding Moor in 1560-61.

Rocks described as marble came from Nidderdale and the "fair quarry of black marble, spotted with white" was seen by Leland at Eggleston by the river Tees. This Teesdale marble was a limestone that polished to resemble marble. It was extracted in thick slabs and had been used in fonts, shrines and altar tables. Jet was found in clefts by the sea at Mulgrave, and at seven or eight other cliffs between Runswick on the north and the Peak on the south, including Saltwick and Black Nab close to Whitby. This was the lightest of all solid stones, making it suitable for bracelets and rings, beads and even salt cellars. John Carlille worked the rock at his house near Whitby Bridge in 1598. Drayton waxed lyrical about jet.

> "the rocks by Mulgrave too,
> my glory forth to set,
> out of their crannied cleves ,
> can give you perfect jet."

Limestone was quarried across the county for lime burning. Camden said that "There is limestone plentifully found here. They burn it at Brotherton and Knottingley and at certain seasons convey it in great quantity for sale to Wakefield, Sandal and Standbridge, from where it is sold into the western parts of the county to improve the soil. It was also quarried for use in mortar. Hull leased lime kilns outside the west wall in the 1560's, which supplied lime in the town for 9s.4d. a quarter. Fuller's Earth, sometimes called Rochester Earth, was a naturally occurring clay, used to thicken cloth, as part of the fulling process. Arthur Dakins of Linton had the profits of a mine, associated with a lease of the manor of East Heslerton. Sherburn close by in Pickering Vale held a "mine of fuller's earth" worth £10 a year in 1639. Raddle, an impure peroxide of iron, apparently used for sheep marking and pencils was worked by a poor "raddleman" who died in 1622 near Braithwell in south Yorkshire.

T62 Masons and other Craftsmen's Daily Wages at York. June. 1563

Candlemas to Michaelmas	without food	with food
freemason, master carpenter	10d	5d
rough mason, bricklayer, carpenter, joiner, carver, tiler, plumber, glazier,		
March to Michaelmas	8d	4d
Michaelmas to Easter	7d	3d
wood hewer,	8d	4d
clinker (rivets)	6d	3d
caulker	5d	2d or 3d
holder	5d	2d
wheelwright, plow wright		
Candlemas to Michaelmas	7d	3d

Salt[13]

Salt was the main preservative for many foodstuffs. Used as crystal or as brine, salt allowed some meats and fish to be kept for months. Salt was used in making cheese, butter and bread. The Lincolnshire coast and Tees-side in Yorkshire had extensive mediaeval saltings. The Yorkshire monasteries had invested heavily in saltings on the south side of the Tees around Coatham. Salt water was gathered in artificial, clay lined, pools, which filled at high tide. It could also be extracted from heaped beach sand. The salt water was boiled in lead pans in small buildings, using peat as a fuel. Once dried in hanging baskets, it was taken inland by pack horse. Mediaeval salt pans were also worked on Scarborough beach.

The end of the Teeside industry awaits an investigator. This may fall within the late 16th century. Newbrough Priory still had a saltcote there worth ten shillings in 1538. A tenement called a saltcote, late of Byland Abbey, with a cottage, barn and three acres,

182

was sold by a London draper to Robert Walls, a Redcar gentleman in 1611. John Lord Lumley's manor of Kirkleatham appears to have had profits in Coatham called "cole raking and salt making" with a coney warren in 1586. Later traditions spoke of salt ways running south eastwards over Blackamoor, down Rudland Rigg, to Keldholme and Malton in Ryedale, and through Saltergate towards Scarborough.

The ancient salt industry of Cheshire supplied south Yorkshire. The brine occurred naturally in springs, drawing on deposits of rock salt, and was being boiled to yield salt before 1086. The Cheshire industry expanded in the 16th century. The salt came over Salters brook into the West Riding, carried on pannier ponies which could bring two to two and a half hundred weight, one hundred and twenty miles in four to six days. Salt ways headed for Wakefield, Penistone, Bawtry, Doncaster and Rotherham.[14]

Salt was also imported to England from the continent on some scale, especially Bay salt from the shores of Brittany and Poitou. The religious wars in France and the Netherlands, gave some stimulus to English and Scots salt production and trade. Whitby had salt houses in 1503 and Saltwick was mentioned in 1519. Undated salt pans at Whitby and Cloughton could fall in the Elizabethan period. New works were erected at Sunderland, supplying salt at 16d a bushel. Ralph Bowes of Berwick had saltings at Bishop Wearmouth using coal by 1587. Bridlington had a salthouse close but John Cook and others had salt houses and colehouses there in 1609. The salt houses may merely be stores.

Thomas Wilkes, a clerk of the Privy Council had a royal monopoly grant of the "making or providing of white salt" in 1585, within the ports of Boston, Lynne and Hull. Several York merchants were already buying salt at Sheilds. Scots salt was delivered to Yarm in 1580. York and Hull protested against Wilkes and the Lord President called the salt patentee before him. Wilkes reduced his price to 14 pence and agreed to ship his salt in York, Hull and Scarborough ships. John Smith renewed the Hull licence in 1599. Scarborough council gave seven year leases of salt pans to merchant William Peacock and others in 1601,and again in 1612.

Coal

The Venetian Soranza said in 1554 that "in the north towards Scotland they find a certain sort of earth, almost mineral, which burns like charcoal and is extensively used by blacksmiths and but for a bad odour which it leaves, it would be yet more employed, as it gives great heat and costs but little. Coal had been mined in mediaeval times at Rotherham, Silkstone, Cortworth and Barnsley in the West Riding. The 16th century traveller learnt that "betwixt Cawood and Rotherham be good plenty of wood, yet the people burn much earth coal, because it is plentifully found there and sold good cheap. A mile from Rotherham be very good pits of coal." Not far away, Hallamshire had plenty of wood and yet there was "burned much sea cole." The coal outcrops gave access to five-foot seams but eastwards there were beds of nine foot.[15]

Coal was often called sea-coal, to distinguish it from charcoal. It was obtained from shafts called day holes and open cast workings. Drift mines were dug into sloping ground, with "adits" to take off water, or a narrow shaft was sunk to the seam. The shaft was widened at the base, as far as was safe from collapse, giving the typical bell pit. The shallow mine shaft was timber lined. The coal was hacked from the face and raised by a pull-wheel or windlass, in baskets called corves, to a hut at the top. Galleries could be excavated outwards from a bell pit, when a good seam offered, but much of the seam had to remain in place to support the roof. Hewers, bearers and a viewer were licensed to dig at Wakefield. Wages were low. Steel picks, iron shod wood shovels, baskets, ropes and iron wedges were the tools of the trade. Water was a common problem but could be drained off by a sough. Crown mines at Rothwell were "drowned with water", giving no product or profit for the nine years up to 1582.

Coal was coming into use alongside charcoal in brewing, brick, glass and steel making, lime burning, pottery, salt and soap making. It was used for smelting and casting brass and for drying malt. The trade was further stimulated by the spread of demand for coal in kitchens and even halls. Coal gave a good fire to roast and boil meat. Some coal was more smokey but it gave a better heat than peat. The new hearth equipment, chimneys, ranges and grates of iron, was partly a response to the spread of coal for house use. John Kaye of Woodsome sank pits at Calverley to supply his own house. Peter Barley of Barlowe in 1578 made a contract for Staveley mine, reserving his house coal.

Coal also came in to Yorkshire by sea. The small shallow mines close by the river Tyne, were being worked out. The industry had moved inland to deeper seams. The Durham collieries needed more capital, more equipment, and not only required wains and horses for transport to the coast but incurred way leave fees. These coalfields supplied London, and north-west Europe. The coal trade from the Tyne rose steadily and massively. Land carriage costs rapidly raised the purchase price of coal but sea transport was cheap, bringing Newcastle and Sunderland coal along the Yorkshire coast and even up river. Sir Hugh Cholmley already brought imported coal from Scarborough, to Roxby Castle near Thornton Dale. The 17th century would transform Whitby and Scarborough into busy ports, building colliers and havens for the collier fleet in adverse weather.

Veins of coal found in the western heights of Richmondshire had not been developed "on account of incommodity of carriage to the lower parts." Sir William Gascoigne of Sedbury opened pits on his Ravensworth estate in Yorkshire late in the century. His mines in County Durham were worth £400 a year in 1607. Durham coal came on pannier ponies into the north part of the Vale of York. Darlington regulated the tethering of colliers' horses in their market place and near their tollbooth. Sir William Eure wrote to William Welbury asking him to send six quarters of malt and two of rye to Wilton "by the colle draughts of Stoxley."

West Riding coal mining began a rapid development. Bishop Barnes had told King Henry VIII of twenty-four coal mines in the Vale of York. Scores of new shafts, outcrop workings and drifts were opened up during the reign. Trial borings, sinking pits and drainage needed capital investment. Concessions were negotiated with the landowners, who sometimes took the initiative. Coal mine owners could make annual profits of £20 to £100. Several held leases or concessions on Crown land, including Henry Farrer at North Owram and Sowerby, Sir Thomas Bland of Kippax Park, John Mallet of Normanton and John Preston of Altofts. Crown rents were low, but rose later in the reign. Edward Careye had rights to work coal at Wakefield for twenty-one years at 26s.8d. a year. Estate tenants normally gained access to cheap coal for their own use.

Small workings in Sheffield Park in the period 1579-1582, occupied between five and eight employees, two to four of whom worked by candle light, at the face, in a deep pit. Loads of three quarters, weighing about eighteen hundred weight were raised. They brought to the surface between 1300 and 1500 loads, which weighed out at some 1200 to 1300 tons in a year. Many days were lost due to damp. New shafts saw flooding, initially drawn off in buckets through the night and day by fifteen casual workers. A bank man dragged the loaded baskets from the face to the pit bottom where they were hauled up. He sold the coal and kept the accounts. They might earn six to nine pounds a year, selling at two shillings a load. This was dangerous work. Henry Smith of Elland was crushed by a rockfall and suffocated in the coal pit in 1601.

Conflicts were common, some taken to the Duchy of Lancaster courts. Esquire Henry Farrer complained of two intruders at Northowram. They made a great deep pit in a close bordering his mine and dug four hundred yards underground, for two thousand horse loads "cunningly drawn up." Then they cut down the heads and pillars of coal supporting the ground, which sank in for a good stretch. Many early mines were made in parkland or open moor, but mines at Seacroft, near Leeds, were put down amid growing corn, and required compensation payments for loss of crops. Richard Gascoigne was prosecuted by the Duchy of Lancaster for mining on Crown land but was able to prove the site was within his own manor.

There were other workings outside the south Yorkshire fields. Sir Stephen Proctor had mines of coal at Grewelthorpe. By the early 17th century coal outcrops were worked at Carlton, Lothersdale and Holden in Craven. Small workings were opened into very thin seams in the limestone hills around Ryedale. Sir Henry Gate had a Crown lease in 1583 of all coal and other mines in Pickering commons and Pickering Lythe at £5 a year. A coal mine, stone quarry and ironstone workings at Cropton Spiers wood was rented at £2 a year in 1583, probably at Coalpit Rigg. York City approached Mr. Cholmley to seek coal at Brandsby, in the Howardian Hills east of the city.

T63 Some 16th Century Coal Workings in the West Riding

Agbrigg/ Morley	Beeston, Bradford, Calverley, Gomersal, Horbury, Horton, Hunslet, North Owram, Ossett, Rothwell, Roundhay, Sharleston, Sowerby, Stanley, Thornhill, Wakefield.
Barkstone	Ledston
Claro	Kirkby Malzeard, Staveley.
Osgoldcross	Glass Houghton, Pontefract.
Skyrack	Austhorpe, Barwick, Garforth, Harewood, Kippax, Leeds, Whinmoor, Parlington, Seacroft, Swillington, Temple Newsam.
Staincliff/Ewecross	Ardsley, Barnoldswick, Barnsley, Briarley, Cawthorne, Darton, Dodsworth, Hoyland, Monk Bretton, Silkstone, Tankersley, Worsbrough.
Straforth/Tickhill	Brampton Bierlow, Brampton, Denaby, Eccleshall, Ecclesfield, Greasbrough, Handsworth, Hooton Pagnell, Hooton Roberts, Kimberworth, Mortomley, Over Cudworth, Rotherham, Sheffield, Swinton, Thurnscoe, Wales, Wath Wentworth, Whiston

New Industries

New industries appeared in Elizabethan England. The Queen's first minister, Sir William Cecil sought greater national self sufficiency, by encouraging new mines and manufactures. He was interested in exploiting known resources and finding new ones. England was a relatively undeveloped country, as far as its industry was concerned but it was rich in important raw materials, including lead, coal and iron, while wood was becoming scarce. The movement of coal from the northern coal field to London was rapidly expanding and some parts of Yorkshire had other local supplies. The tonnage of merchant shipping was increasing.

England had to import the new technology. Skilled foreign workers were encouraged to bring their techniques and skills. Continental know-how was decisive in changing several industries, through Hochstetters' Company of the Mines Royal, and in the new alum, glass and cast iron manufactures. Notable inventions of the period included the printing press, horse and water driven engines for draining mines, the stocking knitting frame, the blast furnace, and furnaces for separating silver from copper ore, and for burning coal or coke instead of wood or charcoal. Some consumer products would be made using established methods, but on a larger scale, including soap, cutlery, stockings, pins and needles. It may not have been an industrial revolution but there were major changes affecting many people in Yorkshire.

Heavy capital investment was necessary in the mining of copper, and iron, for quarrying alum, and in the manufacture of glass and paper, cast iron, guns and gunpowder. Several infant industries suffered long delays before investment could yield a return, with high early exploration and development charges. Only the Crown, the peers, the greater knights and the merchants had the capital, the ready money or the security on which to borrow it. The Italians Spinola and Palavicino invested in English enterprises. An Augsburg mining firm put money into starting the Cumberland copper mines. New organisation and greater working capital was needed to maintain supplies to out workers producing woollens, silk, cotton and linen, for making stockings and the new draperies.

The nobility and gentry were the pioneers in several industries. They owned the woods and the mineral resources. Foreigners were brought in to find them. The Duke of Norfolk had one of the largest and earliest iron works in the Sussex Weald, in the early 1540s. Lord Seymour expanded this in the next decade to produce over two hundred tons a year. Lord Mountjoy in the 1560's set up Canford alum mines and works in Dorset. He wrote that," Some say that I vary from my vocation so far to become a miner." George Earl of Shrewsbury invested heavily in lead and iron extraction and processing, in Yorkshire and elsewhere.

Patents of monopoly, granted for a stated time, were the principal Government device to encourage invention and industrial development. The patentee was given a monopoly for a period of years, usually under fourteen, and he might licence others beneath him. There was little cost to the state. The patentee had to arrange the combination of capital and technical skills, or delegate the task to others. Some grants were made to reward court officials, royal favourites and noblemen. Patents were granted for many projects, not all fruitful, for making mathematical instruments, for printing grammars, primers and other schoolbooks, to paint the Queen's picture, even a patent to print the psalms of David. Reynold Hopton had the patent for making flasks, touchboxes, powder boxes and bullet boxes, for fourteen years. John Spillman had a patent to buy linen rags and make paper. Sir Jerome Bowes had the licence to make drinking glasses for twelve years from 1592.

Prospecting

King Henry VIII had appointed a commission to search for metals. German experts in metal mining used divining and magnetic needles on several Crown estates. The founding work of the earth sciences, Georgius Agricola's "De Re Metallica" was published in 1556. The Queen, in 1564, issued a broad licence covering the northern and western counties, stating that "we have given and granted full power, licence and authority to Thomas Thurland clerk, and to Daniel Hochstetter, a German born, to search for all manner of monies or ores of gold, silver, copper or quicksilver, within our counties of York, Lancaster, Cumberland, Westmoreland, Cornwall, Devon, Glousestershire, and Worcestershire, and within our Principalities of Wales and the same to try out, convert and use to their most profit and commodity." Augsberg invested £20.000 in the first four years.

The grantees sublet parts of the licence to the Earls of Pembroke and Leicester, James Lord Mountjoy, London merchants, Westmoreland gentlemen and others. There was some opposition in Parliament from landowners, but the Exchequer court upheld the Queen's prerogative against the Earl of Northumberland. Hochestetter found copper ore containing silver in Cumberland by 1565 and asked to bring three or four hundred foreign workers to extract it. Mines Royal companies were incorporated in 1568 with the sole right of mining precious metals and copper in the north and west and with sole rights to make battery goods, brass and to mine calamine. By 1579 the Germans had sold out and Customer Smythe took over the works.

It is not clear whether these efforts brought any result in Yorkshire. Young Hochstetter certainly visited Sheffield to gain experience. A number of other royal grants were made affecting Yorkshire, the consequences of which are not known. They may be linked to local developments. The Queen granted mines and quarries at Kirkby Moorside to Richard Bowes, Mary and Christopher Brooke. Sir Henry Gate's licence to work coal in Pickering Lithe sounds like a prospecting lease. A later licence to dig, search and mine for "coles, lead, copper, sulphur, quicksilver, brimstone, slate stone and ironstone", throughout the Honour of Pickering was granted to Henry Lord Danvers early in the next reign. There is some mention of a brass kiln at Pickering.

Vessel Glass

Glass was imported from Italy, Flanders, France, Germany, Spain and the Netherlands, when London merchant Henry Smythe sought a twenty year licence to make "brodeglass" called "Normandy glass" for windows in 1550-53. He intended to bring "certain strangers "expert in the manufacture into England, who could set local men to work, so they could learn the art and eventually instruct others. Something of the kind may have been done. Queen Elizabeth agreed new articles with Jean Carre and Anthony Becku in August 1567 to erect twelve glassworks or furnaces in England "using bracken, briars, sand, pebbles and other things of little worth." In fact, large quantities of wood were also required for the furnaces. The two partners were described as "born in the low countries under the King of Spain."

The partners were licensed "to erect in any place in England, where ever they could agree with the owner of the place, furnaces, buildings and machinery for making glass, for glazing as made in France, Lorraine and Burgundy." For the space of twenty-one years, no one else was to practice the art of glass making, unless employed or licensed by them, on pain of forfeiture of equipment, materials, products and £100. They were to make enough glass for the use of the realm, cheaper than that imported, and to take on a number of Englishmen as apprentices for full instruction in the art of glass making. They were obliged to pay the same duties as merchant importers of glass. The furnaces were to be operating by 1568.

John Carre came from Antwerp. He brought other glass workers to England, some from Lorraine. He arranged to set up a glasshouse at Alfold in Surrey in 1567, but met some opposition from local iron masters and glass traders. He did establish a glass house at the Crutched Friars, London in 1570. His will drawn up in 1572 required his wife and son to assist two sons in law to set up a furnace for small glass. His son was to be taught "the art of making small glass."

It is not clear how the industry spread to north Yorkshire but a John Allain acquired Alleyn close next to the site of an Elizabeth glassworks in 1568 on the west side of Hartoft Dale, though in Lastingham parish. John son of John Carre was buried at Lastingham in 1590. The wife of Amabie the "glasman" was mentioned in the parish register in 1593 and a number of possible French names occur between 1570 and 1590 in Lastingham parish register and in returns of aliens.

Glass vessel furnaces of the late 16th century, with auxiliary furnaces, for annealing and fritting, were found on moorland, south west of Hutton le Hole, and near "glasspitholes" in west Hartoft dale, near the ruined cottage in Alleyn Close, by Raymond Hayes. Sand, fireclay, bracken for lime, and oak timber were all to hand. The winged furnaces were similar to those used in the south of England. The molten glass was gathered on the end of a blow pipe, and by blowing, and shaping on moulds, converted into good quality, well fired bottles, beakers, glasses, linen smoothers, bowls, goblets, and urinals.[17]

William Harrison could say in 1586 "it is a world to see in these our days, wherein gold and silver most aboundeth, how that our gentility, slothing those metals do now generally choose rather the Venice glasses, both for our wine and our beere. The poorest also will have glass if they may, but with the Venice is somewhat too dear for them, they content themselves with such as are made at home of ferne and burnt stone." Yorkshire glaziers remained few in number. Robert Brown a Scarborough glazier agreed a contract to repair the parish church glass for twelve years at £1.6s.8d. a year in 1599. He had a limekiln on the west side of his house in St, Nicholas Street. Thomas England a plumber did the glass repairs, for 2s.6d a year at Malton church in 1609. Barnard Dinnichoff, a Protestant refugee made armorial windows at Gilling in 1585, and was admitted to the York Freemans' Roll a year or two later. He was possibly responsible for others at Otley, Shibden hall, Weston, Fountains Hall and Moormonkton.[18]

Alum[19]

Alum was used extensively in England as a mordaunt that fixed dyes to cloth, and in several other crafts. Production had been almost a papal monopoly, but alum was produced in Turkey, France, Germany, Silesia and Bohemia by mid century. Supplies were imported to England from Germany and Italy. Cornelius de Vos of Liege was granted a patent in 1564 to dig and mine for alum and copperas. Lord Mountjoy replaced him in the patent for working alum in the Isle of Wight and by August 1566 wanted the Queen to advance £6000, promising 150 tons of alum at the end of two years and 150 tons of copperas. Sir William Cecil assigned Mountjoy a tenth of the profits on a patent for making alum. His tenant was Richard Leycolt.

The alum industry of north east Yorkshire may have commenced in the reign of Queen Elizabeth. William Camden said so clearly enough. The facts are less clear and the expansion of the industry came early in the next reign. Alum works were established at Slape Wath near Guisborough on the Skelton estate of John Atherton The site was discovered by Richard Leycolt about 1603-4 and was developed with four furnaces, lead boiling pans, coolers and cisterns. There is a suggestion that the Darcy family began a work at Guisborough in 1600. Another was opened at Sandsend a few years later.

Another alum works was established at Belman Banks on the Chaloner estate. John Chaloner, a man well versed in "De Re Metallica", had prospected at Lambay in Ireland, where he may have had experience with alum. His son Thomas Chaloner left Lambay for Guisborough to run the estate of Sir Thomas Chaloner by 1595. He surveyed the manor in 1602. Sir Thomas was said to have visited the papal alum works at Puzzeoli near Rome and to have noticed similarities of vegetation to works in Germany and a lack of night frost. His step daughter Katherine Leigh was married to Lord Mountjoy.

Salt Petre

Gunpowder was in large part made of nitrates combined with sulphur and crushed charcoal. The only known source of nitrates was urine. Licences to dig for salt petre were issued from 1560. The Earl of Warwick had the licence in 1573, to dig in barns, stables, abbeys and old castles, but not in halls, parlours and shops. He was to spare the little houses of poor men. The "salt petre man" had to find urine soaked earth, in a latrine, pigpen, manure heap, dovecote or fold yard. Latrines are rarely mentioned in houses below the gentry level and not often then. Later centuries offered variations on the theme of "men to the barn and women to the stable." Pot urinals were kept and might be emptied into barrels or lant jars. The salt petre man dug out the best of it, which occurred as a salty white deposit. Richard Hexton, a saltpetre man was licensed in Hull in 1595 and another passed through Malton during the reign.

Iron[20]

Iron extraction was an ancient Yorkshire industry. Monasteries had worked the ores, Byland Abbey at Denby and near Huddersfield, Kirkstead Abbey at Kimberworth, Jervaulx Abbey in Richmondshire, Fountains Abbey in Nidderdale, and Rievaulx abbey in Airedale and Bilsdale. Great mediaeval landowners had profited from iron-working and the heirs of the Bruces in Cleveland, the Laceys about Leeds and the Percys at Spofforth still had pits and bloomeries on their estates.

Bishop Barnes had mentioned the three forges for making iron at Kirkstall, Follifoot and Rothwell Haigh. Brown mine was also exposed in north east Yorkshire's sea cliffs, and may already have been gathered. Another useable iron deposit known as "bog ore" was found where iron bearing water met organic material, and precipitated iron oxide in areas of high moors and wet lowlands.

Once discovered, iron ore might be worked at separate sites along a contour. The ore was usually excavated in bell pits, between five and twelve feet across and from seven to twenty feet deep. The next task was to extract the iron from the crude ore. This had to be washed, crushed into pieces and then roasted on an open hearth, to make it workable. The ore was heated in a clay lined hearth between layers of charcoal. A flue fed the fire, amplified by blasts of air from leather bellows. The fire might be controlled by watering to slow it down. The lumps of ore were reduced to a pasty mass. This was purified by long hammering to give a two foot bloom of iron. The bloomery hearth might produce less than two to three hundred weight a day. Slag tapped from the hearths remained for centuries in extensive "cinder hills".

Water power allowed more effective use of hammers and bellows, in larger furnaces at fewer places, by the early 16th.century. As the industry grew, more woodland was needed, hundreds of acres under coppice management to regularly fuel the furnaces. Sixteen pounds of charcoal were needed to produce a pound of iron from an 8 inch diameter bowl furnace. Rievaulx abbey had 441 acres of coppices before its dissolution. Sir William Bellasis was anxious to sell his woods adjoining Rievaulx Abbey to the Earl of Rutland for his iron works in 1588.

Iron was needed for armaments, ships, vehicles, and for craft and household tools. New technology transformed the iron industry. The bloomery method of making wrought iron directly from the ore gave way to the blast furnace, using much higher temperatures, to produce cast iron objects, as well as pigs of iron, which were sent to a finery forge for conversion into bars of wrought iron. The first English blast furnace was built in Ashdown Forest, in south east England by 1496, associated with a migration of French iron workers to the Weald. The stone tower furnaces spread to other counties in the 1560s, along with the slighter finery forges for making the brittle cast iron into a malleable iron, and chafery hearths where it could be heated again and worked with tilt hammers to forge out more slag. Parish register entries have suggested that workmen of French descent settled in the Sheffield area in the 1570s, linked with the introduction of the blast furnace.

Older style bloomeries and hand forging continued where local need didn't justify conversion. Iron was smelted by the direct bloomery process at the Rockley family smithies, 1500-c1640, south west of Barnsley, using charcoal and ore from well wooded outcrops of the Tankersley ironstone. A smelting hearth and a string hearth had water bellows, worked by a water wheel set in a stone lined wheel pit alongside the bellows house. A statute of the first year of the reign had stopped felling of timber to make "coles for the burning of iron" but exemption licences were given. There had been iron working in Danby Forest in northeast Yorkshire of old. This must have continued since a license was granted to Jordan Russell in 1589. Not until 1615 did a royal proclamation ban the use of wood in all furnaces dictating the complete move to coal as the fuel.

Charcoal blast furnaces and water powered forges were in Yorkshire by the 1580s. Furnaces were near Thurgoland in 1567 and within thirty years at Kimberworth, Wadsley, Heaner near Duffield and Attercliffe. The industry was largely in the hands of the nobility and gentry, among them, the Barnby, Cutler, Rockley, Saville and Wortley families in the area of Leeds, Huddersfield, Barnsley and Sheffield. Hallamshire saw a marked development of metal working promoted by George, Earl of Shrewsbury, who owned seams of ironstone, woods for charcoal, coal mines and the Attercliffe forge, in the township of Brightside Byerlow and other forges in Herefordshire and Shropshire. Matthew Wentworth leased a mine and a delf of ironstone in Emley to supply his West Bretton forge in 1575.

There is some doubt whether the Sheffield area or Rievaulx in north east Yorkshire saw the first Yorkshire furnaces in blast. Bloomery slag marked several valleys near Rievaulx Abbey. The monastery had two bloom smithies, tenanted by a Frenchman

Lambert Seamer, in 1538, one near the house and one at Laskill in Bilsdale. Water powered hammers were used by 1540. Lambert Seamer of Rievaulx in 1558 left all his tools belonging to the smithies at Bolton in Craven, Rievaulx and Laskill to his sons. The Earl of Rutland acquired the Rievaulx estate and installed the first blast furnace in 1576-7, with a casting house, finery hearths, store houses, chafery and a new flood gate on the river. Another forge continued on the old iron working site. The blast furnace was reshaped in 1587 and output raised from 13 cwt to about 22 cwt a day by 1591. Much was sent to York and to London. Inscribed hood plates from Rievaulx survived in 1823. The average net profit rose from £530 a year in mid 1590's to £1000 in the early 17th century.

Lead[21]

Yorkshire Dales lead had been shipped from Yarm and from Boroughbridge down river for weighing at the York crane in the Middle Ages. Some of the prosperity of York merchants was built on the metal. The governor of the fellowship of the Merchants of York in 1511 said "lead is our most principal commodity." Sir John Gresham, the London merchant bought lead from Richmond merchants Ralph Goore and Charles Johnson, during Elizabeth's reign.

Lead was found in Arkengarthdale, Ribblesdale, Wensleydale, Swaledale, Airedale, Wharfedale and below the grits of upper Nidderdale, as well as at Alston Moor. Sir Arthur Darcey and his son Henry mined at Bewerley. They sold out to Thomas Benson in 1573. He was said to make an annual profit of £160. Sir Stephen Procter had Bewerley in 1569 and opened new workings. Other owners were Sir William Ingleby, at Brimham, Sir John Yorke at Appletreewick, and John Sayer esq. at Marrick.

Lead occurred as veins of galena, in vertical fissures and level flatts, among the limestone. When a rake or vein was struck, a stow was built to serve as the top of a windlass and a bell- pit was dug beneath. An adit might be cut in the hillside to drain off water. The ore was broken up with a hammer, crushed, washed, sieved and carried to the bole or furnace, for two stages of roasting, to free the lead from sulphur. Brush wood was used for boles and charcoal for hearths. The bole had a top opening and a chimney and vents at the base to make a blast. Turn boles could be turned into the wind. The lead ran into a stone pig mould at the side of the bole.

An alternative method called "hushing" saw the stream damned, a channel dug to the vein, along which water was released to erode the rock, scour out the loose earth and expose the ore. A second flood trapped the galena at a grating. Hand hammering could give way to the horse wheel and there was a shift from the bole to the ore hearth in the 16th century. Bellows blown ore hearths used peat. A furnace of this kind was made by William Humphrey on the river Sheaf near Sheffield in 1567. They made use of poorer ore and could work all year. Ore hearth sites are known near Greenhow, in Nidderdale, Grassington in Wharfedale, Grinton, Old Gang and Surrender in Swaledale and Arkengarthdale.

Some silver was obtained from ores at Slaidburn, Rimington and Guisburn in Craven. The silver ore from Skelhorn field at Rimington, in Bowland was later reputed to yield twenty-six pounds of silver per ton. It was claimed that Mr Pudsay. a god-son of the Queen worked the Rimington mines without a licence, and had a good store of silver ore. It was said that, "he converted it to his own use - or, rather, coined it, as many do believe, there being many shillings marked with an escallop, which the people of the country call Pudsay's shillings to this day."

> "Oh then he made and thought no ill.
> The Pudsay shilling his debts to pay.
> Still at the mint by Bolton mill.
> The dross of his works is seen today."

The ballad had him pursued by soldiers. He escaped to his god mother, the Queen and craved her pardon on a ship in the Thames.

> "She gave him then her hand to kiss.
> So, while the tears stood in his ee .
> His heart was brought from bale to bliss.
> But no more Pudsay shilling said she."

Cutlery, Pins, Nails[22]

Sheffield cutlery was famous the length of the country. Chaucer's mention of a Sheffield "thwitel" hints at the early fame. There was a scythemill at Holbrook south of Sheffield by 1489. Tradition claimed that the battles of Crecy and Agincourt were won with Sheffield arrows and that they were used at Bosworth field. John Leland said "there be many smiths and cutlers in Hallamshire" and "In Rotherham be very good smiths for all cutting tools." The Earl of Shrewsbury presented a case of Hallamshire whittles to Lord Burghley at London in 1571, "being such fruits as his poor country afforded with fame there from." Three gross of Hallamshire knives appear in some Liverpool accounts in 1589. The "Writing Master" published in 1590, for preparing quills, said "with reference to the pen knife, that a right Sheffield knife is best." Fuller called knives "the teeth of old men" though useful to those of all ages, and said, "some conceived themselves scarce men without them."

There were water driven grinding wheels in at least ten places near Sheffield, between 1520 and 1552. Each water wheel served several grindstones. The Sheffield survey of 1581 showed half year rents of 20s. paid for the north, south, west and east ends of wheels, at the Wicker, Sharowhead, Synder heap Cloughe, Healey Bridge, Walk Milne, Hamer, Marsh, Blackburn and one new built with a house at Waddesley bridge and Morton Rivelin. There were over wheels in the pastures; Greaves wheel, Hyne wheel, and a wheel built at Ecclesfield Moor. A Rotherham cutler acquired "a knife wheel and house lately erected for the necessary grinding of knives" at Aldwark in 1587

Early cutlers used the Tankersley seams of ironstone in Sheffield park Steel from better ores was imported from Spain, Germany and Sweden, with added carbon giving a harder, more malleable metal, which took a better edge. The Earl of Shrewsbury imported fine Spanish steel. William Dickinson his Hallamshire bailiff received six barrels of steel from Bawtry at Sheffield castle in October 1574. William Bankes, a Rotherham ironmonger supplied 600 spruses of iron to an Eckington scythe smith.

Cutlery production in Hallamshire was under the supervision of twelve master cutlers appointed by the manor court. The court assigned trade marks, enrolled apprentices and levied fines for breach of the rules which had been agreed between the cutlers and the Earl. Between 1554 and 1570 the Earl granted sixty-one trade marks to his Master Cutlers. By 1565 when their customs and ordinances were restated, they were "The Fellowship and Company of Cutlers." They would be incorporated in 1624 as the Company of Cutlers in Hallamshire,

The ordinances of the Fellowship restrained masters, servants and apprentices from work in the "science or mystery of cutlers" for twenty eight days after the 8th of August, and from Christmas till 23rd January, when they were to apply themselves to other labours. No one occupying a wheel for grinding knives was to allow any work in these holiday months. Cutlers had to be apprenticed or instructed by their fathers for seven years and were to have only one apprentice. They had to be resident to use a grinding wheel for grinding or glazing knives. Hafters were only to haft knives for residents, other chapmen, hardware men or dagger makers. A new cutler paid five pounds, half going to the Earl of Shrewsbury and half to relieve the poor.

An apprenticeship indenture signed on the tenth of February 1574 saw John Clayton of Lightwood bind himself with yeoman John Urton to dwell with him "after the manner of a servant" from Michaelmas next for four years. Urton would "cause him to be taught, learned and made perfect in the art, craft and occupation of the scythesmith's craft." Clayton paid him forty shillings a year. Urton had to find him six sheep. The apprentice was to make thirty-six scythes a week.

Scythe smiths forged steel between two pieces of wrought iron by hand or by the tilt hammer, hardened, tempered and then ground the scythe at the wheel. Richard Stanyforth of Brynkmlessedge left "2 dossen scythes ready for the chapman" in 1552. Other metal working crafts were spread more widely. Gunthwaite rents in 1588 included two pairs of broad arrows from George Blunt, feathered arrows from a farm at Hunshelf and a thwittle from Thomas Wordsworth of Roughbanks. John Ray mentioned Doncaster daggers. A Ben Johnson play "The Staple of News" acted in 1625 referred to Ripon spurs. There was a saying "as true steel as Ripon spurs". Nail making was long established north of the cutlery area, at Ecclesfield, Chapeltown, and Hoyland, the nailers often part time farmers. Barnsley wire drawers used hard wire to make teeth for cards and fish hooks, soft wire for needles

The York pinners and wire drawers had a guild but Aberford and Sherburn were as famous for pinners. A pinner's epitaph recalled the hazards of ginding.

> "O cruel death to rob this man of breath,
> Who, while he lived,
> In scraping of a pin
> Made better dust
> Than thou hast made of him."

A Statute of 1543 required that "no person shall put to sale any pins but such as shall be double headed and have their heads soldered fast to the shank and well smoothed and the shank well shaven, the point well and round filed and sharpened." Fuller found them "hurtful and useful to fasten our ornaments" but said "many and very good of these are made in Yorkshire the very dust from them is found profitable." Drunken Barnaby recorded the Aberford pinners.

> "Thence to Aberford whose beginning,
> Came from buying drink with pinning
> Poor they are and very needy

Yet of liquor too, too greedy
Have they never so much plenty.
Belly makes their purses empty.

T64 Specialist Metal Craftsmen leaving Wills. 1558 - 1598

Armourer	Beverley, Wakefield, York.
Arrowheadsmith	Darnall 2, Owlerton, Little Sheffield,
Bladesmith,	York.
Brasier	Beverley 4, York,
Cutler	Sheffield 19, Attercliffe, Doncaster, Healey, York 2, Wadesley, Cawthorne, Darnall 6, Shiregreen, Stumperlawe, Neepsend, Wincobank, Tinsley 2, Thorpe (Rotherham), Little Sheffield, Masbrough, Brincliffe Edge 2, Skeath, Brighouses, Osgathorpe Rawmarsh, Bellhouse.
Founderer	York 2.
Goldsmith	Scarborough, Halifax, York.
Hardwareman	Stumperlowe, Sheffield 4, Attercliff, Darnall, Halifax, Walklay,
Ironmonger	Sheffield.
Locksmith	York 5, Malton.
Metalman	York, Hull.
Nailer	Ecclesfield 4, Nether Flockton, Wentworth, Chapelthorpe Worsbroughdale, Nether Shitlington, Wentworth,
Pewterer	York 7, New Malton, Beverley 2.
Pinner	York 2, Sherburn.
Scythesmith	Worsbrough.
Shearsmith	N.Cave, Attercliffe, Sheffield
Shearman	York, Beverley 2, Rygton, Lowthorpe, Keighley, Horsforth, Selby, Hull 2, Leeds 2, Beverley, Swillington.
Sheather	Sheffield 3, Catcliff
Sheathmaker	Swainby, (Whorlton).
Smithyman	Ecclesfield.
Sive maker-	Beverley.
Smithyman	Kirk Heaton.
Spurrier	Beverley
Wiredrawer	Harwood, Hatfield, Barnsley 3, Seacroft, Selby

Clothiers[23]

The York Mayor told the Lord President in 1561 that "one Richard Marshall of the said city, merchant, did lately set up draping in this city and had one woollen loom there of his own, but because he found no gaines at it, he hath left off." There were not above ten weavers in the city for linen and woollen and they were for linen. The four woollen looms were unoccupied for lack of work. "And the cause of the decay of the said weavers and looms for woollen within the said city, as I do understand and learn is the lack of cloth making in the said city as was in old time accustomed, which is now increased and used in the towns of Halifax, Leeds and Wakefield, for that not only the commodity of the water mills is there nigh hand but also the poor folk as spinners, carders and other necessary workfolk for the said webbing may there beside their hand labour have rye, fire and other relief, good cheap, which is in this city very dear and wanting ."

The industry had moved and it had started moving some time ago. King Henry II had once restricted the making of dyed cloth in Yorkshire to York, Beverley, Kirkby, Thirsk, Malton, Scarborough and other Crown demesne boroughs. The Ulnage accounts of 1472 already listed Halifax, Ripon, Leeds, Almondbury, Hull, Barnsley, Wakefield and Bradford as important producers. By 1502 cloth from Knaresborough, Ripon, Leeds, Bradford, Wakefield and Halifax was being marketed in York. A list was drawn up of offenders against laws prohibiting the flocking of cloth in the 1530's. The surviving portion numbered 542 clothiers. Over half were from the parishes of Halifax, Heptonstall and Elland. Other places with more than ten clothiers included Huddersfield, Almondbury, Dewsbury, Wakefield, Leeds, and Bradford, in the wapentakes of Agbrigg, Morley and Skyrack. The clothiers leaving wills 1514-1553 were Leeds 13, Halifax 3; Heptonstall, Bramley, Armley, Ardesley, Sowerby, Warley, Wakefield 1 while dyers were at Beverley, York, Leeds and Wakefield 1. Leland noticed the cloth making at Beverley and Wakefield but at Ripon he said that, "idlesness is sore increased in the town and cloth making almost decayed." Knaresborough had lost out too and by mid century, the weaving of cloth had almost completed its migration from York and Beverley.

A scattering of weavers remained across the county, supplying local needs. Tailors, the "knights of the needle", who made clothing were far more numerous, in villages and towns, everywhere, buying in their cloth and travelling around fairs and gentry houses. The growth of the West Riding cloth manufacture continued, as much in the villages as in the towns. Woollen cloth was the principal manufacture and chief export of Elizabethan England and Yorkshire West Riding its principal part.

The clothiers bought wool from the farmers and supplied it to the houses of workers who washed and carded the wool, spun it into thread and wove it on a loom. The clothiers sold the cloth to merchants and others. The Halifax Act of Parliament passed in 1555 spoke of the "great waste and moors, where the fertility of ground is not apt to bring forth any corn nor good grass, but in rare places and by exceeding and great industry of the inhabitants." This industry had been turned to cloth manufacture, so that "the barren ground in those parts be now much inhabited" Camden thought "there is nothing so admirable in this town, as the industry of the inhabitants who, notwithstanding an unprofitable soil, not fit to live in, have so flourished by the cloth trade (which within these last seventy years they fell to) that they are both very rich and have gained a great reputation for it, above their neighbours.

James Rither exalted the "best common people of this county" saying that "our clothiers, that inhabit all the grounds between Wakefield and Westmoreland are the comliest personages for parts of the body, ablest in substance, best given for offices of the mind and by trading southwards of more civility then their consorts of degree" adding that "the inhabitants of Halifax are planted among our most stony and barren mountains, west from York, somewhat upon the south in the edge of Lancashire, these I say excell the rest in policy and industry, for the use of their trade and grounds, and after the rude and arrogant manner of their wild country, they surpass the rest in wisdom and wealth, enforcing grounds beyond all hope to fertility and ardent for new inventions.

They have a great liberty to inclose and build upon the wastes, mostly crown land. "The same inhabitants altogether do live by cloth making."

Their raw material were bought from and brought by a middleman. "The great part of them neither get the corn, nor is able to keep a horse to carry wools, not yet to buy much wool at once". They "used to repair to the town of Halifax and some other nigh thereto, and there to buy upon the wool driver, some a stone, some two and some three or four, according to their ability, and to carry the same back to their houses, some three, four, five and six miles off, upon their heads, and backs, and so to make and convert the same either into yarn or cloth, and to sell the same and so to buy more wool of the wool driver."

Wool was graded, washed and carded, to take out knots and twists. It was combed and spun into thread. Spinning was done with a cleft stick called a distaff and a spindle. The spinner held the distaff under one arm, propped on a waste girdle, and with that hand drew out strands from the carded wool on top of the distaff and cast it to the rotating upright spindle controlled by the left hand, twisting and winding the yarn. The yarn was woven on a horizontal loom, a framework with warp threads fixed to each end, through which the shuttle was passed with the woof. The clothier took the piece of cloth. The process called fulling, shrunk and felted or thickened the cloth, binding the fibres together by beating the cloth in water with absorbent fuller's earth, which took out grease and dirt. The process, otherwise known as walking had been done by foot, but now at fulling mills, where alternate hammers, tipped by cams on a water wheel shaft, dropped on the cloth in a trough. The wet cloth was stretched on tenters to dry. Loose fibres were drawn off with teazles, raising the nap and softening the surface. The shearman cut off the loose strands and gave the cloth a smooth surface.

When John Pawsone, a clothier of Kirkgate in Leeds died, his inventory was drawn up by four neighbour clothiers. His house held what he called his "office house", a parlour, a chamber, and his "shop and loomhouse". His "leadhouse", and laithe or barn were probably in the yard. The ground floor office house held his only fireplace and was also his kitchen, where he had ample equipment for feeding others. He slept in the parlour, but his three apprentices did not sleep in. His chamber held 43 stone of dyed wool, 15 stones of white wool and some combs, ready for distribution and some alum for dyeing. His shop and loom house held £34 worth of cloth, some equipment for shearing, and five stone of wool, while ten stone of yarn was out at the spinners. He had some madder for dyeing and a loom.

Linen

The emergence of the linen industry may fall in Elizabethan times but this is less clear. This would become the part time industry of a swathe of land from Crathorne in Cleveland down through Ryedale and Pickering Vale in the next century. Yorkshire line-lands are known from the 12th century. Several districts of Yorkshire record early growing of hemp and line. Thomas Anderson grew thirty "beates or shoites of hemp" in 1543 at Hunmanby. Hemp was grown from seed in quantity in Holderness in 1556.

There were signs of early specialisation in Cleveland where a substantial industry would develop. Tithe of line and canvas was taken at Crathorn and Gretham in 1535 and tithe of line and hemp at Hutton Rudby. An Act of Parliament of 1533 required all cultivators to devote a quarter of an acre of land to flax in every sixty acres sown. This was increased to an acre thirty years later. Edmund Metcalf of Rudby in 1558 had three yards of the best lyn. John Stevenson of North Frodingham, in 1577 had a line heckle, a hemp heckle, a pair of yarn windle blades, four scottels two pieces of ground sewn with hemp and line

Hemp grew well on rich manured soil, even on rank weedy ground and produced two crops, summer and winter hemp. Flax was grown on low holmes, sewn thickly to give a tall growth and avoid branching. It was pulled in late July and stacked in small bundles for drying. The bundles were threshed, combed or rippled to remove seeds. The useable fibre was between the core and the sheath. The stalks were steeped in running water, a process known as retting, to rot the woody material. They were trodden, washed, dried, beetled with a heavy wood mallet and scraped with a scutching knife against a board to remove the outer fibres. The flax was heckled to remove coarse fibres, by drawing it through sets of mounted teeth, and combed to make a fine fibre. The tow went to make coarse cloth called harden and the finer fibres went for linen. The yarn was spun on a hand or treddle turned spinning wheel, the yarn wound on bobbins and put on the warp beam of a hand loom. The woven web was exposed to the sun to bleach.

Linen working was well evidenced in Elizabethan Cleveland, hemp working at South Cave. Henry Mawlame at Whorlton in 1583 left "one linen loom and one linen coup with gears" to William Deane, and the rest of his "weaving gear, looms and whole work house" to his son Ralph. Some local weavers had one loom for linen and one for wool. At Richmond Thomas Lee in 1587 had a linen wheel, a line loom and second loom and woollen gear value 12s.7d. By 1598 country websters were taking linen to York. Retting made water courses unfit for cattle to drink. Allerston in Pickering Vale had hemp pits by 1602 and hemp was watered at Byland, Thirkleby and Bagby in the vale of York. Robert Trewman of Pilfytt beamed three webbes of linen cloth in 1605. Linen weaving was recorded at Oswaldkirk, and South Kilvington, flax dressers at Osmotherley, linen drapers Will Hornsby and James Hunter at Kirkby Moorside in the early years of King James I. The linen manufacture would become the principal handicraft of north east Yorkshire until the early 19th century.

Much flax would be imported from the Low Countries and the Baltic, some even as linen yarn. In the 1570's Hull began importing several hundred tons of flax a year. The strong thread was good for canvas, sailcloth, and cobblers twine. Some yarn was also bleached for best quality cloth, itself beetled to give a faint gloss or shine. Henry Best could write in 1641 of "linen cloth bought at Malton off pedlars" who furnish themselves thereof in Cleveland and Blakeymoor, where they buy very much of this sorte, and at New Malton live many at whose houses one may at all times furnish themselves with this kind of cloth." He sometimes also sold yarn to Malton weavers. The town was known for its "linen and huswife cloth"

Knitted Woollens

The cattle districts offered little employment for women or children. This changed as cloth hose was challenged by knitted stockings, caps and mittens. An Act of Parliament of 1571 required every person not possessed of 20 marks to wear a knitted woollen cap on Sundays and Holy Days, when not travelling, or forfeit 3s.4d a day. Kendall and Richmond merchant hosiers bought wool and supplied it to country carders, spinners and knitters, and bought back the stockings, produced in thousands of dozens in the year. The knitted woollen industry was established in Elizabethan times, from

Richmond to Sedbergh, at Keld, and from Wensleydale to Hawes and Dentdale but also at Doncaster.

Richmond corporation required that "no inhabitant of the town shall hire anyone to knit for money, only unless their master or dame do give them meat and drink in their own house during all the time of their service. No one was to take an apprentice for knitting for four years, then keep them for seven. Orphans and paupers were recruited in the apprentice books, the masters given 13s.4d or £1 a year by the corporation. They fed, clothed, lodged and indemnified the Council against the apprentice becoming chargeable to the poor rate. A knitting school was started by burgesses taking a house in St Saviourgate York in 1590. Three teachers taught the craft to poor children, rewarded with coats of the cheapest cloth. Four years later the master was charged for not taking in enough children.

CHAPTER 7
TRADE

Markets and Fairs

The parish churchyards had largely given way, long since, to the market place for buying and selling, whether using money or credit, and for local bartering. All the borough towns had a market. More than a hundred and twenty Yorkshire villages had gained other markets, chartered to local manor lords in the 13th and 14th centuries, and these were usually combined with an annual fair. The market was a weekly event on a regular day. The fair ran for three or more days, once a year, usually including the eve, day and morrow of the feast of a patron saint. The majority were at villages with parish churches.

Many of these markets had ceased to function after the arable and livestock failures in the period 1315 to 1322, the Black Death plague outbreaks of 1348-49 and later, and the population decline of the later 14th century. Only their old market crosses survived, memorials to a vanished past. The survivors adjusted to serve broader areas. There was always some out-of-market trading, and even some use of churchyards. John Leland travelled through Yorkshire and briefly described the places he passed through. He characterised several towns by their markets, in the early 16th century, among them; Sherburn in Elmet, Pocklington, Tickhill, Bawtry and Blyth. Rotherham was a "meatly large market town" and Sheffield the chief market town of Hallamshire, the ancient name for much of Strafforth wapentake. Wakefield had a "fair" area for a market place and Beverley the fairest part of it. He said that the market at Knaresborough was "quick".

William Camden made similar comments in the second half of the century. Ripon fair was much celebrated for cattle and for horses. Malton had a good market, Masham pretty quick and Thirsk was a small market town. There was no longer a market at Patrington in Holderness. Howden was the sole market for Howdenshire. Men said that Wensley lost its market in the more recent plague of 1563. John Taylor wrote that "the reason that, as some think, that nothing is found written in this (parish) register in the year of our Lord God 1563 is because that, in that year, the visitation of plague was most hot and fearful, so that many fled and the town of Wensley by reason of the sickness was unfrequented for a long season, as I find by one old writing dated 1568".

The Tadcaster jury of 1613 were well aware of the trade lost by the collapse of their market. They said that the town was "eight miles from the city of York, Wetherby four miles, Pontefract ten miles, the best market towns adjoining which do vent corn, cattle and victual, albeit it hath anciently been a market town, upon the Tuesday and two fairs in the year which, if it were revived would much better the town and the townsmen are very desirous it may be revived again". Halifax had wool drivers supplying wool to small weavers and clothiers buying cloth but had no organised market in 1555. A proposal for securing a patent for a weekly market and a fair at the prospering town in

1584 was opposed by the lord of the manor, squire Waterton, whose prior claim was admitted in the courts.

A renewed expansion of trading in the late 16th century failed to revive most of the decayed markets. Instead, activity expanded at some of the surviving centres of trade and a few new ventures came into being. Much trading in foodstuffs remained local and a few local craftsmen were a great support to a traditional village market. Many men with a surplus needed to get to market and get home before dark, but the higher prices near a great town, or a seaport, could bring sellers from further afield. The sea or a navigable river made a cheaper highway for bulky goods than any road. New middlemen were seeking goods to buy, which they would take even further afield, not least to the emerging industrial areas, the coal fields and to London. The appearance of cattle breeding and fattening districts fostered short and long distance droving, often to fairs rather than markets. The cattle and sheep were moved alive by road and over the commons.

It is not absolutely clear which markets were functioning in the years 1557-1603. Sedbergh market began in 1526. Queen Mary renewed the Wednesday market and St. Thomas fair at Topcliff. A new market grew informally at Askrigg in Wensleydale. This was legalised after nine years, when Peter Thornton secured a twenty-one year grant from the Queen in 1587, with a remainder to the inhabitants of Askrigg, for a Thursday market and two annual three day fairs, one to start on the fourth day after the feast of St Mark and the other on the third day before the feast of St Luke, paying a rent of 26s.8d. to the Crown.

John Brooke was granted a fortnightly market at Adwalton on every second Thursday between Easter and Michaelmas, with two fairs, after Easter and Pentecost with tolls of a penny for every lamb or five sheep sold. This regularised an informal fair, which had attracted men from Lancashire and Yorkshire. Isabel Countess of Rutland and William Lord Roos were granted a Thursday market, with a yearly fair on Thursday, Friday and Saturday in Whitsun week, in 1595-6, at Warter manor, in the East Riding, but this was an exchange for surrendered rights to a Wednesday market and a fair on the eve, day and morrow of St James Apostle.

T65 16th & 17th Century Yorkshire Markets c1500-1690
C for corn, A for cattle, H for horses

East Riding- Beverley(C), Bridlington(C), Driffield, Hedon, Hornsea, Howden(A), Hull, Hunmanby, Kilham, Market Weighton, North Frodingham, Patrington, Pocklington(C), Warter

North Riding- Askrigg, Bedale, Easingwold, Guisborough, Helmsley, Hovingham, Kirkby Moorside, Malton(C, A, H), Masham, Middleham, Northallerton(A, H), Pickering(C), Richmond(A), Scarborough, Seamer(C), Strokesley, Thirsk, Whitby (cheese & butter) Yarm

West Riding- Aberford. Aldbrough, Barnsley(C), Bawtry(C), Boroughbridge, Bradford, Cawood, Doncaster(A), Guisburn, Halifax(C), Harewood, Huddersfield, Kettlewell, Knaresborough, Leeds(C), Otley, Pontefract(A), Ripley, Ripon(A), Rotherham(A), Sedbergh, Selby, Settle, Sheffield(C), Sherburn, Skipton, Snaith, Tadcaster, Tickhill, Thorne, Wetherby, Wakefield(C).
York

Harrison portrayed the greater Elizabethan towns, as having one or more markets, where all manner of provision for the household could be bought and sold, for "the ease and benefit of the country roundabout". Such towns were themselves major centres of consumption and they stood apart from others. Separate market places were used for different commodities, or for different days of the week at York, Beverley, Pontefract and Doncaster. York had four main markets held three times a week, Tuesday, Thursday and Saturday, for general goods at Pavement and Thursday market, for malt in Coney Street and for leather in the Common Hall. Other markets dealt with fish, pigs and cloth. Scarborough had separate fish and produce markets and undated crosses at one or two road junctions associated with corn and butter sales. Few of the other Yorkshire markets were on that scale. Kirkby Moorside at later dates had separate areas of the one street devoted to selling different commodities, including swine, apples, leather, and corn.

There was little market equipment. The open air cross might give some slight sanctity to the bargains sealed beneath it. Sheffield paid Nicholas Gee for mending and pointing "the market crosse and the Irish crosse" in 1589. Tollbooths or market houses were rare. The lord of a market or his lessee would let stalls in return for a payment of stallage. Shambles for selling fish and meat were rented out and the best market places were paved. Slaughter of cattle was undertaken on site. A bull stake or a bull ring was set in the pavement for securing any bulls, to be baited, an activity believed to make their meat fit to be eaten. Sweeping the floor of the corn market when trading was over was a valued perquisite of the poor at Pickering and other markets.

Borough or manor court officers managed the markets. An Elizabethan judgement said that "The lords of the market town of Thirsk and who are owners of the market place and borough there, have time without memory of man, taken by prescription, all manner of towles of goods, cattle, corn, butter and all other things sold in the same, or at the great fairs held there and also pickage, stallage, and all other pains belonging and accustomed to be paid, and the lords by order from him do provide measures, shambles and all other things convenient for the traders that resort unto the said market, and do pave or causey the corn hill and sweep and keep it clean and in good repair and all the market place and all that belongs to them at his and their proper costs and charges".

Market officers were elected for the year in borough and manor courts. They varied a little from place to place. The bellman would start the market and appraisers would settle values in a dispute. Ale conners or ale drapers, bread weighers, corn, fish and meat lookers were concerned with quantity and quality, as were aulnagers for cloth and leather searchers, who stamped hides and skin with a die head stamp. Toll collectors gathered tolls and stallage. The Kirkby Moorside demesne lessor Richard Maddox took market tolls on swine, beast, sheep and lambs, for stalls and from victuallers. The Doncaster mayor appointed four men with weights and scales to toll all wool sellers in the Summer wool market, at a halfpenny a stone, but the big merchants compounded at sixpence for a pack of fifteen or sixteen stone.

The Justices of the Peace fixed market prices for bread, meat, malt and corn. They also licensed many small traders, the badgers, broggers, corn carriers and maltsters. Harrison thought the system inadequate to control most markets, in the interest of the buyer, without some quality control, expressed in orders for the sweetness of grain and the goodness of other commodities. The state intervened to ease corn prices in dearth years. The Council in the North was told to appoint commissioners to enquire into the marketing of grains and the cause of high prices in November 1579. Orders went to local justices in 1587 to enquire into corn supplies in the hands of farmers, factors, maltsters and bakers and to force corn prices down, by restraining malting and brewing. Private bargaining outside markets was not easy to control.

Standard weights and measures had to be provided and tested. Every market town had a standard bushel but Harrison voiced the common belief that market clerks were so covetous, that when viewing measures, they always provided one too big or too little, so that dealers had one to sell by and another to buy with, and similarly with weights. Breaches of law and order were dealt with in summary 'pie poudre' courts, able to give a quick judgement, before everyone departed. Picking purses was rife rather than the later picking of pockets. On a single day at Scarborough market, several wives from the town and nearby villages had their purses picked, one for as much as two shillings. Stolen goods were often brought for quick sale. Alice Milner of Sherburn came to the port following a maid who stole her goods at Beverley. Ralph Welbank said that she had also stolen a pair of shoes at Hornsey.

Middlemen became more numerous with the growth of long distance trading. Where the seller wasn't mobile, the buyer had to be, or else he must accept the addition to prices made by the middleman. Londoners were attending the Beverley Cross fair by 1502 and James Rither, many years later, said that Beverley was "not to be matched in the north and, as some say, in England, for fish and other utensil of livelihood. Here the Londoners yearly in Spring time continue a fair, supported by the improvidences of York and Hull". Sometimes fairs took the trade rather than the markets but specialisation occurred at both. Howden's annual "great mart" saw the Bishop's manor house and courtyard leased to provide warehouses, stables and shops for London and West Riding traders.

T66 Small Traders who made Wills in Yorkshire 1554-94

Badgers-   South Kirkby 3, Doncaster 2; Thorne 2, Hemsworth 2, Brodsworth, Upper Flockton, Woodkirk, Hartshead, Driglington, Middleton

Carriers-   Wakefield 4, York 3, Beverley 1, Shelfe (Halifax), Harthill, Long Preston

Chapmen-   Leeds 6, Sheffield 2, Wakefield 3, Malton 2, Wrenthorp, Newall (Otley), Doncaster, W.Heslerton, Ardesley, Rotherham, Settrington 2, Markington, Hemsworth, Gisburne, Bransburton, Milnethorpe(Sandal)

Corn driver- Bierley (Birstall), Hipperholme

Corn merchant- York 2, Doncaster

Swine seller- Halifax

Woolman-   Ovenden, Ripon

The annual fairs proved more flexible and suitable than weekly markets for the drover's trade in cattle and sheep, but also for large scale corn trading and some of the small scale trade in many other commodities. The distinction between freemen and others was temporarily abandoned in open trading. Fairs could provide for the rare purchase of cloth or boots, and the exotic, occasional purchase of a luxury from a pedlar's pack, that would otherwise occasion a visit to York or another major town. Some of the best fairs were at those towns. Many payments including rents, some tithes and wages were paid annually. The bargain money given to servants in husbandry at the yearly hiring fairs was there for spending at Martinmas. Fairs were sometimes given their own site. An ancient Pickering fair was held at the castle gates. New horse fairs were outside the borough walls at York, Malton and elsewhere. Hull obtained two extra fairs in 1590 and York a fortnightly cattle fair between Lent and Advent. The Yorkshire fairs, taken together gave York craftsmen as well as the pedlars a regional itinerary and a programme for the year.

T67 Smith's list of Yorkshire's Elizabethan Fairs.

January 25.	Northallerton	(and Wednesdays Xmas to June)
May 1	Ripon.	
May 7	Beverley	
	Skipton on Craven	Whitsun even
	Darington, Bradford,	Whitsun Monday
June 24	Wakefield, Halifax.	MidSummer day
August 1	York, Elland,	Lammas Day.
August 10	Settle	St Laurence Day
Aug 15	Wakefield	the two Lady days
Aug 24	Northallerton	
Sept 8	Wakefield, Gisborn,	Nativity
Sept 14.	Richmond Ripon horse fair	
Sept 21	Malton	
October 18	Thirsk	
October 21	Stokesley	
October 31	Wakefield.	
November 30	Barford	

Cattle trading flourished along the spine of the county. On St. Bartholomew's Day, Northallerton held the throngest beast fair that Camden ever saw. The Rotherham and Wakefield cattle fairs drew sellers from as far afield as County Durham. Sheffield buyers went to fairs at Bedale and Middleham. By the reign of James I, Howden had a great horse fair and up to twenty thousand beasts were said to gather yearly on Bowes Moor. The Earl of Derby proposed a beast fair at Thirsk in 1604. The great wool market was Doncaster, while cloth and yarn were sent to Wakefield, Halifax and Leeds, and to a lesser extent to Bolton and to Ripon.

Shops

The pedlar's pack, the market stall and the shop counter could all place goods before the buyer. Permanent shops, retailing from stock, were largely confined to the towns but were becoming more significant. They cannot be sharply separated in the records, nor in fact, from workshops where craftsmen sold their own wares. The shop was simply a more permanent selling place, built into a house, sometimes a wooden pentice opening out of a ground floor room onto the pavement. A tailor might work in the road outside his house in good weather. Yet, in York, freemen kept shops but not market stalls, while outsiders could buy and sell in the markets but not keep a shop. Anthony Hatfield, a Rotherham yeoman leased to Edward Wood a Sheffield mercer, a mercer's shop with "a pentice fixed to", adjoining the south west corner of the Rotherham churchyard, for twenty one years at 26s.8d. a year. James Coates, a Swinton gentleman, leased a chamber and shop to John Walker at Hunmanby, a village where it is not certain that the market was still functioning. Some town streets had shop rows where the tenants put in their own partitions and shelves.

13 A Tudor Shop

The uneven shop line at Pickering was the result of recorded encroachments onto the market place at different dates. Others were cut backwards from narrow Birdgate into the church yard. The record suggests a slow development of shops over two centuries. Steward Sir David Rawcliffe recorded a new rent for a shop built by William Holyday and demised to Robert Chapman in the Market Place near the churchyard in the late 14th century. Another shop near the churchyard was let for four pence a year in 1435. Matthew Wood took in a waste plot on the south of the Market place in the first year of Queen Elizabeth's reign, sixteen feet by three ells, for four pence rent. The next year Richard Wood rented another new built shop, nine foot by eight foot, at a two pence rent. He was the manor lord at Ebberston Kirkdale. A shop lately occupied by John Smith at seven shillings had been let to Thomas Chapman at six shillings. By 1616, Pickering had at least eight shops, two of them in one house, as well as a smithy, a bake house and twenty-two burgages.

Richmond had shops near the tollbooth by 1492, some still at the under side of the tollbooth in 1556. Another was on the south side of Holy Trinity church while a smith had his "shop" in the castle. Shoemaker Raynold Williams and mercer Thomas Armgill had shops in 1566 and there were fish shambles. The College owned three town shops at Rotherham before 1558, let at five shillings, four shillings and two shillings and four pence. Bridlington market place had three shops in 1546.and four in 1609. St James chantry had a shop at Kilham before 1550 and there were several by the 17th century. The Sheffield book of burgess rents for 1566 mentions nine shops rented at sums from two to four shillings. John Shelden had an out shot for a shop at one shilling and a new house and shop at two shillings. One man owned sixteen shops in Halifax by c1590. Eleven shops appear in the Skipton rental of 1603.

Mercers and Drapers

Mercers and drapers were specialised dealers in textiles. They were not numerous in Yorkshire, but they were present in the main towns. Mercers dealt in silks and other exotic materials. Early in the century, the "new draperies", the lighter, finer cloths made in the Flanders region had made their appearance, challenging the cheaper local woollen cloths. Religious persecution in the Netherlands brought refugees to south east England, where Norwich gained a reputation for the new "bays, says and arras". By 1572 that city had fifteen hundred aliens and there were others at Colchester, including Dutch and Walloon workers. Better off people bought a variety of materials for clothing and for furnishing. Fashion became the "fantastical folly of the nation". A shop kept by James Backhouse at Kirkby Lonsdale in Westmoreland had Spanish silk, French garters, Norwich lace, Oxford gloves, and Turkey purses in 1578.[1]

T68 Yorkshire Drapers Making Wills.

early 16th century	Beverley 5, York 4, Hull 2, Barnsley, Helmsley, Selby, Wakefield, Doncaster, N. Cave, Thirsk, Pontefract, Malton
1554-1568	York 4, Beverley 3, Selby, Hull 3, Bridlington, Wakefield, Gembling
1568-1585	Cottingham, Beverley, York, Hull, Doncaster, Patrington, Ripon, Malton
1585-1594	Beverley 3, York 2, Sheffield 2, Malton 2, Wakefield, Bridlington, Doncaster

The drapers and mercers of the towns bought goods for resale, from merchant wholesalers and clothiers. They were themselves a kind of merchant. Beverley had a company of mercers and merchants. The Bell family of Thirsk, with burgages in Micklegate, Inglorygate and the Market Place were merchants and mercers. Yeoman Christopher Kettlewell tried to break into the trade at Selby, without having served an apprenticeship, "illicitly" trading in mercery for "his own profit". These traders often dealt in far more than the words mercer or draper might suggest. William Wray a Ripon mercer, bought supplies from wholesalers of York, Beverley, Coventry and Norwich, and sold them retail in his Ripon shop to town and countrymen, drawn from a ten mile radius. His stock expanded from cloth, lace, thread, ribbons, pins and buttons, into grocery, with dried fruit, spices, soap, sugar, and stationery.

Many Yorkshire drapers were men of substance. William Calame at York, Matthew Frank at Malton and John Gowland at Bridlington all expected to be buried inside their churches and not in the churchyard. Calame had tenements in Monkgate and Goodramgate at York and leases of others in Minstergarth, Petergate and Gillygate. He had wainscotted his dwelling house. Gowland was a man of property with five oxgang farmholds at Eston and Bridlington besides two cottages, two barns, a laithe and his kiln in Bridlington market place. Mathew Frank had wainscot round his Malton parlour in a well equipped house and could make several bequests of ten pounds each. He left a chest to his servant George Cowper, "once the writings and money had been taken out of it." John Smothing a Gembling draper, who stocked five yards of new frieze, bequeathed a book to Lady Hildyard. Beverley draper Richard Bell gave new made gowns of grey cloth to the needy.

Woollen draper Thomas Jackson of Bridlington had a hall equipped with an iron range, a brass warming pan, brass shovel and tongs, eight chairs and two stools. His parlour held a new oak table and a chair. Three chambers and a garret held feather beds. He had his own malt kiln, a load of manure in the garden, along with turkeys and hens. His stock of thirty firkins of butter may well have been for export to London or the northern coalfield. He had sixty pounds in shipping and a similar sum invested in forty-six pieces of broadcloth. Here was a rich man. The gross value of his inventory in 1626 was £1031.

There were mercers of a similar condition. Christopher Field left a memorial inside Wakefield church. Reginald Harrison a mercer of Stamford paid twenty shillings to take up the freedom at Sedbergh, in c1560, where he was soon on the governing body, known as the first twelve of the borough. Robert Swift the Rotherham mercer advanced his family. He and his wife Anne were remembered on a brass in the church choir. She died aged sixty-seven, he in 1561 at eighty-four years.

> "Here under this tomb are placed and buried
> the bodies of Robert Swifte Esq and Anne his first wife ,
> who lived many years in this town of Rotherham
> in virtuous fame, great wealth and good worship.
> They were pitiful to the poor and relieved them liberally
> and to their friends no less faithful than bountiful.

Bequests hint at the scale of stocks that such men held and sometimes show participation in both trade and manufacture. Mathew Frank's Malton chests held new gown cloth and a doublet cloth of myllane fustian unmade, pillane, calfskins, hose and shirts. William Dawson of Helmsley in 1557 left his father Robert the sale of six dozen caps, with night caps, which he bought at Beverley fair. The price was seven shillings for every dozen caps. He gave Geoffrrey Spensley and George Holiday a pair of capper's shears each, while his father had the rest of his working gear. Jeffrey Wadson of Helmsley left gown cloths of the best sad colour with lining, doublet cloth of black myllane fustian, doublet cloth, a pair of hose cloths of black russells, and another pair of hose cloths of white kersye. John Lemming the merchant draper of Pickering held the two acre Tenter Close, where cloths were hung to bleach. His son called himself a gentleman.

Clothes were a sign of social status and were becoming a means of enjoyment. The shopping expedition was being born. Pin money made its appearance. The third Lord Latimer left a thousand marks for his daughter Margaret' s preferment in marriage in 1542. When he added a nine year lease of Kirkdale parsonage, he said that this was "to buy her pinnes withall". We needn't take that too literally but pins had a new importance. The Earl of Rutland's steward in 1552 paid for a thousand small pins at a shilling and a hundred great pins at three pence. His Countess bought chamblet for women's gowns, Spanish lace, ribbons and hairpins.

Another Countess, twenty-five years later ordered tawny damask for her lords night-gown and gold buttons. The Rutland accounts show regular shopping. She would buy two satin night-caps for Mary, black cony skins for a night gown, and little rarities from Paris at the New Year of 1582-83. Starch was in great demand for ruffs. Other Puritans called starch "the devil's liquor." Lady Hoby at Hackness could write to her husband,

"Deare harte,

Let John Brown buy me at York or send it me by his boy, two pound of starch for I have not left."

Shop goods were as open to theft as those on street stalls. Francis Hill of Kilham complained that Isabel Benneson took a remlet of cloth and a remlet of white frieze out of his shop window. Her husband said his wife brought a remlet into the house but "how she came by it, he knew not." Jane Park took a whole smock and a pair of smock skirts. Matthew Elwick's servant took a web of scots cloth, a cheese and a yard of white carsye thread and resold them to several folk around the town of Scarborough. The hue and cry was raised. She pleaded that she had been persuaded into it. A friend advised her either to cut her own throat or jump in the sea and drown herself.

Grocers

The old guild craftsmen selling their own manufactures had enforced demarcation agreements. The new retailers were tempted to deal in anything which could make money, tending towards the general store. John Green at Glover lane off Petergate in York as early as 1525 offered a bird cage with a cord for twopence, along with a dozen pairs of gloves, bags and purses. The earliest specialised traders appeared for expensive cloths but also in smaller numbers for spices, wines and apothecary wares, where imports in bulk needed to be broken up for many small purchases. Merchants had long traded these wares but the quantities were growing.

Pepper, cinnamon, cloves, nutmeg and ginger were expensive luxuries imported from distant places. The westward movement of Spanish and Portuguese traders across the Atlantic increased supplies. The spice market moved from Venice to Lisbon, Antwerp and Amsterdam. Sugar, once kept for invalids, was eaten as a rich food and blackened the teeth. William Harrison in 1577 spoke of the groceries arriving in English ships, sugar available at 2s.6d a pound, currants or raisins at sixpence a pound, great raisins a penny for three pounds. Pepper was six pence to a shilling a pound but most spices were retailed by the ounce, cinnamon four pence, cloves twopence, ginger a penny and prunes three farthings.

Strange plants including potatoes and sweet potatoes, and some new medicinal and garden herbs, were coming from Ceylon, the Canary Isles, the Indies and the Americas. Yorkshire made its own contribution to the plants in demand for salads with the "mures to be had about Crosby Ravensworth", apparently meaning the sweet cicely. George Fenny the Darlington apothecary had home made preserves but also three boxes of conserve of barbaries, one pot of syrups, and a pot of cherries. John Johnson kept sugar loaves, white sugar, barbary sugar, brown sugar candy, white candy, great raisins, prunes, currants, and biscuits.[2] Several Scarborough merchants delivered sugar. Laurence Rawdon a York merchant trading wholesale grocery could supply two loaves of superfine sugar, weighing twelve pounds fourteen ounces, at twenty two pence the pound, the total sum £1.4s.9d., for the York Lord Mayor's civic gift to Lady Sheffield when she came to King's Manor in 1603.

Vintners and Taverners

The demand for wines was strong among the nobility, the gentry and the town middle class. The Earl of Shrewsbury had Rauf Barber hire carriages for conveying his wines from York to Sheffield castle. Thomas Ellis at Doncaster supplied the Earl's white wine and claret in 1561. Mrs Britten put so much wine and spirit in his venison pasties that they burst in transit. Wine imports combined with wool and later cloth exports, had been the bedrock of foreign trade into France since at least the 12th century. Wine was now brought from Gascony, Germany and the Canary Isles. High import duties and costs of transport made wines expensive. Sweet wines were popular, including sherry or sack, and malmsey from the Middle East. Sugar could be added along with such spices as coriander and savoury. Vintners imported wine by the tun and sold it in barrels, hogsheads, butts and pipes, directly to home buyers or to taverners, who bottled and sealed it for sale.

A few Yorkshire vintners made wills during the reign at York, Hull and Doncaster along with victuallers at York, Patrington, and Pontefract. Those active in the trade became more numerous, and appeared at the smaller towns. The word vintner may also have been used for taverners. The York vintners Thomas Greges and Richard Aynley petitioned the Corporation complaining of others taking up wine retailing, so that "unwholesome and corrupt wine" was being sold. The Council ordered the placing of a garland outside any house selling wine, so that new searchers could examine the wine from time to time.

A 1552 Statute sought to limit the number of taverns retailing wine, and required licensing by Justices or Corporations. It was argued that a recent increase in the number of taverns had made them the resort of misruled people. Those outside boroughs and market towns were to be suppressed. The penalty for failure was £10. London was allowed forty taverns, York eight, Hull four and some other substantial towns two. The London vintners won exemption in 1567 and had some provincial members. York and Hull were each allowed one extra in 1570. Only twenty-three taverns were officially listed in the county in 1574, but vintners are heard of in larger numbers than that. Sir Walter Raleigh was given the right to make licences for keeping of taverns and retailing of wines throughout England and sent his licensing deputies to York in 1583. Vintners would later appear at most major towns.

Wine was readily available throughout at York, Beverley, Hull and Scarborough. Their governing bodies made wine gifts to gentry to secure their influence and at the same time did not spare themselves. The Lady Mayoress of York watching a pageant on Corpus Christi Day in 1554 with the aldermen's wives had much ale, but also six gallons of clary wine and one pottell of sack. The Corporation gave Archbishop Hutton a butt of sack bought from wine merchant George Watkinson at £11.10s. in 1596 and in 1599 gave Lord Thomas Cecil a butt costing £16.10s. brought from the Canaries. Wine sales were not confined to the tavern.

Oliver Degle kept a "victualling end" at Scarborough in 1564. He was charged that over a year he had sold claret wine blended with honey "unwholesome for the Queen's people" at four pence a quart. A whole hogshead was discharged by the bailiffs. He had sold twelve quarts of sack at six pence a quart, contrary to statute. He had kept certain Flemynge in his house, and French wine at four pence the quart". A man of some enterprise, he locked quarts of claret in a chamber, which "did beat the Queen's watch" and he even mixed old and new herring. At the port, William Langdale, William Thompson, Gregory Paicock and Anthony Conyers were charged with selling claret blended with honey, while French wine was sold in the houses of John Fyshe, William Langdale and Thomas Lowson.

Camden thought that English troops campaigning in the Low Countries, with the Earl of Leicester in 1586 acquired the habit of gin or spirit drinking and brought this to England. The tradition gains strength from the phrase "Dutch courage" while Hollands or "hot waters" were popular names for gin. Brandy was spoken of as aqua vitae, or water of life. Spirits seem to have been prepared by distilling a wide range of things including the dregs of the mash tun. An aqua vitae house was known at Barking in 1572 and London had many distillers by 1600. A Yorkshire man J Carter in a will of 1600 left a pot for the stilling of aqua vitae.

T69 Some Elizabethan Vintners in Yorkshire

Scarborough	Richard Thompson
Doncaster	Nicholas Brand, Robert Hackney
Sheffield	Henry Swift, Edward Aproben, Hugh Sponer.
Tadcaster	William Aked
New Malton	Robert Peycock
Ripon	John Morton
Topcliffe	Edward Lockey
Bedale.	Edmund Wales. Luke Lodge
York	Christ Learmouth, Richard Ayneley, Peter Pulleyn, William Gilmyn, John Standeven, William Enrison, John White, George Hunter

Merchants

Gerard Malynes in 1622 wrote that "a merchant deals in the buying and selling of commodities. He deals in "all moveable things, for the back, the belly or the mind, except the holy" An Act of Parliament of 1552 had legalised buying to resell, once a highly suspect activity. The merchant usually traded wholesale and over long distances, exchanging money for commodities and commodities for money, but he didn't himself produce anything. He was several steps away from the man who took his own produce to market, but so were the chapmen, pedlars, badgers and a variety of other middlemen between buyers and sellers. Merchants commonly did a little retailing as well, in the place where they lived. Even the richest York merchants kept shops.[3]

An incomplete but interesting index of the changing location of the merchant community comes from the lists of those Yorkshire merchants leaving wills. Hull, York and Beverley were dominant, but traders at coastal and inland ports were being joined by others. Some merchants formed partnerships but these were rarely permanent. Family connection was more important. Whitby merchant Robert Bushell had his wife's brother dwelling at Newcastle, while John Baxter a merchant of Newcastle on Tyne in 1592 had a house between Baxtergate and Flowergate, at the Yorkshire port. Not all merchants traded to foreign parts, but those doing so had little legal protection. They employed family members quartered overseas or resident overseas factors, paid on commission or factorage, at two and a half per cent on sales and purchases.

The buying and selling of goods within the country may well have exceeded the external trade, but records are hard to find. Much trading moved outside the customary markets and fairs, into inns and taverns. There was important trade within the county. The cloth, cutlery, stocking making and other industrial areas needed grain. So did the graziers. This was gathered from several wapentakes and taken into York, and much was resold to West Riding buyers. Richmond merchants sold foodstuffs into the Dales. York was a populous city drawing on the Ainsty, Bulmer and Ouse and Derwent wapentakes for meat, dairy produce and grain. The city craftsmen and traders served much of the county. Coastal fish were widely resold by York fishmongers. Buttermen went to buy at Swaledale and Wensleydale and pinners to buy stockings at Richmond. Two York merchants brought cargoes from London to Hull in 1565-66 including soap, bedding, haberdashery, oil, wine, alum, currants and raisins.

T70 Yorkshire Merchants leaving Wills. 1500 - 1554

York 16; Hull 10; Scarborough 5, Bridlington 5; Howden 2, Whitby 2, Beverley 2, Yarm 1. York also recorded six fishmongers and Hornsey one, the first specialised merchants.

1554 - 1594

Hull 43, York 38; Beverley 12; Wakefield 3, Scarborough 2, Rotherham 2, Whitby 2, Bridlington 2; Doncaster 2; Birstall, Bessingby, Brampton, Halifax, Hatfield, Hedon, Ripon, Sheffield, Stokesley, Swainby and Wetherby.

It paid to travel, so that you were buying at the point of production. A Basle merchant Andreas Ryff, who did thirty trips a year said "I have had so little rest that the saddle has hardly stopped burning my hind parts". John Isham a Northamptonshire man, who traded from London had mostly bought West country cloth for export to Antwerp, but he regularly visited Halifax to collect "checked kerseys" and wool. He had connections with at least twenty-seven men in Yorkshire. Merchants needed storage, especially for cloth and skins. Leonard Conyers who had Bagdale Hall and the ship Isabel in 1593, also kept a shop and chamber in Whitby Market Place. Merchant Robert Bushell kept a barn at the south end of that town. The Scarborough mansion of merchant William Fish included a shop, a kiln, and a coal house. He had an orchard and he kept a cellar at Long Greece foot near the quay.

The merchant could be seen as a villain or as a hero. Many blamed the high price of commodities on an excess of English merchants, claiming that goods were cheaper when foreigners brought them. They deplored the export of our commodities and the covetous preferment of commodities from other countries, arguing that "all the water of commodity was like to run into their own cistern". Sugar had been four pence a pound but had risen to two shillings and sixpence and raisins once a penny were now sixpence to tenpence. Men were suspicious of the new mercantile spirit that was abroad, with many of "a greedy and covetous humour". A North Grimston gentlemen was charged with "abominable usury." Richard Barer was given the alias, "money God of Roucliffe".

T71 A Merchant's Epitaph; Thomas Legard of Bradford and Bawtry. 1632

"He that could travel through globe and sphere
and teach an expert pilot how to steer,
By card and compass, made by his own hand
To guide his journeys over sea and land
Now in this streate room Thos Ledgard lyes.
A grave rich merchant, provident and wise,
Who venturing for foreign merchandise
At Bradford borne, at Kingston, taught his trade,
His seat of residence at Bawtry made
From whence to heaven, he shall ere long arise.

The proverbial culture enshrined the new preoccupation with risk and reward. "Nothing venture, nothing have" said some, and others "Better one bird in the hand, than ten in the wood". There was caution in "Cut your cloak after your cloth", and in "Enough is as good as a feast", and "All covet, all lose", "A fool and his money is soon parted" and "soon gotten, soon spent". There was warning and there was reassurance.

"He that hath but little, he shall have less". "That penny is well spent that saveth a groat", and "Penny wise and pound foolish" but what of "Spend and God will send" and the wiser "Who so knew what would be dear, should need be merchant but one year".

The merchant's sense of hard won wealth, all too easily lost, and his suspicion of other money makers, came through in a combative testament from the Hull merchant William Gee. "Whereas in the Scriptures, the great God of heaven and earth has called the prophet to say to Hezekie the king to make his will and put things in order for that he must die, so I doe now pray and humbly beseech that great and mighty God to confound and destroy all those men, lawyers and others whosoever, to the devils in the pit of hell, which doth counsel or take upon them to alter this my will".

Merchants making money, turned themselves into gentry, by marrying the daughters of gentlefolk. Christopher Thompson of Scarborough married Isabel the daughter of gentleman Edward Hutchinson of Wykeham. Nicholas Bushell of Whitby wed the daughter of Sir Thomas Fairfax of Dunsley. They bought country manors. Scarborough merchant George Paycocke held Speeton manor as well as his Sandside house in the borough, and had invested in the tithes of Scalby parsonage. Merchant clothier John Armitage bought the site of Kirklees Priory. Whitby merchant Nicholas Bushell bought Bagdale Hall and houses on both sides of Grape Lane from Nicholas Conyers in 1595 and married Dorothy Cholmeley in 1601. Ruswarp Hall is said to have been built for the couple.

London merchant wealth went into conspicuous consumption. The younger wives, "in attire and costly housekeeping, cannot tell when and how to make an end", said Harrison. The male merchant's dress was very fine and costly but conventional, but their feasts had "all manner of delicate meats from every quarter of the country", comparable with those of the nobility. They had "jellies of all colours mixed with a variety of sundry herbs, flowers, trees, march pane, tarts of divers hues and sundry denominations, conserves of old fruits, foreign and homebred candied fruit, suckets, codinface, marmalades, sugar bread, gingerbread, florentines and sundry outlandish foreign confections, altogether seasoned with sugar."

The Yorkshire trader was sometimes judged by what he did with his money, rather than how he made it. Hull merchant John Lister, built Wilberforce House, set back twenty feet behind a brick wall. William Fish the Scarborough merchant wanted burial in the St Nicholas or fisherman's aisle under a great marble stone. There is an epitaph for Robert Dawson, buried at Ripon minster, in 1592.

> "His nature mild, his mind devout,
> His wealth the poor well fed.
> So dead, he lives in spite of death,
> And grave his fatal bed.
> Whom lately Sheriff, merchant, free,
> York's wealthy city had,
> And farmer, chief of Ripon church,
> now Ripon mould hath clad".

Sir William Craven of Burnsall near Skipton, a London merchant tailor, founded London and Yorkshire charities. He was the first to conceive the idea of a Yorkshire University, which he would have sited at Ripon. George Saville grew rich in the wool trade and founded Wakefield Grammar School. He was a "Blackwell Hall man", a merchant selling woollen cloth at the Basinghall Street Hall, near London Guildhall much visited from Wakefield. He died in 1593. William Gee, a Leicestershire man who came to Hull, after fifty years, had been mayor three times. He founded the hospital in Chapel Lane. He gave £80 and twenty thousand bricks to rebuild Alcock's Grammar school. He spent £150 repairing the church, £200 on a market house to store corn, and £1000 on the hospital. John Lowden of London gave a large sum to make loans to Yorkshire carriers. Richard Townend of Blacker who began getting rushes, and setting "sprentes" for birds, gave forty shillings a year for ever to the poor of Worsbrough near Barnsley, from his £1000 estate.

Sir John Ferne, writing for his "Blazon of Gentrie", thought it "wrong for persons engaged in trade, to be granted coats of arms". claiming that "merchandising is no competent or seemly trade of life, for a gentleman". He over stated the divide. You needed money to make more money. Many sons of the gentry sought fortune in trade. The Yorkshire merchant dynasties had names which often betokened gentry origins. Tristram Conyers of Long Westgate, Scarborough was a merchant but of an ancient gentry line. He acquired the manor of Cleeton in marriage to Londoner Richard Cotton's daughter. Many a town business carried such names as Conyers, Mennell, Percy, Saville and their like.

Noblemen and gentry were much involved in trade. Gentlemen held shares in trading companies and lent out money at interest. Indeed, money lending and borrowing is evident in inventories at many levels of Elizabethan society. The Queen's cousin Matthew Earl of Lennox and the Countess Margaret were licensed to buy four hundred scardells of wool at three sacks per scardel and to sell or ship them, paying the Queen five marks the sack. Lord Robert Dudley was licensed to buy a thousand sarplers of wool for three years to process, sell and export, at three sacks to the sarpler. Lord Hunsdon was licensed to buy twenty thousand kerseys for export. The Earl of Cumberland had a patent for exporting cloth and the letters show that he had shipped twelve hundred cloths in one year.

Coastal and Overseas Trade

The main thrust of the Yorkshire export trade was to countries, where we could sell woollen cloth, often to foreign ports whose merchants could take it further afield. The cloth was exported into north west Europe, Germany and the Baltic, even to the Mediterranean. These shipments in large part paid for the widening variety of imports, including groceries, the new draperies, spices, glassware, alum, dyes and wines, received coastwise through London and Baltic raw materials brought in by both native and foreign vessels. The merchants specialising in West Riding cloth, bought directly from their suppliers, at cloth fairs and eventually at cloth halls at Leeds, Halifax and Wakefield There were regular despatches to London for the weekly Blackwell Hall cloth market and to the Smithfield annual cloth fair. When Hull was ordered to fit out a ship for the Crown in 1595, they asked the Privy Council for an order that the three great and rich clothing towns, of Halifax, Leeds and Wakefield, merchants and vendors of cloth, should contribute, being as much interested in the port as its inhabitants.

Hull's foreign trade expanded from mid century. The number of vessels loading and unloading rose in the sixties, as more of the cheap coarse woollens came through from the West Riding. Twenty or more Hull ships went annually to Zealand in the sixties. Hull vessels sailing into the Baltic reached twenty a year, challenging the control of trade by the Hanseatic League. The northern kerseys going from Hull to the Baltic rose six fold between 1565 and 1585, and kept expanding. Ships exporting kerseys returned laden with flax or corn. Several hundred tons of flax came in annually after the seventies. More Baltic and Norwegian ships entered the port with flax, pitch and tar. Tsar Ivan had taken over Narva and some York and Hull merchants opened a trade with the Russians. There were good years and bad. Decay of trade was reported at Hull in 1575 and again in 1585.

T72 Origin of Ships entering Hull from abroad in 1567

Scotland	43
Low Countries	41
France	16
Danzig, Elbing, & Konigberg	14
Spain	4
North Baltic	4
White Sea & Arctic	4
Norway	3

York merchants shipped whatever they could wherever it was profitable to do so. Some lead still came down river. The town had specialist corn merchants, buying in one district to sell in another. A sermon preached in the Minster in 1595 seemed to say that corn profiteering was a sin next to usury. Barley was brought to York for resale in 1567. Much trade was done through the port of Hull. York merchants took foodstuffs to Berwick and Newcastle and brought coal back to Hull. They sent corn and cloth to Emden in Friesland, returning with soaps, hops and other merchandise in 1571. Baltic iron and flax reached the city. Richmond merchants traded lead, moved from Swaledale by pack horse to Low Worsall on the river Tees or to Richmond and Boroughbridge and by river to York and Hull.

T73 Bridlington Harbour tolls. 1591

Farthing	cwt. of hemp, cwt. of beeswax, cwt. of coneyskins
Half penny	quarter of corn, malt, grain, piece of broad cloth, barrel of pitch, of tar, of apples, of onions, etc. 1000 of turfs
Penny	100 of small firspars, barrels of almonds, soap, butter, oil, meal, herring, packet of hops, hogshead of wine, 1000 staves
Penny halfpenny	ton of iron, last of flax
Twopence	100 of fish, weigh of salt
Threepence	100 of firdeals, small fir balks, great fir spars, cwt of wainscot, last of other goods sold by weight, also charged on every ship entering
Sixpence	100 of great fir balks

The revival of a market at Seamer was blamed for some decay of Scarborough trade although barley and malt were shipped to Newcastle. Witnesses from both places agreed that Scarborough was declining in manufactures, shipping and trade. They disagreed about the cause. A royal proclamation licensed the export of corn from the East Riding as prices of corn were low in 1565-6. In 1577-8 eleven winter sailings from Bridlington took out 552 quarters of malt, 477 quarters of barley, and 32 quarters of other grains. This trade was kept up in later years, much going to Newcastle. The inwards traffic at Bridlington was almost all colliers from the north east coal field. Thirty-six vessels brought five hundred and sixty seven chaldrons in 1593-4. Modest quantities of wood, cloth, iron, tar, hemp, flax, beeswax, apples, onions, wine and salt reached the ports.

The Yorkshire Privateer

Spain had formed a highly profitable trading empire across the Atlantic in the new world of America. They were as determined to keep others out as English mariners were determined to break into this trade. As relationships between the countries deteriorated, English privateering was launched as a form of licensed piracy, or commercial war. George, Earl of Cumberland, a man at the peak of Yorkshire society became an out standing organiser and financier of privateering voyages, several of which he led himself. A letter of 1589 describing one voyage, said that they had gone out to "pilfer:" Aubrey said that the Earl had succeeded to his estate in 1570 while very young and "having run through a great part of his very handsome property, he seized on the opportunity of the Spanish war to re-establish himself."

These expeditions went beyond the seizure of foreign shipping. Large numbers of men were carried, small armies, which were landed to seize, steal and ransom whatever could be found. These were business enterprizes, aimed at making a maximum profit. The costs were high, the investment sometimes shared, the risks considerable and the profits on voyages ranged from nothing to vast sums. Between 1586 and 1598 he fitted out ten expeditions, sometimes sailing himself, and conducting some at his own expense. Cumberland was not aboard for the voyage of 1592 when the Queen took heavily from the gains but allowed him a gift of £36.000.

The Earl had some of the largest ships afloat put at his disposal as troop carriers. He took the large royal ship Golden Lion one year, and the Victory on the next voyage. The crew numbered four hundred, and it took over £600 a month to keep Victory at sea. The Queen's ship Garland of 666 tons burthen carried a crew of three hundred and cost £455 in wages and victuals each month in 1591. The ships attacked were mostly merchantmen easily overwhelmed. The cargoes taken were a matter of chance. There were ships laden with Newfoundland fish, valuable cargoes of pepper, ginger and cinnamon, of sugar, wine and oil and Brazilian woods. Cumberland's land campaigns were brief, hasty attacks on lightly defended towns, sometimes with heavy casualties on both sides.

The voyages had all the sense of "adventure" and discovery that fired some English hearts. While anchored for supplies off Sierra Leone in 1586, the men secured an alligator, nine foot long which bowed a sword put in its mouth. They found its back too hard for a sword to penetrate. They burnt a village and stole foods laid out for "idols". They found some women on another voyage, who used tobacco to dye their faces red to make them seem "young and fresh". Contrary winds and lack of nautical knowledge stopped them putting into Ireland in 1589, when a crew held off their thirst by eating hailstones, sucking rainy napkins and putting bullets in their mouths.

CHAPTER 8
TRANSPORT

Travellers

Most people made their short journeys on foot. Long distance travellers were relatively few but they were varied and growing in number. Students went to the Grammar Schools, Universities and Inns of Court. Lawyers, litigants and circuit judges travelled to county towns. Stewards, bailiffs and rent collectors toured the great estates. Chapmen, pedlars and buyers went to the markets and fairs. Fish were walked inland from the coast and cattle drovers took beasts from rearing grounds to lusher pastures for fattening. Church officers went to meetings while higher officials made visitations. The sick went to the healing waters at Bath, Buxton and Knaresborough, and probably many another old holy well, still valued as medicinal. Courtiers, members of Parliament, noblemen and migrants sought out the ways to London. The travelling poor were most numerous of all.

Although the majority of travellers were pedestrians, horse and carriage traffic was increasing. Royalty and the nobility travelled in some style and with changing fashions of ostentation. Princess Margaret rode northwards for her marriage to James of Scotland in July 1503 on "a fair palfrey", followed by two footmen, but with one very rich litter, which could be carried on "two fair coursers, very nobly dressed". She moved from palfrey to litter on entering good towns, or at her pleasure. She was met by noblemen, Lords Latimer, Scrope, Conyers and Percy, with their retainers, along the route. The entourage included a "car", carrying four court ladies, led by six horses and three men. Cardinal Wolsey under arrest at Cawood had travelled with horses and a mule.

Henry Clifford, raised to the Earldom of Cumberland in 1526, rode from Skipton to London with an entourage of thirty-three servants, at a cost of £7.15s.1d. A later Countess took eleven days, on the journey from London to Londesborough, with thirty-two horses, c1640, the expenditure £69.18.9. Archbishop Grindal left London for York on August 1st .1570. He was not much used to horses. Two days later, he was struck with ague and had to rest for ten days before arriving at Cawood on August 17th. He complained of his reception although Sir Thomas Gargrave, Mr Watterton, Mr Saville and four or five others had met him at Doncaster. Mr Aske of that town and Mr Hungate of Saxton took him on to Cawood. The Earl of Huntington as Lord President levied twenty-six horses from York for his journey to Hull in 1573.

Travel for leisure was not unknown. The Abbot of Rievaulx had been wont to visit his Skiplam grange in summer every year, with six or eight monks to hunt and hawk. Great noblemen readily rode to their more distant parks, where new lodges offered accommodation. They moved from one house to another, to let their residences "sweeten", often taking considerable quantities of furnishings, furniture and supplies. Pilgrimage journeys to shrines had once been extensive, often a kind of holiday traffic, in every sense. This had largely ceased, although a Jesuit called Garnett would take

1 LITTER
2. TUDOR CARRIAGE
3 ARMY ON THE MARCH
4 PILLION RIDING.
5. STATE COACH (FROM OLD PRINT)
6 COUNTRY WAGGON
7. STATE BARGE.

14 Tudor Modes of Travel
From 'The Story of Tudor & Stuart Britain' by C W Airne

thirty catholics to St Winifred's, Flint in 1605, nine days each way, over 300 miles, to stay one night.

Gentry and gentry wives visited each other. Mutual hospitality was part of their living standard, providing opportunities for impressive display and shared leisure. Lady Margaret Hoby made short journeys around Hackness, in her carriage, to have talk with her neighbours. She went further to have company with old friends at Linton, her birthplace on the Wolds. She welcomed the Lord President Thomas Cecil to her Hackness Hall in 1601, fresh from visiting Scarborough and Mr. Edward Gate's house at Seamer. Next year she journeyed to stay at Snape Castle, calling on the way on Mr Vaughan at Byland Abbey and Mr. Norcliffe at Nunnington Hall. The 1598 "Book of Serving Men" advised that "if mistress ride abroad, six to eight were to attend, one to carry cloak and hood against rain, one the fan, one a box of necessaries, one to open the gate". A new invention called a coach could reduce the need for so many attendants.

A good horse brought places closer together. Foot soldiers were assumed to make twenty miles a day. Ten miles an hour was common for a horseman on a good road. Sir Robert Carey made a famous ride from London to Edinburgh on 25th March 1603 to give the Scots King James news of his good fortune. This took him 162 miles to Doncaster on the first day. Another ride of 170 miles took him to Berwick and then more to Widdrington. Professional messengers made long journeys and others were taken on for a particular task. John Skaife was a King's and Queen's messenger at York in 1555. The Pickering court accounts recorded "the wages for a man riding from Pickering to Pontefract to give notice to the ministers there of the coming of the audit, as allowed in the preceding years, 3s.4d". Local guides were hired to cross difficult areas like Blackamoor.

Regular posting services needed relays of horses at regular intervals for post riders. They appeared slowly along major roads. York paid John Trew fourteen shillings for the charges of six men and thirteen horses at Pontefract conducting six horses to London in 1569-70. High costs obliged York to reduce its eight post horses to four that year but it was agreed to raise the number to six, to be kept at the charge of the city in 1580. Thomas Randolph as master of the post issued instructions for the post from London to the Northern borders in 1584, charging 2d a mile. Posting routes came off the North road at Northallerton, Thirsk, Easingwold, York and Ferrybridge. Five York men were fined two shillings each for failure to provide post horses for the Countess of Huntingdon at her departure in 1585. A Mr. Brewster was appointed public letter carrier at Scrooby in 1590.

Care of luggage was always a problem. James Knight, a Scot voyaging from Scarborough to Flamborough gave Margaret Thompson custody of his silver whistle and chain, two pair of worsted stockings, half a pound of pepper, his girdle, knife and sheath, and a pair of corked shoes in a chest. Fitzherbert provided verses to help a gentleman's servant not to forget his master's gear at the inn, when they took horse.

> "Purse, dagger, cloak, night-cap, kerchief, shoeing horn, boget and shoes
> Spere, maler, hods, halter, saddlecloth, spores, hat with thy horse comb
> Bow, arrows, sword, buckler, horn, leash, gloves, string and thy bracer.
> Pen, paper, ink, parchment, reedwaxe, pommes, books, thou remember
> Penknife, comb, thimble, needle, thread, point, lest that they gurth break
> Bodkin, knife, lyngel, give they horse neat, so he be showed well
> Make merry, sing and thou can; take heded to they gear that thou loose none"

There was much clandestine traffic overseas, especially by Catholics, who often returned to Flamborough, or the better-known ports. The State required port bailiffs and inland justices to keep a watch for politically suspect travellers. Sir Robert Carr was expected by sea at Bridlington in 1598 and arrangements were made to catch him. The next year, a Nottinghamshire woman, who had met the exiled Earl of Westmoreland at Brussels, landed at Scarborough from Scotland, stayed a night at Widow Constable's house, and next day journeyed to Ness in Ryedale. They brought their son from St. Omer, where he had been two years at a Roman Catholic school.

Tourists

The English traveller, journeying for the pleasure taken in things seen and heard, made his appearance in Queen Elizabeth's reign. Such visitors already showed some familiar characteristics of the tourist role. John Leland early in the century and William Camden toured the north to gather information for their pioneering descriptions of the country. Leland noted such northern "attractions" as the "stony serpents" found at Whitby, said to be crusted over with stone as a result of the prayers of the Abbess Hilda in the 7th century. There were more bullet like stones at Huntcliff containing headless serpents, and stones like sea creatures on Richmondshire hilltops, thought to be signs of Noah's Deluge. Camden was even more impressed by the ammonites of the Cleveland coast, "great stones of several sizes, so exactly formed round by nature, that one would think them bullets cast by some artist for the great guns, for if you break them, you find within stony serpents wreathed up in circles but generally without heads". John Speed was satisfied that the sea had once been on top of the mountains.

Like any tourist today, Camden noted the old castles at Mulgrave, Kilton park, Skelton, Wilton, Kildale and Danby, along with ruinous Whorlton and Harlsey, as he rode across Cleveland. Further south, he found Pickering, Ayton, Slingsby, Gilling, Sheriff Hutton, and Hinderskelfe castles. The Englishman's love of ruins was being born, roused by some sense of mystery and vanished power. At Thirsk he found nothing of the castle, "besides the ramparts". Richmondshire brought castles at Bolton, Middleham, Snape, Tanfield, Richmond, Hornby, Topcliffe and Bowes but Ravensworth was just a high wall and ruins. There was the strong castle at Sheffield, and others at Conisbrough, Tickhil and Almondbury. Local informants claimed that Doncaster still had part of an old tower supposedly destroyed by fire in the year 759.

There was Robin Hood's Bay, with its community, named if not founded by "a kind and obliging robber", Robin Hood's tomb on the great north road, and a dozen Robin Hood's butts and woods around the county. The burial place of the giant Wade was near Mulgrave, between two stones, seven foot high and twelve foot apart. There were the monasteries, fast sinking to ruin and such curiosities, and historic sites as the scene of the battle of Myton, the cross left by the first Anglo Saxon bishop Paulinus at Dewsbury and Hatfield Chase, "where there was special good deer hunting" amid the often flooded areas of Dichemarsh and Marshland. That other main plank of modern tourism, the country house already attracted attention to the family seats at Sowerby, Breckonbrough, Sezzay, the house of the Savilles at Thornhill and many more.

Men loved a marvel but "travellers tales" were already suspect. "A traveller may lie with authority," said the proverb. James Ryther, exploring new ground, found a cave in a rock called "Arthur's Rock" in Lord Cumberland's wood at Giggleswick, reached by a long entry, the forepart like a great door. The old Brigantian capital at Aldbrough daily yielded coins and antiquities of a great city. Not far off, there were "stones like pyramids", which we call the Devil's Arrows. Smith's "Wonders of England" were the baths at Bath, the circle at Stonehenge, the deep caves at the Peak, the Cheshire and Worcestershire salt pits, London bridge and St Paul's church, but he included the Dropping Well at Knaresborough. This turned objects into stone in nine or ten months, if placed in the steadily dripping water, laden with lime. Drayton wrote of Giggleswick "where one a fountain can show, that eight times in a day is said, to ebb and flow."

A scattering of foreign visitors to England recorded their impressions. French travellers were given an escort to Tadcaster Bridge in 1561. A party of Scots visitors came to York in 1583. Meanwhile foreign travel, combined with paid residence at great houses or inns, was seen as an educational experience for young English nobles and knights. A licence was needed to leave the country. France and Italy were favoured and it was famously remarked that "Germany is not the place to acquire the accomplishments of a gentleman". Young Hoby, through the summer of 1548, and until the next spring, was between Padua and Venice, ostensibly improving his Latin, and attending lectures in the humanities, civil law and logic. He met fourteen other Englishmen there and another thirteen elsewhere in Italy. Gilbert Talbot and Henry Cavendish in 1571 found that they couldn't live "so good cheap in France as they lived in Italy".

Those who made a European tour brought back Italian and French influences on their fencing, horsemanship, tennis, billiards and cards, even the single voice singing which would relegate polyphony to the church. Others visited continental spas for their health and would revive those of England. Edward Manners made a tour of Europe in 1571 starting from Calais during which he saw the alum works near Rome. Ralph Eure travelled abroad in 1582-3. George Wandesford was licensed to travel for three years, with Richard Kenyon his schoolmaster and a single servant in May 1597. William Eure son of Lord Eure was licensed in 1599 to travel for three years with two servants, three horses and £60.

Sir William Cecil wrote rules for the conduct and guidance of the Earl of Rutland travelling abroad. A local man Henry Belassis of Newbrough Priory had travelled enough overseas and in his own country by 1657, to claim that England was famous for mountains, bridges, fountains, churches, women and wool. By then, the fountains were becoming known as spas, with medicinal waters "to put into yourselves or you into them". English women were "the fairest on earth". He repeated the advice of Saint Boniface that they had better not go on Pilgrimage to Rome" lest they lure men from the purpose of pilgrimage"[1]

The Travelling poor

An increasing number of poor people travelled for more mundane reasons. They moved to seek the means of survival, either in employment, in charity or to return to their place of origin. A system which had helped the travelling poor had ceased with the abolition of monastery gate houses and hostelries and most of the mediaeval hospitals which had provided a port of call for an overnight stay. Some of the numerous hospitals and other maison dieus in the county had other responsibilities for the sick, the elderly and the poor, but many had offered the traveller some food and accommodation. Together they formed a network of lodgings where the indigent stayed a while and moved on. Only a few survived the dissolution as local almshouses. St. Mary's Abbey

York, Bridlington Priory and other monasteries had been obligated by their founders to provide daily charity at the gate. This had ceased. The sanctuary rights of a few churches, especially Beverley, Ripon and Flamborough, had assisted some others who had committed offences. These had been largely curtailed and would soon be abolished altogether.

Help for poor travellers was still regarded by some as a Christian duty. The clergy still had obligations to provide "hospitality". Broken meats were offered at gentry gatehouses to those who gathered there. One of the best reasons for having a gatehouse separate from the great mansion was to keep the vagrant poor at arm's length. Attitudes hardened as the poor increased. Their appearance on the road could seem threatening. Parliament ordered whippings for fencers, bear wards, common players of interludes, minstrels not belonging to persons of great degree, jugglers, pedlars, tinkers and petty chap men, wandering without licences from justices.

The manor court at Acomb near York took action against locals who harboured any strange women in their houses "being with child", or who entertained vagabonds, suspected persons and pedlars, without the constables consent. Poor people on the move appeared in parish after parish. Two men and a wife taken as vagrant rogues at Kirby Underdale were whipped and sent to Bishop Wilton, whence they had come unpunished in June 1578. A child of Robert Allanson, a Craven beggar was baptised at Thorp Arch in August 1600. Richard Hyrste died near Haycross on Linley moor in snow during February 1568.

A license to beg issued to a Crayke man in 1576, and signed by three justices of the peace and three esquires was addressed to "all Christian people". "The bearer hereof John Lawson, labourer, our Christian brother and neighbour has been visited with long sickness and who has a great sort of poor children and nothing to live upon, but only his handy labour, besides other his misfortunes of the death and loss of the few goods and chattels which he had, being brought to great misery and much indebted, is hereby licensed to travel through the wapentakes of Skyrack and Claro in the West Riding of the County of York for the space of one whole year, to collect the charitable alms of well disposed people". Christians were urged to help and ministers to persuade their parishioners.

A new group of travellers were the "Egyptians" thought to have reached England in the 15th century. One Paul Fa, a native of Egypt, was pardoned for the murder of another Egyptian in 1537. He and other wandering associates were required to leave the realm. A John Faw was in Scotland in 1540, and some others moved from Scotland to England by 1559. Gipsies were apprehended in Oxfordshire in 1562. Joseph Davye an Egyptian was baptised at Leeds in 1567. Elizabeth daughter of Anthony Smawleye in 1572 and John son of John Jackson "an Egyptian. Robert Hue, "egiptia" was at Pickering in 1573. Agnes daughter of "a certain gypsy" was baptised at Wragby in 1574. Philip Bastian of Scarborough joined vagrants called Egyptians for a month in 1579. Gipsies were watched at Sheffield in 1595. Others loitered at Ugthorpe in 1637.[2]

Roads

The greatest movement was local, made by people on foot within the townships, from village farms to fields, commons, meadows and woods in the common field country or around the scattered farms of the dales. People walked wherever they wanted to go, even though horses were becoming more numerous. A husbandman might ride to market, with his wife on pillion behind him but cattle, sheep and other stock had to be driven. A ragged star of ways and paths ran from each village into the fields and meadows, for cultivation and cropping, to sheep washes and watering places, to the mill to grind malt or corn, and reaching beyond, they served as drove ways to moor and carr pastures, and to the places where timber, peat, turf, rushes and litter could be found.

The dale townships, made up of scattered farmsteads, had a different pattern, with individual farm paths, sometimes a low circuit path linking farms together round a dale but with other entry routes to the dales from high moor ways that didn't touch the farmsteads. The greater manors, monasteries and churches had converted some local ways into modest arterial routes, joining a lord's hall and court to his demesne woods and parks, linking an abbey to its granges, or connecting the out townships to their parish church, for baptisms, marriages, burials and church festival services, or the delivery of produce and stock into the tithe barn. Norman boroughs and market villages had opened a few new roads but most traffic from their hinterlands flowed along ancient routes.

The great through roads were often the ancient "king's highways", which, linking the market towns, carried much of the longer distance movement of earlier times, and which had been given a legal status. A through road never existed in isolation. It had destinations and feeder roads. The main Yorkshire roads of Elizabeth's reign had not been planned as a system. They were old roads, adapted to present needs. The inheritance included prehistoric tracks and some paved Roman roads, among the "king's highways", and other "magna vias" or great ways and common ways of the Middle Ages. They were supplemented by fresh drover's ways across old commons, seeking rough pasture and avoiding the traffic and tolls of better known low roads.

Harrison attributed the great Fosse, Watling, Ermine and Icknield ways to the Romans. A number of Yorkshire roads were called Watling Street. The northward tending Ermine Street had come up through the spine of Lincolnshire, crossed the Humber, swept northward through the East Riding to Stamford bridge and on northwards, a direct route through Easingwold, Thirsk and Yarm towards Scotland. The Great North Road paralleled it on the western side of the Vale of York. William Vavasour of Hazlewood recorded the road, as it was in the time of King Henry VIII, through the fifty miles of the vale, over the two Don rivers at Doncaster, the Aire at Ferrybridge, the Wharfe at Wetherby, the Nidd at Walshford, the Ure at Boroughbridge, the Swale at Topcliffe and the Tees at Newsham. This simple dual system, directed towards the northern borders, had been given bye-roads that led to the great fortress and civil town of York.

Many more roads in Elizabethan Yorkshire had once formed the core of the Roman road network, but this had been much altered. A good number were called streets but a "street" road now often showed little more Roman than its name. The word implied paving but on a good natural well drained surface there hadn't always been the need. Paving by people later than the Romans cannot be entirely excluded although evidence is scanty. Many Roman streets remained important through routes, including the Malton Street which crossed the Thirsk-Stamford road south of Birdforth, heading west across the country.

Where ancient metalling showed boldly as a raised way, sometimes due to land shrinkage on either side, the word causeway was used, but short causeways had been made in more recent times, or old ones improved, near major towns and bridges. The causeway from Great Habton and Barugh towards York was a stretch of the Roman road still known as Wade's causeway. Robert Clay in 1502 made a bequest to the Pickering midsyke causey, an unexceptional road in low ground, of no obvious purpose. Others were at Crathorne in Cleveland and Rawmarsh in Strafforth wapentake. Scarborough's stony causeway, sometimes called the Burh Head causeway, ran from Crossgates in Seamer to the castle rock but the town had another unlocated low causeway.

Hallamshire had the "long causey" from Sheffield over Stanedge into the Hope valley and to Buxton, along a Roman Road line, which followed the ridge along Hallamgate and ascended west into Derbyshire.[3] Leland found that the four miles of low ground between Cottingham and Hull had two miles of "causeyway", diked on both sides. He noticed, "the great causeway from Skip bridge towards York", which "hath nineteen bridges, on for avoiding and overpassing cars coming out of the moors". He said that it was made by Mayor Blackburn, with another causeway "without the suburbs of York", perhaps that which linked Micklegate bar with a watering place beyond St James Chapel. Another York "causey" outside Layerthorpe postern led towards the "great causey" in Heworth moor, which was repaired in 1576-7.

The old streets, and causeways would be supplemented by paved trods of single stones set at stepped intervals, or in continuous lines, for pack horses in Blackamoor and in the Pennines. They are sometimes spoken of as causeways in south Yorkshire but trods elsewhere. These flagged paths gave surer footing on hill slopes and in boggy valley ground. Much interest attaches to the causeways and trods. All are of unknown date and some could have been laid down during the Elizabethan expansion of horsed traffic, to carry the products of industry and farming. More research is needed to determine who could have financed their construction and when. Some cross manor, township and parish boundaries, making those bodies unlikely financiers.

Many roads were earthen or grass grown. Country roads over open ground were little more than the route the traveller chose to follow, a right of passage rather than any sure footing. Repeated use, even by sheep, could make a road of sorts and many of the most used tracks on sloping ground became worn in as hollow ways, in parallel series, several feet deep. They can be seen yet, near Eston Nab in Cleveland, above Ampleforth in Ryedale and along the Thurkilsti in Blackamoor. The high moor might offer a ridge way, on firm dry limestone ground, slightly in lee of the crest, and romanticised in the folk lore with such names as Beggars Way, Old Wife's trod, or the Hambleton Street. Their line was often well marked by prehistoric burial mounds, "man" stones and mediaeval crosses, the one visible from the next, making effective way marks. Some were known as "great ways", like one above Rosedale east side, and another rising up Cropton's Fall Rigg. Such roads saw no repair.

There was a rich language of the road. A vast number of tracks carried ancient names, most often ending in "gate". These names usually specified some present or past use, or the destination or character of the road. There were sties for uphill paths, and both wendings and loanings for hedged ways, rising from a valley to higher ground. Egton had a "steean loaning". Long distance routes are suggested by such names as the "lane called hullerbusk or Whitby loaning" miles from that town at the top of Commondale beck in 1577, by "Scarborough street" and Pocklington gate at distant Fimber on the Wolds and a "Scarborough road" recorded in remote Nunburnholme in the 17th century.

Measured miles differed from reckoned miles, by an excess of about one third. Holinshed in 1577 described the method of reckoning a mile by the turns of a wagon wheel, which could make a mile less than seventeen hundred yards. Aubrey wrote of the "Yorkshire way bit" the wee bit extra, an overplus in the reckoning. His advice to travellers in Yorkshire was that on being told there was "So many miles and a way bit" left to go, you had better assume a journey rather longer than you had expected. Travel lore had other local elements. "Cleveland in the clay, bring in two soles and carry one away" and the Craven saying that it is twelve miles to Slaideburn from anywhere. Perhaps some southern critic produced the saying "Shake a saddle over a Yorkshireman's grave and he will rise up and steal a horse".

Harrison gave the mileages for the Berwick, York and London Road, as Berwick to Darlington thirteen, Northallerton four, Topcliffe seven, York sixteen, Tadcaster eight, Wentbridge twelve, Doncaster eight, Tuxford eighteen, Newark ten, Grantham ten, Stamford sixteen, Stilton twelve, Huntingdon nine, Royston fifteen, Ware twelve, Waltham eight, and London twelve. Smith listed some other highways that focused on the city, notably York to Tadcaster eight, Wentbridge twelve, Doncaster seven, Mansfield twenty, Nottingham twelve. He gave the road York to Wetherby seven, Otley thirteen, Bradford six, Halifax six, Blackstone edge six, Rochdale six, Manchester eight, Northwich sixteen and on to Chester twelve miles.

It is difficult to assess which roads attracted greater use. A Quaker 17th century map showed the Great North Road but strongly indicated another northward tending road, much further west, going from Bolsover to Rotherham, Barnsley, Halifax Riston or Bolton, Kirkby Ravensworth, and Barnard castle, with distances marked. The same road is also on a map of c1644.

We get some idea of the roads that they thought important when justices insisted on the repair of some king's highways in the 16th and early 17th centuries. They were not always those which we would expect. The king's highways of Ryedale, included roads linking Sinnington-Keldholme-Kirkby Moorside(1607); Hovingham-Stonegrave carr - Helmsley; (1605) York- Stanegrave way- Kirkby Moorside (1605) and York - North Ings - Kirkby Moorside. Further afield the road ran from New Malton to Scarborough ran by Foulbridge gate instead of through Yedingham. The road from Helmsley to Easingwold went through Ampleforth. The West Riding justices were much concerned with changes in the routes of several king's highways, in one case at least, because of constables charges for carrying cripples on the road. The whole subject needs detailed research.

T74 Some West Riding Highway Reviews by Quarter Sessions
Ferrybridge - Knottingley, Cridlinge, Womersley, Stubbs Walden, Norton, Campsall, Burghwallis, Skellowe, and on the ancient way direct to Doncaster.
Leeds – Roundhay Road, Wetherby, Thorern, Bramham, Tadcaster, York
Leeds Wikebrigg, Seacroft, Kiddall, York
magna via, Halifax-Clarke Bridge, Halifax Old Bank, Beacon Hill, Wakefield, York
Brotherton causeway was decayed running towards Ferrybridge in 1629

Passage Tolls

Road tolls known as "gatelaw" and "cheminage" had been levied on travellers, in forest and other districts, by a few lords of manors, either to limit traffic or to generate income. Some of the old tolls were still valuable. The Master of the Game in Galtres Forest or his lessee, levied gatelaw or cheminage at six shillings for twenty horses, four pence for twenty cattle, two pence for twenty sheep, threepence for every packhorse, and four pence for a wain, during the fence month, a period set aside ostensibly for the protection of the deer and two pence at other times. The foresters took a further four pence a wain, and a half penny for a horse load heading through the forest for York. The city prohibited gatelaw or "guidelaw" in its own liberties and suburbs.

The major towns levied a variety of tolls, which increased as traffic required greater expenditure on road maintenance. York took tolls on coal wains taken through the Micklegate bar. Tolls could be difficult and costly to collect and needed to generate incomes in excess of the collector's wage. The gatelaw in Pickering Forest was not demanded after 1592, because the toll collector was "like to be slain" and one had been. Barwick was leased in 1611 with all the tolls for cheminage. Some tolls were leased separately, and could make a good investment. The Archbishop farmed out the profits of the fairs and market at Ripon, including toll and stallage. Francis Arthington of Tadcaster assigned his lease of Ripon tolls to Miles Staveley in 1597.

Borough burgesses commonly enjoyed toll freedoms in other boroughs by ancient charter grants, but such freedoms were sometimes swept aside. Gabriel Drybeck of Hull was sued before the Council in the North for seizing a Hedon man's beef and mutton, after he failed to pay the tolls. The council decreed that inhabitants of Hedon were toll free at Hull, paying nothing, even when they took their own stalls to Hull market. The Ripon toll collector was brought to book for distraining goods of Leeds inhabitants bringing wool packs through the town. The Leeds men were toll free. When a wain load of peas or beans was taken through the water or over the bridge at Boroughbridge in 1578, its master paid a four penny through-toll. The deputy Queen's bailiff distrained the beans, when Edward Thompson, a resident, took a sack through, but it was later claimed that residents should be toll free.

The tenants of ancient Crown demesne claimed similar exemptions from many tolls. Sir Henry Cholmley pleaded "Pickering liberty" when Scarborough tried to toll his carriers taking coal to his Roxby castle near Thornton Dale. The Easingwold and Huby men were quit of toll, stallage, cheminage, pontage, pavage, picage, murage and passage in Galtres forest. Such claims were often disputed and could not always be enforced. The tenants of Tickhill refused to pay toll and passage money at Blyth, as tenants of the Duchy of Lancaster. The Tickhill bailiff went with them to Blyth market cross, on one occasion, to proclaim their rights.

Road Maintenance

Bequests for road repair had long been seen as good works. They were not as numerous as the sums given for bridges. A few examples may suffice. Robert Hertley of Rotherham in 1521 gave money for paving the lane going to Greasbrough. Wakefield merchant Richard Pymond bequeathed money in 1546 for making and mending the parish highways and bridges. Elizabeth Lord of York left ten shillings to mend Kexby highway in 1550. Richard Harrison of Hunslet left twenty pence each for several Leeds roads. John Gylelyate of Thorpe Arch gave five shillings in 1559 for mending the township highways. London grocer, Thomas Lounde bequeathed £10 to repair highways in Kexby lane, £10 to the causeway between Kexby and Wilton, as well as £10 to his poor Pocklington kinsfolk. Widowed Mary Hardcastle of Womersley gave 26s.8d, each to Wetherby, Walshworth and Tadcaster bridges and 13s.4d to mend Ferrybridge causeway.

The maintenance of through roads had been viewed as the responsibility of neighbouring property owners, rather than road users. Parliament made a significant change with the 1555 Highways Act. This made new parish officers responsible for the repair of the king's highways. This only applied to the through roads leading to market towns. The old responsibilities remained for other roads. The Highways Act required parish constables and churchwardens to call meetings in Easter week for electing two new surveyors of the highways. They had to arrange the repair of highways, using compulsory "statute labour". Farmers with draught animals or a plough, had to provide a wain or cart and two men daily, to work without payment for four Spring days. Other householders had to send labourers, but not hired servants by the year, for an eight hour day with shovels, picks, and mattocks. Fines for not doing so ranged from one to ten shillings. The justices were expected to present highways out of repair. They could compel the use of parish labour and could still order repairs by owners of adjoining lands.

Twice yearly road inspections were required. There was an obligation to remove nuisances, to scour and dry roads and to trim hedges. The surveyors could raise a rate and had to keep accounts. Their first necessity was a quarry for stone. Some areas lacked stone. The best source in Holderness was the sea beaches. The Skipsea manor court elected two men, described as collectors, for the gathering of stones, as well as officers to supervise the mending of the highways. Eight villagers failed to appear for stone gathering one year and twelve the next. A second statute in 1563 even gave parish officers the right to take rubbish stone from a quarry without the owner's permission, and extended the obligation to perform common works to six days.

There was much criticism of the new system. Harrison thought that the six days of activity rarely gave two good days work. Nonetheless, any work done was a gain and the system lasted until the 19th century. Paid labour often replaced the common days. The parish spending of two overseers of the highways for the parish of Rawmarsh in 1558 included payments to several men for such tasks as "bank field gate mending", and "leading a load of rails from Barber wood to the quarry", along with the quarry rent, rivets and nails bought for the windmill gate and allowances paid for labourer's ale. The expenditure for the year ran to £17.10.10d. which had to be raised by a local rate.

Fitzherbert urged the mending of highways on dry Summer days, wherever water had been seen to stand in Winter. The sun could dry a road but it also hardened the mud of wagon ruts. Roadside ditches could drain off winter water. The repair of metalled roads was usually confined to filling potholes with stones, gravel or even earth. The clay lands gave troublesome roads, notorious in Langbaurgh and on the approaches to Scarborough. A Rudstone man claimed that the road from Filey to Scarborough was impassable in Winter. Another man thought the roads from Seamer to Scarborough "very evil and miry in Winter" while a "moor ender" from Goathland said that "no horse could carry a load into Scarborough in winter, unless it was very strong, the roads being so bad". The natural drainage in chalk and limestone areas resulted in a better footing.

The justices would place an increasing pressure on the parishes. Their orders requiring repairs emerged with growing frequency. The highway called Washer lane in Skircoat between Sowerby and Halifax "wanteth mending, being perilous to horses" in 1608. The King's highway from Marske to Yarm in 1610-1612 was in ruin and decay, especially between Eston & Ormsby, and "ought to be repaired by the township of Normanby". That between Normanby and Marton called Ormesby Street "ought to be repaired by the township of Ormesby, it being in the street leading from Marske to

Yarm". The justices had powers to keep king's highways open. But they might allow a diversion. Emparking and enclosures sometimes stopped a road. The Duchy court heard in 1589 that the road heavily used by carts and carriages between Heptonstall and Sowerby chapel had been stopped up. William Oglesthorpe was ordered to lay open a way he had enclosed, leading from Towston to the new close and Gray garth in the Manor of Rigton.

The Highways Act did not stop the flow of road charity, but more was heard of gifts to mend causeways. John Pekerd gave four shillings to the mending of the way in his home village of Staveley. Gentleman Robert Foster of Smawes offered fifty shillings to repair highways about Tadcaster and £5 for mending the causey and highway from his Tadcaster house to Bowebridge. William Creswick, a cutler in 1578 willed six shillings and eight pence to repair of the causeway leading from Sheffield to little Sheffield moor. Parrat Jacques of Finkle Street Selby, in 1592, left a similar sum to byelawmen for his own road to be repaired. John Hoyle of Soyland in 1594 willed a pound to the mending of the way at distant Blackstone Edge. Bryan Bulmer a Hull master mariner in 1563 gave twenty shillings to the highway between Hull and Bilton. Stephen Easby a Pontefract alderman gave 3s.4d. to highways about the town.

The Bridges

Great rivers and minor streams were the principal hindrance to easy movement around the county. The new map makers and the travellers alike made much of the Yorkshire rivers. Holinshed listed the "waters falling into the sea between Seven and Humber", and Drayton produced a Yorkshire map which showed little else. The main rivers were important route ways for boat traffic and their junctions with main roads encouraged major and minor river ports. River crossings by ford, ferry and bridge had always channelled the main route ways. Leland noted the bridges on the routes that he followed. Saxton 's Yorkshire map of 1577 showed no roads but he carefully marked many bridges with fine white lines.

The Great North Road was carried over some of the best stone bridges in the shire, including the five arch "great bridge" at Doncaster, with a gate and chapel at its south end, and the three arch Friars' bridge a little to the north. Wentbridge had a pretty five arch bridge and Ferrybridge seven arches over the Ayre. Castleford had seven arches carrying Watling Street over the Aire. Other great bridges were Wakefield's nine arch bridge over the Calder, with a fair chapel on the east side and the three arch bridge over the Swale at Thornton in the North Riding. The highway linking the north road with York went by the eight arch Tadcaster bridge over the Wharfe. Piercebridge had three arches over the Tees. The three arch Kexby bridge carried the traveller from York over the Derwent into the East Riding. Surprisingly, Pickering had a five arch bridge over a modest stream, but it stood amidst floodable low ground.

York had the busiest bridges, four over the river Foss and one over the River Ouse. There was no bridge crossing the Ouse nearer the sea than York. The city appointed bridgemasters to assist the chamberlains until 1563, two each annually for the Ouse and Foss bridges. The 1554-5 accounts of the two bridge masters, William Wharton a tailor and John Jackson a girdler, showed receipts of £82.13s.2d., set against modest expenditures on repairs. Several great bridges had houses built on them causing fresh problems, but giving useful incomes. Six people made holes in their houses abutting

15 Marsden Moor Pack Horse Bridge

Fossbridge at York in 1575 for sweeping rubbish into the river and grates were nailed at each end.

The old six arch bridge across the Ouse at York collapsed in 1564. A sharp frost, a great snowfall and a sudden thaw raised water levels so high that the weight of ice and floodwater took away two arches and twelve houses and drowned twelve people. It took several years to raise the funds to replace the structure. Alderman Robert Hall's widow Jane gave £100 in 1566 and St George's chapel near the castle was taken down to provide freestone in 1571. Camden spoke with awe of the new five arch Ouse bridge, which included one of the largest arches in Europe. The gradient was steep. The middle most arch was eighty-one feet from the first spring to the arch and seventeen or eighteen feet between the parapets. The bridge shops were rebuilt, the bridge chapel became a bourse and the council chamber was on the bridge. The prison built in 1575 was given an extra arch to support it.

Many minor bridges across the county consisted of nothing more than a plank, or a clap stone, a large flat stone, supported on rough masonry piers. Many would later be replaced for cart traffic. Crossing a narrow bridge was a good test of sobriety. The new "pack horse" bridges were quite different, though still narrow. The best were models of design and construction. They stood tall above the fast flowing streams in moorland valleys, with a high arch to allow an easy passage beneath of water borne debris or rapidly rising waters. Low parapet walls gave free movement of the panniers carried on each side of the pack animals. Sometimes a large stone was placed at one end to rest heavy wicker baskets. The steep angle could be alleviated by a long approach causeway, which also gave a better footing in low and floodable ground. Five packhorses bridges crossed the river Esk in the middle of Blackamoor, all near older fords. Another bridge attributed to the 16th century was at Ivelet in Swaledale.

Bridge Repairs

Bridge building and maintenance were expensive. Merchants and other travellers made many bequests for their support in the late 15th and 16th centuries. The Vicar of Acklam in the East Riding remembered Stamford, Buttercrambe and Thornthorpe bridges with 3s.4d each in 1530. John Waterhouse gave sums for battling parapets at Sowerby bridge, for the amending of Salterhebble bridge and towards a new stone bridge over the river Calder. Merchant Nicholas Blackburn provided sums, against any defect appearing within four years, in the Catterick, Kexby, Thornton or Skete bridges, while York mercer Roger Colynson gave Catterick bridge forty shillings, Greatham bridge six shillings and eight pence, and another forty shillings for making and repairing the road from Ferrybridge to Lideyate and to York.

Ancient bridges at Rotherham, Wakefield and Helmsley had chapels on or near them where the chaplains had collected funds. The chapel of our lady on Rye bridge at Helmsley was given a sheet, and eight pence for a serge by Katherine Tyndale in 1538. Malton bridge had been sustained by a religious guild, which undertook the maintenance. The Statute of Bridges of 1531 gave the justices new powers to enquire into any broken bridges carrying king's highways. Where no individual or corporation could be held responsible, they could tax the town or parish for repairs, or the entire shire for a bridge leading outside the county. District collectors were appointed and county bridge surveyors to spend the money raised.

Antagonism to rate paying would become the strongest political sentiment in the shire. Two collectors were appointed at York to assess inhabitants of the Ainsty wapentake for repair of that part of the Tadcaster bridge in "the county of the city of York". The Mayor threatened dilatory rate collectors with referral to the Council in the North in 1561. Assessments were hard to collect and once collected could stick to fingers Mason Arthur Preston complained that he was unable to get money from the surveyors of Wetherby bridge in 1599. He had to be paid from fresh levies, on a promise to mend the decayed structure.

Sir William Bellassis's claim that bridges were prodigally scattered about, even where they weren't needed, was probably just anti-rate paying sentiment. The opinion gained fuel when the river ran dry beneath Tadcaster bridge in a season of drought. Versifiers waxed lyrical.

> "The muse in Tadcaster can find no theme,
> but a most noble bridge without a stream."

Later came a riposte,

> "The verse before on Tadcaster was just,
> but now great floods we see and dirt for dust."

Abraham de la Pryme reported in another year that high waters had broken down the famous great bridge at Tadcaster. Repairs were needed in 1560 and again for a newly fallen arch soon afterwards, when a rate was levied on the Ainsty. Wains brought the stone from the Tadcaster quarries. Fresh repairs were needed in 1595, along with work at Skipbridge and Ousebridge.

Serious flooding always brought appeals to Quarter Sessions from the much burdened townships. The thaw of 1564 raised waters so high that several bridges were broken on the rivers Ouse, Ure and Skell. Gentleman Cuthbert Fairfax sought help in 1586 for the township of Acaster Malbis, which had lately repaired five bridges. Robert Littlewood and his fellow jurors said "that there are four bridges of stone within the town of Bradford so ruinous and in so great decay, by reason of certain floods which have happened of late years past, that without speedy reparation and amendment, they will utterly fall down and be carried away by the water, to the great hindrance and loss of all the whole country". They wanted a contribution from the broader district. Two justices went to view and assess the sum needed.

The Calder had been made passable with a very fine bridge at Elland not far from Grimscarr. The number of bridges recognised as "county bridges" would increase. A blocked bridge had greater ramifications as trade made areas become mutually dependant. The West Riding justices identified forty-eight of the most considerable bridges to be repaired by the county, leaving any others to the wapentakes and parishes. They presented many of these bridges for repair in subsequent years, among them the four stone bridges in Bradford, Long Royde bridge between Huddersfield and Quarmby, two bridges over the River Laver at Knaresborough, Turnbridge in Snaith parish, Swillington bridge and Humberhead bridge.

The East Riding had few bridges, for it had few major rivers and not all that many minor streams. The Lord President had to ask the York Mayor to make a collection for the repair of Wansford bridge, at the inland port near Driffield, after getting letters from the Privy Council in 1578. The many charges on the East Riding were great, but "those having cause to go or send to London must needs use this passage as their ordinary highway". Malton bridge was maintained jointly with the North Riding, whose justices appointed gentleman Robert Hunter in 1597 to see that carpenter William Solett repaired the North Riding part.

The North Riding justices maintained many bridges. Assessments for "county bridges" were levied for Newsham and Howe bridges on the Rye, and Malton on the Derwent. Yarm, a mediaeval bridge was charged on the North Riding in 1562. Bridge monies came from fifty townships in Bulmer wapentake and fifty-one townships in Ryedale in 1574 to repair Croft and Kirkham bridges. The Fosse, and Essall bridges and Lelam bridge were "newly put on the county". Lelam was given £30 in 1584 and was rebuilt in stone in 1594. Ten pounds was allowed for Sinnington in 1592 and another £10 five years later. Eighty pounds was thought necessary for the decayed Howe bridge "otherwise it should fall as it is very like a greater sum will be needed for rebuilding and the country undone for want of passage". Ten pounds were spent on Bense bridge over the Leven.

A few bridges had endowments of property, given to offset costs of maintenance but the incomes were not enough. Yarm bridge crossing the river Tees, which was tidal as far as Worsell, had received pontage tolls since 1200 and was rebuilt in stone in 1400. The "wardens of the great bridge of Yarm "held town properties chargeable for bridge repair including two burgages on the south side of Westgate let to a blacksmith. The North Riding was charged £95 for its repair in 1562 and another £30 ten years later. James Conyers gave houses that he built on Whitby Bridge to provide rent incomes for its support. The bridge linked the two parts of the town across the river Esk, itself a passage for shipping. The justices repeatedly voted substantial sums for the bridge in every decade of the reign. Evidence was given in 1608 that twenty pounds would be needed to obtain forty oak trees of sufficient size to repair Whitby bridge and another twenty pounds for carriage "because wood is far from us, that will serve for our purpose".

Many lesser bridges were built with timber. Their beams decayed and needed periodic replacement. Considerable sums were spent on scarce forest timber making pairs of jewels, sommers (beams) and planks. The foot planks and the causey of Kirkby Wiske horse bridge were repaired by the local inhabitants. Causeway approaches became more common than stone steps. The construction of a stone causeway leading to a bridge could precede conversion to a stone bridge but this was a major investment. The additional "grece" or stone steps on the west side of Leeds bridge, leading to the tenters, were built in 1583 with stone from Kirkstall Abbey.

Fords and Ferries

The travellers mentioned fords as well as bridges, some even at major river crossings. There was no bridge at Aberford on the north road. St Helen's ford west of Tadcaster carried a major road and had long had a chapel but no bridge. The moor streams in North East Yorkshire, which could rapidly build up water, becoming an obstacle to traffic, had a string of waths, the local name for a ford. Those along the way that marked the boundary between the wapentakes of Pickering Lythe and Cleveland were all named, including Grindstanewath, Bramherewath, West Blawath, Frerwrath, Nether Blawath and Hellewaths. A helle was a flat stone. The Whitby-Guisborough road was shown on Speed's map, running along the sands from Dunsley to Lythe, and crossing a sandy ford at today's Sandsend.

There were ferries on the river Humber for the long crossing to Lincolnshire. Robert Aske had been crossing the Humber by ferry from Brough to Barton, when the boatman told him that that the commons were up in rebellion, the start of the Pilgrimage of Grace. Leland mentioned the three mile ferry from Hull, the usual route to Barton on Humber, "counted by reason of the violent casting of the stream as good a passage as to Golflete". York had a ferry across the Ouse at St. Leonard's landing and another below the common crane in Skeldergate. King Henry VIII had passed over the Ouse by another ferry on the road from Cawood to Wressel. Leland saw ferries below Sutton and Wressell. Myton ferry still crossed the Ouse north of York in 1591. The Moor Monkton ferry over the Derwent had a causeway approach and was leased with the boat in 1584 to William Wiles who was obliged to keep both in repair. A banked way led through floodable lowland to the Hemingbrough ferry.

Horses

"Horses are men's wings, wherewith they make such speed". So said the 17th century writer John Aubrey. As they became more numerous, they were a great focus of interest for their owners. Harrison spoke of horses that served for the saddle, commonly gelded "and now grew to be very dear among us, especially if they be well coloured, justly limbed and have thereto an easy ambling pace". Riding horses were called geldings. Christopher Wyvill in 1579 left geldings to his children. The love affair had begun between the English gentry and their horses. Horse care and management were a

230

major concern for all who had them. The horse gave much work and much pleasure. Men discussed how to get the best from a horse, whether by corrections or cherishings. Correction might be by tongue, rod, bridle, calves, stirrup, spur or the ground. Cherishing was by tickling, or talking.

Yorkshire breeds were becoming well known. Sir Arthur Darcy in 1537 thought that Jervaulx Abbey and its granges, with the "help of their great hardy commons" could have "the best race that should be in England". The royal studs of mares had been kept at Thornbury and around Jervaulx. Men said that "the Jervaulx breed of horses is so good that their like cannot be found in England" and "the breed of Gerlayes, (galloways) was the tried breed of the north". Harrison mentioned the galloways in his list of northern fairs. Gervase Markham said that the little Scots horses called "galway nags" were good hunters.

Blundeville found imported horses more familiar in 1560, the Turkey, the Barbarian, the Sardinian and the Irish hobby. The "Barbs" were small swift and long lived .The term "thoroughbred" came to mean those descended from seventy-eight foundation mares and three Barb, Turk or Arab sires. Aubrey gave English horses "a mediocrity of all necessary good properties, as neither as slight as the Barb, nor so slovenly as the Flemish, nor so fiery as the Hungarian, nor so airy as the Spanish jennets, nor so earthly as those in the Low Countries and generally all the German horse". He added "Yorkshire doth breed the best race of English horses, whose keeping commonly in steep and stony ground bringeth them to firmness of footing and hardness of hoof".

Yorkshire horse breeders and dealers flourished at Ripon and Middleham. Squire Ninian Staveley bred and reared horses at Ripon Park. He left five mares, six young horses, nineteen young colts, three foals, six nags and two geldings in 1559. Aubrey named Ripon first among the nation's notable markets wherein great plenty of horses and colts was bought and sold. Camden said that Malton market was famous for its vent of horses by 1586, as well as eels, corn and farm implements. Mr. Langdale at Sancton in the East Riding gave his uncle "the horse that I bought at Malton". The Earl of Westmoreland left another, a black gelding bought at Malton, to Roger Dalton of Kirbky Misperton in 1563. Brandsby Hall had Turkish horses acquired at Malton fair by 1615.

Small farmers reared horses in the Dales, in Craven and around Blackamoor. At Abbotside, William Parkin of Lund left three mares and a stag worth £3.6.8. In 1557-8, John Warley at Newhouse had horses worth £13.14.4, the grey nag and the foal worth 13s4d, an old mare six shillings and another mare two shillings. James Bradrigge at Brickhill cote had eight mares, a young horse and foals. Mr. Hewerdine of Kirkby Moorside was owed money for nags and horses from Ingleby, Borrowby, Kildale, Guisborough and Newton in distant Cleveland. In 1593 John Radcliffe of Guisborough who owned land at Old Byland, made specific bequests of a grizzled stoned horse, a bay stoned horse called Bay Mennell, an ambling grey colt of three years and a grey colt of two years to be chosen from among his many others. Thomas Metham of Wiganthorpe gave his best breeding mare to his wife, and his own saddle horse to his brother in 1595.

Horsemanship became the essential gentry accomplishment, whether for hunting, racing, travel, tournaments or war. "To ride surely and clean, on a great horse and a rough, was honourable exercise for a man of rank" said Sir Thomas Elyote adding that, "it put a majesty and dread to inferior persons". Roger Ascham reckoned that "to ride comely" was among the virtues necessary for a courtly gentleman. A new literature elaborated the subject. The proverbial culture gained such new wisdom, as "it is a good horse that never stumbleth", "of a ragged colt comes a good horse", and "where saddles lack, better ride on a pad than a bare back". Squire, groom and stable lad alike could talk horses, if they could talk nothing else. Lads would judge a farm by the way they treated their horses. And, life doesn't seem quite the same, once you have grasped the proverb that "A grunting horse and a groaning wife never fail their master".

Fitzherbert, who rode across Grimbald bridge over the Nidd near Knaresborough to buy colts, once had sixty mares and five or six horses, and learnt not to trust horse dealers. He identified ten properties common to "a woman and a horse". The horse had fifty-four properties in all, two of a man, two of a badger, four of a lion, nine of an ox, nine of a hare, nine of a fox, nine of an ass and ten of a woman.

Women well chered, fayr herede, well brestede, cloven cropped, easy at sterop,
and soft bearyng.

Blundeville linked the contemporary male psychology with the character of the horse, relating colour and complexion to temperament. Black, russet or dun went with the melancholic; white with the phlegmatic; sanguine with the bay, and choleric with the sorrel. He approved a balance and liked a star on the face. His writings included some discussion of the four roles of horse breeder, rider, keeper and farrier. Gervase Markham's discourse of 1593 advised how to choose, ride, train and diet, both hunting and running horses. Here were the several paces, the trot, the rack, the amble and the gallop. He preferred the amble, which could be taught with legs strapped, in a new ploughed field. Geldings naturally gambled better than stoned horses.

The horse was often the first bequest in a will. They were named, often with a hint of affection. Mr. Blackburne at Filey bequeathed "Tom Fole" and a white horse called Rollande. Some held very high values. Good horses passed between friends. Mr. Rabanckes gave his brother Samuel the nag that was Mr Rookebies, with a saddle and bridle. Brother in law Thomas Smeton had the bay nag called Dent. James Westrop of Darnecome left his brother Ralph a little stoned nag with a syppe in the nose and a star in the forehead. Anthony Hunter of Thornton Dale in 1561 left an ambling nag to Lord Latimer's daughter Katherine and his nag called Norfolk to Sir Henry Percy. Beverley merchant John Adamson gave his three year old mare to his son.

The local language made the male horse from weaning to four or five years, a colt, the castrated horse a gelding, the stag a young gelding over one year but unbroken, and the stoned horse a stallion. A foal was of either sex until weaned and the filly was a young female. The most common term for a saddle horse was the nag, often called an ambling nag. The hobby was a pony or small horse. Thomas Saville the Welburn esquire in 1588 gave a stoned colt to Sir William. Fairfax's son Thomas and a bay ambling colt of his own breed to Ursula Saville, his daughter in law. Gentleman James Fox of Thorpe le Willows left a sorrel nag, bought off his son Fenton, his Grey Fenton gelding and their saddles.

Horses generated new employment in rich men's houses, for grooms, riders, stablers, farriers, coach and wagon men. The Earl of Northumberland had a corps of gentlemen of the horse and stable servants. He obtained forty-one yards of linen cloth costing twenty-two shillings and a penny during 1585-7 to make sheets and mattresses for the seven grooms of his Topcliffe stable. He bought a horse for his falconers worth seventy shillings and nine bushels of oats for its feed. The Earl of Huntington as Lord President kept thirteen horses and a new coach at York and seventeen horses at Sheriff Hutton. His specialist saddlery kept at the King's Manor included five gilded leather saddles, two trunk saddles, three hackney saddles, a pillion and a flagon saddle. Edward Earl of Rutland left his wife, a coach, a litter, with the horses for both and twelve yeomen's geldings.

The Earl of Northumberland's stable charges in 1585-87 included the purchase of seventeen horses at a cost of £280.4s.4d. During 1598-9 his horses consumed over one hundred and forty three quarters of oats at a cost of £47.11s.4d while hay was another £40.7s.10d . The grooms gathered the stable dung. Iron was bought to bind a pair of wain wheels. The Earl regularly bought hay, straw, oats and horse bread and he paid smiths for shoeing and farriers for healing sick animals. Markham spoke of the "fifty diseases" to which horses were prone, including "spavin" a swelling of the joints. The author of the "Yorkshire Tragedy" used the curse "the spavin overtake thee, the fifty diseases stop thee".

Good saddlery gave comfort to rider and horse. A foreign visitor taking a post horse for Gravesend found the saddle so small, hard, and covered only with bare hide or leather, so uncomfortable for a heavy rider, that he took one home as a rare curiosity. Yorkshire dialect absorbed many terms of saddlery, including the wantey for a horse's belly band. Inventories mention saddles, bitts, frames, stirrups, and snaffles. The hackney saddle was a riding saddle. Fewsters made the saddle trees. A pad was a soft saddle without a tree for a woman or someone aged. Thomas Atkinson the Stillington prebendary of 1571 had both a bay and a grey gelding with saddle and bridle. Yorkshire gentlewoman Jane Metcalfe of Harum Hawe had a side saddle in 1564.

Gentry parks made good horse pastures, given a hay barn for the Winter fodder, gathered in from the woods and low grounds. A Malton draper had stables with hecks, mangers, bayes, racks, stalls and balks at his dwelling, and more balks, sacks and mangers in a separate stable leased at the back gate. James Crosthwaite, the Wigginton rector in 1571 had a bay nag in the stable, with saddle, bridle, breastgirth, housing girth and a collar with a housing cloth. There was hay worth twelve shillings and another bridle and an old saddle that his man used. The Langtoft prebendary kept a horse in the stable at Escrick, and some hay at York .He had a white ambling gelding worth £3.6.8 along with nine other horses, the total value £14.6s.8d.

Tusser described the good, well planked stable equipped with

"key and lock, walls well lined to bear a knock,
rack and manger for litter and hay,
sweet chaff and provender every day".

Yeomen might keep riding horses as well as work horses. Man and woman might ride one horse to market, he in the saddle, she riding pillion. The pillion was a stuffed leather cushion behind a saddle, basically for carrying luggage. Some farmers already used horses to draw and plough, though oxen were more common. Yeoman Gregory Casse of Sawdon gave a black nag and saddle to his brother in 1575. John Lambe of Dunsley in 1597 gave his son John the mare and her foal. William Logan of Skinnergreve in 1584 left his wife a grey ambling mare .

233

Carriages

The first coach in England was an imported novelty from Hungary or Germany for genteel travel. Coaches remained a rarity. The Earl of Rutland had a state carriage about 1555 and the Earl Edward left his wife a "coche". A Bill to restrain the excessive use of coaches was read in 1601.

> "When Queen Elizabeth came to the throne,
> a coach in England then, was scarcely known
> Then, 'twas as rare to see one, as to spy,
> a tradesman that had never told a lie"

Litters remained in use, thought more dignified than the chair, but would be relegated to the aged and infirm. Sir Francis Willoughby asked the Countess of Shrewsbury for her horse litter, with its furniture, for his wife, who was too sick to travel by horse or coach in 1589. The sentiment carried over to coaches which were also thought suitable for old ladies and the very young. They remained slow and had limited upholstery against the jolts. They could be hired in London, and for travelling out one or two days from the city.

One day in August 1599 Lady Margaret Hoby at Hackness wrote "I took my coach and went to Linton" and next day "I took the air in the coach with Mr. Hoby". She entered her diary for Tuesday the 18th September, "After I had prayed privately, I went to breakfast and soon after took my Cotch and went to Malton to salute my Lady Ewre with whom I stayed about two hours; then came to Rillington and went to my cousin Gates house and so home to Linton to supper; after that to prayers and to bed". Her husband Sir Thomas Posthumous Hoby had a coach and three horses at Hackness. Lady Margaret took "a cotch" to London that year.

The Earl of Shrewsbury as Lord President of the Council in the North sent his servant Rafe Barber to borrow wains, draughts and carriages in York to carry his wine and other things from the city and shire to Sheffield castle. His successor the Earl of Huntington, when Lord President, kept "one new coach" of his own at York. Hester Pickering, heir to the fashionable Sir William Pickering at Oswaldkirk received his coach and two coach horses. Sir Cotton Gargrave left the coach, coach horses and a litter worth £20 in 1588. Sir Martin Frobisher at Normanton had two coaches in 1595. Sir Hugh Cholmeley went to public meetings in "a very gentlemanly equipage".

Londoner John Stow said that, "The world runs on wheels with many whose parents were glad to go on foot". There had been a few chariots in the early years of the century, then the Pomeranian coach appeared. He found cars, drays, carts and coaches on the increase in the capital, where streets and lanes were being straightened to accommodate them, although iron shod vehicles were still kept out of the city. He warned of the coachman, riding behind his horse's tail, who "lasheth them and looks not behind him". Traffic was plentiful in other towns. Already there were "parking offences". Peter Harpham at Beverley in 1576 was charged threepence for his cart standing in the street. Wheeled vehicles brought accidents. A stranger was killed by Mr.Slingsby's draught in August 1588.

Great men moved furniture and supplies between their houses as they changed residence. The fifth Earl of Northumberland travelled with seventeen carriages and thirty-six horsemen. All his vehicles were called carriages except the chariot. This was used for shifting wardrobe and other stuff, and is inferred to be a wagon and six. Ox drawn wagons were used by Hugh Cholmeley to move furniture from Whitby to Thornton Dale. The most common carriage for moving the products of farm and industry was the two-wheeled cart. "In England, beside coaches, they use no wagons for the goods but only two wheeled carts which however are so large that they carry quite as much as wagons and many has five or six strong horses draw them." Farmers carried fuel and timber, after fallowing and dunging, in May when there was least to do in husbandry and the roads were at their best. A farm cart had enemies in the sun, wind and rain according to Tusser and a cart shed was essential. York had a little cart made for the whipping of vagabonds in 1570.

Tusser recommended lighter, stronger vehicles, whether tumbrel, cart, wagon or wain, speaking of

> "a strong axle treed cart
> clouted and shod,
> cart ladder and wimbel
> with percer and pod"

Wains might be flat, without sides and have twice the capacity of a cart. The wain blades were its shafts. Some wains were two wheeled, but with long fir pole brakes, for moving timber and brushwood in steep ground. The tumbrel was a one horse tipping coup with sides and ends closed. Long heavy goods wagons became more numerous in flat areas and in the towns. Some had pole draught with horses or oxen stood in pairs, side by side. Others had shafts, in which the fill horse drew behind the fore or trace horses. The axle tree was the bar on the end of which two wheels revolved, while the fellies were curving sections of a wheel rim. Wheel dishing may have begun about now to balance the greater weights carried. Different woods were used for different purposes. Oak was used for spokes, soles, shears and axle trees. Ash for felloes, shelving, rails, everings, spring pole and slivers, elm for naves, shelving boards, sides, hatches and floorboards.

Carts and wains deepened hollow ways up hill slopes, the more so if they were shod with iron. Wheels given iron rims or tyres were described as iron bound. The bound wain or cart was a shod vehicle and there were many of them. The iron rims could cut up roads, mark timber plank and make ruts in stone. York prohibited bound wains from passing over Ouse brig laden with coal, timber, millstones and the like in 1570. Chandler Thomas Hewet was paid five shillings a year to enforce the ban. The Beverley Order Book had prohibitions on burgesses or inhabitants bringing any cart, carriage or wain, bound with iron or having above five nails in a wheel, onto the pavements of the town between twenty fifth October and the feast of the Purification of the Virgin Mary. Offenders were fined 6s.8d.

Henry Fell of Dunnington had two wains, an extra wain body and two pair of wheels valued at seventeen shillings in 1554. William Lacon, the Kirkby Moorside tanner left a wain to his brother in 1564. Thomas Kirkupp a Brompton husbandman had two bound waines, one black filly stag, a two year old and several oxen in 1590. Old and new vehicles stood together in farm yards. The cheaper sledges remained in common use everywhere. Clothier Robert Crossley of Soyland left his son carts, wheels and a sled in 1592. The sledge was still valued two hundred years later for carrying harrows, thorns, and wood, turf and peat, pulled by either horse or oxen. York and Hull sled men in Elizabeth's reign journeyed out into the hill country.

Carriers

Heavy and bulky goods of low value, such as grain, coal, and stone, were moved by water, as close to their destination as possible. Several Yorkshire rivers were navigable for small craft far inland. The river ports and village staithes added a forgotten network for the movement of goods. Beyond them, the expanding transport trades included men on horse and foot, badgers, who resold goods like corn and flour, jaggers, cadgers or carriers, pannier men, pedlars, chapmen, and more specialised wool and corn drivers. The Statute of 1563 for licensing specialist transport men, exempted the north of England so that little is known of their numbers.

York was a focus for the transport trades, with saddlers and spurriers, porters and water men and a dozen other groups. The city admitted twelve inn holders, five victuallers, five saddlers, five mariners, nine pannier men, two porters, four carriers, a spurrier, two water men, and a common herd to the freedom of the city during the first six years of Elizabeth's reign. Porters carried grains, coal and turf around York, Beverley and Scarborough. York had limited their number to sixteen in 1495, setting charges at four burdens for a penny, and three burthens further out into the city. Four score great turfs or a hundred small turfs made a burthen. Numbers fell to nine in 1558 but were made up again to the complement of sixteen, charging a penny for a single burthen taken to the far bars of the city. The labourers' charges for load bearing were revised in 1571, twopence halfpenny for a thousand turves and three pence for a hundred wood, from the common staith to stated areas of the city, including Coney street.

There were long distance carriers from York to London and to the ports. Bishop Barnes said that "the King's high street from London to Edinborrow lieth within half a mile of Hazlewood on the west and the street from London to York on the east, whereby a carrier of York passeth every week to London and another thence to York. A letter to the Earl of Shrewsbury in c1547-51 spoke of several pieces of cloth sent to London by the Derby carrier. His servant wrote from London to Mr. Stringer of Whiston to say he was sending two stag skins by Hobson the carrier in 1584 and he hoped to hear of their safe arrival by the return carrier. This may be Thomas Hobson the famous Cambridge carrier who weekly put up at the Black Bull, in Aldersgate Street, London.

The highway from Rotherham to Mansfield and Nottingham via Mile Oaks and Whiston was described as "the ancient road or London way for carriers". John Taylor's Carrier's Cosmography of 1637 revealed a national network of carrying services linking the major towns, including those with universities. The York carriers lodged at the sign of the Bell Savage outside Ludgate, from Friday till Saturday or Monday. A foot post from York came on the second Thursdays to the Rose and Crown, St John Street. The Wakefield carriers used the Axe, Aldermanby and the White Hart, Coleman Street. Sheffield men were at the Castle, Wood Street and Halifax men at the Greyhound Smithfield.

Local carriers served the different Yorkshire markets. Thomas Preston a Bridlington carrier was paid for work towards pier maintenance in 1538 and Nicholas Waile for hire of a carrier's wain. John Dunston the Wakefield carrier gave five marks to amending the most noisome local highways. Country road carriage costs doubled the pit head price of coal every ten miles or so. York was a coal town but Beverley was a turf town, where certain carriers were licensed as crelers, cadgers or carriers of turves. They were required to carry not less than five hundred on a horse, except Roecliff turves. The horse load cost twopence whether for turf or coals in 1628.

Pannier men seem to have been rarer than might be imagined but the evidence is thin. Henry Sift of Sheffield who in 1522 left forty shillings for highway repair between Sheffield and Heeley, gave his brother a "packhorse with all things belonging" Thomas Fletcher at Robin Hoods Bay in 1538, and Thomas Taylor of York who bought a Bay horse a hundred years later were pannier men who probably dealt with much of the Bay fishermen's trade with the city. Other pannier men were William Storrie at Scarborough in 1552, who left his son his "working gear on the sands". Robert Fletcher of Bridlington in 1546 and Robert Nightingale of Scarborough mentioned in 1616-17, who seem likely to have been moving fish.

The pack horses are believed to have been chapman horses, or galloways, sure footed, rarely higher than fourteen and a half hands. They were later crossbred with Mediterranean animals to give the Cleveland bay. Teams of horses might number twenty, each with a pannier on each side, led by a bell horse. They could cover twenty or thirty miles a day. A packhorse with panniers carried about two hundredweight. The word jagger seems to apply to a man who carried lead ore, salt or other heavy loads on pack horses. Stances for pasture and stopping places were adopted on some principal routes, including pannierman's pool at Thornton dale, pannierman's ing at Foulbridge and pannierman's pool at Rosedale. Scarborough had a pannierman's close.

Other country side carriers were called pedlars, chapmen and badgers. Clement Armstrong had claimed that the country was infested with pedlars and chapmen, sitting in church porches selling trifles from horse packs, foot packs, baskets and budgets, as early as 1525 and Riccal folk saw pedlars selling in the church porch on feasts days in 1519. Their numbers increased but they are not well recorded. They were viewed with some suspicion and many had few assets. Pedlar William Brown of Hull only named his black jacket and doublet, line hose and shirt in his will. A Gildersome badger Paul Backe in 1599 left his brother a buckskin doublet, grey breeches, a cloak and his hackney saddle. Yet Robert Rayner a Hartshead badger was buried in church; left small sums to the poor, and bought a book for the church. Chapmen seemed a wealthier breed. Richard Chowe the Gisburn chapman had a farm and rents in 1588. William More the Settrington chapman wanted four yards of line cloth for his winding sheet, left 26s.8d to twenty poor folk and ten shillings for making a substantial bridge over Settrington town beck. Corn driver Thomas Rhodes of Bierley had a farmhold. Wool driver John Norman of Leathley would be buried inside his church.

Elizabethan Inns

There were traditions of hospitality among the higher levels of society for people of their own status. Travelling nobility, knights and some gentlemen still called at the houses of their peers. There was a hint of this in the young men troubling Bulmer and Ryedale wapentakes in 1575, described as "young gentlemen and others riding and travelling abroad as masterless men, not having whereupon to live, nor using any lawful arts, science or mystery" but who were received in gentlemen's houses and lived idly in market towns. Wealthy travellers had also stayed at monasteries and friaries. The Countess of Surrey stayed at the Stillington prebendal house at York in 1513. King Henry VIII used the King's manor, lately part of St Mary's Abbey in 1541. Monastic gatehouses and some hospitals had sometimes functioned like inns. That at Kirkham Priory remained an inn long after the monastery had closed.

> "If you go to Nun Keeling,
> you find your body filling
> of whig or of whey
> but go to Swine
> and come betime
> or else you go empty away.
> but the Abbot of Meaux
> does keep a good house
> by night and by day "

A wider range of travellers needed overnight accommodation with food for both men and horses. The terms "inn holder" and "victualler" had been replacing the older 'hosteller' at York for some time. The inn could provide food and drink, with beds and stabling but was not alone in supplying such needs. Market places had always had 'wost houses' where a market drinking could be slept off or distant pedlars accommodated. Town inns developed from older hostelries, especially along the major roads. The Wentbridge Inn had welcomed merchants from the Great North Road, in 1487. They travelled on to York to meet the Prior of Tynemouth at the Boar kept by a "hostler" in Castlegate. Outside the towns, the boundary between the inn and the alehouse only became marked as standards of accommodation rose.

The York hostelries were required to have signs in 1503. The city decreed in 1555 that no inn holder, victualler or other inhabitant was to charge strangers above four pence a meal, and he was to have boiled or roast beef. When a visitor called for more, he was to pay more. A horse was to have litter and hay, for a day and night for four pence, if he was from the inn. The lodger was to agree his chamber and bedding with his host, if his horse was sent away from the city. Stable charges were high and good incomes tempted others into the trade. York bakers were ordered to leave stabling to inn holders, and not to take in any horses for feeding in 1575. York innkeepers were required to have lodgings and victuals in 1598 and to lodge none that didn't answer their names.

Harrison thought that London inns were the worst and the best, adding that some other great thoroughfares and "towns of the greatest travel" had twelve to sixteen inns. With London in mind, he said that owners competed in fineness and change of linen, bedding, fine rooms, service at table, costliness of plate, strong drink, variety of wines and well using of horses. The Inns had elaborate signs. Some could lodge two or three hundred people and many horses. There were clean sheets where no man had lodged since they came out of the water. Horse travellers had free beds and were given a key. Hostlers looked after horses, diligent in hope of extra reward, but they were liable to acts of cunning. "Every man may use his inn as his own house" and could decide what services and food to call for.

Southern gentlemen had private chambers or ate alone with friends. A squire with one or two servants attending him might spend five or six shillings for supper and breakfast. Men of poorer condition ate at the host's table and paid 6d a meal. The gentlemen in the north didn't keep to chambers. They ate at the ordinary table together, with choice of meat or fish, each paying no more than sixpence or even four pence a meal. A horse's meat came to twelve or eighteen pence the night for hay, oats and straw and they were commonly put to grass in summer at three pence a horse. Hard riders were put in the stable overnight and given oats in the morning.

The principle that inns were for travellers was stated in 1603. Official post houses were established that year by royal order with a prior right and obligation to supply horses. Once that sort of investment had been made, the inn could have considerable continuity over time. As standards improved Sir Thomas Slingsby could say that "every man loves his inn rather than his house". The Yorkshire innkeeper's greeting was "May god thank thee for making my house your harbour". There was another side to it. Paul Hentze complained of the continual pipe smoking of the English and Andrew Borde of the fleas that stung men in their beds. Tusser knew of lodgers who wiped their scabbard on the curtain, their shoes on a coverlet, who went to bed in dirt and mire, tearing cloths. Others with boots and spurs fouled clean carpets.

> Some make the chimney their chamber pot,
> till it smells like filthy sink.
> Yet who so bold so soon to say
> "How these old houses stink".

What were called the 'thoroughfare' towns attracted the early inns. Folk always gathered at the Darlington inn when "they saw or heard of any coming out of the south, to hear the news". After the collapse of the Pilgrimage of Grace in 1536, thirty or forty gathered with clubs and bats for the arrival of Sir Ralph Sadler. A traveller on the North Road in 1545 spent the night at Darlington and was able to dine at Northallerton on June 20th, have supper at Borough Bridge on the 21st, going on to dine at Wetherby and have supper at Doncaster. He reached London on the 25th. A visitor in the other direction came from Lincoln in 1634, via Newark, to Doncaster's Three Cranes, calling at Robin Hood's Well, where he was charged four pence for sitting in Robin's chair and for a mock knighthood. He rode on to the Star at Pontefract, and with the help of guides to York Coney Street.

Half way house Inns were sited at more remote places on long distance roads. They included the Prioress's inn at Arden near the Hambleton Street. Camden found an inn for travellers in Stainmore. This mountainous waste tract was always exposed to wind or rain. The country around was all "a desert, except an Inn to entertain travellers, in the very middle of this stony waste and near it a fragment of a cross which we call Rerecross, and the Scots call Reicrosse". Tradition has claimed that Blakey Inn, another half way house across the North York Moors dated from c 1588 or had even earlier connections with a mediaeval friarage.

The Earl of Rutland arrived at Scarborough, by sea from Elsinore in Denmark late one July. Mariners carried the nobleman ashore, earning themselves five shillings. My lord's supper at the port and dinner next day cost £6, suppers for other people nine shillings, and mariners' suppers twenty shillings. Musicians received five shillings and the poor ten shillings. Bottles of beer and wine were taken from the waterside to his lodgings and a mariner sold them a fish for a shilling. When they travelled onwards, charges at the Bull in Beverley for supper and breakfast were £6.10s. They rode on for the Humber ferry to Barton on Humber.

Some Yorkshire Inns

The south Yorkshire cloth and cutlery districts were well served with accommodation for travellers. Leland said that an honest and respectable man might dine in Wakefield for two pence. Westgate had the Cock and Swan inn, bearing the date 1593, one of the ceilings having the queen's arms in the plaster work. John Milner, an inn holder with a burgage and a barn in Westgate left his base begotten daughter a brass pot, a pan, a candlestick and eighteen pewter vessels to be set forth by four honest neighbours in 1582. Drunken Barnaby was at the sign of the George and Green in 1634 and Sir William Brereton paid five shillings for supper and breakfast when lodging at the Bull in1635, finding it "an honest and excellent house". It was still mentioned in 1681.

Doncaster had the Dragon Inn, where the landlord had supported the guilds of Our Lady, St. Thomas and the tailors' craft guild, and had kept his books in a little closet under the chamber window in 1505. An inn called the Lyon in Hall Gate, late of the Carmelites was occupied by Alan & Margaret Malster. We hear of the Hind on the Hoop, the New Inn, the Axe, the George hospice and the Hart Inn. During Elizabeth's reign there was the Bull, the Ostrye, the Bear inn, the Cardinal's Hat and the Cock inn in Sepulchre gate. The sign of the Crane rented at twelve shillings in 1546 but was still there in 1627. Thomas Cosyne a Doncaster innkeeper had Dovecote yard near Hall Cross in 1603.

Wills show something of the life of the innholders. The Helmsley inn holder Thomas Dawson in 1565 had ewes, a filly, a hive, a wayne, a cow, and feather beds. His goods were not to be divided, while his wife kept the inn or ostrie in this house. Inn holder Robert Ripley of Ripon was a burgage holder who had bought a house in Stammersgate and left his son all the glass in the house, doors, locks and keys. The George at Tadcaster had old painted glass with the Tudor rose, cupids and an inscription "1592". John Bean the Micklegate inn holder was city sheriff in 1538, Member of Parliament in 1554 and twice Lord Mayor.

York inns saw profit in a fleeting prospect twice in the reign. When Queen Elizabeth postponed a meeting with Mary Queen of Scots at Nottingham in 1562, the tilts were taken down and the feats of arms by young knights cancelled. The meeting was postponed till the period May to late August of 1563. Archisbop Grindall worried about how to receive her and "entertain her according to her dignity". The Archbishop of Canterbury gave advice but she didn't come. She planned another Yorkshire visit. in 1575. Hull ordered the houses painted and gables repaired. York received the court's enquiries about where she would stay, lodgings for her train and places to dine. Brewers were asked what beer they could provide. The visit was called off. Some Yorkshire noblemen and knights breathed again.[4]

T75 Some Yorkshire Inns

Barnsley	Talbot, Marketplace, 1598
Bawtry.	Crown inn 1556-8
	Greyhound 1545, 1595
Beverley	The Bull, perhaps North bar, 1573-4
Catterick	George and Dragon.
Dewsbury	Raven Inn, 1600
Halifax	The Cross Inn 1535, 1585
Harewood	John Harwood, inn holder 1554-5

Helmsley	Richard Rookes, Crown inn Castlegate 1637
	The Castle gatehouse was an inn by 1637
	an old inn, Burrowgate
Hull	The Reindeer, used by the York carrier John Chapman
Northallerton	Swan.1529
Pennistone	White Hart Inn, 1603
Pickering	Robert Parkin, innkeeper. 1610
Pontefract	Star, 1634
Richmond	Cuthbert Cowling inn holder & hosier 1626
Rotherham	Henry Pittes innkeeper;
	Richard Edmondes innkeeper, 1595 1608.
	William Swift's father. the Swan 1568
	Robert Byncliff innkeeper, Talbot in Spark lane. 1584-5
	Bull inn by 1615
Sand Hutton	Thomas Banks. 1606
Scarborough	Oliver Degle, a victualling end, 1564
	John Percy, the Checker, Sandside c1500, later Robert Lacey
	Robert Andrew, inn holder 1595
Sheffield .	James Haldsworth, vintner, mercer, draper of 1564-5. Angel Inn. The Cock Inn of Francis Barlow, chapman and ironmonger 1599. Humphrey Barlow, vintner and grocer .
Tadcaster	The George, of St Nicholas Chantry, Tenant Oswald Warderoppe. The Hart, west of bridge on south side, Edward Marshall. The Swan.
Wentbridge	Michael Fairbank, inn holder with 6 servants at St. Loyes. William Dickinson, lost licence for receiving rogues in 1598
Wetherby	Angel Inn said to have 16C frescoes

CHAPTER 9
MARITIME YORKSHIRE

Fishing communities

Raphael Holinshed made a list of "such ports and creeks as our seafaring men do note for their benefit", on the coast of Yorkshire, in 1596. They ranged from mere beaches to natural bays and artificial harbours. Not all supported a community. They included "Dapnam Sands, Skiningrove, Dysaies, Runswick, Staithes, Robin Hood's Bay, Whitby, Scarborough, Filey, Flamborough, Bridlington, Sister Kirk (Withernsea), Hornsey Beck and Kelsie-cliffe (Kilnsey)". A map drawn and published in Antwerp by Ortelius, but redrawn by Humphrey Lloyd of Denbigh in 1573 showed most of these havens but added Barmston, Patrington and Ravenspurn. Vessels could beach on a rising tide at Ravenser, on the Spurn.

Many coastal communities were devoted to farming and showed little or no sign of maritime activity. Some recorded a single fisherman but then others were fishing communities with no farmland. Scarborough and Whitby were sizeable borough towns but some of the other places, with fishermen, were not even townships. They were newer than that, these communities which specialised in seeking the produce of the sea. Scarborough had been created in the 12th century, as a borough, high above the waterside, and well apart from the older farming village at inland Falsgrave. The burgesses had later bought that manor and so gained control of their field land and commons. They had developed an Undercliff quarter beside the sea with staithes and eventually, further east, a quay protected by a pier.

Whitby and Bridlington began as villages of farmers. The old village of Bridlington was at the old town, inland near its fields, but this was an early parent to a separate port community at Castle Burn, later called Bridlington Quay, a good walk away on the coast. A Norman monastery was sited near the old village in the 12th century and acquired its manor and demesnes. The ancient farming village of Whitby with its earlier monastery had stood next to its fields, on the high east cliff. The village and the fields were absorbed into the new Norman monastery demesne, but a new borough was planted under the cliff, and expanded along each side of the river Esk. With the monasteries swept away in the early sixteenth century, these ports had faced a changing prospect.

The smaller Yorkshire fishing communities were different again, separate from the farming villages, which had mothered them. Flamborough had a small separate fishermen's settlement at south bay. Filey village was on a cliff top south of a ravine, strangely detached from its ancient fields and the church north of the ravine, and yet here, farming and fishing were combined. Fishing communities with no field land had appeared in the later middle ages, at inlets on the hard cliff coastline north of Scarborough. Redcar "a poor fisher town" near Marske sold fish to Rievaulx Abbey in the 13th century, when Sandsend was recorded with fifty or so house plots, separate from inland Lythe. Runswick Bay had at least seventeen dwellings.

242

Seaton Staithes appeared on the coast below cliff top Seaton. Sixteen of the fishermen were summoned to the muster in 1539. Camden found a Skinningrove community thriving from the great variety of fish taken in Queen Elizabeth's time. Robin Hood's Bay was first recorded in the early 16th century, with fifty-one cottages, a herring house and a stable. Leland called it "a fisher tounlet of twenty boats with its dock or bosom a mile in length", reached by a narrow channel between two scars. The houses were packed together on a steep slope. There was neither manor, nor borough nor arable land but they had a small cow close and some rough pasture. Fisherman George Exley kept a 'quie' and no doubt others did the same.

The soft boulder clay coastline below Bridlington was different again, always subject to steady but substantial loss of land to the sea. Filey enjoyed some protection from the Brigg and Bridlington sheltered behind the Flamborough headland and the shallow offshore Smethwick sands. The manor lord of Barmston retained rights to take tolls called flottage, jettage and gate law and claimed freedom from Admiralty jurisdiction. Further south, along the Holderness coast the natural havens were getting fewer, although a small fishing boat could be pulled onto the sands, clear of the sea, at many beaches. The old havens at Easington, Skipsea Hythe, and Ravenser -Odd had long gone. Hornsea Beck, seaward of the farming village of Hornsea was still active, while Withernsea, also known as Sister Kirtk, appeared on Lord Burghley's Holderness map of c 1580 with a navigable creek, since lost to the sea. .

The Fishermen

Cobles and five man boats were the principal local fishing craft. The coble was described as being built of "wainscot", and was designed to work from a beach. It could approach the sands with its square stern first, while the deeper bow kept a firm hold on the water. Two men could easily move the boat on land. A contemporary described Redcar fishermen. They took their cobles to sea through the gaps in a dangerous reef of rocks. Three men commonly went in one boat, "each having two oars, which they governed by drawing one hand over the other". They went out at most times of the year, sometimes twenty to forty miles. Some fishermen had lived aboard their small craft for three days during storms. They returned at ten or eleven in the morning to sell the whole boat's lading for four or even five shillings. It was their custom to change their fellows every year for luck.

Cobles were often owned out right. John Awbroughe of Bridlington Quay owned his "great cobble, the Gregory" in 1558. Richard Raikes of Hull owned an unnamed coble thirty years later. James Conyers of Whitby bequeathed a small coble valued at four marks in 1594. John Marshall of Nether Westgate in Scarborough left his son Robert, a coble and his son in law a five man boat called "Jesus". There were other fishing craft besides cobles and five man boats. They were called "farcostas, northseaboats or northseafares, fishers, ferryboats, and Icelandfares". Some of the distinctions refer more to differences of use than design. John Skinner of Scarborough had shares in one of each.

George Headley in 1575, left "half of my five man boat". William Richardson in 1586 had half a five man boat and half the ship "Marie". William Bratoft of Flamborough left "my half of the coble", and a farmhouse, suggesting that even small vessels could be held in shares. The investment and the risks were commonly shared in the larger vessels. The "Jesus" of Scarborough was a vessel of one hundred and twenty tuns. The tunnage was a measure related to the number of wine tuns a vessel might be thought to carry. Other separate bequests included nets, herring nets and a "Seine net" in 1557. Scarborough fisherman Robert Richardson in 1588, left his sons a quarter of a ship, half a boat and all his coble, together with three herring nets, a small line and a "hanver". He also had a cow and its calf. .

T76 Yorkshire coastal fishermen making wills	1514 - 1552
Scarborough	3
Bridlington & Hilderthorpe	3
Redcar	6
Staithes	1
Flamborough	2
Hornsey & beck	3
East Coatham	1
Estbek & East Rawe (Sandsend)	3
Filey	1
Robin Hood's Bay	4
Skinningrove	3
Sutton in Holderness	1
Withernsea	1

Fishing communities would be thought of as tightly knit. They involved women and children in the work, and they were essential. Thomas Staynerigge of Robin Hood's Bay, in 1548, spoke of his family as "the blood of Staynerigge". When John Beareman, another Robin Hood's Bay fisherman, sought burial in Fyling churchyard, in 1588, he gave his brother George a pair of black breeches, a cassock, upon the same cloth, a petticoat and a 'slepe'. Everything else went to his wife Elizabeth, but he said "There is one little young wench called Margaret Beardman", who was to have those goods his wife would think fit to bestow on her.

Later folklore would record many "superstitions", things done to seek good luck and avoid bad. Where disaster came all too often, it was easy to build up associations with preceding events. The fishing communities rarely had their own chapels yet, though Filey had previously had a Saint Bartholomew chapel in the village, apart from the church which took their tithes. Scarborough had a "fishermen's aisle" in St Mary's church and a chapel in old town. Most fishing villages used churches of the parent village. The rate at which the church tithe was levied had been early re-negotiated at levels well below a tenth, to allow for fishermen's expenses.

Fishing distant shores

A wide variety of fish were caught in offshore waters. What was caught changed with the progress of the year. Thomas Dobie of Scarborough left a quarter of cole fish to his aunt in 1593. Cod was dried as stockfish. Scarborough seems to have dropped out of the distant Iceland fishery but Hull whale fishermen still went to Vardo at the north of Norway, to Greenland, and to Spitzbergen, where whalers from several countries had buildings for rendering whale blubber and packing fin and bone. There were many disputes. Nine ships under Sir John Clere protected the homeward bound Iceland fleet in July 1557.

244

The herring that had once swarmed about Norway and the Sound now came in great shoals around the east coast of Britain. "Winter herring" were taken in April and May off Shetland and Scotland. Some Yorkshire five man boats or "farcostas" fished northwards from Lent onwards. Richard Dennde of Scarborough went fishing in the Shetland seas. When they drew towards the coast of Scotland, the fish were immediately sold, being then at their best. The shoals moved south to the English coasts, and from the middle of August to November, there was plentiful fishing from Scarborough to Thames mouth. The so called "land herring" were brought ashore from June to October at Scarborough. A Scarborough man observed in 1580 that, "the second and best fishing begins at Bartolomewe-tide at Scarborough and so proceeds along the coast". Saint "Bartholomew" was a popular name for local boats.

The Yorkshire fishermen were already part of a broader national and indeed international industry. Since the late 14th century, and perhaps earlier, Yorkshire waters had become hunting grounds for fishermen from many other coastlines. Other English ports sent fishermen to the Yorkshire coast. East Anglian men sold fish in Hull. Distant Aldeburgh ordered in 1598 "that every free inhabitant that shall go after the feast of St John Baptist, fishing into the Skarborowe seas shall pay yearly 2d, for every dole" An Act of Parliament of 1542 spoke of the decay of the east coast fishing towns of England due to the practise of buying fish from the Dutch. A borough order made at Scarborough in July 1584 sought to regulate local purchases of stranger's herring.

Whether Yorkshire coast fishermen were merely out stripped by Dutch expansion or faced an absolute decline is not clear. The Dutch sent four to five hundred "busses" at 'Bartolmewe-tide', to fish for herring, asking leave at Scarborough Castle before fishing off the east coast. They remained for a time at the town as their staple for nets, lines, hooks and victuals. The licensing of strangers may go back to Philip and Mary's reign, when the Low Countries were under Spanish control, and England had a Spanish king. William Camden wryly remarked in 1586 that those of Holland and Zealand were carrying on a very plentiful and gainful trade of fishing for herring, "whereas by an old constitution, they use to get a licence first for it from this castle. For the English always granted leave for fishing, reserving the honour for themselves, but out of a lazy temper resigned the gain to others". That clever man, Doctor John Dee spoke of foreign fishermen abusing our rich fishing about England, Wales and Ireland, "losing us yearly several hundred thousand pounds".[1]

The Hollanders had evolved new purpose –built vessels called busses, which brought a new method of fishing. The busses were large, open- topped, double ended boats. They used drift nets and carried fifteen men and a boy. The fish were quickly gutted, salted and barrelled on board. This made them preserve well for long periods. Other fast ships sailed to meet the busses and transferred the catch, some of which went for quick removal to market. By 1560 they had seven hundred busses and other boats on the Scottish and English coasts, making three voyages a year and taking an average of seventy last of herrings, which they sold for about six pounds. The "Mariner's Mirror" of 1588, showed Dutch busses fishing the Dogger Bank, together with a map of the Yorkshire coast, and pictures of its coastal features as seen from the sea.[2]

Selling Fish

Native and alien fish catches were sold from the boats on Yorkshire shores. Redcar fishermen gave the first chapman a present of a fish. They had a custom that if anyone bid money and was refused, while another outbid him, he could choose to have half the bargain. Fishmongers handled much of the inland and distant trade. These were some of the earliest specialised merchants. They occur singly leaving wills before 1550 at Redcar, Hornsey and Scarborough but there were eight at York and a Wakefield man was active at Robin Hood's Bay. The next half century found them more numerous, still eight at York, but four each at Hull and Beverley, three at Wakefield, two at Pontefract and others at Doncaster, Flamborough, Tadcaster and Leven in Holderness.

The Crown had ancient rights to purchase fish at advantageous prices at Scarborough. Fishmongers acting for the monarch were familiar on the coast buying cheap for the royal household. Many monasteries had once purchased fish at the town. Even now John Starkie of Bridlington was a fishmonger at St. Nicholas Street and Alex Harrison at Newbrough in Scarborough. Richard Harton a London fishmonger had a Scarborough house with wainscot, pewter dishes and candlesticks in his parlour. His son held a local manor but kept houses in London and Southwark. Another London fishmonger arranged for Sir Richard and Hugh Cholmley to mortgage Robin Hood's Bay Cow field in 1626.

Fish were a major part of the Elizabethan food supply. Near the coast, some could be fried in butter and eaten soon after they were taken. Fish could be soused, or pickled, but far more often, the fish were dried, or salted. One part of salt to three of fish gave a lasting store of food. Herring were already familiar, smoked as well as fresh. The fish were carried deep into Yorkshire by land and water. The searchers of the York Company of Fishmongers controlled the sale of all fish brought to the city. They came up river from Scarborough, Whitby, and even Hartlepool. The York fishmongers also went to the coast, or kept partners there, to buy supplies, at most of the smaller havens. Some coastal fishers became York freemen. Any freeman could sell salt or dried fish in open market in Lent, when even Suffolk men rented shops to meet the peak demand. Lincolnshire men appeared and the city knew oysters from Norfolk and salmon from Norway.

A fish landing garth near the Ouse bridge at York was confined to members of the York Fishmongers Company. Strangers had to fasten up and land fish for sale on the bridge itself. They could only cut and sell fish in open market at the fish shambles, but not from houses or shops. Herring and salt fish were sold in bulk at York Pavement. Pannier men from Bridlington Quay, Robin Hood's Bay, Withernsea and York also moved fish inland. The pannier men, "free of the city" of York sold on Wednesdays and Fridays between the gutters on the north and south ends of Fossbridge, while those not free, sold at Walmgate market, at the east end of the bridge.[3]

Pannier men took fish for sale at the fish cross in Malton but John and Ann Frank forestalled the market of panniers of fish, in 1608, buying off fishermen from Runswick or Whitby before the catch came to market. Other Pannier men bought fish at York to take further inland into west Yorkshire. The herring house garth at Selby fish market may well have served as a point of unloading for the south of the county. The earliest herring house at Robin Hood's Bay had belonged to John Smith of Wakefield, a traditional home for Robin Hood, and rather suggestive of an early link between the two places.

A Big Fish

No-one quite knew what the ocean might produce. Near Saltburn, men heard a horrible fearful groaning out at sea. There was talk of the ocean as "a fell and cruel beast desiring to devour men's bodies". There were tales of sea monsters and the makers of the new maps and charts illustrated their coastlines with pictures of fearsome and monstrous fishes. Skinningrove fishermen talked of a merman of the sea who was caught and kept for many weeks in an old house near the sands, till he escaped back to the deep. He fed on raw fishes and nothing else, shrieked a lot but smiled happily on the fair maids among the many who came to see him.[4]

A big fish, twenty yards long, taken at Hessle Cliff in 1551, was seen as a bad omen, thought to be confirmed by the death of the monarch soon afterwards. The Register of the Stationers Company of London for 1595 included an account of "A strange and high fish, driven on the sands at Owthorne in Holderness in February". Into Coatham, in Tees mouth, in October 1615, "came there on land a mighty fish, the length whereof nineteen yards, the body in compass twenty yards, the nose end in compass eight yards, the tail was over the end four yards, and there was betwixt the eyes four yards". Four oxen could hardly draw his tail, which was cut off at ten yards. The stream of oil was like a pretty river. Sir Henry Belassis sold it to John White of Coatham for £120.

Sturgeon, whale, porpoise, seal and grampus were royal fish, reserved to the monarch, although at Filey where the local lord had rights to a whale, only the head and tail were kept for the Queen. Seals were sometimes taken at Filey Brigg, where a spur of rocks rose above sea level. Royal fish had been delivered to the custody of the Abbot at Whitby, until he was replaced by members of the York and Cholmley families as overlords of the borough. The Admiralty court sitting at Scarborough in 1583 fined Christopher Langdale, the Cayton constable, forty shillings for taking a porpoise. Robert Wilkinson of Cayton took another and Robert Usher of Filey was jailed for taking one that had washed on shore.

Seals in great herds "used to sleep and bask themselves in the sun" at low water on the rocks that surfaced towards Huntcliff and Bullfleet Gate in Cleveland. "On the outermost rock, one great seal or more keeps sentinel, which upon the first inkling of any danger, giveth the alarm to the rest by throwing of stones, or making a noise in the water; when he tumbles down from the rock, the rest immediately do the like, insomuch that it is very hard to overtake them by cunning. If it fortune that any unawares hath chosen his sleeping forth so far from the seas, that he is in hazard to become prey unto the pursuer, he then betaketh himself to his arms, flinging the pebbles and sand from his hinder feet with such a tempest and force, that a man had need be well advised before he approaches too near. They fly the sight of men as of those from whom they have received many shrewd turns, where the poor women that gather cockles and mussels on the sands, by often use, are in better credit with them. Therefore who so intends to kill any of them must craftily put on the habit of a woman, to gain ground within the reach of his peece."[4]

Such fish were used with other blubber, livers and fish waste at Scarborough to make train oil in 1597. The licence was held by a group of merchants on a seven years lease, but passed to five cordwainers in 1603. These men vigourously protested when the London widow of the chief yeoman of the Queen's pantry was given a monopoly patent for buying fish livers and making train oil throughout the entire realm. The Borough Bailiffs went to the Exchequer court, arguing that they had always had the making of train oil in the town and that this a was a great help towards the maintenance of both the Scarborough pier and the Scarborough poor.

River Fisheries

Fresh fish came from Inland waterways, as well as from manorial fishponds and mill races, where stationery traps were used rather than the moveable nets of the coast. Holinshed distinguished Yorkshire rivers by the fish they yielded. There was the Ouse "whose water brings forth a very sweet, tart and delicate salmon", and other fish. The Hull river abounded with sturgeon and lamprey, while the Derwent, rising in the moors west of Robin Hood's Bay, in its lower courses, carried "plenty of delicate salmon". The Nidd had good store of salmon, but the Wharfe and the Aire provided only red trout and perch.[5] Crayfish were plentiful in the river Ure and its tributary streams. Camden's editor claimed that they were introduced to the river Yore from the south of England by Sir Christopher Metcalfe. Another tradition was that they were put there by Sir Walter Raleigh on a visit to Nappa some years later.[6]

The great estuary fishings were on a considerable scale. Camden found the Humber an estuary, "best stored with fish of any in the kingdom". The river Tees was fished from Stockton in County Durham, as well as from Coatham and other riverside places, where early monastic fishing rights had passed to others. The valuable Tees fisheries that had belonged to Rievaulx Abbey, with their fish house and fish garth, worth a fifteen pounds yearly rent, passed to the Conyers family of Sockburn. Early agreements provided that none were to fish from Saltholm up the Tees with kiddle nets for taking smelts, sparlin or fry, from St Mark's day to Lammas Day. The fishermen had agreed in 1530 that when seal, porpoise, sturgeon or other head fish lit into a haling net, those present with haling nets would have him, but not if the fish came into other nets.[7]

Permanent river fisheries were numerous along the main water courses. Between 1554 and 1602, inland fishermen made wills at Acaster Malbis, Aike (Lockington), Airmin, Beverley, Naburn, Owthorne, Paulfleet, Thirne, York, Doncaster, Waghen and Newbald near Drax. There were probably many more, who made part of their living in this way. Frameworks of timber, variously known as fish garths, kiddells, fish hecks or fish weirs, were set in the river beds near the bank where there was a good flow. Wings ran to the bank and into the stream, with stakes and stays close wattled to stop the passage of the fish, which were diverted up to the kiddel trap. Eels given to " running" in wind and rain were caught differently. They were trapped in tubular nets, on hoops, tapering to pods, strung from a rope across the river. The Archbishop of York enjoyed a rent of £8 a year from the Cawood ferry and his fishery in the Ouse.

The City of York was much exercised about the interruption to river navigation by the fish garths. They had secured an Act of Parliament "for amending the rivers Ouse and Humber and for pulling down and avoiding of fishgarths, piles, stakes and other engines set in the rivers" in 1531-2. The city had a wide jurisdiction. The Mayor granted licences for fishing the rivers, and a water bailiff annually surveyed the weirs in Ouse, Humber, Wharfe, Derwent, Aire and Don, and removed hindrances. He presented those at court who threw ramell, dung or filth in the Ouse and received half the fines. The Corporation viewed the fish garths in the Ouse and Humber in 1564, the Lord Mayor, the recorder and others making a voyage for the purpose. The six room fish garth at Skelton and the ten room garth at Yokefleet in the Ouse were judged to be nuisances in 1571. York took earlier action against four city fishmongers who confessed to agreeing with the fishers of Acaster and Bishopthorpe to buy all their salmon at fixed prices. Some had gone down the Ouse and bought smelts, lampreys and other fish, forestalling the open market. Others had steeped stock fish in lime water to make it look fair and white.

Fishing in other water courses and in mill ponds, was controlled by manor lords. Many river fisheries were leased out. The Boroughbridge stewards replaced licensed fisheries with leases, requiring payments and a salmon in winter and another in summer for a pair of boats. Roger Portington at Tudworth, had the fishings in Bridge and Sowerdykes, and separate fishings in Langholme, in New Fleet water, and six more streams. Braithmere fisheries in the Marshland were leased with the Hatfield Park pasture agistments in 1558. Elsewhere fishponds were supplied with water diverted from rivers, often but not always associated with mill races. Those at Ayton castle survive as a line of earthworks.

National legislation limited fishing to appropriate seasons and banned the taking of small fry. Manor courts enquired whether anyone killed young brood, spawn or fry of salmon, eels, pike or other fish in mill tails or streams. No-one was to take salmon, trout or pike out of season, or pikes under ten inches, barbell under twelve inches, salmon under sixteen inches or trout under eight inches. Action was taken when weirs in the river Yore were given "ran webs", which killed young fry. The Aldbrough manor court prohibited the taking of kep salmon in kep time.

T77 Some Monastic Fisheries passed to new Owners

Byland Abbey	Gormire fishery, Coxwold fishpond, Oldstead vivaries
Fountains	Eelmare,
Kirkham	Rye fishery from Ryebridge eastwards, Derwent fishery at Firby
Malton	Derwent fishery
Rievaulx	Derwent fisheries.
Roche abbey	Tithe of eels in Hatfield chase
Selby	Fishery of the dam and the carrs, Crowle water with swans .
Warter	Fisheries in Derwent at Wheldrake
Whitby	Esk fishing from Ruswarp
York, Holy Trinity.	Fishery and tithe of others fishery at Drax.
York St Mary	Tithe fish of Hornsea mere. Monkflete and Bradmere

Coastal Harbours

The construction of a pier could give an area of calmer water and protection from high seas in heavy weather. The building of a quay or a staithe made for easier loading and off loading of the larger ships. Only a few of the coastal havens had either piers or quays. Several of the fishing stations had no harbour works at all, though some may once have done so. When a pier was built, the harbour tended to silt up. Heaped rocks, at best set within timber frameworks, were the only available method of pier construction. They were open to frequent breach from the sea's rage, while all timbers were attacked by marine organisms. Stone structures could only be built on dry ground or at prolonged low water.

16 A Tudor Quay Scene

Deep-water anchorages, where goods could be transhipped to another boat or a quay, were rare indeed. Most of the coastal harbours were only accessible at higher tides. As the tide receded, the vessels stood beached on sand. They are portrayed so at Scarborough in a contemporary sketch, a row of ships roped to anchors, high and dry. Whitby was better placed on the small estuary of the river Esk, while Bridlington harbour was fed by a weak watercourse, supplemented by some springs in the harbour mouth.

Each harbour had its own difficulties but the common problem in the time of Queen Elizabeth was the short life of piers and quays without continual and costly maintenance and repairs. The responsibility for maintaining several harbours moved from monasteries to the Crown and to other new owners, bringing crises at Hornsea, Whitby, Robin Hood's Bay and Bridlington. Other havens found the cost of harbour maintenance a heavy burden and repeatedly sought Crown help.

Hornsea Burton had a population of two hundred and forty in 1485 while Hornsea itself had three hundred and forty. Both were sizeable places by the standards of the day. The Hornsea quay had been maintained by St Mary's Abbey, York, partly financed by a levy on masters and owners, each time that fishing vessels put to sea. With the dissolution of the monastery, the Crown became responsible and gave subsidies for repairs. Between 1546 and 1609, thirty-eight houses and a two hundred and forty yard strip of the Hornsea coast was washed away by the sea. One man took twenty tons of stone and two pieces of timber to his Grimsby house in 1556.[8]

250

Bridlington pier was repaired by the Crown using stone from the monastery which wouldn't withstand the surges of the sea, breaking up even when couched with rossell and pitch, and bound with iron and lead. Six hundred loads of timber had to be brought from distant Leconfield and Haltemprice between 1539 and 1545. Neighbouring townships were obliged to send in men to the "common works" on the pier, employed along with labourers on both day and piece rates, carpenters at seven pence a day. Labourers moving wains were paid two pence a load. John Ledum gave money for pier repair at Whitby in 1531. Leland a few years later said that a new key and port was being made from fallen rock. Yet the harbour was in such decay in 1545 that only small ships could get in or out. The bailiff George Conyers claimed that all Whitby vessels suitable for use as ships of war had been sold by their owners, on account of the state of the harbour and the inability of the local inhabitants to mend it. The King spent great sums of money on the pier.

The "suck of the sea" weakened the timber frames or "rooms" holding the stones. At Bridlington the lack of good stone and rotting of timber negated all effort and expenditures and the pier was in great decay again in 1562. The Marquis of Winchester wrote to the Queen in 1568 on the decayed state of the piers of Bridlington and Robin Hood's Bay. He urged leases of Crown property to build up repair funds. He argued that "Your majesty shall understand that the pier of Bridlington and the pier of Robin Hood's Bay in the same country be in great decay, notwithstanding there hath been bestowed in the keeping of them in the king your father's time and yearly since to the sum of four score pound and in timber four score tun whereby your highness woods in that quarter be in manner consumed and yet the said piers presently in as much need of reparation as ever they were and yet they must needs be repaired or the country shall not be served at the ports and yet much of your graces ground and other men's land under the water whereby your rents and other men's shall utterly decay".

The first of several Crown leases of the Bridlington Priory estates was made to a group of townsmen in 1566. This shifted responsibility for harbour maintenance and repair, to the tenants, who were then bound to ensure the safe custody of ships, boats and hoys. They were allowed £100, the old pier materials, the monastery stone and one hundred and twenty trees, together with the tolls, duties and the pier rates. The falling in of the leases suggests that there was little success. Another lease to John Stanhope in 1591, again required maintenance and repair of the ruined pier walls, the jetties, sluices, sunken lockers and rooms. There was renewed decay by 1596. Only in c1630 were feoffees created who bought the manor at Bridlington.[9]

The manorial harbour at Flamborough was in no better case, the pier utterly decayed in 1561. One old chart appears to show two piers and centuries later locals spoke of a mole and old quay rocks. The farm of the anchorage of ships and small vessels "in the port called the pier within the manor of Flamborough included tolls of fish and pannier men and fowling on the cliff". A fresh lease of the "harbour known as a peer" went with the manor to Robert Puckering and others, who were willing to attempt reconstruction the next year. Things were bad again by c1569. The Lennox manor of Hunmanby had groundage of every ship landed within a Filey pier, claiming six pence on every ship and two bushels of coal from every coal ship, supposedly for finding a bushel measure.

Scarborough Harbour Works

A 16th century sketch of Scarborough shows the limited facilities of that ancient port. The projecting pier of no great length, stood on rocks, running westwards from the base of the castle, to form an area of quiet water. The pier carried a small hut and a gun. Of the sixteen vessels in the harbour, four were on the land side of a second, more northerly "island" pier, probably a remnant of an earlier pier. This had timber balks on each side. Eight or nine of the vessels shown were three masted and the town was recorded as having eight "topmen" of between forty and a hundred tons in 1582. Strong, vertical timbers held up a seawall or quay of stone blocks north of the piers, in the general area of Quay street. A line of staithes ran from the quay westwards to West Sand gate, in an area later backed by Staithe Bolts. There was a small turret on the sands well clear of the harbour, and south of the millrace, about which nothing is known.

Many expedients were adopted to finance repairs of the Scarborough pier. Lead blown from two steeples of the church was sold in 1555 and more lead taken from the St. Thomas and St. Sepulchre chapels to raise money in 1562. The Council in the North was petitioned for relief to mend the decayed pier in 1564. The Council urged the Scarborough burgesses to seek local money. The Archbishop as Lord President did authorise an appeal by Master Peacock and Robert Wyvill to the Lord Mayor of York for the well disposed in the City of York to help towards amendment of "part of Scarborough pier or haven now in decay". St Sepulchres church was taken down to provide stone. The petition was sent to Queen Elizabeth, who granted £500, a hundred tons of timber and six tons of iron to rebuild the pier.

The result was a major improvement, virtually a new pier, albeit on the basis of the old one. The "Council in the North", acting for the Queen agreed in 1567, that the Scarborough men would repair and make the pier, not only as long as it had been, but so much longer, "as certain stones at the west end now lieth, which would be twenty or thirty yards longer". They would find ten men working daily for wages until completion within two years. The base breadth was to be raised from thirty feet to forty five feet at least, the top width from nine to twelve feet at least, and the height from sixteen to a minimum of twenty feet.

The cooper was ordered to repair the several "tuns" belonging to the town that year. These were rafts used for moving stone. Scarborough undertook, at its own charge, to lay "great stones of weight five and six tons a piece at least, to lie in height five or six feet or more, all along against the foundation of the outside of the pier, towards the sea, within four years". Every inhabitant was ordered to give three hours labour weekly to the pier and in 1568, members of the common council of the borough were ordered to pay weekly contributions to pier repairs.

Bailiff Nicholas Wolfe gave details of the new Scarborough pier in 1584. This was said to be two hundred and sixty seven yards long, twenty yards broad at the bottom and seven and a half yards at the top. Depth towards the sea was ten yards, and the inside depth nine yards. The pier stood on clay beneath the sand. It had cost the £500 grant from the Queen and over £2000 since. Repairs took about £40 a year. Some rocks had been brought half a mile from the backside of the castle, and others by hand barrow from behind the pier. A crane was used to rear smaller stones with a pair of windlasses and a plank bridge. The master of the works was paid eight pence a tide and sixteen pence a day. The water rose eighteen foot at spring tides and eleven foot at neap tides.

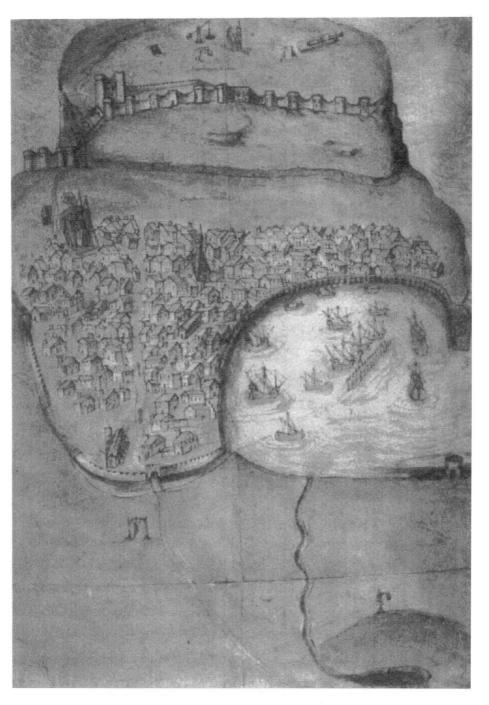

17 The 'Engineer's Plat' of circa 1538. The First Image of Scarborough

A major improvement was a great sea gate, in the pier, which was opened in storms to let the storm water wash out the accumulated sand. The pier was still occasionally breached but was repaired as quickly as possible. A length of thirty-five foot, lately beaten down, had cost £92.10s to repair. They had "petty money" consisting of twelve pence from every ship having a toppe and eight pence from every crayer while every fisherman paid two shillings a year towards the cost of pier maintenance. The new pier was a major construction for the age.

As a result, Sir Thomas Scott recommended using Scarborough men to finish the repair of the damaged Dover pier. Engineer Thomas Dygges thought the Scarborough plan better than the one they had adopted. The bailiffs sent cooper William Newby, two of their best workmen, Henry and Robert Petch and William Forde. Timber was landed at Dover in June, when efforts were being made to get tuns and a chair. Their efforts became controversial. By July, Paul Ive wanted the men of Scarborough discharged. Another critic claimed that "the work of the jetty, proposed by a simple man of Scarborough is very unfit for Dover" He objected to jetties made of rock stone and timber as at Scarborough. He disliked calling in strangers for their opinion.

Pier maintenance remained a continual charge at Scarborough but more improvements were attempted. The key men, Thomas Newton and John Dickinson were told to build the end of the west Scarborough pier, twenty or thirty yards longer for £45 in 1591. They contracted for the "breach of the pier at the Out gate and for repairing the rest of the pier and they also agreed to build up and make a new work at the end, in a substantial manner, as far south as the uttermost part of the stones now lying. They were to finish in four years, in 1598, for the jetty money, received from fishers and crayers". Thomas Butler, the coroner, contracted the next year, to finish the west end of the great pier, as far as outer rocks laying there, within twelve months for £40. Part had been beaten down in 1600 This was a work which was never done.[10]

The Great River Ports

Hull was the great estuary port, free of many of the problems that beset the coastal harbours, but subject to floods, erosion and silting up. Sited at the junction of the old river Hull, near Myton and the river Humber, its origins were as a haven where traders from Beverley and York, transhipped between river and sea going vessels on such a scale as to make this the largest Yorkshire port by 1204. Archbishop Gray founded a borough at Wyke on Humber in 1239, from which large quantities of wool were exported. Meaux Abbey acquired much of Wyke and Myton but sold it all to king Edward I in 1293, who six years later formed Wyke into a free borough under the Crown, as Kingston upon Hull. The burgesses gained privileges similar to Scarborough but the walled town enjoyed better access to a far larger hinterland.

Elizabethan merchants of York and Beverley remained heavily involved in the sea going ships, which met the river traffic at Hull. Both were reached by river ships. Beverley had made an early cut to the river Hull, forming a small river port, south east of the town. All commodities brought into Hull had to be landed before sale. Imported goods were transhipped for Beverley and York in thirty to forty ton keels. Exports were loaded on to foreign as well as English ships. York had a substantial merchant community, which even in Elizabeth's reign played a strong part in county trading and enjoyed privileges at Hull. In the early part of the century, there were ten or more keel boats of thirty or forty tuns on the river Ouse, and some lighters, while the city had two crayers, able to go to sea, of thirty six tons each. The water of Ouse was often so low that they sometimes couldn't pass to Hull. Larger vessels were now trading at sea.

Hull had common staithes and private staithes on the west bank of the river Hull with locked gates, cranes and warehouses, including Danyelstaithe, Horsestaithe, Hornseystaithe, Hurystaithe, Chapelstaithe, Grimsbystaithe, and Rotenheryng staithe. King's staithe was sometimes called a quay and had a latrine. The other staithes comprised a narrow causeway leading to the river bank which ended in a stone and timber jetty. The Corporation had to give much attention to maintaining the haven banks. Seamen loaded ships with the help of catch men, who also supplied ballast from mud banks within the haven. Any one depositing ballast in the river was heavily fined. Fire and candles were banned on ships and staithes after the ship *Dragon* caught fire in 1564.[11]

The York staithes were rebuilt between 1567 and 1570, with the north east part of Ouse bridge set aside for the fish staithe. The St. Leonards landing was a large staithe. The famous York crane was in Cranegarth at the end of Skeldergate. The city still commanded a good deal of inland trade for a wide hinterland. The city fathers stopped keels delivering goods between the city and the mouth of the Wharfe, when lastage, passage and cranage tolls were lost, especially at Tadcaster. The tolls were leased to a new water bailiff. Merchants from London, Kings lynn, Boston and Newcastle bought lead at York. Lead loaded at Borough Bridge came here for weighing, along with wool from the North and East Ridings, and West Riding coal and lime.

River Havens

Small fishing boats and shallow river boats came beyond coastal waters into the main rivers of the shire. The river Tees was navigable for nine miles to Yarm and Stockton. Small craft sailing along the Humber and Trent had access to much of middle England. The river Ouse was tidal, up to a small way above its junction with the river Wharfe, a few hundred yards north of Cawood, but drought, flood and frost sometimes hindered the navigation. Small vessels went on the Ure to Borough bridge, Topcliffe, Ripon, Northallerton, Knaresborough and Bedale. Wetherby could be reached on the Wharfe, and Thorne, Doncaster, and Bawtry by the Don and the Idle.

Loading and unloading places were numerous along the Hull, Ouse, Derwent, Don, Wharfe and other rivers. A few which had some facilities for berthing and storage qualified as river ports. They saw far less storm damage than those on the coast but suffered from flooding and erosion of their wooden staithes. A great tide in the Humber had flooded all the neighbouring country in 1527, the water standing a foot deep in the highest part of Hull. There were river floods in 1550 and in 1571 when high tides, the highest ever known, broke the banks of the Humber and Hull rivers and drove people into upper rooms. The Bishop's manor at Howden was occasionally flooded. The Ouse river banks were eroded by the "Eagre", which was a tidal bore, and by flood waters, and everyday wear and tear. This rise and fall of water made it an advantage to tie boats to staithes at one end only. Many other banks needed periodical reinforcement with breastworks. The eroded coast at Paul was unsafe in1598.

Holinshed named Patrington, Holmes, Keyingham, Paul, Hedon, Hullbridge, Beverley, Hull, Hessle, North Ferriby, Bucke Creek, Wressell and Howden as the river havens of Humberside. Hedon had been a successful 12th century borough and Humber river port, where ships had quartered about the town in sea creeks, but they were overgrown by Queen Elizabeth's time, and the haven was sorely decayed. Vessels still discharged at Patrington haven, linked by a channel to the main river. The staithes at Paul, received fish, brought to dry from Hull, paying twopence a hundred for the privilege. The small inlet villages of low lying Howdenshire, were well provided with staithes. Sandhall, Kilpin and Saltmarsh each had great middle and west staithes while Skelton had north and south staithes. Timber for staithe repair was taken from Howden park in 1561.

There were staithes at Asselby, Wistow, Airmyn, Hatfield and Raincliff, four at Hook, and some at Turnbridge at the confluence of Don and Aire. Staithes west of the Ouse were important transhipment points from the West Riding, not least for taking out woollen kerseys and cutlery. Several Ouse river ports had acquired small boroughs in the Middle Ages. These included Drax, Airmyn and Selby, where the abbey had kept a large barge, a small ship, two punts and a ferryboat. The Abbot's staithe, the quay wall, a stone warehouse, the herring house garth at Ousegate, the CnarGate and Houthwaite landings saw continuing Elizabethan trade. Grain came from Barton on Humber, faggots and turves from Rawcliff while rye was landed at Selby for a Wakefield merchant. Grain moved from Whitgift to Knottingley and to Doncaster staithes. Stainforth was a landing place reached from the Isle of Axholm, where traders hired horses to travel on to Doncaster market.[12]

Bawtry became a significant port. The products of the Sheffield cutlers, and Derbyshire lead workers were brought here over land and loaded on keels and catches. Foodstuffs, Spanish steel and London hides, were unloaded for the inland districts including Nottinghamshire. An agreement drawn up between the Earl of Shrewsbury's officer, Richard Richardson of Bawtry and the freeholders bound the inhabitants not to encourage anyone to load or unload at wharfs other than that belonging to the Earl. They made a bye law banning stacking of goods on the highway to the river Idle. There was even boat building and repairing by 1622.

North Riding villages to the north of York had their landing places. Newbrough Priory had kept a granary at Newton on Ouse. Skelton Hall moor farm formerly of St Mary's Abbey had a road to a wharf on the river. Leland described the river Fosse as a slow stream, yet able to bear a good vessel, but it seems to have become blocked later. Over in the East Riding, the rental for an oxgang in Market Weighton, included rendering two fat hens and carrying a load of coals yearly from Brough Haven to the Earls house at Londesborough.

Ships

England had about fifty thousand tons of merchant shipping in 1560. Ships were of modest size. They were rated on how many wine tuns they might carry. The Gascon wine trade had employed large vessels to carry bulk wine cargoes. The barrel known as the tun held two hundred and fifty-two gallons. Few local vessels reached sixty tons. Coasting vessels were often of small tunnage but ships of fifty to a hundred tons might sail to the Baltic, Bordeaux and Spain. The State recorded the number of larger vessels at the Yorkshire ports, from time to time. Vessels under twenty-five tons were of no use for naval warfare.

Forty three ships belonged to owners at Yorkshire harbours in 1559-60, rising to forty seven by 1572, of which forty were at Hull and among them, the *Talbot*, *Elizabeth*, *Mayflower* and *Primrose* were each of one hundred tons. Hull had more ships capable of keeping the sea than any English port except London, Bristol and Southampton. The 1582 survey listed 1518 ships of which 78% were under a hundred tons and 16,283 seafarers. Yorkshire's contribution was 55 ships of 3,416 tons. Ownership of ships is said to have shrunk at Scarborough. Its councillors claimed that its ships had dropped in number from 50 to 6 while crayers for merchandise had dropped from 20 to 4 by 1575.

T 78 Ships of Scarborough, 1547-53

name	tons	owner	master	men
John Baptiste	80	William Lockwood	.John Gray	10
Mary Grace	55	Wiliam Girdler	Thomas Shakills	7
Mare Kateryn	50	Robert Nightingale.	Wm Kenros	
			Robert Banke	7
Mare James	58	William Kenros	LaurenceBedon	8
Mary Sithe	26	Nicholas Clarke	Nicholas Clarke	3
Fishing boats which cannot sail to any ports without pilots but only fishing seas				
Gabriell	50	Wm Percy &	Richard Denande	6
		Richard Denande.		
Blithe	40	Wm Kenros &	John Stephenson	6
		.John Stephenson		
George	40	John Herwood &	John Bedom	5
		William Kenros		
Bartholomew	55	Richard Conyers.	John Beeford	6
Cudbarte	40	William Lockwood	Robert Craill	6
James of Barwike	20	Sir William Eure	John Battie	6
Thomas	40	William Kenros &	Thomas Londe	6
		Widow Bedom.		
Trinity	50	Fras Kildale, Robt Bank &	John Osten	6
			William Stoxley.	
Christopher	50	Robt Raughton &	Robert Shipperde	5
		Thomas Browne		

Ship building or at least repairs may have taken place at Hull, Beverley, Scarborough and Hornsey. Between 1500 and 1550 three shipwrights left wills at Scarborough, two and a ships carpenter at Hull and one at Dripool. John Peirson the Scarborough shipwright of 1539 owned a great tree lying in Raincliff in nearby Seamer. Between 1554 and 1594, eleven ship carpenters left wills at Hull, one ship carpenter and one shipwright at Beverley, and a single shipwright at Hornsey. Hull had four anchor smiths. Thomas Clarke the Scarborough anchor smith had a pair of bellows in his Key street workshop. York shipwrights were James Croniss in 1570 and Oswald Ewbank in 1590. Although ships were bought from the Dutch, it seems likely that local men could build the twenty to fifty tun fishing boats, fifty to a hundred ton sea going vessels, and the forty to eighty tun river craft. An Amsterdam man, Evart Thomson sold a hoy to a group of Scarborians, in 1598.

Mariners

Mariners, fishermen and river men were distinctive groups, but taken together they formed a small but important part of the county population. The mariners went further afield, crossing the North Sea or the German Ocean as it was called, far beyond the Dogger Bank fishing grounds. Few became prosperous enough to leave wills but the number of men and women involved in the sea was greater than either the wills or the shipping lists suggest. Scarborough alone in 1601 had 35 owners of vessels and thirty-nine masters. Crews varied from three or four up to seven or eight for whaling voyages. Each vessel might make up to twelve voyages a year.

T79 Yorkshire Mariners and River men, who made wills, 1554-1602

mariners	Hull 60, Fishlake 5, York 2, Sculcoates, Sykehouse, Selby, Beverley, Scarborough, Bridlington quay,
keelmen	Hull 2, Fishlake 3
lighterman	Hull
waterman	Beverley 5, Paulflete
shipman	Fishlake 3
shipmaster	Hull 5

The ancient laws of Oleron required a mariner to take one blow from a master. He was fined if he hit back and he could lose the hand. The Hull Shipman's Guild exercised some supervision of mariners throughout the Hull customs port, which embraced the coast northwards beyond Scarborough. The members were skilled master mariners of sea going ships and Humber pilots who could bring a ship in or out of that estuary. They were examined in navigation on entering the guild. The other mariners were under the Trinity House not in it. They could be fined or imprisoned for disobedience or for negligence at sea. A ship's carpenter at Scarborough called his master a knave and was severely punished. The Master of the *Mary Rose* complained of a gunner's disobedience in 1593. He had refused to fire the gun when the master left the ship's side and was imprisoned for twenty-four hours.

Seamen learnt their craft through apprenticeship to other seamen. A few became mates or masters. The master was often agent for the cargo, the mate his deputy. Larger vessels had a boatswain responsible for stowing cargo and in charge of discipline and the ship's gear, a carpenter who did running repairs and a purser who sought freight and paid wages. They were paid weekly, monthly or by the voyage. On the London-Newcastle run a master might get four pounds and a mariner two pounds for twelve days, but many received less. Men had the right to be paid off in their home port and could claim conduct money in case of wreck. The Hull Trinity House settled wages and could compel a master to pay them. Mariners, mostly in their twenties were paid less than farm workers but had free victuals. They were required to stay twelve days after a voyage to unload and load.

Wage disputes were frequent. Three mariners complained against the owners of the *Thomas* for wages to Newhaven in 1584-5 after returning from Malstrand. They were awarded 14s.6d and a chalder of coals each. Trinity house collected the seaman's lowage and stowage money but offered some support when mariners were old, or out of a berth. The Scarborough ship owners and master mariners formed an association in 1602 when they agreed that owners would pay fourpence on completion of a voyage, at any port, to four governors who would use the money for seamen's charity. Master mariners paid a penny a hire for coasting voyages and double for crossing the sea.

258

T80 A list of the number of the masters, mariners and fishermen, belonging to every shire through the realm, certified 1583. [13]

shire	master	mariners	fishermen	total
London	143	991	191	1325
Essex	145	578		693
Norfolk	145	1458		1603
Suffolk	69	198		267
Cornwall	108	626	1184	1918
Devon	150	1915	101	2166
Dorset	85	460	100	645
Bristol	84	464		548
Southampton	25	133	64	222
Isle of Wight	21	94	119	234
York	81	292	507	880
North parts	29	372	450	851
Lincoln	20	195	334	549
Sussex	70	371	122	563
Kent		243		243
Cinque ports.	200	604	148	952
Cumberland	12	180	20	212
Gloucester	19	100	23	142
Chester	85	253	36	374
Lancaster	5	42		48
	4466	9570	3399	14435
			London wherrymen	957
			total	15392

Perils of the Sea

There were always perils at sea. Shipwrecks were already familiar. Indeed, the coast was divided into nine or ten stretches from Humber to Tees whose lords enjoyed ancient rights to gather "wreck". Lord High Admiral Lincoln sent an instruction to the Vice Admiral to respect the right of wreck between Runswick and Yarm of Thomas Darcy and Katherine Conyers, which they held in 1581-2 as descendants of the feudal lord Peter de Brus. Sir Henry Constable had the rights at Barmston. He took his claims to the Court of King's Bench to regain twelve shirts and five cloaks seized from wreckage for the Lord Admiral in 1601. Sir Thomas Hoby enjoyed right of wreck off Burniston where he had a manor. His wife wrote in the Winter of 1603 "This day It was told Sir Thomas that a ship was wrecked on his land at Burniston –thus at all times God bestows benefits upon us, may God make us thankful".

Flamborough Head was a graveyard for shipping. The vessel *Elizabeth* of London was wrecked there in 1581-2. When another ship went down in October 1588, eight drowned men were buried at Flamborough. Osess Napier, the first Ambassador from Muscovy was shipwrecked and arrived in Scarborough. He had come to negotiate commercial agreements and was forwarded to London. Making landfall in a harbour mouth was no easy matter. Adverse winds and storms could drive a ship far from its destination. King Charles of France sent Admiral Verasque with a fleet to Scotland in

259

1572, but the storms drove him into Scarborough, where he was placed in the castle before despatch to London. Six Scottish ships were driven into Scarborough by storm in 1579.

War and piracy frequently threatened offshore shipping. The two are not easily separated. Piracy could be war in peacetime but other attacks were merely a chance of gain seized when it offered. Lord Burghley's chart described bays north of Withernsea and south of Tunstall as "small creeks for landing of fisher boat wherein small ships at spring tides may also enter and do annoyances". He said of Kilnsea on the Spurn that "ships of good burden may ride and land here to the annoyance of the country". There were many attacks on vessels near Scarborough, spoken of as piracy in the 1560s, often against Scottish ships. John Lovelace of Sandwich in Kent used a captured Ostend fly boat to attack a ship of Le Havre off Scarborough. He was pardoned for piracy. Sir Henry Gates notified Lord President Huntingdon of a crayer which had arrived at Scarborough laden with wine and of "suspicious demeanour". The Council ordered it stayed, the cargo sold and the money stored. Peacock of Scarborough was described as a pirate, when he took a ship of Rouen laden with Spanish wares. Hull had wider interests and raised four pounds in 1576 to ransom prisoners taken by Turkish pirates from London ships.

The Privy council ordered the Lord President and seven other commissioners to enquire into Yorkshire coast piracy in 1577. Twenty-two from Scarborough, seven from Bridlington, three from Filey and two from Whitby, were identified as offenders in piracy. The notorious English pirate Robert Scarborough took a French ship *Le Bon Voullor*, carrying twenty-nine tuns of wine, between Dover and Calais. This was the property of a Paris merchant. It was run ashore at Scarborough but the cargo was confiscated by the bailiffs. Robert was taken by Lord Clinton in Lincolnshire the next year. William Hind, alias Eynuis, a Scarborough mariner, was indicted for piracy on the high seas. He and thirty more in the "James" of Cowes, attacked a galley, murdered the crew and stole powder and weapons. He was found guilty of piracy but not murder and was pardoned.

Customs

A variety of early local tolls included plankage for joining ship to shore. Royal grants to the boroughs added murage, for walls and quayage or pierage for harbour works. The Crown had rights of prise, allowing the King's sheriff to take a proportion of any cargo of wine, from before and behind the mast, at favourable prices. Early customs duties were imposed in 1275 on the export of wool and later extended to cloth, with discriminatory rates for foreign traders. Customs charges were extended to imports and as these grew, the duties grew with them, including tunnage on wine and poundage on merchandise. Queen Mary issued a revised book of rates which made smuggling even more profitable.

The government issued a list of ports in 1558, with defined limits, and legal quays where goods could be loaded and unloaded, subject to customs supervision. The Remembrancer's port books started in 1565 and new Customs Houses were established at the head ports around 1572. The chief officers were required to appoint deputies for small creeks, to keep records and to use informers. A small building at East Sand gate was in use as the Scarborough Custom House by 1591. A site at Bridlington Quay was made a legal quay for customable goods, with control from Flamborough Head to

Barmston. The small St. Anne's Staithe north of the Esk at Whitby was appointed the place of unloading for that port.

One Sunday morning in 1579, mariner Richard Peacock was found wounded on Scarborough sands. He died the next day. He had just left York Castle prison after a conviction for piracy. With merchants William and Matthew Peacock, he had assaulted Marmaduke Lacey of Ganton, Ambrose Lacey and Richard Harton of Ruston "going in the peace of God". Matthew felled Harton with a boat's oar. Richard Peacock made at him with a drawn sword. Harton backed against a boat, but drew his sword and thrust it into Peacock. The other side argued that Harton had assaulted Peacock and Ambrose Lacey with a rapier. Lacey was the customs collector. He was pardoned.

Aids to Navigation

Navigation for smaller vessels was largely a matter of following the known coast. Homely advice was relied on for knowledge about dangerous rocks and good anchorages in strong winds. Some found its way into Hull Trinity House pilot books. "You may safely anchor for a northnortheast wind between the pier and Filey bridge, which is a rock that lieth under water at spring tide". Coastal landmarks included churches and chapels. Those at Lythe, Filey, Scarborough castle chapel and others were perhaps sited for that purpose, distant from their villages or any other settlement. Some coastal beacons were visible from the sea. Ingrish Hill at Bilbrough in Ainsty was a land mark for ships coming up the Humber.

Charts and sailing directions were becoming available for the north west coasts of Europe and the Mediterranean. Mercator in 1569 invented his "projection" representing the world as flat, rather than a sphere, with the lines of lattitude shown as parallel lines. A plan of the Humber attributed to Henry VIII's time showed a vanished island outside Spurn point in the Humber, with three masted and single masted vessels in the channel. "A plotte made for the description of the river of Humber and of the sea and seacoast from Hull to Skarburgh in the reigne of Queen Elizabeth" showed the depth of the Humber channel at low water.

The unstable peninsula at Spurn had gained a lighthouse in 1427 and another was proposed in 1590. Hull Trinity house paid for setting up a beacon, perhaps near Paull in 1567. By 1585 they had one buoy in the Humber and intended two more and two beacons. There is a tradition of buoys placed in the Tees at an earlier date . The port of "Dobhome" on the mouth of the Tees was thought very dangerous. "None dare adventure it except in great necessity or when the sea was very calm. It was sounded and lighthouses built either side of the river, so that Newcastle and other ships fearing foul weather could put in, a hundred or more sail with safety". Camden spoke of high turrets with lights erected "within our remembrance."

Unknown waters were negotiated by dead reckoning, by observing the sun, moon and stars and using the astrolabe, the quadrant and the cross staff, the straight edge, dividers, and compass to follow a course on a chart. A Scarborough merchant imported four dozen compasses from Amsterdam in 1512. William Bourne's navigation manual was issued in 1574. A publication by Waghenaer of Holland ignored Whitby but gave the compass bearing for Robin Hood's Bay. Robert Maddeson of Hull in 1589 had a Rochelle compass, Richard Johnson a mariner's cross staff and George Thew a mariner's whistle. Most important to the mariner was how much water was beneath his feet. The sounding lead of seven, fourteen or twenty eight pounds was marked in fathoms of six feet. Tallow on the bottom could check the sea bed. The rise and fall of tides was known and almanacs embodied tables. The inventory of Scarborough mariner Richard Harrisons in 1623 included "one sea book called Waggeyner", and a bible. He also had a fowling piece one dipsey lead (deep sea) with a line and a pair of can hooks.

The Trinity House of Kingston upon Hull had begun as a Guild making payments to sick members. King Henry VIII had given a charter to the Trinity House of Deptford on Strand in 1512 and during his visit to Hull he gave Hull Trinity House a new charter with exclusive rights of pilotage in the river Humber.

Queen Elizabeth's charter of 1581-2 gave the corporation of Hull Trinity house power to govern themselves and seamen of the port, to settle disputes about mariners' wages and to collect dues throughout the havens and creeks of the Hull Customs port. The Board was authorised to "make order for the better and more safeguarding and conducting of all manner of ships and to licence pilots for shipping going beyond Flamborough head and Winterton ness." They could forbid anyone taking a ship beyond these bounds without their licence as a fit pilot. The Trinity House would promote the safety of mariners. They had a monopoly of the Humber pilotage and their licences for pilots to bring ships down the Humber were like the master's certificates of a later age. They set up a warning can near Birkham Sands in 1593, a sort of buoy with chain and anchoring stones, charging vessels from distant ports to sustain it. They set up a great stake in the harbour at Hull and appointed a haven master in 1590.[14]

Sir Martin Frobisher

Martin Frobisher came from Altofts near Wakefield, a son of the manor house. "For lack of good schools", he was sent to the house of his mother's brother Sir John Yorke, a wealthy London Merchant. As a young man, he sailed in voyages to Guinea. He married Isobel Rigatt of Snaith. Many voyages followed, some for trade. but others for privateering, a licensed activity against the ships of other countries which could degenerate into piracy, and was so considered when pursued without licence.

He bought the ship "Matthew", 100 tons, in 1565 from John Baxter, described as a gentleman and town bailiff of Scarborough. She was renamed the Mary Flower and was rigged, trimmed and caulked at Newcastle on Tyne. She left Tynemouth in December 1565 with 36 aboard including Baxter, intending a voyage to Guinea. Driven north from the Humber in a storm, with masts and sails ruined, she had to be beached near Scarborough on Christmas day. The Admiralty bailiff arrested the ship for debts owed by John Frobisher. They stayed for months trying to raise funds for a refit.

There is some suspicion that unlicensed privateering was intended. They were well armed, but had no certain cargo. Martin was examined by officers of the York Admiralty court and his case referred to the Privy council. John borrowed money and took an early opportunity to sail for the West country. The "May Flower" was victualled at Scarborough for a month, with three tons of biscuits, a hogshead of beef, and more butter, cheese and bread. They lay in Bridlington roads a day and half, while John went ashore to call on Mr Boynton at Barmston, whence he bought a sheep, capons, fish and more bread. Contrary winds drove them back almost to Newcastle but they made Yarmouth on May 10th and the Thames by the 14th. At Yarmouth, they were briefly arrested on suspicion of piracy.

Frobisher made many such voyages in subsequent years. He gained fame from voyages in breach of the new Muscovy Company's monopoly to discover new markets via northern sea routes. A voyage with two small ships, the Gabriel and the Michael and a pinnace, took thirty-four men seeking to discover the north-west passage to Cathay under Frobisher's command. They left the Thames on 12th June, 1576. They touched Greenland, lost the pinnace in a storm in the Davis Strait, and saw the Michael turn back. The Gabriel entered Baffin Bay, and lost five men to the Inuit. Those remaining returned to England, bringing an Inuit family captive and a piece of black ore, claimed to be gold.

Claims to have found the north-west passage were not justified, although a Cathay Company was formed. A second expedition with three ships went to find the ore not the passage. They mined ore at Warwick Island. The prospect of riches beyond belief brought out ample investors to finance a third voyage. Fifteen ships sailed in May 1578 and more than a thousand tons of ore was brought back, which proved of little worth. Martin Frobisher had lost his reputation and a good deal of money, including some investment by the Queen.

Frobisher gained brief employment commanding a transport taking troops to Ireland but then vanished from the record for several years, only to re-emerge in Crown employment in the wars against Spain. In 1585 Frobisher was surprisingly appointed Vice Admiral to Sir Francis Drake for the famous raid on the West Indies. Two years later, once again in royal favour, he commanded a fleet of seven ships in the Channel. With the assembly of an English fleet, against the Spanish Armada, in April 1588, Lord Admiral Howard summoned Frobisher. He took command of the Triumph, the largest ship in the fleet.

At dawn on the 23rd of July, he won a tactical victory, with fearless and imaginative manoeuvres, in a close fought action, at a moment of crisis. Frobisher was made commander of one of four parts of the fleet and again fought aggressively and with distinction, in an action, since described as "a close run thing" off the Solent on the 25th. Frobisher led from the front. He was knighted on the Ark Royal and received £4979, share of the prize money. Some he spent acquiring Yorkshire properties. Frobisher was no saint. He has some reputation as an uncultivated and violent man, but he served his country and he served himself, well. He had other fleet commands in later years. He died at Plymouth of a carelessly dressed wound received in an attack on Brest in 1594.

Other northern men captained great ships in the English fleet against the Armada, including Lord Cumberland and Lord Sheffield. A lively legend claims that Thomas Ferris of Glaisdale and later of Hull, sailed in 1588, against the Armada in a ship fitted out at Whitby. It is said that he was chosen on July 27th to go in the fireships, which caused the Armada to scatter, which he piloted and had a hand in setting them alight. Yorkshire with the rest of the nation mustered men for war and prepared the beacons as the Armada moved closer. When the Spanish ships passed Flamborough Head, they were no longer a threat. The English vessels following abandoned the pursuit, as they had no more ammunition aboard for a fight.

CHAPTER 10
TOWN LIFE

Yorkshire Towns

The Elizabethan towns were very small. Only in a few places were the inhabitants more numerous than those in the largest villages or the most populous dales. The difference was that the town houses and their people were concentrated in a small area. The traveller John Leland used the word "town" quite freely, for more than fifty-two Yorkshire places that he passed through during his travels. He relied on the size, appearance and function of a place to separate town from village. Some of his descriptions carry conviction. He said of Leeds that it "standeth most by clothing", while Boroughbridge was "a bare thing".

Camden, travelling and writing half a century later than Leland stressed town markets. Yarm was known for its market, Stokesley was a small market town. Howden was remarkable not for its neatness or resort and Beverley was a town, large and populous. Kirkby Moorside was one of the most inconsiderable market towns; but Malton was a market town famous for its vent of corn, horses, fish and country utensils. We may doubt if his distinction between Guisborough as a small town and Pickering as a pretty large town reflects more than a superficial impression.

London was the outstanding town of England, thought to have had sixty thousand people in 1520, rising to two hundred thousand in 1603, perhaps 10% of the national population and large enough to exert a pull on much of the rest of the country. York may have had ten thousand people in 1600. The county town ranked among the other major cities, with a wide sphere of influence, similar in significance to Norwich and Bristol. In Yorkshire, Hull, Beverley and Scarborough, though much smaller, had long been the next largest Yorkshire towns but Scarborough had seen significant decline, from which it took time to recover, while Leeds, with perhaps three to four thousand people may have overtaken the others.

William Harrison, speaking from the south of England, contrasted a market town of three to four hundred families or households and two thousand communicants with a village of forty to sixty households and two to three hundred communicants. His way of thinking would allow very few towns in Yorkshire. When local contemporaries occasionally mentioned a figure, they rarely reached that level. Sheffield in 1571 held 307 households. Malton was said to have 300 families in 1624. Richmond in 1563 had 340 households and Knaresborough a similar figure. Other figures show different things. A survey showed Pickering with about a hundred property plots in 1598, which is very different. Ripon had 1530 householders but that was for the broader parish not the town.

18 The Shambles, York

T81 William Smith's Contemporary List of Yorkshire towns, (with their streams)

York

East Riding

Beverley (on a man made cree to the river Hull), Bridlington (small river), Hedon (small river), Howden, Hull, Kilham (head spring of river Hull), Pocklington (small river), Weighton (Foulney stream).

North Riding

Bedale (small river into Swale), Guisborough (small river into sea), Helmsley (Rye), Hovingham, Kirkby Moreside, Masham (Ure), Middleham (Ure), New Malton (Derwent). Northallerton, Pickering, Richmond (Swale), Ripley (Nidd), Ripon (Ure), Scarborough, Skipton, Stokesley (small river into Tees), Thirsk (Codbeck), Whitby (small river), Yarm (Tees).

265

West Riding

Barnsley (a small river into Don), Bawtrey (Idle), Boroughbridge (Ure), Bradford (a small brook into Aire), Doncaster (Don), Halifax (a small brook into Calder), Knaresborough (Nidd), Leeds (Aire), Otley (Wharfe), Pontefract, Rotherham (Rother), Selby (Ouse), Settle (Ribble), Sheffield (Don), Sherburn (small brook falling to Ouse), Snaith (Aire), Wakefield (Calder), Wetherby (Wharfe).

Town origins made for different landscapes. York was in a class of its own, with roots in a Roman fort and civil capital. The city had been altered by centuries of later life but remained compact within ancient walls, with modest suburbs along each approach road. The great minster towns of Ripon and Beverley had features derived from the distinctive role of their Anglo Saxon churches with their saintly shrines. Other towns had a large manorial demesne hall enclosure at their core, from which some great Anglian or Scandinavian multiple estate had been administered.

Another group of Yorkshire towns originated as new boroughs, planted by Norman lords in the 12th and 13th centuries. A borough was a new kind of community, with a market, a measure of self government free of the lord's manor, within a definite area of land, with house properties called burgages held at fixed rents, and relying on something other than agriculture for its survival. These were not farming communities. They had small burgage plots, rather than large farm crofts. They remained almost entirely within the new boundaries set by their founders

T82 Yorkshire's Mediaeval Boroughs

East Riding

Beverley, Brough, Hedon, Howden, Hull, Ravenserod, Skipsea, South Dalton.

North Riding

Bootham, Helmsley, New Malton, Northallerton, Pickering, Richmond, Scarborough, Skelton, Stokesley, Thirsk, Whitby, Yarm.

West Riding

Airmyn, Almondbury, Bawtry, Bingley. Boroughbridge, Bradford, Doncaster, Drax, Harewood, Knaresborough, Leeds, Otley, Pontefract, (& Westcheap), Ripon, Rotherham, Sheffield, Sherburn in Elmet, Tickhill, Wakefield.

Some boroughs, like New Malton were founded on sites apart from existing villages, but within the township commons. Other boroughs were grafted onto the end of an existing village, which was itself largely comprised of farmsteads. Such boroughs included Helmsley and Yarm. In such a case village and borough abutted each other. Over time, a prospering borough might acquire a manor as Scarborough acquired Falsgrave, or the distinction between burgess and farmer could become blurred by buying and selling of property.

Scarborough and Pontefract were double boroughs, with new and old alongside each other. A few boroughs added small suburbs beyond a boundary wall or ditch. There was a building or two west of Scarborough's Newborough ditch, outside the gate called a Bar. A suburb called Newbigging formed an addition of village size along one approach road to New Malton. Mr. Ringrose lived "without the bar at Malton" in 1577. The boroughs gained more or less freedom from manorial control. Some lost their freedoms with the passage of time.

Other Yorkshire towns grew from farming villages, in the 13th and 14th centuries, or even later. The manor lord acquired a market but no borough was founded. All these towns had market places but the town which grew from a village had a different atmosphere. It stayed under the control of a manor court.

Large Places and Small

Seventy years after the reign was over, the hearth tax returns do give numbers of households in the townships across Yorkshire. They are not evidence for the Elizabethan age but they do show which were the populous places later. Multiplying households by four to five allows some guess at population. They can be compared with the larger figures for numbers of taxpayers for the poll tax of 1377-1379 and with the numbers of men mustered for military duty in 1584. Each reveals something of the relative importance of places in earlier centuries.

T83 The Larger communities, Yorkshire. 1377-9. Number of Poll Tax Payers

York	4018	Hull	1557	Beverley 2663	Scarborough	1393
Pontefract	1085	Doncaster	800	Hullbank/Cottingham 767		
Tickhill	680	Ripon	654	Whitby 640	Sheffield	585
Wakefield	482	(Kirkby Moorside with its dales	511.			

T84 The Larger Communities; East Riding of Yorkshire. 1584. Number of Able Men.

Hull	716	Beverley	380		
Pocklington	107	Preston	88	Cottingham etc	80
Bridlington	75	Sutton	72		
Hessle	69	Hedon	68	Ottringham	60
Hutton Cranswick	57			Driffield	54
Hunmanby	56	Burton Pidsea	55	Holme	52
Kilham	51	Hornsea	46	Weighton	41
Nafferton	43	Warter	48	Bainton	44

T85 The Larger Communities. Yorkshire, 1673. Number of Hearth Tax Payers

York	2121	Hull	1369	Leeds	1157	Beverley	620
Scarborough	514	Sheffield	482	Halifax	463	Doncaster	415
Wakefield	413	Bradfield	397	Dent	373	Bridlington	352
Sowerby	?356	Ripon	338	Pontefract	338	Whitby	335
Richmond	324	Holme	325	Ecclesfield	306	Bainbridge	292
Cottingham	289	Rothwell	283	New Malton	284	Selby	274
Pickering	276	Keighley	257	Guisborough	267	Sedburgh	240
Quick	248	Thorne	232	Stanley.	246	Bingley	229
Knaresborough	224	Rotherham	225	Bradford	220	Northallerton	214
Thirsk	219	Hatfield	211	Reeth	203	Howden	207
Egton	202	Ovenden	202				

The Town Economy

Towns had a different life from villages. The larger number of people had to have other resources beyond the arable farmland, or the stock pastures that sustained most other Yorkshire communities. There had to be different activities giving employment and earning income. This could come from service to families of wealth or in the past to monasteries. A single wealthy house in any period could generate a great deal of employment and local spending. Tax returns in all periods show that towns had significant middle classes. Many towns in Elizabeth's reign already had a group of resident gentry. Town incomes could come from local administration financed by taxation, from church activity financed by gifts, rents and the tithes of agriculture. More often it was in small craft industries, trade, sea fishing or market services to a wider country district that the town families found their livelihood. These communities were less dominated by the agricultural calendar. There was the weekly market and the annual fair.

A few towns had been freed from monastery or church control. They had adjustments to make. Selby, Guisborough, Whitby and Bridlington had been dominated by monastic manor lords. They were abolished in the years 1536-1538. Urban monasteries had drawn income from wider country areas which they spent partly in the towns. When the control of manor, borough or port passed into lay hands, monastic incomes passed to laymen, who were not always resident. Bridlington and Beverley lost the shrines of saints, which had brought visitors. St. John of Bridlington had been widely venerated. Many monasteries had house property in towns, especially the ports, or enjoyed freedom from toll in local markets. York, Hull, Pontefract and other towns lost monasteries and friaries which had generated activity and cash inflows. Howden's Bishop's palace lost its significance and the role of the church in Ripon and Beverley was dramatically reduced. York remained the only significant centre of church administration.

The dissolution of chantries brought much town property onto the market, and more throughout the reign, as existing leases fell in and Crown sales increased. Chantry endowments commonly comprised small properties, or rents from single houses in the towns, which had been given by small donors long since. When they came up for sale, they were bought in batches by London and local speculators along with similar lands and houses given to sustain hospitals, guilds or lights in churches. The lots were broken up for local resale, or the rents collected annually by a rent collector who put up at the inn. Many properties went quickly to decay, but the change gave some flexibility to the local, urban house markets and an opportunity for profitable investment.

Several Yorkshire towns were suffering from the decay of old crafts with loss of employment and consequent poverty. The 1540 Statute for the re-edifying of towns named York, Scarborough, Pontefract, Hull and Beverley among thirty-six English towns where fallen dwelling houses were not rebuilt. Vacant plots held open pits, cellars and vaults. Other structures were liable to fall and rights of repossession were given to landlords.

Another Act of Parliament of 1554-5 stated that English towns had once been "populous, chiefly inhabited with merchants, artificers and handicraftsmen in good order, the inhabitants set on work and kept from idleness, the children civilly brought up and instructed, prospering in riches and wealth, which supplied great numbers of good able persons for wars and paid fee farms and taxes to the Crown. They were now few in number, less able to pay and liable shortly to come to destruction".

Those who framed the Acts of Parliament found someone to blame in the country traders, dwelling outside towns, who came into them to sell their wares. The Act against Country Retailers of 1554-5 banned country dwellers, not freemen or guildsmen of a town, from selling woollen cloth, linen cloth, grocery, haberdashery, or mercery wares in the towns, except in open fairs. The struggle of urban guildsmen against country traders was one thing. The shift of industries from some town centres to country places, better favoured, was another. The cloth manufacture had long been decaying at York, Beverley and Ripon but was flourishing in the West Riding. Different arguments were advanced for urban decay at Scarborough where the establishment of a rival inland market was blamed for shrinkage from seven hundred householders to four hundred householders over half a century. Leeds, Halifax and Wakefield were in a very different situation. They grew as their cloth trade grew.

The older urban centres still held crafts and service trades, with an impact beyond their boundaries. A small town could thrive if its occupations were demanded in a modest hinterland or by trading up rivers or across seas. A writer of 1569 said that "the town of Kirkby [Moorside] is a market town inhabited all with poor people and they hold their cottages by copy of court roll and they have no lands or other commodities to their cottages". Bridlington was a town that had been dominated by its monastery until 1537 and was said to stand in a far corner of the shire, adjoining to the sea, "where no resort is of strangers, except such as dwell about the same that come to the market there". Bridlington Quay, a mile away had no fields, but was a specialised port community, full of victuallers and with possibilities to realise.

Taxable wealth was concentrated in some towns, partly a result of sheer numbers of people but also of the activities undertaken there. The returns for the taxation called lay subsidies are not available for the whole county, but a sample can show how the tax collectors might have seen a difference between a town and a village. It was notable that Halifax town was not yet outstanding in wealth compared with other settlements in its broad parish.

T86 Lay subsidy collected from the Wapentake of Skyrack 1588

£31.10.8	Leeds
over £10	nil
£7-10	Bingley, Hawksworth
£5-7	Chapel Allerton, Ardington, Barwick, Morton, Powle
£3.-5	Allerton Bywater, Bramhope, Baildon, Collingham, Horsforth, Headingley, Ilkley, Otley, Parlington, Potter Newton, Shadwell, Temple Newsome
Under £3.	Aberford, Awstrop, Adle & Ecop, Alwoodley, Bardsey, Burley, Carlton, Girsley, Garforth, Harwood, Kippax, East Keswick, Menston, Rawden, Roundhaigh, Swillington & Preston, Seacroft, Scarcroft, Thorner, Wike, Weardley, Wigton, Yeadon

T87 Lay subsidy collected from the Wapentakes of Agbrigg & Morley

£25.15.7.	Wakefield
Over £10	Rothwell, Standley, Sowerby
£7-10	Almondbury, North Owram, Quarnby

£5-7	Hipperholme with Brighouse, Halifax, Midgley, South Owram, Thornhill, Wadsworth, Warley
£3-5	Altofts, Bradford, Batley, Barkisland, Calverley with Farsley, Criggleston, Dewsbury, Elland, Holmfirth, Huddersfield, Meathley, Mirfield, Ovenden, Ossett, Stainland, Sandall, Skircote, Walton & Bretton, Wortley
Under £3	Ayckton, Allerton, Bramley with Armley, Beyston, Bollinge, Bolton, CleckHeaton, Cumberworth, Crofton, Clifton, Dalton, Drighlington, Erenden, Eckeshill, Emley, East Ardsley, Fixby, Farnley Tyas, Farnley, Gomersall, Hartshead, Heckmondwyke, Hounsworth, Horton, Hounley Half, Hunslet, Heptonstall, Horbury, Heaton with Clayton, Idle, KirkHeaton, Kirkburton, Liversedge, Lepton, Langfeld, Morley, Marsden, Manningham, Middleton, Meltham, North Byerley, Nether Flockton, Over Flockton, Pudsey, Quick, Rastrick, Rishworth & Northland, Snytall, Shelf, Shitlington, Suthill, Shipley, Sheapley, Sharleston, Slaithwaite, Shelley, S Crosland, Tong, Thornton, Thurstelande, Thorpe on hill, Warmfield, Wyke, Whitwood, West Ardsley, Whitley,

Corporations for Borough Government

Borough towns had a measure of local government, with their own officers, and modest revenues, often including tolls and rents from intermural wastes. The burgesses paid one fixed overall payment to their overlord called the borough farm for whatever liberties had been granted. They held house plots by burgage tenure with fixed rents, which in the fullness of time became low rents. They might have their own borough court although some "manorial boroughs" remained under a manor court, as distinct from "free boroughs". There was a market usually under their own control. They had freedom from villeinage, with its escheats and reliefs. They commonly lacked fuel, stone, and wood but had some grazing in nearby commons. A few major boroughs had bought more extensive liberties and enjoyed extensive local government powers. A few boroughs had lost freedoms and sank back under manorial arrangements.

Other towns had grown from villages, where the manor lord obtained a market charter. There was no borough and they remained under the control of the lord's manor court. Yet the manor court in a large community could gain considerable sway Town and country differences had waned with the replacement of servile villeinage by copyhold and other tenancies. The larger towns made new moves in the 16th. century to secure charters which regularised their arrangements, or which gave a greater measure of local government and the funds to sustain it. The abolition of the monasteries holding the lordship of manors at the ports of Whitby, Bridlington and Hornsea left a vacuum to fill. The Crown seizure of assets belonging to the minsters at York, Beverley, Ripon, Howden and elsewhere, left a financial crisis only resolved by royal grants of former chantry and church estates, to support local government.

Corporations had more legal protection. This was felt to be the more necessary as town ownership of property increased. The process known as "incorporation" gave perpetual succession of office, so that individuals were not held responsible for the misdeeds of the body. They gained the right of sueing and being sued as a body, as well as the authority to hold land, to issue bye laws and to use a common seal, the use of

270

which bound all the townsmen. Incorporation was already under way, at Hull in 1440, Doncaster in 1467, and Pontefract in 1484. It matched the times. Boroughs and manors were replaced or transformed into Corporations, with clear local control by the town elites.

Several major towns took this way to extend their powers and find the funds necessary to deal with growing problems, as earlier church arrangements ceased. Queen Mary's administration made corporations out of some former boroughs. Sheffield sent Robert Swift and William Taylor to London to petition the Queen in 1553-54. Rents previously used to supply three assistant priests for the vicar had passed to the Crown. She granted them to the twelve capital burgesses and the commonalty of the town and parish, not to the vicar and churchwardens. The sequestered chantry, college and guild lands were given to repair the church, bridges, common ways and to relieve poor parishioners. The next year the twelve capital burgesses and the commonalty were constituted a corporation.

The south end of Beverley was a precinct of the Provost and canons of Beverley minster. An Archbishop of York, as lord of the manor, had granted a borough at the north end. The minster Provost and canons were abolished and the Archbishop had surrendered his Beverley manor to the Crown. At the request of the burgesses, Queen Elizabeth granted corporate status to the Mayor, twelve governors and the burgesses in July 1573. They had the power to make and enforce bye laws with a court of record. At the end of the year, the retiring governors chose twenty-six burgesses, from whom twelve new governors were chosen. The outgoing mayor chose a new Mayor. The corporation was allowed two members of Parliament, a recorder, town clerk, court, and a jail. Six years later they gained part of the former minster estates.

The towns had a middle class, traders, craftsmen, and gentlemen who paid the taxes and dominated whatever kind of local government there was, whether a corporation or a burgess court. They struggled to do the same, if there was still a manor court. Very few people paid the taxes. In one form or another, the governing bodies adopted selection rather than election as the main way of filling vacancies, though sometimes with a little of both. This conformed to the nature of town life, where small groups of high status men were indeed dominant. In another day and age, it would be criticised as oligarchy, but that day was not yet. The method gave continuity in local government while allowing a slow replacement of council membership. A petition from Richmond brought a grant of incorporation from Queen Elizabeth in 1576-7. The charter confirmed the existing prescriptive and chartered rights and privileges of the town and said "that Richmond shall be for ever a free borough and that the inhabitants shall be one body corporate and politic in deed, fact and name, by the name of aldermen and burgesses". The aldermen and twelve capital burgesses were to have a common seal. The inhabitants could elect one capital burgess to be alderman, twice a year. James Cotrell was the first alderman. Capital burgesses filled up vacancies in their number from inhabitants of the borough. The aldermen and burgesses could choose two of their number to be burgesses in Parliament at the cost of the town. Ripon would not secure incorporation until 1604.

The new corporations betrayed a strong civic pride. The status of alderman was highly valued, as was that of a burgess in those places where it still brought significant rights. Alderman became a high status, a term of address. There was a preoccupation with civic dignities and a calendar of civic occasions including feasts, often with small rituals. The alderman and merchant, Sir William Knowles gave Hull a chain of gold, of four and half ounces. The mayor had to wear it on holidays and other special days, or forfeit £40. His widow enlarged the chain with £10 worth of angel gold and Mrs Thurscross gave £3 more. Eventually there were 317 links weighing "11 ounce 7 pennyweights and 8 grains". William Gee gave a chain for the mayoress.

The greater towns took some trouble to secure influence in the national and northern councils, and with local gentry who carried weight in high places. Several named the nominees of powerful men to the role of parliamentary burgess, instead of members from their own ranks. Others appointed Recorders to make an influential connection permanent. There were dinners and gifts. The York lady mayoress and the ladies of the city on one occasion gave the Countess of Rutland 5s worth of mayne bread, two gallons of hipocrass, three sugar loaves of seven pounds a piece, two boxes of fine marmalade, a six pound barrel of 'sukker', six boxes of comfits, and two pounds of long comfits.

Beverley entertained Thomas Percy, Earl of Northumberland with gifts on his first visit to the town in 1560-1. This was a two way process. The Earl and Countess enjoyed a shoot at Beverley Westwood in 1568-9, when the Earl made his customary gift of venison to the town governors. Deference to the Archbishop survived his surrender of the manor lordship. Edmund Grindal was consulted by the governors at Cawood in 1570-1 and the newly translated Archbishop Sandes was entertained a few years later. The town courted and consulted Sir Marmaduke Constable of Everingham, Edward Ellerker of Risby, and Sir Christopher Hildyard of Winestead.

Feoffees and Manors

Where an early borough had not gone very far in gaining the power to run its own affairs, or had lost that independence, the situation was little different to towns which never gained borough rights at all, but had remained under the control of a lord of a manor. The Crown adopted different arrangements in such cases, placing the manor lordship in the hands of "feoffees" or trustees, a group of townsmen instead of a single lord. That was a "feoffment". This was done at Ecclesfield in 1549 when chantry land was diverted to lay use. Fourteen feoffees were appointed to administer the land of the former St. Mary chantry, for the benefit of the poor.

A petition from Rotherham to the Crown said that "whereas the town of Rotherham is a great town and not as greatly inhabited with artificers and poor men of occupations and trades and very little ground belonging to the said town and their commons very small for the relief of such a multitude, and for the better relief and maintenance of the said inhabitants such good orders heretofore hath been taken and set down in our Court Leet by the chief lord of the said manor". This was a manor whatever borough arrangements might have existed in the past. Four byelawmen were elected yearly at the great Easter Court by the jury of the Court leet and sworn by the steward to see all good orders and customs observed.

The change came in 1584 when the Queen granted lands at Rotherham, Brinsworth, Marshbridge, Kimberworth and Denaby to four feoffees to be "employed to such uses intent and purposes as shall be agreed upon by the chiefest part of the inhabitants of the town of Rotherham". They were William West and William Blythe, gentlemen, Richard Borrowes and Henry Brown, yeomen. A trust of twelve feoffees would hold the common lands of Rotherham "for the relief of the poor of the town, the maintenance and repairing of bridges, towards discharge of fifteenths, taxes, musters and other common charges". Two were to serve as common graves. The common lands were to be leased for 21 years and rents to be not lower than in 1589. There was a prohibition on speculation.

Bridlington had some status as a port but was never a borough. The monastery that was Lord of the Manor had gone. The Crown's need to unload the high costs of port maintenance at Bridlington led to a series of leases, which did not work too well. The manor of Bridlington was leased in 1566 to twelve Bridlington men led by Thomas Waferer, and in 1581 to esquire John Stanhope. This delayed the grant of the manor to lords feoffees until the next reign. Other small towns remained under manorial government at Stokesley and at Tadcaster where the manor bailiff in 1589, collected the rents, let the demesnes for £120, the two mills for £30, the bake house to a York man for 13s.4d. the quarry for 6s.8d, and the murage and stallage tolls.

Town problems

The towns were full of people, living close together. Beverley had a Kirk Lane house, a burgage divided into eight parts by 1573. Many of the problems in Skipton or Wakefield were the same as those confronting rural manors. The Wakefield burgess court employed a pinder who cleared swine from the streets after five in the evening, taking any that were found, before eight in the morning, to the pinfolds at the ends of Westgate and Northgate. He found unringed pigs grubbing in the Outwoods. The court made orders for folk not to wash their clothes and puddings in the "wavver". They tried to stop people talking in church, people going out of the church to gaze about them and laying timber or winnowing corn in the church yard. Brewsters and tipplers were told not to suffer servants to drink after six o' clock in their houses. The court dealt with quarrellers, brawlers, fighters and spreaders of rumours. They had their own pillory, stocks, gibbet and cucking stool.

There was still a Wakefield manor covering a far broader district than the town. The burgesses reached an agreement, with the farmer of that bailiwick, to have a share of fines gathered, to use locally on necessary works. The Wakefield borough court supervised the churchwardens and bridge masters, laying a rate to pay for highways and bridge repairs. Their sexton was told to keep the clock and ring the bell at five a.m. Each burgess was required to mend the pavement before his door. The fish shambles had to be cleaned out weekly. People were stopped from buying goods in the fields before market started and selling fish from their houses.

Town roads, often narrow, between over hanging timber framed houses, saw much congestion and were the natural place to throw rubbish and to deposit dung heaps. Doncaster at one court heard that sewers in Baxtergate, the St. George Gate well and the privy in the churchyard were out of repair and several dunghills were standing in Fishergate, Sepulchregate and Bardike. The York authorities required inhabitants to sweep in front of their houses and remove the dirt twice a week. By 1583 the streets were to be cleaned three times a week, on Tuesday, Thursday and Saturday. None were to empty tubs or filth in the city but were to bury refuse in their own ground. Trade filth and sweepings were to be carried away as soon as market ended. Each York ward was assigned a place to bury carrion. Wandering swine were impounded in the street at Bootham in 1585. Pigs browsed into Beverley's St. Mary's churchyard, bad herrings appeared in the Walker Beck and in 1574 their court found thirty-four ditches not cleaned. Hull levied fines on pigs kept with in the town walls for more than six days. Pigs might feed on carrion, horse flesh, shamble wastes, and by general scavenging.

Water supply was the greatest town problem. Scarborough was fortunate in having a piped supply, made by friars in the early 14th century, using a rich man's bequest. The water was brought in pipes by gravity, from distant hillside springs to the town, and drawn upon at three conduits. The Council in the North offered two thirds of the cost for a York conduit in 1579. A stranger called Wright, skilful in springs and conduits, was consulted but without result. German technology improved the London water supply in 1581 with a pump operated by a water wheel set in an arch of London Bridge. Another proposal to get piped water for York in 1598-9 proved too expensive. Hull mayor William Gee offered £200 to bring water in lead pipes instead of corrupt ditches into Hull. At Stockton in County Durham the church roof spout water was viewed as a valuable property in 1599.

Fire was a major town hazard, passing easily from one thatched roof to another. York council ordered buckets, hooks and ladders to be kept in churches at the cost of the parishioners in 1575. The St Martins cum Gregory churchwardens bought two ladders in 1585. The corporation sought to prevent fires by settling the number and position of malt kilns in the city. Wakefield secured a water pump and kept long hooks in chambers over Westgate Bar to pull thatch from buildings. Hull Corporation ordered thatched property to be roofed with tiles in 1576-7 and fined owners of haystacks within the walls. Candles were banned in stables and ships in 1585. Leather buckets and iron hooks were provided around the city. Beverley had a great iron crook with a chain for plucking houses down. Serious fires also occurred in villages. The old Ferriby Priory house at Anlanby lost buildings to fire. A brief was grated in 1580 to collect charitable donations for Old Malton because "twenty-eight houses had been destroyed by fire."

The broad ground plans of the towns were static but declining prosperity could create urban wasteland. The removal of urban monasteries and friaries freed sizeable urban plots for other uses. The ruins disfigured the towns until they were themselves quarried for their stone. Others were adapted to make genteel houses and gardens. Scarborough was accused of house demolitions to sell their materials. Town streets needed frequent repairs. The Doncaster great court at one meeting charged several men with broken pavements and foot causeways not made up in Lathegate. York had posts called stulpes to protect passengers from traffic and block alley ways. Beverley kept five great iron chains for blocking causeways when necessary.

Poor people were most numerous in the towns and were first institutionalised there. Beverley complained of being plagued with many paupers and with maintaining eighty orphans. York was continually exercised about growing poverty, relieving many poor weekly and taking action against townsmen who took in under settles. Street crowds were a town phenomena, especially on Sundays and other holy days. Market place preachings offered the church a way to reach people. The street was the place for discourse, for games, for gathering news and not least for the poor to saunter.

Rowdyism easily broke out. Vicar Rowland Taylor of Kirkby Misperton lodged for the night at New Malton in market day and fair time on September 15th 1596. Many strangers were in town. A sizeable group of drunks sought him in Goodman Smith's house. He wasn't there but a clergyman called Lawson sat in a chair before the fire. They punched him, chased him to the inner parlour, where they cast salt in his eyes, grimed him and made his face black. "They made a wonder and scoffed at him as though he had come from hell". They went from house to house, putting rapiers through windows, and drawing wives from husbands. They brought out two naked women from Newlove's house. When they met Taylor going to his lodgings in the Market place, they gave him three hundred strokes with a lash, bruised his head and made his eyes and nose bleed. He told Archbishop Hutton that they would have killed him, but he defended himself with his cloak.

London and Yorkshire

London with its neighbour Westminster was a great European city which grew from 50.000 people in 1520 to near 200,000 people at the close of Elizabeth's reign, largely as a result of inward migration. Here were the Royal Court, and the Privy council and, said Norden, London "above the rest is most usually frequented with her Majesty's royal presence". The Queen wintered at Whitehall. Here was the centre of government, of banking, trade and manufactures.

London was a port. Here came ships from France, Netherlands, Sweden, Denmark and Hamburg. A Roman road system still centred on London. The city wall was breached by Alders Gate, Cripple Gate, MoorGate, Bishops Gate and AldGate, their gatehouse tower posterns closed at night with heavy doors and portcullis. Temple Bar was the western limit of the city. Within the walls, were the stone Limehouse, where executions were done, and prisons at West Newgate and Ludgate. The Tower of London served as a palace, a place of assembly, a state prison, armoury, treasury, mint, archive and it held the royal menageries. London had the palaces of noblemen in Leicester House, and Shrewsbury House, while Westminster had Somerset House, Durham House, the Savoy and the Queen's house at Whitehall, some with large gardens. Lord Hunsdon occupied Somerset House. Lord Dacre had a country house at Chesil.

The river Thames was a main highway, a noisy watercourse connecting the two cities of London and Westminster, and other places up river. Great houses lined the river front, their stairways giving access to state barges, to great men's boats and watermen's wherries kept for hire. The Queen, the Lord Mayor and the livery companies had state barges. Landing places included Queen Hithe and Billingsgate. At the riverside were the Custom House, the Hanse settlement at the Steelyard, the Tower of London and Baynard's Castle.

Overcrowding created slums, as old houses came down in the world. Stables and gardens were built over. Badly paved lanes were lined with over hanging houses. There was garbage in the streets. The suburbs spread beyond the walls among the fields that hedged in the city. Southwark and Bankside held Paris Garden and the five prisons of Kings Bench, Marshalsea, White Lion, Borough Counter and the Clink. Bear pits and theatres were across the river.

Many Londoners were employed in buying and selling merchandise. Areas within the City of London were known for their specialities; Paul's churchyard for booksellers, Bucklersbury for grocers and apothecaries, East Cheap for cook shops, St. Nicholas shambles for butchers and Thames Street for fishmongers selling stock and wet fish. The highway Cheapside-Holborn had Goldsmith's row on the south, with houses four storeys high. Thomas Gresham's Exchange founded in 1566 and made royal by the queen in 1571 had more shops. The mercers and haberdashers were at London Bridge. French and Low Country migrants were among five or six thousand aliens, with an influence greater than their numbers. The fourteen Inns of Court were a virtual university.

London exerted a strong pull on Yorkshire. Up to a quarter of those becoming new London freemen came from Yorkshire and the North. William Atkinson a Scarborough draper died in London leaving merchandise in the south corner of England. Percival Cresswell of Nunkeeling left the lease of a house in Fleet street and houses in the Strand to his wife in 1558. His cousin John was a London brewer. William Kenrew of Scarborough left five shillings to William Baillye against the Three Cranes in Temple Street. for his children and twenty shillings to his apprentice. Richard Farrand a London draper had houses in Beverley and Bristol in 1560.

T88 Yorkshire Lord Mayors of London

Sir William Roche	Whixley	draper	1540
Sir Martin Bowes,	York	goldsmith	1545
Sir Richard Dobbs	Bagby	skinner	1551
Sir William Hewett	Wales. Sheffield	clothworker	1559
Sir John Harte	Kilburn	grocer	1589
Sir Richard Saltonstall.	Halifax	skinner	1597
Sir William Craven,	Appletreewick		1610

London was a land of opportunity. Many younger sons of Yorkshire gentlemen went there as apprentices. An apprenticeship could cost up to 100s. Two illegitimate children of a gentleman called Bigod were left sums of £5 and £3.6.8 to bind them to a craft in London. Edward Osborne of Kiveton was apprenticed to William Hewitt. He is said to have rescued his daughter from the River Thames. His descendants would be the Dukes of Leeds. And London wealth found its way to the country. John Robinson a London merchant bought Yorkshire lands late in the reign and was ancestor to the Robinsons of Ryther, Buckton, Thornton Riseborough and Thicket.

Some Elizabethan Towns in Yorkshire.

Aldbrough (Claro)

Aldbrough once a civil centre for the Brigantes, had shrunk to village scale, but with ample closes around a small green within the ruins of the Roman fort and town of Isurium. The Roman road from London to Carlisle had been replaced by the diversion of the Great North Road through Boroughbridge. Town roads were Aldgate, Brigate Graystonegate, Inskipgate, and Woodgate. There were West, Yorkway and Soursikes Fields, high and low moors, carrs and the ings. Milby wath led across the river Ure. There was a manor house, a tollbooth and a church. The manor extended over Boroughbridge. The Dean and Chapter of York had the vicarage house, seven tenements and four oxgangs of field land. A York goldsmith Thomas Hutton leased the Rectory for thirty years from c 1570.

Barnsley (Staincross)

The manor of Barnsley had belonged to Pontefract Priory, who founded a new town at the junction of the northerly Sheffield-Wakefield road, and the Halifax-Rotherham road, half a mile south east of old Barnsley. The common Aldfield, North, Church and Mill Fields, included Claylands and Brierbutts furlongs, among others. Roads were Eastgate, Southgate, Northgate, Kirkgate, the Causey, High street and Westgate, which held the meat shambles. The chapel had lost its three chantries. The market and a three day fair were granted in 1249. The monastery had owned two corn mills and a horsemill. The market place held the "Talbot" in 1598. The bailiff kept a market measure. There was a "Fair field", a Mayday green, a Grindelstone close, some almshouses near the churchyard and a moot Hall. Money payments were sometimes made at the font in the church. The vicar's tithes and the tolls of the St Paul & St Ellen fairs were let to a layman by 1577. A feast was on August 18. Townsmen included a woollen and linen draper, a clothier, a cutler, and a wire drawer. Coal mines were worked by 1579 and there were coppiced woodlands.

Bawtry, (Strafforth & Tickhill)

Leland found Bawtry a poor, bare, market town on the navigable river Idle. Roads were Top Street, Over Street, Wharfe Street, Church Street, Nethergate, Scot Lane, Bull Lane and Swansty. The farmers worked fields, ings and pastures. The borough had the market stead, on a diversion from the Roman road. A King's highway led to Tickhill, Rotherham and Wakefield and another road to Worksop. The St Mary Magdalen hospital had gone and the St Nicholas chapel had lost its Trinity Guild and chantry. A Tickhill tanner, a Nottinghamshire mercer, and a Scrooby fishmonger were house owners here. The common, burgess and Earl's staithes, on the river Idle, with a new warehouse and a weigh house, made this a busy river port. Teams of forty pack horses brought Totley and Dronfield lead, and cloths from Leeds and Halifax to be sent on river boats down the Idle to Stockwith and along the Trent and Humber to Hull. The Earl of Shrewsbury leased the manor from the crown in 1585. Lord Talbot had a grant of the Bawtry fair tolls and tolls on the river Idle for three lives. He sent 300 tons of lead a year outwards from his staithe. Henry Bigland the Bawtry carrier took wine into Nottinghamshire. There was a maltster and a smith.

Beverley (Harthill)

The town of Beverley had three parts, the minster precinct, the borough and a district along the canal and the road, which linked the town to the river. Archbishop Thurstan was said to have made the cut in the 12th century, giving a passage to the river Hull, and so to the Humber for boats to carry goods in and out. The Archbishops long remained the manor lords, their moated hallgarth house, beyond a wood bridge south of the Minster, but this had passed to the Crown. The borough town had expanded northwards with a market place both long and broad and the great St Mary's church.

The town ditch on the west, north and south, and the Walker beck for much of its length on the east, encompassed much of the borough. The roads across the ditch and the beck had brick built entries known as Newbiggin, North, Norwood, and Kelgate or South Barrs. The Cross bridge carried the main road into the Minster district with its Fish or Wednesday market. Roads were Eastgate, Flemingate, Hengate, Highgate, Keldgate, Ladiegate, Laregate, Lathegate, Minstermoorgate and Walkergate. Lanes included Blackfriarlane, Croft lane, Cuckstool Pitt Lane, Lurke Lane Freere Lane, Grovell Lane, Mackfray Lane, Pighill Lane, Shoemaker Lane, Vicar Lane, Well Lane and Woodlane. There was a small suburb outside the north bar. Gentleman Michael Wharton had a mansion in Beverley park

The Market Place had the cross, a guildhall in TollGavel, the corn hill with its pillory, and sow hill. There were orchards in some of the back crofts. An Act of Parliament of 1535 spoke of many houses in ruin. There had been good cloth making now sore decayed. Even later in the century there was talk of decayed houses and many unemployed. The Corporation was plagued with paupers and maintaining eighty orphans. Others continued to prosper. Beverley had a merchant guild. The Cross fair lasting for fourteen days at Beverley was attended by Londoners. Beverley had merchants, tanners, fishmongers, glovers, fullers, and many other trades. Robert Barbour, a cloth maker rented a tenter on Norwoodhill in 1578-9. A printing press was set up in 1599.

The town had lost the moated preceptory of the Knights Hospitallers in Trinity Lane, the Franciscan Friary outside Newbegin Bar, the Dominican Friary in Blackfriar Lane, and the St. Nicholas, Trinity, St Mary's and St Giles Hospitals. The old rights of sanctuary ceased in 1540, remembered in the sanctuary stones at Molescroft, Hessle, Walkington and Bishop Burton roads. Thirteen chantries came to an end. The Minster became a parish church, it s staff dropping from 77 to a vicar and three curates. Michael Stanhope pulled down the chapter house, sold its roof lead for £100, and took over the provost's house and gatehouse. King Edward VI returned some rents of Minster lands.

Beverley was incorporated in 1573 with a mayor, twelve aldermen and thirteen capital burgesses, annually elected from twenty-six candidates picked by the aldermen. Beverley could make thirty new burgesses in one year, as in 1562, when the town's local government spending was £252.18s.2d against receipts of £297.1s.7d. Both amounts rose into the seventies. Some £76 could be spent in a year scouring Beverley beck, although £54 of this was collected as a benevolence. The new charter cost £223. The Queen in 1579 granted the lands forming the Minster support fund to the town and lands and houses for income to support St Mary's church in 1585. They employed masters of the common pastures, a woodward, and rent collectors, a recorder and a town clerk.

Leland earlier in the century had found Beverley "well builded of wood". The better Elizabethan houses were half timbered, two low rooms and two garrets under the thatch, some with an arched passage, and jettied on four strong corner posts with curved brackets, and with clay and straw infill on woven osiers. Bricks were made at the beck side "tileworks". There were apple orchards in the rear of some houses. Townsmen pastured animals at Westwood, Swine Moor and Figham. Gentry families included Lawson, Ross, Wharton, Freeman, Farrer, Payer and Smales. Thomas Settrington supplied wine to celebrate the accession of Queen Elizabeth.

Boroughbridge (Claro)

The great north road crossed the river Ure at Boroughbridge. The new town grew, as an offshoot from Aldbrough, by 1145, along two roads, one each side of the Fleet beck, with a side road to Aldbrough. The courts for the Liberty and soke of Aldbrough moved to the Borough bridge tollbooth. The roads were High Street, Mickelgate, Fishergate, Watergate, Market Place and Horsefair. St James chapel stood in the market place but had lost its St Saviour's chantry. There was a maison dieu, a grammar school, fulling and corn mills and a bakehouse. Here were sixteen brewers, one beer seller, and an inn. There were valuable fishing rights and goods were sent south by river. The Lemyng's Tak toll was taken at the north end of the town in 1580. Rebels in the 1569 rising met on 20th November, 1569 at Mr Tancred's Elizabethan manor house, sited behind its courtyard and gatehouse. He was executed, despite being a member of the Council in the North. Sir George Lawson had the house in 1580. Eighty died of the plague in 1604.

278

Bradford (Morley)

Leland described Bradford as a pretty quick market town "which standeth much by clothing". Bradford dale was a wooded side valley of Airedale. Elslack Road had been a Roman road. The castle was at Bowling and a market was founded at Bradford in 1251. The borough had 28 burgess houses by 1311. Two more fairs and toll freedoms were granted by King Edward IV. Eight men were already making cloth in 1472. Roads were Kirkgate, Northgate, Southgate, Ivegate, Colliergate, Westgate Street, and Skinner Lane. Bradford beck had corn and fulling mills and a dye house. A school dated from the time of Edward VI. Several clothiers had looms in their houses. There were tanneries and a linen weaver. Many yeoman and husbandmen worked the farming landscape, which included Hallfield, and Hall Ings.

Bridlington (Dickering)

A long street with north and south back lanes ran east towards the inclosed precinct of the dissolved Augustinian Priory. The gatehouse remained near a reduced Parish church, decaying monastic buildings, a large fishpond and "old walls". St John's gate ran south between the ings and the moor, to Bridlington Quay. A 1539 muster had 118 armed men from Bridlington and 22 from the Quay, virtually a separate port-suburb. Timber framed, and cruck houses, lined Westgate (27), St John Gate (18), Kirkgate (3), Nungate (3), and Baylestreet (5) while nine were at the shore. Three in Westgate had dovecotes. There was a common oven, two watermills, three windmills, drapers and merchants. The Crown Manor was leased to groups of townsmen. Nine larger farms held old demesne lands and with about 31 husbandmen worked oxgangs of land in the West, Middle and East Fields, rising towards Huntow moor. The north and south moors gave pasture and whins for house use. The Shippabottoms, Hunters and Brownes were town gentry and the Dyneleys at the Quay. A school mentioned in 1563 was meeting in the church in the 1630s.

Doncaster (Strafforth and Tickhill)

The borough of Doncaster flourished after its foundation in 1194. King Henry VII renewed the charter for a rent of £74.13.11d. The burgesses secured the manor and the Percy estate from the Crown in 1505-6 with the courts for many outlying places, and the Thursday court before the mayor, steward or recorder in the guildhall. Articles agreed in 1568 gave corporation members secret debate and majority voting. A town hall replaced the moot hall in 1575. The constitution was revised in 1589-90. The town had lost a College of Priests, Austin, White and Greyfriars, hospitals of St Nicholas, St Edmund and St James, chantries of St Edmund, St Katherine, St Nicholas, Holy Trinity, St. Mary, St John Baptist and St. Mary Magdalene, and the chapel of Our Lady on the bridge. The advowson of the church passed to the Archbishop.

The mediaeval town had a boundary bardike, penetrated at Gillot, Sepulchre, Sunny and Hallgate Bars. The ruined castle on the north was in a plot that later housed St George's church. The Roman north-south road ran through the town, Marshgate, becoming Frenchgate and Hallgate. Baxtergate linked the road to the large market place, around St Mary Magalene chapel and several encroachments. Other roads were Fishergate, a small precinct abutting docken hill and the river Don Frendlysse Gate,

Hallgate, Laithegate, with a barn of ten posts in 1594, Marketstead Street, Maudlyn Street, Marshgate, St George Gate and Sepulchre (or Spoukers) gate. There were Scot, Meal and Sostange Lanes, a Roper Row and a Ratten row. Butcher Cross was at the principal cross roads, and there were Hall, Hob, Sepulchre and St James crosses. King's highways ran to Bawtry and Maudlyn Ing.

Prominent buildings were the free chapel of St James, Our Lady on Mary bridge, the King's Gaol, a Tollbooth, the butcher and fish shambles, a Guild Hall, a windmill, and Friars bridge. There were sand and clay pits, Diana's temple well, a pinfold, a pillory, a tanhouse, a tenter flat, a wharf and a grammar school, and two corn mills. Timber houses had stone slab roofs. There were strips called lands and selions in three common fields to the south of the town. There were carrs and holmes, but already many small closes.

Doncaster daggers were famous and the town's knitted stockings were reaching London. The town included merchants, mercers, dyers, several tanners, a draper, a corn merchant, millers, badgers, smiths, butchers, chapmen, a vintner and innkeepers, fletcher, cooper, corn merchant, glover, corviser, cordwainers, smith, fishmonger, fisher, glazier, saddler and websters. John Taylor, a draper was in St George Gate and Robert Williamson in Baxtergate. There was a heavy plague in 1582-83. Some 39 people were prosperous enough to pay tax on goods or land for the 1584 lay subsidy.

Halifax (Morley)

Halifax had over 500 houses, and perhaps 2000 people. The larger parish included twenty-three townships, some without a village, where Camden thought there were 12.000 people in 1574. "There were in it more human beings than beasts of every kind". Contemporaries thought Halifax a remarkable place. Camden said that "nothing is so admirable in this town as the industry of its inhabitants, who, notwithstanding an unprofitable barren soil, not fit to live in, have so flourished by the cloth trade (which within these 70 years they first fell to) that they are made both very rich and have gained a reputation for it above their neighbours".

Many clothiers produced kerseys. Small purchases of wool were brought to Halifax market for sale to clothiers who cleaned, oiled and sent them for spinning. Clothier George Bentley was in the Old Hall next to the court House. The town was famous for its byelaw, that anyone found stealing certain things was beheaded. The busy market town in 1585 had a cloth hall, a street of wool shops, old, new and swine markets. Streets were High Street, Cross hill, Southgate and North Gate. Lanes included Back Lane, Bury Lane, Loveless Lane, and Petticoat Lane. Middingstead held a dunghill. There was a Gibbet Close, Potter Clough, Ratten Row, Butchers' Shambles, Milne Cross, a pinfold, "stone trough", well head and cross well. A new corn mill was built in 1590. The town saw epidemics in 1587-88.

The Manor of Halifax, with Heptstonstall was a sub manor of Wakefield, A rectory manor was from 1545 in the hands of the Waterton family. John Bate held the manor and the lease of the rectory in 1601. The manor steward presided over the court meeting at the Moot Hall, employing a water bailey, a pindar and town crier, and dealing with debts and nuisances. The fields were already largely enclosed but intaking from the commons continued late in the reign. There were many copyholders. The vicarage was pillaged and vicar Holdsworth killed in 1556. The church pinnacle was destroyed by lightning two years later. Vicar John Favour brought radical Puritan enthusiasm towards the close of the reign. A new school opened in 1600.

Hedon (Holderness)

The borough of Hedon had acquired considerable liberties in the 12th century. The borough boundary included a broadly east-west village area at the north end and a more regular grid of streets, stretching down to the stream called Hedon haven. A curling road in the north part included Westbrig Gate, Market Hill, with a schoolhouse and a Hall of Pleas, and Sheriffgate. This area was bounded by the Townmoat on the north. The houses were concentrated along a road which cut across this area north-south called Southgate and St Augustinegate and continued southwards to Fishergate and Fleshergate. Its back lane on the west included Wayfarer Lane and Walkergate. Parallel on the east were Back Lane, Magdalen Gate and Baxtergate. There was a Grape lane. Here were St Augustine's chapel and Mary Magdalen chapel.

The southern part had parallel water courses called the haven and the fleet with parallel roads called Walkergate, Sheriff Bridge way and Woodmarketgate. This part of the town had held St James's Chapel, property anciently belonging to St Leonard's hospital at York, and a road called Lighthousegate. There were several bridges. Growth in the size of ships and the development of Hull had rivalled Hedon, but in 1348 the town had gained a charter of incorporation, giving them a mayor, ten aldermen and two bailiffs. Leland in the early 16th century described Hedon as a fair Haven town, sorely decayed, its three churches reduced to one, and with remnants of a castle, but with the sea creeks overgrown.

The town may have made some recovery. The civic authority had a coroner, chamberlains, constables, ale tasters, leather, fire and market searchers. They acquired a new Elizabethan mace. There was a town house, a guildhall, a tannery, two "godluvehouses", a surgeon, John Harrison and a corn mill near Sheriff Bridge. There were Wednesday and Saturday markets as well as fairs. George Painter of Hull founded a coal and turf charity in 1563 and gave monies to the haven and for repairing the Preston road. There was an agreement with the vicar of Preston to find curates for the church in 1564, new charters and ordinances in 1565 and 1584. Holderness wapentake courts were held in the hall at Hedon.

Helmsley (Ryedale)

Helmsley had a small borough grafted on to a village, close by a major Castle, modernised in Elizabeth's reign for the Earl of Rutland. The small burgage plots of Boroughgate and Castle Row contrasted with the farmhouses of Bondgate and Church Row. The large market square, Bridgegate, Ryegate and Pottergate made up the community, which had many cottages as well as burgages and farmsteads. The common Fields extended east and north of the town. The lower slopes included the Swangs, Bellfoot, Leys, Low and Linkfoot fields, and the large Acres field. Helmsley had lost its Our Lady and Trinity chantries, which drew rents from many houses. Some passed to the Steward William Segrave who held 16 burgages and 5 other houses.in 1581. There were over and nether mills, a ruined chapel by Rye bridge, and a Rectory Manor at Canons' Garth where a later Steward John Crossland lived in 1589. The town had a merchant, inns, a glover, a draper and two or three tanneries.

Howden (Howdenshire)

Howden was the market town for a small and ancient, marshy shire. The manor was given to the Bishop of Durham in 1080 and was the focal place of a liberty of Howdenshire. The collegiate church had five prebends and was a peculiar of the Dean and Chapter of Durham with jurisdiction over thirteen places. The church choir and the Bishop's palace fell to ruin in the 16th century. Bishop Tunstall was deprived in 1559 and Bishop Barnes demised Howden manor to Queen Elizabeth. The Prebendal estates and the Bedern mansion passed to laymen. John Gate had the Saltmarsh and Howden prebend houses.

Camden found a quiet, untidy town. South of the church was the Palace, part timber, part stone and brick. The manor porch carried Bishop Skirlaw's coat of arms. There was a park, fisheries, three corn mills, a horse mill, a nail maker, a draper and vintners. Howden dyke had a ferry and a passage ran from the Ouse to the stone bridge at Briggate, where there was a smithy house. There were shops, roads called Hallgate, Applegate, Bridgegate and Flatgate. Thomas Davye was a merchant. The field land was held in oxgangs, in the Spainbrigges and other fields, with meadow in the Ings, Holmes and Northholmbye. There was a hallmoot court with a pinfold.

Hull

Hull's position on the river Humber made the port an outlet for the Ouse-and Trent basins. The town was built in the angle formed on the west bank where the river Hull met the Humber. A brick wall with external ditches encompassed about ninety acres. The walls with gatehouses and numerous turrets, extended along the Humber and made the city into a major fortress. The river was chained from sunrise to sunset and had cranes by 1347. King Henry VIII visited Hull and ordered building of a castle and two block houses on a curtain wall and moat east of the river. An Elizabethan Lord President sent Catholic prisoners to be kept in the blockhouses. Hull was also the normal depository for northern war stores. The old palace of the de la Pole family, enlarged by Henry VIII at King's Place became the armoury.

Leland found the town walls and most of Hull's houses built of brick, made at the tilery near the river. Behind the walls were open gardens, and the west side of the city had many large closes amidst built up streets, far less packed than the east side of the town. Coble stones brought from Iceland as ballast had been used to pave the streets. The St. Mary's and Holy Trinity churches, the Blackfriars tower, and the Carmelites spire were prominent in the skyline but the friaries and several chantries, and hospitals were swept away. Four hospitals remained, along with a grammar school. Some almshouses were newly founded. Camden thought Hull the most celebrated town in these parts, with stately buildings, strong forts, rich fleets, a resort of merchants and with plenty of all things. The dried Icelandic fish, called stockfish, "turns to great gain" and had greatly enriched the town. The cartographer Speed in 1610 said the city had risen to great state.

Earlier settlements of Wyke and Myton had been absorbed within the borough, but the layout was governed by the long Hull street, running just inland from the river with Marketgate as its back lane. Humber street also along that river was similarly back laned by Monkgate. The rest of the town was more open, less given to narrow tofts and crofts. The roads were High Street, Humber street, Beverleygate, Blackfriargate,

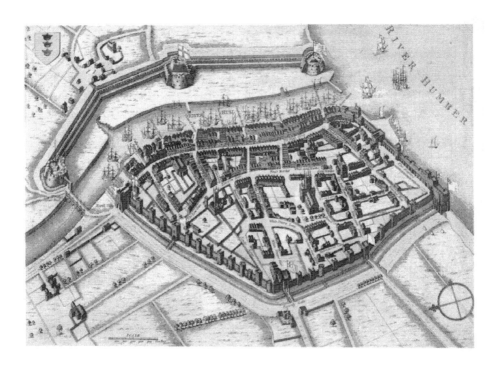

19 Hollar's Engraving of Hull in 1640

Whitefriargate, Hesslegate, Monkgate, Marketgate, Mytongate, Northgate, Aldgate and Posterngate. There were Grimmlane, Kirklane, Chapel Lane and Bishops Lane, Skellgate Lane and Posternlane. The High street had the houses of merchants and such families as the Crowles, Etheringtons and Listers. Those backing onto the river were stopped from holding horses or cows. There was a fish shambles, beer brewers, brickmakers, and cablemaking. The winding of hemp for small cords was done against the straight stretch of the town wall. The corporation met in Holy Trinity till 1577. A grammar school was rebuilt in 1578. Houses were new painted and gable ends repaired when a royal visit was expected in 1575.

Hull was the great port of the estuary and one of the busiest ports of the country, whence Hull and York merchants traded into the Baltic with Elbing, Danzig and Zealand. In 1567, 129 ships of a tonnage of four to five thousand in all entered the port from overseas. Hull had a fellowship of merchants and no burgess not being a freeman of the fellowship could carry wares overseas or to Scotland. Several merchants joined Eastland Company, formed to export dyed finished cloth to the Baltic, bringing back imported timber and tar, hemp, nitre and flax. A customs and weighouse was founded near the warehouses, and counting houses, in High Street. Hull had a customer and a searcher. The riverside had wharfes, cranes, and warehouses. Outside the city walls a bridge crossed the river Hull. There were clashes with Beverley mariners about payments for passing Hull bridge, an ancient agreement having allowed their passage with masts standing.

Kirkby Moorside (Ryedale)

Kirkby Moorside manor, embraced Gillamoor, Fadmoor, Sleightholme Dale, and parts of wooded Bransdale and Farndale. The 12th century castle was on high ground above the village, the 1254 market west of the church. There was no borough. Over a hundred houses in Westgate, Castlegate, Market Place, and Southgate, formed a cross roads. A large burial mound shaped Howe End. The 15th century Neville castle was built high in Castlegate, edging the large park east and a new manor garth south. There were eight tenants at will, eleven tenants for years and many copyhold cottagers without land , who kept cows, in 1567. Sir Robert Constable obtained the old Newburgh Priory church estate.

The Nandikes, Markhams, Hewerdines, and Otterbournes were the town gentry. Henry Neville, Earl of Westmoreland enlarged the park. Christopher Neville left the manor house and the country after assaulting Christopher Rokeby at Gatherley races. His affairs caused some local scandal. He returned to lead rebels with the Earl in the 1569 Catholic Rising, and again had to leave England. Ralph Bowes wed Mary Brook and held the manor, the mansion with its gallery, brewhouse, and dovecote, the manor green court, the mill on the dove and west park, after the Earl of Westmoreland fled the country. His manor courts were held twice yearly. The Market place held Christopher Boyes' shop, a smithy and shoemakers. Southgate had barkhouses for tanners, and Peartree house. There were West, Dove, Howe and High fields, and extensive ings or meadows. Linen making was early established here.

Leeds (Agbrigg)

The village of old Leeds had the manor house on Castle hill above the Queen's mill at the west end, and ran eastwards along Kirkgate. Leeds castle, manor, and the soke mills had passed to the Duchy of Lancaster. The borough chartered in 1207 had been planned around Briggate, the lower end of a wide street from the north to the bridge over the Aire. A compact group of burgages paying 4d yearly rents, expanded northwards. The village nucleus around the church, 200 yards east of the castle, remained a separate manor of Leeds-Kirkgate-Holbeck which had belonged to the dissolved Holy Trinity Priory at York but was now a freehold estate. Leeds Field and Far Field saw early piecemeal enclosures, the furlong names remembered in Ellerflatt, Lady flatt, Halfacres, Long lands, and Meersykes. There were holmes and ings and the Far Moor.

The main streets were Brigate, Kirkgate and Milngate, but Mabgate, further out, already had houses. So did the Headrow, formed from another long distance street, which had cut from west to east across the township. Lesser roads were Boar lane, Buslingthorpe lane, Marsh Lane, Vicar Lane, Woodhouse Lane, Park Lane, and Ratten Row. The Market stead at the north end of the Aire bridge had meat and fish shambles, booths and shops. Burgages had spread from Briggate into Market Place and Head Row. Newton beck entered Sheepscar beck before falling into the river Aire. This was spanned by the Thimble bridge. John Taylor in 1639 thought Leeds had more than 12.000 people.

Leland had said that Leeds "standeth most by clothing". Many cottages had tenters and there were six fulling mills. Here were chapmen, clothiers, a dyer, and drapers, but there were also two water corn mills, tanneries, a windmill, ovens, quarries and clay pits. Nichols Harrison was a piper in Kirkgate. A Leeds elite of principal burgesses included clothiers, many of whom were related by marriage. The manor and borough courts seem to have merged in the previous century, perhaps delaying the move towards incorporation. A clothier presided over the court leet. Four chantries had gone. Leeds bought the advowson of the vicarage for £130 in 1582.and would seek to buy the manor. A new chapel was bought to serve as the Grammar School. There was an almshouse in Kirkgate.

Malton (Ryedale)

A Norman castle overlapped a Roman fort, above the Derwent crossing, distant from Old Malton village. The New Malton walled borough was sited to span the crossroads west of the castle, south of the Old Malton fields. A 1530 muster raised 166 men at New Malton and 66 at Old Malton. The town had no field land but sent beasts up the outgang to pasture on the moor. Burgage plots were in Market Place, Old Maltongate, Greengate, Appletongate and Yorkhousegate. Small suburbs were Newbiggingate and Castlegate which held the water mills. The borough had a court, bailiffs, a pillory and a horsefair, where the Earl of Westmoreland once bought a gelding. A borough guild had maintained the Derwent bridge into the East Riding.

The Burgesses had their own court with two bailiffs and a clerk. Gate tolls went to mend the walls, using stone quarries at each end of the town. There were two chapels, three tanneries, several shoemakers, linen drapers, a merchant, locksmith, blacksmith, apothecary, chapman, coverlet weaver and Robert Fortune's tavern in Appletongate. Henry Wilson worked pewter. Forty-four houses, 3 shops and a bakehouse had belonged to two chantries. The market was well frequented for corn, horses, fish and farm tools.

Lord Eure said the town consisted of 300 families, but "for want of order and government therein, had lately fallen into decay and was extremely misgoverned by the confluence of poor and idle persons". He built one of the shire's largest mansions in the castle grounds after 1591. Borough freedoms may have been extinguished in his time, but the facts are not clear. Robert Butler at nearby Wykeham left his estate to "the Right Honourable my Lord and Master the Lord William Ewrie" in 1580. Town gentry were Constable, Raysinge, Craven, Richardson, Hebblethwaite, Heslerton, Lambton, Suddaby and Hawnsby. Spittal house was still an almshouse in 1591. There was a "bowl alley" a little later outside the north wall.

Northallerton (Allertonshire)

The low lying town was mostly confined to a long broad street between back lanes along the York - Durham road, with the church on a triangular green at the north end. The sixty-six villein farms of 1087 were joined by a 12th century castle, later replaced by a moated palace of the Bishop of Durham west of the church, where Brompton beck joined Turker beck. Borough burgages were established in two rows, east row and west row. The market place gained a 15th century tollbooth, a cross and shambles. Bishop Tunstall secured an additional Wednesday market in the early 16th century.

Carmelite and Austin friaries were dissolved, along with a religious guild, which had its own guildhouse, two chantries, and the large, well-endowed Hospital of St. James. A maison dieu remained. The Manor passed to the Crown. Queen Mary regranted the manor briefly to the Bishop of Durham, but Queen Elizabeth regained it from 1559 to 1566, when the lordship returned to the Bishop but it was held by the Bowes family in 1593. The borough survived. The borough rent was £7 in 1595. The tollbooth rents were leased to laymen. The bailiff was elected in the Bishop's court, and supervised the market and fair, two constables, two ale tasters and two supervisors of meat and fish. There were shops in the tollbooth.

The field land was a broad block within a cultivated belt between the west and east moors. There was an oxpasture. There were water and wind mills. Market town crafts included glovers and other leather trades, a slater, mason, plasterer, weavers, tailor, a merchant and draper Richard Metcalf. Camden found the greatest fair of kine and oxen of most resort that he ever saw in his life in the street on St. Bartholomew's Day. The Sunbeck was crossed by a one arch bridge. There was a well-attended Grammar School, two vintners, a building called "the Queen's House" and an old hospice known as the Swan.

Pickering (Pickering Lythe)

Pickering had a straggling east-west through road, with farmsteads along Eastgate, Hungate and Westgate, stretching to north and south back lanes. The Norman castle was a ruin at the top of Castlegate, holding a chapel used for manor courts. Borough gate and Birdgate had small burgage plots but no borough court survived. Willowgate was a back lane. The 102 ancient house-plots in 1598, were in Eastgate and Hallgarth (22), Hungate (13), Birdgate & Market place (22), Burrowgate (23) and Westgate (23). Six shops were in Market Place and one in Birdgate. Four tanneries and two mills were near the beck. The tenter garth occupied the low land west of the beck. The Market place had a dunghillstead and another was near the churchyard.

Eastgate had a linegarth. A smith's forge was new built east of Potter hill near the stone bridge. The North Mill limepit was let to a glover. Roger Park built a kiln house described as "brasskiln" at Keld Head. Mr Lemming was a merchant-draper with a Hungate shop. Gentleman Gawin Pollard lived in Birdgate. The school of the Virgin Mary chantry and guild was continued in the south chapel of the church. An anchorite's close was in Westgate. Sir Henry Cholmley sold a burgage, 12 houses, 29 cottages and lands in 1598. Esquire William Thornburgh held the Rectory manor, hall and tithe barn at Hallgarth. The stone mansion of the Marshall family was at the west end of Potter Hill and Roger Lascelles mansion was east of Keld Head, where footings remain.

Pickering had an extensive field system, including 194 acres of demesne arable and 76 acres of demesne meadow, now leased to tenants, as were the Duchy of Lancaster manor courts, the market and fair tolls and the mills. Seven coppices of woodland were north of the castle. There were 2376 arable acres in six fields with twenty two oxgangs each, mostly in single ridges, some a mile long. The commons were shared with Newton on Rawcliffe above the town. Outlying farms were at Burton and Keldhead, at Marishes, Blandsby Park, Hunt House and Goathland. A sheepcote was at Yatts. There were a dozen marriages a year. Baptisms rose steadily in the last three decades of the reign.

Pontefract (Osgoldcross)

Pontefract was one of the largest towns of mediaeval Yorkshire. Leland found "a fair large market town and good occupying in it". Eastwards was the Castle, which was the administrative centre of the Honour of Pontefract, the All Saints Church, "the minster of the moors" and the vicar's house in Bailey Place. St Clement's collegiate chapel in the castle had lost its dean and three prebends but the building was repaired.

286

The hill broadened west towards Tanshelf, a separate township, also a borough, with a market place and a windmill. The St John's Cluniac Priory and Monk hill, northwards were divided by a valley from St Thomas's Hall.

Pontefract played a major part in northern politics in many periods. Henry Fitzroy, the illegitimate son of King Henry VIII had used the castle. Lord Darcy had surrendered it to the Pilgrimage of Grace rebels in 1536. Archbishop Holgate, the Earl of Shrewsbury, and a grand jury heard the charges of adultery against Queen Katherine Howard at the castle in 1541 when the King was at Bretton. The Earl of Salisbury brought Scots noblemen for ransom to the castle in1542. Some improvements were made in anticipation of a visit by Queen Elizabeth including a new chapel.

Many religious establishments had gone. All Saints church lost four chantries. The St Giles chapel near market cross, a St Thomas guild, St Thomas Plantaganet's chapel, the St Nicholas Hospital and the Dominican and Carmelite friaries were all abolished. Pontefract Priory went to George Lord Talbot, who built the new Hall in 1591. Thomas Austwick bought the Dominican site in 1601. The Trinity almshouse was retained and a Grammar School. Sir Robert Knolles hospital was augmented by John Mercers will in 1574. Leonard Healeigh's will in 1600, left 20s a year to the poor out of a house in Neat Market. Spacious common fields lay east and south. To the north and west were pastures and meadows. Waterfurlong was in the North field. There was a turf moor but poor coal could be found within the park.

Pontefract kept it ancient borough government with a Mayor and aldermen, a moot hall and a kidcote prison. Street names were Baileygate, Baxtergate, Bondgate, the Booths, Coppergate, Gillygate, Marketstead, Micklegate, Newmarket, Northgate, Penny Lane, or Street Way to Wakefield, Ropergate, Salter Rowe, Southgate, Walkergate and Westcheap. Bondgate Way ran towards Ferrybridge. There were burgages in several streets. The 1560 rental mentioned other houses off Hustcroft, Monkhill, in Salt Row, next to the malt mills, in Fencal Ings and under the castle. Eighty-one property holders paid a rental of £34. 6s.10d. Stephen Esby had the mills and a tavern. House rents ranged from 3d to 2s.6d. Borough traders and craftsmen included a cloth driver, mercers, butchers, a barber, chapman, cloth workers and a rough mason. There were maltings and a conduit.

Richmond (Gilling West)

The walled borough extended north of the inner core of the cliff top castle, as if the borough had started within its walls and burst out beyond the market place and the Frenchgate, Finkle Street and Bar Gates into their three suburbs beyond. The paved Market Place had butchers' shambles, a wool house, a toll booth and Trinity chapel. Bargate with a green ran down towards the bridge and had St James chapel. In rear of Frenchgate was the parish church. There was a Skellgate and Newbiggin. The Greyfrairs walled precinct, with its water conduit was at the north edge of the town. There was a mill below the castle but Kirk Mill and the fulling mill were east of the church. East, West and Gallows fields stretched northwards.

The town had lost St. Martin's Priory, thirteen chantries, the chapels of St James and St Anthony, the Greyfriars, the Whitefriars, and after some delay the St. Nicholas hospital. The chapel at Anchorage hill became an almshouse. The Queen gave some chantry properties to re-endow the Grammar School in 1567 under the burgesses. Ralph Gower living at the Friarage with its gardens and orchard, gave the School land, called

Gower's Paddock. There was some town support for the Catholic Rising in 1569 and a local martyr died in one of the Blockhouses at Hull.

The inhabitants sought an extra fair and a fortnightly cattle market from the Queen in 1567 claiming "the borough is in great decay because of the poverty of the inhabitants". A Charter of Incorporation obtained in 1576-7 replaced the four bailiffs by an alderman and twelve capital burgesses. The burgesses elected two MPs. There were fish, flesh and corn markets. A large trade developed in knitted yarn stockings and woollen caps exported to the Netherlands. Poor children were entered in seven year apprenticeships in the trade. There were town wells, but a covered cistern fed by a conduit from Aislabeck, was erected as a new water supply in 1583. There was a heavy plague in 1597-8.

Rotherham, (Strafforth and Tickhill)

Leland crossed a four arch stone bridge into Rotherham, " a meately large market town with very good pittes of coal a mile away, and good smithes for all cutting tools." The market place adjoined the churchyard. Streets were Bradgate, Doncastergate, Millgate, Wellgate and Westgate, several with burgages. Briggate with three or more shops ran down to the Don crossing. A.schoolhouse was in Jesusgate and the tithe barn was in Warwick street. The king's highway, a 'causey' went to Rawmarsh, and a paved lane to Greasbrough. The common fields in 1615 were Micklehill Field, Canklow Field, edging south into the Moor, Ash Field and Elsemorefield but the names later were St. Ann's and Netherfields to the north-east, Gallowtreehill east of the town, and Canklow Field. Bridge end meadow was on the Don. The moor was 197 acres. There was still timber at East Wood.

Thomas Rotherham Bishop of Lincoln had founded the brick College of Jesus, in 1482-3. When this was dissolved, it had a provost, three fellows, six scholars and five chantry priests, residing within the high brick wall which enclosed the mansion and the two acre garth. Their rental included eleven houses and three shops. At the Dissolution Rufford abbey also had an income of £23.6.8. a year from Rotherham church and £76.13.11 from the manor. This passed to the Earl of Shrewsbury. There were extensive chantry and guild properties including shops, which changed hands

The town had tanneries, a ropery, an inn, merchants and mercers. The Earl of Shrewsbury's bailiff William Whitmore held the market, fair and passage tolls. The mill, the rectory and the tithes were leased to the Swift family. Nicholas Mounteney was a mercer and Robert Swift, another mercer was buried in the choir of the church. Barber Hugh Watson was in Westgate and two corvisers in Briggate. The feoffees of the common lands managed roads, bridges, water, poor relief and appointed swineherds, organ blowers and a bellman. There were market searchers for flesh, fish and ale.

Mary Queen of Scots stayed a week in Rotherham in January 1568-9 some say at Mountenay's mansion in High St; some say at the Crown Inn. On May 17 1570 she wrote to the Duke Norfolk "but I have need to care for my health since the Earl of Shrewsbury takes me to Chatsworth and the pestilence was in Rotherham and in other places". Thomas Cork a vicar presented by George Earl of Shrewsbury in 1573 was accused of some calumnies against the Earl. Plague recurred in 1589 when the feoffees organised isolation huts on the Town Moor and appointed nurses.

The 12th century borough was laid out next to the Crown castle within Falsgrave township. Two "causeways" ran into the town. Streets were Awburghgate, Blackfriargate, Burrwellgate, Cargate, Grayfriargate, Long Westgate, Marketgate, Nedder Westgate, Newburghgate, St Marygate, Paradise Gate, St Nicholas Gate, St Thomas Gate and St Sepulchre Gate. Houses were also at Chamberlay Lane, Dumple, Helperby Lane, Lead Stoupe, Market Cross. Merchant Row, near the Conduit, at Raysing Lane, Sprite Lane, and Tuthill. Below the cliff, houses were "on the sand" as well as in Key Street, at Key End, Sandgate, East Sandgate, near Slutwell, at Bolts and on Sand Hill. Town garths included Swinegarth in St Marygate, Palishill, and Porret lane head, Pillory hill and Limekiln garth

The town had lost a Cistercian rectory manor, which passed to the Conyers family. Also swept away were several chantries, the Grey Friars, Blackfriars and Whitefriars, and the St Nicholas and St Thomas hospitals, although this last became a house of correction. Many monastery and chantry properties in the town came onto the market. St. Sepulchres chapel in low town was closed. The town retained a good water supply to the conduits. Scarborough had been allocated part of Falsgrave fields and commons including field furlongs northwards along Greengate, along newdyke side, the garlands and up to Southfield. Ramsdale and Weaponness were stinted pastures for the town. Falsgrave village held most of the farms, using the How' Wrea, Gilderscliff and Burtondale fields and Falsgrave moor.

Scarborough claimed a decline from 700 households to 400 during Elizabeth's reign, perhaps a fall from 2800 people down to 1600. It was claimed that bakers dropped from 8 to 4, cordwainers 14 to 5, drapers 4 to none, glovers 6 to 3, weavers 14 to 4, butchers 8 to 4, tailors 20 to 9, victuallers 40 to 20, ships 50 to 6 and crayers for merchandise 20 to 4. The establishment of a market at inland Seamer reduced Scarborough market trading and several traders moved shop to the village. It was argued that Scarborough merchants had given up trading fish for trading barley and malt, particularly to the north east coalfield. The facts are not clear. There were 24 victuallers and ale brewers in 1602.

The harbour sustained a few trading ships, eight called topmen in 1582. After the building of the Elizabethan pier, this gave better shelter to the harbour. A wash gate in the pier enabled the scouring of sand from the staithes. The construction of colliers and shipment of coal may already have begun. Coal was coming in for use in gable end chimneys. Some small guilds survived in the food, metal and clothing trades. Salt and train oil were made. A fishing fleet was still active and at least two fishmongers. Three mills were in the valley, and a windmill on open ground. Here were several tanneries, a glazier, maltkilns, a limekiln, herring houses, brewers, a woollen draper in Marygate and a horsemill near the conduit. The port had a new custom house. Scarborough admitted 10-20 burgesses a year in the nineties and formed a strong ship masters' and mariners' association soon afterwards. The town had a rising poverty problem.

The borough was governed by two bailiffs chosen from 44 common councillors drawn from the 37 gentry families and 14 merchants. A number of gentry families resided including papist Thomas Williamson in Long Westgate, the tenant of Northstead manor, William Tancred in Westgate, Robert Lawson at the Chequer at Key End, and John Lacy at his house on the sand. Walter Fish leased the Rectory. Merchant families included Christopher Headley who had the old Dominican friarage. Other merchants were William Conyers in Westgate, John Farrer in Sandgate, William Thompson in Sepulchegate and Thomas Butler in Paradisegate.

Sheffield (Strafforth and Tickhill)

Sheffield's moated castle stood at the junction of the rivers Don and Sheaf, with a draw bridge to the castle folds. A borough was added to the large village and chartered in 1297. The burgesses were given long narrow burgage tofts in Market Place, High Street and Fargate with toll freedom through Hallamshire. The Church had belonged to Worksop Priory. Queen Mary's charter of 1554 divided government between the Manor court , the Town Trustees and the Church Burgesses. The 1571 Easter Book listed 307 households, but that included Darnall and Attercliffe. The Parish register of c1600 suggested about 3000 in the wider parish. A report of January 1615 said there were 2207 people in the town mostly in families of poor artificers, but 725 were begging poor, 1222 children and servants, 100 householders who relieved others and 160 were householders who couldn't.

The Earls of Shrewsbury received Cardinal Wolsey at the castle and later built Manor Lodge, home for Mary Queen of Scots, from 1570 to 1584. The Earl's agent, William Dickinson built a house in High St in 1575 and in 1581 had a new two bay cottage built at the town end. Streets were Waingate, Haymarket, High street with its cutler's shops, Market Place, West Barre street and Balme Green Street. Houses were also in the Farsyde, Prior Row, Castlegreen Street and Water lane. The market place had the court chamber, a cross, a pillory, stocks at one end, the Irish cross at the other and shambles and butchers' shops. Sheffield had an ironmonger, drapers, mercers, a haberdasher, chapmen, hardwaremen and a vintner. The tanhouse rent was £80 a year. Eight shops were under the court chambers. Burgage houses and gardens in 1581, rented at a shilling, cottages and gardens from 1s.8d to 3s.6d and little houses built on my lord's waste upwards from 2d. Our Lady chapel by the Don Bridge became an almshouse.

Cutlers had grinding mills on several streams. Many smiths using local iron but the cutlers imported steel. A grindstone quarry was at Rivelin. Coalpits were near the town. The Earl's manor court granted cutlers' marks, sixty by 1578. Ordinances made in 1567 regulated the trade. There was a Corn mill on a race from the Don, and Pond mill near the sheaf tanneries, also a hopyard, a swinefold, middensteads, town head wells, and Barker Pool. After 1603, there was a Grammar School. The ducking stool was at the whicker.

The west part of the parish had much new inclosure by 1581 including cottages built on the Lord's waste. The Earl's park was 2000 acres but the commons included Crookesmoor-west, Sheffield moor-south and Sharrow moor south west. The long causeway ran away westwards. Many households kept pigs or cattle. Cottages were being built on wasteland and intakes leased. A considerable excess of baptisms over burials in the sixties, was maintained at a lower level in the next two decades but dropped low in the nineties, only to pick up for another decade. There were cruck framed barns and timber framed houses. Dunghill steads were around the streets. Some shops had outshots. The burgery accounts include payment for a yard and a half of red cloth to make the piper a coat.

Tadcaster (Barkston Ash and Ainsty)

Tadcaster's great Percy castle had been reduced to earthworks north of the town. The manor house in the Applegarth was decayed and the demesnes were let to tenants. Town gentry included the Foster, Mawd, Oglethorpe and Neville families. The town had a reduced appearance yet had over 100 houses, mainly west of the Wharfe river, but with a sizeable suburb over the river in the Ainsty. Streets were Bridge End, High Street, Market Place, Kirkgate, Westgate and Washpot Lane. At least 27 houses including the George had belonged to dissolved chantries. Here were inns, a common bakehouse, butchers' shops and the new Oglethorpe school and almshouse near the church.

Roman roads had left a network west of Tadcaster, marked with Stutton, Stump and Emma crosses. Smawes house and grange were alone to the west. The town had an almshouse, a coney garth, a tenter garth and a large parish church. The local quarries gave first class building stone. Carts ran over low moor to the boats landing at Tadcaster bridge and there was a horse pasture. Six common fields containing hundreds of strips extended on each side of the river, which powered three corn mills. The 500 acre high moor was intercommoned between four townships, and the 127 acre low moor with Oxton. A new coney warren was founded during the reign.

Thirsk (Birdforth)

Thirsk township spanned the river. The "long street "or "Micklegate" on the east, was the Roman road linking Stamford bridge to Yarm. The 12th century Mowbray castle was built west of the beck with a westerly motte, and a large bailey running east to the Codbeck and south to a stream. The church was built near Norby to the north. A small square borough was sited over the stream at St James green in the 12th century. Early abandonment of the castle left a moated area north of Castlegate, but saw houses built in the bailey, which became the new market stead. Ingramgate went from it over a stone bridge into Finkle street

The Manor belonged to the absentee Stanley, Earls of Derby, with demesne closes in Woodhill field and cattlegates in Woodberry Howe, tenanted by John Norton, esquire in 1557. Common fields were on each side of the beck, including the near and far West Fields, still with strips in Great Prior Flatt in 1564. Other Fields and furlongs were the north and south Doubergh, the near and far Carlton Butts, the wetlands beyond Norby, stony crofts, and bown crofts. The North Ings were meadow. Dowland woods were mentioned in 1596. The East Moor had 397 acres and the west Moor 346 acres in later days. The Borough bailiff and the lord's bailiff jointly drove the commons for strays among the "multitude of cattle".

Monastery dissolutions brought town properties into new hands. The borough chapel of St. James was closed and chantries of Our Lady, St. John, and St. Anne ceased, the latter with a Chantry house and dovecote in Kirkgate. The Our Lady chantry had long sustained a Grammar School. The church, once held by Newbrough Priory was acquired by the Archbishop, the rectory manor estate with a mill, farmed by the Pinkney family with the tithes of corn and hay in 1596. A parish register began in 1556. A native of Thirsk, John Pybus was hanged for his religion in 1601.

The burgage plots would number fifty-two in the early 19th century. Elizabethan burgesses annually elected a borough bailiff, sworn in by the lord's steward, who supervised the three weekly court. This ruled that every cottage should have four acres and no cottage or house was to hold more than one family without the overseer's licence. Two constables were appointed for the manor lord, the borough and the township, along with two leather searchers and sealers, two field supervisors, pinders, market searchers, four ale tasters, four affeerers and twelve jurymen. Burgesses were toll free and paid no stallage. They could sell both within and outside the Monday market. The lord had the tolls of fairs. Richard and Daniel Bell were mercers while Robert Hoopes was a merchant in 1562. There were several tanners, weavers, shoemakers, a smith, glovers and an apothecary. Forty alehouse keepers were presented in 1637.

Tickhill

Tickhill castle was the focus of the Duchy of Lancaster Honour in the south of Yorkshire. The village worked acres, still dispersed in common fields called Hillgreaves, North, East, South and West Fields. Their furlongs included Riddings, Bagwell Butts, Sheepgatesteil furlong, and the Beanlands. Malpas lane led through ings to the bridge. Beyond were the carrs and high commons to the east, large low commons on the south. There was an oxpasture. Demesne woods were at Old Park and Black Holt. The court rolls for 1597 speak of the management of fields and commons, of timber left in the king's highways, pigs not rung, cattle straying into the seeded fields, and beasts on the common.

St Mary's church was fair and large, but Tickhill lost chantries of St. Crucis, St.Helen, Holy Trinity, Our Lady and Holy Rood, and a guild. St Leonard's Hosptial had closed and the prebend of Tickhill passed to the Earl of Shrewsbury. The Austin Friary with its orchard, stable, kiln, oxhouse, barn, dovecote and coney garth, became a mere farmstead in a valley west of the town. Ninety acres belonging to Grimsby Priory, included Spital and New Chapel closes passed to the town bailiff Nicholas Saunderson. The Abbot of Humberston's cell at Tickhill was granted to laymen.

An early borough had been formed but Leland found the market town very bare in the early 16th century. Roads joined at the market square. Here were Castlegate, Northgate, between two back lanes, Westgate and Sunderland street, the site of gentleman John Sandford's capital messuage. There was a maison dieu, limekiln hill, tanneries, a ropery, three water mills and a windmill.

Wakefield (Agbrigg)

Wakefield Manor was a major lordship of the Duchy of Lancaster, with a castle at Sandal, and other dependencies extending thirty miles through Calderdale to the edge of Lancashire. The great court of the manor embraced a three weekly court baron, a twice yearly court leet and a tourn. Three wards had their own constables. Sir John Tempest, constable and steward of 1565 and the jailer occupied residences within the forty acre park. Another Rectory manor had passed from the Crown to the Saville family. The parsonage changed hands in 1601 for £600 and a rent of £25.

The borough court was separate from the manor court. Burgesses paid sixpence a year for burgage plots in Westgate and Northgate. November courts at the Moot Hall made new byelaws in 1556 and 1579. There was a prison at the tollbooth with gallows and a 'maiden'. There was a marketstead, fish booths and the baker's breadbooths between the churchyard and the manor bakehouse. The church held the clock, the chime and the great bell. The bellman in 1556 was to ring the bells at five and eight in the morning for quarter of an hour and the eight o'clock bell for a quarter of an hour each night.

Leland found mostly timber buildings, but some of stone in a town where "all the whole profit" was in coarse drapery. Camden saw Wakefield as famous for its size, its cloth trade, neat buildings, great markets and the chapel on the nine arch bridge over the river Calder. Prominent were the market cross; the Duchy moot hall and tollbooth, the large new built church, and the Chantry house. The Skitterick stream ran from Eastmoor past Jacob's well beneath Warrengate and as an open stream down Kirkgate through the Softs into the river near Kirkgate bridge. George Savile and his tenants had leys and arable land in St John's field, arable, meadow and pasture in Westfield, Middlefield, and the Crossfield and a close in Wakefield Cliff field. His coney garth was near Northgate bar.

Streets were Kirkgate street, Westgate, High street and Northgate, separately taxed in 1588 at £4.12s.3d; £12.8s11d; and £8.4s.4d. respectively. There was a fair marketstead. Westgate had wealthy houses with warehouses behind. Other roads were Warrengate, Crossgate, Newgate, Begger lane and Stray lane. The high street ran towards Dewsbury. There were quarry pits and the Duchy leased coal workings in 1581. Martin Birkhead, assessed on his wealth at £13, left his initials and crest on a house in Upper Kirkgate.

The substantial men included Martin Birkehead Esq, Richard Clayton, Roger Pollard, Thomas Harrison, Thomas Cave, Robert Kaye, Henry Watkinson in Westgate, and George Saville the manor reeve and Thomas Fleming in Northgate. The elder George Saville gave his sons the stonehouse or George Saville's Newhouse in Westgate. He had bought Haselden Hall and also Pecks Hall in Northgate from Richard Peck in 1572. He also had seventeen houses in Northgate. Both Westgate and Northgate had pinfolds to impound stray animals. A new Schoolhouse was built in 1598 near the market. There were many half-timbered houses.

Whitby

Whitby village had been on the east cliff, where its high fields stretched south eastwards. A Norman monastery was sited nearby, in the 11th century, perhaps including the site of the vanished 7th century Anglian monastery of St Hilda. They were given the manor lordship. Burgage rights and a St Hilda fair were added by King Henry I. Fishermen were active below the cliff by 1129. King Henry II gave port, market and renewed burgage rights to the monastery. At some point, the village fields were absorbed into the monastery demesne, closes 385 acres including the 200 acre high fields. A borough was founded below the cliffs, on the east side, with only the church of St Mary on the high ground above, reached by more than 190 wooden steps. The borough expanded across the river Esk, with houses below the westerly heights but also acquired the old settlement of Flore above, stripped of most of its fields.

Abbot Richard had granted free burgage to the men of Whitby in 1177-89, with four ways in, their own courts to settle disputes, and 5d burgage toft rents. Abbot Peter ended the free borough in the king's courts in 1201 but 24 burgesses kept some borough rights and customs under the bailiffs appointed by the Abbot. The Abbot had rights of 'prise", a proportion of commodities landed for sale. The custom of scot and lot gave the burgesses the monopoly right of buying and reselling goods brought in by sea. Other inhabitants could only buy for their own provision. Some later tolls were granted to the burgesses rather than the Abbot but the lost ground was never recovered. Clashes between monks and the borough men continued until the dissolution of the monastery. The Cholmley family acquired the monastery rights. Their Elizabethan bailiffs, drawn from the Conyers family, living at Bagdale Hall, dominated town affairs.

Whitby was in detached parts east and west of the river Esk, each with its own market place, chapel and staithes. A bridge linked the two and further inland a log path across the sands at low water. Burgages, and cottages, in tofts and half tofts on the east of the Esk lined Southgate, Highgate, Kirkgate and Crossgate, where there was a chapel and the tollbooth over a cellar and a shop south of the market place. Together they formed one long road south wards towards Spittle bridge. Sandgate, with an abbey tollbooth and Grope lane had been built into the river north and south of the bridge and Bridgate. The river was tidal to Ruswarp and the alluvial fitts and sandbanks often dried out.

West of the river was Baxtergate, with a horsemill, near the Callis house chapel and the Blackwell staithe. Two herring houses were on the north side where tofts ran up the slope to Skate lane and to the tofts of the south side of Flowergate. This short road embraced the old hamlet of Flore. The south side of Baxtergate edged the Walker sands and the slike stream, from Bagdale Hall which was outside the borough bounds, in the neighbouring township of Ruswarp. North east of Baxtergate, the west side market place had a marketstede house, and ran east towards St Anne's staithe and west to another Skaitegate. Haggersgate ran north towards the Cragg, with one or two gentry houses.

The town had lately lost the monastery, a chantry chapel, another town chapel, guilds of Holy Trinity, St. Christopher, St John Baptist and, Holy Cross, a hermitage and the Hospitals of St John Baptist and St Michael. St Mary's church remained, inconveniently at the hilltop. Other monasteries had not been well represented, but laymen were able to buy a Grosmont Priory house on the northside of Baxtergate, a Rosedale Priory shop in Flowergate and some plots of the Knights Hospitallers. The Little Marish Priory had disposed of their house to the Lincoln family, early merchants at the port who founded the chantry, for a rent of a thousand herrings. The parsonage was let to distant laymen, including the tithes on gardens and on the pigs that ran around the town.

The pier saw frequent disrepair and the (draw) bridge, part of which carried houses, needed continuous heavy expenditure. Two bridge collectors and two bridge surveyors were annually appointed. Ships and cobles worked from the port and many foreign fishermen called. Three hundred tithe fish went annually to the Archbishop of York for centuries. Fishermen worked the northsefare, holfare, landhering fare, Lentenfare, and took lobsters, coles and codlings. Salt may have been made at Saltwyk and salt houses were sited in the town. The chantry tannery dropped out of use but there were others in Bagdale. An early coal garth was on the west side. By mid century ship owners Richard Cholmley, James Strangeways of Sneaton, Richard Browne, Robert Bushel and Matthew Wilson, were employing thirty-five masters and mariners. Robert Bushell had several ships, built his own salt house, kept a coble at Robin Hood's Bay and wore a gown made in London. Merchants like William Bye, Gregory Annyngson and Robert Bushell could bequeath money to the bridge, hemp for poor fishermen, or chalders of coal for Christmas distribution to the town poor.

Francis Cholmley built a new timber manor house amidst the monastic ruins in the 1580s. Anciently Whitby had been at least a hundred households. The Cholmeley estate at one point included 48 supposed burgages and similar tenements, and another 20 sites, including five shops, two stables, the old coal garth and a limekiln. A conduit may have supplied part of Church street but there was also a St Hilda spring Welgarth, and keldwell, and other water sources. There were twenty alehouses in 1616. The Little Angel upper floor had wall frecoes in a Tudor style. Legend claims the Angel inn was founded in this reign. There were fairs on Midsummer, St Peter's and St. Thomas's Eves with street processions. A farm and a few cottages lingered near St Mary's church. A kings highway ran westwards to Flowergate cross and beyond. Waingate ran up into Bagdale. Moorgate left the monastery site for the south. Alum and coal were about to transform the small port. In 1627 some larger ships were built at Whitby for distant buyers.

York

The visitor approaching York saw the towers of numerous stone churches standing high above the walls and inner and outer moats. William Smith spoke of thirty parish churches in a city that spread on each side of the river Ouse. William Elderton in 1584 thought York the fairest city for merry pastime or company, outside London. James Ryther took another view, crediting York with a lazy abundance, which he thought barely excused the idle inclination of the inhabitants. William Camden in 1586 said that "This is the second city of England, the finest of this region and indeed of the whole north, as well as its principal fortress. It is pleasant, large and strongly fortified, adorned with private as well as public buildings, crammed with riches and with people and famous as the seat of an Archbishop".

The rivers Ouse and Fosse had staithes serving the river port, where lead had long been weighed for trans-shipment south. The principal buildings included the Minster, with its Archbishop's palace and the great prebendal houses in the close. The Crown Castle was decaying and the west castle was a mere earthwork used for musters. The Council chamber on Ouse bridge, and four Guild Halls remained but the city had lost four friaries, three priories, a great abbey, hospitals, bridge and other chapels, a great many chantries and had reduced the number of its parish churches. A quarter of the houses passed out of chantry ownerships into new hands. Many fell into decay.

Palliser has suggested that the population was 8000 in 1548 rising to 11500 by 1600. There was no obvious wave of new building at York. Houses were timber framed, some plastered or lime washed and tiled rather than thatched, with brick chimneys being installed and brick infill for walling. Small one and two room houses may have dominated much of the city. Some individually and others combined to hang street lights. There were private and common wells, but no good water supply system. Stone lined open gutters drained into the King's ditches with in the city, which themselves drained to the moats and the river. There were substantial suburbs at Bootham and St. Marygate, at Gillygate, Monkgate and Micklegate and small suburbs outside Walmgate and Layerthorp postern.

York was a magnet for people, who settled to work, in small industries, in food, clothing, metals, leather and other products. Cloth making had gone but tailors were everywhere. There was a new mint, the bell foundry, and the brick yards and pits near Walmgate. Wholesale businesses were probably on some scale and there are hints that money lending was pioneering its way towards banking. With a thousand beds and

20 John Speed's Map of York 1610

stabling for more than that number, the accommodation and victualling of visitors was a major activity. York was a town of workshops and already a town of service trades. The largest town in the shire consumed many foodstuffs. This was the market place for much of the vale of York. York middlemen bought East Riding corn to sell into the west of the shire. Country goods were exchanged for imports and York manufactures. There were several markets and several fairs.

The county town of a large shire saw the high sheriff's tourns, county elections, county courts and twice yearly assize courts at the Castle. York and Ainsty wapentake together formed a county on their own. The Minster in its close seemed like a separate estate. As head of the diocese of York, the Minster saw the Archbishop, and the city was the seat of the High Commission and several church courts, including the Archbishop's court of Admiralty. The city held the Mint brought here by Archbishop Young. The Council in the North had courts at the King's Manor, its sole meeting place and seat of the Lord President. The legal professions were well represented in the city.

The official role of the city brought the visiting rich from around the shire for a social capital. Eures, Fairfaxes, Constables and Savilles were among those with town

296

houses. Lord Cumberland and Lord Burghley bought properties during the reign. By 1596, there were sixty-four inns. Minster and parish church memorials recall gentry who died here, including Sir Henry Bellassis and his wife. Gold and silver smiths, pewterers and booksellers and shops with luxury imports brought shoppers. Just over a quarter of householders contributed to pay taxes or poor rates. The rich were very rich including Richard Goldthorpe, Robert Brooke, merchants like John Raysing, Dr Lee, John Fearne secretary to the Council of the North and Mint Treasurers George and Francis Gayle.

The long established Corporation ran the city from the Chamber on Ouse bridge. A mayor, twelve aldermen who served as justices, and a common council of 24 craft guild representatives, made up the governing body with two sheriffs, chamberlains, bridge and wall masters, a recorder and a town clerk. The city had four wards named after the main barrs. The Lord Mayor usually drawn from the merchants, was a virtual governor, allowed corn tolls to pay for hospitality, and served by chaplain, clerk, and a range of other officers. "He was a lord for a year and a day, but she is a lady for ever and ay". Parishes within wards had their own wardens, clerks and parish constables and there were some poor parishes. The Minster and the castle were liberties outside the control of the council. The council supervised the guilds.

The corporation asked for remission of the weavers fee farm and still spoke of population decline in 1562. During the 1560s the Corporation got out of debt, raised MP's payments, and made gifts of wine to notables. After property sales, the Corporation was able to buy some country manors. Poor relief remained an increasing drain on the city authorities. They ran several almshouses, workhouses and a house of correction. The city suffered in epidemics of 1558. Infant death rates were high, especially in the first two years of life but the city seemed to see few more epidemics until 1604.

CHAPTER 11
EDUCATION

Not Many Schools

Education is the transmission of the adult culture to the young. This was never confined to the class room, certainly not in the late sixteenth century. We cannot doubt that much was taught at mother's knee, among peers and elders, within families and later at workplaces. There would be early child minding arrangements, always an element in education. We know little of these things in the Yorkshire of Elizabethan times. The church conveyed its message to the young by weekly rote learning and catechism. It seems unlikely that many people saw the inside of school rooms and we can't be sure what contact there was between the young and education in that narrower sense.

Earlier sixteenth century schooling, when recorded, was often in song schools linked to monasteries and collegiate churches or was undertaken by chantry priests at parish churches. Some was clearly at a level beyond the earliest instruction needed in reading, writing and counting. A school was kept in the nave of Kirkham Priory, another at St Mary's Abbey, and one at St. Leonard's Hospital, York. There was a choir school at Bridlington Priory. Skipton chantry had a free school in the parish church, the master a good grammarian with a large number of scholars. The Pontefract school was associated with the canons of the collegiate church. The College of St. Andrew at Nether Ancaster kept a Grammar School, with a schoolmaster paid £5 a year. There were similar schools at Beverley, Bridlington, Rotherham, Halifax, Hemingbrough, Hedon, Helmsley, Howden, Hull, Pennistone, Tickhill and Wakefield.

The College of Jesus at Rotherham had separate masters for grammar, for song and for writing with "accounts". The Grammar man received £10, some gown money, fuel money, free hair cuts and laundry. The writing master received £5.6s.8d. and similar perquisites. Six chorister children were fed, clothed and housed. This seems to have been a petty or elementary school, and a higher school. The Rotherham school for writing and accounts was "for many youths endowed with the light of sharpness or ability, who do not all wish to attain the dignity and elevation of the priesthood, that these may be better fitted for the mechanical arts and other worldly matters."

A number of other schools, or schoolmasters, gained incidental mention, without it being clear at what level they were teaching. Entry to a Grammar School presumed a previous education in reading and writing. Some clergy and parish clerks probably taught these things in petty schools. A yeoman's son attended the Tickhill Friary school for seven years, from age eight into his fifteenth year, while John Gaunt, son of a husbandman, was there from age four to fifteen. He went daily to a kinsman's house for refreshment, morning and afternoon. Thomas Tusser quoted the proverb that "children were better unborn than untaught", else they made fools, fit "neither for prentice, for plough nor for schools".

21 An Elizabethan Grammar School

The monastery, collegiate church and chantry schools were abolished in the years 1536 to 1538, except where specific arrangements were made to continue them. When that happened, there was some emphasis on Grammar School education. This meant that Latin was taught. This was the language used in the church and in large part it was still the language of written administration. Sometimes but not always the Grammar School masters taught the more elementary reading and writing. Sometimes, they seem to assume that scholars would already have those skills.

T89 Some Yorkshire Chantry Schools Retained (with master's salaries).
Acaster College; Aldbrough (£5.3.10), Bolton on Dearne (£4.13.4), Boroughbridge (£5.3.10), Crathorne (£5.4.0), Carlton (£5.4.0), Crofton (£3.19.10), Giggleswick (£4.0.0), Middleton (18s.4.3/4d), Normanton (£2.19.2), Northallerton (£5.1.4), Owston (£4.3.11), Pickering (£1.15.1), Pontefract (£2.19.2), Roston (£4.6.11), Rotherham College, Tickhill (£4.18.11), Sedbergh (£6.0.0), Wragby (£6.16.4).
Pennistone school also seems to have acquired chantry revenues.

T90 A Commission to continue a Chantry School

A commission to Sir Walter Mildmay & Robert Kelway recommended "that the grammar school which had been kept in the chapel of Boroughbridge in the parish of Aldborough with the revenues of the chantry of our Lady should be continued and that William Grey incumbent there should serve as schoolmaster at the wage of £3.2s.6d. and that the chapels of Boroughbridge, Roecliffe and Dunsforth wherein were founded several chantries, being chapels of ease and far distant from the parish church should continue". 11.8.1548.

Early Readers and Writers

The Yorkshire man Miles Coverdale was one of the first to embrace the Protestant faith. He assisted Tyndale in translating the bible into English in 1532 and produced his own translation in 1535. He was an exile in Denmark and Geneva during the reign of Mary, but came home afterwards. He believed in the wider circulation of the scriptures. The printing of the English bibles and of English service books removed a serious obstacle to learning. The bible and one or two other religious books were installed in most churches. The bibles were immensely influential. Tyndale translated so that the poor might read what he saw as the Word of God. He numbered the verses. He spoke of love where another might have used the word charity. Coverdale's text was the first entire bible printed in English. His phrases took hold, for example "sufficient unto the day", and "the valley of the shadow of death".

Yorkshire produced early controversial writers. Sir Francis Bigod penned his "Treatise of Impropriations" in 1534-5. He wanted better use of church revenues, by diverting parish incomes away from monasteries in order to finance a learned preaching ministry in the parishes. Esquire Wilfrid Holme of Huntington wrote "The Fall and Evil Success of Rebellion" in 1537, an account of the Pilgrimage of Grace, which was critical of monks, the worship of saints and miracles. It would be published in 1573. John son of Sir Robert Constable was a noted scholar and Dean of Lincoln. Other scholars and writers briefly held the York prebends, including Thomas Cottesford, William Turner, Alban Langdale and Laurence Nowell, who pioneered Anglo Saxon studies.

Some books appeared in wills and inventories but they were not plentiful. Some were not printed but were manuscript copies. The better educated clergy had books but many priests were ordained without much reading ability or any great skill in Latin. York Minster library was probably the largest collection of books in the north of England, with one hundred and ninety three books in 1536, apart from those used at the Minster. A royal injunction of King Edward VI required additions. Archbishop Holgate made some purchases including the "Annotations on the New Testament" by Erasmus.

Robert Parkin the curate of Adwick le Street wrote a poetical paraphrase of gospel history and a Latin concordance. He carefully bequeathed several books in his will of 1568. The heirs were to sell them and give the proceeds to the poor, if he died young. He gave his Bible and four Latin volumes to his nephew Robert. A parchment book and some moral tracts went to Dean Hudson of Doncaster. The vicar of Brodsworth gained printed sermons, the curate of Melton an index to the bible and three other volumes. James Washington was given Mr Calvin's book. His godson Francis Arthington had "John Harding his chronicle".

300

A few members of the nobility and gentry acquired old books from the libraries of dissolved monasteries. Wressle castle already had a tower called "Paradise", containing a closet of eight latticed squares, each topped with a desk to set books upon. "The Register of Salley Abbey, in a quarto volume of near two hundred leaves on vellum", bore the names Arthur and Thomas Darcy. These words were written in front "Thys booke aperteinethe to Arthur Darcy knight of Salley. Whosoever finds ytt he shall have Xs so he bring ytt agayn to hym and Gods blessyn". Richard Hinchcliffe had helped write the cartulary of Monk Bretton Priory in c.1530. His chamber at Worsbrough held some of the Priory library, and books on physic and grammar in 1558. A copy made in 1560 of the manuscript verse treatise on alchemy by the Bridlington Priory canon George Ripley, found its way to Skipton Castle.

The Petty Schools

The church had some control of education, insisting on rote learning of short statements of the Christian faith. These were taught by the clergy apart from any school. The Bishops were told to licence schoolmasters in 1554, after examining their qualifications at the bishop's and archdeacon's visitations. Teachers had to have a licence to teach. Nonetheless, there were possibly more village schools than were recorded, some of them part time, some Roman Catholic and some with only a fleeting existence. Few had any permanent building outside the church. Officials examined sixty-three schoolmasters in Yorkshire in 1563. A few were rejected as too young. John Nettleton at Ripon was discharged but kept on till a replacement could be found. Unlicensed schoolmasters were reported from time to time. John Lacey at Bradford was found insufficient for the Grammar school in 1570.

Petty schools taught reading and writing, sufficient to read prayers, make out a notice, attend to prices or sign a will. The hornbook was the principal means of teaching reading and writing. This consisted of a sheet of parchment in a wood frame covered with a sheet of transparent horn. This showed the alphabet in small letters and in capitals, and combinations of the five vowels, with b c and d; such as ab, eb, ib, ub, and ob. There was also the Lord's Prayer in English. If making a mark in a parish register or other documents was an indication of a lack of minimal literacy, samples suggest that three quarters of the people were illiterate. Those making wills and their witnesses commonly made marks instead of signing a name.

A steady expansion of educational opportunity continued through the second half of the century. It is remarkable that it was so. At the elementary level, what was offered had limited use. The Bible apart, there was little enough to read in English. At the Grammar School level, the vehicle of teaching was Latin. There was not too much point in most people learning Latin. The content of much that was taught concerned the cultures of long vanished peoples of Biblical, Greek and Roman times. The new Protestant stress on an English bible favoured the teaching of reading in English. Yet. this was the age in which the written word was made relevant to people's lives, as never before. More and more record keeping entered into the managing of estates, parishes, manors and the kingdom. The people attending churches, compulsorily, heard readings from the bible and a few other texts in English every week.

T91 Some Yorkshire Schools (dates mentioned)

Agbrigg/Morley	Almondbury, Bradford, Dewsbury, Halifax (1563), Elland (1563), Heptonstall, (1563), Luddenden (1563), Huddersfield, Wakefield, Illingworth, Ovenden, Crofton, Normanton.
Ainsty	Acaster Malbys (1603), Moor Monkton (1600), Acomb (1603)
Birdforth	Topcliffe (1607)
Buckrose	Acklam (1600), Sledmere (1596)
Bulmer	Hutton on Derwent (1569), Raskelf,
Claro	Ripon
Dickering	Burton Agnes (1563-4), Hunmanby (1563-4), Lowthorpe (1563), Kirkburrn (1636), Garton (1605), Bridlington (1564)
Harthill	Holme on Spalding moor (1563-4), Spaldington (1564), Market Weighton (1576), Beverley (1548), Kildwick (1563), Pocklington (1577), Walkington (1537)
Holderness	Marton (1600), Ottringham (1600), Skipsea (1600)
Howdenshire	Howden (1548), Welton (1586), Eastrington (1567)
Hull	Hull (1551)
Osgoldcross	Norton
Ouse/ Derwent	Elvington (1586), Naburn (1595)
Pickering Lythe	Scarborough (1597)
Staincross	Royston
Staincliffe/Ewecross	Burnsall, Gargrave, Kirkby, Malham, Thornton in Craven, Bolton, Slaidburn
Strafforth/ Tickhill.	Ecclesfield (1564), Worsborough (1560), Tickhill (1576), Sheffield (1564)
Whitby Strand	Whitby
York	Horsefair (1557)

A major contribution to education in the broader sense came with the Statute of Apprentices of 1563. This made it illegal to engage in any art, mystery or manual occupation without having first served an apprenticeship of a stated term of years. Neither the intention nor the results were necessarily educational but they normally were. The Act formalised the connection between master and apprentice long known in the crafts and extended it to cover other occupations. At its best, apprenticeship went far beyond conveying the skills of a craft from an older man to a younger.

Lady Katherine Constable left £6.13s.4d. a year to apprentice a pupil out of Halsham Free School. Robert Newsome, a yeoman of Bolton Percy in 1568, arranged for Alderman Christopher Herbert of York to have the bringing up of his son William, until he was twenty-one. He was to take him as an apprentice and "make him free of the trade which he now useth". Alderman William Robinson would take his other son Richard while Mr Henry Pullen was to have the third son John and "be a means to help him to the place of the office of an attorney". William son of Christopher Spicer of Scarborough put him self apprentice to Abraham Godfrey a Yarmouth fisherman in 1601.

The Grammar Schools

A major educational movement began before Elizabeth's reign and was continued throughout with the further spread of Grammar Schools. They had been linked to the colleges of canons at the minsters of St. Peters York, St. John's, Beverley and St. Wilfrid's, Ripon. Other collegiate churches had similar schools and early Grammar Schools gained mention at York, Wakefield, Scarborough, Northallerton, Doncaster. and elsewhere. There were some breaks in continuity as the Church was reorganised and the number of clergy reduced.

The early sixteenth century saw a strong movement to establish Grammar Schools Many but not all were reformed chantry schools. King Edward VI re-established the Acaster Grammar school out of the possessions of the dissolved collegiate church. Giggleswick had a chantry school founded by John Carr in 1514, confiscated in 1545 and re-endowed by King Edward VI in 1553 at the request of his chaplain John Nowell vicar of Giggleswick.

T92 Grammar School Foundations before 1558

1500's	Bedale 1502	Giggleswick 1507,	
1510's	Halifax 1516;	Topcliffe 1517,	Pocklington 1514
1520's	Ecclesfield 1529;	Bingley 1529,	Settrington1525,
	Whitkirk 1521,	Sedbergh1527	
1530's	Burnsall 1535;	Thirsk 1535,	Walkington 1537,
1540's	Owston 1540,	Rastrick c1540	Almondbury 1542
	Well 1542,.	Middleton 1542,	Pickering 1542,
	Romaldkirk 1542	Kippax 1544,	Birstall 1546,
	Ripon 1546	Long Preston 1546,.	Bolton on Dearne 1548;
	Normanton 1548	Bradford 1548;	Kirkby Malham 1548,
	Gargrave 1548,	Harewood,	Hemsworth 1548,
	Carlton 1549;	Royston	Sedbergh,
	Skipton 1548	Wragby	Topcliffe 1549
1550's	Kirkby Ravensworth1556,		Tadcaster 1557
	Leeds 1552.	Pocklington refounded 1551	

Beverley petitioned the crown in 1552 saying that the parish church was in great decay, while the market town, "having a great number of youths", and five thousand persons, some "apt and meet to be brought up in learning which are not", since there was neither grammar nor any other schools. They asked for the building of a free grammar school, and soon afterwards the Corporation took responsibility for it. Archbishop Thomas Holgate founded secondary Grammar schools at York, Hemsworth and Old Malton in 1546-47. These were nurseries for the new emphasis on the ancient cultures. The masters had to understand Hebrew, Greek and Latin. The boys had to be able to read before entering the school. Education was free, being financed by income from endowments drawn from his own lands. The pupils were expected to attend church services.

Schools could be combined with almshouses. Kirby Ravensworth School and the Hospital of St. John Baptist were founded by John Dakyn in 1556 for instructing youth and sustaining the poor. Bishop Owen Oglethorpe petitioned the Crown in 1557 for a licence to found a Tadcaster Grammar school combined with a hospital nearby. Two wardens and a scholar learned in the art of grammar were appointed. Robert Pursglove endowed Guisborough School in 1561 in combination with an almshouse. Two buildings of two storeys, were built, one for the school, and one for the almshouse for twelve poor people, supervised by two wardens. Halsham school was on the ground floor with Sir John Constable's almshouse above.

T93 Elizabethan Grammar School Foundations

Bedale		Queen Elizabeth
Guisborough	1561	Robert Pursglove
Burton Agnes	1563	Richard Green(vicar)
Gilling	1570	Sir Nicholas Fairfax
Halsham	1579	Sir john Constable
Hull	1583	
Rotherham	1584	Laurence Woolnett
Yarm	1590	Thomas Conyers
Kildwick	1580	
Heath	1585	
Skircoat	1585	Queen Elizabeth
Wakefield	1591	
Yorebridge	1601	Anthony Besson
Easby	1594	Robert Hindle
Normanton.	1592	John Freeston
Wakefield	1591	George Saville
Burnsall	1600	William Craven
Acaster Malbis	1603	John Knowles

Over fifty Grammar Schools served Yorkshire during the reign. They used Lilly's Grammar as the standard text to introduce the classics. There were fresh editions in 1566, 1568 and 1574. Queen Elizabeth repeated the requirement of a uniform grammar, in a proclamation of 1567. Lilly defined the noun, pronoun, verb and participle, and the un-declined adverb, conjunction, preposition and interjection. The pupil learnt the rules of grammar, and went on to make 'Latins', using 'vulgaria', vocabularies, and the double translation system, which involved rendering classical Latin pieces into English and back into Latin. The pupil went on to imitate classical writers by composing essays or verse. The early aim was to speak Latin as well as to read it. Guisborough School used the older pupils to teach English in the petty school. They spoke Latin in their own third and fourth forms but no English. The school ran from six o clock in the morning till seven o'clock in the evening, in summer and to four thirty in winter. Malton school ran from six to eleven and from one to six, from seven to eleven thirty and from twelve thirty to five.

Endowment gave the hope of permanence to a school, whether petty or grammar. The founder's donation might include a building site, a building, or an estate providing income to build or maintain the building or to house and reward a schoolmaster and sometimes an usher. Many schools would vanish in later centuries when inflation reduced the value of endowment incomes. John Knowles bequeathed £100 in 1603 for four feoffees to find a sufficient schoolmaster to teach the youth of the parish of Acaster Malbis and £30 for the poor. Burton Agnes was to buy land worth £200, from which the rents would pay £8 to the master, and leave a surplus to be given to the poor. The Yarm governors, three gentlemen and four yeomen, were to administer lands not exceeding an annual value of £30. Several schools were given corporate status.

Sir John Hart's school founded at Coxwold in 1603 was endowed with £36.13.4. a year. This was earmarked, so that £20 went to the master for his pains and £1.6s.8d. for his livery. The usher would have £10 salary and 13s.4d for clothes. Another schoolmaster had £2.13s.4d. for teaching the "petties", the young children, to read English. Twenty shillings went to the vicar for three sermons; twenty shillings to drinking and repast for the visitors, who were the masters and fellows of Sidney Sussex College, Cambridge. The remainder was used for repairing the school master's house. These expenditures were to be a charge on the manor of Nether Silton.

School founders were remembered beyond their days. Halifax church had a memorial to the Blackwell Hall clothier and bachelor Brian Crowther who died in 1607. He was a chief benefactor, giving £20 a year from Airmyn, to the Free Grammar School and £10 a year to the poor.

> "Some labour hard to leave their children store.
> Some stir and strive to advance their stock in blood
> Some worke for commonwealth which are blessed more
> and happy they that care for churches good
> and leave for pore, for widdowes, orphans ,food."

The legends of the founders included a rags to riches element. It was said of Sir John Harte of Kilburn that "by some means or other, he obtained a knowledge of Latin and afterwards found humble employment at a wholesale grocers in London. His attainments becoming known to his master, he was advanced, became a partner, married his master's daughter, became Lord Mayor of London and was knighted. Since learning had done so much for him, he bought a freehold at Coxwold, then built and endowed a house and schoolroom." The honour roll of past students at Northallerton Grammar school, while Thomas Smelt was teaching, is said to have included Thomas Burnett, master of the London Charterhouse, George Hickes, Dean of Worcester, John Kettlewell, William Palisser, Archbishop of Cashel, John Ratcliffe, physician, and Thomas Rymer.

Secondary bequests were not uncommon. Mercer Reginald Harrison added £20 to the Sedbergh School endowment, to assist two poor scholars, the poorest of his name and kindred having the preference. Sheffield School had two masters receiving support from the capital burgesses by 1564. The school was better endowed in 1602 and received a charter two years later. The Topcliffe school which had been endowed in 1549, received another £10 from John Hartforth of the village and would receive bequests from some London citizens. A Wakefield chapman, left £500 to Otley school in 1603, if they would raise a similar sum.

Some part of the church was the usual schoolroom. Schools newly endowed might get a purpose built structure. St. Peter's School at York used a two storey building with a chimney in the gable end. The Giggleswick school had a two storey building, for high and low schools, with early mullion windows and a front door with raised steps. This foundation of Queen Mary's reign was given an external niche to hold a statue of the Virgin Mary. The second storey at Guisborough School held the master's residence. The class room held four forms. Kirkby Ravensworth Grammar School, on two floors occupied seventy-six feet by eighteen feet. Hull school unusually had a brick building in

1585. Camden found the south chapel of the church used for the school at Pickering, where there are signs of accommodation above. Schools were kept in Wragby church in 1573.

The appointment of the teacher was placed in the hands of governors or trustees. Some were distant patrons. St. John's College, Cambridge had the appointment of the schoolmaster at Sedbergh but not the usher. The Archbishop appointed masters to two of the Holgate schools. The Queen's injunctions required schoolmasters to teach the practices of the Church of England as well as the standard grammar. Bishops and archdeacons were told to exclude Puritans and Catholics from teaching but some of the early wardens and teachers at Guisborough School were Catholics. Sheffield school had a Puritan master in 1564. A Roman Catholic was deprived of his post at Archbishop Holgate's School in 1574. The right to present a suitable master was transferred from the Duchy of Lancaster to the Mayor and Aldermen after complaints of a negligent schoolmaster at Pontefract School. Archbishop Sandys reproved a master for negligence at Pocklington school in 1581. George Dakins bought the advowson of East Cowton for the schoolmaster of Kirkby Ravensworth, when he was "old and decrepit", after ten years service.

Education for Gentlefolk

High born young men and women were sent into service as young people in other households of great men and ladies. The role of servant and companion might not be sharply separated, as the years advanced. What was learnt by the boys could range from personal services, fetching and carrying, to fencing and even estate management. Such accomplishments as hawking, dancing, horsemanship, manners and morals could be acquired by example and precept, from my lord but also from those about him. Some Latin and book learning might come from a tutor. Roger Ascham, as a steward's son from Yorkshire, was placed in the household of Humphrey Wingfield, a Suffolk lawyer, where he learnt Latin and Greek with Robert Bond, read Chaucer and Mallory and learnt archery.

Much was learnt from servants. The Rutland steward bought a sword and dagger for the young Lord Roos and rapiers for him and John Manners in June 1558. Earl Roger studying at Queens College, Cambridge in 1588 wrote to his mother at Winkborne for some blades. John Manners at Helmsley in 1586 received a report from servant John Pulleyn at York saying "Your son is an excellent brave child, and hath that virtue grafted in him, which will bring forth fruit to the commonwealth. My diligence shall not be wanting in performing what I have already begun". Two years later, he wrote "Your son George does well and behaves himself like an honest man, but you write him to learn to write better and rise earlier in a morn. Two hours study in the morning is better than four in the afternoon". Frances Cave wrote to the young Countess of Shrewbury at Worksop in 1603, begging her to take her daughter into her service "if you be not thorowly furneshed wythe wemen". She claimed not to know whether the Countess gave wages but hoped her daughter might have the same as the rest. Grace Flesher wrote to Mrs. Saxey, "Is my daughter able to serve you or not? I wax old and crazy and stand some need of her myself".

Common culture and high culture separated in the 16th century. The idea was abroad that a certain education was necessary for a gentleman, including classroom studies proper to their degree or calling. Education was no longer merely for clerks.

Roger Ascham believed that the rigourously organised study of classical literature was the only possible basis for a liberal education. This could be obtained from a private tutor or at a Grammar School. The gentry agreed and sent their elder sons to Grammar schools, sometimes at a distance, or they employed tutors, who could prepare them to go on to University or the inns of Court. Many earmarked bequests for the education of younger sons, who could look for a career in the church, medicine, law or estate management.

Thomas Constable, a New Malton gentleman, gave Thomas Harwood "who I have brought up," £3.6s.8d. towards his exhibition at school. Sir William Ingleby of Ripley settled £20 a year on his son Francis for "his exhibition and maintenance of his study", hoping he would take to the law. George Saville in 1593 gave maintenance to his nephew George at school till he be fit for University, and an annuity while there. Christopher Wade of Drighlington transferred property to trustees for the expenses of a boy at the University of Oxford. Educational bequests for daughters were rare but Edward Hutchinson of Wykeham, near Scarborough, added another £100 to the £100 already given for each daughter at marriage, to better "bring up and educate them".

Ralph Rokeby in 1565 addressed an essay to his four nephews, which he rewrote near thirty years later. He would rear them on the Bible, Polybius, Tacitus, Plutarch, Commines, Guicciardini, Castiglione and an opponent of Machiavelli. Lord Burghley gave advice to Sir John Harrington at Cambridge in 1578 on reading Cicero for Latin, Livy and Caesar for Roman history "exceeding fine for a gentleman to understand", with Aristotle or Plato for logic and philosophy. He was alarmed at the dowager Countess of Rutland taking young Roger out of University for hunting parties at Belvoir in 1589.

T94 Lord Burghley's Timetable for his son. 1562

7 to 7.30	Dancing
7.30-8	Breakfast
8-9	French,
9-10	Latin,
10-10.30	Writing and drawing
10.30	Prayers and dinner,
1-2	Cosmography
2-3	Latin
3-4	French
4.4.30	Writing
4.30	Prayers and supper.
On Holidays,	The epistle for the day in Latin before dinner and after the gospel.

John Savile born in 1546 at Over Bradley near Elland learnt the alphabet and the English catechism before he was seven, from the clerk and curate of Elland and a master with a degree at Huddersfield. He learnt accidence at Elland and Raistrick, in 1552-3 with Robert Ramsden. The next nine years brought a steady classical programme. He was admitted to Brasenose College, Oxford, in March 1560-61. While at home, during the London plague of 1563, he read Littleton's tenures, Ancient and Modern, the Natura Brevium, John Parkin's book and the Statutes, Magna Carta, Rastall's Abbreviamenta and the Year Books of Richard III, Henry VII, and Henry VIII. He returned to London to attend Clements Inn until 1564-5

T95 John Saville's Teenage Education

year	tutor	Reading
1st Mary .	Richard Gledhill at Elland	part of Aesop's Fables .
2nd Mary	Robert Hutton at Halifax	part of Sacred Dialogues of Castilion
3rd Mary	Huddersfield &Almondbury with Robert Ramsden	Cato's Disticha Moralia
1557-8	Newhall & Elland, John Henshowe	Virgil & Grammatical rules
1558	Robert Ramsden, at Raistrick	Terrence
1558-1561	Richard Best, at Halifax	Metamorphoses of Ovid, Virgil, Horace, the Epistolae Familiares, Amicitia & Senectus of Cicero, History of Europius

A more Protestant emphasis ran through the Instructions given to Mr. Snell for the guidance of his pupil William Slingsby. He was to learn the principles of religion. Daily prayers were to be offered at night, when he lay him down and in the morning when he rose. He was to attend services and sermons of the reformed church when occasion offered. He was not to meddle with servants till his understanding in religion was better. He was always to give God thanks before and after meat, whether publicly or privately. He must spend sometime reading Scripture and other books that taught the good life, and spend Sunday wholly in prayer and other good Christian exercises. Next to religion, he was to apply himself to Latin and to French. The father did most approve of Cato, the morality of Aesop's fables, and then Terrence.

Roger Ascham had been born at Kirby Wiske, the third son of John Ascham, a house steward to Lord Scrope of Bolton. He was instructor in Latin and Greek to the youthful Edward VI and Princess Elizabeth, and possibly Lady Jane Gray. He became Latin secretary to Queen Mary and Queen Elizabeth and professor of Greek in St. John's College Cambridge. The Queen made the Archbishop grant him the living of Wetwang, when he was short of money in 1561. He wrote his influential work "the Schoolmaster" in 1563. This was published by his widow in 1570 and ran to five editions before 1590. "The Schoolmaster" sought to show the right way to good learning, by portraying the ideal tutor and the ideal scholar. Ascham discussed how to judge the aptitude of a pupil, how to encourage the student and how to inculcate the love of learning. He drew on Plato and Cicero. He stressed physical exercise as a part of education. The book was in English, but he set out the double translation method for learning Latin through the imitation of classical models.

Higher Education

There were English universities at Oxford and Cambridge. Their emphasis on providing higher education for the sons of poor men, and preparation for a career in the church was being challenged. There was a new demand for clergy who could preach in English and there was a new demand for a classical education from the nobility and gentry. Endowment incomes supported some students but a rich family or other patronage was an advantage. The Earl of Huntingdon was briefly at Queen's College, the third Lord Eure at St. John's College and the knight's son Hugh Cholmley at Jesus College. William Hopperton, a Hovingham gentleman, sent a son to Cambridge but so did two yeomen called Hayes from Aislaby, near Pickering.

New colleges were endowed. Oxford gained St. John's College in 1555, Jesus College in 1571, a printing press and the Bodleian library. Cambridge secured Emmanuel College in 1584 and Sidney Sussex College in 1596. The first degree dealt with logic, rhetoric, philosophy and mathematics. After four years you went on to study divinity, law or physic. The new Gresham college was founded at London in 1596 to teach the seven liberal sciences.

Trinity College recorded the charges for George Earl of Cumberland in 1571. Here were buttery costs, breakfasts, candles, wood, coal, payments for his tutor's fee, the barber and 4s for the carrier who brought his things to Cambridge. Another man had 4d for taking his stuff to the College. He kept a man-servant, sent his laundry out regularly, had his doublet mended for six shillings, breeches for a shilling, and spent small sums on foot hose and shoes. He hung painted cloths in his study, secured door locks, one for the privy, and made a place to put wood and coals. His horse went to be shod when he was ill. There were payments of 5s to the famous Dr John Caius and 5s8d to an apothecary. Study was evident in his purchase of Tully's Orations, the Colloquies of Erasmus and the Dialogues of Sebastian Castallo, respectively 13d, 20d and 16d. He had pen and ink horn and a sixpeny hour glass on the cupboard desk, with paper, a paper book and a penknife. There was a lute bought for 10s, payments for dancing lessons and bows and arrows. His mother sent him a hawk and the Countess a doe. Goodwife Green brought him some meat for a penny.

T96 Some Yorkshire Exhibitions and Scholarships to University.

1525.	Pocklington.	John Dowman.	5 scholars	St Johns College, Cambridge
1602.	Wakefield .	Thomas Cave,	2 scholars	Clare Hall
1572.	Wakefield.	John Thurleston	1 scholar	St Johns College
1603	Coxwold	Sir John Hart .	4 scholars	Sidney Sussex College

The London Inns of Court also had houses of students where the laws of the realm were studied. Gray's Inn, Lincolns Inn, Inner and Middle Temple offered a legal education, in the native tongue, of some practical use to gentlemen with estates to manage. The register of admissions to the Society of the Middle Temple 1559-1602 listed fifty-three men from Yorkshire, many of them younger sons of esquires and gentlemen, including three sons of Archbishop Sandys and young Fairfax from Gilling. When George Manners wrote home from the Inner Temple garden, he said that would execute his father's precepts, apply himself to his books, use good company and flee the contrary. He would give himself to honest and lawful exercise for the body. He had dropped Mr Blackwell, dancing school, tennis, running, leaping and such like in the fields.

James Rither described young Yorkshire gentlemen. "By the remiss education of indiscreet parents, they fall to rude pastimes before they learn civil behaviour. Their most universal exercise is hunting in which they contend about the cunning of the hounds and speed of their horses. This emulation doth breed in younger men many contentious words and not all true and as this apstire permoeth ready bodies so for the most part it makes rash and unmild minds."

Letters

Letter writing was an emerging art, surviving in official correspondence, letters from masters to their stewards, and between husbands and wives. The curious conventions of written correspondence had already appeared. Sir Robert Plumpton addressed himself in 1503 "to my right hartily and mine entirely beloved wife". Dame Agnes Plompton could write that "in my most harty wise I recommend me unto you". "Dear Hart" was an affectionate convention. Others from Elizabeth's reign, in a variety of letters included a heavy, almost unctuous, formality in opening and closing phrases, such as "my harty commendations unto you", "well beloved brother", "my sister, your bedfellowe", and "most hartie thankes for all your great curtese". They moved easily on to such invocations of the deity as "praying to God to bless you with the gift of the holy spirit", "wishing all your healths to God's pleasure", "the living lord have you in his blessed keeping" and "I commit you to the tuition of the all mightiest". News of death was formally reported as "our cousin departed to the mercy of God".

As today, many letters had very little content but the grittier aspects of life do emerge. John Maude could tell Hugh Saxey of York, of "a very evil customer come to London, my Lord Mayor son of our city, Thomas Robinson, he owes me £30". Anthony Maude could talk of a daughter "being placed in London" and of "horses pastured in the country". Thomas Maude mentions "Mr Cave of Wakefield or some other trusty clothier" and one Cockson who "by some sinister means has intruded himself into the vicarage of Ilkley, presented by Lord Keeper and instituted by the Archbishop of York". Ralph Eure, in August 1581, wrote to "my very good wife Mary Ewre", as he toured Italy, claiming to be improving his Latin and attending lectures in the humanities, civil law and logic. (14)

Books

Most of the "new learning" was old learning newly discovered, but books to serve the interest in classical culture were not yet plentiful. A flood of translations appeared for gentry homes and grammar schools. Scholars worked the written materials of the past, rendering the thought of the ancient Greeks and Romans into English and reworking the thoughts of the authors of the bible. Others turned to more local records, to the world around them and to their own fancy, for material to study. They increasingly wrote on practical matters of day to day work and leisure. The first attempt at a periodical "The English Mercurie" came out in 1588.

John Foster who kept the bookshop, and who did book binding at York from 1580 to 1607, had an inventory of near three thousand books, including theology, law, classics, school and song books. Margaret Countess of Rutland bought "a Hundred Merry tales", "Fortunes" and "Halle's Chronicle" in 1550. Sir William Fairfax had thirty-nine books at Gilling, half in English and the rest in French or Latin. There was St. Augustine but also Tacitus, Plutarch and Machiavelli, along with new books on heraldry and hawking. Robert Rotherforth had books on hunting, hawking and the wars, testaments and Latimers sermons. The Earl of Rutland at York in 1593-4 acquired Thomas Cooper's Thesuarus.

22 A Printing Press

Sir William Pickering was anxious that his "armory and library" go to his daughter Hester. Sir George Clifford, who had been at Cambridge with Whitgift, "had a general knowledge and insight into all the arts and especially the mathematics wherein he took great delight". Lady Hoby read books to her women at Hackness. The Countess Margaret of Cumberland employed Thomas Tymme to translate from the Latin, Dudley Fenner's "Sacred Divinity or the Truth ", some two hundred and seventy pages, sent to her during her affliction in July 1590. She wrote the epitaph on the Suffolk tomb of Richard Cavendish in 1601, and she supported Samuel Daniel, tutor to her daughter Anne, in his scholarship. She practised alchemy, delighted in distilling and spelt as she liked. Henry Constable praised her learning and that of her sister, Lady Warwick.

A varied literature emerged in several different traditions, which could hardly fail to agitate the brains of the thoughtful. Robert Pursglove gave the schoolmaster of Guisborough Grammar School many books, including Josephus' "History of the Jews". Ripon Library gained an Elizabethan copy of the "Nomina Villarum", "a ballad of the Death of the Cardinal", "a little ballet mayde of ye young Duke" and "The Beckley Broadside", a Suffolk town fire story of 1586, put to "Wilson's tune". Catholic books and tracts circulated illicitly. York stationers forfeited unlawful books in 1567. John Goldthwaite lost seventeen Latin primers, five hundred and nine English primers, three accidences, three Geneva grammars and a Latin alphabet.

Robert Parkin, the curate of Adwick le Street, himself the author of a poetical paraphrase of gospel history, left a bible, a heavy stock of bible literature including "Dionysius Carthusianus, a work on the bible in seven volumes", and Mr Calvin's book, when he died in 1568. He gave his godson John, Harding's "Chronicle". Timothy Bright, who wrote a short version of Foxe's popular "Acts and Monuments" had the Hebrew bible, the Syriac testament, Josephus, Plato in Greek and Latin and the standard work on music by Joseph Zarlino.

The Writers

A new secular literature appeared after mid century, in a wide range of subjects. Many writers and thinkers of the day were raised in Yorkshire. Those leaving the county to make their names elsewhere included Roger Ascham, Miles Coverdale, John Fisher and the Saville brothers. Others came into the county to live or fill offices, notably but not solely in the church. Many still wrote in Latin but Protestantism stressed the vernacular. The new translations of foreign books added much to the body of what was known but introduced that excess of respect for the written word, some of it even attributed to God. One of the cleverest men of the age, Bacon recognised the dangers well.

There was a greater curiosity about the universe, nature and human thinking. Many writers did not confine themselves to one subject. Edward Fairfax made translations of Tasso and wrote about witchcraft. Sir Thomas Chaloner translated the "Office of Servants" from Latin, but wrote a "Dictionary for Children" and "a Short discourse on the most rare and excellent virtues of Nitre". A literature based on personal experience slowly found its way. A more practical new knowledge was coming into being, probably not as new as it seems, but more likely now to be written down, and even printed in book form. Gentlemen kept common place books, a man's equivalent of ladies recipe books, with useful information gained from books or experience.

The struggle to separate fact from myth had a lingering obstacle in astrology. Anthony Ascham, brother of Roger, was rector of Methley. Between 1548 and 1558, he produced almanacs with forecasts for the year and a modest herbal. His "Treatise of Astronomy" combined the astrology and the herbal. John Field who lived at East Ardsley, was described as a "farmer, sometimes student in the mathematical sciences". He compiled the first English astronomical tables and the first work to explain the system of Nicolaus Copernicus on which they were based in 1556-58. His better known friend Dr. John Dee wrote the preface.

Sir Henry Saville born at Bradley in Halifax went to Brasenose College Oxford, and was made tutor in Greek and mathematics to Queen Elizabeth, warden of Merton and provost of Eton. This able mathematician founded the Savillian professorships of geometry and astronomy at Oxford and he translated Tacitus. Henry Briggs born at Daisy Bank House near Warley Wood, Halifax went to St John's College Cambridge and became Reader of Geometry at Gresham College, London at its foundation, in 1596. He constructed a table for finding latitude from an observation of the variation of the compass. His best work was done in the next reign. After visiting Napier in Scotland, he proposed an alteration in the scale of logarithms and made the first table of logarithms to the base ten. These converted complex multiplications into simple additions. Aubrey says that he viewed astrology as a system of groundless conceits.

Gentleman Richard Shane of Methley catalogued a botanical garden, compiled a herbal and analysed floral distributions. William Lawson, the vicar of Hutton Rudby wrote "A New Orchard and Garden" the first book on native horticulture, based on experience and the "Country Housewife's Garden".

Two men made significant contributions to legal studies. Henry Swinburne, a York lawyer wrote a manual of law and "a Brief Treatise on Testaments" which ran to several editions. William West of Aston, son of the rector of Hooton Roberts, managed the affairs of the town of Rotherham and the Earls of Shrewsbury. He edited Littleton's "Tenures" in 1581 and produced his "Symbolaeographia" of 1590, which described the verbal tools of the notary and the scrivener. This too made several editions, losing the classical quotations to become a practical handbook.

Several medical men made contributions inside and outside their professional sphere of expertise. Peter Levins from Skerne near Beverley wrote the first rhyming dictionary, with words arranged according to their endings. His "Pathway to Health" of 1587, ran to several editions in English, and embraced cooking and cosmetics. Here was day to day advice on how to know if the brain pan was broken, and treatments for deafness, blood shotten eye, a sauce flamed face, nails falling off, and restoring hair growth.

John Jones, born near Sheffield, vicar at Treeton, translated Galen, and wrote "A Dial for all Agues" and a treatise on the waters of Bath and Buxton. His "The Art and Science of Preserving Body and Soul in Health", touched on breast feeding, weaning, cleanliness, laxatives and the moral education of the child. Timothy Bright, physician and parson of Meathley produced works on hygiene, therapy and he produced the first English system of shorthand in "Characterie". His "Treatise of Melancholy" marks some steps towards psychology. Henry Arthington, a gentleman of Wakefield, writing "Provision for the Poor now in Penury" in 1597, analysed the causes of pauperism and the role of self help. Here was serious social analysis.

CHAPTER 12
HOUSE AND HOME

Homesteads

John Leland, travelling through the shire, before Elizabeth's reign, could say that "the whole town of Doncaster is builded of wood and the houses be slated", while Wakefield was "most of timber, but some of stone" and even Beverley, despite its brick bars, had "houses, well builded of wood". Timber was the principal structural material throughout the county, even in the chalk wolds of the East Riding where it was scarce. The word slate was used to mean thick, heavy slabs of local stone.

Stone work was confined to castles, bridges, monasteries, churches and to relatively few houses. From dates that remain uncertain, perhaps starting in the early 17th century, most domestic timber buildings would be encased in local stone where it was readily available. This might not give roof load bearing walls. if cruck timbers were raised to give a second story. Richard Blome in 1675 could describe Helmsley as "an indifferent built town of slate and stone houses". Chalk, a not very durable stone, was used in the East Riding Wolds where timber was scarce. Everywhere, old timbers were reused, as well as new.

Timber framing and cruck construction were differently distributed around the shire. They will have offered a different living experience. Small rooms and second and third floors came more easily in a timber framed house. The timber framed house was joinered. Posts and studs were fitted to a sill. Oak posts, nine by eighteen inches, were set ten or twelve feet apart. Squared sill timbers were framed lengthways into them. Tie beams were tennoned into the tops of the posts and carried transversely. These carried wall plates, and roof spars. Upper floor beams were framed into transverse beams. On these rested flat joists, the end of which could form brackets for an overhanging storey. Beams were strengthened by heavy curved struts, tennoned, morticed and pegged into the sides of posts. Spaces between main timbers were filled with vertical or diagonal studs, pegged into main timbers to form walls and partitions. Rafters, usually tapering towards the ridge, rested upon purlins, notched onto the main trusses and pinned together with oak pins above the ridge tree. Houses were roofed with one span.

The joinered timber frame house owed more to the house wright than the simpler cruck house. House wrights were recorded between 1554 and 1594. There were five at Hull and others at Alwoodly, Arksey, Arthington, Cawood, Garforth, Stoneferry, and Wombwell, but other wrights were at York, Beverley, Addingham, Bridlington, Broughton in Craven, Cave, Etton, Felixkirk, Howsham, Kirkby and Skelton in Cleveland, Leeds, Leven, Patrington and Rawmarsh, well scattered around the shire. There were sawers at Hull, and York and at Rockley in Worsborough.

Timber framing was the usual method of house construction at York. Some

23 LargeTimber framed house, at the Pavement, York

early houses had their length to the road and were only one room deep, but later houses at right angles to the road had narrow gabled front elevations, and stood two storey, even three storey and were jettied over the street though not to the rear. They survived at Petergate, Stonegate, Goodramgate, Shambles and more rarely in Coney Street, and

24 Cruck Beams were Exposed at Wrelton in 1964

Fossgate.[1] Other towns kept rare survivors, but some country areas used the same building style. Timber frames occurred widely in and around the Vale of York. Bedale houses once had oak posts and studs, not crucks, with upper walling of wattle and daub. Slates were used as well as thatch, implying framed trusses to carry them.[2]

Cruck framed houses were a simpler solution where large timbers were available. The timbers were reused in any reconstruction. Pairs of curved timber trusses met at a ridge beam. The one storey house was covered by thatch or stone tiles. Many were long houses, and could have family at one end, cattle or loom at the other, sharing a common entry, or cross passage, called the threshold, and with its through draught, sometimes used for threshing. There were considerable variations in size. Barns could be similarly constructed. Sub division of the house part could create an inner room, giving the typical three room house. A second storey could be made by inserting upper chambers in the roof, reached by a staircase. The byre end could be given a second entry. The house part could be given a lobby or central entry. Early walling could be replaced by stone. Spout House in Bilsdale once had its firehouse open to the roof, smoke blackened from a central hearth.

Addey gave a good account of the mud walls of an old cottage at Great Hatfield, near Hornsea in Holderness. "The walls are built of layers of mud and straw which vary from five to seven inches in thickness, no vertical joints being visible. On the top of each layer is a thin covering of straw, with the ends of the straw pointing outwards, as in a corn stack. The way in which mud walls were built is remembered in the neighbourhood. A quantity of mud was mixed with straw and the foundation laid with this mixture.

Straw was then laid across the top, while the mud was wet and the whole was left to dry and harden in the sun. As soon as the first layer was dry, another layer was put on, so that the process was rather a slow one. Finally the roof was thatched and the projecting ends of straws trimmed off the walls. Such mud walls are very hard and durable and their composition resembles that of sun-burnt bricks."[3]

The survey taken at Cracowe in Burnsall at Staincliffe in 1586 shows solid well built farm houses. Stephen Kitchen's firehouse held four pairs of "crooks" of ash timber. His barn had five pair of crockes of oak timber lately builded". Other houses had two or three pairs of oak or ash crucks. The room formed within a bay might be seventeen feet by seventeen feet six inches. The keeper of the Bishop of Durham's wood below Osmotherley supplied Thomas Todde with "one crooked tree growing in the loaning there mete to be two pair of siles" in 1602.

Henry Best described the making of an earth floor. You graved it over, with a hay rake or iron wainrakes till the mowles were small then led in water in tubs or hogsheads. You made it soft as mortar, and it lay a fortnight almost as a puddle. As it hardened you beat it down smooth with flat pieces of wood. Floor holes were filled from time to time with coup loads of red clay or fallow field clods. You broke the clods up with a "mell", and shovelled them in. Mud floors could become dusty so they were strewn with rushes or other damp plants. The idea of mixing bullock or ox blood in with a fine clay came from Italy, such a floor would harden and could take a polish. Earth floors were only slowly replaced by boards and that at much later dates.

The houses of the very poor have left little trace in document or fact. Many were probably one roomed hovels. Pictures from much later show one storey houses. The 1620 map of Kildale shows one storey, probably one room houses.[4] Brandesburton was described in 1629 as about thirty messuages and twenty other houses with little yards and crofts. "The houses are very mean, being built of clay walls, wherein there is no timber and the roofs are made of small fir posts and thatched with straw, but in bad repair".[5]

Castles as Homes

The prosperity of the nobility, gentry, merchant and clothier families found an outlet in a wave of rebuilding. Halls, manor houses and town houses were altered or built anew, especially in the later years of Queen Elizabeth's reign and this would continue into the time of James I. William Harrison avowed in 1577 that "each one desireth to set his house aloft on the hill, to be seen afar off and cast forth his beames of stately and curious workmanship into every quarter of the country". Some Yorkshire magnates certainly sought to impress, with a great house dominating the skyline but many more lived in ancestral homes, which they modified to suit a new age. The vast majority of people seem likely to have continued as they were before.

A few great castles had survived in Yorkshire. They had a lingering prestige and were normally close to valued parks and chases. Many more had lost their role and showed mere fragments of masonry or simply earthworks. The early motte and bailey castles had not proved adaptable for more comfortable living. Even good stone-built castles had sometimes ceased to serve as family homes or centres of great estates. Useless ruins and useable buildings could stand alongside each other. Ravensworth castle had a fair stable, but Leland noticed only two or three towers where there had been eight.[6] The great Stuteville castle at Cottingham was reduced to farm buildings, standing behind double dikes and moats. The walls of Malton castle held a farmhouse next to the older earthworks of the Roman military fort, which may have served as its courtyard. Lord Eure would build a great new house on the site, clear of the ruins.

The ancient Crown castles had played a different role and some kept their significance longer. Although rarely used as royal residences and then only for short periods, they remained centres for Crown administration and symbols of Crown power. York castle was sorely ruined and had no good house within but it retained an administrative role. County elections for knights of the shire were held there. Henry Earl of Huntingdon wrote to the justices in 1580 about building a new hall in York Castle, probably for public functions.[7] Robert Redhead, the jailer in 1595 was breaking up the tower and the wall stone for burning into lime.

The Crown castles rarely saw sheriffs or stewards in permanent residence. As administrative centres of some of the great estates, known as honours, most needed a court house and a prison. Sandall castle was maintained in a somewhat better condition as an occasional residence for the Wakefield manor steward. There was a prison with a resident gaoler, and a forty acre deer park containing thirty fallow deer. The Queen ordered the constable to appoint a place in 1561 for keeping the court rolls, with three locks on the door. They had been kept at the church.[8] Sir Edward Carey, son of the Queen's cousin Lord Hunsdon, resided for a time, but later Sir John Saville of Howley had the custody.

The Earl of Cumberland found Knaresborough Castle in reasonable repair in 1538 and still with its great stable. Sir Ambrose Cave in 1561, found only a receiver's lodging and this was replaced by the old court house about 1600. At Pickering castle, only the stone built new hall of 1314 and the chapel were in good repair, although the tower chambers did see some later use. The timber lodges within the inner stone walled court were already in ruins by 1535. Sir Richard Cholmeley as constable had taken the best cut stones from the King's hall, stair stones from a tower, fourteen wain loads of other stone, two loads of slates and tower timbers for use elsewhere. The constables of the great castle at Scarborough preferred to reside in the manor house at nearby Northstead, even though the castle had a useable hall and tower.

The great triple courtyard castle of the Neville's at Sheriff Hutton had passed to the Crown. This was a strong structure built by the first Earl of Westmoreland in 1379 to replace an earlier motte and bailey at a different site near the village church. This castle served the Crown well, virtually replacing York Castle as a royal residence and it was put at the disposal of the Crown's viceroys in the north. There was extensive renovation, on at least two occasions, in the early sixteenth century, once for Henry FitzRoy, the illegitimate son of King Henry VIII who lived here as Duke of Richmond for ten years with a semi royal court, and again in 1537 for the Duke of Norfolk who resided for several months, ruling the north, in the aftermath of the rising called the Pilgrimage of Grace.

Leland said that "there was no house in the north so like a princely lodgings" as Sheriff Hutton with its stately stairs, eight towers, a magnificent hall and great chambers. The Council in the North went on meeting here at least occasionally. Prisoners were kept here after the Wakefield plot of 1541 and Catholic gentlewomen during the Elizabethan Council's campaign against the recusant gentry. A full survey was made for the Earl of Huntington in 1572 by carpenter John Jameson and plumber Richard Peckett. Another £700 were spent on repairs by 1575. There were some garden improvements. The Earl kept sufficient possessions here to suggest that he may often have resided.

318

The modernisation of a castle was one option for a great Elizabethan nobleman. The later mediaeval castles had moved away from the early motte and bailey plans. There were the strong keeps, or tower houses, often standing amidst farm and other buildings. Quite different were the regular, rectangular , walled and towered courtyard castles. These held more private rooms, better service quarters, good fireplaces and simple toilets called garderobes, within compact structures built to better standards. They could still serve in the Elizabethan age. There were other buildings, sometimes called castles, with a mere touch of crenellation, or which stood within some ditch or moat. The term moated manor house has been coined to describe the numerous sites of this kind, often in low ground, where only the earthwork remains, and no-one knows quite what stood within.

Helmsley Castle in Ryedale was a 12th century structure within massive earthworks but with sound masonry, on an accessible site close to the town and a great park. Within the great earthen ditches of the inner court, Edward Manners third Earl of Rutland built an Elizabethan stone hall, and chambers with mullion and transomed windows, oak panelling and good plaster work. A surviving cornice has his shield with sixteen quarterings. Steward William Segrave wrote to the Earl from Helmsley in April 1578 saying "Your buildings at the castle do not proceed as speedily as the mason supposed. The masons work will not be ended before Lammas. The timber is sufficient for making a Gallery in the roof." They were still building two years later. The castle may well have been rather short of servants' lodgings, but the town was close to hand. His son Francis Manners had the timbered Helmsley rectory building.

Sir Francis Knollys described the tower house called Bolton castle in Wensleydale, useable as a prison for Mary Queen of Scots "This house appeareth to be very strong, very fair, and very stately, after the old manner of building and it is the highest walled house that I have ever seen and hath but one entrance thereto. And half the number of these soldiers may better watch and ward the same than the whole number thereof could do at Carlisle Castle".

A small tower house known as Ayton Castle, near Scarborough was only abandoned in 1594, when Lord Eure removed the lead, timber, fireplaces and glass for his new building at Malton. The tower at Gilling Castle in Ryedale proved quite adaptable to the times. The two upper stories were rebuilt on the tower base, but given bay windows and a turret staircase in 1585. Sir William Fairfax's great chamber still has windows inset with coloured heraldry, high wainscot panelling with a painted frieze above, great fireplaces and a rib partitioned plaster ceiling dripping with pendants above the dark oak floor.

The Earl of Northumberland's great courtyard castle at Wressle was recent enough to be left alone. Four corner towers, and a gate tower, four and five stories high were full of lodgings, and service rooms, built in 1380-90. Snape Castle had been built in the early 15th century for John Neville, first Lord Latimer. Dorothy daughter of the last Lord Latimer took it in marriage to Thomas Cecil Lord Burghley who rebuilt the castle in 1587, retaining some structure and a chapel from the older building.

25 The Great Chamber of Gilling Castle

T97 William Smith's list of Yorkshire Castles
Armanthwaite (Danby), Bolton, Bowes, Cawood (Archbishops of York), Conisbrough, Crayke (Bishop of Durham), Gilling, Harlsey, Harewood, Hinderskelfe, Hornby, Hull, Kilton, Middleham, Mulgrave, Pontefract (Crown), Ravensworth (Lord Parr, later Earl of Essex), Richmond, Sandall (Crown), Scarborough (Crown), Sheffield, Sheriff Hutton (Crown), Sigston, Skelton, Skipton, Slingsby, Tickhill, Upsall, Whorlton, Wilton, Wressle, and York (Crown) .

Converted Monasteries

Several monasteries had passed to new owners. A small priory in good repair was readily adaptable for a more modern residence. Some already had an Abbot's or Prior's lodging, of a good standard, some recently rebuilt. A surprising number were allowed to go to ruin. The sites offered rich supplies of stone, and structural timber, and surviving buildings. If anything, there was an excess of buildings. The new owners were not always from the wealthiest class and any decision needed to be taken soon after acquisition. The monastery churches were usually too massive and useless for conversion. Roof lead was a quick profit in prospect and was commonly stripped off for sale. Decay soon set in. The Bishop of Durham's quadrangle manor house at Howden was falling into decay by 1577. James Bishop had removed the lead covered laver worth £20 from the top of the hall and lead from elsewhere. The other old buildings were quarried to build a new house nearby or were adapted to other uses.

The Abbot's house at St Mary's Abbey York had a stone ground floor but had been rebuilt in brick in the late 15th century. The abbey was dissolved in 1539. The Council in the North was installed within a month in what became known as the King's Manor. Monastery ruins fell to disuse towards the river Ouse but Henry Manners Earl of Rutland, Archbishop Young and Thomas Radcliffe, Earl of Sussex, between 1560 and 1572 turned the old Abbot's house round with new windows and used ashlar from the ruins to add the new north west range, complete with a semi-octagonal bay window. The King's Manor was declared to be the permanent home for the council in 1573, with a Crown grant of "the house which of late was called St Mary's Abbey", for meetings of the court of the Council in the North, the occasional residence of the Lord President and the ordinary residence of the permanent members. Henry Hastings between 1572 and 1595, made a Council chamber, on the first floor over a wing and kitchen of the old house, bearing the crest he was granted in 1579 and he added a brick building along the north west precinct wall. Lord Sheffield continued building after 1603.

Newbrough Priory passed to the heirs of Anthony Bellasis, chaplain to King Henry VIII. By 1621-2, the house on the site had twenty-eight rooms besides the chapel, hall, staircase, kitchen, porter's lodge and stable. Many of the rooms held only a bed and bedstead, but twenty-three of them of them were feather beds, while the great chamber had eighteen high stools and four chairs. Much of the north front kept older masonry. It has been suggested that this was the refectory range with a surviving kitchen. The vanishing cloisters may underlie the forecourt.[9] Sir Thomas Gargrave converted part of the monastic buildings at Nostel Priory into a manor house. Robert Strelley made the east range of Egglestone Abbey into a house, perhaps using the refectory as his hall.

Francis Cholmeley built a new timbered house about 1580, complete with an entry porch amidst the monastic ruins at Whitby. The exact site is not known. Lady Scrope may have had separate quarters there during her widowhood. When she died, Francis moved back to his house at Roxby near Thornton Dale. The monastery buildings at Malton, Rosedale, Yedingham and other smaller houses housed gentry families for a time. The details are not usually known and slight ruins remain. The Earl of Westmoreland sometimes addressed letters from Keldholme Priory near Kirkby Moorside. The brick and stone Prior's Lodge at Watton, in the East Riding became a good house for John Farnham. At the sites of other monasteries it is rarely clear what did happen.

The larger monastery granges were on a more convenient scale to improve what there was. Byland Abbey's Thorpe Grange and Wilden Grange were leased to Richard Lascelles for rebuilding. Several gentlemen were occupying Rievaulx Abbey granges by mid century, and others afterwards. Roger Dodsworth, the antiquarian was born at West Newton Grange in 1585. William Eddon was at Skiplam, and Thomas Saville at Welburn. Contemporary descriptions suggest that some improvements were made. Thomas Saville bequeathed to his son Francis, " all the glass pertaining to his house in Welburn, with doors, locks, keys, all the furniture and household implements in his dining parlour, hall and low chamber. Conyers Saville conveyed Welburn manor to John Gibson in 1597, who converted the Rievaulx grange into Welburn Hall.

Elizabethan Gentry Houses

The demand for many small rooms was the dominant theme of the larger scale gentry building construction. The number of lodging chambers and servants' rooms multiplied with a family's prosperity. Other rooms were set aside for specialised purposes. This was not entirely new. Servants had long been part of northern feudalism, as armed retainers in case of need. Now it was less military, more for day to day service. Sir John Neville at Chevet Park had built a half timbered house with twenty-eight main rooms in 1529. There was a hall with a raised dais and a bay window, a dining parlour, great gallery and chapel. Among the numerous chambers were a gilt chamber and king and queen chambers. Special purpose buildings included the brew house, stables, oxhouses, garner and gatehouse. A beam was inscribed "This house was made by John Neville, knight and Dame Elizabeth his wife in the year of our God 1529".[10]

What you built depended on what you had. Several motivations were at work, beside the desire for display. An appropriate body of servants was felt necessary for an acceptable living standard at gentlemanly levels. At the same time, there was a new desire to be apart from the servants. There was a move towards family and even personal privacy in high life, expressed in separate dining chambers, and separate drawing rooms, detached from the traditional hall. There was also a need to show prestigious hospitality to visitors of a similar social station and to reasonably accommodate their servants. Service rooms were given more attention, with a growing conviction that many tasks were better performed in rooms set aside for a purpose. Many modified an older house. Some built anew.

The old tower house at Gilling Castle in Ryedale was altered to hold a dining parlour, new lodgings including the named "great, green, master's, bishops, middle and kitchen chambers" and a low vault. There was a porter's lodge, the far gatehouse, a stable, kiln, dairy and oxhouses, wet garner, pastry, bake house, boulting house, brew house, school house, gallery, new turret, pleasaunce, paradise and an old study. The manor house at Burton Constable in Holderness, "of ancient building" was repaired by

Sir John Constable, but it was given a new addition on the north, with a high turret, great chamber, parlour and many lodgings, a buttery, pantry, wine cellar and common cellar, brew house, bake house, stables, barns, larders, garners and a fair chapel.

The inward looking enclosed courtyard had dominated earlier house and castle plans with multiple rooms placed in buildings set against the courtyard walls. Some Elizabeth courtyards were given an open side, others a walled forecourt with a gatehouse, or a separate arched entry which kept something of the old enclosed atmosphere. The double courtyard was the solution at Ingleby Arncliffe and at Heslington Hall, brick built within easy reach of York, for Thomas Eames, Secretary to the Council of the North.

Hackness Hall, set in a Blackamoor dale appears to have had one closed courtyard, but with a second open court before it. The place would be described in 1608. "Hackness lyeth most pleasantly, environed on all sides with fair woods, hills and dales, pleasant springs, becks and abundance of grass, corn and pasture, whereto belongs an old mansion place or manor in metley repairacon hath hall, parlour, great chamber, chapel, bedchambers, closets and many other lodgings, two kitchens, buttery, pantry ,brew house, kiln, barn, bake house, stables, gild house, little garden and orchard, two water mills, fulling mill, fifty-four acres of demesne, and a dovecote for a hundred doves."

Several new plans abandoned the courtyard. The great house was given a forward outlook, sometimes with some external symmetry, each side of a projecting entry porch, or the simpler balance of a central hall with projecting cross wings. The H and E plans were often more symmetrical outside than inside. Outside appearance could be designed for effect and might cease to reflect the inside arrangements. Most kept a large hall behind the facade. This was reached from the main entry door in the porch, through a screened passage.

The few really great Elizabethan houses chose designs that were more "architectural". They were more open to the view, to see and to be seen. They displayed an impressive frontage of pointed gables, symmetrical facades and such purely decorative features as horizontal mouldings running around the house, at various layers. The roof might be concealed behind a parapet. For their residents, these houses were more outward looking, with many glass windows, to overlook gardens and parks. Sometimes they seemed to have more window than wall. The inner courtyard might remain, but was less of a focal area and it could vanish altogether.

Andrew Borde gave advice on how to lay out a house, with less concern for tradition. He suggested that you could group rooms for the convenience and effective service of the family in the house. "Make the hall of such a fashion that the parlour be annexed to the head of the hall and the buttery and pantry at the lower end thereof. The cellar to be under the pantry set somewhat at a base, the kitchen set somewhat at a base from the buttery and pantry, coming with an entry within by the wall of the buttery. The pastry house and larder would be annexed to the kitchen. The privy chamber should be annexed to the great chamber of estate with other chambers necessary for the building."

There was a notable move to higher rise buildings, with extra floors, reached by staircases, replacing the sprawl of the older manorial complexes. The shift to second floor living would foster the separation of family from servants, when the common hall gave way to the great dining chamber above. The smaller Elizabethan houses lost their open topped hall. An old hall open to the rafters was given an inserted second floor with hearths venting to a chimney. A chamber over the hall is mentioned at Hackness in 1600. The Kirkby Moorside High hall and the timber framed Helmsley Rectory house were given floors with a chamber over the hall. Height brought the accidents that any change does. Earthquakes on 26th February 1574 caused damage everywhere. They shook down the gable end of Hatfield manor hall. Thomas Burnham was killed at Steeton with a fall from the top of a house in 1597-8.

Great houses needed great expenditure. Bryan Stapleton's Carlton manor house cost over £4000 and William Mauleverer's Ingleby Arncliffe £2000. The new building erected at Howley Hall, was said to have cost Sir Robert & Sir John Saville even greater sums. Sir Robert Stapleton in the 1570's at Wighill, started "a palace the model whereof he had brought out of Italy". A contemporary thought that it was " fitter for a Lord Treasurer of England than a knight of Yorkshire."[11] The surveyor Humberstone said that Leconfield, part timber and part stone, was the largest and stateliest house that the Earl of Cumberland had in Yorkshire.

Sir Henry Slingsby who knew the great mansions at Tibbalds and Audley End in the south of the country thought Lord Ralph Eure's house at Malton, Lord Saville's at Howley and Sir Arthur Ingram's at Temple Newsome were the principal houses of the county. The date on Lord Eure's Malton rain head was 1602. and he completed his local estate purchases that year. His son married at Ingleby in 1601 and that house was sold a few years later. The Malton house was said to be large and sumptuous, built round three sides of a quadrangle. The entry hall had a carved wood chimney piece with the Eure coat of arms, while a mantel told the story of Jonah in carved oak. The house had thirty-seven hearths in 1673.

Many houses were not built or developed on this scale. More modest changes could include putting an upper storey into a large cruck house, as at Wyville Hall, Slingsby. A massive chimney was given fire places at each floor level. Many smaller manor houses were new built with a ground floor hall, a chamber over, and modest flanking cross wings, one for service rooms. The Buckingham house at Kirkby Moorside had a modest hall with a chamber over between two slightly projecting cross wings. Examples occur with a single cross-wing giving an L shape plan. Building and alterations continued into the next reign, and good evidence is needed to separate sixteenth and seventeenth century work. Warburton's early eighteenth century sketches showed some of these houses, but often dwarfed by later developments.

Gardens

New gardens were laid out around some of the Elizabethan houses. The arrangements were formal, in styles derived from Italy, with gravel walks, lined by neat dwarf hedges, between beds of flowers, shrubs, arranged earths and stones. They formed one of the pleasurable delights of the age. Alleyways might run between fruit trees in an orchard, leading to arbours with seats and Summer houses. The layout was best seen from the upper floors, the gallery, or even the roof of an Elizabethan house. Lord Bacon praised the courtyard plan, where an inner court could have a garden with a grotto and fountains.

The pioneering gardens came earlier, under King Henry VIII. Dean Higden had built a goodly prebendary house at Ulleskelf which had an orchard and topiary walks. Leland wrote of fair gardens at the Earl of Northumberland's Wressle castle within the moat and in the orchards, including mounts, and topiaries, "writhen about with degrees like turnings of cockilshilles to come to the top without pain". The description may mirror his gardens at Topcliffe, where a 1613 survey of the manor house records gardens, orchards, walks and a hill called Maiden Bower, once a castle motte, which had seven ascending circumferences all quicksette and replenished with some fruit trees.

Elizabethan gardens have not survived. They leave mere shadowy earthworks, if anything at all and little is known about those in the county. Sheriff Hutton castle was given two long ponds or canals, which may have formed a rectangle of formal gardens with the Lady Bridge on a walkway eighty yards long, planked and railed, perhaps even in anticipation of a royal visit. Wentworth Woodhouse was given flower beds each side of a central path in front of the house. Other garden features have been suspected at Byland and at Mulgrave. Lady Hoby delighted in her Hackness garden. She wrote in 1603, "we had in our garden a second summer, for the artichokes bear twice, white roses, red roses and a musk rose set last winter all bear flowers now. Raspberries set fair again and almost every herb and flower bear twice. It is a great fruit year all over, I think the like hath seldom been seen."

New Materials

Where great trees remained, timber was cheaper than stone or brick. Outside the chalk Wolds, now largely devoid of wood, timber trees squared off and jointed one way or another, provided the load bearing framework. Wold chalk was a poor building material of limited life. When John Legard new built his Ganton manor house on the Wold edge, he used local chalk, stone and timber were brought from away. He had "the walls of chalk and stone and covered with slate, a new built kiln house, and a stone dovecote around a courtyard, with two long houses and a long barn of timber forks which had eight rooms" or bays.

Brick was the coming house building material, for walls and chimneys, which would later replace timber and stone over whole swathes of Yorkshire. That day was not yet. The industry was not new. There were brick works making wall, roof and floor tiles at Hull and Beverley in the 14th century, places where the industry remained active but bricks had not spread to the Wolds. The word brick was used by the fifteenth century instead of the earlier wall tiles. Elizabethan brick making was confined to the three largest towns and a few gentry houses, where travelling brick makers would search for a local clay, and make what they needed close to the building site. With no transport cost, bricks were cheap. Heslerton Hall was built in brick between 1565 and 1568.

The clay was dug at Michaelmas, from the alluvial clays of the river banks of Hull and Humberside. It was trodden and chopped to break it up, laid out until Christmas, then turned over to lay again until March. An Act of Parliament of 1477 required the clay dug by the first of November, stirred and turned before the first of February and not made into tiles before March. There was to be no mixing in of chalk, marl or stones. The bricks were formed in moulds and left to dry. A tilehouse kept out the rain and let in a drying wind. The hot centre of the kiln provided harder, better and dearer bricks. They proved an excellent infill for timber framed walling.

The limestone country used thin holed and pegged, heavy stone roofing "tiles" as a defence against fires. A brick roofing tile, sometimes glazed, proved a good fire proof alternative to thatch in the towns of Hull, and Beverley. Bricks from Drax reached St Mary's Abbey, York in the fifteenth century and there were tile houses at Clifton and outside Walmgate Bar soon afterwards. Bricks, ridge and gutter tiles were made to standard sizes. York had brick makers in the 16th century, the furnaces holding twelve thousand tiles, with up to eight firings a year and resident bricklayers. Two brick makers appeared at Rawcliffe in the West Riding with "a close to be digged for brick and tile." The earliest reports at Scarborough were not till 1636 when a lime burner made quantities at a shilling a thousand.

Timber had been the main mediaeval building material. Cladding cruck framed buildings in stone occurred widely but the dates are uncertain. Stone buildings without a wood framework seem to come in the next century. Even a gentleman could opt for timber. Francis Cholmeley succeeded his father Richard at Whitby in 1583. Within ten years, he built Abbey House, being the first of his family to fix his residence there. His descendants blamed his wife for the use of old fashioned materials. "Though the country affords plenty of stone, she would have the sides, even to the ground, all of wood, saying it would serve well enough for their time, as they had no children."[13]

The increased use of local stones would give Yorkshire its building districts. Barnsley and Rotherham had their sandstone. There were millstone grits and limestone further north. The magnesian limestone built the grey and white walls further east, while the vale of York with little stone, kept its timber framing. Brick and stone facades ushered in the age of classical architecture. There was more style, inside as well as out. Both materials took plaster and plaster craftsmen, almost imitating sculpture, made geometrical roof patterns for ceilings. Exterior walls had diamond patterns of coloured brick, and decorative stone or plaster strap work. Classical motifs, entered into decoration. There were pinnacles and pilasters, ogee shape capped towers, flamboyant stone entry porches and detached gatehouses. There was more warmth for many rooms as multiple chimney stacks rose skywards.

Favoured Features

Chimneys were a great innovation, almost an obsession in the many rooms of the great houses. William Harrison said that old men in his village could only recall two or three chimneys in the days of kings Henry VII and Henry VIII. " Now, we have many chimneys and yet our tenderlings complain of rheums, catarrhs and poses". "The smoke in those days was supposed to be a sufficient hardening for the timber of the house" and, "a far better medicine to keep the good man and his family from the quack". Halls were given massive chimney pieces around a vast recess that could hold a tree trunk. Masonry shafts rose on solid bases, receiving other shafts from each flue. Burton Agnes had brick stacks. Even cruck house chimneys were set against the through passage wall, and given a partition to form an ingle nook.

Town chimneys could create neighbour problems. George Cook owning a house in Coney St, York, rented the next property, and built his chimney to project into the other. He was ordered to pay an extra 6d a year rent in 1555, and to remove it at the end of the lease. William Fothergill in 1578 complained of the smoke, air and unwholesome savour ascending from the furnace or beef pan of his neighbour Robert Shawcocke through a chimney under his principal glass window Thomas Ellis of Monk Ward had to remove a chimney in 1582 that was likely to set Monk Bar on fire.

Halls, kitchens, parlours and chambers were given windows. Bay windows were a fashion for great houses, some running the height of the building, and giving each floor pretty retiring places to view the world. Windows could include decorative coloured glass, enlivening a room. The heralds recorded the fashion in 1585. Mr. Kaye at Woodsome hall had fourteen coats of arms displayed and Mr. Aske at Aske hall had a riot of colour with twenty-six.[14] Glass was valuable and moveable. William Kirkby at

326

York in 1558 gave Margaret Lambarne "the window of wood with the glass in the high chamber" and Alison Holme all the glass in the low window. Glass was fragile. A man at York Stonegate set rails in the street before his windows to protect them in 1596.

A set of mullion windows could bring light to a smaller interior, sometimes replacing oiled canvas or horn sheet. Mullions and transoms gave a double set of several panes, two lights high. The wall stonework was grooved for the glass, which was set in grooved strips of lead, with wrought iron saddle bars let into sills and heads. Large windows might have a small part fitted to open. A luxury for the three room cruck house might be a single small pane set to bring light to the ingle nook of the "firehouse" or as we might say, the main living room.

Tapestry, arras work and painted cloths stayed in genteel use but internal roof plastering and ceiling or panelling with oak made decorative interiors. Ceiling was put in halls, parlours, and chambers, the word including wainscot. Panels were small to reduce oak shrinkage. Internal partitions of timber allowed the sub division of rooms. Winestead Rectory in 1579 had "a partition of boards between the hall and the buttery". The wainscot panels kept the heat and excluded draughts better than tapestries, and they prepared the way for the framed picture. There was a vogue for painting on plaster above wainscot level.

A long gallery beneath the roof, running the full length of the house offered space for storage, poor weather exercise, children and music. Galleries seem sometimes to have been made almost casually. Sir Richard Cholmeley employed two masons to add a gallery to Roxby near Pickering, where he lived with fifty to sixty men servants in 1562. He took fourteen wainloads of stone, two loads of slates and a great tree from the Kings Hall in Pickering Castle and stair stones from its tower, apparently with permission of the castellan, the Earl of Westmoreland, his relative by marriage. The Gilling gallery was furnished with sixteen stools, ten and half yards of carpet, a cupboard, a trestle table and two maps. The Newbrough gallery in1622 had a table, a little cheyney table, a couch bed, livery cupboard, four brass candlesticks, pictures and maps.

Staircases replaced the newel centred "vyse", a spiral of triangles of wood or stone. Broad, straight wood flights of stairs, often wide and massive, ascending in short flights of six or seven steps, from landing to landing, were built in a stair well, Treads were low and wide. They were made of solid oak blocks supported by deep stout sloping rails. Many hand rails sat on heavy balusters, ending in a ball or acorn, with heavy, thick, newel posts at each change of direction. Edward Beseley gave his E shaped Skelton manor of c1576, a staircase with square newels, with pierced steeple terminals, carved pendants, moulded rail rests and turned balusters.

Personal pride gained expression in door lintels, carrying initials or names of man and wife, coats of arms and dates, usually for rebuildings. They gossiped when Francis Cholmley's strong minded wife put her name before his on the porch at Whitby Hall. The timber porch at Sharlston Hall was inscribed

"In three things-God and man well pleased
the good loving of brethren,
the love of neighbours,
man and wife of one consent,
In the name of the Lord ,
this house was begun
and by His provision

finished and done.
By John Fleming Cuthbert
and Dorothy his wife,
whose souls I wish
to have angelic life. In anno dom, 1574"[15]

T 98 Some Elizabethan Houses, Built or Modified

Agbrigg   -Heath Old Hall (John Kaye); Linthwaite Hall;Methley park hall (Sir John Saville, 1593); Woodsome Hall, Almonbury (1600); Howley Hall, Batley (Sir John Saville, 1590); Altofts Hall (1582)

Allertonshire.-Norton Conyers (Richard Norton)

Barkstone   -Ledstone Hall (Henry Witham,1588)

Birdforth   -Beningbrough (Raphe Bouchier, RBE 1576); Newbrough Priory (Sir William Belasyse), Colville Hall, Coxwold.

Bulmer   -Wyndham Hall, Crake; Cornbrough villa

Claro   -Swinsty Hall (1575); Farnley Hall (Mr.Fawkes);

Dickering   -Boynton Hall (Sir William Strickland); Burton Agnes Hall (Sir Henry Griffiths, 1601-3); Ganton Hall.(Mr.Legard, 1585); Rudstone Eastgate (1591)

Hang   -Snape, (Sir Thomas Cecil, 1587)

Harthill   -Cave castle 1586, Londesborough (Francis Lord Clifford 1589), Bishop Burton (Sir William Gee, c1603), Leconfield

Holderness   -Barmston, (Sir Francis Boynton,c 1598).

Langbaurgh -Ugthorpe Hall (1586); Ingleby Hall (Mr.Mauleverer, 1577); Ormsby (1588-9, Mr. Pennyman)

Morley   -Oakwell Hall. (John Batte, 1583)

Osgoldcross -Pontefract Hall, (Edward Talbot 1591)

Ouse & Derwent-Heslington Hall (Thomas Eames 1565-8.)

Pickering Lythe-Ebberston Hall (Mr.Etherington)

Ryedale   -Welburn Hall. (Thomas Saville, Sir John Gibson) Helmsley castle (Earl of Rutland, 1563-87, Nunnington Hall (Mr.Norcliffe); Gilling castle, (Sir William Fairfax 1585.) Slingsby Castle (1602-8, Sir Charles Cavendish)

Skyrack   -Arthington (Mr.Briggs, 1585); Baildon Hall, Gawthorpe, 1596) Hawksworth Hall; Middleton Lodge; Rawdon Hall (George Rawdon); Swinsty Hall; Weston hall (Mr.Vavasour); Guiseley Rectory (Robert Moore 1601)

Strafforth   -Ickes Hall (Thomas Reresby, 1587); Great Houghton Hall (Sir Francis Rhodes), Thorpe Salvin (Henry Sandford, 1570); Eccleshall Hall (1602); Thorne (1573)

Staincliff   -Bradley Hall (J.S. 1577) Scothrop manor (1603)

Whitby Strand.-Hackness.(Sir John Constable); Whitby Hall

York   -King's Manor 1560

Fuel for Fires

Turves and peat were the most readily available fuels for family hearths and for kilns right across the county, although a few townships had none. Turf was taken from the top layer of old pasture. Peat was a naturally occurring, partly decomposed, plant material found at waterlogged sites and extracted from a face, something like a shallow quarry. Turf burned brighter than peat. The larger towns imported turf from surrounding areas and along rivers. Turf was regularly landed at the York staithes. Turves dug in the turbaries of Thorne and Hatfield wastes in Summer was taken in small boats to the river Don, whence keel boats carried it to York and Selby.

The high moors of Yorkshire had stretches of ground without grass or heather, but with bare surfaces covering from one to four feet of damp black or brown peat. The names of the workings survive, in Peat Rigg near Cawthorne and Turf Grafts on Hutton Bushell moor. When John Bonvell granted long leaseholds to ten farmers on the west side of Rosedale in 1566 their documents guaranteed "sufficient turf and ling for fuel and roofing". Stainton dale peats were sent into Scarborough. A Westerdale man listed his peat axe, two spades and a turf spade. worth three shillings in his will, along with his six pewter dishes worth six shillings.

The old moors about Huddersfield in the West Riding were far more extensive than they are now. There were agreed places where the tenants with rights of turbary could dig pits for peat and turf. No digging was allowed for turves or sods, within four yards of the highway at Hepworth. At Slaithwaite, the manor lord "with the assent and consent of his tenants" fixed both limits and hours of working. One man from each household was expected to cut turves on the agreed Summer day. Regular roads called turgates were made through the common, for sledges to bring out the turf, which was stacked on edge to dry, until ready for each man's turf house. Two men at Farnley Tyas were fined three shillings and six shillings for digging up more sods than were marked out in 1603. The pits had to be back filled.

Turf was a resource to conserve. Acomb farmers were limited to two cartloads of turves from the common each year, and cottagers one load, with ten shillings fines for any offence. None were to be sold or given away. Four viewers were appointed and paid a shilling to ensure the inhabitants had these quantities delivered. Digging turves on the moor was banned after August 1st. Good turf pits were a matter of dispute between townships. Sproxton tenants claimed rights on Starrett Rigg but some claimed the Rigg belonged to Sandwith grange. Stonegrave men dug turf on Newton Grange moor but had to pay the grange owner for them. A Marske yeoman and a labourer were indicted at Quarter sessions for their assault at Cookhow in Skelton on two other men and theft of turves worth ten shillings in 1566.

Low lying carrs could also yield turf. The Wold edge township of Flixton stretched down into the low carrs where there were demesne and freeholders' turbaries. Fifty cart loads of turf from Folkton carr had annually been sent to Bridlington Priory. Forest laws limited turf cutting. In Galtres Forest, The lord of every manor within the forest was entitled to grave a reasonable amount within his own lordship. None was to be graved up within the Crown demesnes without the licence of the forest justice. Easingwold and Huby in 1566 claimed turf at the Outmoor and within "the most necessary places where the kings highness's game may least have their relief".

Fixtures and Heirlooms

The barely furnished mediaeval Hall with a few moveable trestle tables and forms was being replaced as multiple rooms including private quarters became normal for the gentry, merchants and some other prospering people. Smaller houses saw partitioning, dividing the firehouse from a ground floor chamber. A cruck house might gain a second floor, even a partial floor, a single upper room, like that from the Harum manor house reconstructed at the Ryedale Folk Museum. Here was the birth of privacy.

329

More space and more privacy allowed more possessions. And there was a growing sense that comfort was possible and a greater desire for it. Many wills and the rarer inventories suggest that the richer and middling people had a greater number of items of furniture. There was more interest in having things, both useful and ornamental. More objects were treated as important enough to separately bequeath. There were widely shared values but also a sign of individual preferences. Then there was show, perhaps with fashion hard on its heels.

William Harrison said that "the furniture of our homes also exceedeth and is grown in manner even to passing delicacy; and herein I do not speak of the nobility and gentry only, but likewise of the lowest sort in most places of our south country. In noblemen's houses, it is not rare to see abundance of arras, rich hanging of tapestry, silver vessel and so much other plate as may furnish sundry cupboards, to the sum often times of a thousand or two thousand pounds at the least, whereby the value of this and the rest of their stuff doth grow to be almost in estimable. Likewise in the houses of knights, gentlemen, merchant men and some other wealthy citizens, it is not geson (rare) to behold generally their great provision of tapestry, turkey work, pewter, brass, fine linen and thereto costly cupboards of plate". When he came to the rest of society, he claimed that inferior artificers and many farmers had cupboards of plate, joined beds with tapestry and silk hangings, tables with carpets and fine napery. We may wonder if social distance was lending enchantment to his view.

The better off families of the north had well stocked houses, although most would have seemed empty by 21st century standards. There was a movement to build fittings as fixtures into great houses. Wall panelling, chimney pieces, plastered ceilings and flooring separated people from the framework of a building just as glass separated them from the world outside, while offering them a window to look upon it. Instead of living in a house, it was like living in several boxes within a house. The change must have felt very good.

The bequests made by esquire Francis Metham of Wiganthorpe to his nephew Thomas Metham of Metham included "all the wainscot and sealing in the hall and in both the parlours, the glass in all the windows in and about the house, with all the doors, locks and keys and all frames and shelves, fastened unto the walls or ground", all the brewing vessels in the brew house, stable heckes, mangers and hays, oxstalls and hecks, pales and rails about the house, stoops and rails of stackgarths in the ground." Such fixtures might be moved from one house to another. The church wardens of St Michael's, Spurriergate, York in 1600 "paid to my Lady Beckwith, for certain glass and trellises and wainscot, which is in the house that Mr. Maskew dwelt in and she having the dealing for it, being tutor unto James Mastewe, which said glass, trellises and wainscot is not to remain in the house as other glass and heir looms dothe."[16]

The early "heirlooms" were meant to follow the descent of house property. The heirloom movement probably had several roots. A new pride in personal property was evident in the frequent mention of best and second best possessions, particularly clothing, the ownership of "holiday apparel", and in the street shows of private armour at York, and pewter at Helmsley. The rising sense of family and dynasty merged with pride in the new house which became the family mansion with a life beyond one generation, which could give its owner aspirations to control its disposition beyond his grave. There was the physical difficulty of moving some heavy furniture and the inconvenience of removing fixtures.

Alderman William Beckwith of York left a heavy impress on his heirs in 1584. These things were to remain in his dwelling house "as heir looms for ever". There were the three great presses in the highest chambers, two great tables in the upper hall with benches and forms and cupboards there, one double table in the great parlour below with benches and forms and all the glass, an iron head and three iron backs with chimneys and all sealing in the hall house below, the sealing in the parlour below, two great presses in the high chamber, three stone troughs standing backwards for kye to drink in and a copper pan with holes for steeping beef.

Gentleman John Bonville at Spaunton, a country manor near Lastingham named the heirlooms that he wished his daughter and son in law to keep in the building. in 1582. Many of these could certainly have been moved. There were three tables and six forms in the hall, two tables and four forms in the great chamber, a bedstead, pallet bed, little cupboard and chair in the stone chamber next door, and in the kitchen two great spits, a pair of andirons two long tables. and iron racks. Many yeomen made bequests of things to be treated as heirlooms.

The "Elizabethan room" furnished in one style, was probably very rare. The older generations passed valued furniture and furnishings on to the young, as bequests or as gifts at marriage. It was later recorded as customary for a new bride to take a brideswain, led by an ox, with head and horns ribboned, from her father's house to her new quarters, loaded with household goods and utensils. People made them gifts which were piled up on the wagon during the journey.[17]

New Places for New Things

The great hall of a large house was commonly separated by a screen limiting draughts but containing doorways which led from the entry. The upper end of the hall had the master's chair, his lady's stool and other stools, the high table and a cupboard, sometimes raised on a dais. Boards carried on supporting trestles made the side tables, sited with more forms to sit upon. Livery cupboards or hutches stood at the side. The floor was laid with rushes, sprinkled with sweet smelling herbs. A doorway from the dais end led to other rooms. Beyond the screen doors, at the far end, might be a hutch table or sideboard, where kitchen dishes were placed en route. Built in furniture came to include the screen, aumbries, wall seats, sealing and panelling or wainscot. Tapestries and painted wall hangings only slowly gave way to painted plaster and framed portraits.

The "great chamber" could be part bedroom and partly a room to retire to. The furniture became more elaborate. Thomas Tancred in his Boroughbridge manor house had a standing bed, feather bed, mattress, bolster, two fustian pillows, a pair of linen sheets and a quilt in 1558. There were two little tables, one with a needlework covering, and the other a silk and gold covering. There was one inlaid chair, a low chair, a stool, a long cushion, and three great wall hangings brought from overseas. More could be done here than mere sleeping. The Newbrough Priory chamber had a long table, two livery cupboards, eighteen high and four low stools, two high and two low chairs, a long couch chair covered with red stamell and silk fringed, a long carpet of set work and two cupboard cloths. The fireplace had andirons, fire shovel, and tongs. There were four candlesticks with screws and a chest full of curtains. Almost anything could have taken place here.

T99 Chambers of the Earl of Lennox atTemple Newsham 1565.

Great chamber-

French gown of cloth of tisshew. Childs bearing cloth, velvet with powdered ermine lining; Curtain of crimson taffata; Tester of cloth of silver, embroidered with arms of him and his wife; Two beds of down; Chairs covered with red damask and green taffata; Old cloth of gold; Coat of silver satin; Chair of walnut tree and wrought; Rich cushions; Bankes; Joined stools covered and foot stools; Screen; Pair of virginals; Laver, andirons and fork; Hangings of old imagery; One leg table with bowls; Two tables with trestles; Two old cupboards; Two square tables; Pictures of Henry VIII, Queen Mary,& Phillip; Margaret of Scotland, The Earl, Lady Lennox, Lord Darnley; A pole axe 5s

Lord Darnley's Chamber- andiron, fire shovel, bellow, coffer; round table, three forms, four stools,12 featherbeds

Ladies chamber- coffers, table, cupboard ,close stool, andiron

Nursery- several old tapestries, table ,cupboard, andiron, tongues

Earls bedchamber- tester worth £40 in gold and purple velvet with arms of England, andiron, screen, table, stool.

The "great parlour" could be different again, whether for dining, leisure or reception not always clear, perhaps all three at different times. At Boroughbridge the parlour held a drawing table, three forms, two chairs with cushions, eleven stools, two maps, three pictures, and more cushions. The Newbrough parlour also had drawing tables, two livery cupboards, andirons, and a fire shovel.

In the end, the furniture for any room might become conventional and that change would rename rooms. The great chamber could become a bedroom. Chambers often had names, from colouring or ornament even from a visitor. Things were not always where we would place them. Lady Cecily Boynton had a great carved dresser in her bedchamber. James Thorpe of Ampleforth kept his garnish of London silver in his study. Old tapestries from the main rooms at Whitby Hall soon found their way to a servants' hall. An underused gallery was a natural place for a pair of old organs at Temple Newsome.

Carvings were the main form of furniture decoration in the greater houses. The Burton Agnes chimney carried Faith, Hope and Charity, but the bedroom displayed Patience, Truth, Constance and Victory. The hall showed the wise and foolish virgins and the dining room the dance of death. Wressle Castle had three apartments decorated with poetical inscriptions. The "proverbs in the lodgings" included one urging parsimony. The Earl of Rutland had sixteen suits of armour on a screen by 1638.

Wall decorations included tapestry hangings, often with pastoral or allegorical scenes. The hangings, mentioned even in labourers and widows wills at South Cave, may be cloths used in decoration or curtains. Some painted cloths of no great value appear in wealthy Alison Todd's house in 1591 but also in labourer Richard Sotheran's poor dwelling a year later, listed along with other trifles. Bare walls were sometimes covered with painted patterns. Gentlemen were interested in colour, their commonplace books full of instructions on how to make it.[18]

The tapestries which have survived seem dull today but were once full of colour. Embroidering them was a task undertaken by ladies and their young pupils in country houses. Landscapes were rare, but mythological pictures were common, and popular stories from the bible. Portraits painted on canvas, at first pale faced and with modest characterisation show heads of households. They built into collections as generation followed generation, to hang in halls and long galleries, and give the rising young an awesome sense of family. Holbein was in England from 1526. Sir Richard Cholmley at Roxby had his portrait painted by the Italian mannerist Federigo Zuccaro, in England for only the one year, 1574-5. Sir Mauger Vavasour and his wife were painted at Weston in the Armada year. The wardrobe at Skipton Castle held ten pictures by 1605.[19]

Furniture

Great houses didn't yet have numerous rare objects of furniture, totally lacking in more modest dwellings. They did have more of them, and they had some very exotic pieces. Specialisation in furniture was in its infancy. The many small chambers, usually bedrooms, held little enough, a bed, a chest, perhaps a basin and a ewer. For the rest, there was a range of chairs, stools, tables, chests and coffers, and a variety of cupboards called aumbries, arks, presses, binks, dressers and even cupboards. Much furniture was solid, even massive. More mundane dwellings had some seating and some storage but boards often appear, and with them table boards and shelf boards suggesting much simpler arrangements.

Chairs were rare seats of honour, for men of status, in a great hall but they do appear widely, even occurring in labourers' houses. A "chair of estate" could be virtually immovable, with a cloth of estate behind it. High panel-backed armchairs gained some comfort with cushions. Less robust but more moveable "Andrew cross" chairs were more comfortable, padded or given a fitted cushion on webbing. Pommel tops were replaced by projecting arms. Square joined chairs had rectangular frames, turned supports, scrolled arms and decorative inlaid backs. Turned or "thrown" chairs were made from rods turned on lathes. A three legged chair with a horseshoe back and a wicker box seat was known. William Fish had wanded chairs of ease in 1591.

Stools were numerous. They stood about two feet high, four legged and solidly joinered. They could be cleared away beneath a table. Five stools out of twenty-eight at Temple Newsham were close stools. Most chairs and stools were bare or at best covered rather than padded. Sir John Harrington said they were "so hard that since great breeches were laid aside men could scarce endure to sit on them." The Earl of Rutland in 1558 bought a stool covered with red cloth costing 14s.7d, two chairs of walnut covered with green cloth, two black and one red leather covered chairs. Stammel was bought to cover stools, along with five yards of velvet for a chair, two stools and a long cushion.

Some settles had a fixed position, the stout plank of a fixed bench against the wall with braced forelegs, or were placed in a window recess. Others were given a high back, against draughts and became free standing. We hear of Mr Northroppe's long "croked" settle at Park house, Hatfield in 1556. Standing tables replaced trestle tables for the well to do. The move to private chambers encouraged the making of occasional tables, drawer top tables with an extra leaf, round tables and even games tables with a boxed upper section. Carpets appear on tables rather than on floors. Turkey work was a thick woollen carpet, brightly dyed.

More things meant more storage. The age of lock and key had dawned at the peak of society, at Sheriff Hutton castle in 1537, when vast numbers of locks and keys were purchased at York. It said something about personal possessions. There were storage arks, dishbinks and racks. Chests, were the main storage furniture, notably for clothes, and bedding and could be given inlaid or plain panels. They were sometimes adapted with cushions as seats. Yorkshire inventories included imported "Danske chests " and "wainscot chests". John Watkinson of Hull gave his daughter his Flanders chest. Mr. Bellassis at Newbrough kept a "note of such writings and evidences as are contained in certain "boxes" touching as well my lands and leases as also annuities and other muniments". Robert Vescy of Treeton had one great iron bound evidence chest at Pickhall and a lesser chest with the arms of Vescy engraved upon it, Robert Prudome in Glaisdale had "one great chest which stood behind the cellar door, a little chest which stands at my bed head and a great chest which stands in the loft".

The cupboard began as a board for standing or displaying plate when it was not put away in chests. The board might be given rising shelves above. The lower part was early enclosed with panels at the ends and doors at the front. The livery cupboard had an aumbry above, and a close cupboard with doors below. A livery was the daily allowance of food and drink of one person and the cupboard would hold several. The aumbrey was a hutch on the wall to gather broken meats but became a plate cupboard. The press emerged as a tall, shelved hutch with doors for storing napery, hangings or clothing. Buffets, cupboards and cabinets were the most ornamental pieces, some made of fine woods, rosewood, walnut, oak or inlaid with marquetry.

Rushes were strewn on floors in the wealthier homes though plaited rush mats can be seen in paintings. Paul Hentzner spoke of the Queen's presence chamber at Greenwich with "the floor, after the English fashion, strewn with hay". Erasmus had spoken of the mess on the floor decaying for as long as twenty years. Thomas Tusser had wormwood strewn about. Lord Willoughby paid for monthly renewal of his floor rushes in 1561.

Where inventories have survived, they show great variation in what had been acquired by households. Each was unique. There was no typical case. There were the great households. The Earl of Lennox at Temple Newsham had more than forty beds, twenty tables, thirteen cupboards, twenty-eight stools, fifteen coffers and six chairs. The Earl of Huntingdon had a great standing wardrobe full of tapestry, canopies, curtains, testers, many bearing coats of arms, quilts and cushions, down beds and bolsters. The value of this store was £83.3s.8d.

T100 Furniture of Dame Elizabeth Beckwith at Acaster, Selby.1583

Hall	-table with form, bench with long form, long bench with two plank boards with two inch boards.
Parlour	-new table, new form, and two chairs; stand bed, with feather bed, mattress, pair of sheets, covering, coverlet etc.
Milk house	-board with pair of trestles and 2 shelves.
Buttery	-12 pewter doublers, 4 plate trenchers, 4 saucers, 3 pottingers, one basin and ewer , one pottle pot, 3 chamber pots, a hand basin of pewter, 4 laten candlesticks, a great pan, a brass pot, little kettle, a spit broil iron, dripping pan, basin, ladle, andirons, firepan etc

South Cave husbandman William Tyndale's hall in 1603 held a plank table and two forms, an old aumbrye which was an upright cupboard, an old dishbink and two shelves. His parlour had a stock bed, three chests and a form. His chamber over the parlour held spinning wheels, a large ark, an old chair, an old hogshead barrel and a stock bed. An old servant's bed was in the stable. Labourer Richard Sotheron in 1597 had only a pair of bedstocks, a chest , a presser board, a cupboard and a dishbink in his whole house. Thomas Middleton of Applegarth in Richmondshire had table, cupboard, two chairs and two buffet forms in his hall, and a standing bed in his chamber in 1563. Geoffrey Calvert of West Burton in 1575 had in his hall two meat boards, an old counter, two chairs, five stools, an almery, dishboard, two hanging shelves, a long chest and a board within the chimney. A meat board was worth 1s.2d, a short shelf 4d, a chair a shilling, and a chest 2s.6d.[20] South Cave widow Allison Wetherall's home in 1591 held a spinning wheel, a chair, an aumbry, an old chest, an old ark, a table with two trestles, two tubs, a coffer, a pair of bed stocks, a plank, some little forms, little shelves and little boards. Grasswoman Lettice Lightfoot in 1558 was possessed of an aumbry, a dish board and a pair of bed stocks. That sounds like poverty.

The Bed

The age of comfort had arrived, for the few who were fortunate. This reached its peak in the bed, which for some became both comfortable and secluded. Privacy dawned within the closeable curtains of the four poster bed. The great stand bed stretched between carved head boards and foot posts carved into bulbous pedestals, all together supporting a high tester. The parlour at Winestead had 1555 carved in the bed head.[21] Godfrey Bonville left two carved bedsteads of wood at Gunthwaite to his son in 1580. Even the great chamber at Kirkby Moorside rectory had "its great standing bed". Every chamber had a bed at Sir William Fairfax's Steeton house and in one was his Dames night-cap, flowered with gold. Lord Wharton had two flowered night-caps.

The impressive bed chamber of Thomas Lord Wharton in 1568 had three "brankish hangings bought at London on the walls". His testers, beds and bedding were worth £147.17s.8d. One tester of russet velvet tinsel, fringed with russet silk and gold, with three curtains of russet taffeta were valued at £6.13s.4d. Another, twice decorated with his coat of arms and with eight bull's heads on the valance was valued at £6. He had forty-five feather beds around the house, with bolsters worth £40, fifteen beds of down with bolsters at 30s each worth £45. Mattresses varied from fine to coarse and fustian. There were seventy-three coverlets, numerous pairs of blankets and a quilt of linen cloth made for my lord's back.

There were other sorts of beds. The simple stump beds were like an open box, with no upper structure or curtains. There were moveable trussing or field beds. Servants might have a truckle or trundle bed, low enough to be pushed under greater beds, when not in use. A pair of bed stocks is the most usual bed, kept with the accompanying boards. Even the better beds had no springs, but they might have a criss cross frame of leather strips, or boards for a base, to support stuffed wool mattresses, and feather beds. Other beds were corded. There might be blankets, linen sheets, a bright coverlet, a bolster and down pillows for comfort and warmth. Bed clothes included the cod ware or pillowbere, a case that could be washed. Some kept a spitting sheet by the bed.

Many people willed separate bed stocks or frames. John Nettleton of Knaresborough in1596, had a bedstead, feather or flock bed, mattress, bolster, a cod, a pair of sheets, a pair of blankets, a covering with hangings and two chamber pots, the whole assemblage worth a mere £3.13.4. By 1621, the Belassyse house at Newbrough had beds in most main rooms, except the great and dining chambers, chapel and parlour. Twenty-eight rooms had twenty-three feather beds. The best lodging had a bedstead of "sheyneywood "with tester, valance, five curtains and coverings of crimson damask laid with gold lace. Widow Woolfe of Sledmere had two feather beds and a bolster in 1587. William Cayley of Thormanby had two feather beds, bolsters and pillow beres in 1591 at his Malton lodgings.

Harrison recalled that in his father's time, southern men lay "on straw pallets, covered only with a sheet, under coverlets of dog swain or hop harlots, and a good round log under their heads instead of a bolster". Dog swain was a coarse shaggy cloth and the beautifully named hop harlot was a cuddly coverlet of shreds. If the servants had a sheet over them, they rarely had one beneath to stop the prickling straws of the pallet razing their "hardened hides". After seven years of marriage, a man might buy a mattress or flock bed and a sack of chaff to rest his head on. Pillows were only for women in childbed. Early inventories at South Cave lack beds, merely recording mattresses and bed clothes. Other explanations are possible but it may be that poor people in Yorkshire went to the mattresses each night.

New furniture called for new behaviours. Hugh Rhodes in his "Book of Nurture" of 1577, gave advice on airing sheets. Andrew Borde, in his "Dietary of Health" made suggestions for bedroom behaviour. He thought eight hours of sleep in summer and nine in Winter were sufficient. His advice was "to bedward, be you merry or have merry company about you, so that to bedward no anger nor heaviness, sorrow nor pensiveness do trouble or disquiet you." "In the night, let the windows of your house, especially of your chamber be closed". "Lie a little while on your left side and sleep on your right side. Lie not too hot, nor too cold, and wear a scarlet night-cap of quilt, cotton or pure flock covered with white fustian. When you rise in the morning, rise with mirth". "Have fire in the chamber in the morning to consume the evil vapours. Brush you hose inside and out and flavour the inside against the fire". Once out of bed, "stretch forth your legs and arms and your body, cough and spit".[22]

Sleeplessness was blamed on idleness or weakness of the brain, sickness, anger or fasting, solicitude or reflection, extreme heat or cold in the feet. Andrew Borde's remedy was an ounce of oil of violets, with half an ounce of opium, in women's milk laid on the temples. An alternative was three drachms of each of lettuce seeds, white poppy seeds, or mandragora seeds. Better than all these was mirth as you went to bed.

A widowed Earl of Rutland could speak of his late wife as "my lady, our bedfellow". Lady Katherine Scrope married for the second time a knight called Cholmeley but with a mixture of convention and realism called him "my lord, my bed fellow". Some court interviews were conducted from the bed. Stowe spoke of the new habit of London ladies, of breakfasting in bed, and having broken their fast, they lay upon it. The phenomena of laying in bed wondering whether you had locked the door was already known.

Hearth or Kitchen

Cooking facilities ranged from the well equipped kitchen to the open hearth fire. Central hearths in a single open room, with the smoke lost in the rafters of a cruck house or great hall were once the way of it. When the hearth was moved against the wall of the through passage, in a cruck house, a smoke hood over the fire drew smoke from the hall or firehouse into a fixed chimney. The larger houses were given a flat open hearth set in a deeply recessed and paved fireplace, with a six foot wide arch, five feet high. The cooking might be done with spits but far more often in pots on an open fire.

The equipment of the hearth and the chimney was common to houses large and small. Andirons and firedogs supported a wood fire and gave it under draught. A gallow balk or cross bar was set in the chimney from which pothooks suspended pots over the fire. A cast iron fire back would return the heat and stand the knock of logs. A brandreth would support pots from below. A spit enabled meat to rotate over a fire. There would be a fire shovel, tongs and a poker. A fire cover kept embers alight over night.

Large cooking vessels were necessary in the great households. The "great brass pot" was their oven, with small items suspended over the side in skins like puddings. Richard Simpson at Edstone in 1568 had two great spits, and a great brass pot. John Bonville at Spaunton had four gear spits. The Earl of Huntington had bellows, a brandreth or grid, and spits in 1596. His more specialised cooking vessels included nine brass pots, eight brass pans, two chafing dishes for keeping food warm, a boiling pan, two laten colanders, a grater to grate bread on, and a little brass pan to butter eggs in. Stood about were four hundred salted lings and haberdine "almost lost for keeping". The Borough Bridge manor house had beef pots, dripping and frying pans, chopping and scraping knives, a broiling iron and three bacon flitches.

The yeoman household showed many of the same things. Yeoman Robert Birdsall at Oxton gave his natural son an iron chimney, gallowbalkes, iron reckons and a pair of racks, a steepe fatt, a pair of kiln hairs and a silver pot. Widow Woolfe at Sledmere in 1587 had a spit, cob irons, and a brass pot. Ambrose Tenant of South Cave in April 1592 had a gallow balk. There was bacon hanging in his hall. but he also had a kitchen with three crooks, a brand iron, a pair of tongues and a spit. There were two chairs there. He could pull up a chair before the fire.

T101 Equipment in the Fairfax Kitchen.

furnace pan for beef	10s		
two great bound kettles	26s8d	two lesser bound kettles	12s
three bound pans	13s4d	two little bowed pans	2s6d
two copper lugged pans	1s4d		
two great brass pots	40s		
three lesser brass pots	15s		
one tine pot, three pairs pothooks	4s		
one gallie bawke, three berers, seven crooks and one iron range			40s
two pairs iron racks	16s		
two great square spits, four lesser square spits, three round spitts, two small spitts	26s8d		
two dripping pans	10s		
one iron peel	1s6d		
one brasen morter and a pestle	20s		
two gridirons, one frying pan	6s	three iron ladles	1s6d
one laten skimmer, one grater	2s		
one pepper mill, one pair of mustard querns	6s8d		
three bourdes and a salt pie		3s4d	
boiling pan within a furnace		6s8d	
two latten colanders		3d	
two cowles, 6 tubbs		1s	

one fire shovel, one peele		6d
one grater to grate bread on, one little brass pan to butter eggs in		1s2d

Plate at Table

Food was eaten from wooden trenchers, platters and dubblers and bowls and dishes of pottery, with carved horn and wood spoons. These are rarely mentioned in inventories. Those who could afford to, laid their tables with silver, brass or pewter. Silver was pouring in from the New World. Lord Wharton at Healaugh by 1568 had silver plate worth £473.9s.10d. The Earl of Huntingdon in 1596 had silver and gilt plate worth £194.10s.0. More ordinary houses had brass or pewter.

Silver table pieces were left as separate bequests. Thomas Saville at Welburn left silver salts, a silver bowl and twenty silver spoons in 1588. John Copley of Batley had two great standing cups of silver gilt in his hall. James Fox of Thorpe had "nests of silver goblets". Robert Vescy of Treeton left his son William "two silver spoons which he will choose of my spoons". Some had silver tooth picks. Thomas Swift of Rotherham had a mazer with a cover of silver and gilt with a roebuck on it.

T102 Sir William Fairfax 's Plate at Gilling, 1594
gilt plate

2 gilt salts with cover	one gilt goblet	one square salt with cover
one trencher salt gilt	one gilt salt with cover	4 gilt spoons
one gilt cup	one castinge bottell gilt	two gilt pliverie pottes
5 gilt bowls with cover	one gilt basin and ewer	one great gilt bowl, with cover
one gilt bowl with cover	one gilt standing cup with cover	

(There were also twenty-three items, or groups of items, in white plate including a spout pot, a nest of bowls, two dozen silver spoons, a dozen silver plates, a spice box with spoon, a chaffin dish, water laver, candlesticks, ship basin and ewer, cullander and even four beer pots for the hall. The total value of plate was £393 7s 7d.)

338

CHAPTER 13
FOOD

The Plain Man's Diet

The food of the majority of people was rarely recorded and we might presume that for many there was not much variety to record. There would be marked regional differences in what was eaten, more fish near the sea and rivers, more fowl around the marshland, more meat and cheese in the Pennine dales and Blackamoor, more soft bread throughout the lowlands. The scale and success of farm holdings decreed what yeomen and husbandmen ate and whether they sold enough at market to buy things that they didn't themselves grow. A poor harvest could mean scant food and distress far beyond the ranks of farmers.

Some guidance comes from a corrody from the early 16th century, a pension arrangement, for people in a good way of life. A man and his wife paid money down, for a later living within the precinct of Handale Priory. They were entitled to seven loaves of bread weekly, each loaf weighing two pounds. They had six gallons of convent ale and one gallon of small ale every week. Through the year, they had half a cow, a whole swine, a bushel of oats, a bushel of peas, and one and a half bushels of salt. They were given seven salt fish, a hundred herrings, white and red. They had something from every one of perhaps forty sheep killed in the year and something from every beast. There was the milk of a cow winter and summer and a quart of milk a week from Easter to Martinmas. The couple dined with the convent at every principal feast. There was a pound of candles, four loads of turf and a load of wood.

Bread was the staple food. People ate a loaf a day. Much of what was spent on food went on the loaf. The York Baker's ordinary of 1598 has an illustration of the steps in baking manchet bread. The meal was measured, bolted by hand, kneaded with water, salt and yeast in a dough trough, moulded and weighed, kneaded again, cut into round manchets, pricked and placed in the oven. Gentlefolk commonly ate wheaten bread but many others had rye bread, barley bread, or bread made from mixtures of grain. Wheaten bread included the manchet bread which was white. Beans, peas, oats and acorns were used in years of dearth. Three bakers at York sold coarse meal to the poor, mingled with bran, chesell and evil corn. Others mingled rye, barley, beans and oats together to make a meal for bread in 1589. Wakefield bakers were ordered to keep their ovens for wheat, rye and horse bread between the hours of five and ten.

A bushel of flour would make forty "cast" of manchet, each weighing eight ounces into the oven and six out. Ravelled bread had less wheat and more water and a bushel made thirty cast, with loaves weighing eighteen ounce in and sixteen ounces out. An order for the Berwick garrison for 1553 stated that four quarters of good wheat a day would feed a thousand soldiers. Yorkshire wheat could be bought for 13s.4d. a quarter. Bakers were numerous at York where there was little home baking. There were frequent complaints that loaves were insufficient for the price charged. Occasionally the York bakers' monopoly was removed, allowing in country and part time town bakers. Beverley had some forty-eight bakers in 1574. Scarborough in 1601 had three sworn common bakers but was also supplied by six country bakers.

Wakefield, Otley, Bingley, Helmsley and other small boroughs had common ovens, where bread was taken for baking. Wakefield bakers were required to bake at the common bake house, to bake four pies or pastries for a penny and incidentally to expel loiterers, perhaps seeking warmth. Twenty-five bakers at York, fourteen at Beverley, three at Hull and others at Scarborough, North Cave and Bootham left wills during the reign. Many country manors had a modest common oven where the tenants were obliged to take their dough. This was often rented out to a baker. Freemen might be allowed a bread oven of their own. Quite small villages, like Kildale, Wighill and Easedyke had common ovens. The husbandmen at Ganthorpe in 1563 paid eleven pence at Martinmas and cottagers two pence beyond their ordinary rents for use of the common bake house.

The South Cave farmers' inventories don't mention bread but they do have some stocks of food, usually absent from those of other people. Bacon flitches, and salted meat appear in several houses, along with peas, beans and oatmeal. Among the substantial men, Roger Wilton in March 1582 had twelve bacon flitches and some salt fish. Henry Wright of Faxfleet in October 1593 carried sixty cheeses worth forty shillings and barrels of butter worth thirty shillings. Edward Mounde a South Cave yeoman in July 1606 had five bushels of rye, a sack of barley, three sacks of malt, a frundle of oatmeal, fifteen large and three small cheeses, three pecks of wheat, sixteen cakes of butter, six pounds of swine grease, three bacon flitches and an extra piece in the house.

Through much of the county, oats were more readily available than wheat or rye. Oatmeal was made into a batter with water, salt and yeast, in a wood kit and poured onto a hot bakstone to make oatcakes and other foods. Bakstone quarries are known on the North York Moors and in the Pennines. There were oatmeal makers at Beverley and Holme on the Wolds.

The poor are thought to have had very little meat. William Harrison spoke of southern husbandmen having meat when they could get it. The inflation of the latter years of Elizabeth's reign, meant that meat was eaten ever more rarely. Pigs do appear frequently in Yorkshire inventories and may have been the most common source of meat, eaten as pork or dried into bacon for longer storage. More numerous still were hens, cocks gelded to make capons and geese. We cannot be sure how large a part the wild game played in ordinary diets but the commons were extensive and wild life was plentiful. What meat there was had to be jointed and salted in Autumn for the winter, wet salted in kimlins, large wood tubs in which the meat submerged in brine for three or four weeks.

Town and country butchers supplied the towns. Most of the market towns had one or more butchers. York had a very large number in the trade. The flesh on sale had to be "wholesome for man's body". Occasionally a butcher was charged with selling bad meat or with conspiracy to limit meat supplies and raise prices. York butchers had all "the foreign" butchers searched at every market. Beverley levied 6s.8d. from those who offered meat that was diseased or unseasonable or taken from animals which had died of the murrain.

New legislation in 1563 sought to add Wednesdays to Fridays and Saturdays as days on which fish should be eaten. Visitors' accounts are no guide to local living standards but one described Cleveland as having plenty of sea fish. "For ten shillings you could keep your house here with conger, burt, salmon, trout, soles, turbot, cod, fresh herrings and many other sorts of fish three days together. Their beef and muttons is also very cheap and sweet in taste." "I bought at my last being there, eleven crabs and lobsters for a penny and three score herrings for as much". Salted and dried fish were bought cheap further away from the coast. The stockfish which had been dried rock hard, had to be beaten and soaked in water for two hours.[1]

Fast and hardship were relieved by the occasional feast. When they feasted, the southern husbandmen did "exceed after their manner", especially at bride-ales, and purifications of women, "each one bringing a dish", after consulting with the wife. The host only charged with bread, drink, sauce, house room and fire. Here, they were merry without malice but the talk of the inferior sort "savoureth of scurrility and ribaldry". It was a disgrace to be "cupshotten". This may have been just as true in Yorkshire. Poor folk at York had their best dinners on a funeral day. When William Clithorp of Flamborough died in 1559-60, he left two barrels of beer and ten doles of bread in the church.

T103 Some Food prices in York. December 1561

capon	12d	second best capon	8d	couple of conies	8d
pig	10d	best hen,	5d	mallard	5d
goose	10d	woodcock	3d	teal, plover	3d
6 eggs	1d	12 larks	4d	12 pigeons	8d
gallon of best ale	4d				

Food at High table

John Woodward, house steward to Sir William Fairfax of Gilling and Walton entered his daily, weekly and yearly spending on provisions in account books for the period 1571-1582. The bill of fare was given for dinner and supper for every day of the year. There were contrasts between feast and fast days, for Christmas day, Ash Wednesday, Good Friday and Easter Day, and for Lent which was a time of fasting along with the Rogation or Ember days. Vigils were ignored although the rules were better kept when Lady Fairfax was at home. Friday and Saturday were weekly fast days, with a different diet to the rest of the week.

An ordinary family dinner brought six to eight dishes to table. The food was carefully recorded as it came from the garner, pantry, buttery and larder, and as the returns were checked back again. The pantry held arks and chests for the manchet and some pewter. The buttery was for butts of wine and beer. There were dry and wet larders. The pastry held an oatmeal chest, a moulding board on which to make bread and a boulting tub to sift meal, but there was another separate boulting house with another tub and a great kimlyn for meal.

Guest days brought vast quantities of food to the Master's table. There were always separate bills of fare for the Master, for the "board's end", for the Hall, and on Christmas Day, for those at "the side board". Serving was in messes, a mess believed to be for four persons. Numbers dining varied from thirty to fifty. No priest or chaplain is mentioned so he presumably sat among the servants. Visitors staying a day or two included neighbours and relations of the Belasyse, Vavasour, Constable, Thornton, Cholmley and Dalton families. There was a strict diet when the Archbishop visited on Friday 24th July

1579. We may presume broken meats found their way down the tables, ending with the poor at the gatehouse.

Weekly spending was seven to eight pounds, down to five pounds in Lent and up to twenty-two pounds in New Year week. New Year's day was marked on the 1st of January not March the 25th. The estate probably supplied even more food, which is not recorded under expenditure. Purchases seem to supplement what they might already have, an ox twenty-eight shillings, a cow sixteen shillings, sheep four to six shillings, veal four to five shillings. Herrings were bought by the barrel, white fish by the maze and lune by number. Sea fish cost the household five to six shillings a day. Butter and eggs came daily. Chickens were a penny halfpenny or twopence, geese three pence halfpenny in summer but eight pence in Winter, rabbits two pence to eight pence a couple, salmon or conger cost two shillings, wheat two shillings to two shillings and eight pence a bushel, and beer four shilling and two pence to four shillings and sixpence for a hogshead.

The only drinks were ale beer and milk. There was cheese, porpoise pie and cockles. Sallets and peascoddes are the only green stuffs mentioned. Occasionally, there was a tart of strawberries or prunes. Dulcets are frequent. Puddings only occur once and being followed by boiled beef, were probably suet balls. There were pancakes but not on Shrove Tuesday. Soup or pottage was for fast days and sixteen sorts of fish. Birds eaten included peacock, plover, snipe, woodcock, moor hen, heron, quail, crane, bittern, pheasant, partridge, the occasional cormorant and larks. Thirty pounds of pepper in the year contrast with nine pounds of sugar and eighty-six pounds of currants.

T104 Winter Fare-Gilling Castle Provisions for December

gross   -brawne, mutton, pig, roe, hind, beef, pork, hare, doe, bacon, lamb, kidde, rabbits, goat

fowl in season- bustard, goose, peacock, bittern, godwite, redshank, mallards, woodcock, quales, thrushes, pidgeons, stintes, pullets, crane, stork, turkey, shovelers, knottes, ree, widgeon, plovers, partridges, fieldfares, creluers, larks, turtles, swan, herne, capon, curlew, gull, bayninge, teal, snipe, pheasant, blackbirds, stockdoves, small birds, hermes

Fishes in season -ling, tunnye, sealump, sturgeon, sammon, pike, dace, moppes, dabbes, crabbes, oysters, prawnes, habbberdine, porpus, turnbutt, whittinge, small codde, breme, roches, ruddes, flaunders, lobsters, cockles, shrimpes, codde, seale, thornebacke, haddocke, lamprons, carpe, perches, eeles, sooles, crevices, mussells, perrywinkles.

other foods   butter, milk, cream, eggs, sallett

T105 The Master's Xmas Day Meals at Gilling Castle. 1572

breakfast   brawn and mustard

first course   brawn and mustard, frumenty, boiled mallards, boiled veal knuckle, nemble pies, peascoddes, a chine of roast beef, roast veal, roast swan, roast turkey, roast pig, cold crayne pie, roast capon, baked venison

second course, gillye, roast coney, roast mallard, roast teal, roast partridge, cold turkey pie, roast woodcock and a tart

A scattering of spices found their way to Yorkshire. The sisters at Nun keeling had occasionally enjoyed raisins, rice, almonds, sinfoin, lichorice, ginger and walnuts.

342

Andrew Borde's Dietary of 1542 mentioned imported raisins, prunes from Portugal and the Levant, dates, figs and raisins. The York cook's ordinary of 1606 showed columbine, a kind of ginger from Columbo. Locally available spices may well have included aniseed, bay, coriander, garlic, marjoram, savoury and thyme. Cane sugar came rarely from India or Arabia

T106 One year's spending on spices in the Fairfax household

pepper	30 lb	2s a lb	£3
cloves	1@	11s	16s6d
mace	1@	15s	£1.2s6d
cinamon	2		15s
ginger	2@	2s.8d	6s8d
nutmegs	1		8s
currants	14	4d	18s
great raisins	32	3d	8s
almonds	14		16s10d
prawns	14		9s8d
dates	3		2s6d
lyeres	20		5s10d
anniseeds	20		£1
biscuits & carrroways-	4		6s8d
isingass	1@		5s
saunders	2		3s4d
sugar. 8 loaves (10 lb each)		1s.6d a lb	£6
		Sum £17.4s.6d	

"A book touching the order and government of a nobleman's household" for 1608 shows similar levels of expenditure, suggested for another great Yorkshire mansion of the Constable family. A dietary for a two course dinner offered sixteen varieties of fish, with butter, eggs, and custard. The second course had seventeen more fish items, potato and tart. Fast days provided similar fare for supper, with a first course of fifteen fish, butter, spinach, cucumber, caviare, and eggs. The second course was more fish including sturgeon, together with custard and tart.[2]

There were written instructions telling how a beef might be proportioned into seventeen pieces. Carving meat was a skill, with its own language. You broke a deer, leached brawn, unlaced a coney, reared a goose, lifted a swan, sauced a capon, unbraced a duck, and you disfigured a peacock. You could chine a salmon, string a lamprey, transom the eel, and tame a crab. The tasks of the household servants responsible for food were set out in detail. The yeoman of the garner received all grain, wheat, rye, barley malt, oats, brans, peas and vetches. He turned them so that heat didn't spoil the grain, especially the wheat. After sifting and cleansing from all dust, he delivered malt, and grains to the baker or brewer and provender to the stable. The slaughterman was to kill and cleanly dress the calves and lamb skins, the tongues, feet, tripes, calf heads and feet and lambs heads.

The "catour" was required to look in the country for provisions, "what dainties there be as young chickens, pigeons or such at the first coming of them, best takers of fowl and fish, dead sweet and good". The "catour and slaughterman" together delivered all "caterye" to the yeoman of the larder, including butter, eggs, cream, milk, herbs, oatmeal, fish and meat. He had to make sure it was sweet and well kept. His main task was to provide salt provisions of fish, powdered flesh and all else, as the clerk of the kitchen directed. The yeoman of the scullery checked that the sauces, the vinegar, verjuice and mustard were good. Verjuice was prepared widely, squeezed in a press from the juice of unripe crab apples. The yeoman baker received his corn and the yeoman brewer his malt from the yeoman of the garner, and some went by tally to the miller for grinding. The baker apportioned quantities between manchet and other breads as the household officers required. He also acted as a pantler. The yeoman of the scullery looked to the silver and pewter, gathering in after every meal and checking every other day that the pewter was clean, so that he wasn't "dressing them when the lord was being served".

T107 Thomas Tusser's Advice for the Housewife on Gardening. 1580

In March and in April, from morning to night,
in sowing and setting, good huswives delight:
To have in a garden, or other like plot
to turn up their house, and to furnish their pot.

Herbs and roots for sallads and sauce
Alexanders, artichokes, blessed thistle,
cucumbers, cresses, endive, mustard seed, musk million,
mints, purslane, radish, rampions, rocket, sage,
sorell, spinage, sea holly, sperage, skirrets,
suckerie, tarragon, violets.

Herbs and roots to boil or to butter
Beans, cabbages, carots, citrons, gourds, navewes,
pompions, parsnips, runcivall peas, rapes, turnips

Herbs to still in summer
Blessed thistle, betanie, dill, endive, eyebright,
fennell, fumetorie, Isop, mints, plantine, roses red
and damask, respies, saxifrage, strawberries, sorell,
suckerie, woodrose for sweet waters and cakes.

A banqueting house marked the elevation of feasting to a new pinnacle. King Henry VIII had one at Nonsuch and Lord Bacon built one in his pleasure garden at Gorhambury. The architect Robert Smithson designed banqueting houses at Longleat in 1560 and at Hardwick in the 1590s. Sir Mauger Vavasour at Weston in Yorkshire built a three storey house, at the corner of a walled garden, with fine views from canted bay windows and an open work parapet. There was a staircase tower, decorated with carvings of the Vavasour cock and the Saville owl, and armorials of the main families of Claro wapentake. Another banqueting hall known as the Barden Tower was a complete house, with chambers, kitchen, bake house, brew house, counting house, pantry, buttery, laundry, ewery stored with linen, garners, and slaughter house. After 1570 Lady Clifford often stayed there from Summer into Autumn and George, Earl of Cumberland used it occasionally between 1598 and 1605

Garden Produce

Thomas Tusser in his "Five Hundred Points of Good Husbandry" of 1573 could name twenty-two flowers for physic, one hundred and twenty-seven for summer, twenty strewing herbs for floors, forty seeds and herbs for the kitchen, twenty for salads and sauces and twelve to boil or butter for pleasure. William Lawson who was vicar of Ormesby in Cleveland from 1583 till his death in 1635 managed the vicarage garden for fifty-two years. His book "The Country Housewife's Garden" published in 1617 includes "Rules for herbs and seeds of common use, with their times and seasons, when to set and sow."[3]

Lawson believed that "In the south parts gardening may be more timely and safely done than with us in Yorkshire, because our air is not so favourable nor our ground so good". He used artichokes, carrots, and parsnips, which he considered sustenance for a strong stomach. He used many plants as "pot herbs" including burgage and bugloss, cabbage, chives, endive and succory, fennel, isop, leeks, lettuce, mallows, marigolds, Christ's eye, onions, penny royal and savoury. He distinguished 'caell' and clary for "pottage", lettuce and fennel for salads, time, onions, penny royal and rosemary for use with meat. Leeks could be eaten with salt and bread, strawberries with wine, or sugar and cream.

How far Lawson's contemporaries gardened at their different levels of society is not at all clear. Inventories do not specify gardens but in some areas do list hemp garths, with values from 6s.8d. to ten shillings, usually at the end of an inventory along with the occasional helm or leanto and the hens, cocks, and stack of turf, even geese, at the close of the list. The hempgarth became the normal name for the house yard in parts of the shire. Hemp did well on plots where nettles, thistles and weeds were rife. Sewn in April, it could yield summer and winter crops. To Lawson, paradise was a garden. The hemp garth doesn't sound much like it.

CHAPTER 14
HEALTH

A Different Experience

Queen Elizabeth had scarlet fever at fifteen, many sore throats, smallpox at thirty, migraine, varicose ulcer of the leg at forty, and experienced food poisoning in 1572.[1] Such personal records of health and ill health were rarely made. Lady Margaret Hoby of Hackness who kept herself busy and took daily walks for up to an hour, did keep a diary. She recorded that during fifty-two days of late August and September 1599, she was unwell on at least nine of them. Her ailments varied from being unwell to very sick, from toothache to pain in the head, and loss of appetite with weakness. She had persistent heavy colds. An "inward assault" may not have been physical but she was kept from going in the field for three days by a painful toe. This remarkable lady saw feebleness of stomach and a head pain on different occasions as divine punishment for her sins, yet she frequently visited neighbours to assist with child birth and ran a treatment room for her tenants.[2]

Mrs Ann Thornton of Newton in Ryedale kept a similar record about the middle of the next century. This made her sound almost accident and ailment prone. She was ill on her wedding day, saw children die of rickets and smothering, herself suffered bleeding, miscarriages, a shaking ague, jaundice, smallpox, and spleen, the last after eating a lobster. She recorded such accidents as being thrown when a child, falling in fires and falling out of coaches. She had relations who died of consumption and food poisoning. Her descriptions of the hazards of child birth included the birth of the sixteenth child of her sister Lady Danby. Ten had been baptised and the other six were stillborn, blamed on frights and falls.[3]

T108 Some Hazards of Ann Thornton's childhood
1629. age 3   Fall on a hearthstone giving a one inch head wound.
1630. age 5.   Vomiting after eating poorly boiled beef.
1631. age 6   Small pox and a house fire.
1636. age 10   Fall out of a coach into a river.
1637. age 11   Fall breaking chin bones.
1638. age12   The maid put embers under the stairs, starting a fire.
1639. age 13   Shipwreck.

The town of Patrington in 1587 had eighteen adult deaths and thirteen child deaths. In each year between 1593 and 1601, roughly a third of the deaths in Pickering parish were deaths in childhood. Growing up was a perilous affair. There were old names for familiar conditions. A bloody flux was dysentery and flue was the sweat. The "chin cough" was perhaps whooping cough. There were worms and gripings. Malaria, known as the ague, carried by the mosquito, was seasonally heavy from mid Summer to November, particularly near the still extensive marshy districts. The older years sound more familiar. Sir Henry Saville, ageing at Tankersley, described himself as "yearly decaying from worse to worse". He decided, after advice, "at the spring to enter the new diet" but thought himself liable to expire this year or next. The Earl of Shrewsbury at Sheffield said of his gout in 1585 "his legs and arms are nearly become almost comfortless." He hoped for some relief through physic. Mr Tancred in his old age at Boroughbridge was troubled with the stone.

The idea that human action might promote health and prevent disease was not new, but the search for remedy had out run the search for cause. Useful information was recorded in commonplace books, by some gentlemen. These volumes are full of specific cures which people knew from experience or which they had been told would work. Some awareness of broad causes seems to have awakened in the larger towns. York had made several regulations to improve city hygiene in 1551 including ward refuse dumps, removal of city pigsties, house front sweeping and the twice weekly removal of the dirt. A York city order that none was to cast "dung, mire, filth, and sweepings in Hungate or Hater Lane in 1589-90 was made specifically "for avoiding infections" There was another York order for carrying forth filthy tubs and other filth forth of the city in May 1580 and this was repeated from time to time.

Andrew Borde offered a clear approach to preventive medicine in his "Doctor of Physique" published in 1547 and often reprinted. He identified such causes of ill health as corrupt air, mutual infection, over crowded rooms, street stench, drain stench, blood shed, burials too high in the ground, toilets, unclean houses and beds, corrupt dust, dog sweat, and fleas in beds, while tactfully not excluding "divine punishment". His remedies included diet, cleanliness and avoiding the rushes on the floor. Many people saw ailments as visitations of God, "doubting not that the judgement was on them" in the face of any disaster. If the judgement was associated in the mind with personal sin, then prayer offered a hope of alleviation for the faithful. When Lady Hoby had toothache she prayed and remarkably, after a week the ache was relieved.

There were new threats to health and forgotten causes of accidents There was coal smoke. "Now have we many chimneys and yet our tenderlings complain of rheums, catarrhs, and poses. Then had we nothing but reredosses and yet our heads did never ache. For as the smoke in those days was supposed to be a sufficient hardening for the timber of the house, so it was reputed a far better medicine to keep the good man and his family from the quack". Corn mills had working parts and were marvels of their day, attracting the curiosity of the young, which all too often ended in a death recorded in a parish register. Washing in rivers gave a number of drownings. Grinders of cutlery at Sheffield were seen to die young and they gained bow legs from sitting on the horse at the front of the grinding wheel, or "scimitar legs" from standing on one foot and treading with the other, so that both legs bent the same way.

Inheritance problems required commissions to enquire into the lunacy of Guy Fairfax in 1559 and of Robert Stockdale, a Lockington gentlemen made a ward of the court of wards and liveries in 1595. The Queen commanded twelve members of the Saville family to gather at Tankersley in 1559 to take some stay for Edward Savile's inheritance, he having been found incompetent. by a jury. He was asked how many legs had a sheep. He said two but added that there were two legs and two shoulders and if they had asked how many feet, he would had told them four. A woman described as mad was moved from the York kidcote prison to St. Thomas hospital in 1581. Sixpence a

26 The Plague struck Yorkshire towns throughout the reign

week was allowed by the city authorities and a housewife was told to look after her. A coat of grey at two shillings a yard was provided for the mad woman in the kidcote eight years later. Alice Wright of Grassington who died in 1607 provided for her son John, "a caitiff in body and mean of understanding." The daughter Jane was given discretion to take his portion in her hands, maintaining him in meat, drink, aparrel, lodging and necessaries "according to his society and degree"

Epidemics

Threats to personal survival were abundant in Elizabethan Yorkshire. Deaths in any parish could run low for some years and then came a bad year. While one place suffered, all might be well next door, but there were some years that were bad almost everywhere. Epidemic disorders swept the country, the region, or local districts from time to time. This was not new and it was not peculiar to Yorkshire. George Clapham of Nunnington died at London in the plague of 1543. There was plague at Ripon in 1546. Bad harvests preceded some outbreaks, including the illnesses, reported as "the visitation of my Lord God" at York in 1549, and "the plague of pestilence" early in 1550. When main crops failed, dearth probably made for heavier mortality in the 1550s, in 1586 and again in the period 1594-98.

The sweating sickness of 1550-1551 came to Shrewsbury in April and spread northwards to affect many at Hull and York, some said more men than women. Holinshed said that the outbreak of the "great sweat" made the nation repent - briefly. Death came within twenty-four hours, after a sudden chill, violent perspiration and sleep. Pickering had a bad time from May to August. Aberford, Leeds and Howden were similarly troubled. By 1555 seven York parishes were said to be so reduced that the survivors couldn't pay the tax. Sheffield petitioners in 1554 told the Queen that the fourteen hamlets in that parish were "never void of plagues and other evil diseases". They attributed this to "the great number of poor and impotent persons inhabiting them". There were famine level harvests in 1555 and 1556.

The pestilence of 1557-1559 affected many places and it was said that many wealthy men died in England in 1558. St Olave's parish outside York recorded forty-eight burials in that year and twenty-seven in 1559. Some York registers ceased to be kept and the same was said of Howden. The Earl of Westmoreland penned a letter dated the sixteenth of August 1558 noting that both the City and the Ainsty were sore visited with extreme and fervent sickness. Three vicars of Bishop hill junior died in 1557-58. Thirsk buried one hundred and sixty in 1557-59 but a folio of their register is missing from November 1558 to February 1558-9. The 1557-8 figure of ninety-eight contrasts with an annual average of twenty-six. The pestilence at Kirk Burton took one hundred and twenty from June to October in a period when thirty-seven normally died from a variety of causes. Woodsome, Holmfirth and Scammonden had the sickness but not Honley in 1558.[3]

The plague came to Wensleydale in 1563 driving the East Witton weekly market to a field at Ulshaw. The Queen asked the Archbishops of Canterbury and York to give orders for a day of general prayer and fasting in August on account of the plague. The pestilence of 1563 claimed perhaps a quarter of the population of London.[4] In Yorkshire, Sheffield, York and Almondbury suffered that year and the next. And so it went on. It has been suggested that deaths occurring at one and a half times the moving average were abnormally high while two times that average betrayed a major crisis. Such crises were often confined to one parish but occurred, more widely in the years 1587-88, and 1596-97. After an epidemic had removed the vulnerable, the aged and the sick, lower death rates could follow for several years.[5]

T109 Some Contemporary Reports of Pestilence

1569	Sheffield
1570	Rotherham, Selby, York
1575	Snaith, Howden, Hull
1576	Hull
1576	Blackfriargate.York
1579	Howden & Snaith
1583	Wadworth
1585	Sheffield, Doncaster
1586-7	Chesterfield .
1587-8	Danby
1588	Stammergate. Ripon
1589	Rotherham
1596-7	Leeds
1597-8	Richmond, Bentham, Guisborough
1599	Sowerby, Knaresborough
1603	Newcastle, Tadcaster, Wetherby
1604	Boroughbridge

T110 The Worst Years for Burials in some Parish Registers, 1584-1605

1584,85,86,87,88,89,90,91,92,93,94,95.96.97.98.99.1600.01.02.03.

Parish	1584	85	86	87	88	89	90	91	92	93	94	95	96	97	98	99	1600	01	02	03
Beverley								X	X											
Brompton	X		X	X									X							
Braithwell			X	X			X								X					X
Burton Fleming								X					X							
Collingham			X			X		X								X				
Eston														X	X					
Hedon							X	X												
Humbleton						X		X												
Linton								X		X						X				
Patrington						X		X	X				X							
Pickering			X	X										X	X					
Preston						X											X			X
Roos					X	X														
Tadcaster						X				X										

Towns and even villages commonly segregated infected people, at least in the early stages of an outbreak. Rotherham epidemics saw isolation houses erected on Town Moor. York sited huts outside Layerthorpe postern and on Hob Moor. When the numbers increased, the infected people were confined to their own houses which were marked with a red cross. Those finding it necessary to move about were told to carry a white stick. The villages were ordered to send in grain and some poor relief was given. The approaches to Blackfriargate at Hull were walled up, in 1576, with two little doors left for food deliveries during an outbreak, which seems to have been contained.

When reports of plague at London and Stourbridge reached the city of York in 1563, both visitors from London and departures towards that city were banned. Watchmen posted at the bars excluded people from other stricken towns. Those returning from infected places were quarantined. York escaped heavy mortality that year. City carriers were warned to stay their journeys to London and other infected places again in 1570. The city bars and posterns were locked from nine at night until four in the morning. The common waits kept a daily morning watch every day in the week except Sundays and Christmas. York ordered watches at bars and postern again in February 1579-80. Sheffield was watched for three weeks in 1585 to stop communication with infected Doncaster.

Incoming people and materials were commonly blamed for outbreaks of plague. Soldiers returning from Newhaven were said to have brought pestilence to England in July 1563. York was exercised about goods from Danzig in the late Summer of 1564. Seamen were thought to have brought plague to the Hull Blackfriargate area in 1576. Suspect ships were commonly quarantined by the 1580s. Some said that the plague of 1603 was brought by soldiers returning from the Low Countries, late in the previous year.

The College of Physicians issued comprehensive advice on how to deal with the plague. Suggestions included prayer, humiliations, avoiding goods from suspected places, separation of the healthy and the sick, making graves sufficiently deep, employing searchers to find those infected, shutting their houses for forty days, restricting their movement, privy burials at night, and bonfires.[6] The causes were not realistically known, nor why some were spared and others suffered. A sense of helplessness was often evident in the face of events viewed as inevitable, and often interpreted as "visitations of God".

When plague was suspected at Ampleforth, in April 1591, Sir William Fairfax of Walton instructed his Gilling steward Ralph Pearcie "Be careful to keep the gates well locked and looked to", "I hear that the plague is suspected to be at Ampleforth. Be careful, or it will grow to be contagious to all the country, if good watch be not kept in every town". The remorseless spread of the disease is evidenced in the words of Lady Hoby at Hackness in 1603 "We heard that the plague was spread in Whitby, so great that those who were clear shut themselves up. Later the sickness was feared to be at Robin Hood Bay not far off. Later still, one in the town of Hackness, having been in Harwood Dale, at Mr Bushell's house, whose children were come from Whitby, was fallen sick with three of his children more."

York council tried to recall butchers who had fled the city after one outbreak. They stopped citizens attending Howden fair and refused entry of cloth. Beggars were told not to wander. Men were paid eight pence a week, for six weeks, to deliver food to those isolated behind closed doors and windows. Others were paid twenty pence to bury the dead, sweep out houses and burn clothing. The gravediggers lived at Toft Green house, moving abroad only with white rods or lanterns. The West Riding justices in 1598 made orders that "in regard of the present sickness in the north country, that every constable within this division shall set two or three to watch and ward within their constabulary and shall see the same duly kept as well in towns as in hamlets and that henceforth householders themselves shall keep the watch and ward according to their course and not hirelings as heretofore hath been accustomed."

The impact seemed greatest in the populous towns, because so many were affected. They said that 908 died in the parish of Doncaster from September 1582 to December 1583. The letter P was written in the register against 747 names, the worst impact in June and July. Some relief was raised in the worst years. Malton Register recorded an assessment made throughout the Deanery for the relief of the infected town of Scarborough. The smallest place, Kirkham paid 7d. The West Riding justices levied a rate on the wapentakes to relieve the poor distressed people of Richmond and Guisborough was visited with the plague in 1598.

Physicians

A variety of people offered treatments for many of the other ills of the body. Physicians were thought of as those practising the arts of healing, including physic while surgeons, otherwise chirurgeons, sought the same ends by manual operation and the use of instruments. Professional medicine existed alongside quackery and the difference would rarely be obvious. Qualified specialists in cure were not numerous, nor were they sharply separated from those experts in "the optimistic but incredible", offered as cures in every age. Also present were the "wisemen" and women who practised different traditions of cure, but were the repository of much popular faith. "Never make a physician thine heir", said the proverb. Most people probably never met one and had to deal with most of their own problems, themselves.

Members of the new College of Physicians, absorbed academic learning, which drew heavily on ancient authorities although dissection was allowed by the Queen in 1565 and Dr. Caius widened anatomical knowledge. The College claimed the primacy of

351

physicians over surgeons, blood letters, midwives, barbers, empirics and quacks. The College issued licences but had to deal with many unlicensed medical men.[7] Some well trained practitioners came from abroad. William Butler was licenced but never took the degree of Doctor although he was reckoned "the greatest physician of his time".[8] Peter Turner, the doctor of physic at Bath was licenced to practice medicine in all the cities of the realm. Only a handful of practitioners are known to have been working at the larger Yorkshire towns.

T111 Some Physicians active in Yorkshire

Stephen Tubley	York	1530's
Timothy Bright	Barwick & Methley	1550-1617
Titus Bright	Beverley, & Hull	1580-16
Edmund Dean	York	1572-1640
Roger Lee	York, Pinchonthorpe	1532-1602
Christopher Milner	York	1573
Matthew Lister	York	1599
Richard Remington	Bainton	c1544-1615
Cuthbert Smithson	Richmond	1580-1651
Alexis Vodka	York	15---1626
Peter Levins	Eske	
Thomas Vavasour	York	1570
Edward Lister	Wakefield	1590
Dr Brewer	York	1599

Lady Hoby travelled from Hackness to visit a York physician, who gave her physic and let her blood. Other physicians travelled widely to visit their paying patients. Christopher Milner, the York physician attended a patient at Bolton Percy in 1573. Roger Lee "doctor of physic" practised at York, but acquired the manor of Pinchonthorpe, in Cleveland and lived there. He had a grant from William Stanley, Lord Mounteagle of five marks a year for life, out of Hornby manor. Another North Riding doctor enjoyed an income of £17.4s for the year 1609-1610. His patients ranged from Acomb west of York, into the western fringe of Blackamoor. A gentleman's wife once paid him in spices and on another occasion with three shillings worth of wine and good perry, for letting her blood. He accepted payments in cheese and fish but more often money. His standard rates for his staple treatments were a shilling for a vomit or purge, four shillings for blood letting or an eye lotion, and one shilling for counsel. He may well have adjusted charges to what the client could bear. The Osmotherley shoe maker only paid 2s.6d. for three purges and three powders. Mr. Langdale of Murton paid 2s.6d. for a single vomit. He once prescribed a bath.[9]

Peter Levins of Eske tried to make medical knowledge more widely available. After attending Cambridge University to study physic and chirurgery, he practised physic and taught a grammar school. He wrote the remarkable "Manipulus Vocabulorum", a dictionary of English and Latin words, "set forth in such order as heretofore none hath been" in 1570. His medical book meant for laymen was produced in 1587 entitled "a right profitable book for all diseases, called the Pathway to Health". This was in "the vulgar tongue" being intended for "the unlearned". The main achievements of Matthew Lister, born at Thornton in Craven in 1565, were outside the reign. He gained appointment as physician to Anne, Queen of Denmark on the recommendation of Anne Countess of Pembroke, and was President of the Royal College of Physicians.

Practical relief from illness was certainly sought outside the profession. Although Thomas Tusser advised consulting a doctor, before taking medicine, he disliked physic himself because of its cost. His prescription for health was good broth, good diet, and "keep stirring", but "in sickness seek quiet." Calamy said that Vicar Stephenson at Roos was well skilled in physic, which he administered to the poor for nothing. York Council in 1574-5 "paid Johnston's wife in Skeldergate for healing of two boys heads which was scallded at St Thomas's poor house and stuff for them 4s.6d.". They paid Robert Blake eight shillings for curing a young spaniel and for "stuff" The stuff is presumed to be medicine. They gave a blind man a pass and five shillings to travel to southern parts for the recovery of his sight. Thomas Wilbore from Batley way in 1557 left Agnes Harrison "what I laid forth for her for the healing of her leg". At Hackness Lady Hoby ran her morning surgery, where she dressed a poor boy's leg, saw to Jordan's hand and "dressed the sores" that were brought to her.

Surgeons

Surgeons used physical methods to effect cures. They bled with leeches, extracted teeth and treated wounds. Many surgeons were apprenticed to their art learning to shave, pull a tooth and dress a broken head. Bishops issued midwives, surgeons and barbers with licences to practice but they seem merely to have certified the honesty and good conduct of those who already had experience. The London Company of Barber Surgeons formed in 1540 was also granting licences. York had its own Company of Barber Surgeons. They excluded aliens but only made a modest charge of 6s8d for strangers wishing to practice. They revised their rules in 1592.

The surgeons mainly resided in the towns. Beverley tanner Robert Abbot was treated at the house of Thomas Drye the surgeon in c1556. Henry William Cowling was another Beverley chirurgeon. Surgeon William Woodward tenanted a shop in Scarborough in 1574. Practitioners in the small borough of Malton included George Brown "who named himself chirurgion" and died in William Sleightholme's house in Malton Market place in 1594, Ralph Moyser "chirurgeon", who also died that year and John Taylor an "apothecarie" there in 1599. William Fox of Skipton was described as a professor of surgery and physic in 1589.

The York Barbers-Surgeons Guild Book of c1500, shows something of sixteenth century thinking. The four humours were associated with four human temperaments. People were classified by character types, as sanguine, with blood as the humour; phlegmatic, whose humour was phlegm; choleric with green or yellow bile, and melancholic with black bile. Water, earth, fire and air carried associated attributes in nature. The sanguine was hot and moist, the choleric hot and dry, the phlegmatic cold and moist, the melancholic cold and dry. Here was some sort of a framework for thinking, which lingers to this day. Imbalances could be corrected by bleeding, purging, drugs, herbs, hot or cold foods and a change of diet. Older people going phlegmatic might revert to a children's diet. The thinking was derived from Galen. After Vesalius's textbook of anatomy was printed in 1543 there was some move away from that tradition. It has been suggested that the surgeons writing in English and less hindered by the Galenism of the books, were more open to new methods. The surgeons were necessarily closer to practical action and visible results. The emerging profession included military surgeons and the Vesalian Dr. Caius at Cambridge.

Apothecaries

The apothecaries were few and far between. Where they practised, they prepared and stocked commodities thought to be medicinal. These came to include the new herbs from the West Indies, and fresh preparations from the trees of Eastern Europe. These were converted into the pills, potions, pectoral powders, electuaries, plasters, and comfits that were recommended by the physicians. The College of Physicians had powers to search apothecary wares and could destroy what they disallowed. Apothecaries usually entered grocers or mercers guilds in towns but some were physicians' assistants. They didn't gain a charter till 1617. The Earl of Rutland in London with the Countess and forty-one attendants in 1586, included his own apothecary among them.

The doctrine of "signatures" encouraged a belief in specific cures. Paracelsus had suggested that every plant was signed, meaning that it was. associated in colour, shape, odour, habitat or some other characteristic with a specific disease and hence was a specific for its treatment. Chest complaints were treated with lungwort since the shape of the plant resembled lungs. Other plants were linked to the head, heart, stomach, liver, spleen, womb, and joints.

The household practices of wives and mothers offered the main source of cures for many ills, or at least the means of alleviating their symptoms. Thomas Tusser in his "500 points of Good Husbandry", told his contemporaries –

> "Good housewives provide, ere a sickness do come,
> Of sundry good things in her house to have some,
> Good aqua composita, and vinegar tart,
> Rose water and treacle, to comfort the heart.
> Cold herbs in her garden, for agues that burn,
> That over strong heat to good temper may turn ,
> White endive, and succory, with spinach enow,
> All such with good potherbs, should follow the plough.
> Get water of fumitory, liver to cool.
> And others the like, or else go like a fool
> Conserves of barbary, quinces and such,
> with syrups, that easeth the sickly so much"

The Cleveland gardener, William Lawson noted local remedies, including many specifics. He said of angelica, "the root dried, taken in the fall stoppeth the pores against infection", while the leaves relieved stomach pain. Turnip was "sovereign for eyes", while aniseed would open the pipes. Burrage and bugloss cordial were good for the heart and stomach; and camomile for headache. Chives and garlic had the power of opening. A range of things were just good, coriander good against itches; fennel good for eyes; lilies good to break a boil; parsley good against the stone. "Christ's eye" would clear eyes; French poppy seed would make you sleep. Saffron would expel diseases from heart and stomach. Lavender was "most comfortable for swelling", and radish was a "sauce for clotted stomachs". Lady Hoby read "the new herbal" in 1599.

There was an evident desire among the wise men and women to use exotic substances in medicines, such as fasting spittle, baked powder of worms, women's aftermath, heart of toad, and bull's marrow. A manuscript volume of lore and housewifery kept in the Fairfax family included many homely remedies.[10] This recorded advice for nose bleeding. "Take a toad and dry it in March, put the same into some silk or satin bag and hang it about the neck of the party next the skin and by God's grace it will staunch presently". A toad's heart dried and powdered was a drink for the falling sickness. If you would stop blood, you would "take linen clothes and dip them in the green foam where frogs have their spawn three days before the new moon."

An oyster shell filled with fasting spittle and stood two nights and days in a dunghill, provided a fluid to drop in the ear for deafness. Diagnosis of the king's evil required a ground worm laid on the swelling under a leaf. The worm lived if you were free of the ailment and turned to earth if you were afflicted. The powdered after burden from a woman was a six day cure for epilepsy. Tooth ache might be alleviated, before you could count to twenty, by cutting two or three plantain leaves small, putting them in linen and straining two drops of the juice into the contrary ear. A tooth would fall out when touched with the powder from gendering worms dried on a hot tile.

Elements of astrology and magic entered into many supposed cures. Some were better recorded in the seventeenth century. The wiseman Rogers of Scarborough was reputed to have aids to conception and remedies for barrenness, one involving laying with a sucking boar piglet, reckoned the most lecherous of beasts. His charm against any malignant sickness included a chant, delivered at every full moon. Faith may have contributed something. The Duke of Lancaster's girdle at Pontefract had been thought to help child bearing and his hat to cure head ache. A ring that had belonged to a Hornsea guild and had been used to cure eye diseases, was still in the custody of the curate in 1556. Unfortunately, some one had plucked out the stone.

Spa Waters

The belief in natural waters as a cure for the ills of the body had deep roots in the past. Yorkshire had many "holy wells" dedicated to Christian saints, and some which were associated with older deities. Protestantism broke the official association with the saints, but some quietly retained their dedications. Waters could be drunk or bathed in. The warm baths at Bath were soon brought back into use. Sir William Turner wrote a book on Bath in 1562. Probably other waters stayed in local use to reappear respectably during the 17th century cult of spas. Holy wells used in the Elizabethan age included St Mungo's Well at Copgrove and St Oswald's Well, near Roseberry Topping, between Ayton and Newton in Cleveland. Some thought that if a sick person's shirt or smock was thrown in and floated, then the invalid would recover. Pieces of cloth were torn off and hung from a tree. A spring that came out of the rock towards the crest of the hill also cured sore eyes .

The destruction of St Anne's wells at Buxton in Derbyshire had been ordered in 1536. They were in use again by 1559. The Earl of Shrewsbury built a mansion for visitors with thirty lodgings. Dr John Jones the Derby physician, published "The benefit of the ancient Bathes of Buckstones, which cureth most grievous sicknesses".[11] William Hussey of North Duffield was at Buxton in 1567 and at Bath in 1569. Mary Queen of Scots visited Buxton four times from Chatsworth between 1573 and 1582. The Earl of Leicester was there and Lord Burghley said of the water that "mixed with sugar, I find it potable with pleasure, even as whey." The Catholic exiles the Earl of Westmoreland and Lady Northumberland were at the Belgian spa in 1571.[12]

Captain William Slingsby had visited spa waters in Germany. He drank from a spring near Knaresborough in 1571 and thought that the water tasted like that of the continental spas. He walled and paved the spring. This was the Tewitt well at the west end of the stray. Several years later the physician Timothy Bright, a clergy man of Methley and Barwick declared that the water had healing properties. Fuller thought Knaresbrough springs a mile and a half away in moorland were found by Master Slingsby c 1620.

The Malton spa spring had already attracted attention. It is not clear whether this was the old Well of Our Lady, or the spring later called the spa in Longster's garden. Thomas Brandsby spoke of a "pockie dame (that) had been twice bathed of the pox at Malton" in 1592. A well found in Ripon common was said to have cured many diseases by 1602. Thomas son of John Challoner heard that the mineral spring at Cawdlkell near Guisborough was famed for healing ulcers and cancers but it was already out of fashion by 1604. Places of resort without waters were thought beneficial. York doctors sent patients to Guisborough, on a scale sufficient to make it the first Yorkshire health resort.

CHAPTER 15
LEISURE

Time to Play

Elizabethan life was made acceptable and more enjoyable by "recreation", regular and irregular, at holidays and less busy times. Here were elements of "entertainment", "diversion", "sport", "amusement" and even "pastime". All these words were already known, although they carry rather different ideas of good living. Much that was seen as pleasurable in those days, would be looked on differently in other times. More stood the test of time. The main difference was that theirs was a young world full of children and young people. Many a game played by Elizabethan adults is left to the children in later societies where there are numerous older people. These days, you just can't find anyone for a game of blind man's buff.

Roger Ascham, a famous Yorkshire educator of the 16th century said that "play" was "doing what a man liked, when he liked". Probably everyone had that opportunity sometimes but the leisure pursuits open to the nobility, gentlemen and ladies had always been wider, if only because they could take time when they wished and their incomes were greater. Hunting, hawking, and the horsed military pursuits had been deliberately restricted to their ranks by law and by the scarcity of the animals necessary to pursue them. Gentry chose what they wanted to do and left what they didn't want to do, to paid servants. The exiled Earl of Westmoreland could play tennis with a Spaniard when he lodged in Rouen in 1580. Few from Yorkshire will have seen a courtyard where you could play the game.

A new view was emerging that some activities were more suitable for gentlemen and ladies while others were not. Foreign influences were in play. Sir Thomas Hoby translated Castigliones's "Book of the Courtier" while Sir Thomas Elyot's "The Book named the Governor" ran to several editions. The net was still wide, but some gentler arts and even some book learning were becoming acceptable. The gentry in every age pioneered some new kinds of leisure, while abandoning others. Other English social ranks had to wait for centuries later.

Roger Ascham made a list of acceptable noble exercises "to ride comely, to run fair at the tilt or ring, to play at all weapons, to shoot fair in bow or surely in gun, to vault lustily, to run, to leap, to wrestle, to swim, to dance comeley, to sing and play of instruments cunningly, to hawk, to hunt, to play at tennis and all pastimes, generally which be joined with labour, used in open place and in the daylight, containing either some fit exercise for war or some pleasant pastime for peace."

The state had long tried to limit the pleasurable activities of the other social ranks. It was argued that these distracted from archery, which had contributed much to the nation's military adventures abroad and might still contribute to its defence. An

27 Sports and Pastimes
(From 'The Story of Tudor & Stuart Britain' by C W Airne)

Elizabethan proclamation reinforced the old prohibitions on many games, but exempted those people with £100 a year and upwards. The concern for public order brought similar controls. York had imposed a curfew in 1530, from 8. p.m. on workdays and 9. p.m. on holidays to prevent riotous behaviour by poor labourers and the playing of dice, cards, and other unlawful games in taverns and alehouses. It is not quite so clear how much local authorities enforced such proclamations, or how much others ignored them.

The 1563 Statute of Labourers proclaimed a long working day from March to September, from 5 a.m. to 7 p.m., with two half hour breaks. From mid September to mid March, the working day was virtually from day break to nightfall. Sunday was the traditional "day off work", and for many had probably always been more holiday than "holy day". The workshop controlled labour more tightly, but in house, farm and field, there were busier and lighter seasons of work, dry and rainy days, and there was work which could be done to music and so made easier. There were celebrations, such as harvest suppers, when some seasonal work had been completed.

Special Days

A world dominated by agriculture knew periods of scarcity and others of plenty in each year, as well as dearth in some years. The fasting of Lent had been part of that. The pattern of fast alternating with feast remained unchallenged. The ancient calendar drew on a mixture of Christian, pagan and agricultural traditions, to decree the occasions for major and minor feasting but also structured the seasons, adding small high points to look forward to and enjoy, which rewarded effort, and gave opportunity to meet the basic needs for social life, exuberance, fun, food, foolery and play. Many of the old celebrations were banned or discouraged under the new Protestant religion but something remained.

Church ales and guild feasts vanished. Many saints days dropped from the calendar and saints images were taken out of processions. The number of "holy days" was reduced by a 1536 Act of Parliament. The Convocation of the church ordered every parish to keep its wake or parish fast on the first day in October. That was a step too far and it failed. The twelve days of Christmas, the occasions of Easter week, Whitsun, May Day, MidSummer Day, and many other traditional occasions such as Cocking Monday and Nutcrack night would last for centuries more. Colliers working on piece rates in Sheffield Park not only had Sunday off in 1580 but also a "sick day" for Sheffield fair, and some saints days from the old Calendar. The Elizabethan year included many minor events, rarely recorded, and rather taken for granted at the time. Centuries later, when they were being abandoned, antiquarians noted them down and put them in a bag called "folklore".

There was a change, but mostly it worked to separate the church from its old involvement in people's pleasures. The churchwardens were stopped from holding church ales, banquets and entertainments in the church or churchyard. The Boy Bishop collections, when a lad as a mock ecclesiastic travelled the diocese to raise funds were banned by statute in 1542. Hock collections after Low Sunday ceased. A stronger challenge came with the advent to local power of some Puritans in the 1570s and 1580s. Those who sought to bring "the kingdom of God" into the world, could not leave leisure untouched. They met with determined popular efforts to retain necessary pleasures for more ordinary people. Neither Protestant nor Puritan stifled everything enjoyable with gloom. We hear of those very Puritans singing in the fields. They too had their joys.

Many villages kept their own annual feast day, once associated with a saint, but not confined to communities with parish churches. St Peter's day saw the feasts at Osmotherley, Pickering and Redcar. Shorn of the three day religious element of the night watch on the vigil or wake day, the feast day and the morrow, village feasts survived into later centuries as a single day, for secular celebration. Bells might be rung. There was eating, drinking, sports and dancing. Friends, neighbours and relations gathered and travelling pedlars came for the highlight of the village year. For the Redcar village feast on St. Peter's day, they invited "their friends and kinfolks to a festival kept after their fashion, with a free heart and no show of niggardliness. That day, their boats are dressed curiously for the show, their masts are painted and certain rites observed among them, with sprinkling their bow with good liquor, sold with them at a groat the quart".[1]

Celebration of the great pagan festivals, of Whitsun, Mayday, Midsummer Day and Yule had continued alongside those, like Easter, which had been adapted to serve Christianity. The church had condemned them in the 7th century, still condemned them in the 12th. century and would discourage them again in the 16th century. You don't condemn the extinct. Here was a living tradition of some strength. William Cutter of Flamborough, a husbandman in 1559 wrote in his will that "I will that my boy Chadwayne be sufficiently apparelled at May Day and have two shillings given beside". The Council in the North in 1569 discussed whether to introduce licensing for Summer games. The Puritan, Archbishop Grindal of York, condemned Lords of Misrule, Summer lords and ladies, disguisings, and Mayday celebrations. And yet, maypoles remained widely into the next century and sparingly after that. William Myers still cried Yule in Airmyn church in 1600. People still visited the St John Baptist chapel at Laughton en le Morthen for the Midsummer fair in 1631.

A Sense of Occasion

Special things, rarely done, have great impact. People loved a marvel and rare decorations, disguisings, dances and drama had something of the marvellous about them. Some activities were common to many of these occasions. One was reversing the natural order of things, turning the social order upside down, or allowing an unusual degree of freedom. This was common to St. Nicholas Day, the Summer Lord of Misrule, Kings of Fools, All Fools day and May Goslings. Games where men lifted women, and women lifted men, marked one or two festivals, including Easter, giving a good opportunity for youthful rough and tumble. This could give much fun and familiarity in a young community where marriage was long delayed. The notorious English habit of kissing at every opportunity, noticed by Erasmus, perhaps drew strength from the same root. The return to work after Christmas featured days when men and women splashed each other with water.

Bonfires and bell ringing marked many feasts. Rogation day and rush bearings included processions. Evergreens were collected for decorations on May morning, St Helen's Eve, and for Palm Sunday. The return of families to their homes characterised Trinity, Michaelmas, Martinmas and Christmas. Several days of the year were viewed as prophetic, including St Agnes Eve (January 20), St. Valentines Day, "nutcrack night" and St Mark's Eve (April 24) when you could learn who was about to die. Begging was allowed and formalised in acceptable ways, to finance the food and drink for a feast, by use of the fond plough, wassailing, stephening, thomasing and luckybirding for New Years day.

Games were played on feast days, especially on Easter Monday, Mayday, Whitsunday, Midsummerday and Trinity Tide, not only because many games were banned for most people through the rest of the year. Games were the fun that most people had. Shrove Tuesday was the most notable game day, sometimes thought of as a ball day. Yorkshire Summer games still occurred in 1571 and a Maygame in 1594. The Scotland Street feast on 29th May north of the town of Sheffield probably continued May games. The long twelve day Christmas became a season of games, with the twelfth day as something of a climax. The penalties for playing games under the 1533 Act of Parliament remained in force, but not for the twelve days of Christmas.

A number of feasts and some lesser treats, centred on a particular meal, even a particular food. Egg rents were paid at Easter in many manors, in such numbers that eggs could be boiled and rolled down hills. Nutcrack night saw gatherings round a fire, into which shells were thrown to see which way they flew, the result predictive of whatever questions you wanted to ask. Pancakes, collops, and black pudding marked some of the days in Easter week. The peascod scalding gave a summer evening treat of green field peas, boiled in the shell. Carlings were fried peas, eaten on Carling Sunday, the fifth in Lent and the next but one before Easter. A mell supper could mark the end of harvest. At Brierley they wanted to kill a bull for the harvesters in 1580. William Dickenson, the Earl of Shrewsbury's Sheffield steward gave a rearing supper in May for a new built house, spending £2.6s.8d.

Rush bearings were the occasion for the annual replacement of the litter of the church floor. They shared some of the characteristics of a feast day. Cawthorne chapel had a Summer Sunday rush bearing when flowers and garlands were brought into the church. "Disguised persons" strewed rushes in Rawcliffe church on July 14th 1596. When the minister asked for reverence, one man fired a gun. Two local men brought "a toy called flower of the well" into Hunsingore church during divine service in 1598. Authority disapproved and they were stripped and whipped from the middle upwards through Wetherby. At Aldbrough, they made a night search for "their maumet commonly called the flower of the well". They barrowed it to church in prayer time on January sixth with a piper, horn blowing and striking basins. They crossed the church stile and stopped the minister reading prayers. They were stayed from the church but kept it up in the churchyard.

There were some novelties. The Queen's accession day, November the 17th. the day of her proclamation became an annual anniversary called Queen's day. This was marked with bell ringing and bonfires, and became a patriotic occasion, especially after the defeat of the northern rebellion and the opening of the war with Spain. A thanksgiving day for the Queen on 31st August 1586 saw York streets strewn with flowers and herbs, green bows set up, and houses hung with carpets and coverlets, and all the house plate set forth outside, while men supped at their own doors. Bells were rung and bonfires lit in the evening.

The expanding craft industries developed new feasts. The Sheffield Cutlers feast was on the first week of September, once every three years, quite distinct from the Sheffield Trinity Sunday feast and others at the smaller communities of Little Sheffield, Broad lane, Crook and Attercliffe. The roots of the Bishop Blaize feast in February are not known but it was kept going with processions in the cloth districts into the 19th century.

Playing host was practised in several forms, as municipal feasts for influential visitors likely to be of use on the one hand, and as customary receptions by the great men themselves on the other. There were some great annual patronal feasts, where those higher up the social scale entertained those below them. Dining at the great man's hall was a treasured privilege for some, and was regarded as a duty incumbent on the host. This may even have been a normal feature of manor house life, which had links with later rent, court and view dinners. The Lord Mayor and aldermen of York were conveyed down the river by barge to dine with Archbishop Piers, in August 1594.

The gentry extended hospitality to their peers and it was perhaps expected. There were other expectations of ale allowances when communal work was done, or help given as some relic of feudal obligations. The "arval" feasts at funerals were the best meals some people had when a table was made available for those who called. There were expectations of an invitation to the lord's hall once a year. The Archbishop of York in 1624 invited guests to his Bishopthorpe Hall over the twelve days of Christmas. St Stephen's Day was a Sunday and brought one hundred and three, Monday saw ninety-two from Middlethorpe, Acaster and Copmanthorpe. In the hall on Tuesday were sixty-three including lawyers, members of the York consistory and exchequer courts. Ninety-eight gentry and others appeared on Wednesday, fifty-five more were in the hall on Thursday and on the 3rd of January, the vicars came with the singing men and choristers.

Holy Days and Places

The Protestant Sunday was a direct challenge to holiday custom and was resisted. There was a strong pressure for all to attend church, men, women, and children. The ancient ways of using the church and churchyards were supposed to stop. York Corporation commanded householders to cause two from each house at least to attend sermons in the Minster on Sundays and holy days and banned drinking in public houses on those days. Archbishop Grindal advised ministers and wardens to stop people coming into church from games played outside, and to stop Lords of Misrule, Summer lords and ladies, disguised persons, people from Christmas and May Day games, minstrels, morris dancers and rush bearers coming into church at sermon or service time, to dance and play with scoffs, gestures and ribald talk. None were to walk, talk, behave irreverently or use gaming at such times. A stream of presentments suggest widespread breach of these requirements.

The churchyard was the natural gathering place, offering an audience and an open and almost public ground. Lancelot Stapleton of Wath in 1539 provided for his own burial outside the south choir door of Hovingham church. A stone laying there was to be placed above his grave, somewhat higher, "the more ease for the men to sit on". The clergy tried to discourage use of the churchyard for play and most particularly for the playing of games during service-time. One curate tried to stop Robert Fulbaron bowling in Deighton churchyard on the first of May and was hurt with his dagger. At Osmotherley the vicar and another man fought in the churchyard, as did the parish clerk at Yarm after communion in 1575. Thomas Snawsell and others of Redness were charged in 1602 for playing at football in the church yard of Snaith. The clerk recorded that they "sayeth the use hath bene time out of mind".

The clergy were asked at visitations whether parishioners allowed anyone into their house, or backyard to eat, drink, or play at cards, tables, bowls, and other games in the time of divine service, or during homily readings on Sundays or holidays, as well as whether any absented themselves then or failed to take communion at Easter. They were regularly reminded to take note of any walking, talking or unreverently behaving in divine service time, any gaming or sitting abroad in the street or churchyard, tavern or alehouse during divine service. They were to note any blasphemers, swearers, adulterers, fornicators, bawds or receivers of naughty persons, drunkards and ribalds.

Games were frequently played in church service time despite these prohibitions. On occasion, there was piping, dancing and playing in Aldbrough church while the vicar preached, and dancing at Wighill with a piper in service time. Young people in 1575 made that church yard their common sporting place. Strangers played a game called "penniston" in Topcliffe churchyard and at Hollim the fair was kept in the churchyard as of old. Thomas Savage and Thomas Westby with others not named to the number of twenty, bowled during evening prayer time at Whitsuntide at Howden in 1575. It may be too much to conclude that the moment the preaching began, the young at heart trooped out of the back of the church and resumed their accustomed activities. Or, it may not.

Games

State prohibitions on "unlawful games" found their way into manor court byelaws. The lists of proscribed games and the record of offenders show what was played. They included closh, kailes, half bowl, hand in and hand out, check board, loggeting in the fields, shove groats, and quoits. Breughel's paintings of another country evoke the age better than any such list. They show adults and children swimming, tree climbing, using stilts, playing follow my leader, hide and seek, hoops, dockhorse, piggy back, king of the castle, last at the stile, and hot cockles. Strutt listed "prisoner's base", for two groups trying to touch each other, "barley break" or "last in hell", "hoodman blind", "din is in the mire", and quarter staff. This was a young society where the games later judged as fit for children were played by adults.

Many games were simple enough with no more equipment than human bodies and the natural scene could provide. Barley break and base were catching games. Bones and other waste materials, ready to hand, were used for missile games such as closh, loggats and quoits. A stick thrown at a row of pins was kayles, while closh used a bowl as the missile. A bone was thrown at bone pins or a wood cone in loggats. Nine pins or skittles required better equipment with nine balls rolled to nine holes in the ground. Young Robert Johnson "misused himself" in Flamborough churchyard, when he "did pitch the barre" in 1567.

Most sport was in the open air, at village greens, market places, church and alehouse yards. Permanent game spaces began outside the larger towns, at the alehouse or in the rich man's courtyard and gallery. King Henry VIII had floor-boarded bowling alleys, tennis courts and a cockpit at Whitehall. When Hull leased its Butcroft outside the town walls to Alderman John Thornton and merchant James Clarkson in 1556, it was declared lawful for people to use the Butcroft for such games and plays as were customary before. Other communities similarly set aside a place for their archery butts. Osgodby near Scarborough had a frost fair close. Mexborough had a ball green in 1633. The Vicar of Boroughbridge cited men absent from church at a running or coursing during evening prayer time, on Trinity Sunday in 1597-8. This was clearly organised with " wagers before laid and matches made about the same, betwixt one of the parish of Topcliffe and one servant of Edward Thompson of Burrowbrigg". Many of the town were present. There were Winter sports on the river ice at York.

Bowling could be done in open or closed alleys, on grass or wood. One game had bowls with bias and a jack, the other had skittles. A 1541 statute forbade the keeping of alleys for gain, and suppressed public gaming houses where tennis, bowls, cards, and dice could be played for money. Servants were prohibited from playing bowls except on the twelve days of Christmas and then only in their master's house. Acomb manor ruled in 1553 that "all servants and labourers were not to play cards and bowls". The fine was twelve pence.

Noblemen and those with lands worth £100 a year were allowed to have private bowling greens and bowling alleys. " Jack was as good as his master" and bowls found its way. Thomas Nicholls, the Boroughbridge innkeeper kept a bowling alley in 1563. Roger Ward of Pollington bowled on the Sabbath. Bradford court leet fined two common players of bowls. Twenty Howden men bowled during evening prayer time at Whitsun in1575. Bowls were played at Rufforth during divine service in 1581. Rishworth manor court in 1600 declared that "We pain all those that keep any bowl alleys within their own grounds or doth suffer any to bowl at any time, whether they keep alehouse or not, fine twenty shillings".

Team games were common. Tuts was a kind of baseball, played by Brian Abbay at Bilton in 1575, on Low Sunday at evening prayer time. Three Bilton men played at tuts one Sunday evening during prayers in 1596. There were games called Peniston, pitching the bar, and stool ball, played at Beverley in 1619. Football was played at York in the Winter of 1618. Running at the quintain had been adapted from a knightly exercise into a rustic game, where you struck a turn board with a pole, and a sack could hit the back of your head if you were slow to move. Shovel board was on a bigger scale than shove halfpenny, having a three feet by thirty-two feet arena, with teams trying to get near the far end.

Cards was the most frequently reported indoor game. The Earl of Shrewsbury's ship brought four vats of playing cards on a voyage from Newhaven. The most frequent venue was the alehouse, but homes, shops and barns were used. Common ale- brewer Robert Walker at Acomb in 1570 was ordered not to keep others servants in his house at night or allow card playing and other illegal games. Brewer Thomas Smith allowed three to play cards in his house and was charged four pence for each of them in 1574. Patrick Baynes was fined 3s.4d. "for keeping unlawful company and players of cards and other unlawful games in his house at untimely hours of the night, to the annoyance of his neighbours". Card playing is recorded at Skeffling, Easington and Hinderwell and at alehouses early in the next reign at Malton, Lastingham, Kirby Moorside, Brompton, Goathland, Egton, Scarborough, and Stonegrave, to name a few. Five Ilkley people played unlawful games in their houses in 1584.

Board games included merrills or nine man's morris, the board often carved in choir stalls and on barn barrels. Early Merrills boards have been found at Mount Grace, Kirkby Underdale and Flamborough. A game of shovegroats could be played on a table, chalked for the purpose. Brian Inham at Marston allowed unlawful games in his house at service time in 1594, including "shovgrote or slopdthirsye". Mary the Scots Queen complained of losing the solace of billiards in her English captivity. Queen Elizabeth had played chess with Yorkshireman Roger Ascham. Other indoor games included tables or backgammon, where two tables were combined together, lined and marked with six points, alternately black and white. A games table at Hardwick Hall had backgammon and checker boards. Dice may have been common. Dice games included hazard or main chance. Cheating with false or loaded dice or by sleight of hand was already a fine art.

A State lottery, the "very rich lottery general without any blanks" was advertised by the Privy Council in July 1568. The Queen agreed to the establishment of a rich lottery in London, to raise money for the repair of havens. No-one was to lose more than four pence in the groat. The prizes were listed and safe conducts offered for subscribers to go to London. This ushered in big prize gambling. The lottery was drawn in London between 11th January and 6th May. The "welcome" prizes were £50 in plate, £30 and £20 and the main prizes £3000 and £700. It was proclaimed in Hull and lottery tickets were issued by Gregory Peacock to men from Driffield, Watton and South Cave down to Hull water. There were lottery books at York in 1572.[2]

Children's games and play are but dimly perceived. Toys were made from the materials to hand, hoops and sticks, whips and tops, and wooden dolls. Children were banned from going with clappers at York, on Shere Tuesday and Good Friday. Throwing stones onto the church roof at Harewood, in service time, sounds like mischief. There was one day a year when it was acceptable for small boys to kill cocks by throwing stones while church wardens gave out rewards for the slaughter of many young wild birds and animals, or the destruction of their eggs, since they were seen as pests. The young were employed to keep birds off the crops. Ratting from the stack occurred in every age.

Blood sports

The catching of wild animals, fishes and birds for food remained an important part of ordinary life. For those few with hunting rights, the killing of deer had long since become a sport. The wild boars had been wiped out while several other animals were treated as vermin, including the fox. The monarchs and their nominees had taken the red deer in the royal and baronial forests and chases of the 12th century. After these were reduced in number in the 13th century, the hunt was less frequent in the shrinking woodlands and more frequently confined to the deer hays and parks of those with rights of chase and warren. The deer were kept in and others were kept out, by hedge, wall or fence and sometimes with wild vegetation between great double banks.

Gentry gathered socially to hunt their parks. Sir Henry Saville wrote to his cousin Plumpton of the red and fallow deer hunts at Tankersley and Thornhill and told the Earl of Shrewsbury two years later, that he had been killing stags at Tankersley and Wharncliff with Lord Talbot. The Earl of Sussex welcomed Lord and Lady Herbert, to Sir William Fairfax's Gilling house and park for hunting and hawking in 1569. Many parks had lodges where hunts were managed with refreshments. There were beaters to bring the deer to the hunter, rather than the hunter to the deer, and to give spectators a show. Gilbert, Earl of Shrewsbury annually had many bucks set in a meadow, a mile in compass, near Sheffield townside. All the apron men of the parish went there, and were allowed to kill and carry away as many as they could with their hands. Wakefield sessions in 1600 heard that yeoman Edward Morley of Adlingfleet had taken his greyhound into Hatfield chase to hunt a stag.

28 Hunting was considered suitable for gentlefolk

Hawking was popular with the gentry and hawks were highly valued. The Queen's tenants at Goathland dale were required to promote the hawks that bred at Killing Noble Scar in Newton Dale and to secure them for the Crown. Other hawks were imported from Danzig and Norway. Welburn esquire Thomas Saville in 1587 left his goshwawk and all his "spowdies" to two brothers. Gentleman Cuthbert Gower of Thormonby in Cleveland gave hawks, hounds and greyhounds to a nephew. Sir John Constable of Kirkby Knowle castle bequeathed his best horse to John Manners and his best hawks to the Earl of Rutland. John Crosland kept the hawks at Helmsley. Sir Ingram Clifford of Cowthorpe left all his hawks to George Earl of Cumberland in 1578. On 28th August 1600 Sir William Eure, with gentlemen Richard Cholmeley, William Dawnay, William Hilliard, and Stephen Hutchenson were out with Smythe, Lord Eure's yeoman falconer, in the dales near Hackness.

Animal fighting had a bloody appeal as a spectacle for many people. A bear might be chained to a post and one or more mastiffs sent against him. The bear could vigourously defend itself and was too valuable to be lost, so surviving dogs were hauled off, before any final defeat. The Earl of Cumberland's bear ward danced bears at Beverley market place in 1519. The Queen's bear ward baited at York's Peasholme Green in 1575. Hull paid Lord Robert Dudley's bear wards goodly sums for wine for the keeper of the bears. Bulls were regularly baited at market places, a practice thought necessary to bring the meat to full flavour. The York authorities required all bulls baited in the city before they were killed. Thirsk and Malton had bull rings and Sheffield Market Place a bullstake. A bull was baited at Beverley on the day that the mayor was sworn into office and it was thought remarkable when a bull was not baited there in 1577.

Cock fighting was a popular street sport but became an arena sport for the gentry. Specially bred roosters were pitted against each other in small pits. York Corporation agreed in 1568 to a gentlemen's petition arguing that a cockpit would be an asset to the city and cause money to be spent with victuallers. Friargarth was suggested as a site. Plumpton's cockfights were managed differently from those in Hallamshire. Hare coursing was another countryside sport. Parliament had already prohibited the taking of hares by tracking them in snow. The Duke of Norfolk made rules for coursing with greyhounds during the reign. Hare finders loosed the hares and fewterers the greyhounds.

Harrison considered England the country with the greatest number, excellency and diversity of dogs, ranging from hounds and curs, to mastiffs used for bear baiting and lap dogs. Men valued dogs as servants in their sports and their work. Johannes Caius volume "Of English Dogs" was translated into English in 1576. Their qualities consisted in smelling, sight, swiftness, nimbleness and subtlety. The harriers hunted by smell, the gaze hounds by eye, while the swift greyhound was used to start and hunt both hare, and deer. Spaniels served in hawking, and setters for fowling. There were shepherd's dogs, dog messengers, water drawers, tinkers currs, defending dogs with bite or bark, turn spit dogs, and playfellows.[3] Strutt spoke of butcher's dunghill dogs, pricked ear curs and "bosom comforters". The Maltese spaniels were "meet playfellows for mincing mistresses to bear in their bosoms, keep company in their chambers and lick their lips when they lie like young Dianas in their wagons and coaches". He thought the practice a sure sign of " want of issue".

Horse Races

Race meetings might be merely a small group of gentry running their own horses against each other, on the spur of the moment, and wagering for fortune or fame. Gatherings of gentry, increasingly interested in horse breeding, and possessed of larger stables, gave rise to meetings planned as regular events, which attracted great crowds of other people. Two or three riders were enough and you rode your own horse. Henry Cholmley held scratch horse races outside Whitby parish church during service time, before 1599. He was so addicted to fleet hounds and horses, that he had to take his son out of Oxford and marry him off to an heiress to raise money. Sir William Fairfax at Gilling, said "my Lord of Northumberland and Lady, my Lord of Westmoreland and Lord and Lady Talbot, Ladies Herbert and Wharton and all the principal gentlemen and their wives of this country was here with me a hunting all last week. After divers matches of shooting made amongst us, it happened that my servant Anthony Hanmer struck his own man with a pick shaft".

York was the most likely place for events with a regional attraction. The first recorded horse race was on the Tuesday after St George's day, 23rd April, 1530. A prize golden bell was given by the Lord Mayor, and returned twelve months later, when the winner was obliged to run a horse against all comers, with a wager of 6s.8d. or more. Camden spoke of this annual horse race, run in the Forest of Galtres near York, in 1586, possibly in Clifton Ings. He thought it "hardly credible" what great resort "there was at these races from all parts and what great wagers were laid on the horses". The Earl of Rutland ran and backed horses at the forest races of Galtres against Cholmeley and

Grimston winning £45 in 1595-6. Drake says that it became proverbial "to bear away the bell". Tradition has claimed that the annual Kiplingcotes race on the high Wold of the East Riding, existed in the time of King Richard III. Another account says that it was organised in 1519. The race was mentioned by husbandman Thomas Carter of Helperthorpe, in a court dispute regarding Bainton rectory in 1555-56. He said that he chanced to be "at a horse running at Kypplingcote Eshe (ashes), about Shrovetide last". Articles governing the race were drawn up in 1618. Sir Richard Cholmley is said to have kept horses in training at Kiplingcotes

Camden mentions Gatherley Moor as a place for sports and races in 1586 and Ogilby reported races at the long straight gallop in 1612. The Earl of Rutland lost money there against Whitefoot. The Earl of Westmoreland staying at Keldholme, wrote to his brother in law at Holywell "My old enemies tried to trap me on horse running day at Gaterleymore", in 1569. His brother Christopher came to the moor from Kirkby Moorside to see a horse of his own run. By 1614, there were other meetings. Thomas Meynell wrote of victors taking the Gatherley old bell, the Hambleton silver bowl, the Bagby Moor silver cup, the Studfold silver cup, the forest of Galtres bell, the Hambleton gold bell, and the cups of Thirsk, Knaresborough and Rainton. A Gilling meet in 1569 for "horseraces, hunting and hawking" may relate to the early Nunnington race course. Swift horses were run on the firm smooth sands before Redcar. William Whiting a dyer, John Martin a London draper and Miles Bishop, at Hull agreed a wager of 30s. on a two and a half mile race from Mill Hill, York to Grimston Cross, with two children on horses.

Martial Arts

A few Yorkshire men performed in the tilt yards at London, with some distinction. Robert Carey attending the court in 1586 would remember that "In all triumphs I was one, either at tilts, tournaments or barriers, in mask or balls, I kept men and horses far above my rank". The next year he was sent as an ambassador to the King of Scotland. The Earl of Cumberland took the title "knight of Pendragon castle", when he was made chief champion of the tilt yard for the Queen in 1592, replacing the amorous Sir Henry Lee. A famous portrait shows him in fancy dress for the occasion. His speech detailed fantasies of a Pendragon castle removed by enchantment from Westmoreland to Westminster, of Merlin, of fights with white and red dragons and verses just discovered about "a virgin reigning thirty-three years".

Legislation had long discouraged many games, supposedly to promote archery practice on holidays. Queen Elizabeth continued to issue injunctions from time to time, requiring the maintenance of artillery, which meant shooting with the long bow at the butts. Archery practice was compulsory. A sheaf of twenty-four arrows with flat heads cost 22d in 1559. York residents between seven and seventeen, and from seventeen to forty, were told to have bows and arrows in 1569. The city constables were warned a few years later to make sure that householders bought bows and arrows for themselves, their servants and children. Heworth Moor had archery butts. York Bridge Ings held two mounds of butts, sixty yards apart.

The long bow has been thought of as obsolete, and Flodden the last battle at which it was crucial, but the weapon you have is the one you use. Richard Dunn at Sheffield still described himself as an arrow smith in 1595. Guns were not numerous and powder was not plentiful. An Act of Parliament restricted shooting with guns or crossbows for sport to persons having £100 a year. A statute of Edward VI provided that none under a lord of parliament should shoot with engines in any city or town at a bird or a mark on church, house or dovecote. No-one was to shoot with hail shot or more than one pellet at a time. York had an early shooting match at Palacrofts in 1555. Acomb manor court charged four men for shooting with a gun contrary to the statute in 1572. Robert Ramsden a gentleman of North Deighton was charged in 1598 with firing a fowling piece at geese, using powder and lead pellets called hail shot.

Gentlemen owned swords and regularly wore them but contact with Europe had brought in the more dangerous rapier and more sophisticated contests. Elegant fencing with the point replaced the rougher battling of the English broad sword and buckler. The rapier was light, narrow and dangerous. A dagger supplanted the buckler. Sir Charles Cavendish c1577 practised with a man who favoured the buckler for better defence. He chose the rapier, played it on his ribs and cut his eye. Fencing masters arrived from Europe and books of instructions. A Master of the Fence taught play at weapons to Lord Roos and John Manners in 1557-8. A Scarborough man defended himself with a rapier in 1579, ending Ralph Peacock's life with a five inch deep wound.

Travel and the Resort

The birth of the regional public assembly, conducted primarily for pleasure, may fall into the Elizabethan period. The high sheriff of the county commonly mustered relations in livery to ride with him, in procession, to meet the Assize Judges. The York assize courts continued in the days that followed, also attended by the local Justices of the Peace. A number of gentry families, Goodricke, Saville, Slingsby, Danby, Jenkins, Lister and Ingram appear to have had a second house at York by 1634, perhaps dictated by the emergence of a season. Phillip Constable of Everingham leased his Monk Bar house at York in 1601 for forty-one years, with a proviso that he and his family were to have a lodging parlour, when need arose.

There were regular annual gatherings at Buxton, where we seem to see the birth of the inland social resort, built upon the lure of the warm springs. Thomas Greves wrote to Lord Shrewsbury on August 3 1574, saying that there was no wine there worth drinking. He asked for tips of stags horn for Doctor Beech. The company at Buxton included eighteen strangers, of whom seven ladies, a lady's daughter and two doctors were staying in the one house. Sir Thomas Cecil had had two hogsheads of beer and ale delivered there from Chatsworth. There was another great gathering of ladies and gents at Buxton on August 1st 1576. The Earl of Leicester joined Shrewsbury there in 1580 and two years later the Queen of Scots was twice a visitor to the resort.

An unknown author portrayed the Cleveland market town of Guisborough as a place of resort for the sick, recommended by York doctors about mid century, but the town seems to have taken on all the features of a pleasure resort. The scene was much praised. "The air at Guisborough is so temperate, that partly by reason of the sea, which is three miles off, yet broken by hills lying between the town and it, and the happiness of the seat being a valley mounded on small hills, compassed about with very high mountains, the sides whereof are covered with fair trees, or beautified with green bushes or stately cliffs, intermingled with the downfall of small brooks, which make the most delightful prospect I ever saw".

"The soil in the bottom is fruitful both in corn and grass, the grass is not very long, but so sweet and thick platted, that an acre thereof somereth as many cattle as our best grounds in the heart of England. The ground most part of the year is covered with flowers, whereby the air is so sweet and the earth so good a scent, that gentlemen commonly, when they will delight themselves, say - let us go and pass some days at Gisbroughe and yet there is never a good house in the town to recommend it." Camden added that "This place is really fine and may in point of pleasantness and a graceful variety compare with Puteoli in Italy and in point of healthfulness it far surpasses it."

"The inhabitants are observed by travellers to be well bred and civil, cleanly in their diet and neat in their houses and, which is more, old Doctor Len of York" and "Doctor Howe usually sent his patients to Gisbroughe to lye there to recover their health. The people breed here very long, if they be a while absent they grow sickly. They are altogether given to pleasure, scarce any good husband amongst them, day and night feasting, making matches for horse races, dog running or running on foot, which they use in a field called deer close, where, as if it were in 'campo martio', you shall see from morning to twelve of the clock at night, boys and men in their shirts exercising themselves. Their diet is plentiful from the sea, their beef and mutton is also very cheap and sweet in taste. So is their venison also fair in whiteness and taste surpassing. This makes them content if they have wherewith to live. For the rest, they have a saying, let those that come after us shift for themselves as we have done".

Moving from one place to another for health or pleasure, was the basis of the retreat as well as the resort. Gilbert Earl of Shrewsbury wrote from Bolsterstone to his brother in law John Manners on August 17th. 1587 saying "I have come here to try if a change of air will ease my gout, but return to Sheffield tonight, If you and your brother will come on Saturday you will be heartily welcome and we can confer touching the subsidies and the want of justices." Esquire Richard Norton only spent the Summer at Rilston, but he built a tower in the furthest part near Crookrise.

Spectacles

People liked a spectacle. They had travelled to the Minster towns to see great church occasions. The greater churches and the municipalities had long traditions of providing street drama and public processions. The Beverley guilds had carried the shrine of St John from the Minster to St Mary's on the Monday in Rogation week and on the next day to St Nicholas Church. The Guilds of Corpus Christi, St Aymery and St John had preceded the craft guilds and five more religious guilds. The Guild of St Mary had staged a festival with a pageant on the Feast of the Purification. These religious celebrations were coming to an end.[4]

The towns had sufficient people to make a crowd, a natural street audience, hungry to see anything going on. Travelling entertainers would bring an outlandish fowl, a baboon or an ape, a giant's bone, a fire eater, a puppet play, a woman on a rope, or the tumblers, who appear in illustrations of the time. An Italian took a sixteen foot long serpent into Durham. He claimed that it consumed a thousand people. The Chester pageant showed giants, unicorns, a dromedary, a dragon and hobby horses. The towns could make a spectacle out of the visits of the mighty. York had welcomed King Henry VIII with open air shows, singing and other music at St William's chapel on Ouse Bridge, at Ouse Gate end, near Coney street and at the far end of Coney Street, near the common hall in 1541. The streets were gravelled and the beggars removed. The innholders and tipplers were ordered to have lawful ale pottells, quarts and pints.

They loved a procession and processioners need an audience. Hull planned a parade for Queen Mary's pregnancy but that didn't materialise. Some York petitioners complained to the Mayor and aldermen that there had been "a very rude and barbarous custom maintained in this city and no other city or town of this realm." Annually on Saint Thomas Day, before Christmas, two disguised persons, called Yule and Yule's wife rode through the city. The critics claimed that "great concourses" were drawn together "to gaze and commit other enormities, withdrawing them from divine service and sermons".

The York Sheriff rode through the city, with horsed men on the Thursday after Trinity Sunday, a sort of military parade. Each alderman found six men, four in white armour and two in plate, while the "twenty-four" councillors, found four men each, two in white armour and two with calevers .The city armour was scoured for this parade. The Church High Commission ordered an end to both events. There were public shows of armour at York on St Bartholomew's day, Mayday and Midsummer day. The lord mayor, sheriffs, the 'twenty-four' and the chamberlains according to old custom together fished the waters of Ouse, followed by a dinner, on a July Thursday. Bishop Blaize Day was marked with processions of cloth craftsmen bearing symbols of each trade, at York, and other clothing towns.

Beverley spent money on wine, forty shillings for wait's liveries and badges and two shillings for paupers' badges, when Queen Elizabeth was proclaimed. The city staged a firework display in 1585-6 for Sir Christopher Willoughby, and entertained him and other gentlemen again, that same year when they were at a cockfighting in the town. Hull welcomed Lord President Burghley to the city on an August Sunday in 1601. He was given dinner at the Mayor's house, together with Lord Eure and many knights and ladies. They were "diverted' in the afternoon "with many curious fireworks. One of the engineers planted an old cannon in the Market place and over charged it. The weapon flew into pieces, killing four men and wounding others." The Scarborough Borough Bailiffs in 1602 spent £1.6s.8d on a banquet for Sir William Eure, of which 2s.6d. was for a "lord of misrule" and 2s.4d. for a pound of sugar from Mr. Peacock.

Small scale local events could include ritual movement or dance, to join in or to watch. Dairymaids might dance back from the pasture, led by the neat herd. Tusser mentions reapers crying largesse from their employer and passers-by, with "a lord of the harvest ", ending with a horkey or harvest supper. Lords and Ladies of Misrule were mocked by Phillip Stubbes in his Anatomy of Abuses of 1583. He said that "lusty guts were solemnly chosen in a parish, crowned, given liveries and scarves with bells tied on their legs, handkerchiefs in their hands, and followed by mopsies and bessies with hobby horses, dragons, pipers and drummers to the church." They shared something with the "King of Fools" mentioned on other occasions, and may sometimes have acted as masters of ceremonies.

Rush bearings were the occasions when fresh reeds were carried to a church to refresh the floor. The task was more easily performed with music. A homely disguising took place for rush bearing at Cawthorne, when. gentlewoman Mary Mountney led others to dress up in the chapel, some in women's apparel, and some in visers, to parade the town and shoot guns, in August 1596. Lord Wharton, at Healaugh in 1568 kept a store of "apparell for the revels". There were nine long gowns of dornix, another gown of buckram, laid upon with lace of straw, three fools' coats, six paper hats, two bishops' mitres and two peers' caps, a coat of buckram guarded with straw, two peers' hoods, six wood snowswords with girdles, six beards, eight visors, two fools' daggers, two tip staves and a mace, two drums and one pair of sticks and seven pairs of scarves of red and yellow sarcenet for masking.

Public executions were popular spectacles. The execution of the Earl of Northumberland by axe at York in 1572 was staged on a new scaffold set up for the purpose. His funeral was followed by hundreds, with halts at Leckonfield and Wressle, supposedly with £154 distributed among near fourteen thousand people. A gentry wedding could provide spectacle for the crowd. A Liversedge wedding saw the bride depart on a pillion behind the groom. The company had a play and the company danced from Sunday to the Saturday after. Eight years later when Mary Neville was married, thirty horses had white tassels, and ostrich plumes. There was a ruling made at York that no man was to have more than twenty at the dinner for his marriage.

Pageants

The pageant plays, or mystery plays of the greater towns had combined street spectacle and drama, although rooted in earlier dramatic sequences performed in great churches. York, Beverley and Wakefield had series of plays performed publicly on Corpus Christi Day, a festival which had been proclaimed by Pope Urban in 1264. The costumed members of craft guilds staged the plays on pageants, meaning the mock houses, one up, one down, on six wheels that served as moveable stages. York had some forty-eight plays and Wakefield thirty-two. The York drama told the story of mankind from the creation to the last judgment. The plays were plain spoken and there was probably robust interchange between the performers and the crowd. Christ on the last day was credited with –

> "Man surely ought you for to quake,
> this dreadful day such sight to see
> All this I suffered for thy sake,
> Say man, what suffered thou for me"

Eve has been credited with saying to Adam, in a timeless expression of marital patience, nearly exhausted, -

> "be still Adam, name it no more it may not mend."

A version of the "Noah and the Ark" play was performed at Hull, Wakefield, possibly at Doncaster and in the Beverley watermen's pageant. A hen-pecked Noah was portrayed as terrified at the prospect of forty days afloat with his wife. The Hull Trinity Guild accounts show the play performed on Plough Monday, with women and children involved. The ship on wheels was hung in the Trinity church and the ark kept in a high Street wool house. The Protestants objected to the York plays and an attempt to substitute creed plays was not successful. The Puritan Archbishop Grindal gathered in the texts of several plays in the next few years. Occasionally substitute plays were allowed and alternative mid summer shows during the 1580's. A play by John Grafton was approved in 1584, and performed the next year, advertised for two days by pipe and drum. The pageant of the bakers was borrowed for a midsummer event in 1584. A last attempt made in 1600 was stopped by the mayor.

Groups of male players were licensed to perform plays under the patronage of noblemen. They travelled the country, performing at gentry houses and in towns. This was nothing new. The Shepherd Lord had eleven players at York on Xmas Day and the city paid some Halifax players 14s 11d for St Thomas day in 1510. The city still welcomed Lord Scrope's and Lord Leicester's players in 1565. Fresh legislation in 1572 made any common players, minstrels, fencers, and bearwards, not belonging to a baron or one of greater degree and found wandering without licence, subject to treatment as rogues, by the justices.

James Burbage in 1574 obtained authority from the Lord Privy Seal for himself and three other servants of the Earl of Leicester "to use, exercise, and occupy the art and faculty of playing comedies, tragedies, interludes, and stage plays "Lord Leicester's players received twenty shillings for playing in Doncaster church that year and Lord Monteagle's players were paid ten shillings. Players of Lord Hunsdon and Lord Sussex came to York in 1581 and in 1587 the players of Lord Essex, the Lord Admiral, Lord Chandos, Lord Sussex, Lord Stafford' and the Queen. There were performances in Minster court, the Common hall and at the Merchant Taylors hall in 1589. Use of the Guildhall for plays was stopped after some vandalism in 1592.

Hull prohibited mummers and mystery plays in 1572. Other players resorting to the city were required to pay 2s.6d to the town in 1583. The Hull mayor a few years later denounced "divers lewd persons, players or setters out of plays, tragedies, comedies or interludes" habitually resorting to the city. Those attending any play or interlude in town would now also forfeit 2s.6d. The city saw some drama in Whitefriargate in 1598. and interludes were seen by visitors in 1599. Beverley saw the players of the Queen, the Duke of Suffolk, the Earl of Leicester, and the Earl of Worcester, some more than once.

More informal groups of players, described as "common players of interludes", travelled widely, without official approval, but with gentry patronage. The interludes were short, sometimes religious, and sometimes knockabout, witty even vulgar plays. Their simple plots ranged from the conflict of vice with virtue, to more subtle mockeries, and traditional dramas, like Robin Hood, or St George and the Dragon. Many of the performances were at gentry houses, some being Roman Catholic but public performances were probably more numerous. These players were classed as rogues and vagabonds. Many of the Yorkshire performances that are known were in the next reign.

Interludes at York common hall had to be licensed by the lord mayor from 1578. There were separate performances for the Corporation and for the common people in 1581. Interludes were banned at Hull in 1598 arguably for debauching young people. The St. George play was performed at Sheffield in 1581. A group from the Catholic fastness of Egton, led by Robert Simpson and Christopher Cordiner was active in the period 1595-1616. Christopher Simpson a cordwainer of Westonby was a boy actor by 1595. The later "martyr" Nicholas Postgate was a member in 1616. These players were seen by Sir Richard Cholmley at Roxby. They visited Sneaton, Helmsley, Pickering, Stokesley, Tadcaster, Ripon, Richmond, Northallerton and even Nidderdale. They called at nine or more gentry houses in one year. They performed King Lear in1609 and included Pericles, the Three Shirleys and St Christopher in their repertoire.

The Osmotherley interlude players were active at Christmas 1602 visiting Northallerton, Topcliffe, Hawnby and Bedale. They used a jig by George Ward of Gatenby in 1601 and at other times, such popular pieces as "Ffiliday flouts me",

"Fortune", "Take they old cloak about thee" and "Cobber". Christopher Hutchinson of Hutton Bushell led another group of six or seven players, around the Howardian hills during the reign of James I. Seven players performed the "Robin Hood" play in Brandsby churchyard in 1615. A Sowerby company later visited Gilling, Oulston and Brandsby, the last village enjoying 'the Sheriff and Robin Hood' at a rush bearing in 1615. Yeomen, alehousekeepers and labourers were charged for accommodating and feeding strolling players.[5]

There is no record of other performances of William Shakespeare's plays in the county during the Queen's reign. He did use a local theme, centred on Dale town in Bilsdale. In Henry IV pt ii, act iv scene iii, comes the beheading of Coleville of the Dale for treason in 1405. The play "A Yorkshire Tragedy" has sometimes been attributed to Shakespeare. This was entered in the Stationer's Register on May 2 1608 but was based on a pamphlet entered three years earlier, on June 12 1605 under the title "Two most unnatural and bloody Murthers: The one by Maister Caverley, A Yorkshire Gentleman, practised upon his wife, and committed upon his two Children, the three and twenty of April 1605: The other, by Mistress Browne, and her servant Peter, upon her husband, who were executed in Lent last past at Bury in Suffolk." Tate Wilkinson revived an Elizabethan play at Wakefield Little theatre in 1775 called 'George 0' Green the pinder of Wakefield'.

Music

Musicians were probably more common than we know, principally popular for street dancing. Percy Grave piped in service time at Walton in 1575 and drew people after him. Agnes Cook made a comment about a Kirkby Misperton man Christopher Pinder. She said, "he could play the lute for a gathering, as commonly many serving men could, though he wasn't commonly reputed and taken for a minstrel". Music seems to have been a lure, perhaps itself still something of a marvel. People followed musicians about. Minstrels were banned from playing in Aldburgh, after nine at night except at weddings. No-one was allowed to walk in the Doncaster streets with citterns after nine o-clock.

The larger borough towns had strong musical traditions. They employed bands of three or four musicians called "waits", who kept watch, and were called on for many musical occasions. The minstrels' pillar at St Mary's Beverley shows waits with their silver chains and badges. The town had three in 1577. York waits wore silver collars. Shalmes were bought for four in 1566. A city order issued at York required the common waits to keep their morning watch, with their accustomed instruments, every day in the week, except Sundays, and in the time of Christmas only, "any usage or custom heretofore to the contrary notwithstanding". The group sometimes went to perform at the Earl of Rutland's house. The Scarborough waits had visited Whitby abbey for St. Hilda's day celebrations in an earlier century. Christopher Johnson was made a Scarborough wait in 1598. The Darlington waits played at feasts and weddings and at inns. This may well have been their role everywhere.

A Beverley fraternity of Minstrels claimed a yearly resort of other minstrels, between the river Trent and the river Tweed, since the time of King Athelstan. They met at Rogation time, to choose an alderman, stewards and deputies to collect dues. The

29 The Guild of Minstrels, St Mary's Church, Beverley

"Order of the ancient company or fraternity of minstrels in Beverley" issued "ordinances" in 1555 to regulate standards of performance, conduct, and apprenticeship in their craft. Only a single apprentice was allowed. They required loyalty to the town, excluding outside minstrels and required players not to give tuition to their own children. Beverley fined some foreign minstrels in 1578. They could evict musicians, whose ability declined for "lack of honest usage". Members were limited to performing at weddings in the parish where they lived. The York minstrels guild excluded foreign minstrels from singing or playing any instrument within the city, on church holidays, dedication days, at brotherhoods and at freemen's dinners, with a fine of 3s.4d for offenders.

The great musicians of the day were in the service of noblemen and women. The Earl of Rutland paid a lutenist named Eston for teaching his page to play the instrument in 1558. Roger Manners wrote to the Earl in 1586 assuring him that his daughter's music was not being neglected, saying "I have not forgotten the lady Elizabeth but have the servant to play the virginals with her, when Symonds is away". A year later Edward Paston wrote recommending an organist from Norwich to teach his daughter. William Byrd, an organist to the queen, was tutor to the daughter of the Earl of Northumberland in 1579. Thomas Cutting was lutenist in the service of Arabella Countess of Lennox. Some London barbers' shops had lutes to hand for waiting patrons.

The wide range of musical instruments available appears in the carvings at Beverley Minster. There is the pear shaped lute, used to accompany a single singer. There are single and three string rebecs, the tabor and double pipe, the single manual organ, single and five string harps, bagpipes, shawm, double tambourn, cittern, organistrum, cornam, trumpet, psalterion, tamborine and more.[6] An Earl of Northumberland had a tabarett, a lute, a rebec and six trumpets, which sounds like a band. Wealthy people also bought instruments for playing. The virginals, regals and orpharion were popular. Personal ownership of instruments was evident in gentry and clergy wills. Thomas Brigholme the Fisholme esquire in 1542 had a pair of virginals. Scarborough's Jenkin Lowson left a lute in 1575. Timothy Bright willed a theorbo in a case, and the Irish harp which he usually played. Thomas Saville of Thornhill in 1601 left George Radcliffe his virginals. Thomas Wilson the Danby curate of 1638 had a citherne, treble viol, lute and virginals. Music books helped popularise part singing for madrigals and solo singing accompanied by the lute or virginals.

Three ladies and three men painted on the chamber wall freize at Gilling Castle, set against a background of trellised vines and grapes, roses and honeysuckle, appear more like a house party than a troupe of musicians. The men played violins, while the ladies, sat alternately on benches, playing small lutes, with six music books open before them. Lady Hoby, during January 1600, wrote that "to refresh my self being dull, I played and sung to the alpherion". The great house at Leconfield had a clavicord and virginals. The long gallery was a new haven for keyboard instruments.

The Dance

James Ryther commented on the music of Yorkshire people. He claimed that "by affinity with the Scots and borderers, these people delight in a rude and wild kind of music, to which are suitable rhymes and songs entwined and sung either to wanton or warlike actions". He was speaking of open air dancing. The pipes were the main musical instrument for leading the dance and the county seems to have had many pipers. They haunted alehouses and often appeared at village feasts. Some were mentioned by chance in parish registers. At Bingley were Ralph the piper, leading the dancing in 1595, and Robert Hodgson in 1608. Behind the White Horse Inn was Piper Acre. Frances Bateson was a Wykeham piper in 1587. Thomas Kendall was the Marton piper, and Ralph Theaker was at Hovingham, in Ryedale. The Myton on Swale piper was at Brandsby Hall for Christmas in 1614. A travelling Tollesby piper was accused of sheep stealing at Kildale.

A contemporary misericord showed piglets dancing to a pipe. One has a sow playing a bagpipe. Nafferton and Lowthorpe men marched with their clubs behind a piper to keep order at Little Driffield fair on the Monday in Whitsun week. The organisers of "garries" employing a piper could end before the courts. Piper Percival Graves of Walton played during service time on Sunday May 3rd when nine Wighill men danced. Cuthbert Cowston on two June Sundays saw a hundred dance through divine service with pipe and drum at his Normanby alehouse in Ryedale. Others danced with Laurence Hill at Pickering on a Midsummer day and with Will Ward at Middleton on St. Peter's day.

Dancing was more often in the open air than in doors. Nicholas Breton in "Court and Country" told of the lads and wenches meeting on holidays for dancing with a piper, on the green, in the market house, or around the maypole for the garland, with a kiss at every turn. Thomas Campion spoke of "skip and trip it, on the green, and help to choose the Summer Queen". There was dancing round Helmsley cross. Featherstone in his "Dialogue against light, lewd and lascivious dancing" of 1583 opposed May Day, Mid Summer and Saints day dances. On a Puritan view, "they dance with disordinate gestures, a monstrous thumping of the feet in flaming concupiscence with lust and sensuality". The note of disapproval is there in the alabaster in the Burton Agnes great hall which contrasts industrious ladies with burning lamps, and dancing ladies, with their lamps overturned. The rector of Moor Monkton was said to dance with lewd women, in his great bombasted breeches and ruffs.

Dancing could be done to voices with or without a piper. A ballad was a song to accompany a dance. Thomas Morley in 1597 spoke of "ballet or dance songs which being sung to a ditty, may likewise be danced". One kind was called "Fa La's". Morris dancing teams offered ritual performances of colourful disguise and dance. The male dancers vigorously moved, with rhythmic steps and stamps, through circles, patterns and processings to music, six or eight men wearing clogs, using handkerchiefs, sticks, and hand clapping to give a unique spectacle. The Yorkshire long sword dances saw six or eight men carrying rigid swords, fast walking figures, weaving the swords into a star shaped lock. The rhythm came from a small tabor or drum and the melody from a three hole pipe. Talk of the new dances, and of dance as the new art, suggests that things were becoming more sophisticated. The basse dance where the feet didn't leave the ground was given flourishes, hops and leaps. The haute dance had steps, hops, leaps, jumps, kicks and stamps. The measure was the changed basse, and a variety of fifteen or so dances included the Earl of Salisbury's pavan, the galliard, the coranto, and the allemande.

Ballads

Much popular music was written for dancing. Music printing had been invented at Venice using movable type. Queen Elizabeth granted a monopoly on music publishing early in her reign to two well-known court musicians. Ballad titles were registered with the Stationers' Company from c 1580. The "Broadside Ballads" of the reign were single sheets of wide paper, with or without the music, sold cheaply on street-corners. Over two hundred and fifty broadside ballads survive from before 1600. Where the music is missing, titles must be matched with surviving tunes. Many other ballads published in collections often called "garlands" were originally broadsides. There were nineteen titles for "Cuckolds, all in a row".

There were heroic songs, some about dirty deeds and some that were bawdy. Yorkshire ballads included one about Henry Lord Scrope leading Mashamshire men at the battle of Flodden in 1513. "From Ripon, Ripley and Ryedale, with them marched forth all Massamshire". A ballad written in 1577 has the title "A Brefe Balet, touching the traitorous taking of Scarborrow Castele," imprinted in London, in Flete Street, by Thomas Powell.". There were eight titles for the 1569 "rising of the north" and in 1590 a northern "Lady Greensleeves". One ballad concerns the Earl of Cumberland and his Armada ship the "Bonaventure". Another sang of "the felon sewe", a fierce sow once given to the friars of Richmond by Ralph Rokeby.

There was the "The murder of the two brothers Lewis and Edmund West by the sons of Lord Darcy, John and George." The ballad "Robin Hood turned fisherman" told of the outlaw taking ship as a fisherman, a task at which he failed, but he proved useful with his bow in securing a French treasure ship. He returned to Scarborough, endowed the widow innkeeper with the treasure and built a habitation for the oppressed." Others likely to belong to the shire and the period include "The nutbrown maide and Lord

Clifford", the ballad of the Ellands "the fragraunt flowers most freshe to viewe", "The Pindar of Wakefield" and "York, York for my monie".

The popular ballad "Phillada flouts me" tells of the good things of ordinary life, bags of shreds, crudded cream, whig and whey, bramble cherries, pie lids and crusty pastry, pears, and plums. Men make posies for girls while "wanton Winifred throws milk on his clothes" and another lass "tweaks his nose". Another ballad began "O, man refraine thie vile desyre". Something of the atmosphere can be found in songs sung to accompany the interlude "Ralph Roister Doister".[7]

> "whoso to marry a minion wife,
> hath had good chance and hap
> must love her and cherish her all his life
> and dendle her in his lap
> Roister doister is my name ,
> Roister doister is my name,
> a lusty brute I am the same,
> I must be married a Sunday "

The Alehouse

Alehouses, inns and taverns were the main indoor social centres for town and village alike, away from the family hearth. The alehouse was simply a house where ale was brewed and sold. A tippling house seems to be a. house where it was merely sold. Villages of thirty or forty houses had one or the other, usually run as a part time venture in an ordinary house, by the house wife. It seems likely that there was one public house for something less than every two hundred people. Even little Auburn near Bridlington had a common brewer, who broke the assize of ale in 1563. Bilsdale and Goathland recorded three alehouses each in 1615. A tavern was a house, part of which, sometimes merely a cellar, was used to sell wine. Taverns were confined to the towns. An inn could provide accommodation, food and drink for people and horses. As the largest English county, Yorkshire had more alehouses than any other, by a good measure, but Cornwall, Devon and Middlesex had more taverns.

The towns offered ample chances to make a living or supplement another living by opening an ale house. Occasionally we hear numbers. Beverley had sixty-two people fined for brewing without licence in 1573 and forty-five sold ale with bad measures the next year. In 1596 the council decreed that the town was to be limited to forty alehouses. Pickering hall mote court at an early date presented sixteen wives for selling with mugs and other vessels unsealed and two men who sold ale contrary to the assize. One was John Walker of Burgate, where a cruckhouse sold ale till quite recently and had traditions of gathering travellers for escort across the moors to Whitby. Bridlington in 1538 had twenty-four alehouses and five tipplers and the quay another eleven alehouses. Wakefield had twenty-nine brewsters in 1533 and Scarborough had at least twenty-nine alehouses by 1600. The Aldbrough and Borough bridge court in 1563 recorded two selling beer, and sixteen who brewed ale. The fluctuation in those brewing to sell suggests that market towns had a fringe of temporary alehouses.

Many village alehouses were linked with the manor that had once licensed them under the earlier "assize of bread and ale". Manor courts still appointed ale tasters to ensure that the ale being brewed was of good quality. Villages with several manors

378

commonly had the same number of alehouses, as at Hunmanby and Allerston. Some times it was the manor house or manor farm which became the alehouse, although this could happen at very different dates. Not until 1618 did North Riding justices order that bailiffs of manors and knight's retainers should be licenced. Separate jurisdictions could occur in a borough. A common brewer selling ale outside his house at Malton paid a fine to the Borough bailiff once a year, but brewers who were tenants of the knight's fee or the decayed priory paid no fine. The Deans of York licensed alehouses within their jurisdiction across the county.

Public houses once run or owned by the monasteries, hospitals and chantries had passed into lay hands. Some retained a memory of their past. The numbers seven and three, the cross keys, and a range of other symbols could record such associations in public house signs, but few are reliable and research is necessary in each case. The Little Angel at the entry to Flowergate at the town of Whitby contained ancient structure and the Cross Keys at Malton Wheelgate has a vaulted undercroft. The Whitby Abbot' s house at Goathland became a wayfarers' public house. The "Sign of the George" at Tadcaster, had belonged to the chantry of St. Nicholas. Many such links remain which are unproven.

Church and churchyard drinkings were forbidden. Parish Church alehouses had been common place and some were still managed by parish clergy. Archbishop Grindal in 1571 ordered them to stop. Enquiries were sent to churchwardens with the question – "whether doth the vicar or curate keep any alehouse, tippling house or tavern in his vicarage or dwelling house, or sell any ale, beer or wine". The vicar of Burton Fleming and the vicar of Kilham still kept victualling or alehouses in their vicarages. Rowland Sewell, the vicar of Brompton by Sawdon ran an alehouse. The complaint was not that he did so, but that he and two others at the village had no licence. Will Hallilande kept an alehouse in the Owthorne vicarage in Holderness with the vicar's permission in 1575. A curate at Skelton near York had an alehouse as late as 1613. There was a church alehouse in the vicarage at Whitkirk, an inn at Kettlewell, a brewing alehouse at Ilkley, and others at Darfield, Dewsbury, Kirkby Malhamdale and Adel. The vicar's brother living in Skipton vicarage sometimes brewed ale to sell to his friends.

An order made by the Privy Council required a return of the inns, taverns and alehouses in England in 1574-5, with a view to levying a tax for the repair of Dover harbour. This gave Yorkshire a total of 3941 of which 3679 were alehouses or tippling houses, 239 were inns and 23 were taverns. James Rither wrote to Lord Burghley complaining of growing numbers of York alehouses in 1599.

The alehouses attracted increasing official attention. A Statute of 1552 had required alehouse keepers to be bound by recognizances. This obliged the publican to be bound to a pound and to find two sureties bound for ten shillings each, to ensure the proper conduct of the house. No one was to keep an alehouse without the authority of two justices. The licences were free but had to be renewed annually and could be withdrawn from badly managed houses. Unlicensed alehouse keepers could be punished. It remained lawful to sell ale in booths or houses, at annual fairs without these formalities.

A Recognizance

> "The condicons of this recognizance is first that if all the aforesaid brewers
> and every of them from hensfurth do baik and brew good and wholesome bread
> and drink and sell the same according to the assize and that there be no playing

at carde, dice nor tables in ther houses but only in cristinmas. And they every of them keep two honest bedds for lodging of wayfaring man and have serving men of honest demeanour and that they lodge no vagabonds nor suffer in their houses any man servants nor other in the nights to abide and that they lodge none but such as they know to be of good demeanour and appointment."

T112 Yorkshire Public houses in each Wapentake. (possibly omitting some liberties)

East Riding		inns	taverns	alehouses
Between Ouse & Darwent		-	-	60
Howdenshire	-	-		60
Harthill & Beverley		5	1	268
Holderness & its liberties		-	-	152
Buckrose & Dickering		-	-	179
	Sum	5	1	719
North Riding				
Langbaurgh & Whitby Strand	-	-		126
Allertonshire		3	1	30
Birdforth		2	-	110
Bulmer		1	-	127
Ryedale		17	-	140
Pickering Lythe		-	2	146
Gilling east		3	-	27
Hang east		4	-	60
Gilling west		6	-	48
Hang west		7	-	68
Halikeld		2	-	38
Richmond & its liberties		22	2	22
	Sum	67	5	922(sic)
West Riding				
Barkestone		11	1	129
Osgoldcross & Stanecross		-	-	289
Strafforth & Tickhill fee		-	-	174
Agbrigg & Morley		38	2	600
Skyrack		13	1	192
Staincliff & Ewecross	-	-		254
Claro		18.	2	180
	Sum	80	6	1818
York & Ainsty		86	11	171
Hull and its county		1	-	55
Total		239	23	3674(sic)3679

The Privy Council exerted continued pressure on justices regarding numbers of alehouses and ale prices. Despite this, the North Riding justices in 1609 claimed that most brewster men were brewing without licence and selling ale and beer above four pence the gallon. West Riding men without licences taunted those who had them in 1611. The alehouse keepers sought long opening hours to make their living. Doncaster manor court issued a bylaw warning brewsters and tipplers to "keep no man in their houses after the hour of nine of the clock in the evening", with a 3s.4d fine for offenders. Thomas Smythe in 1580 was accused for allowing other men's servants and children to eat hens in his house in the night time and was fined a shilling.

Ale and beer were vital food but also the main social drink. The commonest social gathering was an "ale". An ale at Lockton in the 15th century saw householders contribute hens to a "mutual meeting" after Christmas where "all night be merry and make good cheer". That was a "scot ale", where the expenses were shared. Other gatherings to raise funds, were called bid ales, church warden ales, or clerk ales, tithe ales, and leet ales. There might be lamb ales at shearing, harvest ales, and Mayday, Easter, Whitsun, Mid Summer and Bride ales. A quart of ale for a penny was the going rate at the end of the reign and small ale was a halfpenny. It was widely believed that the English drank to excess. A new criticism of the practice emerged with the Puritan view that "lewd and idle people consumed money and time in alehouses in a lewd and idle manner".

The alehouse attracted almost every known activity, including much that was frowned on by authority. As talking shops, they were notorious. The Vicar of Muston in 1537 had remarked in the alehouse that the King would be driven from the realm. A Selby man and a Shipton woman were executed in 1576 for "uttering forged promissory notes of the value of fifty guineas" for innkeeper John Learoyd. The West Riding justices in 1598 ordered constables to make a weekly search of alehouses to stamp out dicing and carding and to maintain prices at a penny a quart. A Wetherby widow allowed unlawful games to be played all night and lost her licence. John Banester was discharged from keeping an ale or tipping house in 1589 at York after fiddlers made great disorder at twelve o clock in the night.

London knew heady ales and beers, known as "mad dog", "angel's food", "dragons milk," "go by the wall" and "stride wide". Old ale and new ale were suspect. Agnes Fox told a Rotherham beggar that "she had no other drink but new ale, which he would not drink being so aged a man". He called her an old witch. The standard measures were the potell, the quart, the pint, the gill and the third. Ale was sold from pitchers and jugs into cups, wood mazers, noggins, piggins, bowls and cans. Portable leather bottles went with the shepherd and to the harvest field. Alehouses had jacks, bombards and noggins, the last a small wood mug.

Pleasures of the Home

It is tempting to attribute the "busy fingers" tradition, which lasted among many women well into the twentieth century, to the Puritan movements that made work a virtue and eschewed idleness. They saw spinning on a distaff as saving a woman from being idle. However, the Catholic households where young women were raised in their youthful years learnt the same skills. Bess of Hardwick, Mary Queen of Scots and Lady Cholmeley were all needlewomen. A professional embroiderer drew patterns and filled in the dull bits for Mary. The needle was applied to a range of decorative arts including the freer stumpwork. The sampler was a tool for learning and a display of stitches.

Tobacco came to England from Virginia during the reign. Dealers were numerous by the 17th century as the addiction took hold. Clay and silver pipes were used to take in the smoke made by the burning weed. The Earl of Rutland received twelve tobacco pipes at five shillings in 1599 and paid twenty-five shillings for half a pound of tobacco in

1603. According to Harrison "In these days, the taking in of smoke of the indian herb called tobacco, by an instrument formed like a little ladle, whereby it passeth from the mouth into the head and stomach, is greatly taken up and used in England against rheums and some other diseases engendered in the lungs and inwards parts and not without effect".

Conversation is the universal pastime. We hear little of it, in the nature of the case. As Andrew Borde remarked, "there is nothing that doth comfort the heart so much as honest mirth and good company. A life without conversation is a poor life indeed". Emanuel Van Meteren in 1575, describing English married women said they "keep company with their equals whom they term gossips". Men's wills also mention their gossips. Rowland Scott of Bilsdale in 1558 left his "gossip", the bailiff Thomas Blackett, to be "minister unto" his six under age children and to put the lease of the farmhold to one whom he trusts would occupy it best". Bryan Egglesfield gave Sir Roger Lassells at Kilburn his green ginger spoon as "a poor token of friendship". Some women's wills suggest a network of friends. They made many small bequests to female kin and to others not kin.

Companionship might be extended to animals. George Neville of High Pepperwell in Batley in 1578 had a dog called "Companion"(46). Gentry visitors to Sir Thomas Hoby's household played cards and dice and talked of horses and dogs, every sentence beginning with a great oath. There were much drinking of healths and lascivious talk. Less elevated halls saw their conversation refuelled by a little "eaves dropping". In villages where houses stood open to the green and without a forestead, this was an acknowledged offence. There is nothing like inside knowledge. Acomb manor court presented Elizabeth Fowler in 1574. She had been under John Thackraye's window at night to hear his conversation. Three years later Elizabeth Bankes and in 1583 Agness Bessey listened to hear what was said and done to "carry tales and make debate".

T113 The Pattern of the Year

January.	New Year.	Bell Ringing, Gifts, First footing
	Twelfth Day Eve.	Wassailing, Lamb's wool.
	Twelfth Day.	King and Queen, Games, 12th Cake.
	Distaff day	Flax burning and sousing
	Plough Monday	Fond ploughs
February.	Candlemas.	Processions
	Valentines Day	
March.	MidLent Sunday	Mothers gifts
	Collop Monday,	Eat bacon slices
	ShroveTuesday	Ball game, Pancakes, Throwing at cocks
	Ash Wednesday,	
	Bloody Thursday	Eat black pudding
	Long Friday,	Eat buns
	Carling Sunday,	Eat steeped peas, butter fried
	Palm Sunday,	Carry in evergreens
	Maunday Thursday,	Charitable distributions
	Easter day,	Egg rolling, lifting games
	April Fool's day,	Mischief
	Hocktide,	Catching games
	St Mark's eve	

May	Mayday,	Bonfires, earl and queens dancing
	Rogation,	Perambulations
	Ascension,	Well dressing
	Whitsun,	Games, dancing, bowers made
June	MidSummer eve & Day,	Bonfires, dancing
August	Lammas,	First fruits given
	Harvest home,	Effigies, feast
	Michelmas,	Fairs, rent audits, eat frummity
September	Nutcrack night,	Nutting
October	All Hallows' eve,	Mischief
November	Martinmas,	Hirings, home visits, eat pudding
December	Twelve days of Christmas,	Good fires, evergreens, story telling, feasts, Thomasing, Stephening, (begging gifts for feasts), dances, games, Wassailing, carols, waits.

This was not the "merry england" once favoured by romantic imagination. But, they tried. William Elderton in his verse of 1584 entitled "York, Yorke for my Monie", claimed that the county town was comparable to the capital.

> And when to the cittie of Yorke I came
> I found good companie in the same
> As well disposed to every game
> As if I had been at London.

Samuel Rowlands in 1600 reflected the youthful exuberance of a society where most were young.

> Man, I dare challenge thee to throw the sledge,
> To jumpe, or leape over a ditch or hedge;
> To wrestle, play at stooleball, or to runne,
> To pitch the barre, or to shoot off a gunne;
> To play at loggets, nineholes, or ten pinnes
> To try it out, at football, by the shinnes,
> At ticktacke, Irish, Noddie, Maw and Ruffe;
> At hot-cockels, leape-frogge, or blindman-buffe.

Only the optimist would say that Elizabeth's reign had brought great benefits to the great body of English people. For most, they were hard times, at the start and hard times at the finish, the like of which most of us within the realm can only now strive to imagine. Staying cheerful and having fun has its place in any age. If we cannot quite reach a good sense of their daily life and what that offered, we can take a little heart from the ways they lightened their darknesses.

REFERENCES

YAJ   Yorkshire Archaeological Journal
YAS   Yorkshire Archaeological Society
BIHR   Borthwick Institute of Historical Research
NYCRO North Yorkshire County Records Office
DNB   Dictionary of National Biography
THAS   Transactions of Halifax Antiquarian Society
RCHM Royal Commission on Historical Manuscripts
BL   British Library
NH   Northern History
TERAS Transactions, East Riding Antiquarian Society

Introduction

1   W. Page (Ed). The Victoria History of the County of York. 1913. Vol.3, p415.
2   H.B. Wheatley & E.W. Ashbee (Ed). William Smith. The Particular Description of England 1588. 1879.
3   Description of Yorkshire. (BL Lansdowne MSS 116.9) BIHR Add MSS. 172.
4   E. Gibson (Ed). W. Camden, Britannia. 1586. 1695.
5   G. Manley (Ed). Climate and the British Scene. 1952.
     F.H. Lamb. The Changing Climate. 1966.
6   John Speed. Theatre of the Empire of Great Britain. 1611.
7   L.T. Smith (Ed). The Itinerary of John Leland. 1964.
8   W.J. Craig. James Ryther of Harewood and his letters to William Cecil, Lord Burghley. YAJ. Vol.56 1984, p97 & Vol 57. 1985, p125.

Chapter 1. Government

1   A.G.R. Smith. The Government of Elizabethan England. 1967.
2   R.R. Reid. The King's Council in the North. 1921.
3   The Council of the North, 1537-1637 Book of instructions, notes etc; BIHR
     F.W. Brooks. The Council of the North. 1953.
     The Fauconburg Book. NYCRO. ZDV(L), ZAG.
4   The Journals of the House of Commons.
5   R. Carroll. Yorkshire parliamentary boroughs in the 17th Century. NH Volume. 3 1968, p70.
6   J.E. Neale. The Elizabethan House of Commons. 1949, p74-87.
7   T. E. Hartley (Ed). Proceedings in the Parliaments of Elizabeth I. 1995.
8   Fairless Barber. West Riding Sessions Rolls. YAJ. Volume 5. 1881, p362.
9   William Lee & Daniel Pakeman. The order of keeping a court leet and court baron with the charges appertaining to the same. London 1650.

10	J.S. Cockburn. A History of English Assizes, 1558-1714. 1972.
11	Orders agreed upon by the Council of the North. YAS. Mss 508.
12	H.B. McCall. The Early History of Bedale. 1907, p16.
13	J.W Clay & J. Lister (Ed). The Autobiography of Sir John Saville of Methley, knight, 1547-1607. 2004 (DNB).
14	W.R. Shepherd. The History of Kirby Underdale. 1928.
15	Calendar of State Papers Domestic. 1547-80. p357.
16	S. Macauley. The Lennox Crisis, 1558-1563. NH Vol 41. 2004, p267.
17	G.B. Wood. Mary Stuart in Wensleydale. (In Country Life 22.3.1946).
18	James J. Cartwright. Chapters of the History of Yorkshire. 1872.
	Sir C Sharp. Memorials of the Rebellion of 1569. 1840.
	Miss R R Reid. The Rebellion of the Earls, 1569. Transactions of the Royal Historical Society. Vol 20. 1906.
	The Rising in the North. YAJ Vol 18, p74.
19	Alec Wright & John Mawer (Ed). Stokesley Selection. 1982.
20	John Nicholson. Beacons of East Yorkshire. 1887
21	The names of the Captains appointed by the Lord. Lieutenant for this county of Yorkshire with the numbers of men committed to them and the several places of their charge. YAS Mss 726a.

Chapter 2. High Society and Low

1	W.J. Craig. James Ryther of Harewood and his letters to William Cecil, Lord Burghley. parts 1 & 2. YAJ Volumes 56 & 57, 1984 & 1985.
2	Calendar of State Papers, Domestic, 1598-1601, p272.
3	Dictionary of National Biography.
	Calendar of State Papers, Domestic, Vols 1-6 and addenda, vols 7 and 12.1856-72.
	Acts of the Privy Council of England.
	Historical Mss Commission, Report on Mss. of the Duke of Rutland. Vol.4 1905.
	Historical Mss. Commission. Report on Mss in Various Collections. Vol.2. 1901, p14.
	Arthur Clifford. Collectanea Cliffordiana. 1817.
	D.J.H. Clifford. The Diaries of Lady Anne Clifford. 1990.
	Claire Cross. The Puritan Earl. The life of Henry Hastings Third Earl of Huntingdon, 1536-1595. 1967.
	A.G. Dickens. Clifford letters of the 16th Century. 1962.
	E. Barrington de Fonblanque. Annals of the House of Percy. 1887.
	M.E. James. Change and Continuity in the Tudor North. 1965
	M.E.James. A Tudor Magnate and the Tudor State. 1966.
	Rosamund Meredith. Arundell Castle Mss. 1965.
	C. B. Norcliffe (Ed). The Visitation of Yorkshire in the Years 1563 and 1564 made by William Flower. 1881.
4	T.E. Barker. The Eure Family. 1980 NYCRO Journal. Vol 7, p21.
5	J.Hitchcock. The Misconduct of Lord Latimer. 1977 YAJ. Vol.49, p97.
	Thomas Horsfall. The Manor of Well and Snape. 1912.
6	G.P. Batho. A Calendar of Talbot Papers. 1971.

J.T. Cliffe. The Yorkshire Gentry, from the Reformaton to the Civil War. 1969.

Sir Thomas Wilson. The State of England 1600. F.J.Fisher (Ed).

W. Mark Ormrod. The Lord Lieutenants and High Sheriffs of Yorkshire 1066-2000. 2000.

J.W. Clay (Ed). Dugdale's Visitation of Yorkshire, 3 Vols. 1899-1917.

Sir William Dugdale. The Visitation of Yorkshire, 1665-6. 1859.

Thomas Fuller. The History of the Worthies of England (Ed. P.A. Nuttall). 1840.

A. Browning (Ed). The Memoirs of Sir John Reresby. 1936.

The Memoirs of Sir Hugh Cholmley. 1787.

R.W Hoyle. The Fortunes of the Tempest family of Bracewell and Bowling in the 16th century 2002. YAJ. Vol 74, p169.

C.H.D. Howards. Sir John Yorke of Nidderdale, 1563-1634. 1939.

J. Kaner. The Vavasours of Copmanthorpe and the Court of Elizabeth I. YAJ Vol 72. 2000, p107.

D.M. Meads (Ed). The Diary of Lady Margaret Hoby, 1599-1605. 1930.

R.T. Spence. Londesborough House and its Community, 1590-1643. 2005.

HE Chetwynd-Stapleton. The Stapletons of Yorkshire. YAJ. Vol 8. 1897.

7   Joseph Foster (Ed). Robert Glover. The Visitation of Yorkshire in 1584-5 and 1612. 1875.

8   A Set of Elizabethan Heraldic Roundels in the British Museum. R. Griffin & M. Stephenson. Archaeologia. Vol 70. 1918-20.

9   The Arundel Castle Mss. Hull University. DDEV(2) 68/118.

George Constable. A Book touching the Order and Government of a Nobleman's Household. 1608.

10   John Strype. Annals of the Reformation and Establishment of Religion. 1821 edition.

Chapter 3. Religion

1   A.G. Dickens. Lollards and Protestants in the Diocese of York. 1982.

2   C. Cross. The End of Medieval Monasticism in the East Riding of Yorkshire. 1993.

C. Cross & N.Vickers. Monks,Friars and Nuns in 16th century Yorkshire. 1993.

3   W.Page (Ed). Victoria County History, Yorkshire. Volume 3, p154.

4   A.G . Dickens. The English Reformation. 1964.

D.M. Palliser. The Reformation in York 1534-1553. 1971.

5   J.Purvis. The churchwardens' Book of Sheriff Hutton 1524-68. YAJ Vol.36. 1945, p178.

C.C. Webb (Ed). The Churchwardens' Accounts of St Michael, Spurriergate York. 1518-1548. 1997.

J.S. Purvis. Tudor Parish documents of the Diocese of York. 1948.

6   A.G. Dickens. A municipal dissolution of chantries at York 1536. YAJ. Vol 36. 1944, p164.

J.T. Rosenthal. Yorkshire Chantry Certificates of 1546. An Analysis. NH Vol 9. 1974.

W. Page (Ed). Yorkshire Chantry Surveys. 1892-94.

C.J. Kitching. The Chantries of the East Riding of Yorkshire at the Dissolution in 1548. YAJ.Vol. 44. 1972, p178.

7   A.G. Dickens. The Marian Reaction in the Diocese of York. 1957.

        A.G. Dickens. Robert Holgate. Archbishop of York. 1955.

8   J.S. Purvis. The Condition of Yorkshire Church Fabrics, 1300-1800.

9   W.J. Sheils (Ed). Archbishop Grindal's Visitation of the Diocese of York, 1575. 1977.

10   A.G. Dickens. The first stages of Roman Recusancy in Yorkshire, 1560-1590 . YAJ. Vol.35. 1941, p157.

11   John Strype. The History of the Life and Acts of the Most Reverend Father in God Edmund Grindal. 1710 edition.

        P. Collinson. Archbishop Grindal, 1519-1583. 1979.

12   James J. Cartwright. Chapters of the History of Yorkshire. 1872.

13   H.Holroyde. Protestantism and Dissent in the Parish of Halifax, 1509-1640. THAS. 1989.

14   R. Marchant. The Puritans and the Church Courts in the Diocese of York, 1560-1642. 1960.

        W. Haller. Foxe's Book of Martyrs and the Elect Nation. 1963.

15   A.G. Dickens. The extent and Character of Recusancy in Yorkshire, 1604. YAJ.Vol.37. 1948, p24.

        J.H. Aveling. Catholic Households in Yorkshire, 1580-1603. NH. Vol 16. 1980, p85.

16   C.J. Cox. Superstition in the Yorkshire Monasteries. TERAS. Vol 1. p73, 1893.

        P. Tyler. The Church Courts at York and Witchcraft Prosecutions. NH 1969, p84.

        E. Peacock. A List of the Roman Catholics in the Diocesese of York in 1604. 1872.

        M.Gibson (Ed). Witchcraft and Society in England and America, 1550-1750. 2003.

        P. Crowther. Witchcraft in Yorkshire. 1973.

        R.A. Marchant. The Church Under the Law. 1969.

        J.A. Sharpe Witchcraft in 17th century Yorkshire. 1992.

Chapter 4. Elizabethan People

1   M. Campbell. The English Yeoman. 1942.

        A.H. Dodd. Life in Elizabethan England. 1961.

        G. Edelen (Ed). The Description of England by William Harrison, 1587. 1968.

        J. Guy .Tudor England. 1990.

        D. Hey. A History of Yorkshire. 2005.

        G. Lawton. Collections Relative to Churches and Chapels within the Diocese of York. 1840.

        C.C. Fenwick (Ed). The Poll Taxes of 1377, 1379 and 1381. Part 3. Wiltshire – Yorkshire. 2005.

        A.L. Rowse. The England of Elizabeth; the Structure of Society. 1950.

        L.Stone. The Family, sex and marriage in England, 1500-1800. 1977.

        K.Wrightson. English Society 1580-1680. 1982.

2   Personal papers, Mss notebooks, Richard Blakeborough, 1875-1898, NYRCO. ZVI/2.

3   Elizabeth Burton. The Elizabethans at Home. p235. 1958.

4   Cause Papers. B.I.H.R.

5   William Camden. Remains Concerning Britain. 1674. (John Philipot, Ed). 1870.

6   Henry Best. The farming and memorandum books of Henry Best of Elmswell. 1642. (Donald Woodward. Ed) 1984.

7   The first and second prayer books of Edward VI. Everyman edition. 1949.

8   Gervase Markham. The English Housewife 1615. (Ed Michael Best). 1986.

9   Sir Anthony Fitzherbert. The Book of Husbandry 1534. (Ed W.W. Skeat 1882).

10   Elizabethan Life, Morals and the Church Courts. F.G.Emmison. 1973.

11   Norman Sunderland. Tudor Darlington. 1974.

12   J. Chapman (Ed). Scarborough Records. 3 vols. 1909.Vol. iii. p16.
         Angelo Raine (Ed). York Civic Records. 1939.

13   The Diary of Abraham de la Pryme. (Ed C. Jackson). 1870.

14   R.B. Turton. Henry Jenkins. Y.A.J.Vol.26. 1922, p374.

15   Eileen White. Elizabethan York. 1999.

16   D.M. Palliser. The Age of Elizabeth, 1547-1603. 1983, p35-69.

17   Donald Woodward. Life in Tudor and Stuart England. 1995.
         Angelo Raine (Ed). York Civic Records, Vol VIII. 1953.

18   P.R. Hawkridge & A.Whitlock. Studies in Local History No 4. Aspects of Poverty in Rotherham.

19   W.K. Jordan. The Charities of Rural England, 1480-1660. 1961.

20   A Yorkshire Chapel. G.B. Wood (Country Life 13.2.1964)

Chapter 5. Farming

K.J. Allison. The East Riding of Yorkshire Landscape. 1976.

M.W. Barley. Manorial Bye-laws in East Yorkshire. YAJ. Vol 35. 1890, p35.

W.C. Boulter. Court rolls of Some East Riding Manors, 1563-1573. YAJ. Vol 10, p407. 1938.

K.M. Bumstead. Wills & Inventories in the Bedale area of North Yorkshire. YAJ. Vol.57, p163. 1985.

E.K. Berry (Ed). Swaledale Wills and Inventories. 1998.

Sir Anthony Fitzherbert. The Book of Husbandry 1534. (Ed W.W. Skeat. 1882).

W. Grainge. Vale of Mowbray. 1859.

F. Peel. The Spen Valley. 1983.

H. Speight. Upper Wharfedale. 1900.

E. Bogg. Lower Wharfedale. 1904.

T. Gill. Vallis Eboracensis. 1852.

J.H. Rushton. The History of Ryedale. 2003.

R.B. Turton (Ed). The Honor and Forest of Pickering. Vols 1-4. 1894-97.

G.C. Cowling. A History of Easingwold and the Forest of Galtres. 1965.

A.P. Harris. The Agriculture of the East Rding of Yorkshire Before the Parliamentary Enclosures. YAJ. Vol. 40. 1962, p19.

D. Holland. Changing Landscapes in South Yorkshire. 1980.

R.W. Hoyle. The cattle herds and sheep flocks of the Earls of Cumberland in the 1560's. YAJ. Vol. 73. 2001, p75.

R.B. Smith. Land and Politics in the England of Henry VIII, the West Riding of Yorkshire. 1970

D.M. Palliser. Tudor York. 1980.

M. Pickles & J. Bosworth. Farmhold structure in a district of piecemeal enclosure; the Manor of Askwith from 1596-1816. YAJ.Vol. 63. 1991, p109.

J.S. Purvis. A note on 16th century farming in Yorkshire. 1947. YAJ. Vol. 26. 1947.

G. Redmonds. The Heirs of Woodsome. 1982.

Joan Thirsk (Ed). The Agrarian History of England and Wales. 1967.

1   W.W. Skeat (Ed). The Book of Husbandry of Master Fitzherbert, 1534. 1882.

2   H. King & A. Harris (Ed). A Survey of the Manor of Settrington. 1962.

3   Joan Thirsk. Farming Techniques in The Agrarian History of England and Wales. 1500-1640. Vol. 4, p171.

4   Jennifer Kaner (Ed). Goods and Chattels, 1552-1642. Wills, farm and household inventories from the Parish of South Cave in the East Riding of Yorkshire. 1994.

5   J.C. Drummond and Anne Wilbraham (Ed). The Englishman's Food. 1991, p19.

6   K.J. Allison. Enclosure by agreement at Healaugh.

7   Sir J.D. Legard. The Legards of Anlaby and Ganton. 1926.

8   William Brown , Description of the buildings of twelve small Yorkshire priories at the Reformation. YAJ. Vol 9. 1886, p197.

9   Alice McDonald. The Fortunes of a Family. 1928.

10   Diane Hughes. A study of Rosedale from mid 17th century to mid 18th.century. 1989.

11   A survey taken at Cracowe the 4th of October 1586. Transcribed by Kate Mason in 1989. YAS. (DD/121131/10).

12   T.T. Empsall. Woodsome Hall, Huddersfield. Old Yorkshire, 1890, p99 and Old Yorkshire.Vol. 1 New Series, p165-173.

13   David Hey. The Making of South Yorkshire. 1979, p31.

14   Five Hundred Points of Good Husbandry by Thomas Tusser. (Ed W. Payne and S. J. Heritage). 1878.

15   Henry Best. The farming and memorandum books of Henry Best. 1642.

16   John Philipot (Ed). William Camden. Remains Concerning Britain. 1674.

17   The Arundel Castle MSS. Hull University. DDEV (2). 68/118.

18   Joan Thirsk. The Farming Regions of England (in The Agrarian History of England and Wales. 1500-1640. Vol. 4, p28-40).

    C.V. Collier. Stovins manuscript. TERAS 1906. Vol 8, p197.

18   F.J. Fisher (Ed). The State of England by Thomas Wilson A.D. 1600. 1936.

19   Angelo Raine (Ed).York Civic Records Vol.6, p59.

20   Tudor Royal Proclamations Vol 11, The Later Tudors 1588-1603. (Ed. P.L. Hughes and J.F. Larkin) 1964.

Chapter 6. Industry

J. Blair & M. Ramsey. English Mediaeval Industries. 2001.
J.T. Cliffe. The Yorkshire Gentry, from the Reformation to the Civil War. 1969.
David Crossley. Post Medieval Archaeology in Britain. 1990.
1   Angelo Raine (Ed).York Civic Records .Volume 8, p9. 1953.
2   Statutes of the Realm, 6 Henry VIII. c 4. 1515.
3   Angelo Raine (Ed). York Civic Records.Volume 8, p61. 1953.
4   F.C. Margetts. Records of the York Cordwainers company from c 1395. 1983.
5   Index of Wills in the York Registry. YAS. Record Series. Vols. 14, 19.22 & 24.
6   W. Lee. A History of York made Silver. (Annual Report Yorkshire Philosophical Society. 1965).
7   Ann Bennett. The Goldsmiths of Church Lane Hull, 1527-1784. 1988. YAJ Vol 60, p113.
8   Jane Holdsworth. The Archaeology of York. The Pottery. 1978.
9   B.G. Drummond. Pottery from Rievaulx Abbey. YAJ. Vol.60, p31. 1988.
       R.H. Hayes. Post Medieval pottery at Grimstone manor farm near Gilling. 1978.
10   Jane Hatcher. The Industrial Archaeology of Yorkshire. 1985.
11   K.J. Allison. East Riding Water Mills. 1970, p10.
12   L.F. Salzman. English Industries of the Middle Ages. 1970.
13   David Hey. The Making of South Yorkshire. 1979, p61.
14   Howard Smith. The Saltway Trail. Woodhead to Rotherham. 1979.
15   J.U. Nef .The Rise of the British Coal Industry. 1932.
       G.D.B. Gray. The South Yorkshire Coalfield. (Studies in the Yorkshire Coal Industry. J Benson & R G Neville Ed 1976).
       L. Sterne. An Elizabethan Coalmine (Economic History Review 2nd series Vol.3 1950-51, p97-106).
       J. Uster. Coal Mining in Halifax. (In Old Yorkshire 1885. p269).
16   G.H. Kenyon. The Glass Industry of the Weald. 1967.
17   D.W. Crossley & F.A. Aberg .16th century glass making in Yorkshire: excavations at furnaces at Hutton and Rosedale, NR 1968-1971. (In Post Mediaeval Archaeology. Vol. 6. 1972).
18   H. Murray. The Heraldic Window at Fountains Hall. YAJ. 62 1990, p71.
19   I. Miller. Steeped in History. 2002.
       D. Pybus & J. Rushton. Alum. (In The Yorkshire Coast. Ed. D.B. Lewis 1991).
       R.B. Turton. The Alum Farm. 1938.
20   David Crossley and Denis Ashurst. Excavations at Rockley Smithies, a water powered bloomery of the 16th and 17th centuries. (In Post Mediaeval Archaeology in Britain. David Crossley. 1990).
       R. Spence. Mining and Smelting in Yorkshire by the Cliffords, Earls of Cumberland in the Tudor and early Stuart period. YAJ. Vol 64, p157) 1992.
       C. Collinson. Enterprise and experiment in the Elizabethan iron industry, the career of Thomas Proctor. 1996 YAJ. Vol 68, p191.
       H.R. Schubert. History of the British Iron & Steel Industry. 1957.

21   R.T. Clough. The Lead Smelting Mills of the Yorkshire Dales. 1962.
       A. Raistrick and B. Jennings. A History of Lead Mining in the Pennines. 1965.
       R. Fieldhouse & B. Jennings. A History of Richmond and Swaledale. 1978.
22   D. Hey. The South Yorkshire Steel Industry and the Industrial Revolution.
23   C.R. Norcliffe. The Pawson Inventory and Pedigree. Kirkgate, Leeds. (in
       Thoresby Society, Vol 4).

Chapter 7. Trade

Henry Best. Rural Economy in Yorkshire in 1641. (Ed. C.B. Robinson. 1857).
Fernand Braudel.The Wheels of Commerce. (Civilisation and Capitalism
Volume II. 1979). Translated by Sian Reynolds. 1983.
W. Cunningham. The Growth of English Industry and Commerce in Modern
Times. 1919.
B. Dietz. The north-eastern coal trade, 1550-1750 1986. NH. Vol 22. 1986,
p280.
Alan Everitt. The Marketing of Agricultural Produce. (in the Agrarian History
of England and Wales. Volume IV. Ed. Joan Thirsk. 1967, p466-589).
N.S.B. Gras.The Evolution of the English Corn Market. 1926.
D. Hey. The Making of SouthYorkshire. 1979.
K.L. McCutcheon. Yorkshire Fairs and Markets. 1940.
D.M. Palliser. The Age of Elizabeth 1547-1603. 1992.
D.M. Palliser. Tudor York. 1979
D.M. Palliser. A Hostile View of ElizabethanYork. (In York Historian Vol 1.
1976).
L.F. Salzman. English Trade in the Middle Ages. 1931.
R.H. Tawney & E. Power. Tudor Economic Documents. 1924.
T.S. Willan. The English Coasting Trade. 1938.
T. Willan. The Early History of the Russia Company, 1553-1603. 1956.

1   J.T. Fowler (Ed). The Account Book of William Wray. (In The Antiquary
       xxxii, 1896.
2   N. Sunderland. Tudor Darlington. Part I. 1974.
3   Gerard Malynes. Lex Mercatoria c1622.

Chapter 8. Transport

W. Camden. Britannia, 1586. 1806
John Earle. Some Remarks on the Early Use of Carriages in England, 1628. (In
Archaeologia.Volume 20. Part 1. 1823).
Peter Edwards. The Horse Trade of Tudor and Stuart England. 1981.
Jane Hatcher. The Industrial Architecture of Yorkshire. 1985.
W.B. Rye. England as seen by Foreigners in the days of Elizabeth & James the
First. 1865.
John Stowe. A Survey of London. 1598.
1   Henry Bellassis. An English Traveller's First Curiosity. 1657.
2   Robert Dawson. Yorkshire Romanies. 1996.
3   D. Hey. The Making of South Yorkshire. 1979.

4   Acts of the Privy Council. 1562.
    A. Raine (Ed). York Civic Records. Volume 8. 1953

Chapter 9. Maritime Yorkshire

Calendar of State Papers Domestic. 1547- 80 &1581-90.
Acts of the Privy Council of England.
R. Davis. The Trade & Shipping of Hull, 1500-1700. 1964.
G de Boer. The History of the Spurn Lighthouse. 1968.
B.F. Duckham. The Yorkshire Ouse. 1967.
Robert Fisher. Flamborough village and headland. 1894.
M. Johnson. The mediaeval & post mediaeval port of Filey. 1998. YAJ.Vol.70,
p73
H.E. Maddock. Court Rolls of Patrington Manors. TERAS Vol 8. 1900.
James McDermott. Martin Frobisher, Elizabethan Privateer. 2001.
J.S. Purvis. The Records of the Admiralty Court of York. 1962.
M. Sellers (Ed). York Mercers & Merchant Adventurers 1356-1917. 1928.
T. Sheppard. Early Yorkshire History in plan and chart. 1912. TERAS Vol 19.
T. Sheppard. The Lost Towns of the Yorkshire Coast. 1912.
T.S Willan. The English Coasting Trade. 1938
H. Gee. Yorkshire and the Spanish Armada.

1   John Dee .The petty naval royal, 1577. (in Social England. Ed A Lang. 1903).
2   I. Friel. Maritime History of Britain and Ireland. 2003, p99.
3   A. Raine (Ed). York Civic Records.Vols 6 and 7.
4   Mrs Gutch (Ed). County Folk Lore. North Riding. 1901.
5   Raphael Holinshed. Chronicles of England, Scotland and Ireland. 1587.
6   Mrs. Gutch (Ed) County Folk Lore. North Riding. 1901.
7   Thomas Richmond. Local Records of Stockton and neighbourhood. 1868, p20.
8   J.E. Hobson. A Sketch of Hornsea. 1974.
9   J.E. Purvis. Bridlington Court Rolls and Papers. 1926.
10   J. Binns. The History of Scarborough. 2001, p54.
11   E. Gillette & K. MacMahon. History of Hull. 1980.
12   Paul Hughes. Staiths, the early river jetties of York, Hull and Howden. YAJ.
    71. 1999, p155.
13   T. Hinderwell. History of Scarborough. Extra Illustrated Edition. p242.
14   A. Storey. The Trinity House of Kingston upon Hull. 1967.

Chapter 10. Town Life

K.J. Allison. Victoria History of the County of York. East Riding. 1969.
A.H. Smith. English Place Names of the West Riding of Yorkshire. 8 Vols
1961-3.
J.B. Baker. The History of Scarborough. 1882.
R Barker. Whitby. 2007.
Beverley Borough Records. 1575-1821. 1932.
J. Bilson. Howden the manor house of the Bishops of Durham. 1913. YAJ
Vol.22, p256.
J Binns. The History of Scarborough. 2003.

B. Boothroyd. The History of Pontefract. 1807.

J.R. Boyle. The Early History of the Town and Port of Hedon. 1895.

L. Charlton. The History of Whitby. 1779.

J.W. Clay. North Country Wills. 2 Vols. 1908-12.

T.P. Cooper. Medieval Highways, Streets, Open ditches & Sanitary conditions of the City of York. 1913.YAJ. Vol.22, p270.

J. Crabtree. A concise history of the parish & vicarage of Halifax. 1836.

W.B. Crump. Huddersfield Highways Down the ages. 1949.

F. Drake. Eboracum. 1736.

W. Easthead. Historia Rievallensis. 1824.

Barbara English & Vanessa Neave (Eds). Tudor Beverley. 1973.

R. Fieldhouse & B. Jennings. A History of Richmond and Swaledale. 1978.

E. Gillett and K.A. MacMahon. A History of Hull. 1980.

E.A.H. Haigh (Ed). Huddersfield. 1992

John Harrison. Survey of the Manor of Sheffield. 1637.

S. Harrison. The History of Hornsea. 2005.

W. Harrison. Ripon Millenary Record. 1892.

Jane Hatcher. The History of Richmond. 2000.

D. Hey. The Making of South Yorkshire. 1979.

T. Hinderwell. The History and Antiquities of Scarborough. 1811.

D. Holland. Bawtry and the Idle River Trade. 1964.

W.G. Hoskins. English Provincial Towns in the early 16th century. (Transactions Royal Historical Society. Vol 6. 1956).

N.A. Huddleston. History of Malton and Norton. 1962.

J. Hunter. South Yorkshire: the History and Topography of the Deanery of Doncaster, 2 vols. 1828-31.

J. Hunter. Hallamshire. 1819.

S. Inwood. A History of London. 1998.

J. James. History and Topography of Bradford. 1841.

Joan W. Kirby (Ed) The Manor and Borough of Leeds. 1425-1662 an edition of documents. 1983. (Thoresby Society).

M. Jones (Ed). Aspects of Rotherham. Vol 2. 1996.

A.F. Leach. Beverley Town Documents. 1900.

R.E. Leader. Records of the Burgery of Sheffield. 1897.

J. McDonnell (Ed). A History of Helmsley, Rievaulx and District. 1963.

P. Nuttgens (Ed). The History of York. 2001.

D. Palliser. Tudor York. 1980.

W. Page (Ed). Victoria History of the County of York, North Riding. 2 vols. 1914-23.

D.M. Palliser. A Hostile view of Elizabethan York. 1976. (York Historian Vol 1).

G. Poulson. Beverlac. 1829.

G. Poulson. The History and Antiquities of the Seignory of Holderness. 1840-41

A. Raine. Mediaeval York. 1955.

J. Raine. Testamenta Eboracensia. 6 vols. 1836-1902.

M. Riordan. The History of Northallerton. 2002.

A. Rowntree. A History of Scarborough. 1931.

Patricia Scott. The History of Selby. 2005.

M. Sellers & J.Percy. York Memorandum Book. 1912-73.

Sheffield Museum. Sheffield in Tudor and Stuart Times.

A. Stacpoole (Ed). The Noble City of York. 1972.

J.A. Stow. A Survey of London 1603. (Ed. C.L. Kingsford. 1908).

C.H. Theobald. Extracts from a Doncaster Court Roll of the 16th century. YAJ. Vol 35, p288.

J. Tickell. The History of Kingston Upon Hull. 1798.

P.M. Tillott. Victoria History of the City of York. 1961

T.S. Turner. The History of Aldborough and Boroughbridge. 1853.

J.W. Walker. The Burgess Court, Wakefield. (In Misc 1).

G. Young. A History of Whitby. 1817.

Chapter 11. Education

J. Addy. Pennistone Grammar School, 1392-1700. YAJ. Vol 39, p508.

C.B.L. Barr. York Minster Library. 1980.

J.W. Clay & J. Lister (Ed). Autobiography of Baron Saville. YAJ. Vol 15. p420. 1899.

A.G. Dickens. The Writers of Tudor Yorkshire. 1963. (Transactions of the Royal Historical Society, 5th series, XIII).

A.G. Dickens. Wilfrid Holme of Huntington, Yorkshire's first protestant poet. 1958. YAJ Vol 39. 1956-8, p119.

A.G. Dickens (Ed). Tudor Treatises. 1959.

Dictionary of National Biography.

J.T. Fowler. Ripon Minster Library and its founders. YAJ. Vol 2. 1871-2, p371.

F.R. Johnson. Astronomical thought in Renaissance England. 1937.

J. Lawson. Primary Education in East Yorkshire, 1560-1902. 1959.

J. Lawson. The Endowed Grammar Schools of East Yorkshire. 1962.

A.F. Leach. Early Yorkshire Schools. 2 Vols. 1899-1903.

A.F. Leach. English schools at the Reformation, 1546-8. 1896.

W. Page (Ed). Certificates of the Commissioners appointed to survey the Chantries, etc. in the county of York. 2 Vols. 1894-5.

J.S. Purvis. Educational Records. 1959.

T. Stapleton (Ed). Plumpton Correspondence. 1839.

D.J. Struik. A Concise History of Mathematics. 1965.

H.A.C. Sturgess. Register of Admissions to the Honourable Society of the Middle Temple. 1949.

D.W. Sylvester. Educational Documents, 800-1816. 1970.

W.E. Tate. A.F. Leach as a historian of Yorkshire Education. 1963.

P.J. Wallis and W.E. Tate. A Register of old Yorkshire Grammar Schools. 1956.

Chapter 12. House and Home

M. Airs. The Tudor and Jacobean Country House. 1995.

L. Ambler. The old halls and manor houses of Yorkshire. 1913.

M. Barley. Rural Housing in England. (in The Agrarian History of England and Wales. (J Thirsk Ed) 1500-1640. 1967.

J.J. Cartwright. Inventory of goods of Sir Cotton Gargrave of Nostell in 1588. YAJ. Vol 11. 1891, p279

S.Cooper. Tudor Will Makers of Rotherham. (In Aspects of Rotherham Vol.2 1996).

M. Girouard. Robert Smythson and the Architecture of the Elizabethan Era. 1966.

D. Hey. Buildings of Britain 1550-1750. Yorkshire. 1981

B. Hutton. Timber Framed houses in the Vale of York. (In Mediaeval Archaeology. Vol 17 1973).

C. Platt. TheGreat Rebuildings of Tudor and Stuart England. 1994.

W. Wheater. Some Historic Mansions of Yorkshire. 1888.

1   York. Historic Buildings in the Central area. RCHM 1981. p 12.

2   B. Harrison. & B. Hutton. Vernacular Houses in North Yorkshire and Cleveland. 1984.

3   J. Addy. The Evolution of the English House. p51-2.

4   I.E. Ripley. The Changing Face of Kildale. 1985.

5   G. Richardson. The Emmanuel Hospital Estate Brandesburton, 1600-1919 (in East Yorkshire Historian Vol. 3. 2002).

6   Peter F. Ryder. Ravensworth Castle. YAJ. 51 1979, p83.

7   Mss. of Mrs Harford of Holme Hall, York. RCHM. p348.

8   J.W. Walker. Wakefield, Vol.2. p410. 1933.

9   N. Pevsner. The Buildings of Yorkshire, the North Riding 1966, York and the East Riding, 1972.

10   W.E. Preston. A 16th century account roll of the building of a house at Chevet. YAJ. Vol.32, p326.

11   J.T. Cliffe. The Yorkshire Gentry, from the Reformation to the Civil War 1969. p107.

12   H.E.C. Stapleton. The Stapletons of Yorkshire. YAJ. Vol 8. 1884, p416.

13   J. Binns. The Memoirs and Memorials of Sir Hugh Cholmley of Whitby 1600 – 1657. 2000.

14   J. Foster (Ed). The Visitation of Yorkshire in 1584-5 and 1612. 1875, p477 & 441.

15   Yorkshire Weekly Post. 28.5. 1898.

16   J. Croft (Ed). York Churchwardens' accounts. St Michael Spurriergate. 1600. Excerpta Antiqua, p20. 1797.

17   William Marshall. Rural Economy of Yorkshire. 1788, p309.

18   J. Kaner (Ed). Goods and Chattels, 1552-1642. Wills, farm and household inventories from the Parish of South Cave in the East Riding of Yorkshire. 1994.

19   Dr. E. Auerbach & E. K. Waterhouse. Tudor Artists. Painting in Britain 530-1790. 1953.

20   K.M. Bumstead. Wills and Inventories in the Bedale area of North Yorkshire. YAJ. 57. 1985, p163.

21   J. Miller. Winestead and its Lords. 1932.

22   M. Ayrton. The Bed. 1946, p40.

J. Purvis. Bridlington Charters, Court Rolls and Papers. 1926.

P.F. Ryder. Timber Framed Buildings in South Yorkshire. 1979.

Chapter 13. Food.

1 J.W. Ord. History of Cleveland. 1846.
2 The Arundel castle MS. Hull University Archives DDEV(2) 68/118.
3 W. Lawson. The Country Housewife's Garden. 1617.
   The Northumberland Household Book (Ed. Bishop Percy). 1905.
   P. Brears. Traditional Food in Yorkshire. 1987.
   R.V. Trench. Nineteen Centuries of Drink in England. 1884.
   Report on Manuscripts in Various Collections. RCHM Vol.11. Mss of Sir
   George Wombwell. (Fairfax Family Papers) 1901-14.
   K.M. Longley. Ecclesiastical Tithe Cause papers at York.
   Eileen White. Feeding a City, York. 2000.

Chapter 14. Health

   W. Munck. Roll of the Royal College of Physicians. 1878.
   D.M. Palliser. Epidemics in Tudor York. NH. 1973.
   J.H. Rasch. A Directory of English Country Physicians. 1962.
1 Elizabeth Burton. The Elizabethans at Home. 1958, p165.
2 D.M. Meads (Ed). The Diary of Lady Margaret Hoby. 1930.
3 Charles Jackson (Ed). The Autobiography of Mrs Alice Thornton of East
   Newton. 1875.
4 B.L.Beer. Tudor England Observed. 1998, p49.
5 R P. Hastings. More Essays in North Riding History. (NYCRO).
6 S.J. Chadwick. Some papers relating to the plague in Yorkshire. YAJ. Vol 15,
   p434.
7 A.L. Rowse. The Elizabethan Renaissance. 1971, p287.
8 O.L. Dick. John Aubrey's Brief Lives. 1949.
9 W.R. Le Fanuy. (Medical History Vol 5 No 2. April 1961).
10 The Arcana Fairfaxiana Mss. (In Mrs Gutch. County Folk Lore. Vol 2, p169).
11 E.I. Burton. The Royal Forest of the Peak. 1966.
12 Phyllis Hembry. The English Spa, 1560-1815. 1990.

Chapter 15. Leisure

   Shakespeare's England. 1917. (Clarendon Press. Oxford).
   T. Fuller. The History of the Worthies of England. 1811.
   R.E. Pritchard (Ed). Shakespeare's England. 2003.
   A. Sim. Food and Feast in Tudor England. 1997.
   A.F. Scott. Every One a Witness. The Tudor Age. 1975.
   K. Wrightson. English Society, 1580-1680. 1982.
   J. Graves. The History of Cleveland. 1808.
1 J.W. Ord. The History and Antiquities of Cleveland. 1846.
2 W. Bray. Account of the Lottery of 1567. 1569.
3 A. Lang. Social England Illustrated. 1903.
4 J. Bilson. St Mary's church, Beverley.YAJ.Vol. 25. p359. 1920.
5 R.W. Johnson. Noah at Hull .(In Dalesman May 1963).
   E. Brunskill. The York Mystery Plays. 1963.
   J.S. Purvis. The York Cycle of Mystery Plays. 1957.

A. Raine (Ed). York Civic Records Vol VII & Vol. VIII. 1953.

G.W. Boddy. Players of Interludes in North Yorkshire in the early 19th century. 1976.

6   R.C. Hope. "Notes on the musical instruments on the labels of the arches in the nave of Beverley Minster." TERAS. 1985.

7   G.E.& K.R. Russell. The English Countrywoman. 1981.

S.J.D. Ingledew. The Ballads and Songs of Yorkshire. 1860.

INDEX

Justices of the Peace 8, 9, 10, 40, 201

Katherine Howard, Queen 287
Kaye, John 82, 123, 184,
Kaye, Robert 293
Keldholme 98
Kelholme Priory 322
Kelk, Christopher 71
Kellington 81
Kendall, Robert 96
Kendall, William 101, 276
Kenyon, Richard 219
Kepwick 138
Keswick 16
Kettlewell, Christopher 205
Kexby 107
Keyingham 145
Kiddall 107
Kildale 317
Kilham 106, 134, 157, 206
Kilns 168
Kilnsea 260
Kilnwick Percy 45, 113
king's highways 223
King's Manor, York 3, 321
Kingthorpe 104
Kirby Misperton 28
Kirby Ravensworth 303
Kirby Underdale 220
Kirby Wiske 1
Kirby, William 81
Kirk Burton 349
Kirk Heaton 123
Kirk, Robert 118
Kirkburn 157
Kirkby Grindalythe 149
Kirkby Hill 112
Kirkby Knowle 55, 58, 85
Kirkby Lonsdale 205
Kirkby Malzeard 61
Kirkby Misperton 83, 274
Kirkby Moorside 17, 19, 20, 21, 30, 34, 51,
61, 71, 81, 83, 108, 136, 149, 151, 154, 187,
201, 235, 264, 284, 323, 324, 335
Kirkby Ravensworth 112, 223, 305, 306
Kirkby Underdale 141
Kirkby Wharfe 113
Kirkby Wiske 230
Kirkby, William 326
Kirkdale 98, 99
Kirkham Priory 161, 238, 298,
Kirklees Priory 121, 211
Knapton 131

Knaresborough 6, 16, 20, 21, 39, 49, 88,
89, 90, 123, 199, 215, 219, 232, 318
Knaresborough Forest 148
Knight, James 217
knights' incomes 38
Knights Templar 169
Knolles, Sir Robert 287
Knollys, Sir Francis 20, 319
Knottingley 182
Knowles, Elizabeth 100
Knowles, John 304
Knowles, Sir William 271
Knox, John 80
Knyvet, Sir Thomas 174

Lacey, John 301
Lacey, Marmaduke 120, 138
Lacon, William 235
Laing, William 99
Lambarne, Margaret 327
Lambe, Thomas 100
Langbaurgh xvi, 225
Langdale 180
Langdale, Alban 300
Langdale, Christopher 247
Langdale, Roger 92
Langdale, Sir Lancelot 48
Langtoft 233
Langton 51, 54
Lascelles, Robert 55
Lassells, Sir Roger 286, 381
Lastingham 188, 331
Latimer, Lord 28, 50
Latimer, Lords 36-37
Laughton 360
Lawson, George 279
Lawson, Richard 105
Lawson, Robert 289
Lawson, Thomas 171
Lawson, William 313, 345, 354
Layerthorpe 350
Layng, Will 154
Layton, Richard 171
Lead xix, 191-2
Leaf, John 71
Learoyd, John 381
Leconfield xviii, 30, 35, 108, 251,
Ledstone 88
Ledum, John 94, 251
Lee, Archbishop 68
Lee, Roger 352
Lee, Thomas 197
Leedes, Bryan 113

408

Roseberry Topping 88, 355
Rosedale 81, 91, 117, 122, 130, 168, 178
Rosedale Priory 34, 121
Rossington 88
Rotherforth, Robert 310
Rotherham 14, 41, 84, 87, 88, 111, 129, 166, 183, 192, 199, 203, 204, 206, 236, 272, 288, 326, 338, 350, 381
Rothwell 88, 184
Roxby 58, 179, 224, 322
Roxby castle 184
royal forests 173
Royston 113
Rudstone 25, 87, 178, 225
Rufford Abbey 288
Russell, Jordan 190
Ruston 261
Ruswarp Carr 143
Ruswarp Hall 211
Rutland, Countess of 200, 272, 310
Rutland, Earl of 5, 19, 57, 58, 134, 154, 190, 191, 206, 233, 281, 354, 382,
Rye, River 145
Ryedale xvi, 118, 124, 126, 146
Ryedale Folk Museum 167
Ryff, Andreas 210
Ryther, James xviii, xix, 28, 99, 106, 376,
Ryther, John 218
Ryther, Sir Ralph 132, 148
Ryton 159

Sadler, Sir Ralph 20, 239
Salisbury, Earl of 132
Salmon, Mary 100
Salton in Ryedale 11, 12, 70, 142
Salven, Edward 82
Samwell, Francis 57
Sand Hutton 148
Sandal 31, 113
Sandall castle 318
Sandall, Edward 75
Sandford, John 292
Sandsend 189
Sandwith, Anthony 99
Saunders, Richard 19
Saunderson, Nicholas 292
Savage, Thomas 363
Savile, Edward 347
Savile, George 293
Saville, Anne 102
Saville, Conyers 322
Saville, John 81, 307, 308
Saville, Sir Edward 9, 48

Saville, Sir George 32, 84, 137, 212
Saville, Sir Henry 6, 41, 112, 313, 347, 365
Saville, Sir John 7, 14, 318
Saville, Thomas 83, 232, 338
Saville, Ursula 232
Saxey, Hugh 310
Saxton 215
Saxton, Christopher 124, 127, 137
Saxton, Robert 57
Sayer, John 21, 137
Scagglethorpe 143
Scalby 136, 153
Scalby hay 132
Scarborough xix, 6, 16, 18, 19, 39, 79, 91, 100, 111, 117, 118, 126, 127, 132, 141, 152, 162, 164, 166, 167, 168, 171, 182, 201, 202, 207, 211, 220, 225, 239, 243, 244, 247, 250, 252, 257, 258, 264, 266, 268, 273, 274, 275, 289-90, 307, 318, 326, 340, 353, 369, 371, 377
Scarborough, Robert 260
Scarth, John 29
Schools 298, 301-2
Scotland 3, 19
Scott, Robert 11
Scott, Sir Thomas 254
Scrayingham 94
Scrooby 217
Scrope, Henry, Lord 46
Scrope, John 133
Scrope, Lady Katherine 321, 336
Scrope, Lord 20, 23
Seagrave 50
Seagrave, William 57
Seamer xviii, 34, 48, 70, 148, 167, 171, 213, 217, 225, 289
Seamer, Lambert 191
Segrave, William 134, 281, 319
Selby 9, 22, 45, 205, 226, 246, 256, 268, 381
Selby, Thomas 144
Sellowe, Robert 92
Servants 306
Settrington 30, 59, 66, 82, 117, 134, 159, 169, 179
Settrington, Thomas 278
Sewell, Rowland 379
Shadlocke, William 11
Shafton 124
Shane, Richard 313
Sharlston Hall 327
Sharpe, Bryan 80
Sharrocke, Jane 100

413